NEW BUSINESS VENTURES
AND THE ENTREPRENEUR

NEW BUSINESS VENTURES AND THE ENTREPRENEUR

PATRICK R. LILES, M.B.A., M.A., D.B.A.
Associate Professor
Harvard University Graduate School of Business Administration

1974

RICHARD D. IRWIN, INC. *Homewood, Illinois   60430*

Irwin-Dorsey Limited, Georgetown, Ontario   L7G 4B3

7 8 9 0 MP 5 4 3 2 1 0 9 8

Case material of the Harvard Graduate School of
Business Administration is made possible by the
cooperation of business firms who may wish to remain
anonymous by having names, quantities, and other
identifying details disguised while basic relationships
are maintained. Cases are prepared as the basis for
class discussion rather than to illustrate either effective
or ineffective handling of administrative situations.

ISBN 0-256-01560-0
Library of Congress Catalog Card No. 73–89109

Printed in the United States of America

*Dedicated to
my wife Dagmar
and
my two sons Christian and Michael*

Preface

This book is intended to provide the core materials for a graduate or undergraduate course for individuals who want to start or to purchase a business of their own. As a complement to books, courses, and experiences directed toward developing a career in professional management, this book has been written to serve the needs of individuals seeking to become entrepreneurs. It should also be of interest to those active in related areas, such as venture capital and parts of commercial lending and investment banking.

This is not a cookbook; would-be ventures of any consequence are too complex for a simplistic approach. Instead 15 actual venture situations are presented in substantial detail together with 8 technical notes that deal with the nature of the entrepreneur, legal forms of businesses, tax aspects of ventures, evaluation methods, techniques of purchasing a company, venture capital, real estate, and securities regulations.

The ventures described include a variety of industries, levels of technology and degrees of sophistication. The primary criterion for their selection was that they be the type of situation that has sufficient potential to warrant serious consideration as a career alternative. Each of the cases depicts a wide range of basic problems and issues which an entrepreneur might expect to encounter. Seven major areas receive primary emphasis:

1. Searching for venture opportunities
2. Matching an individual or team with a venture situation
3. Evaluating the potential and long-term viability of a venture
4. Evaluating sources of financing

5. Structuring the financing/purchase of a company
6. Carrying out negotiations
7. Managing operations

In addition, each of the cases contains a myriad of other practical, real-life problems to be considered and acted upon: running out of money, dealing with law suits, selecting a partner, negotiating with government officials, and so on. Those familiar with case method learning will recognize the use of specific illustrations to stimulate the reader's thinking and to develop skills in conceptualization, analysis, and judgment.

The technical notes have been included to provide some of the substantive background and knowledge necessary to anyone working in new venture activities. Because of the highly complex nature of most of this material, it has been condensed and in places over-simplified to make it comprehensible to those encountering it for the first time. The objective is to make the individual aware of the fundamentals of each area and to familiarize him with how they relate to entrepreneurial activities. If he seriously pursues an entrepreneurial career and encounters problems in these areas, he should know when and how to seek out specialized assistance and how to utilize the help he receives.

This material was created for the Harvard Business School course Management of Small Enterprises: Starting New Ventures, which originated under Myles Mace in 1947. Largely because of the efforts of Frank L. Tucker, who taught the course from 1964 until 1969, it developed and expanded to the extent that approximately 480 students took it during the academic year 1972–73. Professor Tucker has been a very helpful source of ideas and inspiration for the writing of this book.

I am particularly indebted to Mike Liles, Jr., of the law firm Bogle, Gates, Dobrin, Wakefield and Long who wrote the note *Securities regulations—A businessman's guide* and who reviewed several other sections of the material. Also, I am indebted to Frederick E. Finkenauer and Clifton H. N. Maloney, graduates of the school in 1966, much of whose research report information on venture capital has been used in the section *Venture capital: What it is and how to raise it.*

I am very grateful to the Bureau of Business and Economic Research of the Graduate School of Business Administration at Michigan State University for allowing me to quote from the work *Enterprising Man* by Orvis F. Collins and David G. Moore with Darab B. Unwalla.

In collecting and putting together much of the material for this book I received the generous help and assistance of a number of people. In the technical areas Henry B. Reiling of Columbia University; Richard E. Floor and Samuel B. Bruskin of the law firm Goodwin, Procter, and Hoar; Robert B. Ray of Nashville, Tennessee; and Robert J. Pavan of the Harvard Business School each contributed to compressing complex subject matter into comprehensible forms. Perry V. Haines, William B. Rodgers, Jesse C. Nichols, Robert J. Gustavson, and Susan B. Aidala provided assistance in casewriting and editing. Proofreading assistance was provided by Mary A. Cafarella. The monumental task of organizing, typing, correcting, and coordinating fell to my cheerful, patient, and hard-working secretary Carole G. Sikkema.

March 1974   P. R. LILES

Contents

Skip

Note

The investor's perspective: *Asset valuations. Earnings valuations.* The entrepreneur's perspective: *Types of cash flows and their different tax treatments. Other considerations causing one type of cash flow to be preferred over another. Two models.* The seller's perspective. Value and purchase price.

Cases
Peter W. Allen, 202
Steve O. Handley, 231
Epicure Products, Inc., 259

Note

I. Introduction. II. Federal corporate income tax: A. *Multiple corporations.* B. *Business expenses.* C. *Accounting period.* D. *Loss carryovers.* E. *Accumulated earnings tax.* F. *Personal holding companies.* G. *Capital gains and dividends received by a corporation.* H. *Consolidated returns.* I. *Small business investment companies (SBIC).* J. *Regulated investment companies.* K. *Corporate tax returns.* L. *Reorganization and liquidation.* M. *Subchapter S. corporations—taxing a corporation as a partnership. N. Sale of mixed assets and installment sales.* III. Partnerships: A. *Family partnerships.* B. *Valuation, splits, and so on.* C. *Expenses.* IV. Inventors. V. Individuals: A. *Individual income tax rates.* B. *Gift and death taxes.* C. *Stock dividends.* D. *Stock options.* E. *Losses on small business stock (Section 1244 stock).* F. *Thin capitalization.* VI. Other taxes.

Cases
Howard J. Forster, 309
Raymond W. Hill, 322

Note

I. Purpose of note. II. Introduction. III. The development process: A. *Economic study.* B. *Preliminary decisions.* C. *Organizing the deal.* D. *Market and investment management.* E. *Liquidation of investment.* IV. FHA financing programs. V. Depreciation and tax considerations: A. *Depreciation.* B. *Depreciation recapture.* C. *Minimum tax on accelerated depreciation.*

Case
Mark Olive, 362

Note

Purchase by an individual: *Purchasing for cash and/or notes. Taxes.* Reorganizations: Corporate mergers and acquisitions: *Type "A" reorganization. Type "B" reorganization. Type "C" reorganization.*

Note
Venture capital: What it is and how to raise it 461

Introduction. Venture capital sources. Raising the initial seed capital for a new venture. Selecting the proper venture capital investor. Legal aspects of raising money. Evaluation criteria used by venture capital investors: *Evaluating the people. Evaluating the venture itself. Presenting a proposal to a venture capital investor.* Investigation and negotiation. Operating period. How the investor realizes his gain or loss. Trends in the venture capital field and their implications for the entrepreneur.

Note
Securities regulation—a businessman's guide 495

Introduction. Definition of a security. Business financing disclosures: *Federally registered offerings. Regulation A offerings. State-registered (instrastate) offerings. Private offerings.* Trust indentures. Acquisitions. Disclosure of material inside information. Manipulation. Regulation of public companies: *Periodic reports. Proxy solicitation. Tender offers and takeover bids. Insider reporting and trading.* Credit regulation. The securities industry. Investment companies. Consequences of violation.

Introduction

Who are the entrepreneurs?

Most American businessmen have at some time in their careers thought about starting their own company. Some have envisioned their own enterprise as an avenue to personal wealth through large capital gains. To them there is a beautiful formula for financial success: (1) Start a small company, preferably in a glamour industry. (2) Generate rapid growth in sales and profits. (3) Then sell out either to the public or to some large acquisitive conglomerate.

Others have seen their own company as an opportunity to do what they really wanted to do: to get close to a sport by developing a ski area, or to reduce a new technology to practical use. Still others have sought an escape from stultifying large-company constraints, politics, or career impasses. In their dreams, their own venture would be a means to gain the top position in a business.

Despite dreams, wishful thinking, and even plans, few people actually take the step of trying to start a company. Why is this? Is there a special breed of man which is particularly inclined to become an entrepreneur? Are there special characteristics or conditions which stimulate entrepreneurial activities?

The basic questions we are asking here are classic ones: Are entrepreneurs born or are they made? If they can be made, what are the ingredients? The conclusions I have reached are that, given a degree of ambition and ability not uncommon to many individuals, *certain kinds of experiences and situational conditions, rather than personality or ego, are the major determinants of whether or not an individual becomes an entrepreneur.*

1

Background

If we examine some of the attitudes in the subculture of American businessmen we find that there are significant connotations to starting a company as a career alternative. Almost everyone gets a glow, a tingle, at the idea of being an entrepreneur. To men in their thirties and forties, the idea of starting a company means "free enterprise" and "opportunity," as reflected in Horatio Alger stories. In value terms of the younger generation, starting a company is a way to "do your own thing." For such businessmen and for many business school students, starting a successful company is a very attractive idea yet only rarely do they seem to consider it a serious alternative. When a possible opportunity presents itself, there is somehow too little time to investigate it properly and too little time to determine whether or not the idea really makes sense. Thus, it appears that *most* would-be entrepreneurs stop before they get started. Unfortunately, there is little information on such people who have had ideas about starting companies but have never pursued them seriously.

We might think that we already know a lot about the entrepreneurs themselves—those who actually go ahead and start companies. Yet, do we really? We find there are people who think of entrepreneurs as being formed by school systems and child raising,[1] by rejecting fathers,[2] or by the business environment.[3] However, efforts to measure and predict entrepreneurial potential are, at best, still in the development stages.[4]

Perhaps one of the best broad-based studies on entrepreneurs was carried out by Orvis F. Collins and David G. Moore at Michigan State University in 1964. Using a series of personal interviews and psychological tests, they reached a number of rather unsettling conclusions regarding people who start their own company:

> Throughout the preceding analysis, obviously we have been having difficulty deciding whether the entrepreneur is essentially a "reject" of our organizational society who, instead of becoming a hobo, criminal, or professor, makes his adjustment by starting his own business; or whether he is a man who is positively attracted to succeed in it. We have, perhaps without intention, regarded him as a reject.
>
> . . . entrepreneurs are men who have failed in the traditional and highly structured roles available to them in the society. In this . . . entrepreneurs are not unique. What is unique about them is that they found an outlet for

[1]William F. Whyte and Robert R. Braun, "Heroes, Homework, and Industrial Growth," *Columbia Journal of World Business,* Spring 1966.

[2]Manfred F. R. Kets de Vries, "The Entrepreneur as Catalyst of Economic and Cultural Change" (Ph.D. diss., Harvard Graduate School of Business Administration, 1970).

[3]Arnold C. Cooper, "Entrepreneurial Environment," *Industrial Research,* September 1970.

[4]Michael Palmer, "The Application of Psychological Testing to Entrepreneurial Potential," *California Management Review* 13, no. 3 (Spring 1971).

their creativity by making out of an undifferentiated mass of circumstances a creation uniquely their own: a business firm. . . .

The men who travel the entrepreneurial way are, taken on balance, not remarkably likeable people. This, too, is understandable. As any one of them might say in the vernacular of the world of the entrepreneur, "Nice guys don't win. . . ."[5]

Several small-sample studies at Harvard and MIT[6] have yielded results different from the Collins and Moore study. Entrepreneurs were not found to be failures. Instead "most of the founders had experienced a generally higher than average level of success in their previous employment. Several had established outstanding records of achievement."[7] These entrepreneurs seemed more typical of the successful, hard-charging young business executive[8] or engineer than a reject figure.

One possible explanation, of course, is that people in Michigan are very different from those in New England. It might be more helpful, however, if we categorized in some detail: (1) the kinds of businesses which are used in studies of small business fatality rates and in the Collins and Moore study, and (2) the kinds of businesses which might be started as alternatives to professional management or engineering careers. The survey-type studies are comprehensive in that they essentially look at *all* companies which are started within a particular period of time. This included a wide range of business ventures: dry cleaners, retail shops, electronics manufacturers, computer software firms, gas stations, and so on. Each of these is used in the computation of a wide range of statistics about the rise and demise of new companies. There should be no reason for us to doubt the aggregate figures or the results of in-depth studies made of these situations. The Collins and Moore study looked at 110 manufacturing firms started between 1945 and 1958 in Michigan but made no further distinctions as to the nature of the business, size, or potential.

If we consider, however, the kinds of ventures which might be of interest to a professional manager or an engineer, the vast majority of the enterprises started each year, and therefore the bulk of those considered in large, broad-based studies, would not be included. A dry cleaning

---

[5]Orvis F. Collins and David G. Moore with Darab B. Unwalla, *The Enterprising Man*, M.S.U. Business Studies (1964), pp. 241, 243–44.

[6]Herbert A. Wainer, "The Spin-Off of Technology from Government Sponsored Research Laboratories: Lincoln Laboratory," Unpublished Master's Thesis, Massachusetts Institute of Technology, 1965; Paul V. Teplitz, "Spin-Off Enterprises from a Large Government Sponsored Laboratory" (master's thesis, Massachusetts Institute of Technology, 1965); and Patrick R. Liles, "The Use of Outside Help in Starting High-Potential Ventures" (Ph.D. diss., Harvard Graduate School of Business Administration, 1970).

[7]Ibid.

[8]Walter Guzzardi, Jr., *The Young Executives*, The New American Library, 1964.

establishment or a small metal fabricating shop is not the basis for the dreams of *these* people. From their perspective (and therefore the perspective of this Note), we should label this subcategory of small business as "marginal firms."

That leaves us with the task of considering the kinds of venture situations which *are* potentially attractive career alternatives. The first, which I have labeled the "high-potential venture," is the company which "is started with the *intention* that the venture grow rapidly in sales and profits and become a large corporation."[9] In its planning stage the high-potential venture is the extreme of personal economic opportunity, the entrepreneur's big dream (Polaroid, Digital Equipment, Scientific Data Systems, Cartridge Television, Viatron), and soon.

Another type of enterprise, less obvious than the high-potential venture, also holds a strong interest for many would-be entrepreneurs. This type of venture we might call the "attractive small company." In contrast to the high-potential venture, the attractive small company is not intended to become a large corporation, probably will never have a public market for its stock, and will not be attractive to most venture capital investors. However, in contrast to the marginal firms, attractive small companies can provide salaries of $40,000 to $80,000 a year, perquisites (company car, country club memberships, travel) to its owner/managers, and often flexibility in life style, such as working hours, kinds of projects and tasks pursued, or geographical location. In this subcategory we find such businesses as consulting and other service firms and some specialized manufacturers.

Both the high-potential venture and the attractive small company are interesting beyond the scope of the benefits they may provide to their founder/owners. In the high-potential venture we find the genesis of the major corporations of the future and therefore the source of a growing number of jobs and other contributions to the economy. The attractive small companies provide less spectacular but stable inputs of a similar nature. Both of these kinds of companies must gain and maintain their position by providing competitive discomfort to the existing corporate giants through innovation, flexibility, and efficiency.

The marginal firms, on the other hand, provide support for their owners/employers but frequently at a lower level than might be obtained by employment if they could or would work elsewhere. However, these people are not likely to seek employment elsewhere because of their difficulties in functioning in larger and more structured organizations.[10]

We can depict graphically these three kinds of small businesses as shown in Figure 1.

---

[9]Liles, "Outside Help in Starting High-Potential Ventures."
[10] Collins and Moore, *The Enterprising Man.*

FIGURE 1

Categories of small businesses (relative sizes are only very rough estimates)

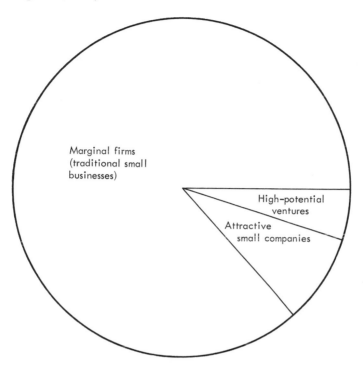

WHAT KIND OF PERSON STARTS A HIGH-POTENTIAL VENTURE OR AN ATTRACTIVE SMALL COMPANY?

Without question, some of the businessmen and engineers who start high-potential ventures or attractive small companies are compulsive entrepreneurs. They cannot function effectively in a large organization. They must be their own boss and they may have known this all their lives. It may seem as if they could have behaved in no other way. But what about the others who started companies? What about the entrepreneurs who are basically well-adjusted people and who had given little previous thought, if any, to the idea of their own company? How did these people happen to become entrepreneurs although most were already successful in the pursuit of a more conventional career? What factors play a leading role in determining who becomes an entrepreneur? Which factors might be largely fortuitous and which might be controlled by the individual?

A basic prerequisite—achievement motivation

Not all people are inclined to take on significantly more than they have to. A high-potential venture or an attractive small company is usually recognized as requiring a tremendous amount of determined effort and commitment. These kinds of activities are not attempted unless an individual is willing to expend more effort and energy than would be required in a more conventional career.

People high in achievement motivation are the people who strive to make things happen[11]—in the laboratory, on the production floor, in the sales office, and in the classroom. Obviously this factor alone is insufficient to determine who starts companies and who does not, but it is a beginning. People without this kind of orientation are unresponsive to the other influences which might encourage starting a venture. However, people with achievement motivation together with other influencing factors may become entrepreneurs.

Achievement motivation can be developed.[12] It would appear unlikely, however, that someone would try to develop achievement motivation in himself in order to start a high-potential venture or an attractive small company. One would expect that it would take a highly achievement motivated person to want to start either of these kinds of enterprises in the first place.

A disqualifying influence—social self-image

The majority of people trying to do exceptionally well in their careers never seriously consider starting a company. Even among the professional managers or career businessmen the number is small. This is not to say that many of these people would not gladly be successful entrepreneurs in their own companies. They are unwilling, however, to take what they see as a backward or downward step necessary to achieve that success.

An acquaintance of mine, Mr. J. H. Hendricks has humorously described in a talk his personal experiences as a graduate of Yale and the effect of this on his thinking about his career. After pondering the success of his noncollege friends from high school:

> It all came clear one night when I was arguing and describing how Charlie had not been able to go to college, but instead after working in a restaurant had bought a second-hand dump truck. That's when it dawned

---

[11]David C. McClelland, "Business Drive and National Achievement," *Harvard Business Review*, July–August 1962.

[12]David C. McClelland, "Achievement Motivation Can Be Developed," *Harvard Business Review*," November–December 1965.

on me that BECAUSE I went to college I could NEVER buy a second-hand dump truck, not even a brand new one with someone else to drive it. When I ran across an old friend, I could not afford to explain that I was the owner of a dump truck. No, I was "with" the ABC Corporation. Not necessary to explain that they are the largest producers of this and that in the world. I was "with" them, and my friend was "with" someone just like them.

Because of recent increasing sentiments favoring personal independence and relevance, we might expect to find in the future a greater general public acceptance of entrepreneurial activities and therefore to discover less and less conflict between this kind of career and a person's social self-image. In this sense, it may be becoming easier for someone to decide to strike out on his own than it has been in the past. Perhaps we shall come to the point where becoming an entrepreneur is recognized as a socially legitimate and even an attractive career alternative.

INFLUENCES ON ENTREPRENEURIAL CAREERS

For the person who has achievement motivation and whose social self-image is not in conflict with starting a company, there are two kinds of conditions which become critical:

1. How *ready* he sees himself for undertaking such a venture.
2. How many *distractions* or *obligations* he sees holding him back.

Note that what an individual does depends upon how he perceives a situation rather than upon what the situation actually is. This is particularly critical in considering a person's readiness or his restraints, because there is no way for anyone to make direct, objective measurements of these characteristics. Instead, a personal assessment of readiness or restraints is going to be a combination of knowledge, insight, judgment, and personal values.

Readiness

In terms of his decision to initiate a company and to try to run it successfully, a person's own assessment of how ready he is probably is a good approximation of how ready he really is. One would not likely find a runner expecting to run a four-minute mile without having some objectively valid reasons behind those expectations. Similarly an individual who believes that he is ready to start a company is probably reaching that decision from some background of experience, exposure, special skills, and industry knowledge. This is not to say that some people do not try to initiate businesses when they are totally unprepared. It would imply, however, that in most instances of this kind the individual himself knows very well that the odds are against his being able to make a go of it.

It might be useful to think of an individual's readiness in terms of levels of specific and general self-confidence. Specific self-confidence in this context represents an individual's feeling of mastery over the kinds of tasks and problems he would expect to encounter in starting a company and making it successful. General self-confidence would be his feeling of well-being and his universal assurance that he can accomplish things.

What people learn through a variety of business and related experience accumulates over time. Most people learn relatively more and learn relatively more rapidly early in their careers when much of what they do and see is new to them. And although the relative rate of learning may diminish over time the cumulative effect is an increasingly competent individual. The evolution of a person's readiness as reflected in his specific self-confidence to master various elements of a venture is depicted graphically in Figure 2.

General self-confidence, which is necessary for someone to want to try something new, is an elusive idea. Most people can identify in their own lives those periods when they were confident and up for doing big, new things. They can also recall other times when they were anxious and uncertain—unwilling to get away from the sure and the known. Given the high degree of uncertainty for most people in starting a company, a high level of general self-confidence is necessary for them to be willing to try.

FIGURE 2

Readiness to start a venture

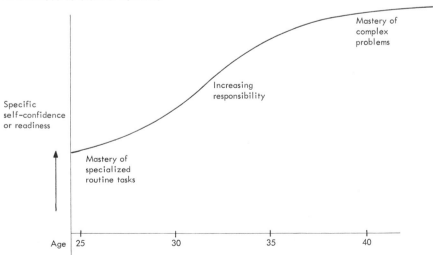

Restraints

Perhaps the most effective restraint on someone who otherwise might start a company is his continuing success and satisfaction in pursuing his present job. Why should anyone want to change if things are going well? Especially with the passage of time, increasing seniority for such people means a larger salary, greater responsibilities, and greater benefits. In addition, an individual develops a personal power base within an organization—key knowledge and skills, confidence and loyalty of associates, and so on—which enables him to assert himself and to be effective. At some point, even in the face of a grave disappointment or disenchantment with the company, it becomes almost prohibitively expensive to resign and pursue another career direction.

A would-be entrepreneur's freedom to break away and start a company also becomes hindered by financial and other obligations typical of the male's life-cycle development in the United States between the ages of 25 and 40. A man gets married, buys a house, and starts to raise a family. He may immediately incur a sizable mortgage and real estate taxes. With children he acquires the cost burdens for their future education. In addition, he assumes responsibility for his family in the event of his death or disability. These immediate and future costs tie him to a schedule of direct expense payments, a plan for savings, and the costs of insurance.

In addition, the usual pattern is for expenditures on living expenses to rise as a person receives promotions and increases in salary. He now has two cars instead of one, a larger house, and takes more expensive vacations. These costs, closely following if not sometimes overtaking income, as a practical matter are only adjustable upward. And until the children have finished school, it is unusual to find sufficient funds for anything approaching financial flexibility.

Other commitments created by marriage and families may do as much to restrict the freedom and flexibility of would-be entrepreneurs as do financial obligations. Few women marry with the intention of becoming nurses and housecleaners for absentee husbands. Moreover, personal relationships among people take time, even the minimum of spoken communication, the ritual of certain courtesies, and the recreational activities people pursue together. Some part of the evenings, weekends, and holidays are expected by the family to be devoted to these activities. The family life-cycle experience usually creates an increasing time requirement upon the husband until the children go away to school. As small children begin to lose physical dependence upon their mothers, the role of the father increases in both depth and scope. In the wisdom of everyday life, "This is the time when the children need a father."

Two other interesting phenomena frequently appear as part of the male career life cycle. The first is an evolution of values as the family, especially children, enters into his thinking. Their security is related to his career security, and therefore his career security becomes more important to him. The time spent with wife and children is more than the minimal to satisfy physical or emotional obligations, but it is a part of a change in the importance he places on what he does—a transition from preoccupation with a career to a realization of new interests in his life.

The other aspect, closely related to a change of values, is a change of pace. The drive, the physical and emotional energy expended by so many young executives in pursuit of a career, is not appropriate to the pursuit of many other interests. Perceived at the office, Joe at 40 is slowing down. Perceived by his wife, Joe is beginning to live. Perceived by himself, Joe is just doing other things—not necessarily enjoying himself more than when he was hotly pursuing his career interests, but rather enjoying himself in other ways.

For starting a company an individual's self-perceived *effective capacity* can be derived from a combination of readiness and freedom from restraints and distractions. The results, depicted graphically in Figure 3, show effective capacity for starting a company typically increases with age, beginning between 25 and 30, as the individual learns rapidly from his early experiences. As a person grows older, however,

FIGURE 3

The free choice period for the would-be entrepreneur

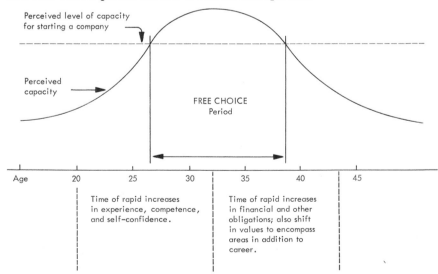

this trend is modified and then reversed as the marginal learning experience becomes less, and the influences of successful employment plus family-related interests and obligations are incurred. If we identify a certain level of capacity as being necessary for a person to be able to act, we can define a certain period—a *free choice period,* so to speak—when the individual sees himself as able to act. During this period the capability, the self-confidence, and the career commitment on balance can be more of an influence than are his economic or emotional commitments and interests in other areas.

The precipitating events

For some people the combination of circumstances is such that they never attain sufficient capacity to start a company. They never reach a free choice period. Their other commitments become too large before they reach a point where they could strike out on their own. On the other hand, there are probably thousands and thousands of people who pass through a period when they could choose to start a company—when they have sufficient capabilities and few restraints—but they don't do it. It would appear that most people need something more—something to help break established ties and to create resolve and something specific to pursue.

Three additional kinds of conditions appear to be major influences on decisions to start ventures. The first, deterioration of job satisfaction, disposes the individual to consider seriously other career alternatives. The second, identifying a new venture opportunity, helps to focus upon what might otherwise be a largely undefined possibility. The third, encouragement to start a company, helps an individual make what becomes a very subjective decision.

1. Dissatisfaction. This element—a negative outlook on his present and future job situation—appears to have a strong influence on the would-be entrepreneur. Relative to his expectations, something disturbs him. A budget for product development is cut back; the right promotion or salary increase does not occur; an addition to his staff is denied. Although entrepreneurs will cite such specific events or unfulfilled expectations as the triggering event which brought them to leave, the reasons are usually more complex. The last straw is but one of a number of disquieting and disappointing incidents which occurred over time and which produced a general feeling of dissatisfaction and perhaps resentment.

Job dissatisfaction for whatever reasons is not an unusual condition. Changing jobs in most instances is the easiest and more common occurrence. Frequently it is the opportunity of another job that triggers a critical assessment of one's current employment situation. The transition from one job to another is relatively quick, and its results—at least in the short term—are predictable. In addition, it usually achieves direct use of special skills and knowledge accumulated in prior positions. The unusual thing is when an individual, instead of expressing his objections in the conventional way by changing jobs, elects to start a company.

2. Identifying a new venture opportunity.   Opportunities for new ventures, like most other opportunities, usually emerge over time rather than suddenly appear. In a technical area, an individual may find or learn of a solution to a particular kind of problem and see the potential for using this approach in areas where it has not been applied before. Or in dealing with his employer's suppliers he may identify key features of purchased products or services which he believes he can handle better or at less cost than others in the business. Or he may discover that there are needs for particular products or services that no one else supplies.

An individual in any part of a business enterprise may see potential opportunities for new ventures related to areas in which he is active. The alternative of starting a company becomes possible only when an individual perceives the basis for a viable enterprise and can see himself playing a major role in it. Whether or not a person interprets a situation as an opportunity is determined to a large degree by his perception of his own ability to take advantage of it.

3. Encouragement and support.   Today when most middle managers or engineers begin to think of leaving their jobs they never seriously consider the possibility of starting a company. Unlike the established training programs and junior positions created by major corporations, there are no recognized patterns or channels for getting into one's own business. A few individuals have the special insights from their fathers' having been entrepreneurs, but the majority do not. For many, any substantial encouragement or help in the direction of becoming an entrepreneur is happenstance or luck.

The inputs which expand an individual's thinking about starting a company may range from an encouraging word to assistance with a detailed plan and analysis. It may be offered in a casual way or directed toward achieving some specific objective of the helper. But in any case it frequently plays a significant initial role.

One source of support comes from other individuals who share in the feelings of job dissatisfaction and would like to join in pursuing a venture or to become part of a team that undertakes such an effort. These people may represent a logical combination of diverse talents and personalities to overcome the problems and inertia of getting the venture started and taking it to a profitable operation. Moreover, they may be known to each other and therefore represent a degree of certainty about how specific tasks will get done. But at the outset, a key role for these people and for others outside the immediate founder group can be to provide psychological support and encouragement. At the initial stage, momentum for the venture originates from talking it up, proposing different ways to solve the problems of starting, and giving helpful criticism to each other.

A wife's reaction to the idea of starting a company is usually a major influence upon how long and how seriously an individual considers starting a company. Eventually, she will be directly affected. Her husband's happiness, her life style and the family's financial future are at stake. I have seen wives who have responded with extreme anxiety at the prospect of their husband's starting a company, and I have seen those who have become a key part of the new venture. At either extreme, the wife's role is critical.

Another source of support emerges from people to whom the would-be entrepreneur goes for help, such as potential suppliers, lawyers, bankers, other entrepreneurs, and government officials. These people help an individual clarify his thinking. They assist in clarifying some of the specific uncertainties associated with starting the venture and indicate their potential role in providing future information, assistance, or service should the venture be actively pursued. The existence of this kind of readily available help is part of the process of transforming an individual idea into a realistic alternative. If these sources of help are not apparent, then real and imagined problems of getting a venture going may appear insurmountable.

WHAT ABOUT RISK?

Up to this point we have not dealt with risk as a factor per se. Entrepreneurs, in fact, have been described as people who *like* to take risks. (I believe the entrepreneurs I know would describe such people as fools.) There is more than a little difference between the person who likes risk and the person who finds risk to be a challenge. Risk covers a multitude of areas, all of which impinge in most instances upon entrepreneurial decisions.

Only when an individual considers starting a company as a serious alternative does his perception of risk become a key factor. Risk in this context has three elements: (1) the perceived "odds" of various good and bad events occurring, (2) the perceived consequences of these events, and (3) the perceived seriousness of these consequences. It should be noted that all three aspects of risk are subjective. The individual's assessment of the risk is what influences his decision.

When an individual is in a free choice stage of his career, and when he is considering starting a company as a specific alternative, the perceived risks in a situation will influence whether or not he goes ahead with it. Below are briefly described four critical risk areas.

Financial risk

The problem most people would think of first is whether or not they can afford to work with little or no salary for a period of several months to several years while the venture is getting started. This is particularly significant for the successful young executive or engineer who has improved his standard of living as he received promotions and salary increases. What would happen to the family budget without the monthly paycheck? How many families are willing to take a severe cutback in their living expenditures?

But this is more a question of financial *sacrifice* than financial *risk*. In most new venture operations the individual will put a significant portion of his savings or other financial resources at stake. This money is risked and will in all likelihood be lost if the venture fails. The entrepreneur may also be required to sign personally on company obligations which far exceed his personal net worth. When such obligations significantly exceed the tangible net worth of the company, the individual exposes himself to the extreme condition of financial risk: personal bankruptcy.

Career risk

A question raised by most would-be entrepreneurs is whether or not they will be able to find a job should they experience a failure in their own company. Obviously, many people who are unsuccessful in their own firms *do* get jobs afterward with major corporations. The question, of course, is how difficult is it to get such a job and how will an employer look upon this kind of prospective employee?

Family risks

As already mentioned, the requirements of starting a new venture frequently consume the energies, emotions, and time of the entrepreneur. As a result, he has little to give elsewhere, and his other commitments suffer. Entrepreneurs who are married, and especially those with children, expose their families at best to the risks of an incomplete family experience and at worst to permanent emotional scars from inattention, quarreling, and bitterness.

The psychic risk

An entrepreneurial effort by an individual has special features which subject a person to high psychic risk. First, everyone, including the entrepreneur himself, identifies the venture with one or two men. The company is these people. In addition, the magnitude of effort required to start a venture has given those activities priority over everything else in their lives—family, friends, and other interests. The greater the commitment, the more the identification with the venture is internalized.

If an individual fails, the experience can be shattering. In addressing the causes of a venture's failure, the entrepreneur himself is always one of the reasons. He planned poorly, he executed poorly, he followed through poorly, or in some way he did not allow sufficient margin for the unexpected. If an individual concludes that his failure in a particular effort was because of an inherent incapacity or inadequacy, he has lost his self-confidence. The risk to an individual is the risk of losing his self-confidence. The individual without self-confidence loses not only his abilities to function effectively in his career or profession but also loses his ability to deal effectively in his personal life. Moreover, once begun, such a process gains momentum and tends to whirl into a relentless downward spiral.

SUMMARY AND CONCLUSIONS

We have examined the entrepreneur who is involved in substantial ventures and have considered what we found in light of traditional thinking that he is a special type of individual—somehow an unusual and uncommon man—a man apart. It is probably true that very successful entrepreneurs *become* men apart. But, at the beginning, when they make the decision to start an entrepreneurial career, they are in most respects very much like many other ambitious, striving individuals. It appears, moreover, that the entrepreneurial interests for those who elect that path are more a function of *external* differences than internal ones—more the result of practical readiness and cost/income constraints than of individual psychology or personality. This is not to suggest that starting a successful company is a game that anyone can play. It is, however, a statement that far more people could become entrepreneurs than ever do so and that the inclination of people to move in this direction could be increased by their increased awareness and recognition of this as a career alternative.

Cases

American Imports

In October 1967 Steve Miller and Jack Wilson, two recent graduates of the Eastern Business School, were actively reviewing their decision to create an imported merchandise store. The two entrepreneurs were having serious second thoughts about their new enterprise. Their corporation, American Imports, was only four and one-half months old. Already it had suffered serious reverses.

The company was the direct result of a business policy report produced in their second year at the Eastern Business School by the two M.B.A.'s. Their report had analyzed the conditions and trends in the importing of household decorator items. In evaluating the various competitive elements of the industry they had decided to organize and finance a retail store specializing in low-cost, quality imported gifts and household decorations. It was their strategy to bypass the traditional channel of distribution for imported goods and procure their merchandise direct from manufacturers overseas. Their type of establishment, known in the industry as an importer-retailer, was to be opened in Washington, D.C., October 1, 1967, in time for the Christmas gift buying season.

The Partners

Steve Miller and Jack Wilson met at the Eastern Business School in 1965. As members of the same first-year section they became friends when they discovered that they shared an interest in the import-export business. Jack Wilson explained:

> We had been section mates in the first year and had been meeting regularly once a week with a small group of entrepreneurially inclined international business-minded second-year students. We talked about the possibilities of developing some import activity in the handicraft area.

16

Both men were convinced that significant opportunities existed in the area of importing goods to the United States from underdeveloped countries.

Steve Miller. After graduation from West Point in 1960, Steve Miller had been commissioned as a lieutenant in the U.S. Corps of Engineers. He had spent a year in Thailand constructing highways. While in Thailand he formed friendships with several local businessmen and became involved in the business of exporting custom-designed hi-fi cabinets to America. In addition, he imported American goods to Thailand through a small company he formed called the East/West Importing Company. Upon completing his military service he entered the Eastern Business School. (See Exhibit 1.)

Jack Wilson. Upon graduation from Harvard College in 1962, Mr. Wilson joined the then recently formed Peace Corps. He was assigned to teach at the University of Teheran, Iran. His ability to speak fluent Persian allowed him to teach English to college level students. In 1964 he was awarded a Fulbright Scholarship for the study of Iranian land reform. Blocked by local political pressure from carrying through his Fulbright assignment, he went to work part-time for a Teheran consulting firm. Commenting on a market research report which he produced for this firm, Mr. Wilson said, "I got very interested in the possibility of developing Iranian handicraft manufacture for export to America. The more I investigated this opportunity, the better it looked. As a result of the report I wrote, they organized a venture which I believe has been quite successful."

In the summer of 1965, Mr. Wilson went to work for the U.S. Information Agency in Beirut. He returned to the United States in time to enter the Eastern Business School along with Mr. Miller in the fall of 1965. (See Exhibit 2.)

The industry analysis section of the business policy report

Miller and Wilson conducted 12 in-depth interviews with companies actively competing within their industry. In addition to using published sources, they spoke to a number of knowledgeable people within the industry. Through their bank they were able to secure Dun and Bradstreet reports on companies which they felt held a significant place within the industry.

Product sources

Manufacturing operations in Europe, the Middle East, and Asia ranged from highly labor-intensive work of hand craftsmen to fairly machine-intensive factories turning out products such as furniture, stainless steel cutlery, and glassware in production runs of substantial volume. The majority of manufacturers sold locally and were not primarily oriented toward export business. They were normally contacted directly by buying agents of U.S. importers and importer-retailers.

U.S. importers were willing to work closely with a manufacturer and be reasonably patient with late deliveries so long as the quality of goods received remained high. A very real weakness within the maker's segment of the industry was that management often tended to take a rather short-run view of the importance of quality control, market changes, terms of exclusive agreements, and loyalty to customers. Importers and importer-retailers frequently complained that many manufacturers would switch customers even on firm orders if another customer offered them slightly better terms. In addition to these problems, in some countries there had been efforts to organize manufacturers into cooperatives and associations. American importers felt threatened by the creation of these manufacturers' cooperatives, since their bargaining position and their ability to make exclusive contracts were weakened. (See Exhibit 3 for history of imports.)

Importer-wholesalers. American importers generally purchased goods from foreign manufacturers and wholesaled these items to jobbers and retailers. Importers bought from a number of sources and carried a much wider spread of products than a single manufacturer.

There was some product specialization by importer-wholesalers and a tendency to carry as many bread-and-butter (staple) items as possible. Sales were handled through company salesmen, agents, and jobbers. Many importers maintained permanent company showrooms in New York and exhibited at annual gift and furniture trade shows. A few importers owned captive retail outlets. Surface freight was the main mode for shipping goods from a foreign maker to the importer-wholesaler, but some items with a high value-to-weight ratio were air-freighted. They normally used truck transport within the United States. Most of them maintained sizable warehouse inventories from which they shipped in-stock items directly to retailers. On the East Coast two-week delivery from importer-wholesaler to retailer was considered standard.

Most importers had their own buyers abroad and/or employed commission agents locally who received 5 percent of the import price for finding and dealing with manufacturers of specific household items. Importers tended to specialize regionally. Within the industry, the trend was for foreign manufacturers to integrate forward in the distribution channel rather than the reverse. Most importers attempted to get exclusive agreements with manufacturers on unusual items. However, these exclusive agreements were difficult to enforce.

The usual method of payment to foreign manufacturers was by letter of credit. Cash payment was due 60 to 90 days after the goods arrived in the United States. Importer-wholesalers' mark-ons ranged from 33 percent to 50 percent on total landed costs of goods.[1] Terms to the retail trade were normally 2/10 net 30. Prompt-paying retail accounts clearly received preference. Most importers maintained some type of customer rating system by which they classified credit history as to promptness of payment.

Trade shows were considered throughout the industry as the most thorough and least expensive way of getting exposure to jobbers and retail store buyers. Buyers attended the trade shows looking for products which they felt would sell in their individual stores. An importer could achieve almost complete exposure to the retail outlets in the United States by showing at a relatively few stores.

Jobbers. Traditionally, jobbers had provided importer-wholesalers with distribution to remote retailers and had had control over selecting the desirability of the customer as a credit risk, either actual or implied possession of the goods, and the responsibility of collection from the retail customers. As retailing imported household goods had grown into a sizable industry, importers and conventional retailers had begun to bypass jobbers whenever possible to improve service and cut costs. In effect, the retailer was moving backward in the distribution channel and the importer was integrating forward, with the net result that the jobber was being slowly squeezed out. In 1967, few importer-wholesalers were interested in acquiring the services of new jobbers; the number of jobbers was at an all-time low; the role historically filled by the jobber had essentially disappeared.

Conventional retailers. The predominant method of merchandising imported goods in the United States was at the time of the industry study through high-priced furniture, gift, specialty, or department stores. The importer-wholesaler served as the middleman between the conventional retailer and the foreign manufacturer. Conventional retailers carried a rather narrow line of imported goods, at a relatively high price. The more successful conventional retailer attempted to maximize his average inventory turnover ratio of imported goods in order to reduce the danger of markdowns.

Importer-wholesalers often provided retailers with working capital in the form of inventory, through trade credit with terms of 2/10 net 30. Many retailers extended their accounts payable to 60 days. In this 60-day time period they could sell the goods and pay their suppliers. The average retailer's markup was 50 percent (a 100 percent mark-on) on his selling price. The financial performance of the average retailer was much less impressive than that of the average importer-retailer. On the

---

[1] For example, if cost was $2 and mark-on was 45 percent, selling price = $2 + (.45 × $2) = $2.90.

other hand, capital requirements were lower for conventional retailers and they avoided the expense, risk, and time-consuming effort involved in direct importing.

In many important markets, conventional retailers were consistently undersold by the importer-retailer with a low-price/high-volume warehouse type of store. As a result, conventional retail buyers were under increasing pressure to develop a more sensitive feel for the pulse of their particular group of customers. They avoided the erosion of their 50 percent markup through excessive markdowns by concentrating on the fast-moving items offered by importer-wholesalers. The net result of this was that a typical retailer, who was inclined to expand his activities, could more effectively supervise the operation of additional stores rather than integrate backwards by taking on the importing function with its higher profitability. (See Exhibit 4 for growth of sales of a typical outlet.)

Importer-retailers. As the industry matured and management had become more sophisticated, retailers were beginning to bypass both jobbers and importer-wholesalers to bring goods directly into the country for resale in their stores. Importer-retailers bought directly from the manufacturers. Initially, their directly imported products were those items which made the most profit, but gradually firms expanded their activities to include virtually all the items offered in their stores. (See Exhibit 5 for survey of stores as of 1967.)

TABLE 1
Industry price structure for Egyptian brass candlestick, 1967 (similar items purchased two ways)

	Purchased through importer-wholesaler*	Purchased direct by importer-retailer
Purchase price f.o.b. dockside (foreign port)	$ .90	$1.00
Freight, duty, insurance	.40	.40
	$1.30	$1.40
Importer's mark-on 43 percent or a 30 percent markup	.56	–0–
Importer's selling price	$1.86	$1.40
Truck freight to retailer	.10	.10
Shelf cost at retail	$1.96	$1.50
Retail markup	1.96†	1.65‡
Sales price	$3.92	$3.15§

*Usually bought at discount.
†100 percent mark-on or 50 percent markup.
‡110 percent mark-on or 52 percent markup.
§Price advantage about 20 percent.

This direct buying abroad entailed numerous risks which were not present in ordering from importer-wholesalers in the United States. It forced retail managers to become proficient at the more complex job of estimating quantities, styles, and types of goods that could be moved through their stores at a profit. Importer-wholesalers, for example, had considerable knowledge as to what was selling well at retail (i.e., hot sellers) which he made available to conventional retailers. This information was quite valuable to retailers in reducing inventory risks. They could further reduce inventory risk by taking advantage of their ability to place small opening orders, with a two-week delivery, to test various items.

On the other hand, importer-retailers had to contend with an average delivery cycle of 120 days. Their purchases might amount to 90 to 180 days of sales for an individual product. In addition, they had to cope with foreign trade customs, languages, currency problems, government regulations, quality problems, short shipments, and financing of goods in transit.

Direct importer-retailers enjoyed a competitive price advantage over conventional retailers. Direct imports were lower priced with higher markups than items purchased from importer-wholesalers. The price policy of importer-retailers was to maintain prices lower than conventional outlets like department stores and furniture stores for comparable quality goods. The industry study disclosed that the average markup of importer-retailers was from 40 percent to 65 percent. Management felt that their typical customer was price-conscious but willing to pay a premium for quality products. However, most merchants continued to sell quality items at lower prices than those of conventional retailers. This pricing and merchandising strategy was justified as an effort to create repeat customers.

The original importer-retailer merchandising concept was to locate the store in a charming, quaint, or romantic setting that would reinforce the "bargain" atmosphere management was attempting to create. Most stores were located on the waterfront to give the impression that merchandise went directly from the ship through the store to the customer.

Cost Plus, a San Francisco store, was the prototype for the early dockside importer-retailers. Their early merchandising strategy was characterized in the trade as "imported items at bargain prices." At the time of the industry study, site location criteria had changed. Desirable locations were on heavily traveled arteries, near a major shopping center, convenient to the suburban shopper and her car. Adequate space for parking and single-level operations were also important. These suburban outlets were felt to build a higher sales per square foot revenue as opposed to the dockside outlets. Better suburban merchandisers were achieving a total inventory turn of four times a year, with in-store inventory turning as often as seven times a year. Less effective merchandisers were turning their entire inventory approximately one and one-half times a year. (See Exhibits 6 and 7 for sales and cost data.)

Industry trends.   In summary of their industry report Miller and Wilson pointed out the following:

> The importance of quality has grown for the importer-retailer to where it is now the most critical feature of the business. There has been commercial acceptance of the more unusual and unique products that would have been characterized as trash or too bizarre a decade ago. The consumer has shown a willingness to pay a premium price for quality items which she can use imaginatively in decorating her home.
>
> The consumer segment had been expanding at a rapid rate, thus making the total market much larger than it was. This growth is being sustained by increasing numbers of people with a background to appreciate these kinds of imported products and by the fact that the appeal of these items is slowly expanding to other groups who are emulating the taste-makers. Department stores have attempted to imitate the importer-retailer's merchandising concepts in recent months.
>
> Industry organization has begun to change within the last three years. Chain stores supported with substantial capital have started with the intent of taking over large market areas. Importer-retailers are actively seeking to combine the purchasing power of their individual stores to wield more power with the manufacturers. It seems likely that this emergence of cooperative buying organizations will materialize and become effective. The final outcome of these trends would be the exclusion of importer-wholesalers from much of their present markets in supplying many firms. Importer-wholesalers, however, would continue to supply gift shops, furniture stores, and perhaps department stores.
>
> Tripling of the present imported product volume would seem feasible over the next five to eight years.
>
> Within the importer-retailer segment of the industry some managements have learned to think about specific products, which are not basic to the needs of the typical consumer, in terms of a finite life cycle. Managers plan on stocking these items until they perceive the life cycle coming to an end.

The consumer.   Miller and Wilson pointed out in their report that the typical purchaser in the importer-retailer's outlet was a woman. Normally, she was a housewife with above-average education. Typically, her husband was a white-collar worker or a professional person. Family income was definitely above average. Most often she purchased items in the store for herself and her home. She did not buy the merchandise for gifts. The typical customer considered this type of imported merchandise store a "fun" place to shop for unique products where something new was always displayed.

In ranking the buying interest of their target consumer they highlighted variety and quality as the most important product features. In addition, their consumer seemed equally interested in shopping convenience and price. The report concluded that if these four consumer interests were satisfied, a decision to buy was often made on the first visit. Return visits were made to the store for repeat purchases. A constantly changing mix of merchandise within the store was underlined as critical to motivating repeat sales.

Designing the first retail outlet

In designing their first store Miller and Wilson were influenced by the example of one of the firms they studied on Long Island. Called World Wide Imports, it was experiencing rapidly growing sales. They were excited about the opportunity which they saw and said so in their industry report. "One such store (a typical importer-retailer) reports profit after taxes of $100,000 on $700,000 in sales, and an investment (total assets) of about $150,000, or a profit of 14.3 percent of sales, and a return on investment of 66 percent."

The two M.B.A.'s quickly settled on Washington, D.C., as their first store location. Washington provided a large potential market with more than two and one-half million people. It was located near a major port (Baltimore) which would minimize inland transportation costs. Jack Wilson was familiar with the Washington market, having lived there. But most important, as he put it, "There are about half a dozen retail outlets carrying part of the merchandise mix that we would stock in Washington. But there is essentially no direct competition in either (1) our price range or (2) our wide selection of merchandise. Although the existing conventional outlets had been able to achieve a relative degree of success . . . the territory is untapped for our type of operation." (See Exhibit 8 for demographic data.)

Site selection. The partners rejected downtown as a location for their first store because the area had been experiencing declining sales for many years. Parking downtown represented a critical problem to the consumer. Finally, rents for large stores were prohibitively high.

After examining the demographic data of suburban Washington, they selected Silver Spring as the location for their first store. The population within 10 minutes' driving time was approximately 150,000. Retail sales in 1965 totaled $152 million. The average family income was $7,600; school years completed, 12.3. The major shopping area in Silver Spring had two large regional shopping centers, one of which was Seven Corners. The partners chose a site near Seven Corners for their store. This site was a large fire-damaged skating rink. The site offered excellent parking and a 10,000-square-foot store on one level. In addition, there were approximately 5,000 square feet behind the store area to use as a warehouse. Commenting on the location Mr. Miller said, "Really, it was an ideal location. The warehouse, the offices, and the store would all be in one building. But more important, there is a great deal of traffic which goes right by our location going toward the shopping center." (See Exhibit 9, analysis of sales by store type.)

Merchandising policy. Quoting from their industry study, Mr. Miller and Mr. Wilson said, "Our basic merchandising concept is to sell quality imported goods at lower prices than the competition, such as it is, recognizing that for many products there will be no effective competition from other retailers in the area. Shopping must be an adventure to the consumer in our store. (10,000 square feet of merchandise would offer such a wide selection that most customers could not see all the items on one shopping trip.) The romance of imported goods and their countries of origin must be conveyed to the customer. All merchandise will be sold on a cash-and-carry basis. There will be no sales discounts to anyone."

Price policy. Their goal was to have a 100 percent mark-on on delivered costs as standard. (This is 50 percent markup.) At all times they intended to underprice gift shops and other types of stores which carried part of their line. The report stated, "It is significant that the most successful popular-price volume warehouse importer-retailers follow this strategy. However, we intend to use higher markups on items which we can get higher prices for without either diminishing our volume seriously or compromising our image." They cited the example of Combined Buying Power, Inc. (a combination buying group) which was frequently able to allow an importer-retailer as much as a 400 percent mark-on on the items it designed and had manufactured itself. Even with a 400 percent mark-on, an importer-retailer could continue to underprice the competition.

Buying policy. As a result of the industry study, the two M.B.A.'s gave up their initial idea of using foreign contacts and business school friends to introduce them to potential suppliers overseas. Instead, they resolved to find a partner in America to help them place their initial purchase orders. They projected an initial inventory of 1,500 products divided into 2,500 different items as a result of different sizes and colors. They estimated that they would place about 30 purchase orders averaging $2,500 apiece, resulting in an initial investment of approximately $50 per product displayed.

Their key procurement decision was to avoid placing any orders with domestic importer-wholesalers. They felt they would need the full 50 percent of their markup during their initial operating period to lower the break even. They intended that their initial orders would cover 180 days of sales. They felt this was necessary because of long (140-day) reorder cycles. This varied greatly, however, with goods from Europe coming within 30 days and goods from India and Saigon often taking as long as 360 days. Mr. Wilson said, "We knew that we were going to be placing orders in May to cover the Christmas selling season of 1967. We forecast sales during that first three months of approximately $110,000. And we knew that January, February, and March were the seasonal low points of this business. We were really just guessing that we were ordering 180 days inventory."

Terms. Both managers felt that the terms of payment offered by their suppliers were critical to their new enterprise's cash flow problems. They planned to use letters of credit to help them finance their business. A letter of credit was an agreement between a U.S. bank and a foreign bank. It stipulated that the U.S. bank guaranteed to transmit specific funds to the foreign bank to reimburse a manufacturer-exporter upon the American bank's receipt of shipping documents. These documents were airmailed from the foreign bank to the U.S. bank, usually 10 days after presentation of documents by the manufacturer. The U.S. bank then presented the documents to American Imports for payment. (At this point, goods were still at sea at least 20 days from port.) From Miller and Wilson's point of view, the terms of payment were very critical. Instead of paying the bank immediately upon receipt of shipping documents, they planned to use short-term financing, which called for payment 60 to 90 days after the goods arrived in the United States.

However, an important drawback to this type of financing was that importer-retailers were required to pay the shipping cost, the custom duty, and the insurance costs at the time the goods reached port. Routinely, goods reached port between 15 and 250 days after shipping documents were accepted. Commenting on this financial problem Mr. Miller said,

> Our biggest initial cash drain will be duty, freight, and insurance. We have to pay it when the ship reaches port. This total amounts to about 40 cents on every dollar of initial cost of foreign goods.[2]
>
> In attempting to secure the needed capital, we quickly realized we must limit the amount of our combined equity position; we decided to take 35 percent initially. However, we required the other equity holders to give us options to repurchase up to 50.1 percent of the stock. Initially, the stock would be sold for $5 a share and our options gave us the right to repurchase it at $50 a share.
>
> Our next step was to attract the owner-managers of World Wide Imports of New York, a Mr. Robinson and a Mr. Sabat, a Syrian national, into our venture as co-principals. They responded to us by saying, "We are very interested, but we cannot put any money into the venture." However, negotiations produced the following results:

---

[2]Initial cost was f.o.b. port of departure. F.o.b. is an abbreviation of "free on board," which means that the manufacturer bears the expenses of packaging the product and getting it on the ship.

1. They were willing to contribute a small amount of money to purchase their original shares of stock.
2. They felt they could help us obtain a revolving letter of credit to buy $55,000 worth of goods on a 90- to 120-day consignment basis.
3. They would provide us with goods, taking no commission for securing them, and furnish us with managerial and merchandise advice.
4. They would be willing to show their store and their financial statements to prospective investors to demonstrate the commercial success possible with such a venture.
5. They also would agree to take back all goods purchased through their sources at cost less back transportation costs in event of failure of our store.
6. They would also agree to put up a note for some undetermined amount of money should the venture get into a cash bind in the months after January 1968.

For these concessions, the two owners of World Wide Imports would receive 17½ percent of the original stock apiece. The position of chairman of the board went to Mr. Sabat. Mr. Robinson would receive the position of vice president in the organization. These positions would definitely not include any salary. It was planned that Mr. Sabat would co-sign the $55,000 revolving letter of credit. However, it was expected that the banks would see our right of selling goods back to World Wide Imports as critical to this agreement.

After concluding their agreement with World Wide Imports, Miller and Wilson determined to seek an additional $60,000 in the form of $57,000 in debt and $3,000 in equity.

The new partners. In their business policy report the two M.B.A.'s summarized the background of their new partners as follows:

Abdul-Aziz Sabat is a 27-year-old Syrian national. He first came to the United States about seven years ago to attend the University of California at Berkeley. While there he became involved in importing Indian handicraft products to the United States. Although he studied business administration for several years, he did not receive a degree. (See Exhibit 10, Mr. Sabat's balance sheet.)

He obviously has had some family money supporting some of his ventures although the extent of this is difficult to determine. However, he has been unable to produce ready cash to put into our present venture.

He said that he sees this venture as a means of gaining more stature or prestige with his suppliers overseas. He obviously is somewhat impressed with the mystique of a business school degree and sees the two of us as bringing some of the "management" into the organization while he and his partner have the buying skills required for success.

He has at times been slighted by other Americans. We think that this past discrimination has rankled him to the degree that he has a very strong desire to be the best in his field and show his past detractors.

Mr. Sabat is a shrewd trading individual with a fast ability with figures. He is a tough bargainer, as we have found out in dealing with him and watching him deal with others.

Both of us feel that he is ethical and trustworthy although we are taking every possible step to protect ourselves against a squeeze-out which could be quite attractive to him.

Charlie Robinson. Mr. Robinson does the merchandising in the store and actually performs the role of store manager—coming in early and leaving late when it closes. Although he is no mental slouch, he has little feeling for financial analysis, as he was rather nonplussed when we showed him our pro forma projections. He does have a feel for the merchandising aspects and the actual operating features of running a store. In appearance, he affects a Hollywood-type image by wearing sunglasses indoors with wild sports jackets. (This may be a carryover from working in southern California where this is a commonly accepted mode of dress in many levels of business.) Again, we both sensed that he is basically honest. He certainly is quite sensitive to anyone even possibly thinking that there might be a possible question of his honesty.

Because of their learning experience in the Management of New Enterprises course at the Eastern Business School, both partners were convinced of the necessity of getting a first-rate lawyer to formalize their relationship with the two prospective partners at World Wide Imports. As a result, they sought out a law firm with experience in organizing new ventures and start-up situations. This law firm helped them draw up the agreement which is presented as the Appendix to the case.

Finding the money

After making the decision to go ahead with their new enterprise, Mr. Miller and Mr. Wilson immediately began looking for equity funds. They contacted three fellow M.B.A.'s and presented their prospectus. All three showed enthusiasm for the project and promised to read it with care. Two weeks later they had failed to hear from any of the three, so they called a meeting. None of the three M.B.A.'s proved to be interested in attending. Wilson said, "Our classmates were a waste of time. But it was worse than that. We found out that one of the three M.B.A.'s we contacted tried to take our real estate in Silver Spring away from us. He got in touch with our landlord and attempted to lease the site we were counting on."

After some additional searching the partners contacted a medical student, Alan Cross, who appeared interested in investing $50,000 in their project for 25 percent equity position. A meeting was arranged in New York for Mr. Cross to see the World Wide Imports operation on Long Island. Miller and Wilson felt that one of their strong selling points was the apparent success of World Wide Imports. In addition, they invited another M.B.A., who had expressed interest in investing, to see the project. This M.B.A., Habib Faridi, was a Persian who had some experience with importing handicrafts into the United States.

The two prospective investors, Mr. Cross and Mr. Faridi, met the M.B.A.'s in New York City in late April. Mr. Cross' father arrived at the meeting in a chauffeur-driven limousine. He proceeded to relate several stories of multimillion-dollar deals and explanations of the various tax dodges which he employed to maximize his net income. The party left to examine the World Wide Imports store. At the store, Mr. Cross' father grilled Miller and Wilson extensively about their operations. About halfway through the meeting he left abruptly.

Alan Cross then demanded additional equity in the project for his investment. He also demanded that Miller and Wilson subordinate their debt to his. And he indicated that he wanted to receive convertible debt which would result in Miller and Wilson owning a mere 15 percent of the company. It appeared that Mr. Cross' father had been coaching his son extensively on what to ask for.

Commenting on the rather ugly situation that developed, Mr. Wilson said, "I was really mad at Mr. Cross. He'd known what the deal was all along. But he thought he had us over a barrel. In addition, he knew he was making a very bad impression on Mr. Faridi, who was also potentially a principal investor. We told him that he could take his new deal and get out."

The equity package.   In spite of the Long Island meeting, Mr. Faridi decided to become an investor. The partners made the decision to go ahead with the equity and debt package which they had been able to negotiate. In addition to their net contribution of $30,000, the most significant investor was Mr. Faridi, who was supplying $47,000 in debt and $2,500 in equity.

As part of the deal Mr. Sabat had promised to supply a loan of $20,000 by January 1, 1968, if it was required by the partners. In addition, he indicated that he could arrange a revolving letter of credit with a New York bank which would enable the company to buy goods and have physical possession of them for 120 days. The amount of this letter of credit would be $55,000. This gave the company almost the full use of the $55,000 worth of purchasing power because managers estimated that 75 percent of the goods would be sold at the end of a 90-day period.

The closing.   At the closing on June 2, several problems arose. Mr. Faridi indicated that he temporarily did not have the cash for his portion of the equity. As a result, Miller and Wilson lent him (on the basis of a gentleman's agreement and a handshake) his portion of the equity, which was $2,500. It was understood that as soon as he reached Iran, he would send a check for $50,000. Whereas Mr. Robinson had his $1,750, Mr. Sabat did not have this amount of cash and asked to be permitted to pay it in the following week. As a result, only four out of the six equity holders provided the necessary funds at the closing. After the closing, Mr. Faridi left for California to visit relatives on the way home to Iran.

TABLE 2
Proposed capital structure at June 2, 1967, closing

	Percent	Shares equity	Equity	Debt
Mr. Abdul-Aziz Sabat	17½	350	$ 1,750	–0–
Mr. Charles Robinson	17½	350	1,750	–0–
Mr. Jack Wilson	17½	350	1,750	$ 13,250
Mr. Steve Miller	17½	350	1,750	13,250
Mr. John Carter*	5	100	500	9,500
Mr. Habib Faridi	25	500	2,500	47,500
	100	2,000	$10,000	$ 83,500
Short-term debt:				
Revolving letter of credit				55,000
			$10,000	$135,000

*A local businessman.

On June 5, the Arab-Israeli war broke out. Miller and Wilson attempted to contact Mr. Faridi but without success. They began to become seriously worried because they had already placed approximately $15,000 in orders for merchandise for October deliveries. After normal efforts to contact him had failed, they resorted to telephoning his home in Iran. Faridi, when he was finally contacted, explained it like this to Miller, "I'm sorry, Steve, but I won't be able to provide you with the $50,000. My family is in construction and a freeze has been put on our assets. The government won't let anybody send any money out of the country."

In retrospect, they suspected that Mr. Faridi had never been a free agent. Because they understood the family structure and cultural traditions of the Mid-East, both men had questioned Mr. Faridi closely on his status as a free agent. They had gambled that because he was 29 years old and quite worldly, his statements were probably true. It was their eventual conclusion upon learning that no asset freeze had in fact existed, that he had simply been told by his family that an investment in American Imports was not a good one and that he should forget about it.[3]

[3] Mr. Faridi's 500 shares became treasury stock. Final equity positions were Miller, Wilson, Sabat, and Robinson, each with 350 shares or 23⅓ percent. Carter had 100 shares or 6⅔ percent. There were 1,500 shares outstanding.

Operating experience at World Wide Imports

The Persian's graceless exit from the venture left it with only $10,000 in capital. A lease had been drawn up by their lawyer for a 10,000-square-foot store in Silver Spring and they had already placed some orders with suppliers in foreign countries. Mr. Miller said, "Frankly, we were desperate. We had felt that we needed about $125,000 to finance our deal. That $40,000 looked awfully small. But it was then that Mr. Sabat really came through for us. He took us down to the National Bank in New York City and to our amazement we were able to arrange a $75,000 letter of credit facility, which was $20,000 more than we had planned."

Both partners were amazed at Mr. Sabat's ability to charm American bankers. Although his personal financial statement claimed a major ownership in an Indian manufacturing firm and an ownership position in a California importer-retailing outlet, these assets alone could not account for his skill and charm in dealing with bankers, according to both men. Mr. Miller reflected, "He seemed instinctively to sense what makes a banker tick. He was amazing. Before we knew what was happening, the banker was acting as if we were doing him a favor." In addition to the letter of credit, Mr. Sabat was able to negotiate a $25,000 line of credit at the Great Eastern Bank in Washington. He signed personally on this second source of short-term debt.

In late May Mr. Miller and Mr. Wilson began working in the Long Island store of World Wide Imports. It was agreed that in return for their help in running the store, the Syrian would assist them in placing their orders for the coming October 1 opening. Mr. Sabat felt that the two M.B.A.'s would be of great assistance to him in rationalizing his operation. As the summer progressed, the two M.B.A.'s received what they called "a liberal education in retailing."

An informal audit. Both M.B.A.'s were surprised to find that in eight months of operations of the Long Island store, there had never been a physical inventory. The gross margin that appeared on the store's operating statement was, by Mr. Sabat's admission, a "guess." About the first of July Mr. Wilson began to do an informal audit of the store's books. He uncovered information which caused him an increasing amount of concern. He found a note payable for $25,000 that was three months overdue. In addition, he found evidence that Mr. Sabat owned $1 million in madras shirts stored in a San Francisco warehouse. Apparently Mr. Sabat had entered the importing business while a student at Berkeley. In the early 1960s a strong demand for madras clothing developed on the West Coast. He had imported and sold madras shirts, making a considerable amount of money. However, his biggest shipment was aboard ship bound for San Francisco when the madras craze died. He refused to accept a sight draft when the ship arrived, claiming that the manufacturer owned the shirts. A lawsuit over the liability for the shirts was continuing at the time of Mr. Wilson's audit.

Mr. Wilson found evidence that Mr. Sabat had borrowed the money to enter his present enterprise from a family friend living in Europe. He was sending 16 percent interest on this loan to a numbered Swiss bank account. This was not listed as an interest expense on the income statement but was disguised as a buying commission. He also discovered that Mr. Sabat had formed a second corporation using merchandise supposedly purchased exclusively for the World Wide Imports Corporation. This act violated Mr. Sabat's banking covenants.

In addition, he was disturbed to find that Mr. Sabat had successfully "squeezed out" the operating partner in the California store of which he owned a portion. He suspected that the success of the Long Island store depended heavily on the cash flow generated by the California store. However, the West Coast partner had left that operation and he was afraid that it was destined to go downhill rapidly. Subsequently, he discovered that Mr. Robinson, Mr. Sabat's American partner in the Long Island store, was stealing from him. At the conclusion of his audit, he came across the fact that Mr. Sabat had created out of thin air the high value of the Indian company and the foreign real estate. He was in a condition of technical bankruptcy.

Remembering the surprise and shock of discovering the real nature of Mr. Sabat's business dealings, Mr. Miller said, "Abdul-Aziz was the most charming, intelligent, sophisticated person that you would ever want to meet. In the two months that we had worked with him on Long Island, he picked up every buzz word that we had learned at the Eastern Business School. To hear him talk now, you'd think he'd spent two years in the M.B.A. program. But his business dealings were far from honest."

About a week after Mr. Wilson had completed his informal audit of the company's books, Mr. Sabat came to the partners with an unexpected proposal. He said that the opportunity existed to increase their letter of credit to $100,000, but to do so he needed $25,000 in cash for a short period of time. He wondered if they might use $25,000 of the cash that they had accumulated for opening a new store to help increase their letter of credit. Because they were aware that Mr. Sabat actually needed the $25,000 to pay off a three-month overdue bank note, they casually refused his request.

Opening the first store. By early August it became painfully clear that the owner of the burned-out skating rink would not complete renovation of the property by October 1st. Faced with the arrival of some $105,000 in imported goods, the partners desperately began looking for another location. They finally found a store in Georgetown. Mr. Miller said, "We were fortunate to get into Georgetown. Really, it was our second choice.

We wanted 10,000 square feet on a single floor location, but we ended up with 4,500 square feet distributed through three floors of an old apartment building. Our rent in Silver Spring was to be $2.25 a square foot. The Georgetown rent was $4.80 a square foot. A separate warehouse was rented at $.90 a square foot. In addition, we were faced with the cost of renovating the space. We hadn't counted on any renovation costs."[4] (See Exhibits 11, 12, and 13 for pro forma data on the Georgetown store.)

Leasehold improvements

. The store location in Georgetown required major renovation. The partners made an agreement with the landlord to share the costs. Jack Wilson explained, "The leasehold improvement decision was our worst mistake. Our landlord agreed to pay $2,000 and we were going to pay $17,000. He suggested a contractor to us and we agreed. We failed to get bids or even a fixed-cost contract. This contractor performed miserably. About mid-September we had to take over and do his job. Steve and I literally worked days, nights, and weekends to get it finished. We finally opened, October 15 and it cost us $28,000. Fortunately we got a $10,000 improvement loan to cover part of the costs." (See Exhibit 14 for October 15 balance sheet.)

Opening day

Miller and Wilson opened for business on October 15. Although renovations were not complete and would not be for another week, they felt they needed the cash from sales. During the morning they sold $125 worth of merchandise. Just prior to noon Sabat arrived to see the store. The three men went to a nearby restaurant for lunch.

At lunch all three men had several drinks. Sabat drank somewhat more than either Miller or Wilson. Recounting the event, Jack Wilson said, "After getting quite a few beers under his belt, Abdul-Aziz began to complain about his deal with us. He exaggerated his contribution and was pretty sarcastic. And then he said he wanted 12 percent additional equity and a salary from our store. He actually threatened to go to our two bankers and take back his personal guarantee on the $75,000 letter of credit and our short-term $25,000 line of credit.

"I literally saw red. Steve sensed what was going on and tried to calm me down. But I came within inches of slugging him. The thing that infuriated me was that he waited until we were at our low point and then tried to squeeze us."

---

[4] At this point American Imports had (1) a letter of credit for $75,000, (2) a short-term 12-month line of credit for $25,000, (3) a leasehold improvement loan for $10,000, (4) stockholder notes for $36,000, and (5) equity of $7,500.

Alternatives

That same evening the partners sat down to consider their alternatives. Both were depressed by the prospect of losing control of their new store to Mr. Sabat. But they agreed that he could cause them serious damage with their bankers. In addition, they doubted if they could reveal the precarious position of Sabat's finances without discrediting their own honesty.

They felt that they had three obvious alternatives. They could sell out to an established chain of importer-retailers. They could go ahead and take their chances with the bankers by refusing Sabat's demands. Or they could give in to him and relinquish some more of their equity as well as salary. They began reviewing their situation with the idea of looking into any additional courses of action and then making a choice.

SUGGESTED QUESTIONS

1. What should Steve and Jack do now?
2. What are the prospects for the company? What will determine how successful it will be?
3. What is Steve's and Jack's bargaining position?

EXHIBIT 1
American Imports
Résumé of Steven R. Miller

Married   6ft.; 170 lbs.   Excellent health

Employment	**EAST/WEST IMPORTING COMPANY**
	Cambridge, Mass.
1966–67	Founded and managed this export business. Primary trade was with several companies in Thailand and Hong Kong. Company acted as export agent for American products.
	STATES MARINE LINES New York, N.Y.
Summer 1966	Assistant to the president, developed a real estate diversification program. Analyzed and assisted in negotiating specific investment proposals. Appraised and analyzed internal marketing studies on proposed new services.
	U.S. ARMY, CORPS OF ENGINEERS
1960–65	Captain, U.S. Army, Corps of Engineers. Served as Assistant Executive to the Chief of Engineers, Battalion Adjutant and as Company Commander. Acted as personal assistant to General William Cassidy, Chief of Engineers. Handled correspondence and public relations. Planned and coordinated administrative and operational functions with Congressional, Department of the Interior and related civilian and military agencies. As Battalion Adjutant in Thailand, budgeted, programmed, and administered the $1.5 million operational budget of a separate Army construction battalion. Constructed 15 miles of two-lane, asphaltic concrete highway in Thailand. Received Army Commendation Medal for distinguished service in Thailand.
Education	**EASTERN GRADUATE SCHOOL OF BUSINESS ADMINISTRATION**
1965–67	Received M.B.A. degree, June 1967. Ranked in the top third of the class after one year. Member of finance, marketing, real estate, and international business clubs. Emphasis on marketing, finance, and management information systems.
	UNITED STATES MILITARY ACADEMY
	West Point, N.Y.
1956–60	Bachelor of science degree in engineering. Dean's list, member of mathematics, debate, Russian and Spanish clubs.
Military	Completed military service.
References	On request.

EXHIBIT 2
American Imports
Résumé of Jack C. Wilson

Married, two children	5ft.10in.; 160 lbs.
Excellent health	

Employment Summer 1966	RAYTHEON COMPANY Lexington, Mass. Acquisitions planning staff member. Financial and market analyses, industry studies, and evaluation of specific companies for the purpose of recommending acquisitions. Assignments frequently resulted in presentations to top management. Subsequent to summer work, performed special assignments as a consultant.
Summer 1965	U.S. INFORMATION AGENCY, American Embassy, Beirut, Lebanon Director of a U.S. State Department-sponsored training program for Lebanese teachers.
Part time 1964–65	IRANO-AMERIC ECONOMIC CONSULTANTS, INC. Teheran, Iran Conducted field study and authored market research report concerning the development of Iranian handicraft exports. Ghost writer for U.S. A.I.D. official, authored several reports concerning Iranian agri-business.
1962–64	PEACE CORPS Iran As a volunteer taught English at University of Teheran, Teheran, Iran and Karaj Agricultural College, Karaj, Iran. Organized extracurricular student activities, including a visiting lecturer series, a technical agricultural publication, and special courses. Extensive travel in Middle East and Indian subcontinent. Fluent Persian.
1961–62	HARVARD UNIVERSITY—M.I.T. JOINT CENTER FOR URBAN STUDIES Publishing assistant in charge of subscriber correspondence and nationwide circulation of international development and urban study publications to universities and other institutions.
Education 1965–67	EASTERN GRADUATE SCHOOL OF BUSINESS ADMINISTRATION Received M.B.A. degree, June 1967. Major courses included marketing, finance, and international business, in addition to required and general curriculum. Member of marketing, finance, and international business clubs. Recipient of competitive Eastern Business School Peace Corps Fellowship.

EXHIBIT 2 (continued)

1964–65	FULBRIGHT SCHOLAR Teheran, Iran Awarded Fulbright grant by Department of State for study of Persian language and Iranian land reform.
1958–62	HARVARD UNIVERSITY Bachelor of arts degree, June 1962. History major. Member of International Relations Council, Latin American Affairs Association, Harvard Glee Club, Winthrop House Music Society, and Phillips Brooks House. Active in intramural sports.
Military	Permanent deferment due to marital status.
References	On request.

EXHIBIT 3
American Imports
Import data* (in \$ millions)

	1951	1958	1959	1961	1962	1964	1965	1966
Total imports (in \$ billions)	10.8	12.7	15.0	14.3	16.2	18.7	21.3	25.6
Wooden and upholstered furniture	n.a.†	16.3	n.a.	n.a.	n.a.	39.5	49.3	60.7
Toys, games, dolls	n.a.	29.0	n.a.	n.a.	n.a.	69.0	82.0	90.0
Glassware	2.6	8.0	11.0	11.5	13.7	18.0	20.5	27.0
Enameled houseware utensils	0.4	1.1	2.0	1.3	1.9	6.0	5.0	3.5
Candles	0.1	0.6	0.9	1.3	1.8	2.2	2.4	3.2
Wood-stemmed matches	0.7	0.8	0.6	0.8	0.8	0.9	1.0	1.5
Artificial flowers	1.7	10.1	17.0	29.0	34.2	46.7	42.0	40.0
Chinaware	13.1	22.8	28.6	26.6	31.2	33.2	36.4	43.0
Earthenware	10.6	22.2	23.2	25.5	27.5	33.3	34.0	42.0
Wool floor coverings	11.2	28.0	41.3	47.1	45.8	38.2	34.9	33.0

*Worthwhile noting from the items selected is the fact that even during the two economic recessions during this period, imports of these items continued to grow rapidly. A tentative conclusion might be that demand for these types of items is not particularly sensitive to fluctuations in the economy. Declines in enameled utensils and artificial flowers are largely explained by the entry of American producers into a market dominated by foreign producers. Floor coverings have had a market erosion by the rapid acceptance of synthetic fibers, mostly of U.S. origin.

†n.a. signifies that comparable totals were not available in the sources.

Source: The primary sources for these statistics were the *Industrial Outlook for 1967* and the various import publications of the Department of Commerce.

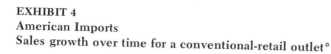

EXHIBIT 4
American Imports
Sales growth over time for a conventional-retail outlet*

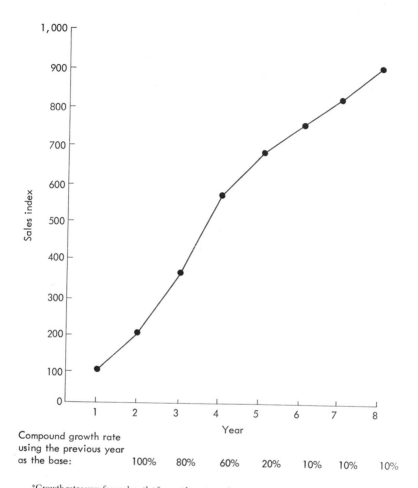

*Growth rates vary for each outlet for a wide variety of reasons. This graph depicts the general sales growth for a "typical" outlet, representing a composite of those that have been observed in the industry. First year sales are given an index of 100.

Source: This graph is a composite of the operating histories of a wide selection of firms in the industry as obtained through in-depth interviews. The authors are grateful to those firms who were willing to release such data. Naturally, this graph is dependent for its accuracy upon the honesty of these individual contributors.

EXHIBIT 5

American Imports

History of the growth in numbers of high-volume, popular price, warehouse-type, importer-retailer stores

Year	Name of company and location	Stores opened during year	Stores closed during year	Stores in operation, end of year
1958	Cost Plus, San Francisco	1		1
1959	Cost Plus (branch), Hayward, Calif.	1		2
1960	Cost Plus (branch) Haywood, Calif.		1*	1
1961	Waterfront Sales, Inc., Atlanta, Georgia			2
1962	Pier One, San Mateo and Richmond, Calif.	2		4
1963	World Imports, Portland, Ore., Dockside Sales, Baltimore; Pier One, Fort Worth and Dallas, Texas	4		8
1964	Price Less, Los Angeles; Pier One, San Antonio, Houston (2), San Jose, and San Leandro, Calif.	6		4
1965	Pier One, Los Angeles (3), Sacramento, Denver, Dallas, Houston	7	2†	19
1966	Cost Plus, San Mateo, Calif.; World Wide Imports, Inc., L.I., N.Y.; Pier One, Phoenix, Ariz., San Diego, Calif.	4		23
1967‡ ...	Pier One, Kansas City, Mo., and St. Louis, Mo.	2		25

Estimated total industry sales in 1966: $10.8 million.

*Cost Plus closed its Hayward branch due to poor results caused by poor management after only 12 months in operation.

†Pier One closed one of its Dallas stores and one of its Houston stores due to poor location and insufficient sales.

‡As of April 1967. In the summer of 1967, World Wide Imports will open a store in Orange County, Calif., and another store in White Plains, New York. Pier One will open 3 stores in the Chicago area before the end of 1967, and add 5 leased department operations to the 10 they currently have in department stores in the Southeast. Adding our operation in Washington, there will be a total of 31 stores of this type in the United States by year end.

EXHIBIT 6
American Imports
Sales growth over time for a typical high-volume, popular price, warehouse-type, importer retailer store*

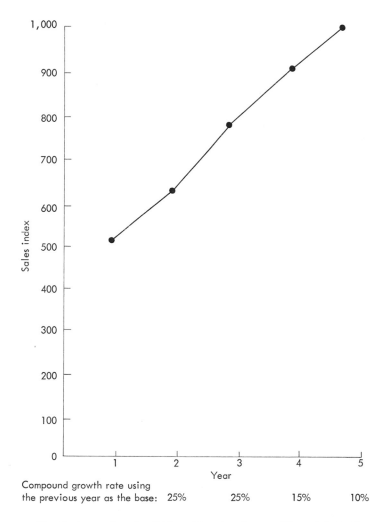

Compound growth rate using the previous year as the base:	25%	25%	15%	10%

*Growth rates vary for each outlet for a wide variety of reasons. This graph depicts the general sales growth for a typical outlet, representing a composite of those high-volume, popular price, warehouse-type, importer-retailer stores who released sales data or whose sales over time were obtained from reliable independent sources. First year sales are given an index of 500, to reflect the fact that in their first year of operation, these types of outlets typically achieve five times the sales volume of the more traditional dockside outlets.

Source: This graph is a composite of the operating histories of several firms in the industry that fit the category described as "high-volume, popular price, warehouse-type, importer-retailing." The authors are grateful to those firms who were willing to release such data. To the extent possible, these figures were checked with independent reliable sources and the authors believe them to be reliable.

EXHIBIT 7
American Imports
Income statement: Showing ranges of performance for selected expense categories for the industry* (importer-retailers)

	Typical	*Industry range*
Sales	100%	
Cost of goods†	60	(45% to 69%)‡
Gross profit	40%	(31 to 55)
Operating Expenses:		
Labor and salaries 8%		(6 to 18)
Rent 4		(2 to 10)
Advertising 7		(0 to 12)
Utilities 2		(0.1 to 3.0)
Insurance 1		(0.5 to 1.3)
Professional services 2		(1.0 to 3.9)
Travel 2		(0.4 to 4.0)
Interest 1		(0.1 to 1.0)
Depreciation of fixed assets 2		(0.1 to 3.0)
Office supplies, maintenance, and		
other expense 2		(0.3 to 2.0)
Total Operating Expenses	31	(20 to 45)
Net Profit before Taxes	9%	(–3 to 30)

*The operating performance of each retail outlet varies by reason of the numerous characteristics that make each a unique operation. Typical performance is shown first, representing a composite of the expenses reported by contributing firms, followed by the ranges that were encountered.
†Includes the cost of transportation to the store.
‡Figures shown in parentheses are not additive. They simply represent the ranges encountered.
Source: This income statement is based on ranges of performance as indicated by the operating histories of a wide selection of firms in the industry as obtained in in-depth interviews. The authors are grateful to those firms who were willing to release such data. Naturally, this income statement is dependent for its accuracy upon the honesty of these individual contributors.

EXHIBIT 8 American Imports

Demographic data on the 29 standard metropolitan statistical areas in the United States with populations above or near 1 million in the 1960 census

SMSA	U.S. rank in population	Total population	Population per sq. mi.	Median income	Median school years completed	Number of high-volume, popular price, warehouse-type, importer-retailer stores
Atlanta, Ga.	24	1,017,188	590	$5,758	11.1	1
Baltimore, Md.	12	1,727,023	956	6,199	9.6	1
Boston, Mass.	7	2,589,301	2,672	6,687	12.1	—
Buffalo, N.Y.	15	1,306,957	824	6,455	10.5	—
Chicago, Ill.	3	6,220,913	1,675	7,342	10.9	—
Cincinnati, Ohio-Kentucky	21	1,071,624	1,468	6,318	10.3	—
Cleveland, Ohio	11	1,796,595	2,611	6,962	11.1	1
Dallas, Texas	20	1,083,601	297	5,925	11.8	1
Denver, Colo.	26	929,383	254	6,551	12.2	1
Detroit, Mich.	5	3,762,360	1,915	6,825	10.8	2
Houston, Texas	16	1,243,158	727	6,040	11.3	1
Kansas City, Mo.-Kansas	22	1,039,493	633	6,317	11.9	4
Los Angeles-Long Beach, Calif.	2	6,742,696	1,393	7,066	12.1	—
Miami, Fla.	25	935,047	455	5,348	11.5	—
Milwaukee, Wis.	17	1,194,290	1,502	6,995	11.1	—
Minneapolis-St. Paul, Minn.	14	1,482,030	702	6,840	12.1	1
New York, N.Y.	1	10,694,633	4,977	6,548	10.7	—
Newark, N.J.	13	1,689,420	2,420	7,149	11.1	—
Paterson-Clifton-Passaic, N.J.	18	1,186,873	2,780	7,431	11.0	—
Philadelphia, Pa.-N.J.	4	4,342,897	1,224	6,433	10.5	—
Pittsburgh, Pa.	8	2,405,935	788	5,954	10.6	—
Portland, Ore.-Wash.	28	821,897	225	6,340	12.0	1
St. Louis, Mo.-Ill.	9	2,060,103	646	6,275	9.6	1
San Bernardino-Riverside-Ontario, Calif.	30	809,782	30	5,890	11.8	—
San Diego, Calif.	23	1,033,011	243	6,545	12.1	1
San Francisco-Oakland, Calif.	6	2,783,359	840	7,092	12.1	3
San Jose, Calif.	29	642,315	493	7,417	12.2	2
Seattle, Wash.	19	1,107,213	262	6,896	12.2	1
Washington, D.C.-Md.-Va.	10	2,001,897	1,348	7,577	12.3	—

EXHIBIT 9

American imports

Sales volume per square foot of importer-retailers* (data collected March 30, 1967)

Single stores	Location and merchandising type	Estimated annual sales	Estimated annual gross margin, 52.5%	Sq. ft. in store	Total annual sales per sq. ft. of retail space	Age of store
Price Less Imports, Inc., ... Los Angeles, Calif.	Located on high-speed, multilane artery near shopping center, with excellent parking, single story, in affluent, densely populated area.	$1,150,000	$602,000	15,000	$76.50	3 yrs.
World Wide Imports, Inc., ... Long Island, N.Y. (Mr. Sabat's store)	Ditto	652,000	342,000	9,600	68.00	15 mos.
Dockside Sales, Inc., ... Baltimore, Md.	Located on waterfront, with difficult access, not near shopping area, excellent parking, multiple story and barge, in poor, thinly populated area.	275,000	144,000	5,500	50.00	4 yrs.
Waterfront Sales, Inc., ... Atlanta, Ga.	Ditto, except there is no barge, there are quite a few other shops, parking is inadequate, and area is being redeveloped.	427,000	225,000	9,000	47.50	6 yrs.
World Imports, Inc., ... Portland, Ore.	Located on waterfront, with difficult access, not near shopping area, inadequate parking, single story, in poor but redeveloping area.	400,000	210,000	10,000	40.00	4 yrs.

*Information volunteered by owner/managers. Accuracy not verifiable in most cases.

Source: Business policy report.

EXHIBIT 10
American Imports
Abdul-Aziz Sabat's personal financial statement
(June 15, 1967)

U.S. Assets:

Cash	$ 5,000
Stocks	15,000
Real estate......................	50,000
Jewelry	25,000
	$95,000

Liabilities:

Personal note	$ 4,500
U.S. net worth	$90,500

Foreign Assets:

Land (market $400,000) at cost (Syria)	$150,000
Clothing factory (net worth) (India)	300,000
Marketable securities at cost (Syria)	50,000
Foreign Net Worth......................	$500,000
Total Net Worth	$590,500

Source: Personal files.

EXHIBIT 11
American Imports
Breakdown analysis (September 30, 1967)

	Imported directly monthly	Percent	Conventional retail methods, purchased from importer-wholesaler	Percent
Breakeven Sales	$17,560	100.0	$26,603	100.0
Variable Costs:				
Cost (f.o.b. maker)	5,619	32.0 ⎫	16,653	62.6
Duty, freight insurance............	2,248	12.8 ⎭		
U.S. truck freight	562	3.2	904	3.4
Markdowns and discounts	351	2.0	266	1.0
Contribution	$ 8,780	50.0	$ 8,780	33.0*

Fixed Costs:		
Wages	$1,985	(2 full-time, 2 part-time clerks)
Miller and Wilson	1,500	(2 full-time, 1 part-time stock boys; 1 window display girl)
Store rent	1,800	(4,500 @ $4.80 per sq. ft.)
Warehouse rent..................	370	(5,000 @ $ .90)
Heat, light, and power	750	(higher in winter months)
Insurance	240	(detailed schedule, $2,880 per year)
Office supplies	150	(estimate)
Telephone	200	(estimate)
Maintenance and repairs	175	(estimate, janitor, etc.)
Truck expense..................	225	(1,500 miles x 15¢ per mile)
Travel and entertainment	300	(air travel and lodging)
CPA and bookkeeping	315	(bookkeeper 2 nights a week @ $30.00)
Interest	440	(7% on $75,000)
Interest bondholders	180	(6% x $36,000 in notes)
Miscellaneous	150	(contingency)
Net Fixed Costs	$8,780	

Discretionary Costs:	
Newspaper advertising (monthly) ..	$3,000

Start-up Costs:	
Advertising and promotion	$ 3,000
Organizing expenses	5,500
Leasehold improvements	28,000
Accrued interest	1,690
	$38,190

*Conventional-retailers' markup was 50 percent of sales price. If American Imports purchased inventory from an importer-wholesaler their cost of goods sold would go up. In order to *continue* to underprice conventional retailers they would have to lower their markup to 33.3 percent.

EXHIBIT 12
American Imports
Pro forma income statement
Georgetown store 4,500 square feet, September 30, 1967 ($000)

	Startup			Total 1967	15 percent*			20 percent			25 percent			40 percent			Total 1968
	Oct.	Nov.	Dec.		Jan.	Feb.	Mar.	Apr.†	May	June	July	Aug.	Sept.	Oct.	Nov.	Dec.	
Sales Georgetown	10.0	40.0	50.0	100.0	10.0	15.0	20.0	20.0	30.0	30.0	30.0	35.0	25.0	40.0	50.0	65.0	370.0
Cost of goods sold (50 percent)	5.0	20.0	25.0	50.0	5.0	7.5	10.0	10.0	15.0	15.0	15.0	17.5	12.5	20.0	25.0	32.5	185.0
Gross margin	5.0	20.0	25.0	50.0	5.0	7.5	10.0	10.0	15.0	15.0	15.0	17.5	12.5	20.0	25.0	32.5	185.0
Operating expense	6.0	9.0	9.2	24.2	8.8	8.8	8.8	8.8	8.8	9.0	9.2‡	9.2	9.0	8.8	9.2§	9.4	107.8
Amortization of leasehold improvements $466/month	.5	.5	.5	1.5	.5	.5	.5	.5	.5	.5	.5	.5	.5	.5	.5	.5	6.0
Net operating expense	6.5	9.5	9.7	25.7	9.3	9.3	9.3	9.3	9.3	9.5	9.7	9.7	9.5	9.3	9.7	9.9	113.8
Advertising	3.0	2.0	2.0	7.0	.7	.7	.7	.7	1.5	1.5	1.5	1.5	2.0	2.0	3.0	3.0	18.3
Total Expense	9.5	11.5	11.7	32.7	10.0	10.0	10.0	10.0	10.8	11.0	11.2	11.2	11.5	11.3	12.7	12.9	132.1
Operating profit before tax	⟨4.5⟩	8.5	13.3	17.3	⟨5.0⟩	⟨2.5⟩	-0-	-0-	4.2	4.0	3.8	6.3	1.0	8.7	12.3	19.6	52.9

*Rules of thumb in the industry on *seasonality* of sales.
†April and September were acknowledged poor months in the trade.
‡Air conditioning caused significant increase in electric bills.
§Extra sales clerks added at Christmas season.
Source: Personal files, Steve Miller.

EXHIBIT 13 American Imports

Pro forma cash budget (September 30, 1967)

	Sept. Prior	Oct.	Nov.	Dec.	Jan.	Feb.	Mar.	Apr.	May	June	July	Aug.	Sept.	Oct.	Nov.	Dec.
Inventory Transactions:																
Orders placed	75.0*	25.0†		30.0	25.0	25.0		30.0	25.0	25.0	25.0		10.0	25.0		
Goods received	50.0	10.0	100.0	—					30.0	10.0	10.0	10.0	30.0	10.0	25.0	—
Landed costs	20.0		20.0	—					12.0				12.0		10.0	—
Inventory on hand	70.0	91.0	100.0	80.0	55.0	50.0	42.5	32.5	62.5	82.5	102.5	87.5	112.0	134.5	114.5	89.5
Cost of goods sold	-0-	5.0	20.0	25.0	5.0	7.5	10.0	12.0	15.0	15.0	15.0	17.5	12.5	20.0	25.0	32.5
Net inventory	70.0	86.0	80.0	55.0	50.0	42.5	32.5	20.5	47.5	67.5	87.5	70.0	99.5	114.5	89.5	57.0
Cash in:																
Capital stock	6.0															
Long-term notes	36.0§	10.0–														
Short-term line credit		25.0#			25.0#											
Cash sales		10.0	40.0	50.0	10.0	15.0	20.0	20.0	30.0	30.0	30.0	35.0	25.0	40.0	50.0	65.0
Total Cash in	42.0	45.0	40.0	50.0	35.0	15.0	20.0	20.0	30.0	30.0	30.0	35.0	25.0	40.0	50.0	65.0
Cash out:																
Landed cost (D.F. and interest)	20.0	10.0	9.0						12.0	10.0	10.0		12.0	10.0		
Operations	-0-	6.0	9.0	9.2	8.8	8.8	8.8	8.8	9.0	9.0	9.2	9.4	9.2	9.0	9.2	9.4
Leasehold improvements	12.0	12.0	5.0	1.0	1.0	1.0										
Organization cost	2.0	5.0														
Bank acceptances		—	—‡	10.0**	45.0**	25.0**					25.0	30.0	25.0		25.0	25.0
Line of credit	3.0	3.0		25.0#												
Advertising		5.0	2.0	2.0	.7	.7	.7	.7	1.5	1.5	1.5	1.5	2.0	2.0	3.0	3.0
Lease deposit								5.0								
Taxes																
Total Cash out	37.0	41.0	16.0	47.2	55.5	35.5	9.5	14.5	22.5	20.5	45.7	40.9	48.2	21.0	37.2	37.4
Net Cash Flow	5.0	4.0	24.0	2.8	⟨20.5⟩	⟨20.5⟩	10.5	5.5	7.5	9.5	⟨15.7⟩	⟨5.9⟩	⟨23.2⟩	19.0	12.8	27.6
Cash Balance	5.0	9.0	33.0	35.8	15.3	⟨5.2⟩	5.3	10.8	18.3	27.8	12.1	6.2	⟨17.0⟩	2.0	14.8	42.4
Extra short-term bank loan (plug)	—	—	—	—	—	+5.2	—	—	—	—	—	—	+17.0	—	—	—

*This is $75,000 letter of credit.
†Assume that goods reach port four months after they are ordered.
‡Assume time draft matures 240 days from order placement.
§Notes to equity owners.
–Leasehold improvement loan.
**Time drafts mature bankers' acceptance agreement.
#Short-term line of credit.

EXHIBIT 14
American Imports
Balance sheet (October 15, 1967)

ASSETS

Current Assets:

Cash	$ 2,000
Accounts receivable*	1,750
Inventory	70,000†
	$ 73,750

Fixed Assets:

Leasehold improvements	$ 28,000

Other Assets:

Leasehold deposit	$ 5,000
Organization expense	1,000
	$ 6,000
Net	$107,750

LIABILITIES

Current trade payable	$ 5,000
Notes payable (banker's acceptances)	50,000
Bank loan	10,000
	$ 65,000
Notes—stockholders	36,000
Equity	7,500
Retained deficit	($ 750)
Net	$107,750

*This was Sabat's portion of the equity.

†This represented $50,000 in initial cost f.o.b. port of departure and $20,000 freight, insurance, and duty (landed cost). The firm had an additional $35,000 on order ($25,000 f.o.b. + $10,000 landed costs).

Source: Personal files.

APPENDIX
American Imports

AGREEMENT made this 1st day of June 1967, by and among Abdul-Asiz Sabat, Charles Robinson, Neptune Imports, Inc.[1] (NI), a New York corporation with a principal place of business at 2763 13th Avenue, Manhattan, New York, and American Imports, Inc. (AI), a Virginia corporation with a principal place of business at 73 Burnside Street, Georgetown, Virginia:

WITNESSETH THAT:

WHEREAS, Abdul-Aziz Sabat and Charles Robinson are the directors, principal officers, and principal stockholders of NI; and

WHEREAS, Abul-Aziz Sabat and Charles Robinson are subscribing for shares of common stock in AI by a subscription agreement of even date herewith; and

WHEREAS, four other individuals, namely Habib Faridi, John Carter, Steve Miller, and John Wilson, are each subscribing for shares of common stock of AI and are, in addition, agreeing to purchase the six percent (6%) notes of AI in varying principal amounts aggregating Eighty-three Thousand Five Hundred Dollars ($83,500);[2] and

WHEREAS, all common stock of AI is to be issued subject to restrictions on transfer thereof, all common stockholders have preemptive rights with respect to further issuance of any class of AI stock, and by agreements by and between the six initial subscribers and AI no additional stock of any class is to be issued at this time; and

WHEREAS, AI is in need of management advice and further financial support in order to promote its business and realize financial success for itself and its stockholders;

NOW, THEREFORE, in consideration of these premises and the mutual convenants herein expressed, the parties hereto agree as follows:

1. Abdul-Aziz Sabat and Charles Robinson jointly and severally hereby agree to procure (at no cost or expense to AI) an irrevocable letter of credit, issued or confirmed by a bank with offices in Boston, Massachusetts, or in New York City, New York, naming AI as beneficiary, being Fifty Thousand Dollars ($50,000) in total amount, and being acceptable in its terms to AI. Credit established under such letter of credit shall be maintained by Abdul-Aziz Sabat and Charles Robinson for a period of five years from the date of this Agreement.

2. AI hereby agrees to reimburse Abdul-Aziz Sabat and Charles Robinson for all drafts upon the letter of credit described in paragraph 1, such reimbursement to be made not sooner than ninety (90) days nor later than one hundred twenty (120) days from the date of payment of such drafts.

3. Abdul-Aziz Sabat and Charles Robinson jointly and severally agree to loan to AI on or after January 1, 1968, the principal sum of Twenty Thousand Dollars ($20,000), provided, however, that AI, by action of its board of directors, authorizes such borrowing and delivers to the lender or lenders its six percent (6%) subordinated note in the form of Exhibit 1 hereto.

---

[1]Neptune Imports was the corporate name of World Wide Imports.
[2]Habib Faridi did not complete his part of the deal, thus reducing the debt to $36,000.

4. Abdul-Aziz Sabat and Charles Robinson jointly and severally agree that they will cause NI, or any subsidiary or affiliate or NI, or any other procurement organization which they now control or may control in the future, to procure and buy goods for the use of and at the direction of AI. Such goods shall be shipped directly to AI at such locations as AI shall from time to time indicate, and shall be billed to AI at the same price as actual cost to NI.

5. However, nothing contained in this Agreement is intended to restrict or limit in any way the right of AI to procure goods from or through any other source, if such procurement is deemed to be in the best interests of AI.

6. AI hereby agrees to pay for all goods procured in accordance with paragraph 4 upon delivery of such goods to AI. Payment will be made to NI or such other organization described in paragraph 4, by check of AI or by draft upon the letter of credit described in paragraph 1.

7. Deleted.

8. NI hereby grants to AI the use of its trade name and style "World Wide Imports" in connection with all AI operations, excepting only the use of such trade name and style in those locations in which NI does business under such trade name and style as of the date of this Agreement.

9. Abdul Aziz Sabat and Charles Robinson hereby agree to provide when and as requested by AI or its officers management advice and consulting services to AI and to its officers, directors, and employees for a period of three years from the date of this Agreement and to apply their best efforts to the promotion of the business of AI and to its financial success.

10. Abdul-Aziz Sabat and Charles Robinson hereby agree that in the event of any default in respect of any of the covenants and undertakings made by them in this Agreement, then the common stock of AI of each of them shall be forfeited to AI for which stock AI shall refund the original subscription price of Five Dollars ($5) per share less their pro-rata share of the organizational expenses of AI.

IN WITNESS WHEREOF, the parties have set their hands and seals to this Agreement as of the day and year first above written.

The Executive Town House

Late on a Wednesday evening during the early part of April 1969, Tom Kershaw and Jack Veasy were reviewing their plans for financing an initial venture which they hoped would eventually become a chain of public town houses in major metropolitan areas. The object of their initial effort was the purchase, renovation, and operation of a restaurant-bar-hotel, the Hampshire House, which was located in downtown Boston. Although they thought their progress to date on raising money had been good, they were still in the process of analysis and negotiations which had yet to produce any funds and which was requiring a major portion of their time. Both men were in agreement that the initial financing was too important to the success of the venture and to them personally for them to neglect it. The closing date was May 1, about a month away, at which time Tom and Jack would lose their $10,000 down payment if they had not secured the necessary financing. But they also felt that there was an urgent need to plan and prepare for changes they wanted to make in the facilities and operations so the venture would be viable from the outset.

Tom Kershaw and Jack Veasy

Tom Kershaw and Jack Veasy first met as members of the same section at the Harvard Business School in the fall of 1960. During the first year they remained just casual acquaintances and went about their separate ways. During the second year they came to know each other better when they were both members of a 10-man seminar. However, it was not until two years after they left the school that they became good friends. When he graduated in 1962, Jack joined a Cambridge consulting firm organized by a professor at the Harvard Business School. Tom went to work for a

50

large chemical company as a salesman and field representative investigating the market potential of products in various states of development. By 1964 he left the company to work for a small manufacturing company in the Boston area where the two men met again and subsequently roomed together for about a year on Beacon Hill.

In 1965 Tom took over the daily operations of a Sugarbush Valley ski lodge which he and a group of friends had bought in the town of Warren, Vermont. About this same time Jack had left his job and with a friend had started a consulting firm. They began work on two large contracts which called for designing computer systems and improving the operational control systems for the client. Jack contributed experience in operational management; his partner contributed experience in building computer models. In 1966 Jack went to Denmark to organize and supervise a contract the new firm had obtained with a large Danish company. When the contract was completed, he decided to remain there and expand the operations of the consulting firm in that country. He felt most European companies had not developed modern management techniques and therefore were potential customers for general business consulting skills which he and his small staff could provide.

In late 1968 Tom and Jack met again in Boston. Tom returned in late 1966 to join the new product development group of a medium-sized development and production firm. By the fall of 1968 it seemed to him that his job, which originally was to be a responsible line position in a critical area of the company, had gradually been made a staff position and he rapidly became disenchanted. He commented:

> The more I thought about it, the more it became clear to me that I was probably going to be most satisfied in a situation where I was doing something on my own or for a very small group in which I had an interest. Ever since high school I have run most organizations I have been with. I finally concluded that I would rather be doing something over which I had a lot of control, even if it was only a very small operation. I was happy with the job, but I felt I could make more money on my own.

During their discussions, Jack observed that his consulting operations in Denmark had reached a point where he would have to commit himself totally to the ideals and ways of life of Denmark if he wanted to continue to grow. Having decided that he did not want to do this, he felt he had to return to the United States.

> I just did not want to spend my life in Denmark, and that's what I felt it was coming to. And I had also concluded by then that I wanted to get out of consulting and into an operating company where I could leverage my skills into a large capital gain. I really didn't care what kind of an operation I went into, as long as it could be packaged and repeated, and eventually be taken public. In a small consulting business there is little leverage; you only make money on the days you work.

In the fall of 1968, the two men pursued various opportunities available to each of them. Tom talked seriously with a group of friends who were about to start a company which would initially provide labels and tape to hospitals and later, after a sales organization had been developed, expand their product line. For joining as a salesman and with the plan that he become sales manager, Tom would have received 3–5 percent of the equity.

Meanwhile Jack followed numerous leads. One idea was to join a conglomerate's management team which would take over a poorly managed company. Another was the formation of a highly computerized distribution company for dental supplies. The three principals (including Jack) would have each owned one third of this company. One of the principals was familiar with the industry and owned a dental products manufacturing company.

The town house concept

During the latter part of October 1968, Tom decided to try to interest Jack in the idea of the two of them going into the business of hotel/restaurant management. After his two years' experience in managing the ski lodge, Tom felt that he related naturally to the business and despite a lack of formal training in the area, it seemed to come as second nature to him. He also saw ample opportunity in an industry where he believed there was little aggressive competition and even less professional management.

The idea interested Jack because even with his limited experience and exposure he viewed the industry as fragmented and with many management problems. He understood that chains of hotels, inns, and eating establishments only accounted for a miniscule amount of the industry revenues which people were predicting would double in total in the next five to six years. The growth potential seemed to him to be possible both internally as a result of the management skills they could contribute and externally as a result of being part of a fast growing industry.

In subsequent discussion their concept began to crystallize and they wrote down their ideas with an eye toward potential investors:

> In Boston's Back Bay/Beacon Hill area and in similar sections of other great cities there stands that proud vestige of the past called the town house. Although most are now converted to lesser uses, they still retain much of the grandeur of the era in which they were built. At the turn of the century, as industries developed, there emerged a particular brand of man, the highly successful businessman with taste, sophistication, and a flair for "the good life." In these private and rather opulent surroundings he entertained his friends and business associates and relaxed by the glow of a fire

with a fine brandy and Havana cigar. As private town houses declined in appeal they were replaced for many by the private in-town gentlemen's club.

The company intends, in appropriate properties, to re-create the subdued elegance of that grand era and to provide the guests with all the amenities of turn-of-the-century town house living. The new businessman in a hurry or at his leisure, entertaining clients or his family, will be catered to with all the graciousness of a long-past era. Emphasis will be placed on quality and service, and every convenience will be provided. . . . Each individualized facility will be operated with only one ambition: to provide the harried but demanding executive with a wide variety of services, to cater to his every need on an individual basis. In total, an executive town house provides an environment reminiscent of an era when quality and service were not as unique as they are today.

Tom and Jack believed there was a large unaccommodated market segment at which to aim a wide range of high-quality services within a multifunction facility. They thought that this market was served inadequately by private clubs (such as the Algonquin, Somerset, Union, and Harvard) because of the small number of people which these operations could handle. They felt the Playboy clubs also had limited facilities and really only sold sex, or rather the illusion of it, to traveling salesmen. The hotels, on the other hand, were too impersonal and did not offer the range of services and facilities which they planned to offer. Tom and Jack thought of the town house as a private club on a public basis. They intended for the town house, a downtown mansion, to have an atmosphere of success. They felt the cornerstone of the concept must be a dedication to the ideal of first-rate service to each customer whether it be a large firm reserving a dining room or a customer ordering a single drink.

The businessman would by no means be the only customer expected to find relaxation and enjoyment within such an establishment. However, Tom and Jack singled him out as a typical customer because the operation of their concept would be directed toward the satisfaction of his needs. They surmised that a town house would appeal to the businessman who wanted a place to go that is distinctively different and connotes success. The combination of the surroundings and efficient service would be intended to attract this type of individual who has both a company expense account and his own money to spend. They felt that if he became comfortable at the town house, he would return often whether entertaining clients or relaxing with his wife or date. Tom and Jack decided to call such a place an Executive Town House.

Central to the two men's vision of the town house and of creating a significant corporation was the idea of the "reproducible unit." The plan was to think through and work out the details of their town house on this first operation. If they decided to go ahead, they estimated it would take six months from the "go" decision to set up their first unit, and then it would require a full year of operating experience to learn the cycles in the business, attend to details, and iron out the kinks. They would then have a highly profitable reproducible unit which they would be able to duplicate in many major metropolitan downtown areas. In this way they thought they could achieve rapid growth through maximum leverage of their own time, ideas, and efforts. They would be able to transfer skills from location to location, build a large chain of facilities, and eventually take the operation public.

The Hampshire House

On November 1, 1968, the two men heard that the Hampshire House, a hotel complete with restaurant facilities and a liquor license, was for sale. Located at 84 Beacon Street across from the Boston Garden at the foot of Beacon Hill, the seven-story former town house and its prestigious location seemed to them to be an excellent vehicle for their concept. (See Appendix A for the location, B for the floor plan, and C for a sketch.)

The two men spent the following week gathering data on the Hampshire House. Having lived on Beacon Hill, they believed they already had a feel for the area. They also checked tax stamps at the Registry of Deeds of the County,[1] received a Dun & Bradstreet report on the operations of the hotel to date,[2] and read industry notes in the files at the Harvard Business School.[3]

On Tuesday, November 18, they inspected the property and talked with the owner who had operated the premises since 1957 but wanted to sell because of business interests in Venezuela. Although the owner had refused to reveal financial information to Dun & Bradstreet and had kept incomplete records because he ran the business on a cash basis, he did give a revenue breakdown estimate (Exhibit 1) and the accountant's records for 1964 (Exhibit 2).

---

[1]When a property is bought and sold, tax stamps representing a small percentage of the amount involved are required by law to be placed on the deed. These records are open to the public at the Registry of Deeds and from them one can ascertain the amount of previous sales and purchases as long as the stamps have not been tampered with.

[2]A Dun & Bradstreet report on a company is usually based on the information that is received from the company itself and is not verified by outside sources. In the case of the Hampshire House the report was prepared from information filed by the Hampshire House with the Massachusetts Commissioner of Corporations. On all D & B reports in small print reads the following statement, "Dun & Bradstreet does not guarantee the correctness of this report and shall not be liable for any loss or inquiry caused by the neglect or other act or failure to act on the part of said company and/or its agents in procuring, collecting or communicating any information."

[3] The Harvard Business School library keeps industry files composed of various reports and articles. Usually the bulk of the file comes from monthly Department of Commerce reports which contain a variety of statistics.

Tom and Jack felt that the present operation probably had revenues of somewhere between $200,000 and $300,000, but how much the owner had been taking out was anyone's guess. They noted a downward trend in operations and the generally run-down condition of the building and decided the owner was probably milking the operation. They believed that this had hurt the business, but not the basic physical structure or the possibility for two industrious individuals to create a profitable town house with better management, renovated and expanded facilities, and a better understanding of the market's wants and needs.

During their inspection of the property, the two men began to make mental plans for the renovations necessary to complete their concept. The sixth floor offered a view of the Charles River Basin, the Public Garden, the Boston Common, and the Back Bay and Beacon Hill areas. They believed this view was a natural asset which could be capitalized on by removing the outside brick from the floor and replacing it with glass panels. In the resulting facility, primary emphasis would be on cocktails but some food would be available: sandwiches for lunch, steak and salad for dinner. The more substantial meals would be served on the first and second floors, nearer the kitchen.

To Tom and Jack the roof seemed like a natural location for a stand-up bar with tables for at least 50 people inside and another 100 outside. They figured that the appeal of outdoor dining and drinking would draw sizable crowds during the summer and that this would help counter the anticipated dropoff in business from the lower floors during vacation season.

In the basement, they planned the addition of a pub with an outside stairwell and entrance. The facility would be modeled after an English pub serving international beers, spirits, and sherries. The objective would be to provide a congenial and comfortable atmosphere with wood panels, leather chairs, authentic fixtures, and English barmaids.

On the first floor they planned to redecorate the entrance hall in a manner consistent with the original town house. The living room needed only a small service bar to allow guests to enjoy a finely paneled living room atmosphere with a blazing fireplace. By refurnishing the dining room in a formal setting, Tom and Jack felt that they could offer meals of a fixed fare, at a fixed time, and at a fixed price from the first sip of sherry to the final sniff of cognac.

Tom and Jack thought that the second floor, consisting of a library and drawing room, would need little refinishing to display its original elegance. The library could be used for reading and relaxing while the drawing room with its hand-crafted walls and Italian crystal chandeliers would provide a suitable atmosphere for friends and business associates to gather for affairs such as exhibitions, recitals, or displays.

The third floor needed painting, decorating, and refinishing and could serve as the corporation headquarters.

The fourth and fifth floors also needed refinishing and some remodeling, but Tom and Jack anticipated that with the necessary effort these floors could provide excellent facilities to accommodate activities ranging from conferences lasting several days to secretaries having their Xeroxing done while on lunch hour. The conference rooms would be convertible to private dining rooms, entertainment suites, or spartan overnight facilities. Available for use would be multilingual secretaries, electric typewriters, duplicating equipment, postage meters, audiovisual aids, a telephone switchboard, personal services such as valet and ticket arrangements, and perhaps even a sauna and billiard room.

To complete all of the above, Tom and Jack drew up the following estimates:

Project	*Amount*
Roof lounge	$ 50,000
Pub	15,000
First and second floors	20,000
Third, fourth, fifth floors	60,000
Elevators	5,000
Architect, designers, and other fees	25,000
Contingencies	25,000
	$200,000

Although they now had "dreamed out" their plans for a town house and the Hampshire House in particular, they were undecided whether or not to take the big step and make commitments. They realized that if they really believed their ideas could work, they should follow up on the Hampshire House since it seemed so ideally adaptable to their concept.

A week later Tom and Jack went to a Harvard football game, still undecided as to whether or not they should pursue the idea further. As they sat in the chill November wind, warming themselves with frequent sips of brandy, the two men resolved that they would follow up on the Hampshire House lead and try to make their concept work.

Financing

As a first step in demonstrating the potential to investors, they drew up pro forma income statements and balance sheets. Relying on Jack's computer experience, they built a sophisticated simulation model of the impact of various operating variables on profits. The model also enabled them to further clarify which elements in their plans were most critical for their success in terms of profits, liquidity, and ROI. The pro forma and model were based on the renovated Hampshire House which they figured would have about six times the capacity of the present operation and be able to accommodate over 700 persons at one time.

Exhibit 3 shows Tom's and Jack's projections of profits before depreciation, interest, amortization, and income and real estate taxes. Estimates were made on the basis of three possible approaches: the expected level of business, industry averages (based on square feet), and a minimum level of business. Exhibits 4, 5, and 6 give some of the assumptions behind these figures.

The owners had mentioned during early conversations that they wanted $800,000 for the Hampshire House. Tom and Jack believed that the owners had received other offers but that none of them were as high as $700,000. They thought the owners would accept $650,000 if they could make a firm offer quickly and not give the owners an opportunity to play off the possible buyers against one another. The two lawyers they had retained agreed that this tactic might succeed if they could act quickly. On December 10, Tom Kershaw and Jack Veasy delivered a written offer to the owners for $650,000. They gave the owners 10 days to accept, explaining that the offer would be withdrawn after this period. The men expected to put $10,000 down immediately which they would invest personally. They offered another $75,000 at the closing.

By buying the existing corporation, the men expected to get essentially ownership of the building and the liquor license. Since receivables and payables almost balanced out and inventory was negligible, the entire net worth of the corporation existed in the license and the building (owned outright with no mortgage).

They also began to investigate the possibilities of obtaining a mortgage on the building, and conversations with local banks indicated they would be able to get this financing. Thus, with a second mortgage from the owners, their financing plan had looked roughly as follows:

	Use		Source
$650,000	purchase Hampshire House	$565,000	mortgages
200,000	renovations	10,000	personal equity
$850,000		$575,000	

They figured that the initial working capital would result from the staggered and delayed outflows for renovations but that they would still need a minimum of $275,000 of outside equity. With the offer made, Jack Veasy returned to Copenhagen to finish up his business and to wait for a telegram from Tom as to whether or not they were in business. On December 19, the owners agreed to the terms and price of the offer; they would sign a purchase and sale agreement and expect to close by May 1, 1969. This would give the partners five months to arrange mortgage commitments from the banks, to organize their new firm, and to raise the additional $275,000 in equity capital. Shortly before Christmas, Jack received a telegram from Tom, "Go." He returned to Boston in early

January, and the two men began to formalize their ideas for raising the necessary capital. They met with the owners periodically over the following three weeks, and on February 4, 1969, signed a purchase and sale agreement which specified a closing date of May 1, 1969. They also made the required $10,000 downpayment.

The two men then began their search for equity capital by talking to various contacts they had made since leaving the Harvard Business School and to people suggested by the two lawyers they had retained. In addition, they talked to private individuals, investment bankers, private syndicates, and traditional venture capital organizations. Their intention was to give up about 40 percent of the company for the $275,000. They believed this would permit the outside equity investors to make an attractive ROI if their projections for the Hampshire House were correct; the really large return of this risk money, however, would come from having equity in the additional locations which would be financed internally from the cash flows of the original Town House.

The men had several individuals and groups express interest in putting money into the venture. Tom and Jack felt that despite the very rapid pace of events these investors were impressed with their understanding of the critical elements of the plan, the sophisticated nature of the simulation model, Tom's experience in managing a hotel operation, and the fact that both men were experienced in operating small, start-up situations.

A small, newly formed investment company offered to raise the entire $275,000 by a Regulation A offering. As evidence of their intentions to follow through, this group indicated that they would immediately provide $50,000 to guarantee the deal. The group's proposal was to sell 20 percent of the company to the public for $300,000, take 10 percent themselves and thus leave Messrs. Kershaw and Veasy with 70 percent. The proceeds of roughly $250,000 after expenses would go to the corporation. Numerically, Tom and Jack thought the offer was extremely attractive, but it had posed several questions and problems. The timing was at the tail end and height of the frenzied new issue market. Although they believed that the investment group could have brought the deal off, Tom observed, "The group represented the worst of what was going on at the time . . . the 'you take this one and I'll give you one next week' attitude of pushing issues on the market."

Tom and Jack decided that if they were to commit to a financial organization, it should be to a firm with which they could build a long-term relationship and which would be capable of providing counsel for later financings and an eventual public offering. They believed the group in question did not have the ability to help them in the later stages of the company's growth. Nevertheless, it appeared that the money was literally waiting to be siphoned off the market. By using this investing group, Tom and Jack could have been off and running while retaining a very large percent of the venture. After much deliberation they turned down the offer.

A second private group expressing interest consisted of the former management team of a small operating company. Their company had recently been acquired for cash, and these individuals were anxious to put their money to work in a venture capital situation. Again, however, Tom and Jack declined the offer because they thought that this group could not assist in later financing.

Tom and Jack figured they could afford to set their criteria for investors very strictly because their search seemed to be progressing well despite the fact that it was time-consuming and far from complete. On the strength of their earlier relationships in the Boston area, they had exposed their ideas to two well-known local venture capital organizations and were encouraged by the fact that one of the two expressed some interest in the deal. Although the firm sought a more lucrative arrangement than the two men wanted to offer, the firm indicated that they would reevaluate the proposal should Tom and Jack want to do so at a later date.

During the course of two months or so, the two men felt that they had interested several individual investors in the possibilities of their ideas. This they felt was beneficial because they believed a small group of private investors might be the best source of capital at this early stage. To enable individuals to take a depreciation shield on the building, the two men developed a slightly restructured version of their original financial plan. First, a limited partnership would be set up to take in the equity needed to support a mortgage on the building. Ownership of the building in this manner would provide a return to the investors in the form of a cash flow through the rental of the building and a tax shield from the accelerated depreciation which could be taken. The second entity would be the operating corporation which would generate profits from the various service areas—bar, restaurant, hotel, and so on.

Except for the large amounts of time both of the individuals had been required to spend on getting together the investors, the men had felt they were proceeding satisfactorily. In early April, however, a partner from a small but very aggressive Boston-based investment bank said he would be interested in handling the entire financial arrangements. Although Tom and Jack still believed they could eventually raise outside money on their own, the task was going to take more time. They saw in this offer the chance to put the financing task in the hands of professionals and to free up time for dealing with some of the many operational and other problems which had to be solved.[4] They had postponed the tasks of arranging for the renovation of the building, hiring staff, and making

---

[4] One such problem which cropped up while exploring their ideas about the Pub was the various city agencies whose approval would have to be obtained before the Pub could be licensed and operating.

changes in some of the suppliers, and other operational problems until after the money had been raised. By early April they were becoming anxious to attend to these areas and were seriously considering placing the burden of finding the rest of the money on the investment banker. They also saw in this arrangement a chance to build a longer term relationship with a known investment house. It appeared to them that the most difficult task in accomplishing their ideas was putting together the deal and that it would not be as difficult to run a small business —unless they thought of it as a "small business."

SUGGESTED QUESTIONS

1. What should Messrs. Kershaw and Veasy do now?
2. What do you think of their concept for a venture? How would you go about evaluating what they plan to do?

    What are the key elements in a *successful* restaurant/bar operation?
3. How would you evaluate the progress to date in getting the operation started? What priorities should be given the tasks remaining to be done?

EXHIBIT 1
The Hampshire House
estimate of revenue breakdown by former owner

Dinners/week	200	
Average revenue per meal...................	$5	$1,000/week
Lunches/week	400	
Average revenue per meal...................	$3	1,200
Total revenue from food.....................		$2,200/week
Assuming food is 40 percent of revenue:		
Total revenues		$ 5,500/week
Total revenue for 52 weeks..................		275,000/year
Assuming room revenue......................		25,000
Total		$300,000/year

EXHIBIT 2

The Hampshire House

Profit and loss for the year ending September 1964 by former owner

Sales income:			
Rooms	$ 10,844		
Food and beverage	233,571		
Other: (employees' food)	2,084		$246,499
Cost of goods sold:			
Beverage	$ 32,000		
Food	39,896	$71,896	
Departmental wages:			
Beverage	$ 11,370		
Entertainment	6,882		
Kitchen and dining	27,165		
Porters	10,407		
Office and reception	8,548		
Miscellaneous, labor	4,277		
Checkroom	3,138	71,787	
Departmental expenses:			
Beverage			
Bar supplies	$ 1,329		
Licenses	2,775		
Bar expenses	715	4,819	
Kitchen			
Dishes	$ 2,900		
Kitchen expenses	4,867	7,767	
Hotel supplies	$ 3,389	3,389	159,658
Total			
Gross Operating Income ..			$ 86,841
Administrative and general expenses:			
Flowers	$ 413		
Cleaning	5,058		
Laundry	3,844		
Office	396		
Payroll tax	4,300		
Union	296		
Sewer tax	237		
Telephone	1,986	$16,530	
Advertising and business promotion:			
Promotion	$ 1,255		
Advertising	447	1,702	
Heat, light, and power:			
Gas	$ 516		
Heat and light	8,761		
Water	525	9,802	
Repair and maintenance		$4,020	
Total			$32,054
Gross Operating Profit			$ 54,787

EXHIBIT 3

The Executive Town House

Comparison of three pro forma income statements for full year's operation[*]

	Expected		Industry statistics[†]		Minimum	
Sales						
Dining room	$378 ⎫					
Cocktails	72 ⎬		429		360	
Banquets	351 ⎭					
Roof	256		600		300	
Pub	120		110		50	
Rooms	108		63		40	
Total		1,285.0		1,202		750
Cost of goods sold						
Food and beverage	329.6		340		210	
Labor	203.9	533.5	385	725	180	390
Gross Operating Profit		751.5		477		360
General and administrative		280.4		227		150
House Profit.....		471.1		250		210

[*]Prepared by Messrs. Kershaw and Veasy, November 1968.
[†]Based on square feet.

EXHIBIT 4

The Executive Town House

Assumptions for year's sales forecast by Messrs. Kershaw and Veasy

1. Pub

Do a moderate off-the-street trade—using estimates for smaller bars in the area.

2. Lunch

At the outset, same volume as current (300/week).

Maximum: 50 (lounge)+50 (dining) x 5 days x 2 (turnover)=1,000 lunches.

500 lunches/week over summer.

Expected volume reached in November =750 lunches/week.

3. Dinner

Initial volume same as current (1,000/month).

Maximum 2,100 dinners/month.

4. Banquets

Maximum 4,000 servings/month @ $7.50/person.

Buildup: March–April—20%, May—30%, June—50%, July–August—10%.

5. Cocktails

Maximum volume: 2,000/month x $3 =$6,000/month (noneaters).

6. Roof

Lunch:	Fall/winter: 350/week x 4 weeks @ $3=$4,200.	
Dinner:	Winter: 500 maximum @ $4 x 4.3 =$8,600/month.	
	Summer: 50% of winter	
Cocktails:	Summer: 1,000 drinks/week = $4,300/month.	
	Fall/winter: 2,000 drinks/week =$8,600/month.	

7. Rooms

4th and 5th floors:	18 rooms @ $20 x 30 days=		$10,800
3rd floor:	$150 for 30 days=		4,500
		Maximum:	$15,300
Capacity:	Summer—30%;	Fall—50%;	Winter—70%

EXHIBIT 5
The Executive Town House
Assumptions for labor expenses by Messrs. Kershaw and Veasy

			Per week	Total per week	Per month (4.2)
ROOF					
Minimum:	15 hrs./day×7 days/week×2 people =210 man-hours @ $2.00/hr				
Expected:	Waiters 2.5	15 × 7 = 105 @ $2.00	$525		
	Bar 2.0	15 × 7 = 105 @ 3.00	630		
	Cook 1.0	15 × 7 = 105 @ 3.00	315		
	Hostess 1.0	15 × 7 = 105 @ 2.00	210		
	Cashier .8	15 × 7 = 105 @ 1.00	80		
				$1,760	$7,500
ROOMS					
Minimum and expected:	Maids—2 @ $75/week			150	700
DINING ROOM					
Kitchen					
Minimum:	Chefs—3 @ $200, $100, $110		$410		
	Dishwashers—2 for $140		140		
				$ 550	
Expected:	Chefs—4 @ $200; 2 @ $100		$600		
	Dishwashers—3 for $200		200		
				$ 800	
					3,400
Waiters					
Minimum:	2 for lunch:	3 hrs./6 days @ $2	$ 72		
	2 for dinner:	6 hrs./6 days @ $2	144		
				$ 216	
Expected:	2 for lunch:	3 hrs./6 days @ $2	$108		
	5 for dinner:	6 hrs./6 days @ $2	360		
				468	
					2,000
LOUNGE					
Minimum:	Bar 1/15 hrs./6 days @ $3.00		$270		
	Waitress 6 hrs./ 6 days @ $2.00		72		
				$ 342	
Expected:	Bar—Same		$270		
	Waitress 3/6 hrs./6 days @ $2.00		216		
				486	
					2,000

EXHIBIT 6
The Executive Town House
Industry averages*

First and
Second floors . .864 sq. ft. @ 16.6 sq. ft./seat   52 seats
        52 seats @ $11/seat/day
        25 days/month = $14,000/month
        12 months = $171,600/month for food only
        Assume food 40% of revenue,
          total revenue per year $ 429,000

Rooms $2,863/room
        22 rooms, per year $ 63,000

        1,000 sq. ft. @ 16.6 sq. ft./seat
        60 seats @ $11/seat/day
        30 days/month = $19,000 per month
        12 months = $237,600 per year
        Assume food 40% of revenue,
          total revenue per year $ 600,000

Pub . . . . .750 sq. ft. @ $0.50 revenue/day/sq. ft.
        25 days = $9,400/month
        12 months per year $ 110,000

      Total per year $1,202,000

*Based on statistics in *Trends in the Hotel-Motel Business–1967*, Harris, Kerr, Forster, and Company; and statistics from Hilton Hotel operations.

Appendix A

Location of the Hampshire House

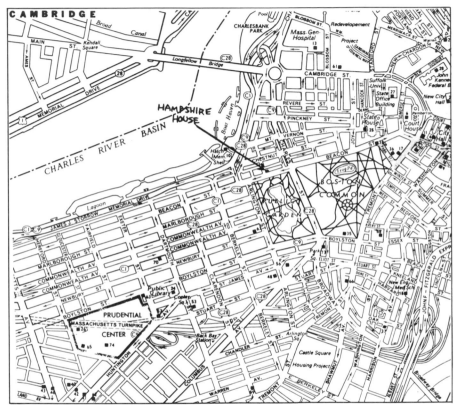

Appendix B

**Floor plan of the Hampshire House
Basement**

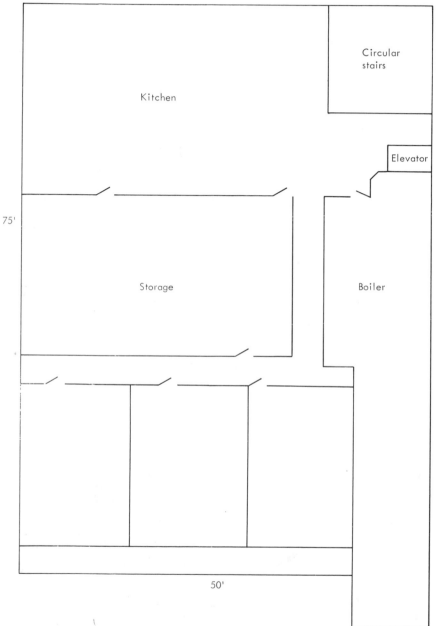

Appendix B (continued)

First floor

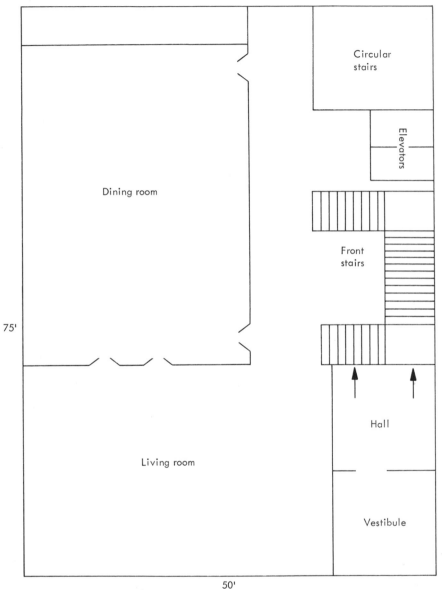

Appendix B (continued)

Second floor

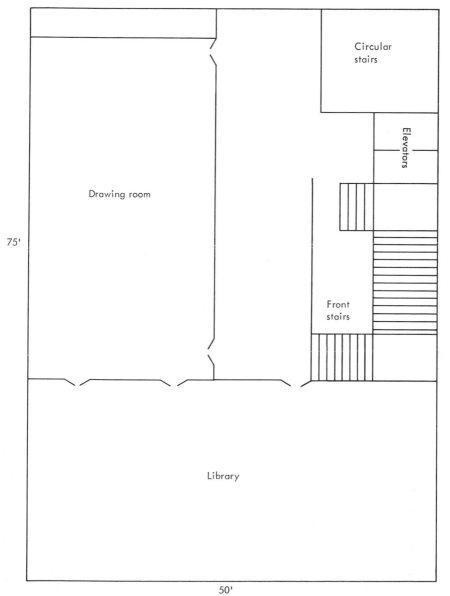

Appendix B (continued)

Third floor

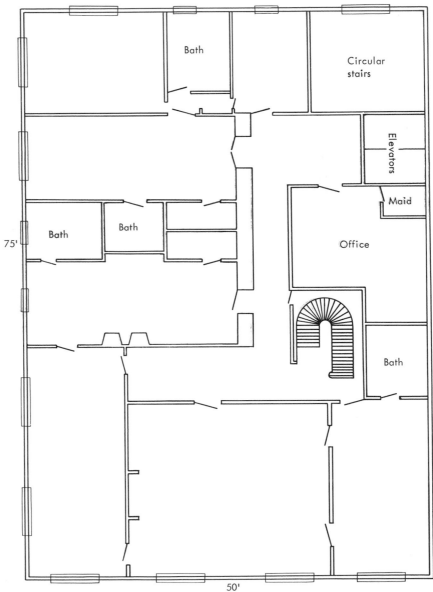

Appendix B (continued)

Fourth floor

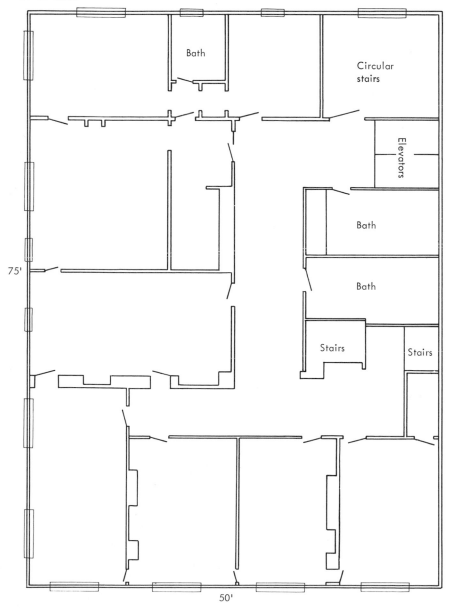

Bath

Circular
stairs

Elevators

Bath

Bath

75'

Stairs

Stairs

50'

Appendix B (continued)

Fifth floor

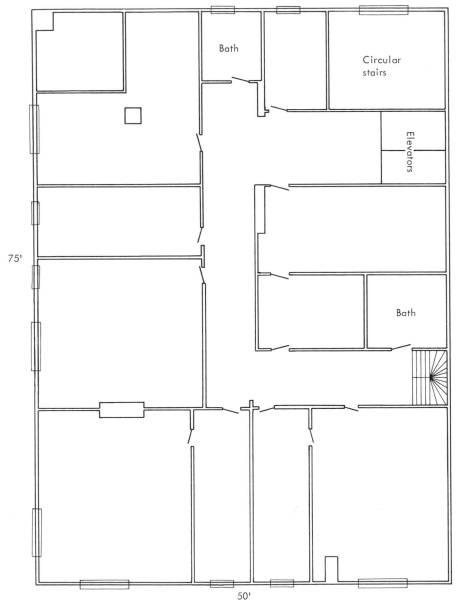

Appendix B (concluded)

Sixth floor

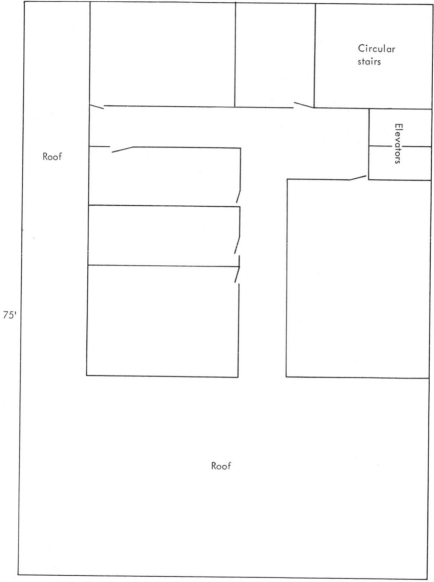

Appendix C

The Hampshire House

Note

The legal forms of business enterprise

Introduction

This note aims to increase the student's familiarity with various legal aspects of starting a company. The particular focus is on that decision which the entrepreneur must make at the outset of his venture—*the form of enterprise with which he will conduct his business.* This Note catalogs and discusses the factors (such as liability limitation, tax treatment, and continuity of operations) which the entrepreneur should consider in choosing between the proprietorship, corporation, and partnership.

This Note does not intend to be complete, encyclopedic, or minutely technical. Rather, it is an overview, but one which will apprise the entrepreneur of the specific issues critical to the threshold organization of the firm. Thus armed with issue-spotting ability, the entrepreneur should be better able to judge when and where he needs more advanced legal advice.

If the entrepreneur does start a company, it is inevitable that he *will* need such advice. Before entering into the main body of this Note, a few words should be said about how to obtain advice.

There are four rules regarding legal advice that the entrepreneur should keep in mind:

1. Get a lawyer.
2. Get the best lawyer available.
3. Base the choice on the lawyer's reputation, particularly in the area of new ventures. Avoid choosing a lawyer merely because he is a friend or (worse) a relative.
4. Attempt to understand as many of the legal issues as possible.

1. Get a lawyer.   It is almost always necessary for an entrepreneur to obtain legal help at the early stages of starting a venture. The entrepreneur will be faced with an array of legal problems which only a lawyer can handle: choosing the form of organization, drafting the incorporation papers or partnership agreement, registering the enterprise in the states in which it intends to do business, preparing the income tax returns, and so on. Nor will the entrepreneur's need for special legal advice cease after the business's early days. Business enterprise and the laws governing it are inexorably intertwined. The entrepreneur will need a lawyer throughout the operation of his business. But his subsequent problems will be fewer and smaller if he can begin with competent legal help.

2. Get the best lawyer available.   Bad legal advice may be worse than none at all because the effects may not be known until it is too late. Usually, an entrepreneur does not learn how good or bad his legal assistance has been until he has had need to call upon a particular clause or section in a document signed several months or years previously. Needless to say, a great deal can hinge upon whether or not certain kinds of things were anticipated when the agreement was originally made. The best lawyer is the lawyer who anticipates the things that can go wrong.

Good lawyers are expensive and busy. In theory, there is a $50/hour (and higher in New York City) meter ticking as he listens, talks, or works on the project. For the entrepreneur, however, the meter does not always get turned on during early discussions and the initial start-up tasks. Although it is difficult to be specific about legal fees for a hypothetical task, the most simple and straightforward incorporation should cost about $300–$500; if there are complexities, the fee may be a multiple of several times one of those figures. The entrepreneur will probably have to meet the costs of legal fees *in cash* rather than in stock of the new venture. (Actual payments, however, frequently may be delayed.) Although some lawyers will take their fee in stock, many frown on this practice because it detracts from a position of objectivity.

Good lawyers are also busy—generally very busy (one might begin to wonder how good a lawyer is if he is not close to unavailable). He may take days or weeks longer than planned or anticipated to do the work needed. When faster service is necessary, the entrepreneur must be prepared to push for it—no easy task when the new venture's account is relatively a very small one, and probably not yet a paying one. Given this demand on a good lawyer's time, the key to attracting and holding his attention may be his personal interest in the entrepreneur, and/or the venture. For a lawyer generally involved in more routine affairs, a venture start-up situation can be a refreshing change.

But the critical point: despite the expense (both in money and time), a good lawyer is worth it to the entrepreneur. It will be one of his best investments.

3. Base the choice on the lawyer's reputation, particularly in the area of new ventures. Avoid choosing a lawyer merely because he is a friend or (worse) a relative. How does the entrepreneur choose a lawyer? The "testing" procedure is generally limited to a careful examination of the lawyer's previous experience and performance with other individuals in situations similar to the one planned. Or, in other words: choose based on reputation in the area of starting new ventures.

While the good lawyer who knows little about new ventures is preferable to the bad specialist, the lawyer experienced in start-ups or acquisitions is in a position to provide valuable help beyond the confines of technical legalities, particularly if the entrepreneur is an inexperienced individual. This type of lawyer has had repeated close-hand exposure to a wide range of start-up problems. He can provide the novice with a wealth of insight and assistance.

A very brief background on individual lawyers and law firms can be found in Martindale and Hubble, a directory published annually by the American Bar Association. The specialists in new ventures can be located by making inquiries of a senior partner in the firm, of other people who have started ventures, and of people in related professions. The entrepreneur who has successfully started a firm will probably have strong opinions about the outsiders who worked with him, and he usually will be willing to share his experiences. Similarly, a banker (such as a loan officer) who has contact with ventures would be in a position to know what lawyers are frequently involved with these kinds of activities.

It has been said many times before, but the point must be made again: a lawyer should not be selected because he is a neighbor, friend, or relative, and therefore is convenient and inexpensive. Although at the beginning a minimum amount of legal knowledge may be helpful, the knowledge and skills which are of major importance in starting a venture are not common to the entire population of the profession. The classic error is made by the entrepreneur who gets his brother- in-law involved because he is a lawyer, because he is handy, and because he has the time to sit and talk. Then when major decisions have to be made, the entrepreneur discovers—too late—that the relative knows virtually nothing about the alternatives for a legal organization or about structuring a purchase and sale agreement. And by then, the working relationship has usually developed to such a degree that getting another lawyer is a very embarrassing election.

Finally, since the entrepreneur and his lawyer may be working very closely together, particularly at the outset of the venture, it will be helpful if the lawyer's expertise is accompanied by a reasonable match in personal chemistry. Do the parties involved hit it off together? Frequently, an early meeting during which the entrepreneur describes what he is trying to do can be a useful means for an initial acquaintance and some mutual exposure. Where there are signs or feelings of possible incompatibility, the relationship can be broken off easily before it really begins.

But this last consideration is really minor compared to the main question the entrepreneur should ask in choosing a lawyer: can he do the job? A good reputation indicates that he can.

4. Attempt to understand as many of the legal issues as possible. Lulled into security by a fine lawyer, the entrepreneur will be continually tempted to abdicate responsibility for legal matters by delegating them to his counsel. This abdication is dangerous because it may cause the entrepreneur's decision-making power to atrophy. The role of the lawyer is only to inform and to advise. It is the entrepreneur who must make the final decisions on the basis of information and advice provided by the lawyer. He cannot make many decisions wisely if he does not understand the crux of the legal issues.

A major difficulty for the inexperienced is the welter of strange terms and phrases which are scattered throughout most legal documents. The novice in this kind of reading should be persistent in getting some understanding not only of *what* is contained in such documents, but also *why* these provisions have been included. If an entrepreneur cannot find the time or take the interest to read and understand the major contracts into which his company will enter, he should be very cautious about being an entrepreneur at all.

The point is that entrepreneurial activity does not end with the establishment of the venture. *The essence* of entrepreneurial activity is that it calls for ongoing, rapid decision making—and such decision making will inevitably involve legal questions. If the entrepreneur has not allowed his legal sense to develop early in the game, he may not be able to make the rapid-fire choices that will be often required of him later on.

THE LEGAL FORMS OF BUSINESS ENTERPRISE

There are six basic business forms:

1. Sole proprietorship. The sole proprietorship is actually the *absence* of a legal form of business organization. It is the noncorporate ownership of a business by one individual.

2. General partnership. An association of two or more persons to carry on as co-owners of business for profit. A *joint venture* is more limited in scope and duration, but otherwise is basically identical to a general partnership. It is treated the same for tax purposes.

3. Limited partnership. A business association formed by one or more general partners and one or more limited partners, the latter having their liability limited to a definite amount. To achieve and maintain their limited liability status, the limited partners cannot participate in management.

4. Joint stock company. An association of individuals who have joined for the purpose of profit and have contributed common capital which is represented by transferable shares held by the members. In essence, the joint stock company is a corporation whose members (in most states) have unlimited liability. (Uncommon)

5. Corporation. A business corporation is a legal entity which is created under statute, composed of individuals under a common name. Limited liability and succession of ownership is possible.

6. Business or Massachusetts trust. An unincorporated organization created for profit under a written instrument or declaration of trust and managed by compensated trustees for the benefit of persons whose legal interests are represented by transferable certificates of participation. Unlike a corporation, however, the holders of these trust certificates do not elect the board of trustees. (Uncommon)

The fine spun differences between the six forms of enterprise may be interesting from an academic standpoint. For the majority of new ventures, the corporation is the most suitable form. Each entrepreneur, however, must make this decision for himself. Seven considerations will affect his choice:

A. Organization requirements and their costs.
B. Liability of owners.
C. Continuity of the concern.
D. Transferability of interest.
E. Management and control.
F. Attractiveness for raising capital.
G. Tax treatment.

This Note will discuss each of these considerations in turn and will indicate how each can affect the ultimate choice of enterprise form. A comparative summary table of the seven business forms and the above considerations is shown in Table 1 at the end of this Note.

A. Organization requirements and their costs

In very few instances will the expense of organization be a significant consideration in selecting the form of enterprise. Even the fees associated with the most expensive form, the corporation, become insignificant when amortized over several years and deducted from taxable income.

The following sketch, however, is for those entrepreneurs for whom even this small organizational cost is important. The order is from least to most expensive.

1. Sole proprietorship. An individual "creates" a proprietorship by the simple act of starting a business. If he is trading in his own name, no registrations, agreements, taxes, or fees are required. If the business is conducted under a trade or assumed name, he may have to pay a filing fee, but such fees are usually small. Thus, the proprietorship is the cheapest form to establish— cheap because it generally costs nothing at all.

2. Massachusetts (business) trust. A Massachusetts trust is established by a declaration of trust. The cost of the legal services needed to draft such a declaration is usually the only expense. No filing fees or taxes are required.

3. General partnership. Creating a general partnership can be either very cheap or more expensive—and, as with most things, you get what you pay for. That is, the more expensive organization form will usually prove to be the more convenient in the long run.

As a legal form of enterprise, the proprietorship is available only to a single individual. When two or more individuals combine as co-owners of a business, they have automatically satisfied the textbook definition of a partnership. As with the case of the proprietorship, no registration or filing fees are required unless the partnership's business is conducted under a trade, fictitious, or assumed name. Similarly, no formal, written partnership agreement is required. Thus, the creation of a general partnership can cost nothing at all.

The hitch lies with the partnership agreement. Although underlying state statutes may deal with aspects of partnerships, unlike a corporation, whose ground rules are established by state statute *and* the mandatory articles of incorporation, a partnership's form is shapeless, infinitely flexible—and therefore, a potential source of infinite trouble. As we shall see later in this Note, matters such as division of the firm's profits, rights of the partners vis-à-vis each other, and even the continuity of the partnership itself are all determined by the partnership agreement. In a partnership, *everything* depends on that agreement. It is perfectly possible to operate with another partner on no more than a verbal agreement and a handshake. But in most partnerships, where there are several partners, some of whom are strangers to each other, a written partnership agreement is a comforting source of explicit and readily visible ground rules. Naturally a lawyer will be needed to help draft such an agreement. Also naturally, the expense associated with such a lawyer will make this form of enterprise more expensive than the sole proprietorship.

4. Joint stock company. This form is very similar to the general partnership. But unlike a general partnership, which can be created without a written agreement among the partners, a joint stock company *requires* formal, written articles of agreement among its members. In most states, the legal drafting costs of such articles will be the only expense, since no statutory authorization fees or taxes are levied. Thus, the legal organization and expenses are similar to a general partnership.

5. Limited partnership. The creation of a limited partnership, unlike that of a general partnership, requires strict compliance with statutory requirements usually calling for: *(a)* two lists, one of the general and one of the limited partners; *(b)* a written partnership agreement; and *(c)* a filed certificate indicating the rights and duties of the parties among each other. In addition, to notify the public of the existence of partners whose liability is limited, some advertising procedure may be necessary. Because of its greater complexities, expenses will usually exceed those of a general partnership of the same size and scope.

6. Corporation. A business corporation is created *only* by statute. In general, satisfying the statute requires: *(a)* registering the name and articles of incorporation, *(b)* compliance with the statutory procedures of the state of incorporation, *(c)* the payment of filing fees, *(d)* the payment of an organization tax usually based on the amount of the corporation's capital, and *(e)* the payment of fees in all other states in which the corporation registers to do business. Thus, organizing in the corporate form may be the most expensive. These costs and subsequent annual costs, however, vary considerably among states.

B. Liability of owners

Frequently a critical consideration in the selection of a business organization is the entrepreneur's desire to minimize his liability stemming from his business. No matter which legal structure is used, creditors always have first claim on assets before *any* equity capital is withdrawn. When these assets do not cover liabilities, the owners can be compelled to meet creditors' claims out of their own personal assets. The extent to which they will be required to do so varies with the type of organization. As is the case with taxes, the difference in liability among the organizational forms depends on the concept of *the entity*.

Briefly put, the corporation is an entity—the proprietorship and the partnership are not. As Chief Justice John Marshall declared in 1819,

> A corporation is an artificial being, invisible, intangible, and existing only in contemplation of law. Being the mere creature of law, it possesses only those properties which the charter of its creation confers upon it, either expressly, or as incidental to its very existence.[1]

Marshall's emphasis is on the limitations of the corporate existence. Our emphasis here is on the advantages. The point is that while proprietorships and partnerships serve only as *conduits* to flow business earnings through to their owners, a corporation is a separate, legal "person" which is taxable (a disadvantage), but which also absorbs liability (an advan-

---

[1]*Dartmouth College* versus *Woodward*, 4 Wheaton 518.

tage). We can see how this works by proceeding through the various forms, examining the extent to which their owners are personally liable.

1. Sole proprietorship. An individual proprietor is personally liable for all debts of his business. There is no distinction made between the individual owner and the business entity. Thus, even if the owner has assets *outside* the business (for example, house, car, stocks, cash), these assets may be seized by creditors to satisfy the debts of the business.

2. General partnership. The same rules apply as with a proprietorship: each partner is fully responsible for all debts incurred by the partnership or the other partners acting in what appears to be the firm's business. In fact, such personal liability to existing creditors continues even after the firm has been dissolved. Regardless of the amount of capital contributed, general partners share profit, loss, *and* liability equally *unless* there is a specific agreement to the contrary. Thus, if one partner has to satisfy debts of the partnership out of his personal assets, he has the right to recover from those of his partners who did not pay their agreed share of the loss.

It is important to note that a specific agreement providing for an assumption of personal liability on other than an equal basis has validity *only among the partners themselves.* That is, it does not limit a partner's liability to the outside public doing business with the partnership. Such an agreement merely establishes the right of one partner to proceed against another who has not met his stipulated share of the partnership debts.

Because of this unlimited liability, the entrepreneur dealing in a potentially dangerous product or service will probably want the protection afforded by the corporate form. But in addition to incorporation, there are other methods of limiting liability in a partnership:

(a) Insurance. Insurance can cover a businessman for certain well-defined risks such as public liability, workmen's compensation, and tort claims.

(b) Reluctance of creditors to move against personal assets. Unless the liability is very large, historically, creditors have been hesitant to seize personal assets because of the legal expenses and the ill will which accrue.

(c) Putting personal assets in someone else's name. Unlimited personal liability has little meaning if there are no assets against which creditors can make claims. Thus, a transfer of those assets not needed by the business to the businessman's wife (for example) will put them beyond the reach of creditors. Indeed, if the property is owned by the wife, it can, under some conditions, even be leased to the business with no fear of liability. Two caveats: (1) if the transfers to the wife or other party were made with the sole intention of defrauding creditors, the courts will allow creditors to attach such property; (2) the wife or other

party may become involved in legal difficulties of her own, thereby exposing transferred assets to *other* creditors.

(*d*) *Special contracts.* If a creditor will accept such a limitation (and it is unlikely), liability can be limited by contract to the partnership assets. However, such a sign indicates financial weakness on the part of the partnership, and a creditor will probably refuse such terms.

(*e*) *Inactive partners.* An inactive partner is one who lends capital to a partnership and receives a share of its profits, but exercises no management control over the operations of the firm *except* to the extent needed to protect his loan. Such an inactive partner is in a superior position to the actual partners and gains his protection at the other partners' expense. Although this type of arrangement may give the inactive partner an advantage vis-à-vis the other partners in the firm, it does not limit his liability to claims outside the partnership.

3. Joint stock company. Members of a joint stock company also have unlimited personal liability. As in the case of a general partnership, an attempt may be made to contract with creditors to limit this liability to company assets, but such attempts are usually ineffective. However, some states will allow the members of a joint stock company to limit their liability upon compliance with extremely strict procedures of *notice* to the general public. But this route is a dangerous one.

4. Limited partnership. This form of enterprise gets its name from the presence of "limited" partners—partners whose liability extends only to the amount of capital they have invested in the partnership. There must be *at least one* general partner in a limited partnership, but in most other respects, a limited partnership operates like a corporation, while avoiding the double taxation inherent to that form.

There are dangers, however. For the limited partners to retain their protection from personal liability, two procedures must be followed.

(*a*) *Notice.* In order to protect creditors who might otherwise assume that all of the members of a limited partnership were general partners, an elaborate and thorough public record must be filed listing the limited partners and the amount of their potential liability. This notice requirement is normally satisfied by a registration at the local courthouse. The Uniform Limited Partnership Act, which is in force in most of the states, sets out the information which should be included in such a registration.

(*b*) *Behavior of limited partners.* In order to retain his limited liability, a limited partner must act like a limited partner—i.e., he must avoid engaging in the day-to-day management of the firm. The purpose of this rule is to protect creditors, who would naturally consider a man participating in the active management of the partnership to be a general partner.

5. Massachusetts (business) trust. In general, the beneficiaries of a Massachusetts trust are not personally liable for debts incurred by the trust. But the trustees, unlike the directors of a corporation, are personally liable. These rules, however, vary from state to state.

6. Corporation.   The corporation, as a legal entity, limits the financial risk of its owners to the amount of capital invested. Creditors can make claims only against the assets of the corporation. As an entity or fictitious "person," the corporation can sue or be sued, and can hold, buy, or sell property in a common or firm name. The corporation as an entity unto itself is thus separate from its shareholders. This is the bedrock distinction between the corporation and the other forms of enterprise. Although the other business organizations have generally acquired by statute a status as a separate legal entity for some purposes (e.g., a partnership can hold property in the partnership's name), this entity status is by no means as wide ranging as the corporation's (e.g., the property of a Massachusetts trust or a joint stock company is still held in the name of the beneficiaries of the trust).

But the entrepreneur may not be able to take full advantage of the corporation's protections against large liabilities. Usually, loans to a newly formed corporation require the personal guarantees of the company's owner/managers to assure repayment of the loan. Such personal guarantees, of course, expose the entrepreneur to personal liability for that loan.

In addition, the courts will disallow the protection afforded by the corporate shield in those cases where the corporate form is being used to defraud creditors. In a doctrine known as "piercing the corporate veil," the law will rule that the corporate shell is merely a sham, that the owner/manager's assets and the corporation's are identical, and that the individual owner is personally liable for debts incurred in the corporation's name.

C. Continuity of the concern

What happens to a business enterprise when one of its participants withdraws or dies? As we will see, the answer depends on both the nature of the participant and the type of enterprise. And the answer has important consequences, for a liquidation forced by the death or withdrawal of a participant can involve a substantial loss—as, for example, in the case where a sole (1) proprietor might have a valuable franchise terminated at his death whereas a corporate entity would maintain it.

1. Corporation.   The corporate form of doing business provides for the greatest degree of continuity. Neither the death nor withdrawal of the shareholders or managers will affect the legal existence of the corporation. There may be practical problems, however, particularly in a closely held corporation where there is no ready market for the corporation's stock. Therefore, to avoid stranding a decedent shareholder's heirs with an estate consisting of unmarketable securities, provisions should be drafted into the corporate charter requiring either the remaining living shareholders or the corporation itself to redeem the shares held in the decedent's estate.

2. Joint stock company. Because a joint stock company is not dissolved by the death or withdrawal of its trustees or managers, this form of enterprise achieves the same degree of continuity as the corporation.

3. Business trust. Again, the degree of continuity is identical to that of the corporation, since death or withdrawal of beneficiaries or owners does not affect the existence of the trust itself.

4. Limited partnership. In general, the partnership form of enterprise is particularly vulnerable to deaths or withdrawals of its participants. The limited partnership form is somewhat more stable. There are certain rules to keep in mind:

(*a*) A limited partnership is automatically dissolved by the death or withdrawal of one of the *general* partners *unless* the partnership agreement specifically provides to the contrary or *all* of the members consent to continuance.

(*b*) The death of a limited partner does not dissolve the partnership, and the partnership agreement can empower a limited partner to substitute a new limited partner in his place.

(*c*) Unless otherwise specified in the partnership agreement, a limited partner can withdraw his capital six months after he has given notice to the other partners.

5. Partnership. So flexible in other ways, the partnership form of enterprise is at its worst as regards the factor of continuity. Basically, the rule is that the death or withdrawal of one of the partners *automatically* terminates the partnership. However, entrepreneurs should not despair of using the partnership form, for the all-powerful partnership agreement can correct this flaw in continuity merely by providing to the contrary.

Indeed, appropriate provisions in the partnership agreement can mold the partnership into a form including much of the same continuity as that of a corporation. To wit:

(*a*) One of the most effective means used against withdrawal prior to the expiration of the specified term of the partnership is to provide penalties for such withdrawal. This can usually be accomplished by the agreement's allowing the remaining partners an option to purchase the withdrawing partner's interest at a discount.

(*b*) If withdrawal is *not* discouraged, but continuity is desired, the conflict may be solved by providing in the partnership agreement that any of the partners may sell or assign his partnership interest. In this case, a partnership interest would resemble stock in a corporation.

(*c*) The partnership agreement can insure the continuing existence of the partnership despite the death of a partner. Usually, the method used is for the agreement to provide for an option or absolute obligation of the remaining partners to buy the deceased partner's interest. The purchase is made at a price determined by some prearranged method of valuation (such as valuation by appraisers, periodical valuation by the partners themselves, capitalization of earnings, or book value). Where the remaining partners are not likely to have the resources to pay a substantial sum in cash, the use of life insurance can be an effective solution.

(*d*) Where the partnership is a personal service business and tangible assets do not contribute materially to the business, the purchase of the deceased partner's interest may not be appropriate. In this case, the agreement can provide for the estate or heir to continue as a partner for a given amount of time. During such time, of course, the estate or heir would be entitled to the deceased partner's share of the profits.

In sum then, it is always wise to provide for continuity in the partnership agreement. If no such provision is in evidence, the death or withdrawal of a partner can necessitate a forced liquidation of the partnership, a situation which is likely to cause financial loss to the remaining partners.

6. Sole proprietorship. Although individual proprietorships, unlike corporations or partnerships, have no time limit on their existence, they are obviously not perpetual since the death of the proprietor dissolves the business.

D. Transferability of interest

Unrestricted transferability of interest in a business enterprise may or may not be desirable. On the one hand, participants in the enterprise may want the right to consider all potential new members and be able to refuse those considered unattractive, for whatever reason. On the other hand, these same participants probably want to be able to leave the enterprise freely and quickly, without subjecting the sale or assignment of their interest to the potentially capricious scrutiny of the other participants. These two desires are the polar extremes and may be charted:

Desire to screen new members	Desire to be able to sell or assign one's individual interest at one's own choosing
● ←	→ ●

Depending on which of these conflicting desires is greater, an organizational form can be chosen either to bridle or to give free reign to transferability.

1. Sole proprietorship. The sole proprietor has complete freedom to sell or transfer any part of his business. Limitations on transferability of interest arise when individuals who have joined together decide that prospective participants must be screened by the established group. Since the sole proprietor is by definition working alone, he is free to do what he wants with his business.

2. Joint stock company. Ownership interest in a joint stock company, like stock in a corporation, is freely transferable. An additional benefit is that, unlike the case regarding corporations, such transfers do not disturb control.

3. Business trust. As with the ownership interest in a joint stock company, the beneficial interests in a business trust are freely transferable without disturbing control.

4. Corporation. The corporation offers extreme flexibility in the transfer of interest. The ownership of corporate property may be divided into any number of combinations of shares with varying rights regarding income and assets. Shareholders do not need the consent of the other shareholders in order to sell or give away their interests, but such transfers can be restricted by agreement as we shall see. Unlike the cases of the business trust or the joint stock company, such transfers have the *disadvantage* of potentially modifying the control of a corporation through the power stockholders generally have to elect directors. On the other hand, these voting rights (rights not provided by ownership interests in either the business trust or the joint stock company), make it likely that such shares will be more liquid.

Thus, we can see that the corporate form of enterprise exists at the pole of free transferability of interest. As such, the corporate form offers no insurance of control to the original stockholders—especially in the situations when an individual shareholder dies or sells his stock, or when new stock is issued. To the participants in a small corporation, this lack of say-so regarding new shareholders can be a matter of deep concern.

The courts have held reasonable, and therefore valid, restrictions which are designed to promote efficiency in management by placing conditions upon the introduction of outsiders into the corporation as shareholders. Examples are restrictions which give the corporation or shareholders an option to purchase the stock at a specified price or the right of first refusal. In effect, an option or right of first refusal assures that all of the shareholders will have an opportunity to veto the admission of a new shareholder.

5. Limited partnership. As a form of enterprise, the limited partnership is the perfect compromise between the desire to have veto power over prospective new participants in the business, and the desire to have free transferability of ownership interest. It lies *between* the two poles. The general partner in such an arrangement can only transfer his interest with the consent of all the other general partners. The limited partner, on the other hand, can sell his interest without such consent. Since a limited partner is by definition one who cannot actively participate in the management of the business, the substituted, new limited partner is merely one who is entitled to the share of the profits which would have been due his predecessor.

Thus, the limited partnershp form can permit the active managers of a business (the general partners) to keep out undesirable new managers, while at the same time allowing the investors in the business (the limited partners) to transfer their interests.

6. Partnership. Without an express agreement to the contrary, a partner may not sell or assign his interest in the partnership without the consent of all of the other partners. If the corporate form lies at the pole of totally free transferability, the partnership form is at the opposite pole of complete veto power. Thus, a partner will never have an undesirable new partner forced upon him against his will, but he may have to see the partnership liquidated in order to dispose of his interest. Of course, the partnership agreement can be written to permit free transferability of partnership interest.

E. Management control and regulations

If the entrepreneur is a skillful administrator, he will probably want to retain as much control over his business as he can. He will thus try to avoid intervention by either the government or other would-be managers. How do the six forms of enterprise stack up against these criteria?

1. Sole proprietorship. A sole proprietorship is the most free form of business organization. There are no formalities limiting the owner's control. He can make all of his own decisions. Because he is operating alone, the sole proprietor is the single locus of authority in the business.

With respect to government regulation, the sole proprietor is also unhindered. He can normally conduct business in his own or any other state without the sort of registration and qualification procedures typically required of the other forms of enterprise. This rule of thumb is subject only to compliance with general statutes regarding trading under an assumed or fictitious name. And, too, there are a few exceptions of businesses which require special licenses. But in general, control and supervision by federal, state, and local authorities affect the sole proprietor no more than any other individual.

2. Partnership. It is inevitable that the addition of associates will chip away at the single entrepreneur's control of his business. In a partnership, for example, the majority rules (one vote per partner) *unless* the partnership agreement states otherwise. To be practical, however, it is unlikely that our hypothetical entrepreneur will be able to attract partners who will abdicate their voting rights. In addition to this simple voting power, a partner can make his weight felt (and thereby exert a sort of *indirect* control) in several other ways: he can threaten to withdraw, an act which would force dissolution of the partnership. But more important (because it is a day-to-day matter), because each partner is an agent of the partnership, any one partner can bind the entire partnership in a business arrangement, even if it is contrary to the opinions of the majority. To see how this works, look at this example: Mr. X thinks that his contracting partnership should buy a new truck. His proposal, however, is voted down by the other three partners. Mr. X ignores the vote against him and buys the truck, representing to the truck dealer that he is acting not for himself as an individual but for the partnership. Despite the vote of the other partners, the partnership is legally bound to pay for the truck.

Because of the delicate webs of control (both direct and indirect) operating within the confines of a partnership, it is critical *(a)* that the partners get along with each other; *(b)* that certain areas of authority are carefully spelled out, especially in the partnership agreement; and finally, if all else fails, *(c)* that provisions for penalties be drafted into the agreement for acts which are in derogation of the majority vote.

Like the proprietorship, the partnership is relatively free of government regulation and restrictions. A partnership may be operated with a minimum of formality. This freedom can be a definite advantage over a corporation. Usually, a general partnership is not required to publish financial statements and is free to trade anywhere.

3. Limited partnership. With respect to management control and government regulation, the limited partnership, as it does in so many areas, exists as a halfway house between the freedoms and dangers of the general partnership and the restrictions and safeties of the corporation. In the limited partnership, we get a hint of the separation of ownership from control, although the separation is not as distinct as it becomes in the large corporation. In a limited partnership, the general partners have control of the business. Indeed, if a limited partner participates in the management of the business, he loses his limited liability and becomes liable as a general partner. The Uniform Limited Partnership Act does, however, allow a limited partner to participate in a few acts without loss of his limited partnership status: he may vote on the admission of a new partner into the firm and may use partnership property for private purposes.

It should be recalled that in order to protect creditors, a limited partnership requires a thorough registration proceeding. The purpose of such a proceeding is to inform prospective creditors of the scope of authority among the partners by indicating which are to be general partners and which are to be limited partners.

4. Corporation. With the corporate form of enterprise, it is necessary to distinguish between two kinds of control: *(a)* the *legal, formal control* that resides with those who own the majority of the voting stock; and *(b)* the *working* control exercised by those who actually manage the day-to-day conduct of the corporation's business. The same group may possess *both* types of control, and in a small, new corporation, this possibility is a likely one. Typically, the founding entrepreneur will retain a majority of the voting stock in the new enterprise. If he also is the principal manager of the business, he has both types of control well in hand. His position is strengthened by the fact that disgruntled minorities cannot exert the type of indirect control possible in a partnership. Their withdrawal will not force dissolution; their capricious acts cannot bind the corporation.

But the larger the corporation becomes, the more likely there will come into existence that separation of ownership and control which characterizes the giant modern businesses. When the entrepreneur is no longer the principal executive officer, he is reduced to the status of a typical shareholder-owner whose only influence on the management and control of the corporation is indirect—through the election of a board of directors. This intermediate board in turn elects the chief operating officers, and it is they who have the working control of the business.

In such a situation, marshaling effective minority opposition can be difficult. Voting rights are normally (but not necessarily) allocated on a one-vote-per-share basis, but if the stock is widely held, even a *minority* interest in control of the company can be difficult to dislodge because of the lack of an organized opposition.

What solutions are available to the entrepreneur who needs equity capital, but wishes to retain control, or at least to retain management participation similar to that of a partnership? Several:

(a) *Nonvoting stock.*   If nonvoting stock and voting stock are issued in appropriate proportions, control on the basis of proportional equity contributions can be avoided. Nonvoting stock is not allowed in Illinois.

(b) *Cumulative voting.*   In most cases (as long as the number of directors to be elected at each election is sufficiently large), cumulative voting will assure representation on the board of directors since it allows each shareholder to cast all his votes for one director rather than spreading them equally among the number of directors to be elected.

(c) *Preemptive rights.*   Preemptive rights allow a shareholder to purchase a pro rata portion of any stock issued in the future; thereby insuring the preservation of his existing voting control by preventing dilution of his interest. A rigid rule requiring such rights can, however, prove to be a nuisance.

(d) *Classification of shares.*   Allowed in most states, classification of stock can insure representation on the board by entitling each class of stock to elect a specific proportion of the board. If the state requires that all classes of stock be allowed to vote for all the seats on the board, each party can receive the same number of shares to assure equality of vote—

but those who have advanced the most capital can be given stock of a different class bearing higher dividend and liquidation rights.

(e) *Voting trusts and pooling arrangements.* In a voting trust, legal title to the stock is issued in the name of a trustee who votes the deposited stock in accordance with the trust agreement. Thus, during the term of the trust, a shareholder can be assured of maintaining proportionate representation. A pooling arrangement accomplishes the same purpose as a voting trust, but avoids statutory formalities. In pooling agreements, the parties agree to elect certain persons (or each other) as directors. Courts in a number of states look with disapproval on various forms of voting trusts and pooling arrangements.

(f) *Shareholder agreements.* Although the above suggested devices help to insure representation on the board of directors, a minority interest would still have a difficult time exerting any real control over the operation of the corporation, since on the board a mere majority rules. Thus, representation may not be enough. But shareholder agreements requiring unanimity for all shareholders' or directors' resolutions have historically been struck down by the courts. The rationale is that such agreements would require the corporation to be governed like a partnership, and the courts will not allow an enterprise to operate as a disguised partnership with limited liability. There are some states, however, where such stockholder agreements *are* valid.

With regard to government regulations, the corporation is particularly trammeled by formalities with which the other forms of enterprise do not have to contend. Briefly, the corporation must act in accordance with its charter and bylaws, hold meetings of stockholders and directors, keep accurate books of accounts and minutes of meetings, register in states other than its domicile before transacting business in those states, and file financial information and tax reports.

5. Joint stock company, and 6. Business trust. Because the board of trustees of a joint stock company or of a business trust, unlike the board of directors of a corporation, is not subject to recall by annual elections, the members or beneficiaries of these organizational forms have less control over the management of business than do shareholders in a comparable corporation. Thus, there is great continuity of management control lodged with such trustees. However, these trustees can be held accountable to elections if either the joint venture agreement or the trust certificate so provides. In such cases, these forms of enterprise resemble a partnership. Finally, in many states, these two forms have been statutorily classified as corporations, with the attendant rules governing that form having authority.

Vis-à-vis the government, it should be remembered that both the joint venture and the business trust require registration documents, but post-filing regulations are few.

F. Attractiveness for raising capital

The entrepreneur is almost always concerned with the need to raise capital for his firm's requirements. He should consider this need in his choice of organizational form, since some forms are clearly more suitable for enticing capital investors.

1. Sole proprietorship, and 2. Partnership. Because of the unlimited personal liability incurred by investors in sole proprietorships and partnerships, these two forms are the *least* attractive for raising equity capital. They are particularly unattractive to the very class of investor who is most desirable—the wealthy private individual. Few wealthy individuals are willing to expose their entire personal fortunes to the vagaries of a struggling small business. Should the enterprise fail or be subject to heavy legal damages, such an investor would be unlimitedly liable for debts owed, and his personal assets could be entirely wiped out. Thus, if an entrepreneur contemplates large capital needs which he himself cannot meet, he should avoid the sole proprietorship or the general partnership.

3. Joint stock company. Joint stock companies are somewhat more appealing to an outsider than are partnerships, since the investor need not participate in the management, and since the shares are transferable. On the other hand, as in a partnership, an investor is unlimitedly liable for debts incurred by the business. So, in general, this is not an attractive form for capital-raising purposes.

4. Business trust. The business trust would seem to be a relatively useful form for enticing equity investors. Such capital contributors are afforded the protection of limited liability, and they do not have to take part in the management of the business. But the general lack of familiarity with this form of enterprise is likely to make money raising difficult. It is really known in few places outside of Massachusetts.

5. Limited partnership. Because of the limited liability afforded the limited partners in a limited partnership, this form is very attractive to wealthy investors. An additional advantage is that such investors can remain passive, as they are, in effect, stockholders. The limited partnership is somewhat more flexible than the corporation: e.g., profits and losses can be divided in various manners among the general and the limited partners, with no requirement that the division proceed strictly according to the amount invested. While variances in profit distributions can also be achieved in the corporate form by means of various classes of stocks possessing different dividend rights, the process is more rigid. The limited partnership, for these reasons of flexibility, has, of course, become a very popular form in real estate ventures. There is one *drawback* to the limited partnership form regarding capital raising—the blocks of ownership are much less liquid than shares in a publicly held corporation.

6. Corporation. The corporation is the traditional business form for raising equity capital. Shares in a corporation offer: *(a)* limited liability, *(b)* a proportional interest of the total profits, *(c)* marketability, *(d)* liquidity, and *(e)* flexibility to divide shares. Nevertheless, one should be aware that small companies may find these attributes are theoretical when there is a thin market.

There is generally a statutory minimum of capital required in many states for a corporation (and sometimes for joint stock companies and business trusts when they are treated as corporations), but the requirement is usually only a nominal one.

G. Taxes

The choice of organizational form for *most* businesses usually comes down to a choice between the corporation and the partnership. Such a choice may be controlled by the considerations we have been discussing—i.e., tax matters may be incidental to a more fundamental need of the enterprise, such as limited liability. Increasingly, however, the difference in tax liabilities between partnerships and corporations is proving to be the dispositive factor. A complete summary of tax law relating to businesses is, of course, beyond the scope of this Note, which concentrates only on those tax rules which will affect the initial choice of organizational form.

1. Taxes on operations: The importance of the entity. The major difference between the taxation of partnerships and proprietorships on the one hand and corporations on the other can be summarized in one word—entity.

Corporations (and any associations taxed as corporations) are taxed as separate entities. The income stream is then taxed again when it is distributed by the corporation to its shareholders in a nondeductible form such as dividends. The result, of course, is a double taxation on the same income stream, as the diagram in Figure 1 indicates.

In contrast, neither a proprietorship nor a partnership is a taxpaying entity. These organizational forms serve only as nontaxable *conduits* of income and deductions. The confusion surrounding this point results from the fact that the partnership and the proprietorship *do* have a legal identity distinct from that of their partners or owners. But such an identity constitutes only a reporting entity for accounting purposes.

Thus, even though the partnership itself is not subject to taxation, it is required to calculate and report partnership income for the purpose of determinig the distributive share to which each partner is entitled. Such a return is *only* for informational needs however. It is the individual partners (or owner in the case of a proprietorship) who pay tax on their pro rata shares of income and expense items. They report these items on their individual returns as if they were each in business as individuals.

FIGURE 1

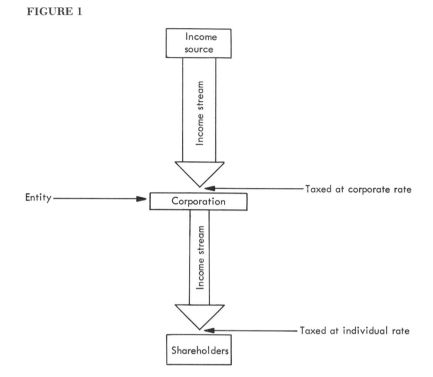

To emphasize the role of the partnership as a mere conduit, we can note that a partner is taxed on that share of the partnership's current income to which the partnership agreement entitles him—*regardless of whether such income is actually distributed at the immediate time.* As opposed to a corporation, there can thus be no unreasonable accumulated earnings tax levied against a partnership, since the current distributive shares are immediately taxed. On the other hand, it may create cash flow problems for the individual in that taxes may become due on occasions when no cash is received.

For this disadvantage of immediate taxation, whether or not he has actually received his distributive share, the partner receives a significant advantage: the character of each income and expense item reported by the partnership is preserved when passed through to the partner. That is, a capital gain to the partnership will be taxed as a capital gain to the partner. Even charitable contributions and foreign tax credits retain their character when passed through to the partner. And losses from the partnership can be used by the partner to offset against other income. This conduit approach is opposed to the corporate situation where income is "cleansed" and loses its character when passed on to the shareholders. The result there, of course, is that *all* income to shareholders is taxed as ordinary income, and losses cannot be used to offset other income until the shareholder sells his stock or the corporation is liquidated. The diagram in Figure 2 summarizes the conduit approach to partnership taxation law.

FIGURE 2

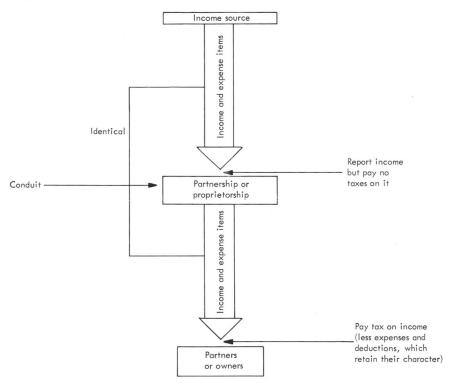

As we have seen, the crucial disadvantage of the corporate form of doing business is the inherent double taxation. To minimize this effect, businessmen have often tried the following measures:

(a) Paying high salaries to the owner/manager (tax deductible to the corporation).

(b) "Thin stock": investing in a company with a high proportion of debt as opposed to equity (debt provides a tax free return of capital to the investor, and prior to its repayment, the interest is deductible by the corporation).

(c) Making leasing arrangements with shareholders (shareholder ownership of plant and equipment permits tax free [to the corporation] repayment of money to the shareholders).

The tax commissioner rules on the "reasonableness" of the above. The term is difficult to define precisely although some basis for reasonableness can usually be established. For example, in determining whether a salary is excessive, comparisons might be made with other individuals with similar responsibilities in the same industry. In the case of stock, a rough rule of thumb is that a 3 to 1 debt/equity ratio will not be challenged.

A better way for a corporation to avoid double taxation is: elect to be taxed as a partnership. Such a choice (Subchapter S election) is permitted only in certain instances. The electing corporation must *(a)* be a domestic corporation; *(b)* have only one class of stock outstanding; *(c)* have 10 or fewer nonalien shareholders (only individuals or estates), all of whom must consent to the election; and *(d)* not have more than 20 percent of its gross income from "passive income" such as interest, dividends, rents, royalties, annuities, or gains from the sale or exchange of securities.

After such an election, a stockholder in the Subchapter S corporation includes on his personal income tax returns his pro rata share of the corporation's distributed or undistributed income or loss—as in the case of a partnership.

Another possibility for the businessman is to operate in the partnership or proprietorship form in the early stages of his business, switching to the corporate form when profits become higher. The reverse (i.e., the change from a corporation to a partnership) is also possible; but the shareholders are treated as having exchanged their stock for corporate assets, and the fair market value of the property received in the liquidation is matched against the basis of the stock to find the taxable gain or loss.

A corporation may also issue its stock as Section 1244 stock, which permits any loss incurred by original owners (on the sale, exchange, or even worthlessness of the stock) to be treated as an ordinary rather than a capital loss.

Finally, one should also be aware how a particular organization is classified by the Internal Revenue Service (IRS) for tax purposes. Determining the classification is not automatic, especially in the more hybrid forms of organizations which possess attributes of more than one organization form. The Internal Revenue Code divides the ordinary business entities into four general categories:

(a) Individual or sole proprietorship.

(b) A *partnership* which includes not only common law partnerships, but syndicates, groups, pools, joint ventures, or other organizations which are "not a trust, estate or corporation" under the Internal Revenue Code.

(c) A *corporation* includes certain associations, joint stock companies, business trusts, and certain partnerships possessing specified corporate attributes.

(d) A *trust* under state law generally includes those businesses which do not resemble a partnership or corporation in nature or activities. These generalities can be somewhat clarified by reference to the regulations and decisions of the courts in typical factual situations. The aid of a lawyer is essential.

For most practical purposes, a proprietorship, partnership, and trust (which distributes its income) are all nontaxable conduits—as opposed to the corporation, which is a taxable entity.

2. Initial organization. At the time of formation of the business, state and local taxes in the form of license fees are usually imposed on the type of business rather than the form of organization. If they are levied on one form and not another, or are recurring, they are usually nominal, and thus of little significance for this discussion. (In a few states there are fairly sizable annual franchise fees for corporations. Federal income tax consequences, however, *are* of importance.

(a) Sole proprietorship. With this form, commencement of business incurs no additional income tax for the individual. Similarly, there are no taxable gains or losses attributable to those assets which are assigned to the proprietorship. And, as with other forms of business the owner is entitled to deductions for items used in the business such as automobiles.

(b) Partnership. The crucial distinction to make here is between contributions of property and services. Contributions of *property* to a partnership do not constitute taxable transactions, even though the market value of the contributed property may increase or decrease as a result of the partnership formation. Such property contributions may even be made in installments (i.e., with some transfers occurring after the partnership has been established) without incurring tax liability.

On the other hand, the general rule is that tax liability accrues when a partner receives a share in the partnership capital in exchange for *services* rendered. Such a "service partner" must report ordinary income in that year. If, however, the service partner is not credited with a percentage of contributed capital, but only given the right to a share in future partnership income, no tax liability is incurred.

(c) Corporation. The acquisition of stock for cash entails no immediate tax consequences: gain or loss will not be recognized until the new shareholder disposes of his stock (or until it becomes worthless). But the transfer of *property* to a corporation in exchange for stock *is* a taxable transaction to the extent that the stock he receives has a greater value than the property he contributes.

However, the founders of a new corporation can generally postpone such a tax by complying with the "nonrecognition" provisions of the Internal Revenue Code. Section 351 provides for tax free incorporation when at least 80 percent of the voting stock outstanding is controlled by the transferers. There are other, more detailed requirements which also must be followed, and the entrepreneur should consult his lawyer to avoid incurring immediate tax liability. Such liability is, of course, only postponed by compliance with 351 and not avoided altogether, for any appreciation in the value of property transferred should eventually be reflected in the value of the stock received and the gain taxed when that stock is subsequently sold.

As with a partnership, ownership interest in a corporation is a taxable event when it is received for services. The stockholder is considered to have received income in the amount of the value of the stock he received for his services and in the year that the stock, or promise of the stock, was received.

3. Retention of earnings and withdrawal of profits.

(a) *Partnerships.* As we have explained, partners do not need to withdraw the profits of the partnership in order to be taxed. They must include in their reported taxable income their distributable share of the partnership income for the taxable year—whether or not it is withdrawn. The partnership agreement is controlling as to the amount of that distributive share, as well as to the amount of particular losses, deductions, or credits to which the partner is entitled. Special IRS rules and doctrines govern how income and expense items may be allocated.

(b) *Corporation.* As opposed to a partnership, the earnings of a corporation are not taxable to the shareholder until they are distributed and received. Eventually, earnings distributed in the form of dividends will be taxed at the shareholder's individual tax rate.

In addition, taxable dividends may be paid in media other than cash and, unlike partnership distributions, need not be made in proportion to stock ownership. Such property is frequently distributed with the value disguised to provide for bargain purchases by the shareholders. But in such cases, the differential from fair market value is taxed as a dividend.

Where considerable earnings are anticipated, it may appear that the corporation form has immediate tax advantages—the corporation can receive the income stream (taxed at the relatively low corporate rate of 22 percent on the first $25,000 of profits and 48 percent on additional amounts) and hold it, thereby forestalling the individual's taxes. Ultimately, the shareholder can reap his profits through the sale of his appreciated stock or through a corporate liquidation—both events taxed at capital gains rates.

What attempts to prevent this scheme from working? *Two tax rules:*

(1) *Accumulated earnings tax.* It may seem logical for a corporation to accumulate earnings and only distribute them when the shareholders have little other income or have experienced outside losses. But the corporation may be liable for an accumulated earnings tax if it accumulates earnings for the purpose of avoiding income tax to shareholders

rather than for the reasonable needs of the business *and* if the accumulation is larger than $100,000.

Accumulations are usually considered unreasonable if they are used for the personal needs of the shareholders, for loans to shareholders, for loans having no reasonable relation to the conduct of the business, for investment in properties or securities unrelated to the business, or even for protection against generalized or unrealistic hazards.

(2) *Redemption treated as dividend.* A particularly difficult part of the Internal Revenue Code sets forth the rule that any distribution in redemption or cancellation of stock which is nothing more than a disguised attempt to distribute earnings and profits will be treated as an ordinary dividend—and thus, as opposed to a legitimate redemption (taxed at capital gains rates), will be taxed at ordinary income rates.

In passing, the entrepreneur should note that receipt of stock dividends or rights is normally not taxable as a dividend. Such a distribution merely transfers surplus to a capital account.

4. Withdrawal of capital and liquidation. The sections concerning capital withdrawals, liquidations, and redemptions are among the most treacherously difficult in the Code. Only a bare sketch of the outline of these provisions can be given here. It cannot be emphasized enough that the entrepreneur should consult his lawyer before making any major moves.

(a) Partnership. Since the partnership, like the sole proprietorship, is not treated as a separate entity for tax purposes, the withdrawal of assets from the business is not a taxable event. Partners generally realize no gain on a current distribution or withdrawal *unless* the money received exceeds the adjusted basis of his partnership interest. In such a case, the gain is a capital gain. Thus, in a distribution of capital, the partners, like the proprietor, are considered as receiving what they already had.

In liquidating the partnership, either of two things may happen: (1) the partnership's assets are sold and the money distributed to the partners; or (2) the partnership's assets are distributed to the partners in kind.

For tax purposes, the sale of the partnership's assets results in capital or ordinary income or loss depending on the nature of the assets. Such income or loss will then be included in each partner's share, and the actual distribution produces no additional tax. If (2) is followed, each partner receives his proportional share of the assets and realizes capital gain to the extent that any money received from eventual sale exceeds the partner's basis for his partnership interest. The distribution and sale of inventory and accounts receivable generally do not result in capital gains.

(b) Corporation. The situation is not as clear-cut for the corporation. Partial liquidations versus dividends: The critical distinction is between a redemption treated as a partial liquidation and a redemption treated as

a de facto dividend. The significance inherent in this distinction is simply put: partial liquidations are accorded capital gains treatment; dividends are taxed at ordinary income rates.

In broad terms, a selling shareholder has three methods whereby he can obtain capital gains treatment for the redemption of his stock—i.e,, three methods for effecting a valid partial liquidation:

(1) The distribution will not be treated as a dividend if it is a "substantially disproportionate redemption of stock" with respect to the shareholder. The precise rules require the shareholder to own, after the redemption, less than 50 percent of the voting stock, and to have his own stockholding reduced by more than 20 percent by the redemption.

(2) The distribution will not be treated as a dividend if it is "in complete redemption of all stock of the corporation owned by the shareholder" (i.e., a complete termination of the shareholder's interest).

(3) The distribution will not be treated as a dividend if it "is not essentially equivalent to a dividend." This general test, however, is not of much help, since the courts will almost invariably refer back to the single most important criterion: how disproportionate the transaction is. However, there are some rulings which illustrate that even though a redemption is not sufficiently disproportionate to qualify as a "substantially disproportionate redemption (see 1)," it may still be disproportionate enough to satisfy this nonequivalence test.

The burden of proof in all of these cases will be on the shareholder to prove that the redemption was a partial liquidation and not a dividend.

Sale of corporation. The technique of a *sale* of a corporate business is of vital concern since it may mean realizing tax twice— at both corporate and stockholder level—if the assets rather than stock interests are sold. If the shareholders sell the corporation itself by selling all their stock in the corporation outright to a third party purchaser, the corporation realizes no taxable gain or loss but the shareholders do. Or if the buyer is unable to buy out the entire stock of the corporation, the stockholders may sell the part the buyer can afford and have the corporation redeem the balance. The sellers generally realize capital gain.

But if the corporation sells all the assets and distributes the proceeds to the shareholders in a complete liquidation, both the corporation and the shareholder will be liable for the appropriate capital gain or loss unless the sale by the corporation was pursuant to a plan of complete liquidation adopted within 12 months prior to the sale. An alternative to avoid the double tax would be for the corporation to be completely liquidated and the assets distributed to the shareholders who would then sell them. The corporation realizes no gain on the liquidation (the corporation must not have acted as the sales agent), and the shareholders have a capital gain or loss on the liquidation. This produces a "stepped-up" basis which in part determines the gain or loss when they later sell the assets.

Collapsible corporations. Collapsible corporations first came into being in the movie industry. Having agreed to work for low salaries, the producer, director, and leading stars would form a corporation to make a picture—a corporation that would be liquidated (or "collapsed" to use the pejorative) after the picture was finished, but *before* it had been released to distributors. At that point, the corporation's value would be the one picture which had only an estimated value. That estimated value would then be attributed to each of the shareholders, who would report any excess over investment as a capital gain. In this way, income that was potentially ordinary was converted to capital gains.

After similar practices were adopted in the real estate industry and other businesses producing one-shot, expensive products or services, Congress cracked down. Now the Code blocks such conversions of ordinary income on corporate income-producing property to capital gain by premature sales of stock or premature distributions to shareholders. If the sale or distribution occurs before the corporation realizes "a substantial part of the taxable income to be derived from the property," the corporation is said to collapse, and the proceeds of the sale will be classified as ordinary income.

REFERENCES

Bittker, Boris, and Eustice, James. *Federal Income Taxation of Corporations and Shareholders.* Boston: Gorham & Lamont, 1971.

Deer, Richard E., chief reporter. *The Lawyer's Basic Corporate Practice Manual.* Associate reporters: Anderson, John T.; Choka, Allen D.; Garling-house, John G.; Scott, Myrl R.; and Simpson, Russell G. Philadelphia: Joint Committee on Continuing Legal Education of the American Law Institute and American Bar Association, 1970.

Federal Tax Handbook. Englewood Cliffs, N.J.: Prentice-Hall, 1972.

Internal Revenue Code. Chicago: Commerce Clearing House, 1973.

Smith, Dan. *Tax Factors in Business Decisions.* Englewood Cliffs, N.J.: Prentice-Hall, 1968.

Tax Choices in Organizing a Business. Chicago: Commerce House, 1969.

U.S. Master Tax Guide. Chicago: Commerce Clearing House, 1973.

TABLE I

	Organizational requirements and their costs	Liability of owners	Continuity of the concern	Transferability of interest	Management control and regulations	Attractiveness for raising capital	Taxation
Sole proprietorship	Minimal expense and organization requirement	Unlimited personal liability	Dissolved at death of sole proprietor	Free to sell or transfer	Complete freedom of management; minimum formal regulation	Related directly to the individual's ability	
General partnership	Minimal expense; no registration or filing fee; written articles of agreement not required although advisable	Unlimited personal liability	Can be dissolved at death or withdrawal of a general partner	Consent of all general partners required	Generally management by majority; minimum formal regulation	Related directly to the individual's ability	
Limited partnership	Statutory requirements usually include written agreement and statement of general and limited partners; exceeds cost of general partnership	Limited partners; liability equal to amount invested; general partners: unlimited personal liability	Limited partners: death or withdrawal does not affect; general partners: death or withdrawal can dissolve partnership	Limited partners: have right to sell; general partners: consent of all general partners required	Limited partners: not allowed to participate in management; general partners: generally management by majority minimum formal regulation	Limited partners: limited liability a strong advantage in raising capital although share may not be liquid	Often the most important and complicated criteria; hinges on concept of taxable entity
Joint stock company	No statutory requirements but generally written articles of agreement; organization and expense similar to general partnership.	Unlimited personal liability	Continuity of business despite death or withdrawal of member	Ownership interest freely transferable but without disturbing control	Greater continuity of management control by board of trustees which is not subject to annual election; less formalized than a corporation	Generally more than partnership and less than corporation	
Corporation	Requires and costs the most; articles in-corporation, statutory regulations, filing fees based on capital structure; require ments in all states where do business	Liability limited to amount invested	Continuity of business despite death or withdrawal of shareholder	Transferability through shares of any combination of assets or income	Management control in hands of board of directors influenced by votes of shareholders; require greatest formality and regulation	Generally, the most attractive form	
Business or Massachusetts trust	Requires declaration of trust	Generally, beneficiaries: limited liability; trustee: unlimited personal liability	Continuity of business despite death or withdrawal of beneficiary or trustee	Beneficial interest freely transferable but without disturbing control	Greater continuity of management control by board of trustees not subject to annual election; less formalized than corporation	Generally, more attractive than partnership and less than corporation	

Cases

Ar-Tech Packaging

Late in April of 1969 Bob D'Amore (see Exhibit 1 for résumé) was wrestling with the possible consequences of decisions that he would have to make during the next few days. Bob had started a company during his first year at the Harvard Business School and he believed the operation had progressed reasonably well. Now, in his second year of business school and only a month away from graduation, he had to decide whether to attempt to acquire another small company as the first step in expanding the scope of his present business. In considering the acquisition he thought he needed to analyze this particular situation not only as it related to his existing company but also as it affected a number of other plans and ideas that he had had. Bob also had to admit to himself that he could not ignore the fact that in the spring of 1969 M.B.A.'s were being exposed to a wide range of job offers, some of which Bob thought could be an excellent and lucrative stepping stone to pursue his goals without the immediate risks inherent in an entrepreneurial situation. Bob felt a certain extra pressure on him as he had begun his career as a businessman at the age of 32, five to ten years later than his classmates because of an extended military experience. He knew that for better or for worse he was likely to follow whatever path he now chose for a number of years.

Bob D'Amore

Having graduated from the U.S. Military Academy at West Point in 1958, Bob had realized after three years active duty that he did not want to make a career of the Army. Nevertheless, it was another six years before he actually applied for and, with a great deal of hassle, received his discharge. During this time he had served with the Army Signal

Corps as a rated parachutist, been the youngest company commander of a line company in the Army, and risen to the rank of major. What finally prompted him to seek a discharge was a long series of correspondence which he had carried on from Vietnam in 1966–1967 with his brother-in-law, Arthur Aulenback (see Exhibit 2 for résumé). Art had lamented the corporate game he had been playing as an employee of a large corporation. As an alternative Bob had proposed that Art go into business with him. Art accepted. Bob decided, however, to prepare himself by first attending Harvard Business School.

The search

Bob began his search for a new enterprise almost immediately upon entering school. His first step had been to take stock of his own and his partner's objectives. Art stated his very simply; he wanted to get rich quickly. After nine years in the Army and no business experience, Bob's immediate objective was to find a situation where he could gain experience and build a track record for return on investment. Eventually he hoped (and wrote down):

> to build a business conglomerate whose worth will be measured not only in market value, but in terms of its scintillating interest, and the personal development its challenges will accrue. . . . I have no real time or net worth schedules by which to measure my progress. Each step I take will be an end in itself, and I will attempt to avoid becoming locked into a "good thing" at some plateau because it is making money. Rather, I will judge my success by the ratio of new ideas to old ones used up. Should the ratio ever decrease—then I'll know that it is then time to turn to the arts, and try some writing and painting.

To aid him in filtering the possibilities Bob developed a number of criteria:

--Minimum required investment (Bob and Art had practically no capital and Bob had already stretched his personal credit in order to pay his business school bills. He believed he would not be able to buy an already operating business).
--Requires highly innovative *general* technical competence.
--In a growth market segment and avoids head-on competition with larger firms.
--Maximum exposure to other businesses and opportunities.
--Open-ended to horizontal and vertical integration for growth and strength.
--Attractive to potential investors whose business influence could be used advantageously.
--Attractive as an acquisition by a larger firm to leave an "out" if interests change.

With the above criteria in mind Bob uncovered the following possibilities:

Computer software
Foreign auto repair
Industrial real estate
Automotive speed shop
Industrial packaging

After evaluating the possibilities, it appeared that industrial packaging best met the criteria. This choice was much encouraged by the fact that Art had extensive experience and contacts in the industry which would help balance Bob's lack of business experience and the demands placed on his time by the M.B.A. program at Harvard. A review of Dun & Bradstreet reports on the packaging houses and corrugated sheet plants in Massachusetts showed impressive growth to Bob in every instance. Many of the firms had initial capital investments ranging from $7,000 to $25,000 and in less than 10 years were doing a quarter to over $1 million in annual sales without significantly diluting the original equity. Bob found, though, that profits were harder to pin down as most firms seemed to be understating them or negating them altogether by salary withdrawals and accelerated depreciation of rapidly expanding equipment assets. Nonetheless he thought the industry offered a particularly good fit for himself and Art.

Thus by Christmas of his first year, Bob had decided not only to create his own firm together with a partner (see Exhibit 3 for the partnership agreement), but he had also chosen the industry in which to do it. During the cold New England winter months ahead, he began to distill his plans.

Ar-Tech Packaging

After study and consultation with Art, Bob began to define more specifically the segment of the industrial packaging industry that his firm, Ar-Tech Packaging, would go after. The solid fiberboard or "chip board" (commonly called cardboard) houses that handled industrial shippers were almost nonexistent since they had been displaced by corrugated shippers. It appeared that those chip board houses that remained fought in a hotly contested market for point-of-purchase boxes such as those for baked goods, cereals, and so on, selling basically paper and labor in an extremely price-sensitive market. Bob felt that the more successful houses dealt in colorful point-of-purchase containers for large accounts, particularly cosmetics and pharmaceuticals. Entry in this market was difficult because the equipment required large capital outlays, and selling would require a highly trained and knowledgeable sales organization. Therefore, Bob decided not to deal with chip board except in a brokerage capacity as an extra service for important customers.

On the other end of the spectrum, he had no intention of competing with the corrugated giants like Allied Container or West Virginia Pulp and Paper. Instead, Bob's initial strategy was to attack the market segment that the larger corrugated houses did not want: users who bought short runs of corrugated containers (generally less than 2,000 units) and who therefore could not take advantage of the economies of scale in the manufacturing process that the large production houses had built in. The larger houses sold the corrugated sheet in bulk to the smaller houses to do these jobs. Bob guessed that the larger houses were interested in seeing that the needs of this small-order segment were met with corrugated sheet so these customers would become accustomed to its use.

To differentiate from other short-run houses, Bob wanted Ar-Tech to be a service-oriented packaging house which would offer complete analysis of packaging problems and provide packaging design and consultation as well as the packing itself. He wanted to concentrate on those customers who wanted more than just a box—those who wanted and needed an engineered shipping container to protect a delicate product or to improve efficiency in packing and shipping. Of course, these customers would have to pay for more than just paper and labor; they would also have to pay for ideas.

Bob planned to aim this product mix at two major target markets. One would consist of the plethora of electronic firms that had sprung up in the eastern Massachusetts area; the other would consist of the New England produce growers and packers. Bob considered the small electronics firms particularly attractive. Because their products were sensitive to damage in shipment and because they had high unit price, Bob surmised that the manufacturer would be willing to pay for the kind of high-quality packaging and design which Ar-Tech intended to supply. Bob anticipated approaching these firms on a technical sales level by contacting the engineers who actually designed and built their "babies." The initial sales approach would be made to people on the technical level with emphasis on their problems related to packaging. Then, in consort with these people, the purchasing departments would be approached with proposals reflecting Ar-Tech's and the company's ideas. This sales method would vary markedly from the more standard wine-and-dine tradition of the industry and the sizeable kickbacks given to buyers, a practice which Art believed to exist at a number of companies. The only thing Ar-Tech would offer purchasing agents was to make them look good by saving money for the company through design and delivery.

Bob had continued his research during the spring of 1968 and decided that there were remarkable similarities between the packaging problems of the electronic manufacturers and produce growers. The grower's product was also highly susceptible to damage. Additionally, he normally shipped a major part of his produce on small trucks, and consequently he had to be able to stack his containers 10 to 12 deep without their collapsing. Heretofore, the growers had used wooden crates costing approximately 52 cents new (22 lbs. capacity) and 17 to 23 cents used. These crates varied in price and availability and generally were difficult to set up and stack evenly.

During this time Bob also noted two unusual pressures in the produce industry. One was that in the spring of 1968 the federal Department of Agriculture ruled that wooden crates could not be reused for certain produce. The other was that the commission agents who bought the growers' produce were paying more than $1 per square foot per *month* for their stall space in the South Boston Market and thus wanted the growers to ship in square containers that could be stacked to the ceiling. Bob believed this was an opportunity to which he could respond. His research led him to believe that a die-cut corrugated box which was strong enough to meet all criteria, required no taping or switching, and stored flat until set up could be sold for 25 to 33 cents each. He estimated that the total sales potential in the eastern Massachusetts/New Hampshire area would run over $1 million and full manufacturing cost would range 16 to 20 cents. Ar-Tech could bring its own expertise to bear by designing interior package/display trays for higher priced fruit, such as strawberries and blueberries, and handy carrying trays for tomatoes and corn, and so on.

Summer vacation 1968

By the time June rolled around, Bob had determined what equipment would be needed and was anxious to find a location for Ar-Tech and to complete the financial arrangements. He wanted to begin the operation over the summer vacation between his first and second years of business school.

Thus far Ar-Tech had $8,000 in equity capital, half of which Bob had raised by borrowing from friends and relatives and the other half of which Art had contributed from his savings. With original equipment needs estimated at $7,000, though, Bob wanted an additional $10,000 in debt for working capital and other expenses. After denial for the loan by a bank, Bob went to the Small Business Administration which was very encouraging and stated that Ar-Tech could expect to hear within eight days of receipt of the paper work. This Bob had submitted June 16th, but it was not until October that one of the SBA's representatives contacted Ar-Tech to begin preliminary investigations. In the meantime, Bob had continued talking with the bank which on August 1 lent Ar-Tech $3,500 on a note signed personally by Bob. The banker seemed to have been swayed by Bob's repeated hammering about his own fantastic earnings power. He reasoned that he could always go out and land a job and pay the loan off within a few months. Conventional wisdom of the business school dictated that he not sign the note personally, but to Bob this did not seem particularly apropos since his net worth was substantially negative. In September the bank lent an additional $6,500, making a total of $10,000 on Bob's signature. Part of his approach to the banker this second time had been that the only way Ar-Tech would ever be able to pay back the original $3,500 was for the bank to keep giving him more money until that point in time when the cash flow became positive.

During the summer Bob also contacted an investment firm about the possibility of obtaining private investment capital. He considered the response encouraging, but his capital needs were small and securing outside equity would have been costly. He decided to reserve this source until it could be optimally exploited.

In June, Bob had also turned his attention to finding a location for Ar-Tech. Proximity to the corrugated suppliers did not seem critical since they would deliver without extra charge within 25 miles. However, the intended foam supplier in Lawrence was notorious for his inability to deliver to small accounts.[1] Bob decided a location northwest of Boston between routes 128 and 495 would be accessible to both the foam supplier and the potential market's center of gravity.

The first week in June Bob contacted an industrial realtor and gave him the following list of requirements:

--Proximity to Route 128 and quick access to either Route 3 or Route 93 for north-south mobility.
--3,000 to 5,000 square feet suitable for manufacturing with a loading dock to facilitate volume material handling.
--Semi-skilled labor force available.
--Class A fireproof building.
--If possible, an area that was appreciating to facilitate subleasing the premises in the event of moving (or liquidating).
--Price negotiable but as close as possible to $300 per month.
--A landlord with empathy for new enterprise.

The realtor showed Bob about a dozen places. It became apparent that the price requirement had to give way to the other six on the list, but far worse, Bob realized that he already had suffered a serious setback. Because of the prolonged telephone strike, firms were delaying moves until they could get telephones installed at their new locations. Bob could not find space available earlier than August. Not only would this

---

[1]Bob intended to use various foams for the interior of his packages. He believed that foam instead of excelsior and shredded wood would be necessary as interiors for the sophisticated package Ar-Tech was expecting to design and sell.

hamper the plans to have Ar-Tech running before school began again in September, but it would also force the company to miss the produce growers' major harvest and box purchases. In particular, the area's largest corn grower was understood to be converting from wood to corrugated.

Eventually, 5,000 square feet in a two-year-old building in a new industrial park was leased for occupancy on August 16, 1968. The site in Woburn was a mile from the junction of routes 93 and 128, 20 minutes from the foam supplier and an hour from all proposed customers. The monthly rental of $550 ($1.32 per square foot) was judged to be well below the area average. Two weeks before the move-in date of August 16, Bob was able to talk the owner into letting him use 150 square feet tucked away in a corner to begin the setup of his die press.

Operations and the second year of the M.B.A. program

From mid-August until the beginning of classes in late September, Bob spent most of his time organizing and managing the shop while Art concentrated on sales. At night the two of them designed packages and worked up sales quotas. Bob characterized this period as having an *unbelievable* array of problems which might have been avoided had they been able to start from other than a "standing start" (i.e., by buying an ongoing business). When the previous tenant had left, he took *all* the wiring and switchboxes with him. For two months Ar-Tech was not able to have a phone installed. Prospective customers were very wary and skeptical of depending on a new firm as a supplier. In general Ar-Tech lacked credibility. Often Bob had no way of knowing what price to charge other than by "gut feel."

In some areas Art's professional reputation appeared to have helped. The primary suppliers of raw materials extended Ar-Tech a total line of credit of $5,000. (Standard practice dictates that many new firms pay cash.) Bob and Art also selected two other smaller packaging firms with whom they felt Ar-Tech had the best fit (i.e., did not compete for the same customers and had different manufacturing capabilities). These firms were approached and operating agreements were reached which might be construed as a reciprocal protection of accounts and a pooling of resources to provide a full line of service to respective customers. This reduced Ar-Tech's raw material inventory requirements and broadened the sales base through the other company's outlets. One of the firms had several active salesmen who began to sell Ar-Tech's specialties.

For the first two months following the August 16 start-up, sales totaled almost $5,000 which paid all expenses and generated a small surplus in terms of receivables. However, in terms of cash Ar-Tech was not able to collect $1,100 from one customer. School began again and Bob found himself working under a new schedule. He had to arise early enough to open up the plant and then drive to school in time for his first class. After classes, he would return and run the shop until 9 or 10 P.M. By the time he arrived home, there seemed to be little time left for his wife, children, and cases in preparation for the next day's classes.

At Ar-Tech one full-time employee was hired (Bob's 19-year-old brother) and a part-time helper. Nonetheless, with school and Art on the sales road much of the time, Bob felt that workmanship suffered and that some of the customers who had originally been impressed with the products were becoming disenchanted. As a result, Bob and Art spent more time in the plant, and although they believed they had improved quality and reconvinced some of the customers, sales effort and thus sales declined in October, November, and December. (See Exhibit 4 for an operating statement for this period and a balance sheet as of December 31, 1968.)

Sales began to build up in the new year and from January to mid-February 1969 they approached $4,000 (see Exhibit 5). However, the cash position which had been continually low only got worse as receivables went up. During February and March it became so critical that Ar-Tech concentrated on jobbing for other packagers, using their materials to reduce payables and pushing orders that would use up existing inventory.

This pace continued through most of the spring of 1969, and it was not until Bob was forced to allot some time to write his research report that he was able to raise his head out of the maelstrom of business and academic frenzy and look around. By then Ar-Tech had many repeating customers: Polaroid, Raytheon, Furcor, National Research Corp., Acoustics Research, Instrumentation Labs, Mechanics for Electronics, Anacon, Image Optics, Hickock Teaching, Aritech, Fenwal, General Laser, Precision Components, Scott, Mathatronics, Dynisco, Inland Controls, and Cambosco. All these companies produced the high-margin delicate electronic components that Ar-Tech had originally sought to package. Bob believed that Ar-Tech was developing a reputation for superior technology with these accounts. The evidence for this was that competitors were beginning to steal Ar-Tech's designs and to raid accounts, and Bob could keep tabs on this since most companies used the same foam supplier.

The performance of Ar-Tech seemed to be improving in the spring of 1969 and Bob found time to compile the operating statistics breakdown for March and May and a balance sheet (see Exhibits 6 and 7). In looking at the figures, though, he was not unaware that he had taken no money home in 1968 and that $75 a week take-home seemed likely for most of 1969.

Bob also felt that Ar-Tech had developed three proprietary processes:

1. The ability to die-cut triple-wall corrugated. (This material is a substitute for ¼-inch plywood and has a bursting strength of 1,100 pounds per square inch.)
2. The ability to die-cut beaded polystyrene foam which is universally molded or cut by saw or hot wire. ,
3. The ability to cover flat corrugated sheets with fancy embossed paper that will not crack or wrinkle after being made into a container.

He also thought that they had a good idea on how to manufacture transparent plastic corrugated from rolls of polystyrene, polypropylene, or polyethylene. At the time, Japanese firms were producing it and shipping it, literally packages of air, halfway around the world.

Bob also noted a trend that in more and more purchasing departments people were becoming more and more interested in a total packaging system with emphasis on the functional performance of the package and punctual delivery. This meant that there was a movement away from buying components from several sources or from brokers who must go to several sources themselves to secure the various components of a package. With this trend in mind Bob tried to persuade some of the major corrugated manufacturers in the greater Boston area to have their salesmen seek orders which contained both corrugated and foam. Ar-Tech would be able to process the foam, and the corrugated houses would be able to offer a packaging system. Otherwise, this business would be lost to the brokers. Eventually Bob interested a large corrugator with sales of over $16 million in this arrangement. As a result, the large corrugator's salesmen brought in $20,000 of orders for the months of March, April, and May.

The brokers for packaging materials generally were the distributors who serviced shipping departments with tape, twine, paper bags, and so on, and who had recently begun to offer more intricate assemblies to their customers as an additional service. This included foam and carton combinations. The trend on the part of customers who increasingly wanted to buy all their packaging needs from the same source also affected Ar-Tech. As an additional service to customers Ar-Tech found themselves supplying customers with tape, twine, paper bags and other items. Bob felt that he could build his marketing strategy on this trend. As Ar-Tech took away the high-margin shipping supply accessories from the brokers, it would be able to increase its sales coverage and thereby reduce the coverage of the brokers who were existing on large profit spreads and low volumes. Bob felt this strategy was sound since he had lined up a dependable source of shipping room supplies. Because Ar-Tech looked at these materials as an additional customer service and not the main producer of profits, the company would virtually be in a position to control the brokers' markups with its own pricing strategy.

At the same time, Bob decided to abandon the produce growers' market which he had originally felt had a high revenue potential for Ar-Tech. The generally grim economic plight of the farmer seemed to be continuing, and as a result, growers were trying to squeeze credit out of every available source. Because Ar-Tech had always been in a cash bind and because growers were purchasing boxes for reasons of credit available rather than technical innovation, Bob decided not to pursue the market.

Gildham Container Corporation

In early April of 1969 Bob was presented with an opportunity for an acquisition. After a series of discussions Bob found that he could acquire the Gildham Container Corporation in Lowell, Massachusetts, for $16,000. The acquisition seemed attractive for a number of reasons. Gildham was a sheet plant that manufactured corrugated cartons which complemented the Ar-Tech line. It had every piece of equipment that Bob had originally wanted for Ar-Tech but had been unable to purchase because of his limited financial sources. The present owner had a similar but larger operation in Connecticut and had started Gildham about a year ago as an expansionary effort. Exhibit 8 gives the balance sheet after six months operation in December 1968. At that time, Bob ascertained monthly sales of corrugated boxes were as high as $11,500 (Bob, however, considered one-fifth of this to be bad accounts), but the owner had decided to curtail the operation when his principal contract ran out and had lost money since then. Bob attributed this loss to the almost complete lack of management by the owner who was in at least three other ventures that Bob knew of. Because of his overextension, the owner had curtailed operations in December and now seemed susceptible to Bob's proposition, which was based on the long-range benefits that the sale of Gildham to Ar-Tech would make available to him and his Connecticut operation.

The proposal was to move Ar-Tech from Woburn to Gildham's location in Lowell and add the sheet plant operation to Ar-Tech's specialty line. Ar-Tech would purchase the equipment and inventory only and sublease the building. The present owner could continue to operate Gildham as a sales outlet for both his Connecticut operation and Ar-Tech who would pay him a 5 percent commission. An advantage of this proposed setup for the Gildham owner would be that the ongoing nature of Gildham's name and continued operation of the plant would facilitate collecting his high receivables. Furthermore, Ar-Tech would complement his Connecticut operation by allowing it to expand into the technical specialty design market. The Gildham owner had developed sales outlets that covered southern New England, but he was now losing the high-margin technical specialty market because he lacked the capabilities of Ar-Tech. It seemed to Bob that the Gildham owner had a great deal to gain and little to lose in revitalizing the company and his interests by selling to Ar-Tech. And it was with exactly such reasoning that Bob talked the owner into offering to sell at a price lower than the market value of the inventory and machinery (at least $5,000 lower after selling expenses, Bob determined). This purchase plus some allowance for working capital was to be financed over 39 months at the then current prime rate (7½ percent) with a $5,000 balloon payment at the end of the period. Bob worked out these payment figures to make them be less than the anticipated depreciation. He also knew the man was in a bind for $16,000 which he owed a bank and thus felt the amount he was offering would strike a responsive chord. Of course the real benefit to the man would be if Bob could help him with his half million dollar Connecticut operation. The rent for subleasing the Gildham facility would be $.55 per square foot (including heat) versus $1.32 per square foot which Ar-Tech was paying at the time.

Bob calculated that with the addition of Gildham's plant and equipment, sales of over $35,000 would be possible with only the addition of labor. Fixed costs could now be spread over double the sales volume, and labor costs would be reduced by both division of labor and more use of efficient production and materials handling equipment. In addition, the manufacturing back-up of the foam supplier was available.

Bob decided that the probable path to follow if Ar-Tech did acquire Gildham would be to improve earnings and negotiate with the foam supplier to invest in about 10 percent of Ar-Tech. With these funds Ar-Tech could purchase another company, Nicefit Plastics, which was located in the same building complex as Gildham. Nicefit performed vacuum forming on plastic sheets and concentrated on low-margin, high-volume commodity items such as small plastic lids, covers, and cups for the fast food industry. Because Nicefit was losing money on sales of about $120,000 per year in this highly competitive industry, Bob believed it could be acquired for well under book value with liberal financing arrangements from the present stockholders. Once acquired, Bob thought the appropriate strategy would be to sell off any assets not needed for immediate business needs and to cull out all the nonprofitable accounts which were taken to fill out machine capacity. Ar-Tech would then use the facility to produce plastic interior packaging. This would consist of functional or highly styled inserts and trays which would help fill out the present industrial line as well as provide an entry to the commercial point-of-sales packaging market.

Bob also thought they would have the potential of developing a method of vacuum-forming expanded polyethylene foam which would prove to be a technological breakthrough for low-cost molding of this material in packaging applications. The resulting product could also be used as a high finish, extreme strength to weight ratio structural component that could be formed at very low costs. Bob immediately thought of two applications for such a product: full monocoque construction of compact autos and boat hulls.[2]

Nevertheless, despite the apparent attractiveness of Gildham (see Exhibit 9 for a combined pro forma of Gildham and Ar-Tech) and potential expansion through Nicefit, Bob felt compelled to seriously reconsider his goals and strategy. As he had written in his research report, the goal of his packaging entrepreneurial venture was:

> My personal goal is to develop in the next year, the best possible return on investment track record . . . to get into that sphere where an entrepreneur can make new things happen where the limits are set only by knowledge and courage . . . requires power. That power will come from demonstrated performance, and accumulation of assets at the progressive echelons—the base being Ar-Tech.

Bob sensed that if he followed the Ar-Tech, Gildham, Nicefit path the demands on his time and energy would be severe. In effect, he felt the decision to follow this path would both commit and lock him into this strategy for at least a couple of years as a means of obtaining his goals. Therefore, he had to be sure that this was the best possible route for him to follow.

He believed he had never really given full consideration to the alternative of building both experience and a track record by working for a large company for a few years and then striking out on his own. Perhaps there were unforeseen pitfalls and mistakes that he would make given his complete lack of business experience that would best be made at someone else's expense while employed with them for a training period. He had recently become painfully aware of this line of thinking as he saw his classmates walk around at school with numerous job offers averaging almost $15,000 a year. And at home he realized his decisions were affecting his wife and three children to say nothing of how he would pay off his school loans. As the wife of a major, his wife had been accustomed to socializing with colonels' and generals' wives and to the security of the Army. At that time the family had always had some money and benefits; now Bob was struggling to take home $75 a week. When his wife asked him why there was no money now, Bob found that the answer, "We have plenty but it is in inventory and receivables," was rarely satisfactory.

---

[2]Full monocoque construction is the use of the foam as a sandwich between two layers of fiberglass. Like plywood, the strength of these materials joined together is greater than the sum of the individual strengths of the parts.

Although Bob almost intuitively shied away from the idea of accepting a job offer with a large firm, his wife did not. She noted that all the salary offers which Bob received, in addition to being many times his current take home, were substantially above the average of his classmates. In fact, the best offer out of the five that he followed in any detail was for $20,000, not including such fringe benefits as profit sharing and easily obtainable mortgage money. Not only was the position lucrative, but he would be general manager of a $6 million division with profits of $1.5 million. Also, he would be responsible for new product development. This alternative began to weigh on his mind heavily.

He also wondered if he continued with Ar-Tech whether he would have time to pursue as acquisitions or ventures several ideas or companies he had become familiar with but which were not related to the packaging industry. One such company was Game Makers of America, which Ar-Tech supplied with shippers, store displays, and some general consulting. Game Makers of America was a fledgling toy company with $64,000 in assets. Bob felt the primary strength of the company was an extremely imaginative game inventor and 25 patented games. The company had no sales but was in the process of readying a word game called "VOKAB" for promotion. Bob believed the game was a good one and everyone he knew that had played it, enjoyed it and stated they would buy it. The company, however, had difficulty in effectively organizing to promote VOKAB and developing the other games for marketing. Bob had considered offering to reorganize their marketing efforts in time to meet the coming Christmas selling season and program the development of several more games in exchange for a negotiated percentage of their stock. He also liked the idea of working with the president of Game Makers who was also a senior partner in a small certified public accounting firm. As such, Bob believed the president had excellent access to investment capital and was in a position to learn of and review many acquisition opportunities.

Another venture Bob was exploring was the establishment of a venture that would market digital on-line process control systems for manufacturing and data communications. Bob, who contributed his relevant military experience, had been working on the idea with a systems analyst who worked on the original development of the COBOL and BASIC programming languages from machine assembly language. The systems analyst was reputedly a recognized authority on closed loop systems. Bob thought that with the aid of some local think-tank electronic firms (Ar-Tech customers) they could overcome the instrumentation and servo-mechanism barriers which were associated with on-line control systems. He also knew of authoritative estimates which indicated that as much as 15 percent of all U.S. capital equipment expenditures in the next 10 years would be spent on on-line digital control systems if the measurement and response problems could be resolved. There would be a need, Bob thought, because the increasing intercommunication of computers was rapidly overloading existing and projected common carrier communication facilities. Users could not afford leased-line wide-band facilities for medium speed (2,500 to 12,000 bits per second) data communication channels (IBM spent almost $1 million for data communication service last year), but instead had to use regular, low-speed phone circuits which operate at teletype speeds (less than 100 bits per second) or mail tapes. This could force the operation of many scattered computers in a company's system rather than inexpensive consoles tied into large centralized data banks.

Bob entertained the idea of engineering and marketing a computer-controlled nationwide system that employed leased wide bank trunks[3] between major relays using proprietary modern equipment over telephone loops[4] at high speeds (90,000 to 125,000 bits/second—magnetic tape output speed). The messages would be automatically coded for security. They would employ time division multiplexing[5] techniques in conjunction with pulse position modulation fed into the proper trunk at computer output speeds (up to several million bits per second) for automatic relay until it reached its destination. Although this would not be a real time system, Bob intended that the user perceive it as such because of the electronic speeds employed. The user's computer could operate at tape output speeds with any other computer on the system, and the cost of the trunks, and so on, would be spread over many users which was not then possible. The system would be designed to give the user absolute security due to simultaneous telephone voice contact between users. Bob believed that such a communications system would be critical to successful implementation of the much heralded computer based "cash-less societies" and the like.

He figured that there were three alternatives possible for creating the high-speed trunks:

1. Lease exclusive trunks from the Bell System.
2. Multiplex the data onto existing TV and microwave links.
3. One communications satellite (expensive) and many microwave systems (inexpensive) feeding from the satellite.

Bob was well aware of the great amounts of capital and cooperation of the common carrier that would be required. The systems analyst, Bob's associate in exploring the idea, had taken a position which would give

---

[3]A trunk is the circuits linking central offices or relays together.

[4]A telephone loop is the circuit linking the subscriber to a central office or relay.

[5]Multiplexing is a system whereby a single circuit can be used for more than one channel of communication. A simple example in telephone would be using one pair of wires for two distinct, separate, and simultaneous transmissions.

him more widespread exposure to the commercial software market as preparation for the venture. Meanwhile, Bob had planned to begin the required research until capital could be established to hire additional engineers.

In addition to the other possible ventures and Ar-Tech itself, in the back of his mind, Bob held the desire of ultimately developing and marketing an innovative sports car to fill the void between the present U.S. Corvette at $5,000 to $8,000 and the high performance imports at $14,000 to $19,000. (See Exhibit 10 for a sketch.) With little number pushing Bob realized that he would not want to be dependent on the earnings from such an undertaking. In fact, this appealing market segment that he saw had financially broken many ambitious firms. Bob thought it was unlikely that such a venture would be a profitable operation in and of itself. (See Exhibit 11.) But someday when he could afford it, he thought the operation could do very well if it were tied in as a promotional vehicle with a retail automotive product such as an oil additive or performance accessory.

By now it was late April and although Bob was running between his house, the plant in Lowell, and the business school in Boston while writing his research report and studying cases, his mind was really pondering his strategy for attaining his goals. He wondered whether Ar-Tech packaging was the best nucleus for a business conglomerate and what he should do with his other ideas.

SUGGESTED QUESTIONS

1. What should Mr. D'Amore do?
2. How would you evaluate the performace of Ar-Tech Packaging? (A little quantitative analysis will give you some additional insight.) What is its potential for the future?
3. How well does this company match the goals and objectives of Bob D'Amore? What should be his time horizon?
4. What do you think of the partnership agreement?

EXHIBIT 1
Ar-Tech Packaging
Résumé of Robert D'Amore

Marital Status	Married, three children	Age: 33 years

Education 1967–68	HARVARD GRADUATE SCHOOL OF BUSINESS ADMINISTRATION Candidate for the degree of master of business administration in June 1969. Main concentration in marketing and application of new technologies to business, with secondary emphasis on entrepreneurship. Courses include marketing management, advanced computer applications, advertising, technical innovation, and small manufacturing enterprises.
1965–66	U.S. Army Signal School: Advanced Communications Engineering.
1959	U.S. Army Signal School: Automatic Data Processing Systems.
1954–58	UNITED STATES MILITARY ACADEMY West Point, N.Y. Bachelor of science degree. Courses stressed mathematics, physics, and mechanics. Electives in economics of national security. Dean's list. Academic coach. *Pointer Magazine,* acolyte, French, and ordnance clubs. Lacrosse, boxing. Designed floats and displays for 1957 Army-Navy football game.
Work experience 1968	AR-TECH PACKAGING Owner: Founded firm July 1968. Innovative packaging for industry.
1963–1964	U.S. ARMED FORCES INSTITUTE Instructor, aircraft powerplants, three nights per week.
Military	Major, Signal Corps. Responsible for overall communications systems, planning, and programming, Vietnam 1966–67. Developed and implemented improved Army Division Communications System, 1964–65. Parachutist. Awards include Army Commendation Medal and Bronze Star. Inactive reserve.
Background and interests	Raised in Massachusetts. Attended public schools. Active in community activities. Interests include auto racing and design, bridge, free-lance cartooning, and sports.

EXHIBIT 2
Ar-Tech Packaging
Résumé of Arthur F. Aulenback

Marital status	Married, two children	Age: 33 years

Military status   Honorable discharge from 182d Infantry Tank Co. U.S.A.R.

Education   Graduated Arlington High School, Arlington, Massachusetts, 1957

Work experience   RAYTHEON COMPANY
Final Test Shipping 1957–59; packaging of electronic equipment to government specifications.

Hawk Documentation 1959–60; assisted a packaging engineer in the design, construction, and documentation of corrugated and wood containers and cushioning for various parts of the Hawk missile which also entailed drop testing and inspection.

Industrial Engineering, Packaging Engineering Section 1960–62; independent and original design of corrugated containers and their interior cushioning materials for protection of electronic equipment during handling, shipment, and storage. Worked with corrugated (various types), polyurethane, polyethylene film, styrofoam, barrier materials, tissues (various types), hairflex, and all types of preservative packaging materials.

WEST VIRGINIA PULP & PAPER COMPANY
Manager Packaging Service Center for division 1962–68; responsible for supervision, direction, and administration of the Packaging Service Center whose function is to provide superior design skills; a high level of technical knowledge pertaining to the design, manufacture and performance of corrugated products, and the corrugated packaging machinery and the problems this machinery creates for corrugated products; and communicative skills to translate this technical knowledge to the staff and customers and/or prospects.

EXHIBIT 3
Ar-Tech Packaging
Partnership agreement, July 20, 1968

The undersigned hereby enter into a business partnership on this date, to do business as "Ar-Tech Packaging," hereafter referred to as the business. The business will generally concern itself with the design, manufacture, and sale of industrial shipping containers, although it may at the discretion of the two partners enter into any business activity.

The undersigned partners will initially deposit in the business checking account matching sums of money, which will be the business' equity capital. Each partner will own 50 percent of the business, and control will be divided respectively, with any debated decision requiring the concurrence of both partners. Should an impasse develop, and compromise be unacceptable to both partners, then the following "buy or sell" conditions will be employed:

He who considers himself the offended partner will offer to buy the other partner's half of the business at some equitable figure, not to be less than the normally accepted book value of that half of the business. The other partner will have the option of accepting the offer or buying the offering partner's share at a like price. Should the book value be disputed, a certified audit is to be performed with both partners sharing equally the expense of such an audit. In order for the surviving partner to make a valid offer for the business, he must be able to assume all the liabilities accruing to the business, completely freeing the other partner from any and all obligations, including prior personal guarantees and other personal assets previously pledged to creditors of the business. Should the so-called remaining partner be unable to make and perform a valid offer, the other partner will have the option of buying at the same price provided it is no less than book value, and he can free the selling partner from all obligations. If neither partner can do this, then a settlement agreeable to both must be negotiated. If this is not possible, then the business is to be liquidated or sold as advantageously as possible with both partners sharing equally in the resulting gain or liability. Such a sale must take place within 60 days of the establishment that neither partner can buy out the other, unless both partners agree to an extension.

Both partners must concur in assuming any liabilities not considered normal trade credit for materials or services connected with a valid work order in process at the business.

In the event of the death of either partner, the surviving widow or the estate will be paid in cash, and/or notes, at her or its option, at least the book value for her husband's share of the business, as determined by a certified audit. The surviving partner will, upon payment, own all of the business. Neither partner will sell, nor assign any of his part of the business without the consent of the other.

Should either partner put more equity capital into the business and the other partner does not match that amount, he will give the "majority" partner a personal note for one half the difference in their individual invested capitals. In this manner, ownership will remain split evenly.

The business will be incorporated at some future date, and this agreement will be terminated effective the date of incorporation, unless sooner superseded by subsequent written agreement.

EXHIBIT 4
Ar-Tech Packaging
Operating statement (July 22, 1968—December 31, 1968)

Net Sales............................		$9,019.45
Cost of Goods Sold:		
Raw material	$3,557.19	
Purchased parts..................	2,765.93	
Direct labor	1,407.30	7,730.42
Operating margin		$1,289.03
Selling and administrative	$1,700.00	
Rent	2,420.60	
Repairs	187.00	
Insurance	255.69	
Interest	333.13	
Miscellaneous and depreciation	1,037.86	5,934.28
Net Surplus (deficit)		($4,645.25)

Ar-Tech Packaging
Balance sheet (as of December 31, 1968)

Cash	$ 2,745.33
Accounts receivable.................	4,529.42
Inventory	800.00
Prepaid and deposits	750.00
Plant and equipment	7,004.00
Total Assets	$15,828.75
Accounts payable	$ 2,250.00
Accruals..........................	224.00
Notes payable	10,000.00
Owners' equity	8,000.00
Earned surplus (deficit)	(4,645.25)
Total Liabilities	$15,828.75

EXHIBIT 5
Ar-Tech Packaging
Balance sheet (as of February 9, 1969)

Cash	$ 1,174.96
Accounts receivable	4,982.95
Inventory (including work in process)	2,141.00
Prepaid and deposits	821.00
Total current	$ 9,119.91
Plant and equipment	8,518.02
Total Assets	$17,637.93
Accounts payable	$ 3,437.71
Accruals	52.33
Total current	$ 3,490.04
Notes payable	10,000.00
Owners' equity	8,000.00
Retained earnings	(3,852.11)
Total Liabilities	$17,637.93

Note: Owners' salary draws have been treated as expense.

Ar-Tech Packaging
Income statement (July 22, 1968—February 9, 1969)

Net sales		$12,799.15
Cost of Goods Sold:		
Raw materials and purchased parts	$ 8,501.45	
Labor	1,817.84	
Utilities	300.28	
Shipping	158.83	
		$10,778.40
Operating Margin		$ 2,020.75
Selling and administrative	$ 2,070.00	
Interest	393.83	
Rent	3,254.60	
Miscellaneous	15.11	
		$ 5,733.54
Net Surplus (deficit)		($3,712.79)

EXHIBIT 6
Ar-Tech Packaging
Spring 1969 operating statistics breakdown as percent of sales

Raw and purchased materials	42.6%
Equipment maintenance and depreciation	1.9
Supervision and labor	20.1
Rent, power, phone, general maintenance	4.2
Cost of Goods Sold	68.8%
Sales commission	1.9
Gross Operating Margin	29.3%
General and administrative	11.8
Net before Taxes	17.5%

EXHIBIT 7
Ar-Tech Packaging
Balance sheet (as of April 24, 1969)

Cash	$ 560.87
Accounts receivable	5,780.39
Inventory:	
Raw material	410.00
Work in process (full cost)	6,160.00
Prepaid and deposits	355.00
Total Current	$13,266.26
Net plant and equipment	8,418.00
Total Assets	$21,684.26
Accounts payable	$4,683.11
Accruals	113.00
Total Current	$ 4,796.11
Notes payable	$10,000.00
Owners' equity	8,000.00
Retained earnings	(1,111.85)
Total Liabilities	$21,684.26

Note: Owners' salary draws have been treated as expense.

EXHIBIT 8
Ar-Tech Packaging
Gildham Container Corp. unaudited balance sheet as of December 31, 1968
(after six months of operation)

Cash	$ 5,175	Accounts payable	$19,068
Accounts receivable	20,842	Accruals	94
Inventory	4,773	Notes, bank	16,000
Total current	$30,790	Notes, other	4,747
Plant and Equipment:		Capital stock	4,000
Machinery	$19,829	Retained earnings	7,555
Leasehold	1,064		
Total	$20,893		
Less depreciation	346		
Net	20,547		
Organization expense	127		
Total Assets	$51,464	Total Liabilities	$51,464

EXHIBIT 9
Ar-Tech Packaging
Gildham Container Corp. pro forma monthly income statement:
Combined operations (Gildham's December 1968 and Ar-Tech's
April 1969)

Sales:			
Corrugated		$11,500	
Less commissions @ 5%		575	
Net			$10,925
Specialties		$10,000	
Less commissions.......................		520	
Net			9,480
Total Net Sales			20,405
Cost of Goods Sold:			
Raw materials		8,600	
Purchased parts..........................		1,250	
Miscellaneous materials		262	
Direct labor		2,420	
Total Cost of Goods Sold			$12,532
Operating income:			7,873
Selling and administration..................	$ 230		
Utilities and rent	630		
Depreciation	200		
Interest	184		
Truck	110		
Insurance	77		
			$ 1,431
Net Pre-Tax Profit to Partnership ...			$ 6,442

EXHIBIT 10
Ar-Tech Packaging
Luxury high performance sports car: The Celerime
Full MONOCOQUE mid-engine V-8

EXHIBIT 11

Ar-Tech Packaging

Pro forma operating statement for luxury high-performance sports car

Sales (5 cars per week at $11,500 each)........		$2,870,000
Less dealer commission		$720,000
Net Sales.............................		$2,150,000
Cost of Goods Sold:		
Raw materials and parts	$690,000	
Direct labor and supervisory	415,000	1,105,000
Gross operating margin		$1,045,000
Rent and utilities	$150,000	
Selling and administration...................	170,000	
Advertising................................	150,000	
Development and racing	500,000	
Interest	140,000	$1,110,000
Net Pre-Tax Profit		($ 65,000)

APPENDIX

Ar-Tech Packaging Company
Electronic industry sales ($ millions)

	1964	1965	1966	1967	1968	1969*
Total	16,525.0	17,714.0	18,989.6	21,411.4	23,122.1	24,665.0
Federal (Dept. of Defense, NASA, FAA, AEC)	9,844.0	9,551.0	9,810.0	10,932.0	10,659.0	10,789.0
Consumer (TV, radios, phonographs, tape recorders, hi-fi components, guitar amplifiers, organs, automotive, etc.)	2,550.0	3,079.5	3,445.6	3,847.7	4,174.0	4,395.5
Industrial (Total)	4,131.0	5,083.5	5,734.0	6,631.7	8,289.1	9,480.5
Test and measuring instruments	454.0	535.0	576.0	648.5	684.4	769.0
Medical equipment	209.0	216.5	230.6	260.5	366.3	406.9
Nuclear instruments and equipment	104.0	129.6	138.2	113.4	123.8	141.2
Computers and related equipment	1,850.0	1,945.2	2,145.1	3,118.9	4,134.0	4,787.2
Communications equipment	1,121.0	1,213.9	1,382.5	1,288.8	1,625.2	1,849.2
Lasers and equipment	—	22.4	33.6	51.9	55.2	71.6
Closed circuit television	24.0	26.0	30.6	69.1	91.8	108.2
Dictating services	35.0	100.0	100.1	103.5	110.0	114.4
Power supplies, OEM	—	50.0	67.5	72.0	77.0	86.0
Industrial operations electronic equipment	334.0	768.9	934.8	905.1	1,021.4	1,146.9
Optoelectronic instruments and equipment	—	75.0	95.0	—	—	—

*Estimate, January 1969.
Source: *Electronics Magazine*, January issues, 1965–69.

Terry Allen

In December 1970, Terry Allen was reconsidering his plans for the immediate future. Since March of 1966 he had been pursuing a venture in the tool and equipment rental business and had now pushed the company through what he thought was the most difficult period of the corporate life cycle, start-up and acquisition. While he had been pursuing the rental venture, Terry had developed another idea and company, Merchants Welcome Service, and toward the end of 1970 he was spending an ever-increasing amount of time with it. He now found himself in a serious time bind. The formation, promotion, and development of a new idea were proving irresistible yet he still wanted to capitalize on the effort that had gone into Green Mountain Rentals. He was now having to question whether he could run both operations and not risk everything. He believed that the rental company would probably bring little on the market now should he try to sell it but sizeable appreciation could come as soon as the company entered a stage of growth and established a history of profits.

Background

At the age of 15 Terry Allen announced to his parents that he would thereafter be financially independent. This declaration did not originate because he had already accumulated wealth or because his parents had little money. In fact, Terry had no money, and his father, a college professor, could have financed his education. But in 1955, at the age of 15, Terry's lifetime goals were to attend Harvard Business School and to become a millionaire.[1] Announcing his financial independence seemed

---

[1] In 1970 Terry Allen was still setting goals at the beginning of each month, ranging in categories from the sales volume of his businesses to the number of books he would read, sets of tennis he would play, and times he would go out for dinner. At the end of the month he would write a one-page analysis of his activities in light of his objectives.

like a logical beginning and the following summer Terry took some initial steps toward his goals.

He earned several thousand dollars through a variety of efforts. A 170-house paper route was a mainstay of his activity all through high school, as was collecting scrap paper.[2] In the summer he started a lawn mowing service with a machine he rented for $9 a month. Its use was so great that by the end of the summer he had almost worn the rubber tires down to the metal rims. The rental agency complained that the machine had been worn out in three months, but Terry took full responsibility. He refused to let the agency speak to his parents and he refused to pay more than $27. That summer he also ran a carnival every other Friday which he figured netted him $40–$50 per show. One of the main attractions was his 50 pet snakes which he also took to camps and parks in the area for a paid lecture.

In 1957, his senior year in high school, Terry turned down Harvard College to attend Wesleyan University because the scholarship was larger there, and as he planned to attend Harvard Business School, six years seemed too long to be at one university. While at college and during the intervening summers he never had fewer than two jobs in addition to being active on the campus socially and athletically. He also played semipro baseball at night during the summers. For four years he washed dishes in his fraternity for his meals. Usually the upperclassmen switched to waiting on tables, but Terry elected to remain at what was thought to be the more demeaning task of washing dishes because that job took less time to earn a meal. Time, he felt, was his most important asset.

During his junior year he sold paperback books because the campus bookstore had refused to sell them. He later calculated that three out of four Wesleyan students had purchased *Love without Fear* from him. At the end of the academic year he was left with several thousand books in inventory, but by then the campus bookstore had decided to carry paperbacks so he liquidated his entire inventory to them at cost.

His senior year he happened to see a do-it-yourself kit to make paperbacks into hardbacks. The idea and the potential of the product fascinated him, and he quickly made a trip to New York to talk with the manufacturer. For the purchase of $2,000 inventory he was given a franchise for the New England area. The four salesmen that he hired contributed the $2,000 and the inventory was quickly sold and more reordered. Terry then discovered that a prime market was the veterans' hospitals since the public frequently donated paperback books to them. He sold this market nationally on a one-shot basis with a direct mail campaign.

---

[2]Because the market for scrap paper fluctuated between $.30 and $1.00 during those years, Terry would hoard it in anticipation of the best possible conditions for selling. This policy led to an accumulation of three tons in his family garage at one point in time.

Although it was difficult to pin down exactly, Terry figured that the book ventures of the last two years in college probably netted him a couple thousand dollars apiece. It was a little easier to figure the $1,000 of his scholarship money that he lost in the stock market.

At Wesleyan Terry majored in economics, and it became one of his serious pursuits. He worked with one of his professors on a Ford Foundation grant to study "Change in Negotiated Wage Rates in Union Settlements." They developed a wage rate index which they believed more accurately reflected actual wages and eliminated inaccuracies in measurement from overtime and shift in job categories. Nonetheless, when Terry's professor was called to testify in Washington during steel strikes, Terry decided not to attend because of his personal antiunion sentiments.

Terry graduated from Wesleyan in 1961 and after another active summer entered the Harvard Business School. His first year he concentrated on his studies, but by the second he began to branch out. He started and ran what he believed was Boston's first roommate matching service which produced some income.[3] He also became New England area chairman for the Small Business Club, a position which meshed with his fervent but largely intuitive and unexplainable desire to move to and work in Vermont. He mounted a job campaign by writing every firm with over 40 employees in the State of Vermont. The effort netted him four job possibilities. After a few days' deliberation he accepted a job in Rutland, Vermont, as assistant to the president of Carris Reels, Inc., a manufacturer of plywood reels for wire and cable.

Terry received his M.B.A. degree from Harvard in 1963. He particularly remembered his professor's advice in the Management of New Enterprises course. There were three basic steps to consider in order to become an entrepreneur. First, money is no obstacle; second, decide what business you want to be in (look through the Yellow Pages of the phone book for an idea, if necessary); third, just go out and buy whatever business you have chosen. He had emphasized the first point, since money could always be found to back a venture because so many people had it who did not have the ideas or energy to invest it. Furthermore, having any money at all could limit the imagination. For example, if a person had $5,000, he would look for a business he could buy with that amount; but if he had no money, he would not be confined by financial limitations and could look for a much larger business to buy.

Two weeks after he arrived in Rutland Terry learned that the local 180-student schoolhouse on four acres of land was being sold at a sealed bid auction. With visions of a skiers' lodge he submitted a bid of $4,810 which he based on the fact that a schoolhouse in a nearby county one third the size had sold for $1,600. Thus 3 x $1,600 = $4,800 plus an extra

---

[3]Later, when he moved to Vermont, he lost about $1,000 as the absentee owner/manager before he dissolved the firm.

$10, so that he would outbid anyone using the same logic. His bid won and he had seven days to produce the money. (He considered calling his former professor since he had no cash available.) After discussing the idea with his boss and a few of his boss' friends, he raised the money in one day and retained 50 percent of the equity for organizing and undertaking the management of the project.

Terry spent his nights and weekends converting the old schoolhouse, now called Chateau Ecole, into a skiers' dormitory by investing an additional $13,000 in loans on the strength of his partners' signatures. After looking around he found the best place to buy the 140 beds he needed was in Baltimore. If he ordered 180 beds, he could get a rock bottom price of $40 apiece. Feeling sure that he could sell the extras, he ordered 180 and timed the purchase so that for a $20 tip, one of the Carris drivers, who was making a delivery in the Baltimore area, would freight the beds to Rutland. Several nights later at a cocktail party he sold the extra 40 beds for $60 apiece. (He even contemplated selling the entire lot at a profit but decided against it because he was afraid that he would not be able to get another shipment before the ski season started.)

After six months in Rutland, Terry married Leslie Pratt, a native Rutlander. The newlyweds' first home was Terry's 140-bed ski domitory with a 12-burner kitchen range. At nights and on weekends Terry and his wife ran the operation and broke even the first season. In subsequent seasons young couples were hired to run the ski lodge.

After a year with Carris Reels, Terry decided to go into the real estate business for himself. His work as assistant to the president had been interesting in the production and cost control areas, but he felt that by nature he was a promoter and not a manufacturer. Also there was the unavoidable fact that there seemed to be scant possibilities for advancement in a closely held private company with a young president who had a son.

For the next two years Terry spent most of his time dealing in real estate.[4] His plan was to generate a steady income through commission sales and to make larger gains by buying from the local inhabitants and selling to out-of-staters. He spent many nights and weekends renovating and repairing buildings for this latter activity and even attempted to build two shell homes but "lost his shirt." He also found that "the occupational hazard of the job was that I fell in love with many of my listings and by the end of the two-year period I owned 21 buildings." On these he had personally signed mortgages of almost $200,000. In addition to these negative cash flows he also had a $250-per-month cash drain in repay-

---

[4]Terry was asked to be a director of the Rutland Cooperative Savings and Loan Association in early 1965. He enjoyed this position and when the president died a year later, Terry was elected to the position because, according to his own assessment, "I was the only one who ever showed any deep interest or asked any questions at the directors' meetings."

ments of his college loans. Thus, although he averaged an income of about $30,000 a year for the period, cash was always scarce. He enjoyed his success but his interest began to wane because the work did not seem particularly stimulating or elevating. Both years he met his goals by October of the year and had difficulty motivating himself to perform after that time. He also was fond of taking long vacations, and found that when he broke away from day-to-day operations, he had to start all over again by acquiring listings and making contacts when he returned.

Green Mountain Rentals

Terry's growing dissatisfaction with real estate led him to purchase a franchised rental store called Taylor Rental Center in March of 1966. In his renovation and repair activities Terry had rented equipment from the Taylor Center, which was the only rental store in the area. The owner/operator was anxious to retire and had continually tried to interest Terry in the purchase of the store. He had opened the store three years before and subsequently had sales in 1963, 1964, and 1965 of $4,000, $10,950, and $16,700, respectively. He had run the business on an all-cash basis, and it was difficult for Terry to pin down the profits. Eventually, however, Terry purchased the business for $27,000 with terms of 10 percent down and the balance payable over two years.

The owner agreed to stay on for two months to teach Terry the business, after which Terry continued to work full time in the store for the next year. He drew no salary and used the cash generated to buy more equipment and to pay off the note on the business. To maintain an income, Terry continued to teach school three nights a week and to sell real estate on the other evenings and on Sundays.[5]

In April of 1967, Terry opened a second Taylor Rental Center in Barre, Vermont, a town with a population of 15,000. Nearby Montpelier added another 9,000, making it the largest population area in the state with no rental store except for a paint store which rented a few tools on the side. He made the $35,000 investment personally in the store and rented the assets to the company for $618 per month.

In both stores he had day-to-day managers which allowed him to oversee both operations and draw a salary of $12,000 while tending to his dwindling real estate holdings. He also found time to attend the American Rental Association Convention in New York City in the fall of 1967 against the advice of his Taylor Rental Center franchisor, who thought conventions were a waste of time and money. Terry returned feeling that his eyes had been opened to the great potential of the industry and the fact that equipment was generally available at 20 percent less than his

---

[5]Since graduation from business school, Terry had always taught school on a part-time basis at night, finding it enjoyable and highly profitable on an hourly basis.

franchisor was charging. Ties were severed with Taylor, with whom they had a verbal agreement to buy all their equipment in exchange for using the name. He changed the name of the company to Green Mountain Rentals, Inc.

In March 1968, Terry noticed in an industry magazine a distress sale of a rental store in Hamden, Connecticut, whose sales had plummeted from $40,000 in 1965 to $20,000 and an operating loss in 1967. Terry bought the assets for $18,000, $5,000 down and $13,000 on an unsecured note. He moved the location and spent a week with the newly hired manager cleaning, repairing, and sorting the equipment in the daytime and sleeping in the store at night. He then rented an apartment in Hamden and supervised the operation for the next two months. The store recorded sales of $32,000 in its first year of business.

Although the Barre store had not quite shown a profit, Green Mountain Rentals started a second store from scratch in Glens Falls, New York, in August of 1968. The town was rapidly growing and had a population of 30,000 and only one rental store. To finance the operation, Terry borrowed $20,000 against the Hamden operation. The fact that the opening of the Glens Falls store was poorly timed (just after the busy summer season and a year before they would be listed in the phone book) was compounded by the fact that some of the equipment was delivered late.

Terry finished a busy year by acquiring his fifth store, which was located in West Hartford, Connecticut, in December 1968.[6] A deal was structured whereby Terry paid $15,000 down and $45,000 over 10 years at 7 percent simple interest. The $15,000 was raised by selling 3 percent of Green Mountain to his family and a friend. The store in West Hartford maintained a business which was over 90 percent in the party equipment line (china, glasses, tableware, chairs, tables, linens, and portable dance floors). The intent of the acquisition was to move the store to a nearby but better location in West Hartford so that it could continue renting equipment and at the same time allow other Green Mountain stores to offer a line of party equipment and other accessories.

This acquisition was also part of Terry's overall plan to ease the cash flow problems which resulted from the seasonality of sales (Exhibit 2). After June (school graduation), December (holiday season) was the best

---

[6]Terry was president of the Rutland Chamber of Commerce for 1968. In June of 1968 he was appointed to the $9,000 a year post of Executive Secretary of Vermont Higher Education Facilities Commission. The responsibility of the commission was to administer and evaluate proposals for three federal aid programs. With the full-time assistance of an administrator/secretary Terry felt he was able to do a top-notch job by working four to five hours per week and attending the commission's annual meeting. He even received several commendation letters from Washington which he believes resulted from his spending $11,000 less than his $34,000 budget. In his spare time Terry wrote (actually he dictated it while driving his car between stores) a 100-page book entitled *Advertising and Promotion Ideas for the General Rental Store*. Using a direct mail campaign, he sold 500 copies at $8 apiece to more than cover his eventual out-of-pocket costs of $1,000 to print 1,000 copies. Later, in a second mailing at $10 per copy, he increased his total revenues to $8,000.

operating month for the West Hartford store and its party line. Another measure was to acquire 16 snowmobiles for renting during the winter months. Terry also acquired all the equity in Chateau Ecole and merged it into Green Mountain in 1968.

In April 1969 Terry noticed an advertisement in one of the industry journals for a rental store in Manchester, New Hampshire, which was for sale by the owner, who had fallen ill. After a few weeks Green Mountain acquired the store, its sixth, by borrowing the downpayment.

The rental industry

With six stores in his operation Terry decided to concentrate on operations in 1969. His first chance to consolidate some of the knowledge he had acquired about the rental industry came when he was preparing Green Mountain's annual report in 1968. He was particularly enthused about the possibilities of putting a successful company together in a fragmented mom and pop industry which would be the antithesis of his Harvard Business School education. In the report he put together the following industry study:

> The equipment rental industry is a post-World War II phenomenon which has flourished predominantly on the West Coast. The do-it-yourself trend created the demand for consumer-type tools and equipment on a rental basis, and increased specialization and cost of contractor equipment encouraged the growth of the industrial and commercial demand for rental equipment.
>
> The rental industry has matured on the West Coast while it is still in its infancy in the East. The average Californian rents $20 per year for personal property (i.e., not counting real estate), while the average New Englander rents less than $1 per year. A population of 20,000 within two miles of a store can generate $50,000 in rental sales in the West, while over 50,000 are required in the East, according to industry sources. The city of Burbank, California, with a population of 90,000 has 13 rental stores, each having over $100,000 worth of inventory, and each apparently flourishing. On the other hand, Manchester, New Hampshire (over 100,000 population), has only one rental store, and this store has less than $40,000 in inventory.
>
> In contrast to the West, where independent stores predominate, the greatest part of the rental industry in New England involves three franchise operations. United Rent-Alls is the oldest and largest franchisor in the country. They have started perhaps 40 stores in New England during the last 15 years, and all but a handful have dropped their franchise. The first full-line Taylor Rental Center was started in Rutland, Vermont, in 1963, and Taylor Rental Centers number over 100, but most of them are tool rental sidelines in hardware stores or lumber yards. The third, and fastest growing, franchisor is the A to Z subsidiary of Nationwide Industries, Inc. Across the country, they are averaging a new store every 72 hours and will certainly become the largest franchisor in the country within two years.

The franchisor earns a net markup of $5,000–$10,000 upon initially setting up a franchise. In addition, substantially all future equipment purchases must be made through the franchisor. Nationwide and A to Z also charge a royalty (franchise fee) on rental sales as well as making a profit on sales of rental contracts to franchisees. The Taylor Rental Center franchisor, Dealer Supply Co., charges a higher mark-up on new equipment, but no franchise fee. Once a franchisee becomes established, he generally finds that he no longer needs the services of the franchisor and, in many cases, will drop the franchise in less than five years. Even the Taylor Rental Center franchisor, with no franchise fee, has experienced more than 10 stores "going independent" or being purchased back by the franchisor (who provides financing) in their five years in existence.

The great majority of the franchise stores are "mom and pop" type operations with less than $50,000 in total inventory. The large rental operations are exclusively "independent" (i.e., not franchisees). Every spring, when the growing franchisee plans his purchases for the busy summer season, he must face the decision whether or not to pay the extra $2,000 on every $10,000 in purchases and/or the franchise fee on the increased rental volume, or become an independent. If a franchisee does not grow significantly, these considerations are not as important to him.

Equipment rentals versus automobile renting

The automobile and truck rental business are firmly established throughout the country. Car rentals are supported by expensive national advertising. New automobiles may be rented at virtually every Esso station. With this much interest and activity, there surely must be some profit in this kind of rental.

How does the car rental business, which is firmly established in New England, compare with the equipment rental business, which is just beginning to become a part of the New England scene? On the average, a car rents for approximately 1/200 of its cost per day. In other words, a $2,000 car will rent for about $10, plus a charge for mileage which approximately covers the variable costs of operation (gas, oil, repairs, depreciation, etc.). On the other hand, the "average" item in the equipment rental industry rents for approximately 1/20 of the original cost. Many items are even higher. A lawnmower, for example, costs $39 and rents for $6 per day, or 1/7 the cost. Variable expenses are approximately the same as car rentals as a percent of original cost.

The following chart shows a representative sample of rental rates compared to original cost for various items. Certainly, many of these items do not have the widespread or year-round demand of automobiles, but when this equipment is not being used, it is not depreciating, either. In fact, as inflation continues, rental inventory is often an excellent hedge against higher prices. A rental operator is often able to sell equipment which he has been renting for five or more years at his original cost or more. During this period, if he is a typical rental operator, he will average 100 percent return on original cost per year on all his equipment. For a car-renter to achieve this record, he would have to have his car out on rental 200 days out of 365 each year, which hardly leaves any time for the inevitable repairs.

In summary, the equipment rental industry, which has established a firm foothold in the West, has just started to grow in the East, led by three major franchisors. Green Mountain Rentals has more branch operations than any store in New England, but is not as large as some single store (mostly heavy equipment) rental operations around Boston.

Number of daily rentals necessary to recover full cost of equipment, 1968 (miscellaneous representative items)

Item	Cost (in dollars)	Daily charge	Number of days to recover cost
Santa Claus suit	9.00	$ 4.50	2
Post hole digger	5.00	1.50	4
Wine glass	.27	.06	5
Rotary lawn mower	39.00	6.00	7
Staple gun	8.00	1.00	8
Banquet table	20.00	2.00	10
Porta-crib	15.00	1.50	10
Power pull	22.00	2.00	11
Lawn spreader	17.00	1.50	12
Wheel barrow	24.00	2.00	12
Wooden chair	2.60	.20	13
Lineoleum roller	28.00	2.00	14
Roto tiller	172.00	12.00	15
Gas chain saw	188.00	12.00	16
Paint sprayer	77.00	4.50	17
32′ ladder, aluminum	55.00	3.00	19
Ditch pump	140.00	7.00	20
Electric cement mixer	96.00	5.00	20
Submersible pump	75.00	3.50	22
Tandem bicycle	76.00	3.00	26
Appliance hand truck	57.00	2.00	29
Two-wheel trailer	360.00	5.00	72
Camper trailer (caravan)	336.00	5.71†	60
Wheelchair	68.00	1.00	68
Belt vibrator	60.00	.71†	86
Floor sander	390.00	4.00	98
Portable TV	120.00	1.14†	105
80 C.F.M. air compressor	2,266.00	20.00	114
One section, scaffolding	39.00	.15*	260

*At monthly rate.
†At weekly rate.

Having armchaired the industry and the past year's performance in his annual report, Terry turned to action to improve his company's operations.

After sharpening his computer programming skills in a night course, he rented a terminal and joined a time-sharing system to aid him in his nighttime task of bookkeeping and to provide more information on inventory and rates of return. He numbered every piece of equipment in his stores and was able to generate rates of return and repair listings monthly. Terry found that the information was useful in purchasing equipment, but once the decisions were made, there was little further use for the information, especially now that he was no longer acquiring sites. As for monitoring repairs and out-of-stock items, he believed the cost of generating the information on the computer was prohibitive so he shifted back to detailed reports from the managers.[7] He also kept track of items not carried but asked for. Sometimes he found that a sufficient return could be generated if an item, such as a self-propelled ditch digger, was purchased and rented out of all six stores.

Terry spent two days a week on the road visiting his managers whom he had recruited through newspaper advertising. Their salaries averaged around $9,000 a year and their backgrounds were fairly similar. They were all around 40 years old, non-high school graduates, and mechanics for most of their careers. All had at one time or another owned and operated gas stations, and most had gone bankrupt at some point in their lives. They still valued working for themselves which Green Mountain offered to a degree, but they were all hesitant to go out on their own financially again. Terry attempted to appeal to their motivations by instituting an incentive program whereby they earned bonuses of 25 percent of everything over budgeted profit and 50 percent over a second higher hurdle. In this way he felt he bridged some of the distance between absentee owner and owner/manager. This seemed necessary in an industry where the major competitors were franchised "mom and pop" operations run by people who did not value their time as much as running their own shops.

Having attended to internal operations, Terry turned to drumming up additional business by contacting new homeowners who were a great source of business in the first few weeks of occupancy when they particularly noticed home maintenance needs.

Merchants Welcome Service, Inc.

In his efforts to contact new homeowners, Terry first tried the Welcome Wagon, a national service organization which contacted new residents in communities with "words of welcome" and gifts and notices from merchants. At a cost of $1.10 per introduction Terry felt the service was too expensive especially since Green Mountain would also have to pay for introduction to new apartment dwellers, a market segment they were not particularly interested in. Also, Welcome Wagon did not make contact until six or eight weeks after the new residents had moved in,

---

[7]He refers to this experience with time-sharing as a "$10,000 lesson."

which was past what Green Mountain felt to be the critical period of rentability.

Terry decided to perform the function himself, to dig out the information on new community residents from the Registry of Deeds, the Mortgage Association, and the Real Estate Association and to approach them by mail, which was less expensive, but served his purposes just as well as one of the Welcome Wagon's hostesses. He soon found that a mailing which cost him $.09 per letter and offered a discount of $3.00 produced a 10 percent response rate with an average rental order of $11.25.

The idea seemed so beneficial for Green Mountain that Terry found himself wondering if he could leverage his efforts by selling the idea to other merchants. The first seven noncompetitive merchants that he approached immediately subscribed to the idea of having their own messages included in Terry's mailing at $.10 per introduction. Buoyed with success and optimism, Terry charged $.20 apiece to the next 10 merchants and then raised his price to $.30. Eventually, he bound each merchant's message into a book of coupons which typically offered a discount or free introductory offer. These served as an incentive to lure the new community residents to the merchant. He called the service and company Merchants Welcome Service, Inc. By early 1970[8] Terry was mailing books of coupons which grossed $6 from the merchants for each mailing at the rate of 40 a month in Rutland County, which had a population of 50,000. The costs were difficult to measure because of his own time, overhead, and by-product pricing since he was making the mailings anyway. He surmised, though, that his total out-of-pocket expense associated with a mailing was $.75.

To Terry the possibilities for further entrepreneuring of the idea seemed endless, not only in the form of his coupon book, but also in the form of a personalized letter service, or just the addresses he generated. Those who were less optimistic noted that "Terry Allen can sell anything, but can anyone else sell the Merchants Welcome Service?" To test this hypothesis and also to generate rentals for his store, Terry designed literature (Exhibit 3) and hired a salesman to cover Glens Falls, New York. Within three weeks the salesman had sold 40 merchants at $.25 per introduction. This meant that Merchants Welcome Service would gross $10 every time a coupon book was mailed in the Glens Falls area, which averaged about 40 new out-of-county, home-buying residents a month.

Encouraged by the results of the Glens Falls test, Terry became anxious to push the plan further. Not only did the potential of this new venture lure him, but he calculated the business would take very little capital to begin. On the other hand, Green Mountain Rentals was lever-

---

[8]In December 1970 Green Mountain's Hamden manager quit, and Terry took the opportunity to close that operation since eight stores had opened within five miles (some at better locations), and a price war had begun.

aged so greatly that opportunities for further expansion were limited and all available cash was being used. He felt he already had provided his most significant contribution to Green Mountain in terms of financing, purchasing, and location analysis. Yet if he could focus his attention on the fine tuning of the organization, the payout of the loans, and the development of a profit history, he would probably then be able to reap the greatest capital appreciation for time spent. Consequently, he was loath to sell Green Mountain and he did not feel there was sufficient cash flow to hire a manager. As he looked at the statements for the last five years on Green Mountain (Exhibit 4) and industry statistics (Exhibit 5), he wondered whether he could pursue both ventures.

SUGGESTED QUESTIONS

1. What should Terry Allen do?
2. How would you compare and contrast his two current operations? Which do you think should receive most of Terry's effort and attention? Why?
3. For whichever of the two ventures you prefer, what specific things should Terry do to improve his situation? How much money do you think he can make, if any, in this activity?

EXHIBIT 1
Terry Allen
Green Mountain Rentals, Inc., summary of buildup

Location	Date	Method obtained	Rent or purchase space	Previous year's sales	Gross cost or investment	Terms	
						Down	Approx. $/mo.
Rutland, Vt.	March 1966	Acquisition	Rent	$16,700	$27,000	$ 2,700	$ 500
Barre, Vt.	April 1967	Start-up	Rent	—	35,000	—	618*
Hamden, Conn.†	March 1968	Acquisition	Rent	20,000	18,000	5,000	1,200
Glens Falls, New York	August 1968	Start-up	Rent	—	30,000	—	480
West Hartford, Conn.	December 1968	Acquisition	Purchased building for $40,000	60,000	60,000	15,000	500
Manchester, N.H.	April 1969	Acquisition	Rent	45,000	38,000	10,000	891

*Terry Allen owned the assets in his own name and leased them to Green Mountain for $618 per month.
†Closed down in December 1970.

EXHIBIT 2

Terry Allen Green Mountain Rentals, Inc., per cent of annual income per month (based on 1965–68 figures)

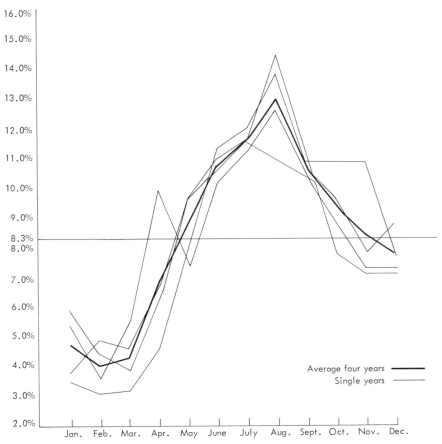

EXHIBIT 3
Terry Allen
Green Mountain Rentals, Inc.

a unique marketing service designed to provide the missing link between the merchant and the new. home owner . . .

merchants welcome service, inc.

program:

When a person purchases a new home in a town, he receives a valuable booklet of certificates with his name and new address inscribed on an attractive cover. Each certificate contains a discount, gift, or word of welcome from a local merchant.

Certificates in the booklet are offered only to non-competing merchants in a particular area. Except for restaurants, as soon as one type of merchant subscribes to the Merchants Welcome Service Program, the service is not offered to other merchants in the same basic business in that area. Consequently, Merchants Welcome Service participating merchants are the first of their type who are introduced to the new homeowner. The welcome extended by these merchants is usually a lasting one.

As an alternative to the certificate program, Merchants Welcome Service offers a letter service. Families who have just purchased a new home are sent personal letters of welcome or the merchant's stationery. Using an automatic typing system, each letter and envelope is individually typed and sent to the merchant. He personally signs, stuffs and mails the letters along with any special advertising material he may choose.

Each month (or in some cases, each week) participating merchants receive a list of all families in the area who have received certificates or letters. This list is useful for special mailing campaigns as well as to verify that the newcomers were actually contacted on behalf of the merchant.

Merchants Welcome Service has the capacity, the people, and the experience to provide its introduction service in a highly efficient and tasteful manner. Whether through welcome certificates or personal letters, the merchant who is selected to participate in Merchants Welcome Service will be favorably remembered by new homeowners for having extended his hand of welcome.

merchants welcome service, clark building, natick, mass. 01760 617 / 655-2724

EXHIBIT 3 (continued)

concept:

When families move to a new community they establish new spending habits. Usually the first stores they patronize when they move are the ones they continue to patronize in the future. Most of these early spending patterns are based on accidental circumstances because the family does not have an *incentive* to select specific stores.

Merchants Welcome Service has designed a new type of program to provide the *incentive* for new homeowners to patronize those merchants who are selected to participate in our program.

The basic concept of this service has been recognized for many years. Most welcoming services, however, have been unable to reach the newcomer shortly after his arrival and offer the service at a sufficiently low cost-per-contact. Merchants Welcome Service has researched and tailored a program that overcomes the shortcomings of other introduction services.

The *Information Center* of Merchants Welcome Service knows when and where people are going to move, often before they do so. Consequently, the Merchants Welcome Service Program is able to contact new homeowners long before other welcoming services. This time advantage is vital, for once a newcomer arrives, a lost day could be a lost customer.

Market research has shown that homeowners are better customers than apartment-dwellers because they are usually in higher income brackets, have more discretionary income, spend more on home improvement projects, and are likely to stay longer in one place and become permanent customers. Accordingly, Merchants Welcome Service caters exclusively to new homeowners, and excludes apartment-dwellers from its introduction service.

These advantages, coupled with the fact that the Merchants Welcome Service Program usually costs a merchant 50% to 80% less per introduction than competing welcome services, explain why this service has been received enthusiastically by merchants throughout the country.

EXHIBIT 4
Terry Allen
Green Mountain Rentals, Inc., operating statements

	1966	1967	1968	1969
Gross income	$22,237.89	$44,275.23	$123,035.96	$278,386.81
Cost of goods sold	1,540.67	947.45	1,530.83	6,471.23
Net Income	$20,697.22	$43,327.78	$121,505.13	$271,915.58
Operating expense*	17,473.62	33,940.46	98,642.69	222,240.62
Lease payments*	—	6,562.89	8,983.28	21,525.77
Interest	—	1,597.37	5,365.02	16,240.10
Depreciation	5,411.73	6,611.30	13,876.88	37,454.35
Total expenses	22,885.35	48,712.02	126,867.87	297,460.84
Gross profit (loss)..................	(2,188.13)	(5,384.24)	(5,362.74)	(25,545.26)
Tax	—	—	—	—
Net Profit (loss)..............	$ (2,188.13)	$ (5,384.24)	$ (5,362.74)	$ (25,545.26)
Chateau Ecole Net Income (loss)	—	—	$(298.11)	$4,204.97

*Terry received no salary in 1966 although he did receive $6K of expenses. By 1969 he was receiving about $30K, which included salary, lease payments the company made to him, and expenses. Expenses included total payment of his and his wife's auto expenses, health insurance, medical bills, life insurance, and some entertainment expenses.

EXHIBIT 4 (continued)
Balance sheets

	1966	1967	1968	1969
Cash	$ 122.44	$ 8,267.89	$ 3,804.65	$ 5,703.52
Accounts receivable	1,811.65	4,620.88	24,427.77	60,166.73
Due from stockholders	539.40	—	10,095.43	10,435.15
Other	—	1,102.20	7,088.52	5,872.34
Total Current Assets	$ 2,473.49	$13,990.97	$ 45,416.37	$ 82,177.74
Land	—	—	4,000.00	4,000.00
Building	—	—	15,147.55	55,147.55
Rental equipment	34,626.62	49,278.56	189,189.52	268,330.55
Shop equipment	—	—	3,969.23	9,680.15
Office equipment	—	—	4,791.51	2,145.41
Service vehicles	—	—	8,958.17	13,670.28
Leasehold improvements	—	—	5,231.98	6,910.67
Mortgage loan	—	6,923.19	—	—
Total	$34,626.62	$49,278.56	$231,287.96	$359,884.61
Less accumulated depreciation	15,361.46	21,972.76	36,635.88	75,027.93
Fixed Assets—Net	$19,265.16	$27,305.80	$194,652.08	$284,856.68
Prepaid interest	—	—	13,594.42	16,776.91
Other	—	—	4,005.48	5,371.76
Total Assets	$21,738.65	$48,219.96	$257,668.35	$389,183.09
Notes payable (1 year)	—	—	65,602.13	78,099.21
Accounts payable	442.99	5,622.41	28,055.42	42,834.79
Mortgage payable (1 year)	—	—	537.84	3,018.48
Accrued expense and other	2,272.26	1,122.54	3,334.09	11,140.34
Total Current Liabilities	$ 2,715.25	$ 6,744.95	$ 97,529.48	$135,092.82
Long term Notes payable	—	27,835.85	101,110.68	126,283.53
Mortgage payable	—	—	11,098.68	51,365.62
Total Liabilities	$ 2,715.25	$34,580.80	$209,738.82	$312,741.97
Capital stock	20,300.00	20,300.00	21,600.00	23,300.00
Paid in surplus	—	—	33,551.22	86,351.22
Deficit	(1,276.60)	(6,660.84)	(7,221.69)	(33,210.10)
Total Capital and Liabilities	$21,738.65	$48,219.96	$257,668.35	$389,183.09

EXHIBIT 4 (continued)

Operating statement—1970

Rental income		$248,349.21
Merchandise income		7,575.97
Miscellaneous income		7,449.13
Equipment sales		2,892.20
		$266,266.51
Cost of merchandise sold	$ 5,303.18	
Cost of equipment sold	2,024.54	
Total cost of goods sold		7,327.72
Total Income		$258,938.79
Depreciation	$ 33,600.00	
Taxes, property	3,858.59	
Taxes, payroll	875.36	
Taxes, licenses and others	1,813.75	
Accounting	642.81	
Bank service charges	486.86	
Dues and subscriptions	705.35	
Freight	564.68	
Insurance	6,829.44	
Interest	13,037.83	
Lease payments	19,259.22	
Legal and auditing	2,554.20	
Postage	2,495.88	
Rent	25,294.00	
Telephone	7,380.94	
Delivery	1,717.81	
Advertising	2,245.10	
Auto repairs	611.00	
Bad debts	10,500.00	
Credits and refunds	3,365.62	
Employee benefits	4,378.44	
Travel and entertainment	4,038.64	
Gas and oil	3,191.03	
Laundry	2,264.73	
Miscellaneous	4,827.33	
Office supplies	1,635.42	
Over and short	58.19	
Employee bonus	2,117.71	
Repairs and maintenance	12,773.58	
Subrents	830.12	
Supplies	2,875.12	
Utilities	5,629.50	
Wages*	104,857.75	
Total Expenses†		$287,317.00
Net Loss		($28,378.21)
Chateau Ecole Net Income (loss)		$3,817.14

*In 1970 Terry received about $18K in salary, $10K in lease payments, and $7K in expenses.
†$20K of Green Mountain expenses had been spent towards the start-up of Merchants Welcome Service.

EXHIBIT 4 (continued)
Balance sheet—December 31, 1970

Cash		$ 5,236.45
Accounts receivable		39,235.76
Due from officers		8,795.16
Mortgages receivable		1,717.41
Prepaid interest		10,767.07
Rental equipment	$270,308.48	
Accumulated depreciation	95,781.64 ✓	174,526.84
Shop equipment	6,968.58	
Accumulated depreciation	3,093.45 ✓	3,875.13
Office equipment	5,430.18	
Accumulated depreciation	976.98 ✓	4,453.20
Land		9,000.00
Real estate	54,827.55	
Accumulated depreciation	2,559.19	52,268.36
Furnishings	320.00	
Accumulated depreciation	69.33	250.67
Service vehicles	13,670.28	
Accumulated depreciation	4,337.61	9,332.67
Merchandise inventory		3,282.09
Leasehold improvements	7,577.74	
Accumulated depreciation	1,809.73	5,768.01
Deposit with utilities		2,225.00
Investment*		1,000.00
Total Assets		$331,733.82
Accounts payable		29,666.42
Chattel mortgages		191,799.50
Real estate mortgages		43,200.00
Accrued expenses		6,681.20
Accrued sales tax		3,506.84
Total Liabilities		$274,853.96
Common stock		23,300.00
Paid-in surplus		86,351.22
Earned surplus (Loss)		(52,771.36)
Total Net Worth		$ 56,879.86
Total Liabilities and Net Worth		$331,733.82

*Merchants Welcome Service.

EXHIBIT 5
Terry Allen
Industry statistics* expense ratio analysis comparison table (percent of gross income)

		\$25,000	51–	101–	151–	201–	301–	Over	Average all
	From	\$25,000	51–	101–	151–	201–	301–	Over	*Average all*
	To	\$50,000	100	150	200	300	500	500	*firms*

Rental income categories

Number of firms

	18	20	13	8	4	3	3	69
Gross income	100.00	100.00	100.00	100.00	100.00	100.00	100.00	100.00
Cost of sales	8.50	14.79	5.80	30.54	36.34	27.46	2.99	14.57
Adjusted gross income	91.50	85.21	94.20	69.46	63.66	72.54	97.01	85.43
Fixed Expenses:								
Occupancy	8.83	7.13	3.35	4.03	2.16	3.33	5.57	5.98
Supplies	3.18	2.57	2.94	1.68	1.35	.31	3.88	2.60
Insurance	2.36	1.88	2.17	1.83	1.79	1.77	2.99	2.09
Tax and license .	2.36	1.52	2.54	1.48	2.17	2.64	2.67	2.06
Telephone	1.16	.80	.79	1.03	.87	.65	1.44	.94
Legal and audit .	.63	.72	.84	.76	.56	.38	.56	.69
Utilities	2.10	1.17	1.13	.69	.57	.37	.78	1.26
Total	20.63	15.77	13.76	11.50	9.48	9.44	17.90	15.62
Variable Expenses:								
Wages and salaries	29.22	28.10	27.35	24.86	23.53	28.31	31.16	27.76
Repairs	6.49	6.61	8.73	4.63	6.31	6.58	10.85	6.92
Miscellaneous . .	4.03	1.75	4.97	2.55	3.43	2.22	4.29	3.23
Advertising	5.25	3.93	3.62	3.15	1.79	1.61	2.27	3.83
Interest	3.70	1.97	2.78	.93	1.54	1.69	1.85	2.42
Gas and oil	2.54	1.47	3.34	2.05	1.09	1.36	1.62	2.16
Total	51.23	43.83	50.79	38.17	37.69	41.77	52.04	46.32
Total Expenses: . .	80.36	74.39	70.35	80.20	83.51	78.67	72.93	76.51
Profit before depreciation . .	19.64	25.61	29.65	19.79	16.49	21.32	27.07	23.49
Depreciation . . .	20.94	15.33	18.48	10.57	11.70	13.94	12.65	16.45
Total	101.30	89.72	88.83	90.78	95.21	92.61	85.58	92.96
Profit to Gross (before taxes) . . .	(1.30)	10.28	11.17	9.22	4.79	7.38	14.42	7.04
Profit to Equity (before taxes) . . .	(2.34)	24.34	20.42	23.33	14.17	20.85	34.66	16.22

*Source: American Rental Association Survey, 1964.

Thomas Kane

In July of 1963, Thomas Kane was reviewing his efforts to purchase the Wilson Body and Equipment Co., Inc., of Cincinnati, Ohio. The owners of the firm, Frank and John Wilson, had agreed in principle to sell their firm to Tom Kane and his partner Scott Hanson. After extensive negotiations the two partners had submitted an offer for an installment purchase, only to have the two brothers refuse it at the last minute and demand cash, $300,000 for the nonliquid assets of their company. Irked at having his installment purchase offer refused after time-consuming negotiations in which an apparent understanding had been reached, Mr. Kane had immediately countered with a suggestion for a modified cash purchase, which to his surprise appeared to be agreeable to the brothers. In reflecting on his proposal Tom was concerned about its feasibility, and particularly about raising the necessary $300,000. He also wondered how his partner would react.

Thomas Kane

Tom Kane was born in 1933 and grew up in Manorville, Long Island. His father had become a patent broker, who specialized in bringing European ideas and techniques to the United States and Latin America, after graduating from Harvard Business School, class of 1921. He had accumulated stocks and warrants in return for his services, which were worth over a million dollars. Wiped out in the panic of 1929, at age 30, he set out to repay his debts and raise his family, on Long Island, commuting to Wall Street. In 1963 Tom Kane's father worked for a firm that specialized in trusts which owned stock and bond portfolios. He worked with customers who had bond portfolios over $100,000 in value.

Tom Kane attended Harvard College, where he received an A.B. in economics in 1955. He financed one third of his college education through his own earnings from summer jobs. During the summer he operated two milk routes on a seven-day-a-week basis for a local dairy. His routes included 250 customers. The job included sales, delivery, and bill collecting responsibilities. Commenting on his experience Mr. Kane said, "The initial value of this work was in learning to apply myself from day to day without having any free time. . . . it was my first serious experience in responsibility, and was my first practical introduction into the workings of simple business situations."

During high school Tom Kane had worked for a florist after class. He had learned the techniques of growing delicate hybrid delphinium flowers. While at college, in addition to his summer milk routes he became a specialized flower grower. He acquired an acre of land from his father and planted it with hybrid delphiniums. He sold cut flowers to the New York Wholesale Flower Association for an average revenue of $200 per summer.

Following his graduation, Mr. Kane served two and a half years as an officer and navigator in the Air Force. Flying in B-47 jet bombers, he was given enjoyable assignments in Europe and the Mediterranean. Commenting on his military experience Mr. Kane stated:

> I went into the service determined to get the most out of it that I could. I was eager to fly and was frustrated that I couldn't get into pilot training. As a result in my spare time I took private flying lessons. By the time I got my navigator training finished I had earned my commercial pilot's license. I was so stupidly eager back then that I didn't take any leave time, prior to my active duty assignment, and as a result I accelerated ahead of my class, by about 30 days. As a result I was the only one who had the fun of combat ready flying in B-47's.

Following the completion of his military service Tom Kane moved to Boston, Massachusetts, and applied to the Harvard Business School. During the spring and summer of 1958 he lived with his older brother, who was a Harvard M.B.A. working at Arthur D. Little, Inc. He worked for the City of Boston as a real estate appraiser. Although he was accepted at Stanford Business School he was rejected at Harvard. Recalling the impact of his rejection by the school Mr. Kane said, "The next morning when I woke up with a terrible head, I was upset. I called Chaffee Hall, the Dean of Admissions, and told him I wanted a chance to talk to him. I went in and told him in so many words that they had made a mistake. I admitted that my college performance had only been average. But I insisted I had benefited from my Air Force experience, and was ready for H.B.S." As a result of his conversation and a written request for a second evaluation of his application, Mr. Kane was admitted to the school.

During the summer of 1959 following his first year at the school Mr. Kane was married. His wife had graduated from Cornell and then enrolled in the education school at Boston University for her master's. During his second year at Harvard she taught school to provide income.

During his second year at Harvard Business School Mr. Kane concentrated on the area of corporate finance. He remembered creative marketing strategy as his most enjoyable course. Mr. Kane wrote his final report for the Management of New Enterprises course. It dealt with the opportunities to operate profitably a marina located on a lake in upper New York State. He used the facilities of the Small Business Placement Program to find a job with the Cincinnati (Ohio) Mfg. Co., a manufacturer of industrial equipment. Summing up his M.B.A. experience Mr. Kane said, "I felt that I needed to develop skills in both the marketing and finance area. As it turned out finance was especially important for someone who wanted to buy a small business. As a result of my work at the school I felt competent to handle the financial side of business. This is something I don't think you can pick up on the job when you are working for a specific firm."

The Cincinnati Mfg. Co.

The Cincinnati Mfg. Co. was a manufacturer of industrial equipment, pumps, and machine tools. At the company Mr. Kane found a management team made up of engineers, who appeared to lack a variety of management skills. They were weak in administration, marketing, and finance, while they were strong in production and engineering. It was these weaknesses that attracted Mr. Kane to the firm. Concerning his position with the company he said:

> I went with the company without a title, without knowing what my salary was going to be, or knowing whom I would really work for. It may sound crazy but the opportunity in a company that looked so "open" to any kind of improvement was very interesting to me. After I got into the company I found that I was operating as a "free agent" type of staff consultant to the executive vice presidents for the principal functional activities, and to the president also. I worked on a project basis. [See Exhibit 1 for more personal data.]

In addition to his work with the members of top management Mr. Kane worked within the industrial equipment division, the pump division, and the machine tool division on a variety of projects. The firm's 2,000 employees and geographically separated plant sites made it obvious to him that Cincinnati Mfg. Co. needed some type of data processing capability, as opposed to its existing system of hand-produced records and documents. He worked hard without much success to get this idea adopted. He was frequently involved in market research on the firm's nationally distributed products. He also worked on the problem of systematically allocating factory burden by product line to establish the actual contribution of various products to fixed costs.

> Probably the most important project which I have worked on for Cincinnati Mfg. Co. was a series of detailed analyses of burden rates on the various product lines. Here is a company doing $30 million in sales and they really didn't know their costs. As a result they were thinking about spinning off some of their products which in fact produced excellent margin for them. On the other hand they had products which they viewed as big money makers which my analysis showed to be losers. I wrote many reports on this situation, and some progress toward proper use of the cost information has occurred.

Mr. Kane characterized the role which he played at Cincinnati Mfg. Co. as one in which he offered, "constructive criticism to top management on the way the company was operating." He felt that in the early 1960s he was the only person who was willing to say, "I don't agree with you," to top management, and then put his reasons down on paper. He felt sure that his approach to the job was appreciated by the president and some of the other members of management.

The management of the company was, according to Mr. Kane, very conservative. The company had no long-term debt of any kind in their capital structure. In addition they held cash reserves of from $3 to $4 million. By 1963 Mr. Kane recalled that there were some signs that the past conservatism of management was changing and that a younger, growth-oriented man was in line for the presidency within the next two to three years.

During the three years that he worked for the Cincinnati Mfg. Co., Tom Kane began to speculate on the possibility that he might purchase his own firm. Although he felt that the Cincinnati Mfg. Co. was an exceptionally fine firm and offered him very good opportunities for a successful career, he had always dreamed of having his own company. His experience with the commercial flower business had convinced him that he had the capacity to own a small business, if the situation was right. Tom felt that the greatest drawback to going into business for himself was his small financial resources. It was at this point that he met Scott Hanson, another employee of the Cincinnati Mfg. Co.

Scott Hanson

Tom met Scott Hanson while working on a marketing project for the Heating Products Division. Scott Hanson was some 15 years older than Tom. He was the division's sales manager at the time. Scott's business career had begun when he was a partner in a small engineering firm, the Smith-Hanson Engineering Company prior to 1955. The firm had developed a dust collecting device as a proprietary product. Sales had grown to over a million dollars. At Mr. Smith's retirement and because of inability to finance growth, the firm had been sold to the Primary Metals Co. Scott joined Primary Metals as sales manager for his product. Five years later the dust collector product line was resold to Cincinnati Mfg. Co., Heating Products Division. As a result of the sale, Scott found himself an employee of Cincinnati Mfg. Co., with a personal net worth of about $120,000. He was hoping to invest about $100,000 in small business ownership.

Their work brought the two men into contact with each other and they learned of their mutual interest in owning and operating a small business. As a result of their association they learned to respect each other's ability and judgment. According to Tom, Scott Hanson was a very well-spoken individual who could make a very effective presentation of any type. His strongest skills were in the area of sales, sales management, and in design engineering. He felt that these skills complemented very well his own abilities in the area of administration and finance. (See Exhibit 1.)

The partnership

In January of 1963, Mr. Kane and Mr. Hanson made the decision to form a partnership, and began to look for a small business to purchase. Tom, unlike Scott Hanson, did not have any appreciable amount of cash to invest in the project. He had only recently repaid his student loan to Harvard. However, he wanted to have a 50 percent ownership in any property acquired. Because of previous experience at the Smith-Hanson Engineering Company, where he had been a minority owner, Scott Hanson agreed, but asked him to try to raise at least $6,000. The two men decided to invest a maximum of $100,000 in a small business. Tom would borrow $44,000 from Scott. The loan was to be in the form of a demand note, repayable in $400 monthly installments. There was no penalty for missed payments. Interest would be 6 percent.

Tom was able to raise the required $6,000 through a series of fortunate circumstances. When he had moved to Cincinnati in 1960 he had purchased a home. His wife's father, who was a successful doctor, offered to help Tom with the $4,500 downpayment necessary. Three years later Tom discovered that he had purchased the house for a very low price as the result of a depressed housing market. His home was revalued by the mortgage company for a price $10,000 over the purchase price. This allowed him to increase his mortgage by $5,000. By using the cash value of his life insurance and a small savings account Tom was able to raise the additional $1,000 required. His $6,000 coupled with his note for $44,000 enabled him to contribute $50,000 to the equity of a possible purchase.

The business broker

Tom Kane and Scott Hanson decided to begin visiting possible small businesses during their lunch hours and after work. They decided not to leave the Cincinnati Mfg. Co. unless they could actually buy a small business. They contacted two business brokers to help them. Jones and Associates was a business brokerage firm with headquarters in Cincinnati. They failed to produce a company for Tom and Scott with the exception of an industrial clay pipe manufacturer located in Wisconsin. Low margins in this industry made it unattractive to the partners.

On the other hand, the partners used the services of a Mr. Sam Benson, a part-time business broker and full-time insurance salesman. Tom described him as,

> A real character. Sam must be at least 65 years old. He knows Cincinnati and Columbus like the back of his hand. He has made a specialty out of selling key man insurance to small businessmen. And through his extensive contacts he has developed the ability to locate companies for local businessmen. He dragged us out to see a company every two or three days. A lot of them we just drove by. We saw about six or seven companies which we really looked into.

Tom believed that Sam Benson had excellent financial connections with local banks.

The partners outlined in detail to Sam the kind of company that they wanted. They instructed him as their broker to find them a manufacturing company with a proprietary product line, with an established niche in the market, so that it would have a going concern value. In addition, they wanted a firm large enough to support both of them. In retrospect Tom said, "Despite our detailed instruction as to what we wanted I think that Sam showed us everything he could get his hands on."

They looked at a company that manufactured aluminum storm windows and doors. They looked at a small metal stamping firm. And they looked at the Eastern Lumber Company, for which they decided to make an offer. It was a lumber company which had branched out into manufacturing prefabricated cottages, cabins, and garages. It also was a distributor of lumber products. It enjoyed sales of about $850,000 a year. At the time they saw the firm, negotiations were already in progress with another potential buyer. They offered $170,000 for the firm, on an installment purchase basis, with $50,000 in cash.

The purchase proposal to the Eastern Lumber Company cost the two partners more than $2,000 for professional fees. They were extremely disappointed when their offer was rejected in favor of the other buyer. However their lawyer and their accountant agreed to apply their costs against a future purchase. This was in mid-April 1963.

The Wilson Body and Equipment Company

Several days after the Eastern Lumber Company deal fell through Sam Benson told Tom that the Wilson brothers might be willing to sell their company, which was an installer and distributor of special truck bodies and related equipment, with sales of $1,018,000 in 1962.

A week later Tom received word that the brothers were seriously interested. At the first meeting between Tom, Scott, and John and Frank Wilson, the owners gave Mr. Kane a large number of financial documents detailing their firm's past operations. (See Exhibits 2, 3, and 4 for financial documents.)

In a 10-day period following the meeting with the two Wilson brothers, Tom worked very hard to pull together an analysis of the company's past operations, its market position, and the truck body industry to enable his partner and himself to make a decision on the company. At the end of the 10-day period they decided to offer the Wilson brothers an installment purchase. (See Exhibits 5, 6, 7, 8, and 9 for the documents Tom Kane produced.)

The Wilson brothers

Frank Wilson was 56 years old at the time of the negotiations; John was 52. Their father had established the Wilson Body and Equipment Company in 1905. Frank Wilson was the president of the corporation, but Tom observed that they operated the firm essentially as a partnership. Frank Wilson supervised the production shop while John was in charge of administrative matters, finance, and sales. The company did not have an engineering department. John did the design work required for the custom bodies, by hand-sketching production drawings, or using drawings shown in competitors' advertisements. (See Exhibit 10 for an organization chart.)

Frank Wilson. Frank Wilson did not participate in the negotiations to sell the company, preferring to leave them to John. Both partners observed that Frank ran the production shop in a very autocratic manner, with all 35 men in the shop under his direct supervision. Commenting on the production situation Tom said, "The shop covered 67,000 square feet. At times when we were out there we saw Frank literally run from location to location to solve problems and make decisions. It appeared to us that he was overextended. His office was piled high with papers, which from the dust on them looked like they had been there for some time."

However, Frank Wilson was obviously very well liked by the men in the shop. In fact Tom was told that in the trade Frank Wilson was very well liked while John Wilson was almost universally disliked. It was

Frank who had good relationships with all the customers although he wasn't in charge of sales.

John Wilson. In describing John Wilson, Tom said, "We were very much impressed with John, right from the start. He seemed to have handled his side of the business in a very competent manner." The partners were especially impressed by the financial and cost information that John showed them, and also by the obvious detail of the figures. Although John was an individual who hadn't finished high school, he seemed to have an extremely good grasp of administrative techniques and selling methods. They estimated that he also was very greatly overworked.

Both partners were impressed that the company's operating statement was broken into four separate profit centers. And Tom used the detailed figures available to him to compute the marginal contribution of each one of the profit centers to cover period costs. At one of the negotiating sessions John briefly showed them a job cost system which he had personally designed. It was, according to Tom, "a surprisingly sophisticated system."

Marketing. Tom Kane spoke to a number of people in the Cincinnati area in an attempt to establish the Wilson Company's market share in the truck body business. The results of these inquiries were inconclusive. Commenting on the company's market share Tom said, "Just driving around the streets of Cincinnati we could see that from the back of every truck that went by it looked like another Wilson body, because the mud flaps all said Wilson, which meant it was sold by the company. It seemed that six out of ten trucks had the Wilson name on them so we felt sure the firm had a dominant share of their market."

John Wilson estimated that his firm sold at least 50 percent of all the special truck bodies in Cincinnati and approximately a third of the truck bodies and equipment sold in Columbus through the company's branch office in that city.

He also told the partners that Wilson marketed its products on a regional basis, although sales were concentrated in Cincinnati and Columbus. The Columbus branch did approximately $200,000 a year in sales, with one full-time salesman and the manager selling. He said that his firm sold to public utilities, municipalities, and produce companies who sold the supermarket chains, in both cities.

Tom discovered that the truck body and equipment industry was cyclical, showing similarity to the construction industry. The demand was strongest in the spring and early summer. However he felt that the Wilson Company had balanced these seasonal sales by acquiring exclusive distributorships for snowplows and wrecker truck bodies which sold well in the fall and winter months. As a result overall sales were relatively level.

He believed that Wilson's past sales showed a reasonably good correlation with national trends in the truck body and equipment industry as reflected by SIC category 3713. In addition, sales tended to follow the overall economic cycle. For example, they reflected the 1951 boom, the 1953 recession, the recession in 1958, and so on. (See Exhibits 11 and 12.)

Tom reported that Wilson was a custom shop principally installing a variety of equipment on truck chassis. The firm was an exclusive distributor for a variety of truck bodies and related equipment listed in Table 1.

TABLE 1
Wilson Company exclusive distributorships (May 1963)

1. Service bodies (power and light company trucks, telephone company trucks)	4. Van bodies
	5. Power lift gates
	6. Snow plows
2. Dump truck bodies and hydraulic units	7. Wrecker bodies
	8. Hydraulic cranes
3. Platform bodies (used on flat bed trucks)	9. Winches

Source: Company catalog.

In addition to their exclusive equipment distributorships the company custom fabricated a limited number of van bodies and about half of the wrecker bodies which they sold, special platform bodies, and a few special dump bodies. In analyzing the four profit centers on the Wilson income statement Tom was aware of the fact that a majority of the custom sales, about $200,000 in an average year, were for van bodies. These van bodies were not fabricated at Wilson but were purchased as component parts and assembled in the shop.

The repair and paint job sales were largely made to past customers for truck bodies or equipment. The repair business was largely related to the hydraulic equipment the firm sold, and was seasonal, being strongest in the late fall and winter. The painting was done on customers' used equipment to prolong its useful life. Both the repair and painting work were labor-intensive and high-margin sales.

Mr. Wilson had for many years used direct mail to advertise the various types of equipment which the company distributed. John Wilson claimed that many of the brand names had become the preferred quality product in the area. Tom guessed that a considerable amount of awareness on the part of past and potential customers existed for the firm's 20 distributed products.

Summing up his investigation of Wilson's market position, Tom estimated that the average national return on sales dollars for truck body installers was 1.8 percent after tax and only 2.2 percent before tax. He prepared the short report that appears as the Appendix to summarize his analysis.

The shop.   The shop was located in an old brick building with high ceilings and largely open area. Tom saw some sheetmetal cutting and bending equipment and a few machine tools. But most of the work appeared to be hand work. The truck bodies were scattered all over the shop floor on steel sawhorses. The inventory of truck bodies and equipment appeared to be composed of a small number of large items. Tom found the hardware inventory hard to evaluate, in a cursory examination; it consisted of fittings like tail lights, bumpers, locks, and hinges.

The Machinists Union represented the blue collar employees in the shop. Mr. Kane did not request access to the union contract. The partners assumed that relations with the union were satisfactory.

The installment purchase proposal

During the latter part of the month of May and throughout the month of June, Scott and Tom negotiated with John Wilson in order to arrive at a satisfactory installment purchase contract. The parties finally agreed on a contract which required the partners to purchase a third of the brothers' stock in return for $100,000. There were 746 shares issued of which 50 shares were treasury stock. The partners were to receive options to purchase the remaining shares over a 10-year period following the date of sale. The Wilson brothers were to be given five-year employment contracts with the firm at $23,000 apiece plus expenses. A management contract was to guarantee the new owners control of the firm.

Two days prior to the scheduled signing of the installment purchase contract, John Wilson called Tom and told him that he and his brother had decided that they wanted all cash for their company or the deal was off. He said that his accountant had convinced him of the desirability of selling the nonliquid assets of his firm for approximately $300,000 in cash.

Reasons for selling.   The Wilson brothers told Tom that they had decided to sell their company in order to retire and devote time to other opportunities. Frank was a vice president of the King Pin Bowling Alley and Lounge of Cincinnati. Both Frank and John were officers of the East-West Corp. which owned the Wilson building, which it leased to the corporation for $8,520 a year, and the property occupied by the Columbus branch for $125 per month. Dun & Bradstreet reported that East-West Corp. was also engaged in the business of wholesaling automotive bodies and parts.

Tom believed that there was probably some conflict between the Wilson brothers. For example, several times he witnessed a situation in which John countermanded one of Frank's orders to the production personnel. In each case John had made the sale as he was familiar with the customer's requirement, and Frank had misinterpreted the paper work. Sam Benson told Tom that the two Wilsons had been rumored to have had difficulties in the past. In 1960 they had considered selling the company, but had subsequently taken it off the market.

Later on, reflecting back on the negotiations, Tom commented,

> In these situations you always wonder about the owners' reasons for selling. The information that you have about the company is usually incomplete. And it can be misleading or even wrong. When it came right down to it we were hard put to find a really good reason why they should want to sell out to us. And it was particularly unsettling that at the last minute after they knew that we were committed very deeply, they should change their position and demand cash.

Mr. Kane's counter offer

In the heat of the moment of John Wilson's rejection of the installment purchase and his demand for $300,000 cash for the company Tom proposed the following basis for a deal, subject to Scott's approval:

A. The existing company would be liquidated, with the fixed assets, inventory, name, goodwill, personnel, and lease on the Wilson building going to the new owners in return for $300,000.[1]

B. The Wilson brothers were offered a one-year employment contract at $15,000 apiece. They were to agree to sign a noncompetition agreement with Mr. Kane and Mr. Hanson good for five years.

C. The lease on the building was to continue for five years at the $8,520 amount. The option to renew would be granted for two consecutive five-year periods at an annual rent of $12,500. At the end of the first five-year period the new owners had the option to purchase the land and building for $150,000.

D. The cash and accounts receivable of the company were to go to the Wilson brothers and were to be used to pay off the current liabilities, in the liquidation of the firm.

E. Operations of the firm were to suffer no interruption, as it would continue to do business under the same name as before, at the same location, with the same personnel.

F. The exact valuation of the assets would depend on an independent audit, by a certified public accountant, purchase price to equal book value.

When Tom telephoned Scott about the rejection of the installment purchase proposal, Scott was discouraged. He said, "We might as well give up on this thing, Tom. It's going to be the Eastern Lumber situation

---

[1]Subject to adjustment after audit.

all over again. We will never be able to raise $300,000 in cash. I guess we just aren't going to find a company to buy and that's all there is to it."

In proposing a cash purchase Tom knew that he and his partner only had $100,000 to invest. To retain 51 percent control, the total equity would have to be limited to $195,000; this would leave $105,000 of the initial capital of the firm to be raised in the form of debt. He had some confidence in Sam Benson's ability to find a banking connection for placing the debt, perhaps in the form of a term loan. But he wondered if it could be for the full amount. (In the purchase of the Eastern Lumber Company Sam had found a bank loan for the partners.) In addition Tom hoped that there was a chance of his selling a portion of the equity to some of the members of top management at the Cincinnati Mfg. Co.. His close association with them had encouraged him to believe that they thought well of him and his ability. However he was not sure how they really would feel about his leaving the firm.

Finally, Tom was acutely aware that he did not have any experience in operating a company of the Wilson variety. And although he had three years of experience in a staff job in making recommendations to line personnel, he wondered how he would perform when it came to implementing his own decisions. He also realized the situation which he had encountered at the Cincinnati Mfg. Co., with its 2,000 employees, would be quite different from those at the Wilson Company with a total payroll of less than 50 people.

However both Scott and Tom agreed that they could make some important changes at Wilson. The production shop clearly needed to be rationalized and supervised on a different basis. They expected significant savings in production costs as a result of improved administration in this area. Scott felt that all of Wilson's products were very likely in need of a redesign. He felt that good blueprints and better design could further cut production costs. Tom believed that Wilson could expand its sales efforts in the equipment area. He especially saw an opportunity for increased sales of cranes and hydraulic equipment for lifting on special use trucks. He planned to initiate a selling effort in the small towns around Cincinnati if he became involved with the Wilson Company. (See Exhibits 13, 14, and 15.)

Tom's wife had not expressed any serious objections to his plan to purchase the Wilson Company. "I guess coming from a medical family she has gotten used to the idea of being your own boss and dependent on your own ability to make a living," he said. He felt that she would back him up. But he noted that his family with two children and its present comfortable home required that he generate a minimum income of at least $11,000 to $12,000 a year.

With these thoughts in mind Tom sat down to evaluate the many factors in the situation and to decide whether or not he and Scott should firm up the proposal he had previously suggested to the Wilson brothers.

SUGGESTED QUESTIONS

1. What should Tom and Steve do about their counterproposal to the Wilson brothers? What is your evaluation of the original offer to buy?
2. What potential exists for the Wilson Body and Equipment Company? If Tom and Steve buy the company, what should they try to do to achieve this potential? What are the biggest problems they will face, and how should they deal with them?
3. How would you evaluate Tom's and Steve's search for a company to buy, and their specific investigation of the Wilson Company?

EXHIBIT 1
Thomas Kane
Personal data

Scott Hanson. Age, 47. Presently employed at the Cincinnati Mfg. Co. as sales and product manager of the Air Filtration Section of the Heating Division. The Air Filtration Section was recently acquired by the Cincinnati Mfg. Co. (1962) from the Primary Metals Co. where Scott Hanson was responsible for sales and marketing in the subsidiary company.

Previous to his work at Primary Metals Co., Mr. Hanson owned and operated a company in conjunction with another investor. The company, the Smith-Hanson Engineering Co. was the original developer and manufacturer of a proprietary dust collecting device. It was this device that was subsequently purchased by Primary Metals Co. in 1955.

The Smith-Hanson Engineering Co. was created prior to World War II. During the war the company designed and fabricated "Lindsey" truck bodies and other equipment similar to the products of the Wilson Company under contract to the U.S. government. Scott Hanson activated a series of patents covering dust collection devices, following World War II. The result was a proprietary product line of dust collection devices, which was experiencing sales of $1 million and was almost equal in size to the Wilson Company.

Scott Hanson is a mechanical engineer by training and education. He is a registered professional engineer in Ohio. He has 25 years of sales, marketing, and production experience behind him. He also belongs to various engineering societies related to his specific interests and activities.

Thomas Kane. Age, 30. Presently employed at the Cincinnati Mfg. Co. as manager of marketing services. Marketing services is largely a financial and administrative function, as well as a marketing function. Tom Kane joined the company in 1960, after completing his education. He has an A.B. in economics from Harvard College and an M.B.A. from the Harvard Business School. He is active in the Harvard Club of Cincinnati as treasurer and program chairman (1962). He was the moderator of the executive training program from 1960 to 1963.

Source: Thomas Kane's private records.

EXHIBIT 2
Thomas Kane
Wilson Company balance sheets

	Dec 31, 1959	Dec 31, 1960	Dec 31, 1961	Dec 31, 1962	May 31, 1963
ASSETS					
Cash	$ 38,130	$ 50,693	$ 32,255	$ 34,928	$ 32,535
Accounts receivable	97,943	104,172	81,438	78,847	112,865
Inventory	161,351	149,333	182,231	200,895	193,165
Total Current Assets	$297,424	$304,198	$295,924	$314,670	$338,565
Fixed assets	131,067	120,743	105,725	102,227	101,681
Prepaid-deferred	9,239	10,411	10,447	6,846	8,729
Cash value life insurance	22,431	24,157	29,025	31,003	37,003
Other assets					
Total Assets	$460,161	$459,509	$441,121	$454,746	$485,978
LIABILITIES					
Due banks	$ 45,000	$ 25,000	$ 15,000	$ 5,000	$ 5,000
Notes payable	24,000	12,000	12,000	12,000	12,000
Accounts payable	40,203	44,787	15,221	36,375	46,154
Accruals	15,332	8,764	13,581	13,129	7,710
Taxes (except federal income)	—	4,704	10,763	11.197	12,355
Federal income taxes	5,960	13,240	6,609	5,285	3,642
Undistributed earnings	2,109	—	4,100	—	—
Total Current Liabilities	$132,604	$108,495	$ 77,274	$ 82,986	$ 86,861
OWNER'S EQUITY					
Common stock (less treasury shares)	104,500	104,500	96,075	94,500	94,500
Capital surplus	—	4,649	4,649	4,649	4,649
Earned surplus	223,057	241,865	263,123	272,611	299,965
Total Liabilities	$460,161	$459,509	$441,121	$454,746	$485,978
Net working capital	$164,819	$195,711	$218,649	$231,683	—
Current ratio	2.25	2.81	3.83	3.79	—
Tangible net worth	$327,557	$351,016	$363,845	$371,759	—

Notes: Inventories valued at cost. Accounts receivable are net less reserve, $1,829. Fixed assets are net less depreciation, $150,500. Annual rent, $10,020. Fire insurance on merchandise, $500,000; machinery and fixtures, $50,000; and buildings, $300,000. Notes payable are due wives of officers, bear 6 percent interest, and are not subordinated to creditors claims. Contingent debt, $5,075, was settled in January 1962.

Source: Company records.

EXHIBIT 3
Thomas Kane
The Wilson Company income statement (1957 to 1963)

	1957		1958		1959	
Sales:						
Custom body	222.7	26%	295.0	35%	256.3	30%
Equipment	415.6	50	396.8	47	408.1	47
Repairs and paint	175.5	21	138.6	16	176.7	20
Miscellaneous parts	24.3	3	18.1	2	26.8	3
Net	838.1	100%	848.5	100%	867.9	100%
Cost of Goods Sold						
Materials:						
Custom	75.8		108.4		87.2	
Equipment	285.9		276.2		286.8	
Repairs and paint	37.3		26.6		45.3	
Miscellaneous parts	17.0		13.5		20.8	
Total	416.0	50%	424.7	50%	440.1	51%
Direct Labor (shop)						
Custom	47.1		58.7		53.3	
Equipment	22.4		20.5		25.6	
Repairs	45.3		34.3		47.6	
Miscellaneous parts	—		—		—	
	114.8	14%	113.6	13%	126.5	15%
Prod. Shop Overhead:						
Freight in	15.2		12.7		12.6	
Subcontracts	13.2		14.1		14.5	
Indirect labor and						
sup. in the shop	71.8		66.4		72.4	
Shop exp.	75.7		81.2		81.9	
Total Cost of Goods Sold .	706.7	84%	712.7		748.0	
Gross Margin	131.4	16%	135.8	16%	119.9	14%
Sales:						
Salaries and commissions	21.3		22.7		23.3	
Expenses	17.4		19.4		11.4	
	38.7		42.1		34.7	
General and Administrative*:						
Salaries	46.1		44.3		42.0	
Expenses	28.7		32.7		25.8	
Total	74.8		77.0		67.8	
Operating profit	17.9		21.7		17.4	
Other income†	—		—		—	
Less federal tax	5.8		6.8		6.0	
After-tax Profit‡	11.9		14.9		11.4	

*Discounts and interest expense were included in General and Administrative prior to 1962.
†Discounts of $8,000 less interest expense.
‡Figures may not add due to rounding.
Source: Wilson Company records.

1960		1961		1962		5 months 1962		5 months 1963	
229.2	23%	349.4	40%	389.8	38%	158.1	38%	163.2	33%
513.5	53	323.7	37	385.4	38	163.2	39	229.2	47
198.6	20	169.4	19	199.0	19	79.1	19	77.8	17
37.3	4	35.6	4	44.6	5	17.5	4	18.8	3
978.6	100%	878.1	100%	1,018.8	100%	418.0	100%	489.1	100%
90.7		149.2		185.1		72.9		74.3	
354.1		239.9		289.6		115.2		159.9	
42.0		32.5		43.0		14.6		16.1	
22.4		26.4		32.6		11.7		13.3	
509.2	52%	448.0	54%	550.4	54%	214.4	51%	263.6	54%
42.4		52.3		63.5		23.5		23.7	
34.1		15.7		21.6		7.7		11.7	
53.4		44.5		52.7		19.9		20.8	
.3		1.2		.6		.3		.3	
130.2	13%	113.7	13%	138.4	14%	51.4	12%	56.5	11%
14.1		9.6		14.8		6.1		7.5	
19.2		18.0		16.5		6.4		7.0	
71.7		71.9		71.8		27.1		28.5	
83.8		77.9		82.7		34.9		36.8	
828.2		739.1		874.6		340.3		399.9	
150.4	15%	139.0	16%	144.2	14%	77.7	18%	89.2	18%
25.5		31.7		40.6		17.0		16.7	
13.7		17.9		12.9		5.7		6.5	
39.2		49.6		53.5		22.7		23.2	
47.2		47.0		46.7		19.1		18.3	
30.8		29.0		33.1		22.7		25.3	
78.0		76.0		79.8		41.8		43.6	
33.2		17.2		10.9		13.1		22.4	
—		—		6.6†		2.8†		3.3†	
13.3		6.6		5.2		n.a.		n.a.	
19.9		10.6		12.3		n.a.		n.a.	

EXHIBIT 4

Thomas Kane

Data relating to purchase of assets (from May 31, 1963, balance sheet)

ASSETS	Cost	Depreciation	Total
Inventory:			
Lumber	$ 5,458		
Paint	1,701		
Hardware	98,478		
Equipment	80,857		
Work in process	6,671		
Total	$193,165		
Fixed Assets:			
Leasehold improvements	$145,955	$69,850	$76,105
Shop machinery and equipment			
(Cincinnati)	48,380	48,278	102
Shop machinery and equipment			
(Columbus).......................	15,489	11,858	3,631
Trucks	17,059	9,060	7,999
Office furniture and fixtures			
(Cincinnati)	6,420	5,380	1,040
Office furniture and fixtures			
(Columbus).......................	3,259	1,677	1,582
Automobiles	15,616	4,394	11,222
Total	$252,178	$150,497	$101,681
Other Assets:			
Prepaid insurance	$ 6,570		
Prepaid tax	605		
Prepaid interest	122		
Miscellaneous	1,432		
Total	$ 8,729		

Note: Mr. Kane believed that the leasehold improvements of the Wilson Co. building were reasonably valued. Both the office and shop of the old building appeared to have benifited significantly from the renovation. He also noted that the cars and trucks owned by the company were recent models and in running condition.

Source: Wilson Co. records.

EXHIBIT 5
Thomas Kane
Summary of financial data Wilson Co.

Years	Sales	Profit before tax and officers' salaries (approx.)	Working capital	Net worth	Depreciation
1948	$ 475,881	$82,000	$101,603	$201,841	$ 7,838
1949	373,146	56,200	109,970	203,611	9,138
1950	486,240	77,000	128,997	225,865	n.a.
1951	625,094	69,000	179,183	244,197	12,132
1952	527,003	58,400	163,941	250,950	12,051
1953	599,225	52,400	159,855	246,056	11,838
1954	717,018	73,000	170,153	262,036	12,414
1955	801,429	64,300	159,768	280,115	15,794
1956	969,247	74,400	90,137	294,552	12,115
1957	838,174	69,700	120,710	311,453	22,561
1958	848,567	84,600	160,552	314,979	21,970
1959	867,976	75,100	164,891	329,667	20,014
1960	978,614	93,800	195,711	351,017	19,341
1961	878,117	61,400	218,649	363,847	17,925
1962	1,018,827	59,900	231,683	371,760	14,478
1963* ...	489,057	45,100			
1962* ...	417,962	33,700			

*Data is for five months.
Source: Thomas Kane's private records.

EXHIBIT 6
Thomas Kane
Inventory turnover

Year	Cost of Goods sold	Year-end inventory	Inventory turnover
1954	$581,049	$118,234	4.8
1955	671,085	114,166	5.8
1956	816,829	125,609	6.5
1957	706,662	130,200	5.4
1958	712,717	140,528	5.1
1959	748,066	161,351	4.7
1960	828,200	149,333	5.5
1961	739,140	182,231	4.0
1962	974,630	200,895	4.4
1963*	399,220†	193,165	5.0

*Data is for five months.
†Annualized—$959,000.
Source: Thomas Kane's private records.

EXHIBIT 7
Thomas Kane
Average days in receivables and payables, monthly information (in thousands)

Month ending:	Net sales (in dollars)	Working days	Average sales/day	Total accounts receivable (in dollars)	Days receivables = accounts receivable/ sales/day (in days)	Total accounts payable	Days payables = account payable/ sales/day (in days)
1961							
Jan.	55,600	21	2,640	74,100	28	$55,600	21
Feb.	83,600	20	4,170	82,100	20	54,400	13
March ...	66,700	22	3,030	81,000	27	52,900	17
April	77,500	20	3,860	86,500	22	56,200	14
May	52,200	22	2,380	75,500	31	58,000	24
June	81,800	22	3,700	83,900	22	71,000	19
July	64,600	20	3,220	74,700	23	62,800	19
Aug.	101,100	23	4,580	101,900	22	72,900	16
Sept.	76,400	20	3,820	101,200	27	67,600	17
Oct.	77,800	22	3,520	78,600	22	64,600	18
Nov.	82,600	21	3,920	85,400	22	59,200	15
Dec.	80,700	20	4,040	?	?	?	
1962							
Jan.	88,400	22	4,020	71,700	18	49,900	12
Feb.	56,800	19	2,980	67,200	22	57,900	19
March ...	89,700	22	4,070	75,600	18	53,000	13
April	86,100	21	4,100	82,900	20	43,800	10
May	97,000	21	4,610	92,100	20	48,000	10
June	94,600	21	4,500	92,700	20	65,100	14
July	123,200	21	5,850	137,600	23	60,100	10
Aug.	84,600	23	3,660	100,900	28	44,400	12
Sept.	62,400	19	3,290	73,800	23	38,200	12
Oct.	67,100	23	2,290	71,700	31	40,700	17
Nov.	131,300	20	6,530	108,700	17	50,300	8
Dec.	66,800	20	3,340	70,700	21	50,400	15
1963							
Jan.	110,900	22	5,410	78,600	14	44,200	8
Feb.	71,800	20	3,590	80,400	22	44,600	12
Mar.	85,700	21	4,070	84,800	21	41,100	10
Apr.	115,200	21	5,480	106,400	19	56,600	10
May	105,500	22	4,790	112,400	23	57,300	12
June	113,400	20	5,670	123,500	22	56,600	10

Source: Thomas Kane's private records.

EXHIBIT 8

Thomas Kane
Direct and period costs allocated by product line (1962)

	Custom body		Equipment		Repair and painting		Miscellaneous parts		Total	
Gross sales	$403,048		$399,832		$212,332		$48,263		$1,063,474	
Net sales	389,805	100%	385,372	100%	199,047	100%	44,603	100%	1,018,827	100%
Direct Costs (variable):										
Material	185,132		289,605		43,059		32,623		550,418	54.0
Direct labor	63,555		21,586		52,669		557		138,368	14.0
Direct shop overhead*	23,040		23,590		12,395		2,730		61,755	6.0
Selling direct*	2,975		2,950		1,546		346		7,817	} 2.3
Administrative direct*	5,880		5,807		3,040		682		15,409	}
Total Direct	$280,582	72.0	$343,538	89.0	$112,709	56.0	$36,938	83.0	$773,767	75.9
Marginal income	$109,223	28.0	$41,834	11.0	$86,338	43.0	$7,665	17.0	$245,060	24.0
Period Costs (fixed):										
Period shop O/H*	$ 46,618		$ 47,400		$ 24,500		$ 5,500		$124,018	
Period selling*	17,600		17,430		8,582		2,050		45,662	
Period administration*	24,513		24,400		12,650		2,840		64,403	
Total Period	$ 88,731		$ 89,230		$ 45,732		$10,390		$234,083	
Profit or (loss) before other income expense and taxes	$ 20,492	5.3	$(47,396)	12.3	$ 40,606	20.4	$(2,725)	6.1	$ 10,977	1.1
Other income	—		—		—		—		8,551	
									19,528	
Other expense	—		—		—		—		1,966	
Income before tax	—		—		—		—		$ 17,562	
Federal tax	—		—		—		—		5,285	
Net Income									$ 12,277	

*All intangibles are prorated by "net sales dollar."
Source: Thomas Kane's private records.

EXHIBIT 9

Thomas Kane

Income statement showing gross profits and allocation of sales and administrative costs on the basis of net sales dollars (1962)

	Custom body		Equipment		Repair and painting		Miscellaneous parts		Total	
Net sales	$389,805	100%	$385,372	100%	$199,047	100%	$44,603	100%	$1,018,827	100%
Cost of Sales:										
Materials	185,132		289,604		43,058		32,622		550,418	
Direct labor	63,555		21,586		52,669		556		138,367	
Shop overhead*	85,329		28,981		70,714		747		185,772	
Total	$334,016		$340,171		$166,441		$33,925		$874,557	
Gross margin	55,789	14%	45,201	12%	32,606	16%	10,678	24%	144,270	14%
Selling:										
Variable	2,975		2,950		1,546		346		7,817	
Fixed	17,600		17,430		8,582		2,050		45,662	
Administration:										
Variable	5,880		5,807		3,040		682		15,409	
Fixed	24,513		24,400		12,650		2,840		64,403	
Total Sales and Administrative Expense	$50,968		$50,587		$25,818		$5,918		$133,291	
Profit or (loss) before other income or expense and taxes	$4,821	1%	$(5,386)	1%	$6,788	3%	$4,760	11%	$10,979	1%
Reallocated total sales and administrative expense	58,902		58,521		12,909		2,959		133,291	
Profit or (Loss) before Other Income or Expense and Taxes	$(3,113)	(1%)	$(13,320)	(3%)	$19,697	10%	$7,719	17%	$10,970	1%

*Shop overhead was allocated at 135 percent of direct labor, in the financial documents supplied by John Wilson. In order to arrive at a figure for profit by product line Tom Kane had to allocate sales and administrative expense by product line. He used net sales dollars to make this allocation. However upon reflection he felt this method of allocating sales and administrative expense was unfair to the repair and painting and the miscellaneous parts section of the business. He cut sales and administrative expense allocated to these two sections of the business by 50 percent. The results of this second method of allocating sales and administrative expense are shown at the bottom of the table.

EXHIBIT 10
Thomas Kane
Wilson Co. organization (prior to May 31, 1963)

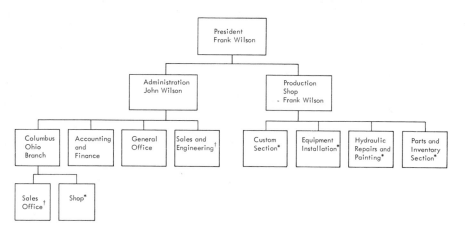

*There were 30 to 35 men in the shop who belonged to the Machinist Union in Cincinnati and 6 to 8 men who belonged to the union in Columbus.

†Three salesmen worked out of Cincinnati and one out of Columbus.

Source: Casewriter's analysis.

EXHIBIT 11
Thomas Kane
Industry data for truck and bus bodies, SIC 3713 (for sale separately, for
assembly on purchased chassis—not complete trucks or buses)—[in millions]

	1954	1955	1956	1957	1958	1959	1960
Value added adjusted....	$116.2	—	$152.1	$144.1	$145.6	$157.6	$172.7
Value of shipment*......	232.5	—	300.7	290.3	338.0	362.8	394.8
Cost of materials	116.3†	—	148.6†	146.2†	193.0†	207.5	223.7
Materials as percent							
of shipments	50%	—	50%	51%	57%	57%	57%
Value of inventories	$ 39.9	$50.3	$ 55.4	$ 53.7	$ 61.2	$ 67.3	$ 68.5

*Growth rate of approximately 10.5 percent.
†Estimate.
Source: U.S. Dept. of Commerce.

EXHIBIT 12
Thomas Kane
Projected sales through 1970 (in thousands)

	1964	1965	1966	1967	1968	1969	1970
Company trend (June to June),							
assume 7 percent rate.	$1,150	$1,215	$1,300	$1,350	$1,420	$1,500	$1,660
Industry trend calendar year,							
assume 10 percent							
growth rate (use 1962							
as starting point)	1,135	1,270	1,397	1,537	1,691	1,859	2,045
Average of company and							
industry sales.	1,152	1,242	1,348	1,448	1,555	1,679	1,815

Source: Tom Kane's private records.

EXHIBIT 13
Thomas Kane
Possible corporate goals for growth and profitability to apply to Wilson Co. if purchase proposal is accepted (May 20, 1963)

Memo:

After much preliminary review and consideration, this memo is prepared in order to summarize my thoughts (some of which are borrowed from others) and recommendations for action for the next 12 months.

Simply stated our long run corporate goal primarily involves a program of maximum growth, consistent with sound financial and other practices. Probably the single greatest limitation to our growth rate will be limited financial resources. Therefore careful planning and selection of only the most promising projects is most important. The criteria of (1) potential total sales dollars, (2) rate of return, and (3) quickness of return on investment are all essential for the evaluation of proposed ideas.

For these reasons it clearly seems wisest to engage in projects which can be accomplished with the maximum use of present talent and plant capability. They should also be selected on the basis of those projects which will least change the present basic mode of operation. Because of a number of potential possibilities within the truck body and equipment industry, which can be acted on as soon as the decision is made to proceed, it is recommended that we postpone all eventual diversification possibilities, such as development of a "package dust collector," until time and opportunity are more favorable.

Within the present truck body and equipment industry, there exist three major areas of opportunity for evaluation and action. They are (1) the sale of special cranes and lifting equipment for standard truck bodies, (2) custom bodies for vans and special use trucks, and (3) tool or utility carts for in-plant use. These opportunities were pointed out by Mr. John Wilson as market areas which he has known about for some time, but was not able to pursue because of limited resources and time.

Source: Thomas Kane's private records.

EXHIBIT 14
Thomas Kane
Pro forma sales and earnings and balance sheet (June 29, 1963)

Income statement

	Year 1	Year 2
Estimated sales*	$1,190,000	$1,190,000
Estimated before-tax income (before adjustments).	$ 30,000	$ 30,000
Less adjustment:		
One year of management duplication†	(30,000)	–0–
Salary reductions	9,000	9,000
Plus added interest expense on $105,000	(6,800)	(6,800)
Profit before tax	$ 2,200	$ 32,200
Cash Flow from Depreciation	$ 11,400	$ 11,000

Balance sheet (90 days after purchase)

ASSETS		LIABILITIES	
Cash	$ 35,000	Current payables..............	$ 66,000
Accounts receivable	71,000	Short-term note‡	40,000
Inventory	200,000	Long-term note	105,000
Fixed assets	100,000	Capital	195,000
	$406,000		$406,000

*First year sales forecast at 17 percent greater than 1962, based on first 5 months.
†One-year employment contract for the Wilson brothers. Tom assumed their present combined salary was $46,000. He estimated that his salary would be $17,500 and that Scott's would be $19,500, or $37,000 combined.
‡Mr. Kane assumed he could get a $60,000 line of credit.
Source: Mr. Kane's private records.

EXHIBIT 15
Thomas Kane
General economic conditions, May 1963

GENERAL BUSINESS CONDITIONS

Business has moved up in recent weeks, breaking away from the plateau in production and trade which stretched from mid-1962 through the early months of this year. To be sure, part of the advance represents the bunching of business deferred from past months because of strikes or uncommonly cold weather. Some of the activity—building of protective inventories against overhanging strike threats—is borrowing from the future. Nevertheless, much of the improvement is clear gain.

Not only are many signposts of economic activity once more pointing upward, but confidence has also rallied. Most observers in business and government have raised their sights on the outlook for 1963. Businessmen, encouraged by the Administration's understanding of the need for better profits as an essential support to increased production and employment, have been adding to their capital investment plans for 1963, and now expect to push beyond $40 billion for the first time.

An essential part of this upgrading of expectations has been the emergence of better feeling between business and government. The business community was especially heartened by President Kennedy's willingness to let the forces of supply and demand determine whether selective price increases for steel products would stick. Sentiment has been further helped by the prospect of income tax rate reductions. As evidence of the hopes raised among investors, the Dow-Jones industrial stock price average by late April had risen within 2½ percent of the record high set in December 1961. Underlying all this is a steady flow of business statistics which have, in most cases, turned out better than expected.

Favorable business developments

According to preliminary estimates by the Council of Economic Advisers, the gross national product reached a seasonally adjusted annual rate of $572 billion in the first quarter, up no less than $8.5 billion over the fourth quarter of 1962. The widespread worry over a recession starting last fall or winter proved to be a false alarm.

Practically all the major indicators of the nation's economic health gave plus readings in March, and preliminary April figures were also favorable. Department stores reported an excellent Easter season, and retail sales generally maintained a substantial 7 percent gain over a year earlier. Auto dealers continued to move cars at a near-record pace. For this year through April 20, sales were 11 percent ahead of the corresponding 1962 period and within 2 percent of the peak sales year, 1955.

Industrial production has been picking up. As measured by the Federal Reserve index (seasonally adjusted, 1957–59=100), output broke out of its narrow eight-month range of 118.9 to 119.8 and rose to 120.4 in March. The index

EXHIBIT 15 (continued)

appears to have advanced somewhat further in April. The inflow of orders for durable goods continued strong during March, and backlogs again increased.

Employment (seasonally adjusted and including the armed forces) exceeded 71 million persons for the first time, and the unemployment rate receded from 6.1 percent of the civilian labor force in February to 5.6 percent in March. However, this reduced level of unemployment—equal to the average rate for 1962—is still considered excessive and it remains a powerful factor in the Administration's tax cut proposals.

Increases in capital spending

Many businessmen have been reviewing and expanding their capital expenditure plans for 1963. According to the latest survey, taken in March and April by the McGraw-Hill Department of Economics, outlays for plant and equipment are scheduled to exceed $40 billion in 1963—a rise of 7.4 percent over the $37.3 billion spent for this purpose in 1962 and 8.4 percent above the previous high in 1957 of $37.0 billion.

Source: First National City Bank of New York, *Monthly Economic Letter*, May 1963.

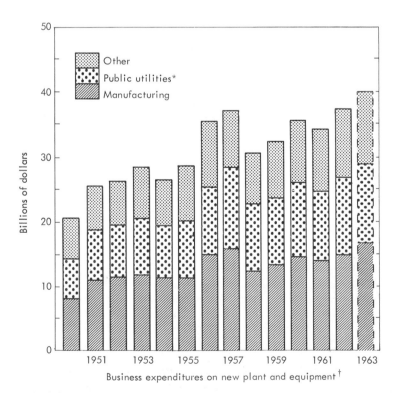

Business expenditures on new plant and equipment[†]

*Includes communication and transportation.
[†]Source: 1950–62, U.S. Department of Commerce and Securities and Exchange Commission: 1963 (anticipated), McGraw-Hill Department of Economics.

APPENDIX

Review of the Wilson Body and Equipment Company
(May 5, 1963)

General

Wilson assembles, as a franchised distributor for various companies, and manufactures in its own right truck bodies, trailers, and related equipment. The company was started by the father of the present owners, and has constantly but slowly grown in its 50 or so years of *continuously profitable operation*. Sales since the postwar period have grown at the rate of 7 to 8 percent a year. 1962 volume was slightly over a million.

Plant

The company moved to its present location on 17th Street about five years ago when the East-West Corp. (owned by the Wilson brothers also) purchased the building and leased the facilities to the Wilson Company. Wilson under its lease altered the existing plant and now utilizes from 60 percent to 70 percent of the 67,000-square-foot building which occupies a 97,000-square-foot lot. About 10 years ago Wilson Company established a branch operation for assembling bodies in Columbus. The Columbus branch has progressed so that now it contributes about 20 percent of Wilson's sales volume. Because of improved business Wilson has been recently engaged in negotiations for the expansion of the Columbus facilities.

Profits

Wilson has always operated as a family company and as such has provided the owners with good incomes plus many perquisites taken through the corporation. The company has generally increased its payout in income and other benefits that under the tax laws could be taken through the corporation, and has added personnel as sales volume and corporate income indications would allow. In years where such expenses did not increase and sales volume improved significantly so that the company operated further beyond the "normal" position above the breakeven point, profits improved considerably. For example in 1960 sales increased 14 percent over 1959 and profits (including officer salaries) increased 24 percent. More recently in five months of 1963, sales increased 18 percent over the same period in 1962, and profits increased well over 70 percent. Part of this more recent profit improvement is apparently also due to increased sales of the more profitable segment of the equipment business.

Company size and other

Wilson Company is the largest company in its line of business in Ohio outside of Cleveland. It is respected as being the leader in the southern region of Ohio. The company has maintained the highest of financial ratings in all respects. The primary banking connection has been the R & L Trust Company who through

Mr. John Ford, Senior Vice President, has had their business for more than 20 years. The R & L has indicated specific interest in continuing a similar relationship in the future.

The Wilson Company sells its product lines to a diverse group of industries and includes most of the major manufacturers, service, and civic organizations in southern Ohio.

Future growth

Because of the satisfactory income and employment experience of the company, the owners have not particularly attempted to have the company grow beyond its normal pace with the total economy, and in particular have not undertaken to pursue the more complex (but more profitable) custom body business, nor to diversify into related and other product lines. Because of this, over the last 15 years, Wilson has grown, although successfully, at a rate of 7 percent to 8 percent a year in contrast to the overall industry rate of growth of more than 11 percent. Specific indications suggest that increased attention to special body and equipment business will favorably expand present types of sales and profits in the near future.

Greater growth and diversification are clear possibilities through progress in related fabricated metal products and through steps into new areas which can easily utilize presently available facilities and skilled personnel. The possibility of acquisition as a route to sound growth is also an active consideration.

The longer run objective of professional managerial effort applied to the aim of maximum return on the stockholders' equity is the dominant underlying interest. Profit improvement appears very evident in the near future through internal improvements and increased utilization of the excellent facilities which are available under an extremely favorable lease and option to purchase. Long-term profit potentials appear greatest through specific aims to develop proprietary product lines and capability in an effort to diversify from major dependence on the competitive and relatively low margin assembled truck and body business.

While Wilson is today a sound company and the leader in its field, the application of careful and consistent effort to well-planned objectives should greatly increase total corporate capability and significantly increase the rate of return on invested capital.

From Thomas Kane's private records.

Tru-Paint, Inc.

On April 19, 1961, Warren G. Hamar received a telephone call from John Dublois, a finder, about a company which was for sale. After being reassured that he would receive a finder's fee of 5 percent of the purchase price, Dublois indicated that he would bring the information over to him in the morning. Dublois apologized for not thinking of Mr. Hamer earlier but only six days were left to submit a bid.

Mr. Dublois appeared early the next morning at Hamer's office with the three pages of information contained in Exhibit 1.

A quick check of the competitive situation with the Tru-Paint president disclosed that in the specific field of liquid paint dispensed in tubes for use in home decoration, Tru-Paint's sales were larger than any of its six competitors. Of the six competitors, only three distributed their products through the house party plan. (See Appendix.) In the more general home hobbycraft and industrial markets, Tru-Paint had to meet intense competition with firms of significantly greater sales and resources.

There were certain aspects of the purchase which made Mr. Hamer apprehensive about the deal. First, the manner in which the company was being sold was very unusual and the time period allowed to evaluate the situation was very short. Second, no assurance could be given that the present management would stay on, and Mr. Hamer did not want to become actively involved in the management of a small company such as Tru-Paint. Finally Mr. Hamer was worried about the restriction on contacting the company's distributors and the effects of the company's sale upon their continued loyalty.

Not wanting to commit a significant amount of his assets to the venture if he decided to undertake it, Mr. Hamer contacted a former associate,

177

Mr. Blake. Mr. Edmund J. Blake, Jr., was a vice president of P. W. Brooks & Co., a medium-sized Wall Street investment banking firm which had specialized in unit financing programs, primarily in the utility and chemical industries during the past 55 years.

On Friday, April 21, Messrs. Hamer and Blake met with Mr. Henry L. Aaron, president of the E-I Mutual Association, and with Mr. Joseph Reimann, president of Tru-Paint, Inc. The company's office was in one corner of a large, basement room in an old commercial section of the city. The entire production facility consisted of vats and tanks for mixing and filling the ball-point tubes and a shipping area for packaging the tubes after they were filled. The history of the company, presented by Aaron and Reimann, is summarized in Exhibit 2.

SUGGESTED QUESTIONS

1. What should Messrs. Blake and Hamer do?
   a. What is the company worth?
   b. If you decide that they should buy the company, describe your reasoning in detail.
      (1) Outline in detail the bid they should make. Describe your reasoning.
      (2) What should be their plan for the company should they be successful in acquiring it?
   c. If you decide that they should not try to buy the company, describe your reasoning in detail.
2. What additional information, if any, would you try to get? How?

EXHIBIT 1
Tru-Paint, Inc.
Information and terms and conditions relative to proposed sale by E-I Mutual Association of its wholly owned subsidiary, Tru-Paint, Inc.

Tru-Paint, Inc., is located at 82 Main Street, West Orange, New Jersey. It manufactures and distributes on a nationwide basis, liquid paint dispensed in ball-point tubes. The product is sold under the registered trademarks "Tru-Paint" and "Liquid Embroidery"; and is used primarily for hobby work of a decorative nature. It bears the Good Housekeeping seal of approval. In addition, Tru-Paint, Inc., manufactures or has manufactured for it a line of products accessory to its paints.

The product is distributed chiefly on the so-called party plan basis, with distributors located at various points throughout most of the United States.

The company has operated under its present ownership for the last five years, during which the volume and profit have steadily increased.

Terms and conditions of sale

1. Cash bids will be received up to and including April 24, 1961.
2. Bids shall be accompanied by a 5 percent deposit.
3. Bids shall be firm until 5 P.M., May 24, 1961. Acceptance may be made by a telegram filed before that date and hour or by letter postmarked prior to that date and hour.
4. Seller reserves the right to reject any or all bids.
5. Closing shall be at Seller's option between June 19 and June 23, 1961, inclusive.
6. Inspection of plant facilities is invited.
7. Bids shall be submitted subject to the understanding that Seller's distributors may not be contacted by or on behalf of Bidder and that any violation of this restriction shall result in automatic forfeiture of deposit.
8. Audited financial statements for 1957, 1958, 1959, and 1960 are annexed.
9. All bids shall be submitted to:

> Henry L. Aaron, President
> E-I Mutual Association
> 670 Q Street
> West Orange, New Jersey

Please mark the envelope "Confidential." All inquiries shall also be directed to Mr. Aaron, who may be reached by telephone at Redwood 5-1234.

EXHIBIT 1 (continued)
Copy of audited statements: Balance sheet

	1960	1959	1958	1957
ASSETS				
Current Assets:				
Cash.........................	$ 90,094	$ 89,790	$ 81,844	$ 70,639
Note receivable...............	23,902			
Accounts receivable (less allowance for doubtful collections)	63,107	45,505	35,746	28,091
Inventories...................	91,079	75,704	59,050	59,261
Prepaid expenses	9,090	6,130	4,700	2,239
Total Current Assets	$277,272	$217,129	$181,340	$160,230
Furniture, fixtures, machinery, and equipment, motor vehicles .	$ 22,669	$ 17,604	$ 15,328	$ 15,148
Less: Accumulated depreciation	13,944	10,323	9,645	6,437
	$ 8,725	$ 7,281	$ 5,683	$ 8,711
Covenant not to compete, foreign license agreement, patents, etc.	$ 82,180	$122,180	$192,180	$193,180
Less: Accumulated amortization	24,566	52,264	51,915	35,963
	$ 57,614	$ 69,916	$140,265	$157,217
Goodwill......................	70,000	70,000		
	$413,611	$364,326	$327,288	$326,158
LIABILITIES				
Current Liabilities:				
Note payable		$ 27,500	$100,000	$175,000
Accounts payable and accrued liabilities............	$ 22,397	19,683	11,781	9,993
Federal income tax payable	71,249	60,966	46,889	32,589
	$ 93,646	$108,149	$158,670	$217,582
Capital Stock and Surplus:				
Authorized 1,000 shares of common, no par value—				
issued and outstanding	$ 2,000	$ 2,000	$ 2,000	$ 2,000
Earned surplus	317,965	254,177	166,618	106,576
Total Capital Stock and Surplus	$319,965	$256,177	$168,618	$108,576
	$413,611	$364,326	$327,288	$326,158

Sales   52 million now

EXHIBIT 1 (concluded)
Copy of audited statements: Statement of income and surplus

	1960	1959	1958	1957
Net sales	$688,327	$597,603	$481,350	$466,580
Cost of goods sold	431,975	359,956	288,188	289,519
Gross Profit	$256,352	$237,647	$193,162	$177,061
Selling, shipping, general, and administrative expenses	87,362	78,893	67,692	64,788
Operating Profit	$168,990	$158,754	$125,470	$112,273
Other income...................	1,972	1,614	4,706	6,453
	$170,962	$160,368	$130,176	$118,726
Other Charges:				
Provision for amortization	12,301	12,801	16,952	17,452
Interest	624	4,121	6,293	9,185
	$ 12,925	$ 16,922	$ 23,245	$ 26,637
	$158,037	$143,446	$106,931	$ 92,089
Provision for federal income tax	71,249	60,966	46,889	32,589
Net Profit for the Year	$ 86,788	$ 82,480	$ 60,042	$ 59,500
Surplus January 1, ...	254,177	166,618	106,576	47,076
Add: Partial disallowance by Treasury Dept. of amortization of foreign license agreement, patents, etc.		12,452		
		$179,070		
Deduct: Additional federal income taxes		7,375		
		$171,697		
Dividends $23 per share..........	23,000			
Earned Surplus December 31	$317,965	$254,177	$166,618	$106,576

EXHIBIT 2
Tru-Paint, Inc.
Background of the company (summarized) as described by Messrs. Aaron and Reimann

Tru-Paint was organized in 1948 to exploit the possibilities of the ball-point paint dispenser. The company was the original manufacturer of ball-point paint dispensers and paint compounds suited to this use. The company originally utilized both manufacturer's agents and direct contacts to sell their products through large retail outlets. By 1954 Tru-Paint sales through the retail outlets had grown to over $1 million.

By 1953, however, the large paint manufacturers were introducing competitive products with by-product pricing. The company foresaw that additional competition would create a substantial decline in the company's profit margins. This factor coupled with disagreements within the management group placed Tru-Paint on the sales block. Thus, in early 1954, the original owners were approached by E-I Mutual with a purchase offer.

E-I Mutual Association was founded in 1949 by the son of Thomas A. Edison, Mr. Theodore Edison, then president of Edison Electric, as an experiment in labor management relations. It was his thesis that if employees became stockholders in companies, they would be more sympathetic to the needs of the stockholders and the management of their own company. He set up the association with about $1 million worth of stock in Edison. The original intent was that E-I Mutual should invest these funds in small companies, but by 1954 it had sizable investments in American Telephone and Telegraph, General Motors, General Electric, and other blue chip stocks. An employee of Edison could purchase one share of E-I Mutual $3 dividend stock at $10 a share for each year that he worked for the company up to a limit of 15 shares. If, for any reason, his employment was terminated, the emloyee had to sell back to the association one share of his holdings each year following separation at the same $10 per share price.

In 1954, Mr. Joseph Reimann, as president of E-I Mutual Association, learned of the availability of Tru-Paint and recommended that E-I Mutual purchase 100 percent ownership for some $300,000. The membership voted and approved this recommendation. Subsequently, Mr. Reimann became president of Tru-Paint.

Mr. Reimann realized that the Tru-Paint's distribution system needed to be revamped and it was his idea to market the company's products under the home party plan. By 1957, the company distributed its products to the consumer market primarily through independent distributors under the home party plan. In developing its distributor organization throughout the United States, Tru-Paint entered into exclusive territorial franchise agreements with its distributors.

Tru-Paint supplied kits consisting of its line of paint-filled ball-point tubes, various accessories such as embroidery hoops to hold the stamped materials taut, and sample pieces of fabric printed with a design on which the novice could practice. The distributor was free to make his own arrangements with other suppliers to sell at the same parties, products such as stamped textiles, glass and leather to which the Tru-Paint line of color tubes could be applied. The distributors were also free to create and manage their own organizations of demonstrators. The growth and selection of the independent distributors for Tru-Paint

EXHIBIT 2 (continued)

could be characterized as somewhat haphazard. Vast differences in population, size of territory, and normal trading areas were noticeable between distributors. By 1960, the company had 17 exclusive distributors.

Prior to the end of 1960, several of the company's distributors had indicated an interest in purchasing Tru-Paint if E-I Mutual decided to sell its interest.

In 1959, the company's products were awarded the Good Housekeeping Seal of Approval by *Good Housekeeping* magazine.

APPENDIX

Tru-Paint, Inc.

Party Plan Selling

There are three basic methods of house-to-house direct selling in which a salesman demonstrates and sells his products in a prospective customer's home—cold canvassing, coupon advertising, and party plan selling. The differentiating characteristic between these forms of direct selling is the method of generating prospects.

In cold canvassing a salesman, without first having made appointments, systematically knocks on every home or apartment door of a street until he encounters an interest in his product. If invited into the home, he demonstrates his product and attempts to make a sale.

Coupon advertising generates potential customers by means of reader service coupons attached to advertisements and promotional materials. When a reader of an advertisement or promotional handout sends in a reader service coupon requesting more information about a product, a salesman is sent to the reader's home to demonstrate and sell the product.

The party plan generates prospects by encouraging housewives to hostess a coffee and doughnut party for her friends; the stated purpose of the party to the guests being the opportunity for the company salesman to demonstrate and sell the company's products. The incentive for the housewife to hostess a party is the prospect of receiving a gift certificate from the company's hostess gift catalog which usually includes both company and noncompany home products. The value of the hostess's gift is a function of the dollar sales resulting from her party, the number of people who attend, and the number of additional hostesses recruited from the party.

For example, a Tru-Paint dealer (salesman/woman) might start developing a prospect-customer list by persuading a friend or relative to hostess a Tru-Paint embroidery party for a hostess gift. At this party the dealer would exhibit the range of materials to which Tru-Paint could be applied, available predesigned patterns, and all the necessary accessories needed to accomplish Tru-Paint embroidery. The dealer would receive from this party (1) a commission from the sales that were made and (2) leads on additional hostesses for future parties. Thus the party process frequently tends to snowball because of the "friends have different friends" phenomenon which can generate a constant supply of new prospects for the distributor as well as producing a customer list for potential repeat sales.

The major advantage of home selling is that it focuses the attention of potential buyers only on the company product being sold. This elimination of competing products tends to make closing a sale easier than is possible in the more competitive environment of a retail outlet where similar and substitute products are displayed. Some advantages of the party plan over cold canvassing and coupon advertising as a means of home selling are: (1) less sales resistance is met in the home because the hostess is sponsoring the product to her friends and the guests know in advance the selling purpose of the party; (2) customer and prospect lists grow faster and each sales call generates a larger sales volume since more than one family attends each party and hears each sales presentation; and (3) its respectability is generally greater in the eyes of the public because of its non-abrasive prospecting and straightforward selling approach.

Companies and products that employ the party plan selling method exclusively or in addition to cold canvassing and coupon advertising are:

Cosmetics

Studio Girl, Inc.

Mary Kay, Inc.

Fashion Two Twenty, Inc.

Vanda-Beauty Counselor, Inc.,
    a subsidiary of Dart Industries

Vivian Woodward, Inc.,
    a subsidiary of General Foods

Apparel

Beeline Fashions, Inc.

Queensway to Fashion, Inc.

Dutchmaid, Inc.

Joya Fashions,
    a subsidiary of Jewel Fashions

Lingerie

Claire James, Inc.

Penny Rich, Inc.

Household products

Tupperware Home Parties

Stanley Home Products

Note

Evaluating a going company

When confronted with the problem of evaluating a company, an individual frequently experiences difficulty deciding which approach or method makes the most sense. His uncertainty may be increased by the fact that different approaches or methods may result in very different values. The objective of this note is to assist the reader in determining the validity and appropriateness of various methods of valuation which might be used in a given situation. Also, we shall attempt to clarify the separate but related questions: What is a company worth? and What can it be purchased for?

Evaluating small, privately held companies is an uncertain art at best. In placing a value on a going business there are innumerable factors which might be brought into play—assets, earnings, net worth, market share, patents, and so on. Which of these factors should be considered for determining value will depend upon a host of conditions surrounding the specific situation.

The appropriateness of any method of evaluation also depends to a large extent upon the perspective of the valuator. Depending upon his needs, and in some cases upon legal guidelines, different people will, and should, approach valuation problems in different ways. Two kinds of situations requiring one to place a value on a company—pricing an initial equity offering and establishing estate taxes—will *not* be pursued here. Three other perspectives, however, we shall consider in some detail:

1. Making an investment by purchasing a company.
2. Buying a company as part of an entrepreneurial career.
3. Selling a company.

It should be noted that the perspectives of an investor and an entrepreneur are not mutually exclusive; one might be either or both.

THE INVESTOR'S PERSPECTIVE

Although there are numerous examples of variation from this norm, investors are primarily trying to earn a return on their investments. To do this they must earn interest, receive dividends, and/or sell their investment at a higher price than what they paid for it. The investor is not only concerned with how much he can make but also with how little he might lose.

The two traditional investor's approaches to evaluating a company deal with assets and earnings. The first, asset valuation, is usually an indication of the investor's exposure to risk. If within the company there are assets whose market value approximates the price of the company plus its liabilities, the immediate downside risk is low. In some instances an increase in the value of the assets of a company may represent a major portion of the investor's anticipated return.

Asset valuations

Book value. The easiest asset valuation that a prospective purchaser can examine is the book value. In a situation replete with variables and unknowns it provides a tangible starting point. However, it must be remembered that it is only a starting point. The accounting practices of the company as well as other things can have a significant effect on the firm's book value. For example, if the reserve for losses on accounts receivable is too low for the business it will inflate book value and vice versa. Similarly, treatment of asset accounts such as research and development costs, patents, organization expense, and so on, can vary widely. Nevertheless, the book value of a firm provides a point of departure when considering asset valuation.

Adjusted book value. An obvious refinement of stated book value is to adjust for large discrepancies between the stated book and actual market value of tangible assets, such as buildings and equipment which have been depreciated far below their market value, or land which has substantially appreciated above its book value which stands at the original cost. An adjustment would probably also reduce the book value of intangible assets to zero unless they, like the tangible assets, also have a market value. The figure resulting from these adjustments should more accurately represent the value of the company's assets.

Liquidation value. One step beyond adjusted book value is to consider the net cash amount which could be realized if the assets of the company were disposed of in a "quick sale" and all liabilities of the company paid off or otherwise settled. This value would take into account that many assets, especially inventory and real estate, would not realize as much as they would were the company to continue as a going concern or were the sale made more deliberately. Also, calculation of a liquidation value would make allowances for the various costs of carry-ing out a liquidation sale.

The liquidation value, it should be noted, is only an indication of what might be realized if the firm were liquidated immediately. Should the company continue its operations and encounter difficulties, most likely a subsequent liquidation would yield significantly less than the liquida-tion value calculated for the company in its current condition.

The liquidation value of a company is not usually of importance to a buyer who is interested in the maintenance of a going concern. One would assume, however, the liquidation value would represent some kind of a floor below which the seller would be unwilling to sell because he should be able to liquidate the company himself.

Reproduction value. The current cost of reproducing the tangible assets of a business can at times be significant in that starting a new company may be an alternative means of getting into the business. It sometimes happens that the market value for existing facilities is consid-erably less than the cost of building a plant and purchasing equivalent equipment from other sources. In most instances, however, this calcula-tion is used more as a reference point than as a seriously considered possibility.

Earnings valuations

The second common approach to an investor's valuation of a company is to capitalize earnings. This, it would seem, involves multiplying an earnings figure by a capitalization factor or price earnings ratio. Of course, this just begs the two questions: (1) Which earnings? and (2) What factor?

Before these questions can be answered, it is helpful to consider just what one is trying to represent by various approaches to earnings valua-tions. First, *capitalization of earnings* is a somewhat misleading term because it implies that earnings are an appropriate measure of return to the investor. In most cases, if the assumption is that funds produced by the venture will be reinvested, it is more meaningful to use cash flow (internally available funds) or dividends/interest/tax benefits (externally available funds) as a basis for comparing alternative investment oppor-tunities.

However, most investment decisions related to small companies are made on the basis that the stock will appreciate and that the future public sale of stock at a price higher than the purchase price will be the primary source of gain to the investor. The price of the stock, however, is only *influenced–not determined*—by earnings, dividends, or cash flow. As many investors have learned through glorious and/or bitter experiences, the prices at which publicly traded stock can be bought and sold is determined by supply and demand.

Using future earnings as a factor in influencing future stock prices, it is generally expected that for a company in a given industry, the price of the stock, i.e., the price at which supply and demand are equal, will reflect, among other things, the level of the company's earnings and the rate of growth and stability of those earnings. If earnings, the rate of growth of earnings, or the stability of earnings should increase, it would follow that the price of the stock should also increase. Predictions of future earnings are therefore used as a means for predicting future stock prices and thereby become a means for the investor to estimate the return on his investment.[1]

Another treatment of earnings for evaluating a company is to use them as one of the means of comparison with similar publicly held companies to get an idea of the going rate or current cost to the investor for this kind of investment. Here the argument is that if a company needs capital and an investor wants to invest, the investor should expect that what he will get for his investment should bear some relationship to the current market price of similar companies. This approach, however, implies two questionable assumptions:

1. Investors would consider earnings in closely held companies the same way they view earnings in publicly held companies.
2. Such small companies are readily comparable.

The question of *which earnings* relates to three basic kinds of earnings figures:

1. Historical earnings.
2. Future earnings under the current owner.
3. Future earnings under new ownership.

Obviously, an objective assessment of all three might yield the same value but this is unlikely.

Historical earnings. The logic behind looking at historical earnings is that they can be used to reflect the company's future performance; there is no logic in evaluating a company on the basis of what it has earned in the past. As will be discussed below, however, historical earnings should be given careful consideration in their use as a guide to the future. It is intended that they provide concrete realism to what otherwise would be just best guesses.

Historical earnings per se rarely can be used directly and an extrapolation of these figures to obtain a picture of the future must be considered a rough and frequently a poor approximation. To gain benefits from the

---

[1] It should be noted that in some situations factors other than earnings may be more relevant to the future selling price of a company. If, for example, an investor has as his strategy to build a distribution system which would become attractive as an acquisition by a manufacturer, gross sales may be a more useful measure of what the firm might be willing to pay than would earnings.

information in a company's financial history of past operations it is necessary to study each of the cost and income elements, their interrelationships, and their trends.

In pursuit of this study it is essential that random and nonrecurring items be factored out. Expenses should be reviewed to determine that they are normal and do not contain extraordinary expenses nor omit some of the usual expenses of operations. For example, inordinately low maintenance and repair charges over a period of years may mean that extraordinary expenses will be incurred in the future for deferred maintenance. Similarly, nonrecurring "windfall" sales will distort the normal picture.

In a small, closely held company particular attention should be given to the salaries of owner-managers and members of their families. If these salaries have been unreasonably high or low in light of the nature and size of the business and the duties performed, adjustment of the earnings is required. An assessment should also be made of the depreciation rates to determine their validity and to estimate the need for any earnings adjustments for the future. The amount of federal and state income taxes paid in the past may influence future earnings because of carryover and carryback provisions in the tax laws.

Future earnings under present ownership.   How much and in what ways income and costs are calculated for future operations depends to a large degree upon the operating policies and strategies of management. The existing or future owners' approach will be influenced by a host of factors: his ability as a manager, his economic objectives, his noneconomic objectives, his Weltanschauung, and so on. In calculating future earnings for a company these kinds of things must be considered and weighed.

A calculation of value based upon the future earnings of the company should provide an indication of the current economic value of the company to the current owner. To an investor, including the present owner as an investor, this figure should provide an economic basis for *that* individual's continued activity and investment in the company. (As we shall discuss later in this Note, there is usually more to a potential seller's position than just an economic analysis of his own future as an investor.) To an investor who anticipates a change in management with his investment, a calculation of value based upon earnings from the current owner's continuing with the company is *not* a meaningful assessment of the value of the company to the investor.

Future earnings under new ownership.   These are the earnings figures which are relevant to the investor who is investing in the turnaround of a dying company or in the reinvigoration of a stagnant one. The basis for his figures—his assumptions, relationships between costs and income, and so on—will probably show significant variance from the company's past performance. Plans may be to change substantially the nature of the business. The evaluation and investment decision may also involve large capital investments in addition to the purchase price of the company.

It is the future earnings of the new operation of the business which are helpful in determining the value *to him* of the company as these are the earnings which will influence his return. Most likely these kinds of projections will have large elements of uncertainty, and he may find it helpful to consider high, low, and most likely outcomes for financial performance.

The multiple. Assuming that the primary return to the investor is anticipated to result from sale of the stock at some future date, the investor asks himself the question: Given the anticipated pattern of earnings of this company, the nature of the industry, the likely state of the stock market (!), and so on, what will the public or some acquisitive conglomerate be willing to pay me for my holdings? In terms of some multiple of earnings, what prices are paid for stock with similar records and histories? Again, we are likely to come up with a range of possible answers. Looking at figures for New York Stock Exchange companies—a far less volatile securities market than over-the-counter trading—we find that for the period 1961–70 the average of all price/earnings ratios for all stocks ranged from 22.9 to 13.7. Some individual securities, of course, had ranges far exceeding the averages. To estimate with any degree of confidence the future multiple of a small company is indeed a difficult task. In many instances working with a range of values might be more helpful. This great uncertainty for a potential investor in estimating both a small company's future earnings *and* future market conditions for the stock of that company in part explains why his return on investment requirements for this kind of an investment are so high.

THE ENTREPRENEUR'S PERSPECTIVE

This viewpoint we shall consider in depth. Traditional approaches to evaluating a company have placed the principal emphasis upon earnings. Assuming that the company will continue in operation, the earnings method posits that a company is worth what it can be expected to earn.

But this approach is only partially useful for the individual entrepreneur who is trying to decide whether or not to invest in a business, for by evaluating the situation only in terms of *company* earnings, this method ignores the critical factor in which the investor/entrepreneur is interested—*the cash flow from the venture which will be available to him.* In addition to personal or subjective reasons for buying a business, the entrepreneur's chief criterion for appraisal will be return on investment (ROI). Because an entrepreneur's dollar investment is sometimes very small, it may be useful to think of return more as a return on his *time,*

[ROI (time)] than a return on his dollar investment [ROI ($)]. To calculate the latter return, the entrepreneur must calculate *his individual* prospective cash flow from the business.

It is therefore necessary to separate the concept of the individual, who is seeking a personal return, from the concept of a corporation, which is seeking a corporate return. This latter involves cash flows *to the company* and, other things being equal, has implications for the individual owners only in proportion to their share of the company. But as we shall see, net cash flow to the individual owner/manager has a host of possible inputs.

Types of cash flows and their different tax treatments

There are six basic ways for an individual owner/manager to get cash flow from a venture:[2]

1. Perquisites (benefits, such as a car or country club membership, which are incidental to the job but in addition to the provided salary).
2. Return of capital via debt repayment.
3. Return of capital via sale of the company (sale of stock or liquidation).
4. Capital gain via sale of the company (sale of stock or liquidation).
5. Interest and salary.
6. Dividends.

Now, if all tax considerations were removed, and if all other things were equal, there would be no reason for the owner/manager to prefer any one of these types of cash flow to any other. But in fact, tax considerations are very present, and the differences in the tax treatment of the various classes of cash flows can become a major consideration in determining the value of a situation for the prospective entrepreneur. Taxes paid to the government significantly reduce the amount of cash available to the owner/manager. He will thus pefer the types of cash flows which will minimize such taxes. With this criterion in mind, he will rank the classes of cash flows in the order of preference listed above.

1. Perquisites. Perquisites are not literally cash at all, but can be considered cash equivalents in terms of their direct benefits. Business-related expenses charged to the company, (e.g., company car and country club memberships) are received by the individual and are *not taxed* at either the corporate or personal level. Their disadvantage is that they are limited in absolute dollar terms.

2. Return of capital via debt repayment. This class of cash flow is a *tax*

---

[2]A seventh, depreciation and loss shields made available to individuals, is primarily cash flow sources made available to wealthy investors.

free event at both the corporate and personal level. An additional advantage to this type of flow is that it can occur while enabling the entrepreneur still to maintain a continuous equity interest in the company. Its disadvantage is, of course, that it requires him to make the original investment.

3. Return of capital via sale of the company. If the owner/manager sells all or part of the business, the amount he receives up to the amount of his cost basis is a *tax free* event at both the corporate and personal level. Since a sale of his interest is involved, however, it is evident that, unlike a return of capital via debt repayment, the owner/manager does not maintain his continuous equity interest in the concern. Also, like a cash flow based on debt retirement, an original investment is necessary.

4. Capital gain via sale of the company. When capital gains are realized in addition to the return of capital, no tax is imposed at the corporate level, and the tax rate at the personal level is less than for regular income.

5. Interest and salary. Both of these items constitute personal income and are taxed as such at the personal level. However, no tax is imposed at the corporate level.

6. Dividends. As a means of getting cash from a venture, dividends are the least desirable as the resulting cash flow has undergone the greatest net shrinkage. Dividends incur taxes first at the corporate level (at the 22 or 48 percent rate as income accrues to the corporation) and then again at the personal level (at the personal income tax rate as the dividend payment accrues to the individual). At the maximum corporate income tax rate of 48 percent and the maximum personal income tax rate of 70 percent, we can see that this devastating double taxation can reduce $1.00 of pre-tax corporate profit to $.15 after-tax cash flow to the individual—an 85 percent reduction in available cash flow.

We can diagramatically summarize how tax considerations affect the six types of cash flows to the individual. Using $1.00 as the initial flow, we can calculate the resulting net after-tax personal cash flow for an individual in the 30 percent tax bracket. See Table 1 (pp. 194–95).

Other considerations causing one type of cash flow to be preferred over another

The reader will recall that we began the tax section of this Note with the following proposition: "Now, if all tax considerations were removed, and if all other things were equal, there would be no reason for the owner/manager to prefer any one of these types of cash flow to any other." We have already seen that tax considerations are anything but removed. We will now examine those circumstances when all other things are *not* equal in order to determine what other considerations

TABLE 1
Getting cash flow from a venture for an owner/manager in the 30 percent tax bracket

Capital transactions

Return of capital:

Debt repayment	Cost basis	Capital gain	
Repayment of debt: $1.00	Sale of company (sale of stock or liquidation) at cost basis: $1.00	Sale of company (sale of stock or liquidation) at *greater than cost*	

Sale: e.g., $2.00
↓
Less: Cost basis: e.g.,$1.00
↓
Equals: Capital gains: $1.00

Less: Capital gains tax (e.g., 15%): $.15

Net Personal Cash Flows	$1.00	$1.00	$.85	$1.00
	Return of capital: Debt repayment	Return of capital: Cost basis	Capital gain	Return of capital: Cost basis

might cause the owner/manager to prefer one class of cash flow over another. For the purpose of this analysis, we can group the six basic types of cash flow into three larger generic groups:

1. Income type flows.
2. Debt repayment flows.
3. Flows created by sale of the company.

1. Income flows (salary, interest, dividends, and perquisites). The greater certainty and more immediate timing of these types of cash flows

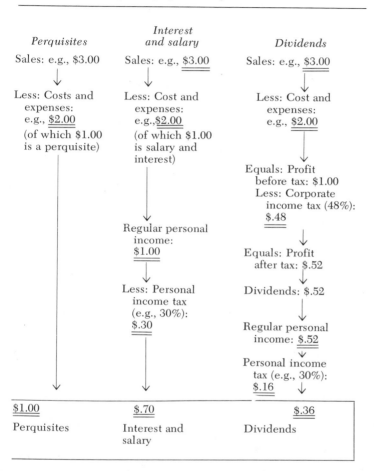

Day-to-day operation of venture

Perquisites	Interest and salary	Dividends
Sales: e.g., $3.00	Sales: e.g., $3.00	Sales: e.g., $3.00
Less: Costs and expenses: e.g., $2.00 (of which $1.00 is a perquisite)	Less: Cost and expenses: e.g., $2.00 (of which $1.00 is salary and interest)	Less: Cost and expenses: e.g., $2.00
		Equals: Profit before tax: $1.00 Less: Corporate income tax (48%): $.48
	Regular personal income: $1.00	Equals: Profit after tax: $.52
	Less: Personal income tax (e.g., 30%): $.30	Dividends: $.52 Regular personal income: $.52 Personal income tax (e.g., 30%): $.16
$1.00 Perquisites	$.70 Interest and salary	$.36 Dividends

makes them particularly attractive to the individual. In situations where a company is closely held by the owner/managers and where they anticipate a long term or indefinite involvement with the business (with no concomitant urgency to maximize their return whenever they do leave the business), these types of cash flows are especially practical. This kind of situation is typically found when the entrepreneurs enjoy the work and life style associated with the venture. The reader should recall that because of their favorable tax treatment, salaries and perquisites are favored over dividends.

However, when there are outside investors, they are usually seeking capital gains on an appreciated stock. Therefore, in their eyes, high salaries and perquisites for the entrepreneur are inappropriate. The outside investors usually want to enter a situation where the entrepreneur will be kept "hungry" until he finally achieves his rewards in capital gains—at the same time that the outside investors achieve theirs the same way.

2. Debt repayment flows. Return of capital in the form of debt repayment is an attractive device for getting money out of a venture without paying personal taxes. It is appropriate, however, only where as a practical matter the money is available to be withdrawn from a venture either through internally generated funds or through refinancing. Usually in the rapidly growing company, there are continuing requirements for more funds, and the owner/manager may consider the cost of replacing his debt investment in the company to be prohibitively expensive.

3. Flows created by the sale of the company. The cash flow created by selling the company at some future date is the traditional way that the entrepreneur seeks to achieve his personal financial gain. What is meant here is net *realized* cash flow, not the financial fantasy produced by "paper profits" occurring when an owner/manager holds restricted stock after going public in an attractive new issues market.

However, predicting the amount for which stock in a small, unlisted company can be sold at some future date is not an easy task. First, there is the uncertainty related to financial *performance* which results from management's efforts to deal with product performance, demand, competition, operating efficiency, and so on. To indicate this uncertainty, the pro forma operating projections are sometimes cast in terms of "most likely," "high," and "low" expectations of financial performance. Second, there are also additional uncertainties related to the *demand* for a company's stock at a given point in time. Demand may be considered in terms of stock market conditions at a particular time, or it may be appropriate to evaluate demand in terms of the interest of acquisitive conglomerates. Finally, the price which someone might be willing to pay for a company's stock even when the company is growing rapidly, may depend upon a number of factors other than simple historical earnings per share: e.g., rate of earnings growth, type of industry, market share, and so on.

Thus we see that the figure used in a valuation analysis based on cash flows generated by a sale of the company is necessarily imprecise. Indeed, in most instances, a range of possible selling prices and selling dates might be more useful to provide an indication of the sensitivity of the various components affecting the eventual sales price. In any event, thinking of the situation as we have outlined above should be a useful approach.

Negative cash flows and present value

The entrepreneur must also take into account his negative cash flows. Three types of negative cash flows are particularly important:

1. Cash portion of the purchase price.
2. Deficient salary.
3. Additional equity capital.

Frequently the most critical aspect of the cash portion of the purchase price is that it must be small enough for the entrepreneur to be able to pay it in the first place. In this kind of situation the seller finances the purchase of his company by taking part of the purchase price in the form of a note. The seller then receives cash later on from future earnings of the company or from its assets. Of course, the less cash he is required to put up the more cash the entrepreneur has available for other uses and the greater the opportunity he has to produce a high ROI ($). On the other hand, too much initial debt may hamstring a company from the start, thereby hurting the venture's subsequent financial performance and the entrepreneur's principal source of return—be it the cash he withdraws from the company or the funds he receives from eventual sale of the company.

The significance to the entrepreneur of a negative cash flow based on a deficient salary is self-evident—he has a lower income for personal use than he could get elsewhere. But the effect of requirements for additional equity capital is more subtle: faced with an immediate equity requirement for working capital or fixed assets, the owner/manager may be forced to seek outside investors, thereby diluting his equity (and diminishing his current and eventual cash flows) and also introducing the possibility of divergent goals in the financial and other aspects of the company's operations.

At this point in our analysis it will appear obvious to some that the next step for the entrepreneur is to find the present value of the cash flows he predicts for the venture. In other words, he should discount the value of future cash flows to arrive at a value of the venture in terms of cash today. We shall see, however, that in many respects this approach raises more questions than it answers and therefore its usefulness to the analysis is questionable at best.

The essence of the problem is that present value is basically an investment concept utilizing ROI ($) to determine the allocation of a limited supply of funds among alternatives, whereas the entrepreneur is faced basically with a personal situation where the measure ROI (time) is key.

In investment analyses utilizing present value the discount rate is selected to reflect uncertainty associated with cash flows—the higher the uncertainty, the higher the discount rate and consequently the lower the present value of the cash flows. In the corporate context there is usually a minimal ROI ($) criteria for noncritical investments to keep the ROI ($) greater than the firm's cost of capital.

For the individual entrepreneur, however, the decision to buy or to start a company is fundamentally a subjective one. His ROI (time) for this kind of decision is measured not only in terms of dollars but also in terms of what he will be doing, who his associates will be, how much time and energy he will have to expend, and what his life style will be. Different kinds of ventures present different *kinds of return* for ROI (time). As cash to the entrepreneur is an important enabling factor for *some* of the things the entrepreneur is seeking, it is important that he calculate what these cash flows might be and when he can expect them. However, because decisions affecting cash flow also affect the other returns to the entrepreneur and because these other returns may be at least as important as the financial returns, a present value calculation is not really appropriate.

In thinking about the attractiveness of a particular opportunity an entrepreneur rarely has similar situations as alternatives to compare. More than likely his decision is either to go ahead with a venture or to stay where he is until something else comes along. Perhaps the most useful way to think of his position in a particular decision situation is to compare it to an individual looking down a corridor which, if he elects to go that way, will provide him with a possible range of opportunities— opportunities to achieve different levels of financial and other rewards with their accompanying risks and sacrifices.

Two models

Tables 2A and 2B below combine elements of the above discussion to show two simplified models of cash flow evaluations. The situation shown in 2A depicts the present value analysis of the kinds of cash flows usually associated with an *attractive small company* which the entrepreneur intends to pursue indefinitely and to take out his economic rewards accordingly. Table 2B depicts kinds of cash flows usually appropriate in the present value analysis for a *high-potential venture* with which the entrepreneur plans eventually to make a large capital gain.

THE SELLER'S PERSPECTIVE

For the owner who is strictly an owner-investor, the outlook should be very similar to that of the purchaser-investor: most elements of the situation can be evaluated purely in economic terms. For the owner-manager, however, there are also likely to be personal, noneconomic

TABLE 2 A
Cash flow evaluation for a long-term venture involvement

Cash flow		Periods						
		t_0	t_1	t_2	t_3	t_4	t_5	t_x
Positive				—	(1) Perquisite (2) Excess salary	(1) Perquisite (2) Excess salary	(1) Perquisite (2) Excess salary	(1) Cash from selling out
Negative	(1) Entrepreneur's cash portion of purchase price		(1) Deficient salary	—	—	—	—	—

TABLE 2 B
Cash flow evaluation of a venture pursued for capital gains

Cash flow		Periods			
		t_0	t_2	t_2	t_x
Positive					(1) Cash from selling out
Negative	(1) Cash portion of purchase price	—	(1) Additional working capital (owner's investment) (2) Deficient salary	(1) Deficient salary	—
Indirect negative......		—	—	(2) Additional equity capital (ownership dilution)	—

considerations which can play a major role in how the individual perceives the value of his ownership. This is most often the case when selling the company is an act of retirement by an individual who has spent the greater part of his career in the business and has built and molded the company. Usually this person sees the company's success largely as a measure of life. In such instances continuity of such things as the company name, product quality, customer value, employee security, company image, or other items may become more significant than additional dollars in selling price. In cases where the owner-manager is to remain with the company, his future role will be an additional point of concern.

The problem for the entrepreneur in such situations is determining what kinds of things are of value to such individuals. Whether or not the owner-manager is willing to sell at all may depend upon how well he believes these noneconomic needs of his are going to be met.

In negotiating with an owner-manager who has noneconomic objectives, the would-be new owner of the company can concede noneconomic items in return for concessions on price or terms. However, most noneconomic items in fact cost something, either directly, such as payments or obligations for future payments in retirement benefits for employees, or indirectly, such as constraints upon labor costs in operations from an agreement to keep the company at its existing location. Therefore, as part of the preparation for negotiations the prospective purchaser should anticipate both the noneconomic factors and their related costs so he can make knowledgeable trade-offs in the actual negotiations.

VALUE AND PURCHASE PRICE

By this point it should be becoming clear that the value of a company to a person is not necessarily what he will have to pay for it or have to sell it for. The other party's value is also a factor. For a sale to be possible, the would-be seller's value must be less than the would-be buyer's. But the differences may be substantial, and at what price the transaction occurs if it occurs at all, will depend upon their relative perceived strengths and, even more so, upon their skills in negotiations.

A difference in values does not necessarily mean that someone is foolish or has made a mistake. It frequently reflects differences in what the two different parties have to bring to the situation. A seller may believe that he is getting a very good price for a company while a buyer believes he is getting the company for well below what he thinks it is worth. The one individual may have greater abilities or other resources to make a success of the business whereas the other may equate a high dollar value with some noneconomic things.

Two particular kinds of related situations are worth mentioning. The first involves *different assessments of the same business.* Here values are derived because of differences in expectations about what is going to happen. The differences in expectations may be the results of different levels of skills, different access to resources, or different information about the specific company or industry. The familiarity of the current owner to the business and his own operations in particular would appear to give him a decided advantage on this latter point, therefore the warning *caveat emptor.*

The second kind of situation is where the difference in evaluations occurs because of *assessments of different businesses.* Here the potential buyer sees greater opportunity in some new activity. An extreme example would be where a person buys farm land from a farmer with the idea that he can drill a producing oil well on it.

Finally, consideration must be given to special pressures on the parties from the conditions which surround them. How badly does the buyer want to buy and how badly does the seller want to sell? More precisely, to what degree does the current owner feel that he *must sell to a given would-be purchaser,* and to what degree does the would-be purchaser feel that he *must buy this particular property?* For example, if the owner of a business badly needs cash or if, because of poor health, he can no longer operate the business, he may be willing to sell at a price even less than what he believes the company is worth. Similarly, if a potential buyer has had a life-long dream of being in a particular industry and he knows of just one company in that industry currently on the market, or if a company is seen to provide a missing key element (such as location, salesman, product, or technology) in a larger scheme, the would-be purchaser may be willing to pay more than what he sees as the individual company's value.

In all three of the above situations certain information about the other party—his valuation and the reasons behind it—could be crucial in influencing the selling price were this information available to the other side. Therefore, in addition to making one's own evaluation, it is *key* to assess whatever information one can obtain about the other party to determine his probable position.

REFERENCES

Helfert, Erich A. *Techniques of Financial Analysis.* Homewood, Ill.: Richard D. Irwin, 1972.

Mace, Myles, and Montgomery, George. *Management Problems of Corporate Acquisitions.* Boston: Division of Research, Harvard Business School, 1962.

Cases

Peter W. Allen

On August 1, 1963, Mr. Peter Allen, general manager of the welder division of the Thomson Electric Welder Company (Thomson) was reviewing his plans for another try at purchasing the division from the parent company. Because the primary interest of the owners of Thomson lay in the activities of the other two divisions and because the welder division had recently been unprofitable, a program for liquidating the assets of the welder division was currently underway. Mr. Allen knew he would have to make an offer quickly if he were going to acquire the division as a going concern.

Peter W. Allen

Mr. Allen was born in Niagara Falls, New York. In 1944 he entered Dartmouth College, but subsequently transferred to Case Institute of Technology in Cleveland, Ohio, where he received his B.S. degree in mechanical engineering in 1948.

Shortly after graduation Mr. Allen persuaded three friends to join him in finding a way to make a round-the-world sailing trip. Each had done a little sailing in small boats on Lake Erie. Through a *Yachting News* classified ad they found a 52-foot, 1934 vintage cutter yacht which had sunk and which an insurance company would sell them, afloat but not restored, for $4,500. On August 15, 1948, they set sail from Connecticut with Boston as their first stop.

The entire voyage lasted more than a year but the group got only as far as Acapulco, Mexico, because of lengthy stops at Boston, New York, Miami, Bermuda, and Panama where the travelers worked at various jobs. During the periods on shore Mr. Allen worked as a Fuller Brush salesman, greeting card packer, construction worker, and Panama Canal guard. At Acapulco the boat was sold for $7,500 and Mr. Allen and his friends returned home.

After the trip Mr. Allen spent two additional years at Case taking graduate courses in industrial engineering. In 1951 he went to work for Federal Machine and Welder Company in Warren, Ohio, as a designer and sales engineer of special machinery. In 1956, he became assistant chief sales engineer and in 1958 he became chief draftsman with responsibility for scheduling and coordinating production line startup. "I found at Federal that about every two years I would get to where I knew what I was doing in that particular job . . . first as a designer, then as a sales engineer and assistant to the chief sales engineer, and then as chief draftsman. Every time I got to that point I found myself trying to do something about it. Generally I just went and said I wanted to do some thing different and generally they [the company] did something for me."

During the fall of 1957 Mr. Allen read *How I Turned $1,000 into a Million in Real Estate–in My Spare Time* by William Nickerson and decided to investigate real estate investment opportunities in Warren. Through a broker he located a house which could be purchased for $7,000 and at the same time found an individual who was willing to pay even more for the house but who could not obtain credit. Mr. Allen bought the house for $7,000, sold it the next day for $10,000 on a land contract agreement,[1] thus assuming for $3,000 the credit risk the bank was unwilling to take.

In the fall of 1960 Federal Machine and Welder Company was acquired by a competitor, McKay Machine Company. In the organizational changes which subsequently occurred, new people were brought into the Federal management group above Mr. Allen. As he perceived the new situation, his opportunities for continued advancement in the immediate or medium-range future had been considerably reduced by these developments. During the winter Mr. Allen contacted several competitors about employment. Two years earlier one of these companies had offered him the position of sales manager at a salary approximately 20 percent above his then $12,000 salary at Federal, but he had declined. In January 1961, he also contacted several employment agencies in NewYork but only received replies from two medium-sized firms with openings for junior engineers. Mr. Allen was dissatisfied with all of the alternatives open to him and discontinued his inquiries. He decided that if he were going to relocate he would have to do something to change his basic direction.

Mr. Allen was then 36 years old. While engaged in activities of a

---

[1] A contract in which the buyer agrees with the seller to make monthly payments toward the purchase of a house but does not receive title from the seller until all payments have been made. In this situation Mr. Allen obtained a mortgage from the bank to purchase the house from the original owner and then arranged for the new purchaser to make his payments to the bank to apply against the mortgage.

Warren community theater group he had met a girl whom he had married in 1954 and by 1961 there were five children. The Allens were living in a six-room rented home in an upper-middle income section of Warren. Mr. Allen had about $1,000 in savings and $4,000 in other assets.

In March of 1961 Mr. Allen applied to the M.B.A. program of the Harvard Business School and within several weeks received a letter of rejection from the Admissions Board. He then wrote to inquire whether or not he should reapply the following year. The business school director of admissions answered that perhaps he should visit the school to discuss the situation. In May Mr. Allen and his wife drove to Boston and after several hours of discussion were told that Mr. Allen would be admitted to the M.B.A. class starting in September.

In 1962 during the summer following the first year at the business school, Mr. Allen went to work for the Thomson Electric Welder division of Seton, a Textron subsidiary formed in the 1950s from a knitting mill, a defunct steamship line, and an electric welding equipment manufacturer. (The original merger arrangement had been made to take advantage of a tax loss carry-forward situation.) The products of the welder division were very similar to the products of Federal Machine Company in Ohio where Mr. Allen had worked previously. "It wasn't the sort of summer job which consists of a three-month project. Within a few days of my joining the company I was quoting prices on custom design production welders and other equipment." Mr. Allen's salary was $600 per month.

When he had first arrived in Boston in August 1961 Mr. Allen had purchased a $15,200 house in Holbrook, Massachusetts, for $3,000 down and taking up the previous owner's notes for $140/month. In June 1962, soon after starting at Thompson, he had found another house closer to work, and with the promise of the $3,000 equity in his Holbrook home and some carefully prepared pro forma statements of income, Mr. Allen persuaded the bank to give him a $19,500 mortgage even though he would be starting school full time again in September.

When the second year started Mr. Allen arranged his courses so all of his classes would be in the morning. He then was able to continue his job at Thomson from two to five each weekday afternoon and all day on Saturdays. "By the last half of the second year you really don't have a serious time problem. I could have studied awfully hard and probably have made better grades . . . and starved. But I decided to keep my job and kind of slide through the last part of that year."

Mr. Allen knew that the electric welder division had not been doing well. In November 1962 he learned from the then general manager that plans were being made to sell the two stamping divisions and the welder division to the president, also an Harvard Business School graduate, and the controller, who had financial backing for the deal from an investment corporation headed by Royal Little. It was the general manager's understanding that if the company were sold to this group the welder division would be sold off or its assets liquidated. When the sale of the company to the president and controller occurred in December, Mr. Allen inquired whether or not the welder division was for sale and, if so, what price range they were asking. The new owner's estimated value of $900,000 was considerably more than the approximately $500,000 which Mr. Allen thought the division was worth.

Mr. Allen still wanted to pursue the possibilities of purchasing the division, however. "Before going to business school I would never have thought of trying to do something like this. But by the middle of the second year I thought I could. It was the type of thing in which I felt I could make use of the full range of what I had been learning."

For a course on business policy Mr. Allen had written a paper on the welding industry and one on Thomson. These papers included information on welding processes, welder manufacturers, the welder division of Thomson, and sales figures for Thomson and the welder industry. With the knowledge of his professor, Mr. Allen used his business policy paper as Appendix I of his Management of New Enterprises report,[2] which described his evaluation and plans for purchasing the welder division. The section entitled "Report" at the end of this case shows parts of Mr. Allen's report, which also contained evaluations and projections based on conditions in the division as of early March 1963. (Note: Exhibits 1 and 2 *of the case* show revised estimates made by Mr. Allen to reflect his evaluation of the situation as it had changed by the summer of 1963.)

Among the major problems in the acquisition was finding a source of funds, as Mr. Allen had a negative personal net worth at this time. A classmate at the business school introduced Mr. Allen to a small venture capital group, Northeastern Development Corporation, which was then engaged primarily in real estate and development operations, but was interested in investing in a manufacturing operation. Northeastern Development had been active in the Boston area for several years and could provide excellent introductions to banks who would consider providing debt financing for the acquisition of the welder division.

After numerous discussions between Mr. Allen and Mr. Price of Northeastern Development during the preceding months, it was informally agreed in March that if Mr. Allen could arrange for the purchase of the company for approximately the $450,000 indicated in his report, Northeastern Development would furnish $39,000 of the $40,000 equity money required and the bank with whom they worked would supply the debt money secured by certain assets of the acquired company. Northeastern Development would not be in a position to put additional money

---

[2]The paper was an optional part of the course.

into the company. Mr. Allen would give a note for $1,000 in equity money and would become president at a salary of $15,000 per year which would be reviewed as the company progressed. For what the two equity contributors were bringing to the deal, Mr. Allen was to receive 1,000 shares of common stock at $1 per share and Northeastern Development was to receive 2,000 shares of common stock at $1 per share and 37,000 shares of 5 percent callable preferred stock at $1 per share.

On March 31, 1963, the welder division's five salesmen were changed from salaried company employees to manufacturers' representatives on commission. All but 6 of the 40 production workers were laid off.[3] The union contract expired around this time and although a strike was discussed, the union accepted a new contract which provided for severance pay for the departing workers and wage increases for those remaining. At one point Mr. Allen had discussed the situation in some detail with the union steward and had been of the opinion that a strike by the union might have been best at that time to force immediate disposal of the company by the owners while it was still a going concern. The general manager was terminated and Mr. Allen was selected to replace him at a salary of $12,000 per year which Mr. Allen negotiated to $15,000 per year. Around the same date Mr. Allen had learned that the new owners had entered active negotiations for the sale of the building and were discussing an auction date for the sale of the production equipment.

In May the building was sold and the floor space for the company's operations was subsequently reduced from 22,000 to 12,000 square feet. During June approximately two thirds of the company's production equipment was sold at public auction. The company had retained one of each major type of production machinery, drying ovens for the transformer coils, and other special equipment used in manufacturing.

Mr. Allen believed that the events to date had not decreased the basic potential for realizing the plans essentially as he had outlined them in the Management of New Enterprises report. In examining the situation critically, however, he recognized several significant problem areas.

Sales.   The sales representatives were seriously demoralized at the change in their position from company agents to manufacturers' reps; and one had discontinued any active effort to sell the line. Mr. Allen planned to continue the men as manufacturers' reps if he purchased the company. The morale situation had been made worse by the cutback in the production force, the sale of the building, and the well-publicized auction of the production equipment. Several inquiries expressing con-

---

[3]Late in April two large orders had been received and consequently several of the laid-off workers had been rehired. At the end of July 1963, these men were still with the company. The company personnel in July 1963 consisted of 15 direct shop workers, 2 indirect shop workers, 1 purchasing agent, 1 shop supervisor, 2 lab and servicemen, 4 direct engineers, 3 sales engineers, 4 office and accounting personnel, and Peter W. Allen.

cern about the company's actions had been received from customers who depended upon the company for parts and servicing of their equipment.

Capacity. Although Mr. Allen realized that the company had been operating significantly below capacity in the past several years, he felt the reduction in production equipment by 65 percent and floor space by 45 percent was more drastic than necessary to adjust to demand. Also, if any more production workers were to be rehired, the union contract required that they be recalled on the basis of seniority until April 1964. Mr. Allen knew of several individuals whom he definitely did not want to have back with the company.

Personnel. Most of the key people in the welder division were in their fifties and although they had shown themselves capable of a reasonable standard of performance, Mr. Allen wondered if they could and would accept the work and responsibilities which would be necessary to turn the company into a profitable growth situation. Mr. Allen had noted that many people had developed rather lax working habits, and he was not sure how they would react to a relative youngster pressing for more and better work.

On the technical side, there were only two employees other than Mr. Allen who had had formal engineering training. Mr. Allen knew that new and improved products would have to be introduced before long if the operation was to remain competitive.

Competing bids. Although he had not heard directly, Mr. Allen knew that a former general manager was also trying to work out a plan to buy the division. Mr. Allen also strongly suspected that other companies in the welder business had approached the owners of Thomson about purchasing the division.

Other. In addition to the economic aspects described above, Mr. Allen also had things of a more personal nature to consider. At 39, with his experience and M.B.A. training, he was still an attractive item in the job market. He believed, however, that a delay of two or three years in trying unsuccessfuly to turn around a failing company would begin to place him in a significantly less flexible and less attractive position. In the few interviews he had had at the business school Mr. Allen had noted that the orientation had been naturally toward younger, less experienced people than himself but that Ford had offered him fairly early a position of immediate responsibility in their production machinery buying department at a salary of $12,000. Mr. Allen was reasonably confident that he could obtain a higher offer from Ford or another company in a similar position.

Further, Mr. Allen knew that he would be experiencing increasing financial demands as his children grew older and he was well aware that a venture of this type, even if successful, might produce very unpredictable cash flows. In addition, although his wife had been very patient and understanding during their financial cutbacks while at the business school, Mr. Allen knew that she would very much prefer seeing him in a more stable situation. She was also apprehensive about Mr. Allen cosigning $190,000 in notes to the bank.

If he were still to have a chance to purchase the division Mr. Allen knew he would have to act immediately. Exhibit 1 shows Mr. Allen's revised pro forma income statement prepared on June 19, 1963. Exhibit 2 shows Mr. Allen's revised figures for valuation of the company, funds source, and payments schedule prepared on July 23, 1963. Exhibit 3 shows an excerpt from the First National City Bank of New York *Monthly Economic Letter* of May 1963. Both Northeastern Development and the bank had informally agreed to the plan for purchase of assets outlined in Exhibit 2. Mr. Allen believed the price of $311,000 would be high enough and the schedule of payment acceptable to the owners if no significantly higher offers had been made.

SUGGESTED QUESTIONS

1. Advise Mr. Allen whether or not he should try to purchase the welder division.
2. What are the key elements of his decision?
3. How would you evaluate the specific proposal he has outlined for the acquisition?
4. What are the key elements to the company being successful?

EXHIBIT 1
Peter W. Allen
Pro forma profit and loss (July 1, 1963, to June 30, 1964) ($000)

	1963						1964						Total
	July	Aug.	Sept.	Oct.	Nov.	Dec.	Jan.	Feb.	March	April	May	June	
Sales	100	60	60	60	60	60	60	60	60	60	60	60	760
Cost of Sales:													
Variable @ 60 percent	60	36	36	36	36	36	36	36	36	36	36	36	456
Fixed	5	5	5	5	5	5	5	5	5	5	5	5	60
Total	65	41	41	41	41	41	41	41	41	41	41	41	516
Gross margin	35	19	19	19	19	19	19	19	19	19	19	19	244
Operating Expense													
Variable (comm.)	8	5	5	5	5	5	5	5	5	5	5	5	63
Fixed	12	12	12	12	12	12	12	12	12	12	12	12	144
Total	20	17	17	17	17	17	17	17	17	17	17	17	207
Operating profit	15	2	2	2	2	2	2	2	2	2	2	2	37
Depreciation													5
													42

Exhibit prepared by P. W. Allen, June 19, 1963.

EXHIBIT 2

Peter W. Allen

Valuation, funds source, and payments schedule (000)

Valuation		Offer	Basis
Accounts and notes receivable		$108	Gross book
Inventory:			
Raw material.................................		24 ⎫	½ gross book
Stock parts and subassemblies		35 ⎭	
Work in process		89	Gross book x 1.17 (equivalent to 43% add-on less 18% discount)*
Finished goods		—	Taken on consignment
Machinery and equipment:			
Plant†	$40		
Lab†	30		
Office†	8		
Name, drawings, and patents†	50	125	See schedule A
Total Assets.............................		$381	
Less-payables		70	Gross book
Net.................................		$311	
Funds source schedule:			
Surplus cash from previous year.................			
Sale of stock			
Operations: Profit and depreciation..............			
Total cash available			
Needs:			
Cash for operations			
Closing costs................................			
Available for downpayment			
Payment Schedule:			
Terms of sale‡			
Surplus cash			

*Historically sales had amounted to 143 percent of work-in-process book value. It was Mr. Allen's intention to divide with the sellers the 43 percent excess over gross book after a deduction of 8 percent for sales commission, e.g.

Sales price	143% of gross book
Less 8% commission	8
	135% of gross book
To be received by the buyers..............	18
To be received by the sellers	117% of gross book

†Appraisal was obtained by outside auctioneer.

‡$200 payment plus three notes for a total price of $311,000. Assume 6 percent interest on notes.

Exhibit prepared by P. W. Allen, July 23, 1963.

	Timing			
		Financing		
Immediate	*Year 1*	*Year 2*	*Year 3*	*Sources*
$ 86				Bank loan at 80% of book @ 8%
	$ 5 20	$ 5 10		} Decrease in inventory
44				Bank loan at 50% of offer @ 8%
60				Bank loan at ½ sound value if less than liquidation value† (8% interest)
— 40 —	— 42	26 — 21	27 — 22	See Exhibit 1
$230	$67	$62	$49	
(25) (5)				
$200				
$(200)	(41)	(35)	(35)	Total $311,000 over three years
—	$26	$27	$14	

EXHIBIT 2 (concluded)
Schedule A machinery and equipment details (000)

	Serial number	Original cost (shop)	Net book value, 6/30/63	Proposed purchase price, 6/30/63
Plant machinery (such as lathes, drills, borers)			$84.0	
Laboratory welders and equipment				
(1) F-4 250 KVA flash welder	18777	$26.2	2.3	
(1) F-3A 150 KVA flash welder	18827	15.9	2.3	
(1) F-1A 30 KVA flash welder......	19610	7.8	6.5	
(1) FOB 10 KVA flash welder......	18831	2.6	0	
(1) #700 projection welder	19479	3.6	1.6	
(1) H frame projection welder	none	3.0	1.1	
Subtotal.....................		$59.1	13.8	
Office machinery			18.0	
Total.....................			$115.8	$125.0

EXHIBIT 3
Peter W. Allen

Increases in capital spending

Many businessmen have been reviewing and expanding their capital expenditure plans for 1963. According to the latest survey, taken in March and April by the McGraw-Hill Department of Economics, outlays for plant and equipment are scheduled to exceed $40 billion in 1963—a rise of 7.4 percent over the $37.3 billion spent for this purpose in 1962 and 8.4 percent above the previous high in 1957 of $37.0 billion. Evidently, businessmen boosted their investment plans about a billion dollars in the two months following the January–February survey by the Department of Commerce–Securities and Exchange Commission. This had come up with a figure of $39.1 billion.

It took a long time to get plant and equipment spending above the old peak set in 1957. As shown in the accompanying chart, manufacturers plan to spend $16.1 billion in 1963, a rise of 9.5 percent over 1962, but scarcely more than was spent in 1957. Among the individual industries planning sizable increases in investment over 1962 are autos (23 percent), steel (27 percent), fabricated metals (29 percent), and nonferrous metals (34 percent). Less than one-third of the 1963 outlays is scheduled to go into expansion of capacity; the balance will provide for modernization and replacement of present facilities of which 22 percent is reported as technologically outmoded. Participants in the survey indicated their investment planning is geared more closely to long-term growth prospects than to current sales or utilization of capacity.

From what is already known of plant and equipment expenditures in the first half of 1963, it is clear that a marked expansion in capital spending will be required during the second half to meet the goals set for the year as a whole. Present indications are that the fourth quarter rate will be about 10 percent higher than it is now in the second quarter. Here, then, is an expansionary force which can help offset any softening that may occur later this year in the current high rates of steel and automobile production.

*Source: Excerpted from First National City Bank of New York, *Monthly Economic Letter,* May 1963.

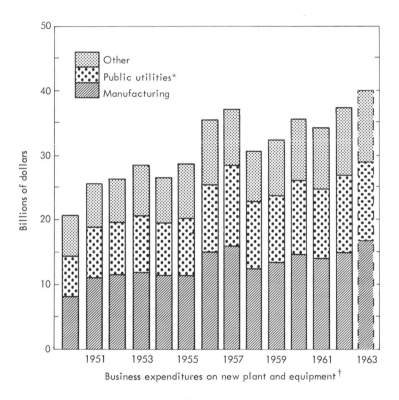

Business expenditures on new plant and equipment †

*Includes communication and transporation.
†Source: 1950–62, U.S. Department of Commerce and Securities and Exchange Commission; 1963 (anticipated), McGraw-Hill Department of Economics.

REPORT

A prospectus

Thomson Electric Welder Co., Inc.

by

Peter W. Allen
March 15, 1963

Because I have a desire to acquire control of a manufacturing concern, plus a strong interest and substantial experience in the resistance welding industry, and because I feel that a real opportunity exists for the creation of a profitable company in New England offering a needed product, I propose to form a new corporation known as Thomson Electric Welder Co., Inc., created to purchase the assets of the Thomson Electric Welder Division of the Thomson Co. and to operate as an independent producer of resistance welder machinery and related products. I offer the following information to those who may wish to join me in this venture as stockholders or suppliers of debt financing.

Present owners

The Thomson Electric Welder Division is presently one of three divisions that make up the Thomson Co. The other two divisions are located in Michigan and produce metal stampings for the automobile industry. The Thomson Co. came into existence on January 1, 1963, when a management group purchased the three divisions from the previous owners and formed the new company. This group is anxious to dispose of the welder division as their interests lie with the other two plants. Appendix I gives the history of the company in greater detail.

Future potential

The forecasts are based on an assumption that the national economy, and particularly the machine tool industry, stays at the level of activity of recent years. Actually, it is likely that there will be substantial improvements in machine tool sales in the coming years, as new and proposed tax laws favor increased capital goods spending. Also, the last peak in Thomson's sales (and in machine tool sales) occurred in the early to middle fifties and in several more years replacement of that equipment should generate increased sales. Thomson has single shift plant capacity for about $1,800,000 in sales per year. Due to the fixed and variable cost relationships, sales increases above the breakeven point of $850,000 will generate pre-tax profits at the rate of about $.35 for each sales dollar of increase. In view of this, a prime company objective will be to work for controlled growth at about 10 percent increased sales per year through improved products, competitive pricing, and new products to meet the needs of Thomson customers. It is apparent from the projections in Exhibits IV, V,[1] and VI that a growth rate of about 10 percent per year is the practical limit with the financial structure proposed. This growth rate assures adequate cash balances and debt repayment plus allowing some investment in new equipment.

Sales program

A drop in sales is expected for the first year. This is due in part to the fact that all company employed salesmen have been changed to a manufacturer's representative status. These men (five in number) are currently devoting efforts to obtain other lines, and the result has been a slowdown in inquiries. Also, the morale of these men has been severely damaged by this change and the present uncertainties about the continued existence of the company.

The policy of the new company would be to retain the manufacturer's representative relationship with these men, but to undertake a strong effort to build their morale by offering fullest technical support, competitive prices, and the promise of new products to fill out their lines.

In addition, a sales analysis program will be instituted to pinpoint the sources of sales and to direct efforts of the sales force towards these sources. Sales potential for a given customer cannot be measured accurately by past history. Sales of machines to a good customer can be spaced several years apart and so a look at past history is not an effective way to tell where sales will be coming from in the near future. Sales patterns are probably more accurately determined by evaluating customers' potential needs and growth trends. A program of this sort will be undertaken.

The Thomson sales strategy will be to regain the New England–New York areas as its prime market and work toward developing customers in this area. Thomson will regard its task as that of supplying resistance welder and other assorted equipment to its customers so that Thomson can become a source for a complete installation. There is a prime opportunity for this approach with transistor manufacturers, as discussed further below.

New products and developments

Several steps can be taken to improve the present product line:

1. Dry boxes and related items. Currently there is no manufacturer of transistor welders who is capable of equipping his machinery with a dry box (to provide a special atmosphere during welding). These items are subcontracted, or more often the customer buys the welder and ships it to a dry box builder for installation of this equipment. The technology is not difficult and with a little effort Thomson should be able to obtain a large portion of this business. The dry box and its associated vacuum oven, and high vacuum pumping system, can double the cost of the installation so that there is a sales potential of about $200,000 or more that is obtainable.

2. Flash welders. The Thomson patents on the synchromatic flash welder control mechanism expire in about three or four years. It is possible to make significant, patentable improvements in this mechanism giving a more flexible control and a lower cost. Development of these improvements will protect

Thomson's flash welder position and provide ammunition for a sales promotion campaign that should generate considerable additional flash welder business. Thomson flash welders are presently overpriced, and the new developments coupled with the planned price reductions on this line will bring flash welder prices in line with competitors so that Thomson will be able to offer a machine that is widely accepted as a superior product at a competitive price.

3. **Other products.** In searching for other products that will fit Thomson's marketing and production capabilities two alternate criteria will be considered. First, a new product should be an item that is not now being produced effectively in the New England area, and is sufficiently complex that a geographical factor in determining market areas will be important. (The effect of geography on Thomson's present product line is discussed in Appendix I.) As an alternate to this, a product that is sufficiently unique that geography is of no importance in determining market areas will be considered. Industrial applications of the laser is an excellent area for search in this second classification. Laser welding technique is a technique that is potentially usable by many of Thomson's present transistor customers in the fabrication of microminiature electronic packages. However, an investment in developing metallurgical and other skills would be required and this could not be undertaken immediately.

Pricing

Exhibit VIII[2] shows a contribution analysis by product line. This analysis shows that to achieve planned profits in the first year a total contribution of $312,000 will be required and that $214,000 of this can be obtained by following current pricing policies on parts and noncompetitive segments of the machinery line (transistor welders, brake shoe welders, some specialized flash welders). The balance can be obtained by quoting on price sensitive negotiations at prices designed to produce a contribution of 27 percent. This would amount to a 16 percent price reduction if estimates were perfect. However, some allowance should be made for imperfect estimates of costs, and so a 10 percent price reduction seems to be justified. This would reduce contribution to 33 percent and bring prices in line with competition.

The company's policy will be to meet competitive prices in all bidding situations where distances or other factors are not important and so long as a contribution of at least 27 percent can be obtained. This will result in substantial price reductions in many cases and should be helpful in improving morale of sales personnel.

Personnel

The president of the new company will be the writer, Peter W. Allen. A resume is attached. Other operating personnel will largely remain with the company. These include the following key people:

Merrit Whitney—middle fifties; Vice President. Many years experience in New England and with Thomson selling resistance welders. Is widely known throughout the area and is highly regarded as an expert in the field of resistance welding.

Jack Means—late forties; Plant Superintendent. Many years experience in the
 Thomson shop and as shop superintendent.
Justice Martin—middle fifties. Many years of experience in sales engineering
 and engineering at Thomson.
Frank Lester—early fifties. Experienced welding engineer recently hired from
 National Electric Welder Co.
Sam McDonald—middle thirties. Experienced sales engineer recently hired
 from National Electric Welder Co.

 The above is a partial list of employees with valuable technical experience in
the field of resistance welding and special machinery. The company has excellent technical capabilities.

Facilities—history and products

 Appendix I attached describes in detail the industry, the market, and
Thomson's place in the market. In other parts of the report are a customer's list
and selected bulletins describing the products.[3]

Backlog

 The backlog is currently at about $165,000 and includes $150,000 in machinery orders. All current orders are for proven equipment of a standard, semistan-
dard type, or similar to equipment built previously.

Merger and acquisition possibilities

 The machine tool industry has been operating below capacity for several
years. The resulting shakeout has undoubtedly created opportunities to acquire
machine tool manufacturers at distress prices. The opportunity thus presents
itself to acquire companies of this sort, liquidating assets as necessary until a
combination of sales has been built up that matches the remaining capacity. A
program of this sort for Thomson would consist of acquiring other smaller
manufacturers on a stock exchange basis in an attempt to build the sales volume
up to a better relationship with plant capacity. An approach to several smaller
concerns would be desirable in order to insure that present owners held a
relatively larger share of stock than any one new partner. Such a program could
generate a very rapid rise in profits as sales climbed above the breakeven point.

---

[1]Part of Exhibit V has been included in this case.
[2]Exhibit VIII has been included in this case.
[3]These have been included in this case.

EXHIBIT V (b)
Breakeven calculation

	Fixed costs	Variable costs
Cost of sales:		
Material		30.0%
Direct labor		12.0
Factory overhead	$108	8.0
Direct engineering............		4.5
Subtotal	$108	54.5%
Operating expense:		
Engineering	$ 30	
Administrative	38	
Accounting	27	
Sales..........................	75	9.0
Subtotal	$170	9.0%
Other:		
Interest	$ 30	
Total	$308	63.5%

$$\text{Breakeven} = \frac{308}{1 - .635} = \$845,000$$

EXHIBIT VIII
Contribution analysis

Basic sales goals	$850,00
Associated fixed costs (Ex. V)	306,00
Associated planned profit (Ex. V)	6,00
Total to be Covered by Contribution	$312,00

Sources of contribution	Percent contribution	Expected sales	Contribu earnec
Parts*	50%	$150,000	$ 75,00
Contract machining †	29	30,000	9,00
Noncompetitive welders ‡....................	43	300,000	130,00
Total			$214,00
Balance needed to achieve planned profit			$ 98,00
Sales needed to achieve goals		370,000	
Total		$850,000	

Percent contribution needed $\frac{98,000}{370,000} = 26\%$.

Allowable price cut 43% – 26% = 17%.

*Parts are priced at twice manufacturing cost.
†Assuming $7/hr. average selling price and $5/hr. variable costs.
‡Based on current pricing formula.
  Note: Some business is now being taken at less than a 43 percent contribution due to lowered prices. Also an allowance shou
be made for estimating errors. The average price cut on competitive items should probably be about 10 percent. Greater cuts wou
be justified in individual cases.

RESUME of PETER W. ALLEN

43 Elm Crest Road Telephone 245-4937
Wakefield
Massachusetts
Married, five children 5 feet 10; 175 lbs. Good health

Job objective

--*To obtain a responsible management position* in a small- to medium-size manufacturing firm producing products of a technical nature.

Education

1961–63

HARVARD GRADUATE SCHOOL OF BUSINESS ADMINISTRATION
--*Candidate for degree* of master of business administration in June 1963. Second-year program emphasis is on production and factory management. In top third of first-year class. Education financed largely through personal savings.

CASE INSTITUTE OF TECHNOLOGY
Cleveland, Ohio

1944–48

--*Received degree* of bachelor of science in mechanical engineering cum laude, January 1948. Took extra courses in physics, mathematics, and aerodynamics.
--Member of Theta Tau honorary engineering fraternity, Phi Delta Theta social fraternity, and vice president of graduating class.

1950–51

--*Took additional post graduate courses* at Case in industrial engineering.

Employment

1962

THOMSON ELECTRIC WELDER CO.
Lynn, Mass.
--Employed at this company during summer after first year of business school and currently on a part-time basis as a sales engineer and design engineer. Duties include machine design, estimating and preparation of proposals for bids. Company products are resistance welders and special machinery.

FEDERAL-WARCO DIVISION,
MCKAY MACHINE CO. Warren, Ohio
--This company was formerly known as the Federal Machine and Welder Co. Products are stamping presses, resistance welders, and other special associated machinery.

1958–61

--*Chief draftsman.* Duties were supervisory and included scheduling of engineering work load, supervision of designers, coordination of engineering with other departments, purchase and followup on machinery bought from other manufacturers, design review with customers, and production line startup and tryout activities.

‑‑Was involved in such projects as automatic feeding and welding of transistors, automatic lines for fabrication of washing machine tubs, and various special welding and forming machines.

1956–58   ‑‑*Assistant chief sales engineer.* Duties consisted of preparation of proposals on special machinery, customer negotiation at all stages, and supervision of other sales engineers in these areas.

1951–56   ‑‑*Designer* of special machinery and later sales engineer preparing proposals on special machinery.

Military   ‑‑*Served in Navy* in officer training V-12 program during World War II. Discharged at end of war before completion of training. No present service obligation.

Recent community activities   ‑‑*Member of board of directors* and twice president of active community theatre organization engaged in profitably operating its own theatre. Member of board of directors of local chapter of American Welding Society. Directed a highly successful publicity campaign for this organization. Member of Junior Chamber of Commerce. Associated with introduction of Junior Achievement to Warren, Ohio.

Interests   ‑‑Present recreational interests include theatre, sailing, and skiing.

Early background   ‑‑*Grew up* in Niagara Falls, N.Y. Attended public high school. Member of National Honor Society, and president of high school fraternity. Active in scouting as Eagle Scout, Sea Scout, and member of the Order of the Arrow. Father was engineering executive in packaging machinery industry.

‑‑Undertook a two-year deepwater sailboat cruise through the Caribbean and around Central America with three comrades in 1949 and 1950. During this period worked for short intervals as door-to-door salesman, shipping clerk, construction laborer, and Panama Canal guard.

Patents   ‑‑*Inventor* of a device for sorting steel-backed silver switch contacts. Also have developed a flash welder control system which will likely result in patents.

References   ‑‑Will forward personal references on request.

5 November 1962

Customers—Thomson Electric Welder Co.

Custom Engineered Welders
The Budd Co.
General Electric Co.
Electrolux Corp.
American Motors Co.
Peerless Manufacturing Co.
Foxboro Co.
Bendix Aviation Corp. (Friez Instrument Div.)
Sonotone Co.
A. D. Little Mfg. Co.
Morrison Machine Co.
Westinghouse Electric Corp.
Ford Motor Co.

Standard Products Welders
Gilbert & Bennett Co.
Pittsburgh Steel Co.
American Steel & Wire Co.
Sheffield Steel Corp.
Colorado Fuel & Iron Corp.
Chevrolet Div. of General Motors Corp.
Kelsey-Hayes Co.
Chrysler Corp.
Raybestos
    Div.—Raybestos-Manhattan, Inc.
Budd Co.
RCA Victor
Pittsburgh Plate Glass Co.
Perfection Stove Co.
Zippo Mfg. Co.
Northern Pacific Railway
Metals & Controls Co.
Minneapolis-Honeywell Regulator Co.
Mesta Machine Co.
Hot Point Co.
A. C. Gilbert Co.
Electrolux Corp.
Simonds Saw & Steel Co.
General Electric Co.
Westinghouse Electric Corp.
Reynolds Metals Co.
Bailey Co.
Leeds & Northrup Co.
Echlin Mfg. Co.

Aircraft Welders
Ford Motor Co.
Rohr Aircraft Co.
Aluminum Cooking Utensil Co.
No. American Aviation
Convair Division
Anemostat Corp.
Bendix Aviation Corp.
Douglas Aircraft Co.
Ryan Aeronautical Co.

Spot, seam and flash
Surface Combustion Co.
Ingersoll Div. of Borg Warner Corp.
American Machine
Moore Corp.
Solar Aircraft Co.
Fenton Steel
W. R. Ames Co.
American Saw & Mfg. Co.
Bourne Products Co.
Bell & Gossett
Bohn Aluminum
John Wood Mfg. Co.
Metal Fabricators Co.
Sexton Can Co.
Metal Products Div. of Thompson Ind., Inc.
Baltimore Air Coil Co.
Reynolds Metals Co.
Copco Steel & Die Co.
Convair Co.
Cooper Alloy Co.
Ceco Steel Co.
Cleveland Twist Drill Co.
Millers Falls Co.
Wasco Flashing Co.
Westinghouse Electric Corp.
General Electric Co.
J. S. Thorn Co.
Michael Flynn Co.
Alcasco Products Co.
Sunlight Metal Co.
Aluminum Home Products Co.
Soule Steel Co.

Foreign shipment welders
Cosa Corp. of Japan

Henry G. Thompson & Sons Co.
Sprague Electric Co.
Sylvania Electric Co.
Raytheon Mfg. Co.
Pratt & Whitney Div.—United Aircraft Corp.
Robertshaw-Fulton Thermostat Co.

Kito Mfg. Co., Japan
General Electric Co., Puerto Rico
Westinghouse Corp., Roseberry, Australia
Arc Engineering Supply Co., Johannesburg, S.A.
Esso Standard Oil Co., Venezuela, South America
Mitsubishi Co., Japan
Crittal Mfg. Co., England

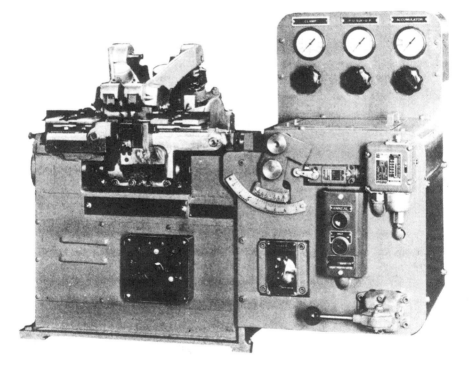

The Thomson Model FOB-10 KVA with synchromatic push up, air operated alligator clamps, and ball bushing platen mounting. Excellent for rods, wire, rings, and small sections. Superior for steel, stainless steel, copper, aluminum, copper to aluminum, brass, bronze, titanium, and all other weldable metals. Rugged, simple, easily adjusted, and economical. The design, construction, and field-proven performance of this welder reflects Thomson's years of experience in making resistance welding machinery.

APPENDIX I
The resistance welding industry
and
Thomson Electric Welding Co.

THE RESISTANCE WELDING INDUSTRY

The resistance welding process is one of the least known and yet one of the most important industrial techniques in use in the American economy. The process is used to permanently join metal stampings for automotive, appliance, and other industrial and consumer products. The equipment used in resistance welding is comparatively expensive. Prices range from several thousand dollars up to as high as a hundred thousand dollars for a machine. The equipment is often special in nature and highly automated. This is because the resistance welding process lends itself well to mass production techiques such as use of automatic transfer equipment and automatic feeding. The manufacture of equipment for this industry can be a challenging and rewarding career as one becomes involved in a field that is of fundamental importance to the American economy and also offers unlimited opportunities for imagination and ingenuity.

The process

The resistance welding process is relatively unknown outside of the industries involved in its application. It is often confused with arc welding, but there are fundamental differences between this process and the arc welding process. The basic technique in making a welded joint is to pass a high level of current (5,000 to 100,000 amperes) through a concentrated area of metal for a very short period of time and while maintaining the joint under pressure. The high current level very rapidly heats the joint to the melting point due to the electrical resistance of the material. However, the molten metal is contained by forces applied thru the current-conducting electrodes until the metal cools and solidifies. The process is very rapid and a spot weld may be made in about 1.0 to 1.5 seconds. The characteristics of the process described, such as the rapidity with which a weld can be made and the absence of an arc, make the process suitable for high production welding of sheet metal parts such as automobile stampings, metal desks and cabinets, wire fencing and a multitude of other applications.

There are five basic resistance welding techniques—spot, projection, seam, butt, and flash welding. The most common is spot welding. This method results in the formation of round fused nuggets, or spot welds, roughly ¼" in diameter. Welds can be made one at a time on standard machines or a larger number of welds can be made simultaneously with multi-head machines. Automobile floor pans and refrigerator back panels are generally spot welded.

Projection welding is a variation of spot welding technique wherein dimples are pre-formed in one of the two metal stampings so as to permit making a number of welds simultaneously with flat or contoured current-carrying dies. A well-known example would be the joining of a handle on a Revere Ware kitchen piece to the body.

The seam welding process is related to spot welding in that a series of closely spaced spot welds are made by feeding flat stock through a pair of opposed rotating wheels. Oil drums, pails, and ammunition boxes are typical examples of this welding process.

The butt welding process is used to join small bars or rods end to end. In this case the two pieces are butted under pressure and current is passed through the joint until it is soft. Additional pressure then forges the two pieces to make a weld. Curtain rings are often butt welded.

The flash welding process is similar to butt welding but differs basically from all of the previous processes in that the welding heat is developed by a very violent arc rather than by the resistance of the metal itself. An arc is struck between the two pieces to be welded and allowed to "flash" until sufficient heat has been built up to forge the parts together. This technique permits welding large sections up to several square inches in area. Typical applications include joining of strip in steel mills, welding of tire rims, or welding aluminum window frames.

The welder manufacturing industry

The welding machine industry is a capital goods industry and welding machines would be classed as machine tools. Users of resistance welding machinery are also generally users of stamping presses, roll-forming mills, and other high production machine tools.

The welding machine manufacturers can be divided into two groups. There are approximately eight or ten leading manufacturers, most of whom are members of the Resistance Welder Manufacturers' Association. This association reports annual sales of its members totaling in the order of $30 million per year. There are perhaps as many as 20 other manufacturers not members of the association producing about another $30 million of the machinery a year. For the most part, these other manufacturers are small and serve local areas. In addition, the major users of the process, in some cases, build their own equipment so that the total market for machinery is probably in the neighborhood of $70 to $80

TABLE 1
Comparison of resistance welder industry with
machine tool industry (000,000)

Year	RWMA sales*	Machine tool sales†
1953	$24	$1,191
1954	22	892
1955	31	670
1956	48	886
1957	31	844
1958	20	411
1959	25	413
1960	29	508
1961	25	507

*Resistance Welder Manufacturers' Association.
†National Machine Tool Builders Association—cutting machine tools.

million per year. Sales vary from year to year in the same general pattern as the machine tool industry. (See Table 1.)

In addition to welding machine manufacturers, there are a number of manufacturers of specialized components for the resistance welding industry. These include builders of control panels, specialized air cylinders, and welding transformers.

The market

The principal market area is the Midwest, running from Cleveland to Chicago. This area includes a major portion of the automobile stamping plants and the large appliance manufacturers, plus a number of smaller companies making parts for these people. Most of the larger equipment builders are located in this area. Because of the high production rates encountered, much of the equipment sold to these larger customers found here is special in nature.

The welder business in the Midwest is highly competitive. Further, delivery is often a very important factor, particularly in the automotive industry. In general, in order to compete successfully in this part of the country as a resistance welder manufacturer one must be able to offer highly competitive prices, high levels of skill, and the ability to move fast and meet delivery promises.

The market for machinery in other parts of the country includes a larger pecentage of smaller companies. Smaller resistance welding manufacturers have appeared in several of these areas to service these customers. There are several companies in the New York City area supplying equipment for a number of small users there. California is another market and there are several manufacturers in that area. New England is also a market typified by smaller users. Thomson Electric Welder is the only machinery builder in this area. As production rates are generally lower and runs shorter, one does not find the need for special machines in these other parts of the country. Thus, a greater percentage of the machines sold are standard machines, usable for a variety of applications.

The user of resistance welder machinery is concerned primarily with achieving a certain assurance of quality and service. He thus selects as bidders for his applications those manufacturers whom he regards as most effective for him in these two respects. Most of the nationally known major manufacturers would qualify with most users with respect to quality because of their reputation. However, a user will often work with the nearest manufacturer more closely because of the importance he places on service. In situations where reputation and service are reasonably equal among several equipment builders, then price becomes an important factor and the pricing will be very competitive. This situation prevails throughout the Midwest.

It can be seen that there is a definite geographical orientation to the market. The customer's estimate of his service needs will often lead him to favor the closest suppliers of equipment. This factor becomes extremely important when the equipment is special in nature and it is expected that continuing contact between the customer and the builder will be required in the development of the machine and tryout and debugging process. It follows that it would be very difficult for a manufacturer outside the Midwest area to compete in that area in the sale of special machinery. A manufacturer from outside the Midwest with a quality reputation, however, could expect to compete successfully in the sale of equipment where service and customer contact would not be an important factor, as for example standard machines. However, prices would have to be competitive with local manufacturers. On the other hand, users in New England tend to turn to the only manufacturer in this area, Thomson Electric Welder Co., because of the service advantage. The manufacturer nearest Thomson of comparable reputation is in Warren, Ohio, approximately 600 miles away.

Characteristics of welding equipment manufacturers

The manufacturers of welding equipment can be divided into two groups. One of these groups would be made up of the larger nationally known companies. Manufacturers in this group have annual sales of approximately $1 million per year or more, and build a full line of standard machines and a variety of special machines. Most of these companies are located in the Midwest. These companies all sell nationwide, using manufacturers' representatives and company salesmen. The major part of the sales, particularly for special machinery, is in the Midwest.

Although all of these nationally known companies build a full line of machines, each company tends to specialize and develop an expertise in a particular line. This occurs because customers, as discussed above, feel that quality is so important that they tend to favor the more successful manufacturer of each type of machine. Also, as a manufacturer specializes he gains a price advantage in reduced engineering costs on future equipment of the same type.

The Thomson Electric Welder Co. may be considered a member of this group. Although its sales are low compared to the others, its reputation is national and the company maintains sales outlets throughout the country. Thomson has specialized in the flash welder and transistor segments of the industry and is widely regarded as the leading manufacturer of machines for these applications.

The other group of manufacturers consists of smaller companies that do not have national reputations. These companies will generally not manufacture a full line and will sell largely in the geographical area around them. In their area, these companies generally offer equipment at lower prices than the national manufacturers, as these companies are much smaller and do not carry the overhead required to maintain a national selling effort. In view of the local nature of the operations of these companies and their limited scope in equipment offered, they cannot maintain a reputation or compete with the larger manufacturers outside their own areas.

Technological change

The resistance welding process is an old one. It was first invented by Elihu Thomson (founder of Thomson Electric Welder Co.) in 1884. The basic technique was fully developed by World War II. There has been no significant technological change since that time except in certain specialized areas. It is highly unlikely that any other process can be developed for joining sheet metal as efficiently and rapidly as the resistance welding method.

The technical change that does occur revolves around the development of specialized machines and improved components. None of these changes are of such a nature that they supply a material advantage to a manufacturer in other than some special segment of the business.

To the writer's knowledge, there are only two significant patents now in force. One of these relates to a method of using a three-phase power supply for resistance welding machines. This patent is held by Sciaky Brothers in Chicago. The other patent covers an improved flash welder control mechanism and is held by the Thomson Electric Co. These two patents provide significant advantages for their owners in the areas where they are applicable.

The technology of resistance welding is rather widely known among the large users in the Midwest. This results in the use of detailed specifications on new machinery and a great deal of involvement of the customer in the design of the equipment. On the other hand, in other areas of the country, the customer is often unfamiliar with the basic technology and will generally allow the manufacturer to supply equipment that he deems suitable.

THOMSON ELECTRIC WELDER CO.

The Thomson Electric Welder Co. is made up of three divisions, two located in Michigan, and the third, a parent division, located in Lynn, Massachusetts. The Lynn Division manufactures resistance welders and the other two produce metal stampings for the automotive companies.

History

The Thomson Electric Welder Co. was founded in 1884 by Mr. Elihu Thomson, the inventor of the resistance welding process. Mr. Thomson was associated with the company for many years. He was also a member of the M.I.T. faculty, active in many other scientific areas, and a holder of a number of patents.

In the early 1930s Thomson bought out the Gibb Electrical Co., a competitor in the manufacture of resistance welders, located in Bay City, Michigan. The Gibb operations were moved to Lynn and for a time the company was known as the Thomson Gibb Co. At about this same time the metal stamping operations were started in a building vacated by the Gibb concern in Bay City. Over the years this metal stamping operation grew substantially and now consists of two separate companies, the Rolled Products Division and the Welded Products Division of Thomson Electric Welder Co.

In 1959 the three Thomson divisions were purchased by Seton Corporation, a corporation which had been organized by Textron to take advantage of certain tax situations. The company has operated under this arrangement until the present date. At the moment a management group associated primarily with the two metal stamping divisions is in the process of negotiating the purchase of the three Thomson divisions from Seton. It is expected that this negotiation will be completed shortly. This group plans to sell or liquidate the Lynn division. The remaining portion of this paper is concerned only with manufacturing at the Lynn division.

Product history

For many years Thomson built a full line of standard and special resistance welders. Since World War II the emphasis has been placed chiefly on standard machines, as Thomson has found that it cannot compete with other leading manufacturers in the Midwest due to its geographical location.

Table 2 is a breakdown of sales by territory and by product line. It can be seen from this exhibit that flash welders are an important part of the Thomson sales. Thomson has been able to establish a strong reputation for flash welders throughout the country, largely as a result of the development of a superior control mechanism. The Thomson flash welder can do welding jobs that cannot be done on competitors' machines, such as joining copper and aluminum bus bars. It also can do a more effective job on other applications such as aluminum window frames. The Thomson flash welder, however, offers no real superiority for many common applications involving the welding of steel parts.

Thomson has also developed a line of welders that are used by transistor manufacturers. This development has been largely due to the concentration of transistor manufacturers in the northeast part of the country, so that Thomson was a natural source for them to turn to. Thomson's competitive advantage in this

TABLE 2
Thomson product distribution by area where sold and by type

Area	Percent of total welder sales	Product	Percent of total welder sales
New England	24	Transistor welders	19
Mid-Atlantic	16	Flash welders	39
South Atlantic	10	Standard general	
Midwest	41	purpose welders	21
Export	6	Special welders	18
Other	3	Other	3
Total	100	Total	100

Breakdown by area for each product type (in percent of total sales)

Area	Flash welders	Transistor welders	Standard general purpose welders	Special welders
New England	4	17	47	64
Mid-Atlantic	0	40	21	16
South Atlantic	13	8	11	0
Midwest	77	22	21	0
Export	6	10	0	20
Other	0	3	0	0
Total	100	100	100	100

Note: Above results taken from an analysis of machinery sales for a 10-month period in 1962. Parts sales not included.

business chiefly lies in some measure of experience and an advantageous location. There are no significant technical differences in the equipment supplied by Thomson and competitors for transistor welding.

As shown in Table 2, Thomson sells throughout the country and has representatives in all significant marketing areas. Greatest sales occur in the Midwest and the New England and New York areas. Midwest sales are largely for flash welders, while the sales in the East are for other standard machines, transistor welders, and some special machinery.

At the present time, Thomson prices are generally higher than competitors' and this has resulted, in the opinion of the writer, in a reduced share of the market over recent years. See Table 3 for sales and profits in past years.

TABLE 3
Thomson Electric Welder Division
recent sales and profits (losses) (000)

Year	Sales	Profit before taxes
1953	$1,851	$404
1954	1,539	305
1955	1,119	110
1956	1,595	139
1957	1,483	101
1958	1,103	(38)
1959	1,284	93
1960	1,321	(46)
1961	954	(79)
1962*	1,080	(91)

*Estimated from 10 months' data.

Operations

Inquiries are normally received either directly from customers or from sales representatives or salesmen. Quotations are then prepared for these inquiries. The preparation of a quotation involves a determination of the type of machine to be quoted and the determination of a price, either from standard pricing or by making an estimate of the material and labor and applying a pricing formula. It is often necessary for a sales engineer to visit the customer to work out in detail what is to be quoted. Also, depending on the complexity of the job, it may be necessary to make several quotations over a period of time and before an order can be obtained.

When an order has been received, it is turned over to the engineering department. This department releases standard parts and designs new equipment as required. The engineering skills required for designers are not particularly unique—i.e., a machine designer experienced on other types of equipment can fairly easily transfer his knowledge to the design of resistance welders. Engineering supervision, however, must be well versed in resistance welding techniques and applications. The electrical engineering requirements consist of the design of welding transformers and machine relay control systems, both of which are fairly straightforward.

The manufacturing facilities of Thomson are typical of a job shop type machine shop. There are facilities for welding and machining virtually all the components used on resistance welders. There are also facilities for building transformers and for testing the finished equipment.

Steve O. Handley

On Monday, February 8, 1971 Steve Handley was discussing the financial statements of Modern Industries, Incorporated, with his associate Ed Irwin in the larger of the two rooms that the company used for offices. "Ed, we are going to have to be real salesmen if we are going to get someone to invest on any basis in a company with a six-month's loss of $35,000 and a net worth of $17,000. And I have the feeling that an auditor isn't going to try to increase the value of that inventory for us."

Ed shook his head. "If we can't get rid of the royalty payments, we can't raise the money anyway. What we really need is to get this alternating current (A.C.) unit ready and get ourselves out on the road and do our selling there."

Background: Post business school experience

After graduating from Harvard Business School in June of 1969, Steve Handley had accepted a job in Seattle, Washington, with the Tech Data Systems Division of Logitech, Ltd., a small firm with its home office in Natick, Massachusetts. As vice president and general manager, Steve had been given the task at Tech to work with two scientist-engineers who had developed an information system which could be used as an inexpensive credit check on credit card users each time a credit card purchase was made. Steve had the responsibility for the entire marketing program and for setting up the layout for high-volume production of the system whose sales in early 1969 had been at the rate of approximately $1 million per year.

For the first six months work had gone well and by January 1970 manufacturing operations had been transferred and set up in a

231

13,000-square-foot facility with total out-of-pocket costs of approximately $50,000.

During this period Steve had been kept informed of the parent company's pending $2 million financing which had been "going to close within the next couple of weeks" for more than two months. Early in February he was told by telephone that he should drastically reduce all cash expenses immediately because the continuing delays in the financing had produced a severe financial strain. In short, the parent company was almost out of cash.

Over the next several months Steve had cut back operations and had attempted to learn when he might expect more funds to be available. Late in July, he received a telephone call from a vice president at the New England office of Honeywell, Inc., whose receivables contained approximately $250,000 owed by Logitech. In addition to mentioning this debt, the Honeywell vice president mentioned that his company had an interest in a contract in which Logitech was to supply a major airline with an automatic vending system for tickets. He further indicated that Honeywell was interested in Logitech, but because Honeywell wanted more of a management type of president (as opposed to a promoter), they wanted to talk to Steve about the possibility of taking over operations. If this were done, Honeywell would be in a position to provide money to pay off creditors and to supply working capital for the company. Steve then flew to Boston, discussed the situation further with Honeywell, and on August 20th met with the Logitech president and presented his proposal. At a rather stormy session the president turned down Steve's plan, and the next day Steve returned to Seattle.

About a week later, however, Steve received a telephone call from one of the directors who thought that in the interests of everyone concerned Steve should present his proposal to the board again. Steve then flew to the director's home-town for the weekend and then to Boston where after three days of discussions, which from time to time became very emotional and bitter, Steve was promised the resignation of the president and the board should he be able to raise the financing. Steve then contacted the vice president at Honeywell to learn that Honeywell was no longer interested in Logitech. On September 4, 1970, Steve returned to Seattle to look for a job.

The search

Steve first drew up a resume (see Exhibit 1) and with it approached several friends—bankers, business acquaintances, and so on—who could provide introductions. Through them, Steve located two companies, one in consumer goods and the other in peripheral computer equipment, each of which was seeking a vice president of marketing and was prepared to pay someone with Steve's background and experience around $35,000/year. Steve refused both offers. At that point he decided that he was psychologically unemployable and that he should seek out a situation where he would be in charge and not have his future depend largely upon someone else's abilities.

Steve began by calling on financial sources in the Seattle area to see what kinds of deals they would finance and by talking to people who might have leads to businesses that needed management and financing. These individuals included bankers, finders, venture capitalists, consultants, stock brokers, and other people who were "centers of influence" in the business community. In early November a trust officer at one of the banks introduced Steve to Ed Irwin, a graduate of the University of Washington Law School, who was also looking for a company. The same age as Steve, Ed had practiced law for a year and a half, had spent a year with Boise Cascade setting up a Plastics Division, and had subsequently left with one of the group vice presidents to start a venture which never got financed. At the time Steve met him, Ed was in debt by about $60,000 from an unsuccessful venture which he had started while in law school and was looking for a situation of his own. (A copy of Ed's resume is shown in Exhibit 2.)

After a number of discussions, Steve and Ed decided to join forces and see if together they could find what they were looking for. Steve saw in Ed a complementary personality. Ed was much more of an optimist, much more of an aggressive person, and was therefore more inclined to plunge into things. Steve believed that he himself was more conservative and would be more inclined both to look more carefully at details and to move more slowly into a new situation. Together they would make a good team.

By mid-January, three situations had been located which showed sufficient promise for further investigation. The largest was a keyboard manufacturer, Mastertron Computer Equipment, which produced a memory/logic keyboard for the data processing industry and had achieved an annual sales volume of approximately $3 million. The company was considerably underfinanced, however, and was trying to raise $1 million while also seeking new management—including a president. Steve and Ed had obtained a nonexclusive finder's agreement with the company which would provide, if Steve and Ed were instrumental in obtaining the financing, a 5 percent fee. Because of the large size of this company, however, Steve and Ed had about concluded that any management/ownership deal which they might work out would involve very limited equity and stock options and very limited control. On the other hand, because the company appeared to have huge potential growth, it remained attractive.

The second company, Wood Specialty Products, was a firm owned by two friends which did approximately $2 million in annual sales. Because the company had no debt and a net worth of over $700,000, Steve had first thought that it might be possible to buy all of the company based upon the future profits and the immediate leverage available from the company's balance sheet. After looking at the company's manufacturing operations, however, it appeared that buying lumber was a key factor in the company's success and that this expertise had been developed by the current owners over a period of many years. Steve and Ed concluded that they could not possibly develop the skills needed for buying lumber soon enough to assure that the company would not suffer wide variations in product quality and/or severe reductions in operating performance.

The third situation was a small company, Modern Industries, Incorporated, in business for approximately four years, and managed by the inventor of the company's products. The company had been in financial difficulty and its marketing efforts had been reduced to almost nothing.

Modern Industries, Incorporated

Modern had been founded in September of 1966 to produce and market a direct current (D.C.) power converter, the Dynamote, which had been developed by Mr. Frank R. Schneider. Schneider had little formal technical training, but had worked several years as a technician. The original converter was designed to obtain 1,200 watts of 110 volt direct current from the alternator of a truck or car, and it was intended to compete with other sources of auxiliary and remote electrical power.

Since early 1968 when initial sales of the product had been made, approximately 5,000 units of the converter had been sold. During that time, Mr. Schneider had continued product development, and by December 1970, he had designed one model of the power converter to produce 3,600 watts and had expanded the product line to include an alternator-powered arc welder, a hot start with battery charge, and a power inverter to transform vehicle alternator output to 60-cycle alternating current (A.C.) with up to 3,000 watts of power. Prototype models of the inverter had been used to operate a small air conditioner and other tools and appliances but the device had not yet gone into production. A price list of the Dynamote power systems is shown in Exhibit 3.

Modern had originally come to Steve and Ed's attention on December 17 at a meeting with one of the principals of International Business Development Corporation (IBDC), a small firm established to provide assistance and a limited amount of capital to fledgling companies. At that meeting the Modern situation had been described as ready for rapid growth if the right management could be found. The IBDC representative had indicated that they would assist in getting Frank Schneider to step down as president and to agree to an equity incentive for the new president. It was also revealed at this meeting that IBDC had just completed for Modern a private placement of $35,000 in debt with warrants thereby relieving the company's current financial problems. Upon further inquiry Steve and Ed had been shown monthly projections of the company's performance for the following year. (See Exhibit 4.) These figures indicated that operations would be profitable after accumulating a three-month loss of $18,095 and that profit before taxes for the year would be $261,440 on total sales of $907,500.

On January 4, Steve and Ed met with one of the principals from IBDC, Al Bond, and indicated that they would like to arrange to see Frank Schneider. They also wanted to see how they might be able to participate in the ownership of the company, should it look attractive. Al had expressed some concern at the prospect of both Steve and Ed coming with Modern because of the additional overhead burden it would create. He indicated, however, that some kind of six-month to one-year option could be arranged for, roughly 30,000 shares at $2.50 to $3.00/share. Ownership of the company, Al explained, was as follows:

	Shares
Frank Schneider	52,000
Jim Guhlke*	52,000
IBDC	40,000
Int'l United	5,500
Other stockholders	24,000
Recent investors (warrants)	(35,000)

*A founder with Frank Schneider and formerly a vice president of Modern.

In addition, there was a royalty agreement which provided for Schneider, Guhlke, and IBDC each to receive 2 percent of sales.

On January 8 Steve and Ed had gone to see Frank Schneider at the company's offices, a rented property in a commercial section of a suburb just north of Seattle. The buildings had originally been built as a two-bedroom ranch-style house but subsequently had been converted to provide a reception room, two offices, and a "laboratory" upstairs and a large storage room, production area, and assembly section in the basement. As the assembly space was located in what formerly had been a double garage, receiving and shipping were handled through the large doorway at one side. Most of the parts, including chassis, electronic components, and brackets, were subcontracted to outside vendors and only assembly, testing, and the production of a few special items were done by Modern. The largest item produced in-house was a special transformer which was wound on a small transformer winding machine, lacquered by hand and dried in the oven of a three-burner efficiency kitchen stove which had been left in the house by the previous occupant.

Frank had received Steve and Ed cordially, and they thought he had been open and responsive to their questions. They learned that prior to starting Modern, Frank had been active in a venture set up to distribute a special automobile oil filter similar to one which had been advertised for many years in *Popular Mechanics* and *Mechanix Illustrated.* Before that, Frank had served for 12 years as a full-time minister for the Assembly of God church.

In answer to their questions about the company's products and competitive power sources, Frank explained that only one other company had attempted to make a similar product, and that it had only D.C. current capability. Before he had developed the original converter, few people had thought of existing automotive alternators as sources for electrical power beyond the requirements of the vehicle's own electrical system. Consequently the other auxiliary and remote power sources had been designed and developed either as generators to be connected with belts and pulleys to the motor of the vehicle (called "piggyback" generators), or as portable, gasoline-powered generator combinations which could be transported in the back of a car or truck. The latter had the advantage over vehicle-mounted power sources in that it could be left on location while the vehicle was being used elsewhere. It had the disadvantages, however, of costing approximately twice as much as Modern's and being much larger and heavier than the inverter system. It also required periodic mechanical maintenance. The mechanically connected power sources were approximately 30 percent more expensive than Modern's, and they were inclined to incur maintenance problems primarily because of failures in the mechanical clutch between the generator and the vehicle's motor. Fitting an additional generator under the hood of a vehicle also made this system difficult to install.

Over the past three years Modern had tried a number of different kinds of distribution systems, none of which had been particularly successful. Frank's partner and co-founder, Jim Guhlke, had originally sought to establish a "pyramid" system of distribution which, not unlike the sales organizations for life insurance companies, would involve several "layers" of salesmen and overrides[1] which would provide strong incentives for "upper level" distributors to recruit and train other distributors. This type of sales organization had been used when the two men had been in the business together distributing oil filters.

After this approach had been attempted several times with little success, Jim had surveyed the Seattle area for various specialty dis-

---

[1]Overrides provide for an individual to receive a commission on sales made by people under his direction. For example, 10 field salesmen may receive a commission of 5 percent of the sales they generate, and their sales supervisor may receive an additional 1 percent of total sales by his group. In addition, the regional sales manager may receive .5 percent of the sales generated by the sales groups of six sales supervisors.

tributors in certain industries: automotive, marine, and so on. Then, with the help of IBDC in May 1969, Modern had made an exclusive agreement with the Engine Accessories Operation of Fairbanks Morse, Inc., a part of Colt Industries. In this agreement, Fairbanks Morse had committed to the purchase of 3,000 units for May through December of 1969; 12,000 units for calendar 1970; and 18,000 units for each year thereafter with cancellation of the agreement being the penalty for nonperformance. Because sales had not approached the minimums prescribed in the agreement it was soon renegotiated; the minimums were omitted and Fairbanks Morse became a nonexclusive distributor. In September of 1970 Jim had left Modern to set up a wig importing and sales business in Seattle where he planned to establish a pyramid system of distribution for his new venture.

After their initial discussion with Frank Schneider, Steve and Ed had made inquiries among Seattle distributors that carried Modern's product line. Although each of the distributors said that they liked the Dynamote, none of the four they visited knew much about the equipment. Only one could install the unit for a customer; the others referred buyers to garages in the neighborhood. Two of the four were uncertain about the differences between alternating and direct current and consequently were not sure about the types of tools or appliances which could be used.

The two partners had difficulty in determining which markets might have the greatest potential for the Dynamote and related equipment. Distributors had reported sales to a wide range of end users including line crews, construction companies, and marine repair yards. To get some feel for the total market potential, Steve gleaned information from the public library, as shown in Table 1.

TABLE 1

Trucks in use in agriculture, construction, and utilities and services	6,385,000
Power boats above 16 feet in length	1,300,000
Current annual production rate on mobile homes	450,000
Current annual production rate on travel trailers	150,000
Current annual production rate on truck campers	130,000
Current annual production rate on camping trailers	100,000
Current annual production rate on motor homes	30,000

The two partners had also discussed Modern and the other two situations with several local bankers (see Exhibit 5).

Steve and Ed had talked to Frank Schneider again on January 18. This time they had inquired more directly about how Frank regarded his situation at Modern and whether or not he might be interested in having them involved in the management of the company. They also asked about the ownership of the company and the royalty agreement which had been set up at the time of IBDC's initial association with the company. (A copy of this agreement is shown in Exhibit 6.) Ed had summarized in Table 2 what he had concluded from the meeting.

TABLE 2

Jim Guhlke	1.	Has 52,000 shares.
	2.	Wants to keep 10,000, but is willing to sell 42,000.
	3.	Needs $24,000 cash.
	4.	Will trade 30,000 Modern shares for Frank's shares in the wig company.
	5.	Has 2 percent royalty rights.
	6.	Owes Frank $0.20/wig sold in the new business.
Frank Schneider	1.	Is willing to trade Canadian company shares to Jim for 30,000 Modern shares.
	2.	Will release 2 percent royalty.
	3.	Will release $0.20/wig royalty.
	4.	Has provided collateral for $35,000 loan.
	5.	Wants all the shares he can get.
	6.	Will sell 30,000 shares received from Jim and loan money to company.
	7.	Now owns 52,000 shares.
Int'l United	1.	Now owns 5,433 shares plus options to purchase 21,732 shares @ $2.50/share (assignable).
	2.	Will sell 5,433 shares for $10,000 and will release options.
IBDC	1.	Owns 40,000 shares.
	2.	Has 2 percent royalty rights.
	3.	Looking primarily for growth of company and maximum appreciation on stock.

Based on the above Steve and Ed put together a possible deal which would provide them with a significant equity position in the company.

TABLE 3

1. Modern issues 2,000 shares each to Schneider, Guhlke, and IBDC for cancellation of royalty agreement.
2. Schneider exchanges Canadian company stock with Guhlke for 30,000 shares of Modern stock.
3. Handley and Irwin buy 30,000 shares of Modern from Schneider @ $2.00/share (money from bank?)
4. Schneider lends money (all or part) to Modern @ 8 percent (?).
5. Handley and Irwin buy 7,000 shares from Guhlke @ $2.00/share.
6. Handley and Irwin buy 5,433 shares from Int'l United.
7. Handley and Irwin get five-year options on remaining treasury stock (21,732 shares) at $2.00/share.

Starting the next day, Steve and Ed made frequent visits to Modern and discussed with Frank the problems of the company. They estimated that the recent lack of marketing activity would cause revenues to be low in the immediate future. With Frank, they went over the cost of purchased parts, labor, and variable overhead for each of the items in the product line. They also inquired about Frank's immediate plans for product development and learned that Frank anticipated that the major portion of the next three months would be spent in bringing the A.C. unit into production. With these things in mind they visited several potential sources of capital and discussed with them the Modern situation. One source had expressed a strong interest in the company if payment of the 6 percent royalties could be discontinued and had indicated that a straight Section 1244 equity investment would be appropriate.

Over the weekend of January 30–31 Steve and Ed discussed the Modern situation in detail. Basically they thought it was attractive both in terms of the potential business which could be developed and the specific contributions they would be able to make. Frank Schneider, they concluded, was a capable, practical designer who could develop additional products with the objective of performance and reliability, rather than the engineer's traditional goal of perfection. In all of their discussions, Frank had repeatedly shown a concern for development and production costs of the equipment he designed. And finally, both Steve and Ed believed that Frank was very anxious to have them join him in the company so they could work on the marketing and administrative aspects of the business while he got back to the design and development work.

The size of the actual demand and how to penetrate the different markets were the two major question marks. Steve believed that lack of product knowledge had severely limited sales thus far. One approach would be to select the major markets in each industrial area and to locate the strongest distributors serving each of these segments. Another approach would be to seek out distributors who dealt primarily in auxiliary-type power equipment and to select the strongest of these. Or they could devote their major efforts toward working with the Fairbanks Morse system already established. Regardless of which way they decided to go, a program would have to be developed to make that approach effective.

On Sunday evening the two partners put together pro forma operating and cash flow statements for high, low, and expected sales levels. They both concluded that the 4 percent in royalties, assuming Frank would give up his 2 percent, would be a major drain on the company and would provide a serious handicap when additional capital had to be raised. (Copies of the pro forma statements are shown in Exhibit 7.) In addition, they concluded that a direct investment in Modern would involve greater risk than they had previously anticipated and that it would not be wise to make as large an investment as they had originally planned.

On the following Wednesday, Steve and Ed met with the two princi- pals of IBDC and proposed that Steve would become president of Modern and that both he and Ed would work at Modern with low salaries ($15,000 each) but with bonuses based on profits. They also proposed that IBDC give up its 2 percent royalty on sales and that Steve and Ed would buy 5,000 shares each at $2/share and each be granted five-year options on 35,000 shares of Modern stock at $2/share. After several hours of discussions some agreement was reached on salaries and options, but no agreement was reached to cancel the royalty agreement, an item which the IBDC people seemed very unwilling to negotiate. Steve and Ed left the meeting with the understanding that a draft of the agreement would be made up and sent to them. A copy of the agreement which Steve received the following Friday, is shown in Exhibit 8.

On Monday, February 8, Steve and Ed met at Modern's offices to go over the company's unaudited 1970 financial statements which Steve had completed over the weekend. A copy of these statements appears in Exhibit 9. Although for December 31, 1970, the company had shown a cash balance of $25,123, the cash balance was now less than $500 be- cause of cash purchases for parts to assemble the new A.C. unit.

Steve's thoughts were scattered by the ringing of the telephone. As Steve talked, Ed doodled several rows of dollar signs on the desk pad. After a few minutes of mostly listening, Steve hung up and threw his pencil on the desk. "Well, if that doesn't beat everything! Now we aren't going to be able to issue 1244 stock. Or we are going to have to do without the options because you can't issue 1244 unless you have only one class of stock and the options are treated as a second class. George says he checked it out, too. You *know* no one is even going to sniff at making an equity investment in this thing if they can't write it off against regular income should we bomb out. And without more money in here, we won't be able to do anything. How big a gamble do you want to take on this one?"

SUGGESTED QUESTIONS

1. What should Steve and Ed do?
2. What is the potential for this company? (How do you make an evaluation of potential in this situation?)
3. What are the key elements for this company to operate successfully? Where should Steve and Ed concentrate their efforts?
4. What should be done to get the buy-in/financing deal back on the tracks?

EXHIBIT 1
Steve O. Handley
Resume of Steve O. Handley

3702 East Prospect	Married
Seattle, Washington 98102	5'9"; 160 lbs.
206-329-8484	Excellent health

Work experience
1969 to present   LOGITECH, LTD.
Vice president and general manager of Tech Data Systems Division in Seattle, Washington. Responsible for all aspects of division operations including marketing, research and development, manufacturing, and finance. Division engaged in the design, manufacture, and marketing of communications oriented data processing systems with sales of approximately $1 million in 1969.

1964–67   IBM CORPORATION
Data Processing Division marketing representative for IBM in Atlanta, Georgia. Managed sales territory consisting of computer users in manufacturing industries. Directed or participated in feasibility studies, systems design, and installation of IBM 1400 and System/360 disk, tape, and card oriented data processing systems for accounting, production control, and inventory control applications. Achieved over 100 percent of sales quota for each of three years.

1961, 1963–64   IBM CORPORATION
Marketing representative trainee. Classroom and on-the-job training to become marketing representative. Included work in programming, systems design, applications, and sales techniques.

1961–63   U.S. ARMY
Lieutenant. Data processing plans and operations officer. Highest ranking officer in Controller Section Data Processing Division, Fort Bliss, Texas, employing approximately 50 military and civilian personnel. Data processing applications included financial, inventory, and personnel accounting. Awarded Army Commendation Medal and Citation. Received honorable discharge.

Summer work
1968   IBM Corporation, Waltham, Mass. Worked as an assistant to branch manager in the areas of marketing and personnel planning. Also acted as a consultant to marketing representatives in sales situations.

Part time
1968   Working through Business Assistance Program at the Harvard Business School. Consulting to Black corporation starting a temporary employment business.

EXHIBIT I (continued)

Education
1967–69   HARVARD BUSINESS SCHOOL
Received Master in Business Administration degree in June 1969. Second-year emphasis directed toward finance and manufacturing. Electives include management of lending, capital asset allocation and management, manufacturing policy, small manufacturing enterprises. Elected Student Association representative for first and second year. Member of Finance, Marketing, New Enterprise Clubs.

1957–61   GEORGIA INSTITUTE OF TECHNOLOGY
Received Bachelor of Mechanical Engineering degree in June 1961. Alfred P. Sloan Foundation Scholar. Elected to Tau Beta Pi, Omicron Delta Kappa, Pi Tau Sigma, member of Sigma Alpha Epsilon. Elected to Student Council two years, senior class secretary. Who's Who among Students in American Colleges and Universities.

Personal background   Grew up in Waycross, Georgia. Attended public schools. Active in athletics and student government. Summer jobs in construction work. Interests include reading and outdoor sports.

References   Personal references will be forwarded upon request.

EXHIBIT 2
Steve O. Handley
Resume of Edward C. Irwin

1411 East Ward Street
Seattle, Washington 98102
Telephone: (206) EAst 3-2344

Objective:

General manager or assistant general manager of a small or medium-size company.

Experience:

Developed a complete new division for a major (sales of $1.75 billion) international company. Started with development of strategies for product lines, manufacturing and marketing, as well as "selling" them to top management; then searched out companies and products which fit the strategy and negotiated acquisitions for the division. Developed all financial "justifications" (pro formas) and operating budgets, and hired the people to staff the division.

Developed and managed into existence a new manufacturing company. Included market research, feasibility studies, pro forma financial statements; "selling" the concept to initial investors; selecting and hiring technical and management employees; selection, purchase, and development of manufacturing plant, machinery, and equipment; product pricing and marketing programs; registration and actual sale of public stock.

Helped small manufacturing company expand and diversify its product lines. Developed and installed new transportation system for their products, which increased reliability of deliveries, and produced a 30 percent savings in transportation costs.

Produced feasibility plans for outdoor leadership training organization to enter sporting goods market on a commercial basis. Analyzed markets and competition and prepared development plan including organization, staffing, approach to the business, and marketing plans.

Education:

B.S. Mechanical Engineering—University of Washington
Honor graduate

Law Degree—University of Washington
Emphasis on business planning, taxation, and antitrust.

References
will state:

Mr. Irwin is intelligent and highly motivated, and an energetic self-starter. He provides impetus to turn plans into action; he is keenly analytical; he has a high sense of loyalty, is perceptive, sensitive, and empathetic, is socially poised, a good leader, and is capable of managing a medium-size company.

Personal: Age: 31. Happily married. Height: 5'9". Weight: 160 lbs. Health: excellent. Active private pilot. Handball player and backpacker.

EXHIBIT 3
Steve O. Handley
Dynamote price list

Model	List price	Product description
104*	$249.00	Power inverter—1,200 watts, 60 Hz AC
105*	298.00	Power inverter—2,000 watts, 60 Hz AC
106*	398.00	Power inverter—3,000, watts, 60 Hz AC
1—CH*	49.00	Control head—power inverter remote control for models 104, 105, 106
204	99.50	Power converter—1,800 watts, 110 volts D.C.
204-A	124.00	Power converter—1,800 watts, 110 volts D.C., with battery charge
204-B	143.50	Power converter—1,800 watts, 110 volts D.C., with automatic throttle (pneumatic)
205	168.00	Power converter—1,800 watts, 110 volts D.C., with automatic throttle (pneumatic) and battery charge
206	208.00	Power converter—2,400 watts, 110 volts D.C., with automatic throttle (pneumatic) and battery charge
207	298.00	Power converter—3,600 watts, 110 volts D.C. with automatic throttle (pneumatic) and battery charge
300†	174.00	Arc welder
301†	274.00	Arc welder—includes 100-amp alternator
302†	348.00	Arc welder and power converter—1,200 watts, 110 volts D.C.
303†	448.00	Arc welder and power converter—1,200 watts, 110 volts D.C., includes 100-amp alternator
304	49.80	Welding cables and stinger—(one 20', one 30' cable; stinger; ground clamp)
400	198.00	D.C. power supply—250 amp
	148.00	D.C. power supply—165 amp
	98.00	D.C. power supply—70 amp
	78.00	D.C. power supply—40 amp
	48.00	D.C. power supply—10 amp
500	248.00	Hot start and charge
600	35.00	Automatic throttle control—single-speed pneumatic
601	68.00	Automatic throttle control—dual-speed pneumatic
602	36.00	Automatic throttle control—single speed electric
700	68.00	Automatic engine start control

*To order with control head, add code letter suffix "CH" to the basic serial number.
†Specify make of vehicle and type of alternator used.
  Note: The above prices are f.o.b., Seattle, Wash. Each unit includes: mounting hardware and wire for standard installation and one-year warranty.
  Source: Dynamote Power Systems Modern Industries, Inc. 17711 15th Ave. N.E. Seattle, Wash. 98155 206/364-5858

EXHIBIT 4

Steve O. Handley

Modern Industries, Inc. one-year estimate for 1971 (December 1, 1970)

	Jan.	Feb.	Mar.	Apr.	May	June	July	Aug.	Sept.	Oct.	Nov.	Dec.	Total year
Management fee	900	900	900	900	900	900	900	900	900	900	900	900	10,800
R&D technology-production	650	650	650	650	700	700	700	700	700	700	700	700	8,200
R&D engineering-application	1,000	1,000	1,000	1,000	1,200	1,200	1,200	1,200	1,400	1,400	1,400	1,400	14,400
Operations marketing	750	750	750	1,450	1,450	1,450	1,450	1,450	1,500	1,500	1,500	1,500	15,500
Secretarial-bookkeeping	465	465	465	500	500	500	500	500	500	500	500	500	5,895
Payroll W/H-ind. ins.	305	305	305	370	395	395	395	395	415	415	415	415	4,525
Field service	–	–	–	300	300	300	300	300	300	300	300	300	2,700
Advertising-printing	500	–	–	500	500	500	500	500	500	500	500	500	5,000
Travel, other (sales)	200	750	750	1,500	1,500	1,500	1,500	1,500	1,500	1,500	1,500	1,500	15,200
Liability insurance	60	60	60	60	60	60	60	60	60	60	60	60	720
Key man insurance	60	60	60	60	60	60	60	60	60	60	60	60	720
Materials/labor test units	100	200	200	200	200	200	200	200	200	200	200	200	2,300
Professional services	500	250	250	250	250	250	250	250	250	250	250	250	3,250
Office supplies	50	50	50	50	50	25	25	25	25	25	25	25	425
Telephone	175	175	200	250	250	250	250	250	250	250	250	250	2,800
Rent	375	375	375	375	700	700	700	700	700	700	700	700	7,100
Capital equipment/tooling	–	–	–	–	1,000	–	2,000	–	1,500	–	–	1,500	6,000
Loan interest	–	–	600	–	–	600	–	–	600	–	–	600	2,400
Production manager	750	750	750	825	825	825	825	825	825	825	825	825	9,675
Payback A/P	3,500	3,500	3,500	3,500	3,500	3,500	3,500	3,500	3,500	3,500	3,500	3,500	42,000
Labor/materials	6,000	12,000	18,000	24,000	30,000	36,000	42,000	48,000	54,000	54,000	54,000	54,000	432,000
Royalties	450	900	1,800	2,700	3,600	4,500	5,400	6,300	7,200	7,200	7,200	7,200	54,450
Total Costs	16,790	23,140	30,665	39,440	47,940	54,415	62,715	67,615	76,885	74,785	74,875	76,885	646,060
Sales	7,500	15,000	30,000	45,000	60,000	75,000	90,000	105,000	120,000	120,000	120,000	120,000	907,500
Net Profit (Loss)	(9,290)	(8,140)	(665)	5,560	12,060	20,585	27,285	37,385	43,115	45,215	45,215	43,115	261,440
Cum. Profit (Loss)	(9,290)	(17,430)	(18,095)	(12,535)	(475)	20,110	47,395	84,780	127,895	173,110	218,325	261,440	261,440

Source: IBDC.

EXHIBIT 5
Steve O. Handley
Letter from banker

Seattle First National Bank
South Everett Branch

January 21, 1971

William P. Marks
Manager

Mr. Edward C. Erwin
1411 E. Ward Street
Seattle, Washington 98102
   and
Mr. Stephen O. Handley
3702 E. Prospect
Seattle, Washington 98102

Dear Ed and Steve:

I very much appreciated and enjoyed your visit of last Monday and an opportunity to discuss with you your proposed business ventures. Our discussion left me with the impression that you are logical, well organized, and thoughtful in your approach.

I have given some thought to our discussion, and I might offer a few additional comments for your consideration. In looking through my notes, it appears to me from a financial, production, and marketing standpoint, that you should give your primary consideration to Wood Specialty Products. Although their product is not along the line of your backgrounds, I think that you would personally gain more from this company, with a greater degree of probable success, than you would from the other companies discussed.

Secondly, I think you should consider finding a financial person to join your group, particularly somebody well schooled in equity finance. Should you wish to pursue this suggestion, I might be able to put you in touch with one or two appropriate people. I think the addition of a financial person would be highly desirable for any of the ventures and of particular importance should you decide to get involved with Modern Industries or Mastertron Computer Equipment, as both of these companies have very definite needs to seek equity financing. In any event, I am sure that you realize that good financial control and information is a prime ingredient in making any company a success.

Thirdly, and after you have decided which company you wish to get involved with, I would suggest that you acquire an option for the equity interest involved, and then go to work for the company for six months prior to exercising that option. While both of you are well educated and have good corporate experience, neither one of you has encountered the experience of running a company on your own. There are differences between successful individual company management and ability to operate a section of a larger corporation. Furthermore, association with the company for a six-month period prior to the investment of money should confirm or deny your impressions of your desire to operate the company and leave a way out before you are in too deeply.

Fourth, your absence of substantial liquid assets to personally invest in an enterprise is going to present some problems, and necessitate some equity partners in any enterprise in which you become involved. I have reviewed your situation with a few parties who have money to invest in such things, and I can give you some encouragement that you would probably be able to gain some equity participation partners on a noninvolvement basis.

I hope these few comments and suggestions will be of some assistance.

Please stay in touch.

Sincerely,

W. P. Marks

WMP:rp
Encl.

EXHIBIT 6
Steve O. Handley
Royalty Agreement

AGREEMENT

AGREEMENT entered into this 1st day of October 1968, between MODERN INDUSTRIES, INC. a Washington corporation, "Modern" herein, INTERNA-TIONAL BUSINESS DEVELOPMENT COMPANY, a Washington partner-ship, "IBDC" herein, FRANKLIN R. SCHNEIDER, an individual, and JAMES A. GUHLKE, an individual.

Modern's primary activity at present is the manufacture and sale of an auto accessory known as a power converter. In the future, Modern may develop, manufacture, license, or sell other products, processes, ideas, or technology which may or may not be related to the product line now being handled by Modern.

IBDC is an organization which has supplied, and which will continue to

EXHIBIT 6 (continued)

supply Modern with business know-how intended to assist Modern in such general management functions as obtaining capital, surveying markets, distributing product lines, and formulating long and short range programs for exploiting proprietary products.

Franklin Schneider and James Guhlke, who are the President and Vice President respectively of Modern, were the joint inventors of the power converter, and helped Modern to incorporate and get its business activity underway, and have devoted, and will continue to devote, their time, skill, talent, and energy to expanding and enhancing Modern's corporate activities.

This agreement shall not apply to products invented or owned by Schneider and Guhlke other than the power converter, unless Schneider and Guhlke by specific written instrument agree to make any such product available to Modern. Schneider and Guhlke are presently working on an A.C. power converter. They agree that any patent acquired for the A.C. power converter, or the right to manufacture and sell it, shall be transferred to Modern on a royalty or commission basis, but in any event Modern shall not pay therefore an amount greater than two percent (2%) of the gross sales therefrom to Schneider and Guhlke, each.

In exchange for, and in recognition of the services, ideas, inventions relating to the D.C. and A.C. power converters that have been, and that will be provided to it by IBDC, Schneider and Guhlke, Modern agreed, in an informal agreement, to pay each two percent (2%) of its annual gross revenue for a period commencing October 1, 1968, and ending September 30, 1978. This instrument is the formal written embodiment of the informal contract previously made by the parties.

NOW THEREFORE, in consideration of the mutual covenants herein contained, and for the know-how, inventions, and services that have been, and that will be, provided to Modern, the parties agree as follows:

1. *Payment of percentage of gross revenues.* Modern shall pay an amount equal to two percent (2%) of its total gross revenue during the term of this agreement to each of IBDC, Franklin Schneider, and James Guhlke, for a combined total of six percent (6%) of gross revenue to all three parties. As used herein, "gross revenue" shall mean all income of whatever nature and from whatever source received or accrued by Modern, directly or indirectly, in connection with its corporate activity or operations. Gross revenue shall include amounts for orders received by Modern before the expiration of this agreement and accepted within one hundred eighty (180) days after its expiration. Gross revenue shall not include amounts received for sales which prove uncollectible, or amounts received for items sold which are later returned and for which the customer is reimbursed, and where such amounts are included in gross revenue, appropriate adjustments will be made.

2. *Term of agreement.* The term of this agreement shall commence on October 1, 1968, and end on September 30, 1978.

3. *Method of payment and books of account.* The percentage of gross revenue payable to three of the parties herein shall be paid no later than the tenth day of each month following the end of each quarter that amounts are payable pursuant to this agreement. The first quarter that amounts are

EXHIBIT 6 (continued)

payable pursuant to this agreement shall begin on October 1, 1968, and end on December 31, 1968, and the last quarter that amounts are payable under this agreement shall begin on the first day of July 1978, and end on the 30th day of September 1978. Modern agrees to furnish IBDC, Schneider, and Guhlke each with a copy of a quarterly statement of gross revenue, and Modern further agrees to give them reasonable access during regular business hours to all its corporate books and records, which books and records shall be kept by Modern at its principal place of business.

4. *Method of payment.* Payment of the percentage of gross revenue to which IBDC, Schneider and Guhlke are entitled shall be by check drawn on Modern's funds; each check shall be mailed or delivered to each party entitled thereto at the address specified in Paragraph 14 and on or before the date specified in Paragraph 3.

5. *Duties of IBDC.* In addition to the assistance IBDC has already given to Modern, IBDC shall continue to assist Modern by giving such managerial assistance and advice to Modern as may be necessary in the opinion of IBDC to assist Modern in achieving its corporate programs and purposes. In no event shall the amount of gross revenue payable to IBDC by Modern hereunder be decreased or terminated in the event that the quantity of managerial assistance given Modern by IBDC is reduced or terminated, it being agreed by Modern that as of the date hereon, the amount of gross revenue payable to IBDC pursuant to the agreement between the parties hereto has already been fully earned.

6. *Duties of Schneider and Guhlke.* It is contemplated by the parties that Franklin Schneider and James Guhlke shall continue serving as officers of Modern throughout the term of this agreement. Should their employment as officers be terminated for any reason, whether by resignation or otherwise, the percentage of gross revenues payable to them shall not be decreased or terminated, it being agreed by Modern that as of the date hereon, both Schneider and Guhlke have earned full right to the percentage of gross revenue that is payable to them.

7. *Licensing agreements to affect payments.* During the term of this agreement, Modern may license the use of its technology or the manufacture of one or more of its products. In the event that Modern enters into a licensing or similar type arrangement with some third person or persons, Modern will make appropriate adjustments to the percentage of gross revenue payable to IBDC, Schneider, and Guhlke. In making the adjustment, Modern will accurately estimate the amount of gross revenue that would have been generated had the technology or product not been licensed, and had Modern itself manufactured the product or used the technology, and the amount of gross revenue as so estimated will be added to the amount of gross revenue actually received or accrued in the quarter for which the amounts are payable. IBDC or Schneider or Guhlke shall each have the right to challenge the accuracy of any estimate of gross revenue made pursuant to this paragraph. In the event that Modern is unable to satisfy the party making the challenge, final determination of the estimate shall be made by arbitration in accordance with Paragraph 8 hereof.

EXHIBIT 6 (continued)

8. *Arbitration.*   In the event any dispute arises hereunder, the parties agree to submit the same to arbitration, to be held in accordance with the rules of the American Arbitration Association then prevailing. Each party hereto shall have the right to select one arbitrator, who together may select a fifth arbitrator, and the decision of the majority of arbitrators so selected shall be final.
9. *Reimbursement for expenses.*   Modern recognizes that the other parties hereunder may, in the course of performing their duties hereunder, incur expenses in connection with their duties for such items as entertainment, traveling, hotels, gifts, and similar items. IBDC, Schneider and Guhlke shall be entitled to reimbursement for all expenses reasonably incurred by them in performance of their duties hereunder, and said expenses shall be reimbursed over and above the amounts payable as a percentage of gross revenue.
10. *Sale of business.*   This agreement may be assigned by Modern in the event of a bona fide sale or transfer of ownership to another person, firm, or corporation, provided, however, that the assignee shall assume in writing all of the obligations of Modern under this agreement, and provided further, that IBDC, Schneider, and Guhlke agree to said sale and the accompanying assignment. At least thirty (30) days prior to any such proposed sale or assignment, Modern shall notify the other parties to this agreement in writing of its intention to effect such assignment.
11. *Governing law.*   This agreement shall be governed by and construed according to the laws of the State of Washington.
12. *Modification of agreement.*   This agreement constitutes the full and complete understanding and agreement of the parties, and supersedes all prior understandings and agreements, and can not be changed or terminated orally.
13. *Assignment by IBDC, Schneider, and Guhlke.*   Modern agrees that the rights granted hereunder to IBDC, Schneider, and Guhlke may be assigned and transferred to any third parties, and shall inure to the benefit of any such third party assignee.
14. *Notices.*   All notices, correspondence, checks, and other information required to be sent hereunder shall be mailed to:

International Business Development Company
10306 Northeast 10th Street
Bellevue, Washington 98004

Modern Industries, Inc.
17711 15th Avenue Northeast
Seattle, Washington 98155

Franklin R. Schneider
17711 15th Avenue Northeast
Seattle, Washington 98155

EXHIBIT 6 (continued)

James A. Guhlke
17711 15th Avenue Northeast
Seattle, Washington 98155

Any party hereto may change his address given above by giving notice thereof in writing to all the other parties.

IN WITNESS WHEREOF, the parties hereto have caused this agreement to be executed on the day and year first above written.

INTERNATIONAL BUSINESS DEVELOPMENT COMPANY

By: ————————————————————————————

International Business Development Corporation, Sam Scimeca, its president.

MODERN INDUSTRIES, INC.

By: ————————————————————————————

Franklin Schneider, its president

————————————————————————————

Franklin Schneider, individually

————————————————————————————

James A. Guhlke, individually

EXHIBIT 7

Steve O. Handley

Steve and Ed's pro forma income statement (1971)

	Jan.	Feb.	Mar.	Apr.	May	June	July	Aug.	Sept.	Oct.	Nov.	Dec.	Total
Sales—high	3,900	10,000	20,000	30,000	40,000	50,000	55,000	60,000	65,000	70,000	75,000	80,000	558,900
Cost of goods sold and royalty @ 4%	1,840	4,400	8,800	13,200	17,600	22,000	24,200	26,400	28,600	30,800	33,000	35,200	
Gross Profit	2,060	5,600	11,200	16,800	22,400	28,000	30,800	33,600	36,400	39,200	42,000	44,800	312,860
Sales—medium	3,900	7,500	15,000	20,000	25,000	30,000	40,000	50,000	55,000	60,000	65,000	70,000	441,400
Cost of goods sold and royalty @ 4%	1,840	3,300	6,600	8,800	11,000	13,200	17,600	22,000	24,200	26,400	28,600	30,800	
Gross Profit	2,060	4,200	8,400	11,200	14,000	16,800	22,400	28,000	30,800	33,600	36,400	39,200	247,060
Sales—low	3,900	5,000	7,500	10,000	15,000	17,500	20,000	25,000	30,000	35,000	40,000	45,000	253,900
Cost of goods sold and royalty @ 4%	1,840	2,200	3,300	4,400	6,600	7,700	8,800	11,000	13,200	15,400	17,600	19,800	
Gross Profit	2,060	2,800	4,200	5,600	8,400	9,800	11,200	14,000	16,800	19,600	22,400	25,200	142,060
Operating Expenses:													
Salaries		6,400	6,700	6,700	6,700	6,700	7,500	7,500	7,500	7,500	7,500	7,500	
Payroll taxes and benefits		1,300	1,400	1,400	1,400	1,400	1,500	1,500	1,500	1,500	1,500	1,500	
Field service		300	300	300	300	300	500	500	500	500	500	500	
Insurance		120	120	120	120	120	120	120	120	120	120	120	
Professional services		250	250	250	250	250	250	250	250	250	250	250	
Office supplies		75	75	75	75	75	100	100	100	100	100	100	
Telephone		200	200	300	300	500	500	500	500	500	500	500	
Rent		350	350	700	700	700	700	700	700	700	700	700	
Sales expenses-travel		2,000	2,500	3,000	3,500	3,600	3,600	3,600	3,600	3,600	3,600	3,600	
Advertising and printing		500	500	700	700	1,000	1,000	1,500	1,500	1,500	1,500	1,500	
Miscellaneous		200	200	300	300	500	500	500	500	500	500	500	
Interest		400	400	400	400	400	400	400	400	400	400	400	
Management fee		900	900	900	900	900	900	900	900	900	900	900	
Depreciation		100	100	100	150	150	150	200	200	200	200	200	
Total Operating Expense	8,000	13,095	13,995	15,245	15,795	16,595	17,720	18,270	18,270	18,270	18,270	18,270	191,795
Net Profit before Taxes:													
High	(5,940)	(7,495)	(2,795)	1,555	6,605	11,405	13,080	15,330	18,130	19,930	23,730	26,530	121,065
Medium	(5,940)	(8,895)	(5,595)	(4,045)	(1,795)	205	4,680	9,730	12,530	15,330	18,130	20,930	55,265
Low	(5,940)	(10,295)	(9,795)	(9,645)	(7,395)	(6,795)	(6,520)	(4,270)	(1,470)	1,330	4,130	6,930	(49,735)

Source: Steve Handley's records.

EXHIBIT 7 (continued)

Steve and Ed's pro forma cash flow (1971)

	Jan.	Feb.	Mar.	Apr.	May	June	July	Aug.	Sept.	Oct.	Nov.	Dec.
1) High Sales Forecast:												
Cash expenses*		12,095	12,995	14,245	14,745	15,545	16,670	17,170	17,170	17,170	17,170	17,170
Purchases		3,500	4,000	8,000	12,000	16,000	20,000	22,000	24,000	26,000	28,000	30,000
Cash out		15,595	16,995	22,245	26,745	31,545	36,670	39,170	41,170	43,170	45,170	47,170
Revenue†			10,000	20,000	30,000	40,000	50,000	55,000	60,000	65,000	70,000	75,000
Operating net cash flow		(15,595)	(6,995)	(2,245)	3,255	8,455	13,330	15,830	18,830	21,830	24,830	27,830
Pay past due A/P		3,100	3,100	3,100	3,100	3,100	3,100	3,100	3,100	3,100	3,100	—
Total Cash Flow		(18,695)	(10,095)	(5,345)	155	5,355	10,230	12,730	15,730	18,730	21,730	27,830
Cumulative Cash Flow		(18,695)	(28,790)	(34,135)	(33,980)	(28,625)	(18,395)	(5,665)	10,065	28,795	50,525	78,355
2. Medium Sales Forecast:												
Cash expenses*		12,095	12,995	14,245	14,745	15,545	16,670	17,170	17,170	17,170	17,170	17,170
Purchases		3,500	3,000	6,000	8,000	10,000	12,000	16,000	20,000	22,000	24,000	26,000
Cash out		15,595	15,995	20,245	22,745	25,545	28,670	33,170	37,170	39,170	41,170	43,170
Revenue†			7,500	15,000	20,000	25,000	30,000	40,000	50,000	55,000	60,000	65,000
Operating net cash flow		(15,595)	(8,495)	(5,245)	(2,745)	545	1,330	6,830	12,830	15,830	18,830	21,830
Pay past due A/P		3,100	3,100	3,100	3,100	3,100	3,100	3,100	3,100	3,100	3,100	—
Total Cash Flow		(18,695)	(11,595)	(8,345)	(5,845)	(2,555)	(1,770)	3,730	9,730	12,730	15,730	21,830
Cumulative Cash Flow		(18,695)	(30,290)	(38,635)	(44,480)	(47,035)	(48,805)	(45,075)	(35,345)	(22,615)	(6,885)	14,945
3. Low Sales Forecast:												
Cash expenses*		12,095	12,995	14,245	14,745	15,545	16,670	17,170	17,170	17,170	17,170	17,170
Purchases		3,500	2,000	3,000	4,000	6,000	7,000	8,000	10,000	12,000	14,000	16,000
Cash out		15,595	14,995	17,245	18,745	21,545	23,670	25,170	27,170	29,170	31,170	33,170
Revenue†			5,000	7,500	10,000	15,000	17,500	20,000	25,000	30,000	35,000	40,000
Operating net cash flow		(15,595)	(9,995)	(9,745)	(8,745)	(6,545)	(6,170)	(5,170)	(2,170)	830	3,830	6,830
Pay past due A/P		3,100	3,100	3,100	3,100	3,100	3,100	3,100	3,100	3,100	3,100	—
Total Cash Flow		(18,695)	(13,095)	(12,845)	(11,845)	(9,645)	(9,270)	(8,270)	(5,270)	(2,270)	730	6,830
Cumulative Cash Flow		(18,695)	(31,790)	(44,635)	(56,480)	(66,125)	(75,395)	(83,665)	(88,935)	(91,205)	(90,475)	(83,645)

*Cash expense = Operating expense − [Noncash expense + Accrued expenses].
†Assumes accrued royalty.
Source: Steve Handley's records.

EXHIBIT 8
Steve O. Handley
Stock purchase and management agreement

This agreement is between MODERN INDUSTRIES, INC. (Modern) and
EDWARD C. IRWIN and STEPHEN O. HANDLEY (Managers). As parties
hereto they agree:

1. Stock purchase. Managers each agree to purchase from Modern upon
execution of this agreement and Modern agrees to sell to each Manager 5,000
shares of the common stock of Modern Industries, Inc., at the price of $2.00 per
share.

2. Employment as managers. Modern employs Irwin and Handley as its
General Managers in charge and control of all its business operations and affairs,
subject to the supervision, direction, and approval of its Board of Directors.

3. Compensation. Modern will pay each Manager and Managers will accept
as compensation for their services:

(a) A salary of $1,250.00 per month each beginning February 1, 1971, and
payable each month thereafter until this agreement terminates or until a
Manager's services are terminated as provided in this agreement.

(b) A bonus payable to Edward C. Irwin, Stephen O. Handley, and Franklin R.
Schneider, share and share alike, based on "net profits" before provision for
federal income taxes as follows:

Net profit	*bonus*
$ 0–$250,000	none
250–500,000	5%
500–750,000	4
750–1 million	3
1 million–1.25 million	2
1.25 million–1.5 million	1
In excess of $1.5 million	1

"Net profits" shall be determined upon generally accepted accounting principles. The bonus shall be determined and paid upon "net profits" before deduction or allowance for federal income taxes and without allowance for depreciation. Bonuses shall be paid within three months after the end of the fiscal year of
Modern.

4. Stock option. Modern grants to each Manager the option to purchase
35,000 shares of the common stock of Modern Industries, Inc., at $3.00 per share
as follows:

(a) At the end of the first year of employment with Modern each Manager shall
have the right to purchase 10,000 shares.

(b) At the end of the second year of employment with Modern each Manager
shall have the right to purchase 8,500 shares.

(c) At the end of the third year of employment with Modern each Manager
shall have the right to purchase 8,500 shares.

(d) At the end of the fourth year of employment with Modern each Manager
shall have the right to purchase 8,000 shares.

The right to purchase the number of shares stated shall accrue at the end of each year of employment as stated. The option to purchase such accrued shares may be exercised by either Manager at any time after the year in which the right to purchase the shares has accrued. The right to exercise the option for any accrued shares shall terminate January 31, 1976. If the employment of a Manager is terminated as provided in this agreement, the option to purchase stock shall terminate for the year in which his employment is terminated and any year or years thereafter. A Manager whose employment has been terminated may exercise the option to purchase those shares which have previously accrued to him under this option for prior years of employment, if he exercises the option on or before January 31, 1976. A Manager may exercise his option to purchase by written notice to Modern accompanied by cash payment for the stock subject to the option.

5. Termination for cause. Modern may terminate this agreement as to either Manager on 30 days written notice in the event of any of the following:

(a) If, because of mental, physical, or other disability, Manager shall be incapable for a period of _____ days from fully performing any or all of his obligations and agreements hereunder.

(b) The failure, refusal, or neglect by Manager to perform any of the services required by this agreement.

*(c)*If Manager commits an offense involving moral turpitude under federal, state or local laws or ordinance, or conducts himself publicly or privately in any manner which offends against decency or morality, or causes him to be held in public ridicule or scorn.

(d) In the event Managers do not obtain and continue sources of capital to meet the needs of Modern based on the estimates of business and growth plan prepared by Managers, which estimates and growth plan are incorpoated herein by reference, or if the business of Modern does not develop in accordance with such estimates and growth plan.

6. Noncompetition. For a period of 12 months after Managers employment hereunder terminates for any reason, they will not directly or indirectly engage in the production, manufacture, or distribution of any products being produced or distributed by Modern, or any of its subsidiaries or affiliates, for his own benefit or for the benefit of any other person. Managers shall not sell any such products to persons purchasing products from Modern or any of its subsidiaries or affiliates, at the time of termination of their contract hereunder until the above specified 12 month period has passed.

7. Confidential nature of employment. Managers will keep all matters concerning the business of Modern and its subsidiaries and affiliates confidential following their termination of employment. Managers agree to keep confidential all plans and methods of manufacture and distribution and production of products, accounting, and financial information; production, customer, and supplier lists; and information concerning management and control of the various activities of Modern and its subsidiaries and affiliates.

8. Term. The term of this contract shall be for five years beginning February 1, 1971, and terminating January 31, 1976.

9. Arbitration. In the event of a dispute under this agreement, parties agree to arbitrate the matter. Managers shall jointly select one arbiter. Modern shall select a second arbiter. The two arbiters so selected shall select a third arbiter. The three arbiters shall hear the matter in dispute and their decision shall be binding on all parties. The losing parties shall pay the expenses of the arbitration.

10. Successors and assigns. This contract shall be binding upon the heirs or personal representatives, successors, and assigns of the parties hereto.

11. Entire agreement This contract represents the entire agreement between the parties, any other or prior understandings, agreements, and contracts being hereby cancelled without any further liability whatsoever on either party.

DATED this _____ day of _____ 1971.

MODERN INDUSTRIES, INC.

By ————————————————   ————————————————————————

                                        Edward C. Irwin

                                        ————————————————————————

                                        Stephen O. Handley

EXHIBIT 9
Steve O. Handley
Modern Industries, Inc., statement of income (unaudited)

	12 Months to June 30, 1970	6 Months to December 31, 1970
Sales:	$150,817	$ 26,159
Less: Royalties	8,853	1,616
	$141,964	$ 24,543
Cost of Goods Sold:		
Beginning inventory	$ 17,161	$ 53,400
Purchases	79,600	17,876
Freight	1,179	1,002
Labor	12,970	4,593
Indirect manufacturing expense	4,847	520
	$115,757	$ 77,391
Less: Ending inventory	53,400	67,441
	$ 62,357	$ 9,950
Gross Profit	$ 79,607	$ 14,593
Operating Expense:		
Salaries—administrative	$ 27,090	$ 15,060
Salaries—secretarial	5,625	2,914
General office	2,120	1,731
Travel and entertainment	7,650	7,222
Auto expense	4,374	3,078
Depreciation and amortization	1,016	560
Legal and accounting	4,366	2,125
Payroll taxes	4,753	1,608
Business taxes	1,749	578
Telephone	1,749	1,028
Insurance	1,515	1,039
Management fee	9,895	5,400
Research and development	2,996	6,808
Miscellaneous	4,990	1,650
Contributions	2,508	
Advertising	509	1,289
Literature	808	1,986
Interest	2,447	2,317
Bad debts	2,580	
Commission		2,948
	$ 88,740	$ 59,341
Net Loss	$ 9,133	$ 44,748

ASSETS

Current Assets:		
Cash	$ 10,283	$ 25,123
Accounts receivable	6,383	4,086
Inventory—at cost	53,400	67,440
	$ 70,066	$ 96,649
Fixed Assets:		
Manufacturing furniture and equipment	$ 3,099	$ 3,099
Office furniture and equipment	2,291	2,291
	$ 5,390	$ 5,390
Less: accumulated depreciation	(1,834)	(2,171)
	$ 3,556	$ 3,219

EXHIBIT 9 (continued)

Other Assets:		
Trademark and patents	$ 1,910	$ 1,910
Organization expense	330	330
	$ 2,240	$ 2,240
Less: Accumulated amortization	(1,455)	(1,679)
	$ 785	$ 561
Total Assets	$ 74,407	$100,429

LIABILITIES AND STOCKHOLDER'S EQUITY

Current Liabilities:		
Accounts payable	$ 17,656	$ 39,432
Accrued expenses	4,128	2,180
Royalties payable	719	
Management fee payable	1,800	
Notes payable—officers	28,919	1,191
Notes payable—bank		5,000
	$ 53,222	$ 47,803
Long-Term Debt:		
Notes payable		$ 35,000
Stockholder's Equity:		
Paid in capital	$ 96,004	$137,193
Retained earnings	(64,686)	(74,819)
Current net loss	(9,133)	(44,748)
	$ 21,185	$ 17,626
Total Liabilities and Stockholder's Equity	$ 74,407	$100,429

Epicure Products, Inc.

On March 1, 1969, Bill Hamilton was taking his last hard look at whether to join Epicure Products, Inc. (EPI), and what arrangement to propose to the president, Winslow Burhoe, if he did decide to join. EPI was a fledgling manufacturer of high-priced enclosed loudspeaker systems for the consumer market which were sold separately or as part of high fidelity component systems by retail hi-fi equipment dealers. The company was essentially a two-man firm producing one product carrying a retail price of $109. It was currently selling this product through two commissioned agents to dealers in New England and New York City. Sales since the company's incorporation on October 1, 1968, had been approximately $5,000.

Bill had been meeting with Win Burhoe on several evenings and Saturdays over the past three weeks to learn all he could about the company. He had also made a sales call for the company in Worcester and had accompanied Win to the Stereo Store in Cambridge for a meeting with the floor salesmen. The Stereo Store was the only dealer besides one small dealer in New York City which was actively selling EPI's product.

Bill thought that it was now time to make a decision about EPI, and expected to contact Win the following day.

Bill Hamilton

Bill Hamilton was graduated from Yale University with a B.S. in industrial administration in 1966 and went immediately for his master's degree in management at the M.I.T. Sloan School of Management. During the three summers preceding his graduation from Sloan, Bill

259

worked in manufacturing positions, two of them with United Home Products, a large household products producer. Although he enjoyed this experience, Bill began to develop a keen interest in marketing at the Sloan School. He took the three marketing courses available at the school, as well as a consumer behavior course at the Harvard Business School, and wrote his master's thesis in the area of consumer behavior. A copy of Bill's resume is shown in Exhibit 1.

In the spring of 1968, with the required coursework of the second year behind him, Bill decided to leave Sloan and finish his thesis in his spare time. Married the previous year, he was anxious to have some income, rather than go any further into debt. Bill was unsure of what career path he wanted to follow, and decided to return to United Home Products in the Plymouth, Massachusetts, plant. He had very much enjoyed the last summer's job at this plant as foreman of a small work group in the detergents packing department. Another key factor in his decision was his interview with the marketing people at United Home Products for a position in brand management. They turned him down, implying he was more suited for manufacturing than for marketing. At the time he commented to his wife, "This is the first time I have ever been turned down on something for which I feel qualified. But maybe they are right; perhaps I am not the marketing type after all."

With his first position as an industrial engineer in a soap packaging department at Plymouth, Bill soon realized that manufacturing management was not for him. He felt he lacked the technical background and interest in engineering and plant management to perform optimally, and in addition found factory life extremely monotonous. He commented at the time, "It seems the world is going by, while I spend all my time within these same four walls." In December 1968, he learned his next position was to be shift supervisor in another department, which meant he would be working two weeks on the day shift alternating with two weeks on the night shift. Finding this distasteful, he decided to try to leave before training for the new job began.

With about a month and a half to look for a job part time, Bill decided he would look only at marketing positions. He found opportunities in sales and in marketing research, but both these jobs seemed too narrow to him. He thought that becoming assistant to a marketing manager in a medium-sized company would be a realistic position for someone with his limited marketing background and would give him the overall marketing viewpoint he wanted to learn. Nevertheless, he found no suitable openings, particularly because he and his wife wanted to remain in the Boston area. He also found it difficult trying to convince someone he had marketing talent when his resume included only manufacturing work experiences.

In early February a professor at M.I.T. advised Bill to look at a small company, EPI, which was in its start-up phase. The president was looking for someone to work in sales and marketing. After his first meeting with Win Burhoe, the president, he commented to the professor:

> I never thought about a small company, let alone an *infant* company, before. But since meeting Win the other night in his tiny factory, with classical music blaring loudly through the EPI speakers I have become intrigued. It strikes me that this could be a chance to get totally immersed in a situation, and at the same time, the company could have great potential. There have been a number of hi-fi companies which have grown from one man's idea into sizable concerns, and EPI might be able to do the same.

With this initial positive reaction, Bill decided to look further at the company and at the high-fidelity industry.

The high-fidelity component industry

In his investigation over the next three weeks, Bill could find no published data on the high-fidelity component industry, so he had to rely on information Win Burhoe provided as well as what he picked up from his several visits to hi-fi dealers. Win had formerly worked in a manufacturing and design capacity for the two biggest loudspeaker manufacturers, Acoustic Research (AR) and KLH Research and Development Corporation.

Bill learned that hi-fi components could be set within a larger industry, which might be thought of as "sound reproduction systems," comprising such things as portable record players and AM-FM radios selling for under $50 as well as complete stereo consoles (i.e., the various elements of a stereo record playing component system, all mounted by the manufacturer in an attractive piece of wooden furniture) selling for over $1,000. Component systems were characterized by the physical separateness of the different functional pieces, which the user connected by wires to carry the power and signals, and could cost the consumer anywhere from $200 on up to $2,000. Dollar for dollar, components were considered by dealers and sophisticated listeners to be far superior to consoles, because there was no expensive furniture involved. However, the majority of women greatly favored consoles because of their attractiveness and ability to blend with other household furnishings.

Generally hi-fi components were sold by independent dealers who specialized in just higher quality components. Phonographs, consoles, automobile tape systems, radios, and most component systems selling under $250 were sold in a variety of outlets including department stores, TV and appliance stores, camera stores, and even car accessories stores.

A few department stores and TV and appliance stores had separate departments carrying high-quality hi-fi component systems.

Bill found that a "component high-fidelity system" had many alternative forms, but dealers claimed the most frequently purchased system, presuming the consumer was buying his whole system at once, was a turntable or record changer with cartridge, a stereo "receiver,"[1] and two speakers (see Exhibit 2 for pictures of this equipment and other component items). What was regarded by dealers as a good system might consist of a changer and cartridge retailing for between $50 and $125, two speakers between $50 and $125 each, and a stereo receiver costing $200 to $250. An "excellent" system was priced anywhere from $600 to over $1,000, and generally the consumer was paying for more power and control features in the receiver, more control features in the changer, and greater sound output and power handling capability in the speakers. Generally the quality of sound reproduction improved with higher price, although Win believed this was not the case for some loudspeaker systems. He claimed that because nearly all consumers and most dealers had an unclear concept of what a high-quality loudspeaker should be, there were some inferior loudspeakers sold at high prices.

Hi-fi dealers carried several lines of each audio component to cover the various price ranges and to accommodate varying consumer tastes. Bill learned there were two types of hi-fi dealers: those who sold merchandise on the basis of price (the discounters) and those who sold on the basis of heavy salesman demonstration followed up by customer service. This distinction was made clear to Bill when the proprietor of the Stereo Store, a nondiscounter, commented that if EPI ever sold to Cambridge Radio, a known discounter in the Boston area, he would never buy another speaker from the company. Generally, the discounters carried the older lines of merchandise with proven brand names, although many established manufacturers prevented discounting on their lines by selecting dealers very carefully and by using fair trade agreements in states where they were legal.

There was usually a heavy investment of the retail salesman's time in selling a component system to the uninitiated consumer. Often the selling process stretched over several visits by the consumer, who might visit another retail store in the interim. As a result, salesmen in nondiscount stores tried to emphasize those lines which they knew discounters did not handle.

The Northeast corridor, the Chicago area, and California accounted for the majority of dealer hi-fi component sales. Discounting tended to predominate in the New York City market, the most concentrated area of hi-fi component sales, and it accounted for probably half of the Boston area sales. However, Win had heard that discounting accounted for the

---

[1]A one-piece unit containing amplifier, preamplifier and AM-FM tuner.

minority of sales elsewhere. Bill figured there were probably between 500 and 750 dealer locations in the U.S. (some dealers had multiple locations) which sold higher priced equipment. In the greater Boston area, for instance, besides the Stereo Store and Cambridge Radio's three stores, there were five other discount stores, and nine nondiscount stores. In Worcester, a city of 250,000, there were by contrast only two small stores, both of which were primarily nondiscount oriented.

Sales for the industry were highly seasonable, with a large majority of retail sales occurring between September and January.

The high-fidelity component industry was subject to continual innovation. One trend which seemed to be developing was for a manufacturer to sell a "compact" consisting of a changer mounted on top of a receiver, with two remote speakers This packaging tended to cut down on the number of separate components and the clutter of connecting wires, and also meant one manufacturer enjoyed the sale of the complete system. KLH Research and Development Corp. had been popularizing this trend with a recognized high-quality line of compacts selling between $200 and $400. However the majority of hi-fi systems sold still consisted of separate components, and most of these comprised a receiver made by one manufacturer, a record changer by another, a phono cartridge by a third, and speakers by a fourth.

Component hi-fi seemed to be regarded as a small industry. Bill found several people making the comment that as yet the industry was too small for an RCA or GE to become seriously interested in it, but that someday it would be large enough for their entry. In fact Zenith and Motorola were already manufacturing lower quality component systems at less than $200, but such equipment was not sold through the hi-fi dealer. The industry consisted predominantly of small companies, with the largest U.S. manufacturers thought to sell between $10 and $20 million of equipment. However, large Japanese firms like Sony, Sansui, and Pioneer were becoming strong in this market, particularly in receivers and tape recorders. The industry was considered by all to be a "growth" industry, but the rate at which it was growing was unknown.

Component manufacturers sold directly to dealers through their own sales force, by the use of independent sales representatives, or by a combination of the two methods. Independent agents commonly carried a line of receivers, one or two speaker lines (when they covered different price ranges), a cartridge line, and perhaps a record changer, tape recorder, and/or headphone line. Agent commissions were a standard 5 percent. The dealer margin structure on components was usually 40 percent for speakers, and between 33 percent and 40 percent on the other types of equipment. Bill learned from Win that some manufacturers raised their margins in the spring in an attempt to stimulate sales in the slower months of the year.

As far as loudspeakers in particular were concerned, Bill noticed in his visits to dealers and his scanning of the high-fidelity consumer magazines that there were at least 20 brands of loudspeakers marketed. Win felt the largest companies were AR and KLH, each selling about $10 million of loudspeakers a year. He thought AR sold a slightly larger volume of speakers, but KLH was a significantly larger company in terms of total component sales because of its compacts. Win did not think any other loudspeaker marketer had even half the loudspeaker volume of an AR or KLH.

Win suggested that perhaps seven or eight of the other companies including many of the Japanese firms offered speakers merely as line extensions, with their main strength being in receivers or tape recorders. These companies, and some other manufacturers bought speaker drivers[2] from OEM driver manufacturers and mounted them in wooden cabinets which they also purchased. Nearly all speaker systems had at least two drivers, a "woofer" for low frequencies, and a "tweeter" for high frequencies. Some loudspeakers had one or more "midrange" speakers for middle range frequencies.

Only six or seven loudspeaker system manufacturers including AR and KLH actually manufactured their own speaker drivers. Win said that manufacturing one's own drivers allowed for greater quality control, potentially lower cost on low-volume, high-quality units, and maintenance of secrecy on proprietary designs and methods of manufacturing. Win felt his own ability to design high-quality drivers was a unique art. He said that the number of good designers for high-quality speakers in the whole United States could be counted on one hand.

Bill found that there was by no means a consensus among consumers or dealers on what was the best speaker sold. The theoretical objective of a loudspeaker, and in fact a complete high-fidelity system, was to reproduce sound exactly as it was recorded from the original music. In fact most of the good quality amplifiers, tape recorders, and cartridges were quite close to the theoretical optimum of a "linear transducer," i.e., translating sound input signals into output signals of the same proportionate amplitude over the complete range of audible frequencies.[3]

Many loudspeaker systems, on the other hand, were known to add a "coloration" to the sound (i.e., certain portions of the audible frequency range were boosted and others attenuated), and each type of speaker had its following among dealers and consumers. Speakers also differed in their distortion levels. Distortion was the inexact reproduction of certain frequencies, and the most common form of distortion in loudspeakers was imprecise reproduction of bass frequencies. Rather than reproduce

---

[2]Drivers are the actual speaker elements assembled from a permanent magnet, wire coil, metal frame, paper cone, and other parts.

[3]The range of audible frequencies for humans can be as wide as 20 Hz to 20,000 Hz, although most people hear within a much narrower range, such as 40 Hz to 13,000 Hz.

xactly all the audible bass frequencies (i.e., around 30 Hz to 2,000 Hz) peakers with distortion tended to resonate at certain frequencies, muddying" the reproduction of other frequencies. Bill learned from Win however that speakers with a good deal of bass distortion still found ready market. This was because bass distortion gave the impression to ll but the most perceptive listener that the bass was louder on these peakers than others. Since many consumers, particularly the younger ock and roll enthusiasts, liked "a lot of bass" in their music, this distorion sometimes helped to sell the speaker.

Win regarded AR and KLH speakers as having good sound quality for he money. Distortion levels were very low, and sound reproduction was airly linear throughout the audible range. An independent testing group vhich was highly regarded by knowledgeable consumers had given heir highest rating to the AR4x, and also gave a great deal of support to he AR2ax and AR3a. (See Exhibit 3 for price levels and other specificaions of AR, KLH, and EPI speakers.) Win was sure the AR4x enjoyed the ighest sales of any speaker in the United States. Among the KLH line, hose dealers who handled it considered the whole line to be of good uality, but the most popular speakers were the Model 17 and the Model ̄. Win estimated that the Model 17 was probably the second biggest elling speaker in the United States. The KLH line also included the nost expensive speaker sold in any quantity in the United States, its Model 9, at $1,140 per stereo pair. This speaker used an entirely different lectromechanical design for sound reproduction from other speakers, ·alled the electrostatic principle. However, the company appeared not o be pushing this model, and Win believed it was because of quality and nanufacturing problems.

AR and KLH offered an interesting contrast to Bill in terms of marketng strategy. AR used a "pull" strategy using heavy advertising in the ii-fi consumer magazines to attract customers as well as its long-standing eputation from the independent test ratings. The company also had 'listening rooms" in Harvard Square and Grand Central Station where ·nly AR products were displayed, and none were for sale. AR sold to any lealer with good credit, and it allowed dealers to discount to the custom-·rs. Dealer margins were 33 percent. AR sold to dealers using its own actory-based sales force. KLH relied on a dealer push strategy, and upported dealers by having only a limited number of franchises in each ιrea to eliminate discounting, having a 40 percent or higher margin tructure on its products, and assisting dealer promotion by display and ·ooperative advertising allowances. KLH did very little hi-fi magazine ιdvertising, and used as its sales force, a combination of regional salesnen and sales representatives.

Bill could see from dealer lists that AR had 500 dealers, while KLH ιad about 150. There was some overlapping of coverage by the two nanufacturers.

Against this industry backdrop, Win said that he had a speaker system which improved on the existing AR and KLH designs, in terms c linearity of sound reproduction, and that his design could be manufac tured at low cost when volume grew. He believed his chief desig improvement was in "dispersion," the ability of a loudspeaker to gener ate sound in a wide arc, rather than "beaming" it directly forward Although Win knew his speaker to be superior to other systems along thi attribute, he suggested to Bill that a major problem was that dispersion was not a well-known or well-understood concept among hi-fi retailer and consumers.

Win Burhoe

Bill was able to learn a good bit about Win's background during thei several meetings. Win related that he had lived all his life in the Bosto area, and after primary school he attended Boston Latin High Schoo which Bill knew was a prestigious public high school. After graduatin, in 1953, he went on to study music, electronics, and physics at th University of Massachusetts. However, he soon found the tedium c college life not to his liking. He commented jokingly to Bill, "I learne how to play ping pong, and it was all over after that."

A stint in the Army, employment as a Boston taxi driver, and eventu ally work as a store manager in an ice cream chain were differen activities he pursued after leaving college. Win felt the latter experienc was invaluable to him in learning some of the disciplines of business:

> The control and reward system for the ice cream chain was based on one simple measure of performance: gross sales divided by wages. I had the highest rating for all stores, and it was because I moved quickly and had my employees hustling. It was there that I learned how to work hard mentally and physically for long stretches of time.

During this period he developed a friendship with a physics doctora student at Harvard, who taught him basic electronics and physics.

From 1961 to 1966 Win worked for Acoustic Research, Inc. (AR) ir Cambridge. AR in 1954 had introduced the "acoustic suspension" loudspeaker system, a product which revolutionized the high-fidelity industry. With the acoustic suspension design it became possible tc produce in a relatively small cabinet enclosure (one to three cubic feet the complete range of audible frequencies with minimal distortion Previously, mammoth enclosures were used for enclosed loudspeake: systems, with some expensive ones ranging up to 10 or 15 cubic feet. The only sacrifice with acoustic suspension speakers was that their "effi ciency," i.e., their ability to turn electrical power into sound, was lowe: than for traditional speakers. However, more powerful amplifiers of higl quality were being developed at reasonable prices, which could be coupled with the less efficient acoustic suspension speakers for a great improvement in sound reproduction over previous systems. At about the same time, the high-fidelity component manufacturers got a tremendous boost from the development of the stereo record, which necessitated stereo reproducing systems with two amplification channels and two speakers.

Win spent the first year at AR in electronic design. In the last four years, however, he worked exclusively in loudspeaker design. He said much of his time was spent on development of speaker drivers for the AR4x and AR3a.

Win left AR in 1966 to start a TV repair business with a friend in Somerville. Win performed all the repair work while his friend spent his time on pick up and delivery and customer relations. After a short time Win became dissatisfied with the operation and decided to go back to work in the loudspeaker field, but this time with KLH Research and Development Corporation, which had been founded by an ex-employee of AR in 1957. Win spent a year and a half at KLH in production and quality control, but did not get into any speaker design work for the company.

Drawing on his speaker design experience at AR and the knowledge he had acquired about speaker manufacturing at both AR and KLH, Win decided in late 1967 to start his own loudspeaker company. He commented to Bill on his motivation for the company:

> I wanted to try my hand at creating and building an organization. It could have been in any business, but I chose loudspeaker manufacturing because it was a business I knew, and I had a design I thought was excellent at very low cost. I was less interested in the possible monetary gain to be obtained from a business than the challenge and satisfaction of building an organization of people who would grow with the business.

Start of the company

Win also related to Bill the history of the early months of the company. Some of the things he covered were as follows:

He spent the first six months developing the designs for the loud-speaker system, trying out various methods of manufacturing, and checking on the capability of suppliers. Win felt that his design could potentially out perform the AR3a and that he could eventually price the product to compete in the same price range as the AR4ax. In the beginning he did all the manufacturing and testing himself in the same building as his former TV repair business, a small building renting in Somerville for $150 per month. All his designing was centered around one product, which he called the EPI Model 100. The design consisted of two drivers, a woofer, and a tweeter, along with a simple crossover[4] mounted in a one cubic foot wooden cabinet enclosure made of walnut veneer plywood, the standard material of the industry used for high-priced loudspeaker cabinets. Each of the drivers was an assembly of about 10 separate parts, including metal stampings, magnets, speaker cones, and so on. During the summer of 1968 Win hired Charlie Doherty, a production man whom he had gotten to know while at KLH. Charlie took over the functions of purchasing, assembling and testing of prototypes, improving production methods, and final assembling and packaging of finished Model 100's. Win hired another person part time to assemble the woofers and tweeters on a piecework basis.

Early versions of the Model 100 were sold to friends for $75 each. Some of these speakers "blew out" (the wires of the speaker coils melted from the heat) or had other mechanical problems, but Win felt he was able to learn from these how to make the speaker elements stronger. Win decided to have a 10-year warranty on all parts and labor for any defective speaker.

Win attempted several sales trips to dealers in New York City and in the process met Bob Dunkel, an independent sales representative for one of the successful U.S. stereo cartridge manufacturers. Impressed with Win's AR and KLH backgrounds, Bob offered to represent the EPI speaker in New York City at a 10 percent commission. Bob suggested the retail price be raised to $119 with a wholesale price of $72 to dealers. Bob and Win then made the first EPI dealer sales—a half dozen speakers to each of two small independent hi-fi dealers whom Bob had known for years. This was in November of 1968.

The following month, Win made what he thought was his most important sale up to that point—a dozen speakers to the Stereo Store, a large and very popular hi-fi store among the young college group, located in Harvard Square. The proprietor was again impressed with Win's credentials and decided to try the line. However he felt because of the speaker's size the retail price should be dropped to $109, with a corresponding drop in the wholesale price. KLH was the Stereo Store's biggest speaker line, and the proprietor also felt $109 filled a natural price hole between the KLH Model 17 at $69 and the KLH Model at $134. A key factor in the proprietor's decision to carry the EPI product was a comparative test, conducted by an independent testing laboratory, which he paid for himself. In the test the EPI Model 100 provided more accurate sound reproduction than a very popular loudspeaker manufactured by one of

---

[4]"Crossovers" are necessary in any loudspeaker system containing two or more drivers. The purpose of a crossover is to control the distribution of electrical energy from the amplifier to two speaker drivers in the frequency range where they overlap, i.e., in the range where they both can produce sound. In some loudspeaker systems the crossover consisted of complex electronic circuitry, but in the EPI system the tweeter and woofer were so well matched that the crossover consisted of a simple capacitor.

the major speaker companies which retailed at a significantly higher price. The testing company refused to allow use of the results for promotional purposes however.

Win adopted the $109 retail price and structured it so that dealers would have at least a 40 percent margin on the product. Dealer cost was set at $66, with a discount of 10 percent on orders of two dozen or more speakers, and a 5 percent allowance for cooperative advertising. He set trade terms at 5 percent 10 net 30.

The Stereo Store proprietor also suggested Win get in touch with Steve Thompson, age 40, his personal friend, who was sales representative in New England for a small but prestigious tape recorder line, and who had been manager of one of the bigger New England hi-fidelity stores. Steve was struggling with just this one line and was looking for others. Win hired Steve at 10 percent commission as representative for New England because of his background, his interest in the EPI line, and because he seemed filled with enthusiasm and ideas on how to sell the company's product.

In December, Win had a reorder from both the New York City dealers and finished the initial three months of corporate operation with sales of $2,500 including private sales. In January, he had additional orders from the Stereo Store and one of the New York dealers.

However, Steve Thompson had reported difficulties in selling the EPI Model 100's to new dealers, and in the month of January had managed to sell only four speakers on consignment to a small dealer in Wellesley. It was at this point Win decided to hire someone to help in the central selling and marketing activity.

Other information

Bill also learned that Win was currently talking to one of the small Boston banks about a $15,000 Small Business Administration guaranteed loan. Win had prepared a pro forma balance sheet (see Exhibit 4) as one of the requirements for the application, which Bill was able to examine. Win said he felt sure the money would be raised, but that the processing would probably take another three or four weeks before the money was in his hands.

Stock in the company consisted of 1,350 shares of class A voting stock issued to Win, his father, Charlie Doherty, and Bob Dunkel. Win held personally 720 of the shares, while Doherty and Dunkel held small amounts. The most recent purchase price was $10 per share. Win had also created a Class B nonvoting stock of which he held 150 shares. Five hundred shares had been sold the previous month for $5 per share to Dick Reesman, age 39, a free-lance electronics designer with work experience at a number of New England electronics firms. Win was anxious to have Dick's participation in the firm because he felt he had the ability to design a high-quality amplifier and tuner and could design the electronic portions of a compact which EPI could eventually market. Win was thinking of having a compact on the market by the summer of 1970. Dick had also been issued an option on 75 shares of class A common stock at $10 per share.

Issuance of stock to Doherty, Dunkel, and Reesman was according to Win's philosophy of having employees committed to the company through partial ownership. When Bill asked him if he could invest some of his own money in the company, Win said it was not necessary, but would be welcome. In the short term, Win was adamant about maintaining voting control as he felt he was the only person who knew in what direction to move the company.

On two Saturdays Bill had a chance to accompany Win on visits to dealers. The first Saturday they went to the Stereo Store where Win talked to the six floor salesmen about the distinctive features of the EPI Model 100. Besides demonstrating the Model 100, Win and Bill also carried in two 6-foot-high speakers with four 1½ square foot faces, each weighing 150 pounds. Each face contained the same woofer, tweeter, and cross-over used in the Model 100, and the effect was a speaker radiating sound in all directions and capable of handling large amounts of power. In the last two weeks Win had designed these speakers for his own interest, but found their effect so pleasing that he thought dealers might also enjoy them.

The salesmen liked the sound of these "Towers" as Win called them, although they joked about the unfinished exterior appearance of the units. Bill could see that several of the salesmen liked the EPI Model 100 very much, but the others, including the sales manager, mentioned they thought the retail price was too high at $109. In an attempt to raise the salesmen's appreciation of his product, Win had instituted a policy of providing two Model 100's free with every Stereo Store order of 24, until all salesmen had a pair personally.

There was also a dealer from a hi-fi store in Buffalo visiting the owner of the Stereo Store that Saturday who sat in on Win's product demonstration. When Bill asked him what he thought the speaker's retail price should be, he said $75.

During the next week Win and Bill agreed they would both find it useful if Bill tried his hand at selling for EPI. He telephoned two dealers in Worcester and arranged for appointments the following Saturday. He was surprised to learn that neither dealer had been contacted by Steve Thompson on EPI's behalf. That Saturday morning he and Win took the two "Towers" on the roof of Win's station wagon and a half dozen Model 100's inside and headed for Worcester.

Much to Bill's annoyance, the first dealer they visited said he was not really very interested in hearing the new product, and said they would be wasting their time by bringing in the speakers for demonstration. However, the second dealer, a small store carrying KLH and a few other lines, was more receptive. Early in Bill's pitch, the proprietor asked him and Win to bring in the products for a listening demonstration, as he was anxious to play some of his favorite demonstration records with the equipment. He was very impressed with the "Towers," crude as they appeared, and liked the EPI 100's also. He understood fully Win's technical description of the speaker's features. At the conclusion, he decided on the spot to order a half-dozen speakers as a trial order, and paid cash immediately.

As Bill rode back to Boston with Win, he thought of the day as a success, but wondered if perhaps the second dealer had purchased speakers simply because he liked their sound personally. Bill also thought that with the store's small size, the potential volume for EPI there would be slight.

Bill also had the opportunity to observe the complete operation at the EPI factory, from manufacture of woofer and tweeter subassemblies on through final assembly and testing of the finished speaker system. He felt he knew enough of the costs to get a general feel for the cost structure of the business. Win paid to a part-time man $5 for each completed woofer and $5 for each tweeter. The cabinets were purchased for $7 each from two men moonlighting to make cabinets only for EPI. The cost of the other materials was about $10, including tweeter and woofer parts, crossover, fiberglass for the inside of the cabinet, outside packing materials, glue, and so on. Charlie Doherty was paid $150 per week for his various duties and Win thought that about one fourth of his time was spent on activities directly related to the Model 100's. Bill noticed that he put in tremendously long hours. There were only a half-dozen speakers as finished goods inventory, which Win explained was necessary to conserve working capital. Stored in various places around the factory were a large number and variety of early prototypes and older design Model 100's traded in for more recent units.

Bill thought he was aware of all existing overhead costs, which included the $150 rent, telephone and utilities of $100, and depreciation of $60 per month. In addition to these, he anticipated other costs would develop: Win was not drawing a salary, and Bill knew at some point this would change. A friend of Win's was currently performing minimal bookkeeping chores and answering the telephone, and Win promised he would start paying him "when the company could afford it." Win was also negotiating for a lease on some very sophisticated testing equipment which he knew no other loudspeaker firm possessed. The lease was to be $390 per month. Other cash drains Bill considered were the interest and principal payment on the anticipated bank loan and the possibility of advertising in consumer hi-fi magazines.

As Bill was thinking about his final decision, he had a few other things to consider. Although he thought Win had not actively been interviewing other people for the sales and marketing position, chances are he was about to begin, if he had not already. Bill's personal financial situation consisted of $2,000 in savings and a $2,500 school loan payable to M.I.T. over the next eight years. Bill's wife was working as a secretary and was pregnant, with the baby due in July. His current salary at United Home Products was $12,000. He looked upon the EPI position as a great opportunity and felt that he could struggle along for a few months at some point with little or no salary should the company sustain continued losses. At the same time, he felt he would have a difficult time finding another job if all he would be able to point to was five or six months' duty on a sinking ship.

SUGGESTED QUESTIONS

1. What are the important factors in Bill Hamilton's decision of whether or not to join Epicure Products, Inc.?
2. Should he join the company? If so, what arrangement should he propose to the president for joining the firm?
3. What is the potential of the company?

EXHIBIT 1
Epicure Products, Inc. (A)
Resume of William J. Hamilton

25 Park Drive	(617) 266-5192
Apartment 2	Married
Boston, Mass. 02215	5'10", 170 lbs.
Birth: May 29, 1944	

Work experience

1968—   United Home Products Company
Industrial engineer and assistant to the department manager in the operation of a soap processing and packaging department at the Plymouth, Mass. plant. Work included budgeting, cost analysis, methods improvement, and other industrial engineering functions as well as assisting the department manager in the day-to-day operation of the 16-man department.

Summer work   United Home Products Company
Summer of 1967 spent working at Plymouth plant as line supervisor in detergents packing department. Summer of 1966 was project engineer on cost and quality problems at Philadelphia plant.

Bonney Forge Company, Inc.
Summer of 1965 worked in production control and accounting departments of small Allentown, Pa., forgings company.

Education

1966–68   Sloan School of Management, M.I.T.
Received an M.S. degree in management, February 1969, having completed all necessary requirements in September 1968. Courses of special interest were marketing management, marketing research, management information technology, financial management, a marketing-oriented management information system for the Corning Glass Company, Corning, N.Y., and consumer behavior. Thesis title: "Consumer Behavior as Risk Taking; a New Model and New Hypotheses." Received fellowship first year and wrote chapters of a probability and statistics text. Worked as research assistant during second year.

1962–66   Yale University
Received B.S. in industrial administration. Graduated magna cum laude and elected to Phi Beta Kappa. Varsity lightweight crew, four years; captain, 1966.

Military status   1Y, due to near-sightedness.

EXHIBIT 2
Epicure Products, Inc. (A)
Stereo high-fidelity components

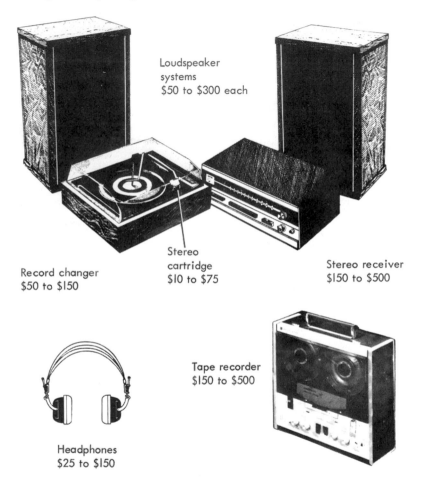

Loudspeaker
systems
$50 to $300 each

Record changer
$50 to $150

Stereo
cartridge
$10 to $75

Stereo receiver
$150 to $500

Tape recorder
$150 to $500

Headphones
$25 to $150

EXHIBIT 3
Epicure Products, Inc. (A)
Specifications and list price of selected loudspeaker systems*

Loudspeaker system	Drivers	Dimensions(D x W x H)			Suggested list price
EPI Model 100	2	9"	x 11"	x 21"	$ 109.00
KLH 22	2	7.5	x 10	x 18	54.95
KLH 17	2	9	x 12	x 23	69.95
KLH 6	2	12	x 12.5	x 23.5	134.00
KLH 5	4	12	x 14	x 26	179.95
KLH 12	4	15	x 22.5	x 29	279.00†
KLH 9	Electrostatic	3	x 30	x 66	1,140.00‡
AR 4x	2	9	x 10	x 19	57.00§
AR 2ax	3	11.5	x 13.5	x 24	125.00§
AR 3a	3	11.5	x 14	x 25	250.00§

*Data copied by Bill Hamilton from manufacturer specification sheets.
†KLH Model 12 and Model 9 are both floor models. All others listed above are of common bookshelf design.
‡KLH 9 price is $1,140 per pair.
§All AR speakers are subject to substantial discounting by the dealer.

EXHIBIT 4
Epicure Products, Inc. (A)
Balance sheet (February 28, 1969)

ASSETS

Current Assets:		
Cash		$ 4,070
Accounts receivable.................		2,520
Inventories		8,378
Total Current Assets		$14,968
Other Assets:		
Operating equipment	$6,876	
Less: Depreciation.................	286	
		$ 6,590
Organization expense		300
Total Assets		$21,858

LIABILITIES AND NET WORTH

Current Liabilities:		
Loans payable		$ 6,850
Accounts payable		4,300
Total Current Liabilities		$11,150
Net Worth:		
Common stock		
Class A Voting*....................	$10,000	
Class B nonvoting†	2,500	
	$12,500	
Deficit	(1,792)	
Total Net Worth		$10,708
Total Liabilities and Net Worth		$21,858

* Authorized 6,375 shares no par value; issued and outstanding 1,350 shares.
† Authorized 1,125 shares no par value; issued and outstanding 650 shares.

Note

Tax aspects of new venture activities

I. INTRODUCTION

This note is prepared to highlight various federal tax aspects of the financing and operating of a new business. The Note is not intended to be a comprehensive treatment of taxes. State and city income and other taxes (see Part VI below) can also be significant; such taxes are not considered in this Note. The reader should also be aware that both the items subject to federal tax and the provisions of the tax law may be changed during any session of Congress.

Because of the complexity of the tax structure and the problems of applying it to a specific situation, a qualified legal counsel skilled in taxation should be consulted when situations concerning taxation arise, particularly in connection with the formation or acquisition of a company. However, because taxes often have a major influence upon business decisions and the form of transactions, a general knowledge of taxation is invaluable to the entrepreneur.

References to Bittker and Eustice[1] indicate the use of the most thorough and understandable textbook dealing with the relationship between corporations and shareholders.

II. FEDERAL CORPORATE INCOME TAX

The Internal Revenue Code will be described as it generally applies to all corporations. It is a fact, however, that the treatment of income and

---

[1]Boris I. Bittker and James S. Eustice, *Federal Income Taxation of Corporations and Shareholders* (Boston, 1971).

276

expense of different kinds of businesses is far from uniform, e.g., the depletion allowance given to oil, gas, and other extractive industries.

Corporate income tax rates. The normal tax rate is 22 percent on all taxable corporate earnings. An additional tax (surtax) of 26 percent is applied to income in excess of $25,000 thus giving an effective tax rate of 48 percent on earnings over $25,000. An example will clarify the application of this "step" rate structure:

Corporate income tax on corporate earnings of $100,000

First $25,000 x 22%	$ 5,500	Tax payable
Next $75,000 x 48%	36,000	Tax payable
	$41,500	Total tax on $100,000

In sum then: 22 percent on the first $25,000; 48 percent on all earnings over $25,000

A. Multiple corporations

Prior to the Tax Reform Act of 1969, there were two chief advantages in dividing an economic entity into two or more corporations:

1. Surtax exemptions. Because the first $25,000 of a corporation's income is exempt from the 26 percent surtax, management could lower the total amount of tax paid by the *overall* enterprise by using the multiple corporation form of doing business. Each individual corporation would then be benefited by having its first $25,000 in income taxed at a rate of only 22 percent plus a special multiple corporation surcharge of 6 percent for an effective tax rate of 28 percent. An example will indicate the savings made possible by such corporate proliferation:

	Single corporation	Two corporations A	Two corporations B
Earnings	$75,000	$37,500	$37,500
Taxes:			
Single (.22 x $25,000 + .48 x $50,000) .	29,500		
Two (.28 x $25,000 + .48 x $12,500) ...		13,000	13,000
Total Taxes......................	29,500	$26,000	
Savings in Taxes		$ 3,500	

Similarly, $8,500 in tax savings could be achieved merely by splitting a single, $75,000-earning corporation into three $25,000-earning corporations—a savings amounting in this example to 11 percent of the overall entity's profits.

2. Accumulated earnings exemptions. As will be discussed in Section E below, each corporation is permitted to retain a minimum of $100,000 of earnings without becoming subject to an accumulated earnings tax. This $100,000 credit could be expanded by the use of multiple corporations, each with its own $100,000 exemption.

Even before the 1969 act, the use of multiple corporations was always subject to scrutiny by the IRS. In particular, if the multiple corporation form had no valid business purpose other than tax avoidance, or if the individual corporations were not actually engaged in significant business activity, the courts would disallow the two previously mentioned tax advantages. But evidently such subjective tests were found unreliable, for the drafters of the 1969 act initiated an absolute phaseout of the multiple corporation tax benefits—with or without the presence of a valid business purpose or significant business activity among the individual corporations. The gradual diminishing of tax benefits is to continue through 1974. Beginning in 1975, the component members of a multiple corporation group will be limited to *one* $25,000 surtax exemption and *one* $100,000 accumulated earnings tax credit for the entire group.

Even in the wake of the 1969 act, there may still be some tax advantages of multiple corporations. Bittker and Eustice suggest that separate accounting methods and piecemeal sales of portions of the overall business activity are facilitated by the use of the multiple form. But, in general, the authors admit that tax advantages in this area now exist on "a substantially reduced scale."

Before and after 1969, there has always been one major tax *disadvantage* of multiple corporations: an operating loss from one corporation may not be used to offset the operating profits of another corporation as would be possible when earnings are reported on a consolidated return. (See Section H below.)

B. Business expenses

Legitimate business expenses are, of course, deductible from gross profits in the computation of taxable income. Thus, the designation of items as "expenses" is a way of reducing corporate taxes. Normally, the small business owner has wide latitude in treating certain expenses which may affect his personal income. But extreme positions, whose evident motivations are tax avoidance, will be frowned upon by the IRS and the courts.

The most common example of both the leeway regarding expense accounting and the polar positions to be avoided is the case of the entrepreneur's salary. He could pay out his corporation's profits to himself as dividends, but since dividends are not deductible to the corporation and are income to the shareholder, he would subject the income to both corporate and personal taxes (rates on personal income range from 14 percent to 70 percent). He would rather adjust his salary upward. Salary receives favored tax treatment in that it is taxed at a maximum marginal rate of 50 percent (except where the employee has substantial "preference income") and it represents a business expense to the corporation which would lower its taxable income. Thus extracting money as salary instead of dividends avoids the corporate tax and may lower the marginal rate at which the money is taxed to the shareholder-employee. But if the IRS finds the amount of such a salary to be unreasonable, the unreasonable portion of it will be disallowed as a deduction to the corporation.

On the other hand, the smaller company owner may elect to receive a low salary and allow earnings to accumulate in the corporation, anticipating that he can eventually realize these profits at capital gains rates through a subsequent sale or liquidation of the company. However, once again extreme positions are penalized—in this case by the penalty tax on unreasonable accumulations of earnings over $100,000. (See Section E below.)

1. Depreciation. *(a) Methods:* The three most commonly used depreciation methods are straight line, declining balance, and sum-of-the-years' digits.

-- Straight line. The easiest way to explain this method is by example. Using straight line, an asset with a useful life of 10 years depreciates at the uniform rate of 10 percent of the difference between cost and salvage value per year, a 20-year asset at 5 percent a year. Thus, the flow of tax-deductible expense is spread evenly over the asset's life.
-- Declining balance. The most commonly used of the accelerated methods of depreciation, the declining balance procedure employs a percentage rate based on what would be the appropriate straight-line rate, and then applies this rate each year to the undepreciated balance. Again, an example is easier. In *double*-declining balance (which, for tax purposes, is the maximum rate allowed under any circumstances), 200 percent of one year's comparable straight-line percentage is used. Thus, on a $10,000 machine with a 10-year life and a salvage value of $2,000, the maximum rate would be 20 percent (200 percent of 10 percent). The first year's depreciation would therefore be $2,000 (the amount on which depreciation is computed is not reduced by salvage value but the asset cannot be depreciated below its salvage value). For the second year, the 20 percent rate would be applied to the remaining balance of $8,000 ($10,000 − $2,000) to yield a depreciation expense of $1,600. Under this method, there will always be an undepreciated balance.

The practical effect of this method is to write off about two thirds of the cost of an asset with no salvage value during the first half of its life, thus generating more cash flow during the early years. But this method may be changed to straight-line depreciation of the balance at any time, and this changeover is usually made as soon as straight line gives higher depreciation charges than declining balance.

——Sum-of-the-years' digits (SYD). Here, a fraction using the years of remaining life as the numerator and the sum of the years of total life as the constant denominator, multiplied by the depreciable amount (the difference between cost and salvage value), gives the depreciation in any one year. For a $10,000 machine with a 10-year life and no salvage value, depreciation in the first year would be 10/55 (10 = years of life remaining; 55 = sum of 1, 2, 3, ... 10) x $10,000, or $1,818. For the second year, the depreciation expense would be 9/55 x $10,000 or $1,636.

Generally, the SYD method yields smaller deductions than the double-declining balance method in the first years, but when there is no salvage value it quickly catches up and passes that other accelerated method. The choice between these two methods depends thus upon the estimated period for which the asset will be held, salvage value, and other less specifiable considerations.

(b) When the methods may be used for tax accounting:

——Not depreciable.   Land, goodwill, brand and trade names.

——Straight line.   May be used with any property, new or used, equipment, or buildings.

——Declining balance.   In general, is allowable when depreciation is assumed to be greatest in the earliest years, and in specific, only where the useful life is three years or more. The availability of the specific declining balance rates are as follows, each as a maximum:

125 percent—used residential buildings with a remaining life of at least 20 years. Note that this is an exception to the general rule that only nonaccelerated methods can be applied to used buildings (used office buildings, for example).

150 percent—new buildings purchased or built after 1969, new equipment acquired before 1954, or used equipment acquired after 1953.

200 percent—new residential buildings, or new or rebuilt equipment acquired after 1954.

——Sum-of-the-years' digits.   Allowable where the useful life is three years or more.

(c) Additional depreciation deductions:

——First year write-off.   When equipment has a useful life of at least six years, any business is permitted to charge off in the first year 20 percent of cost up to $10,000 *in addition* to the regular depreciation on the balance. Thus, if the Jones Company buys a drill press with a 10-year life for $10,000, it can deduct $2,000 in the first year, plus any form of depreciation it chooses on the remaining $8,000.

--Asset depreciation range system (ADR). Since early 1971, businessmen have been able to increase their depreciation deduction on new and used equipment placed in service after December 31, 1970, by 25 percent or more. Under the asset depreciation range system, a taxpayer can choose to reduce the guidelines for economic lives announced by the IRS for depreciating equipment (*not* buildings) by as much as 20 percent. Even though the total amount of depreciation deductions is unchanged, shortening the depreciable life raises the amount of each annual depreciation deduction and thus produces tax savings more quickly than smaller annual deductions spread over a longer period of years.

(d) Two pitfalls—recapture and preference:

--Recapture. Simply put, what would normally be a capital gain on the sale or disposition of depreciable property is taxed as ordinary income to the extent that it represents a recoupment or recapture of prior depreciation taken. With regard to equipment the full amount of depreciation previously taken can be recaptured as ordinary income whereas with regard to buildings only the difference between accelerated and staight-line depreciation is recaptured as ordinary income (residential rental property receives additional favorable recapture treatment).

This situation arises when the book value of a capital asset decreases faster than its corresponding market value. For instance, some vehicle rental companies have depreciated their autos at an accelerated rate (40 percent the first year using the declining balance method on a five-year life). In doing so, a $3,000 car depreciates $1,200 in the first year, and $720 in the second. At the end of the second year, the automobile may be resold for $1,500 or $420 higher than the book value (basis) of $1,080. The $420 is subject to recapture. Thus, if equipment is eventually sold, depreciation does not avoid ordinary income tax. But by postponing such a tax, it does provide some time-value-of-money advantages to the business.

--Preference. As will be explained further in section V(A) below, the 1969 Tax Reform Act established a new tax of 10 percent on certain items of income and deduction for both the individual and the corporate entity. One of the principal items of tax preference applicable to a corporate taxpayer is the excess of accelerated depreciation on buildings and certain leased equipment over straight-line depreciation. A basic exclusion of $30,000 is allowed plus an additional deduction equal to the amount of income tax owed for the year. After that, the individual or corporation must pay a flat 10 percent on the excess.

(e) Special five-year life items.   Several items fall into special categories which permit depreciation over five years, in most cases a period significantly shorter than the item's useful life. Such items include certain railroad rolling stock, expenses for rehabilitating certain low-income rental property, certain coal mine safety equipment, and certain child-care facilities.

2. Investment credit.   The Revenue Act of 1971 restored the 7 percent investment credit for property acquired after March 31, 1971. The investment credit allows a deduction from tax liabilities of as much as 7 percent of the investment cost of new or used depreciable equipment having a useful life of seven years or more (the credit is reduced and eventually eliminated when the useful life of the asset is less than seven years). Note that unlike a business expense which constitutes only a reduction of gross income, such a credit is subtracted *directly* from the amount of taxes payable.

The Code also provides for a recapture of any investment credit taken prior to that date on an "early disposition" of the asset involved. In other words, if the property upon which this credit is based is disposed of before the end of its useful life, a prorated part of the credit will be recaptured by adding to the tax liability in the year of disposition.

There are other rules involving the investment tax credit. (1) It cannot exceed the first $25,000 of the overall tax liability plus 50 percent of the balance in any one year. (2) But if a portion of it goes unused, it can be carried back three years or carried forward five years against past and future tax liabilities. (3) Finally, the credit is independent of depreciation and does not affect the basis of the depreciable property. Thus, if Jones Company buys a drill press (assuming a 10-year life) for $10,000, it has an investment credit of $700 in addition to a deduction for the first-year's depreciation regardless of the chosen method of depreciation.

3. Depletion.   Depletion is essentially a method of recovering the value of natural deposits exhausted during the course of an extractive business. Like depreciation, it is a tax-deductible expense. There are two methods of charging off depletion:

(a) *Cost depletion method.*   The operation of the cost depletion method resembles depreciation of capital assets. An estimate is made of the quantity of the deposit (i.e., proven reserves) and of the cost of the deposits or its value on March 1, 1913, if acquired or inherited before that date. From these a depletion cost per unit (e.g., per ton, per pound) is derived. As the mineral is sold, the units sold times the depletion cost per unit yields the depletion deduction for the year. Each year the depletable base of the property is reduced by the depletion deduction taken.

(b) *Percentage depletion.* Applicable to most minerals and natural mineral combinations, this method frequently permits recovery of much more than cost. The deduction is a percentage *of gross income.* It may not amount to more than 50 percent of the net taxable income computed without regard to the depletion allowance. Typical percentage depletion allowances, based on gross income, range from 22 percent for oil and gas wells (down from the pre-1969 rate of 27 1/2 percent) to 5 percent for minerals such as clay. Most depletion allowances are in the range from 10 percent to 15 percent. Finally, percentage depletion is based on the conservative receipt of income from the raw product if marketable in that form (whether or not marketable at a profit) and *not* the value of the finished product—e.g., none of the value added to raw clay in brick making can be used in figuring the depletion allowance.

The depletion deduction may be calculated by either the cost or the percentage method. Normally that method is used which yields the highest allowance. There are two caveats, however: (1) Although percentage depletion is allowed even after the cost of the property has been recovered, the excess of percentage depletion deductions over the adjusted cost basis of each item of depletable property constitutes a tax preference item potentially subject to an additional 10 percent tax. (2) Any cost or percentage depletion deductions taken are considered as reductions in the cost basis of the property—in effect, the basis for determining gain or loss on sale is adjusted downward.

4. Organizational expense. A corporation may elect for tax purposes to amortize its organizational expenses over a period of not less than five years. Such an election must be made by the end of the first year of doing business, and a statement to that effect must be attached to the tax returns along with comments, descriptions, and the dates of these expenses, as well as the number of months over which these expenses are to be deducted.

The expenses must have been incurred before the end of the tax year in which the corporation actually begins the business for which it was organized. In addition, the Code sets up *three criteria* for defining a legitimate (and therefore, tax deductible) organizational expense:

(*a*) an expenditure incident to the creation of the corporation;
(*b*) an expenditure chargeable to the capital account; and
(*c*) an expenditure of a character which, if expended incident to the creation of a corporation having limited life, would be amortizable over such life.

To help further, the Internal Revenue Service's regulations, which help to explain the finer points of the Code, lists several examples of legitimate, amortizable organizational expenses:

(*a*) legal services incident to the organization of the corporation,

(b)   necessary accounting services,
(c)   expenses of temporary directors,
(d)   expenses connected with organizational meetings of directors or shareholders, and
(e)   fees paid to the State of incorporation.

The principal organizational expenses which are *not amortizable and deductible* are those related to stock issuance or transfer of assets, such as commissions, underwriting fees, and even certificate printing costs. The rationale behind this prohibition is that these expenses, as Bittker and Eustice put it, "do not create an asset that is exhausted over the life of the corporation."

Finally, *re*organizational expenses may also be amortized for tax purposes to the extent that they are directly incident to the creation of a new corporation as in the case of split-offs or consolidations.

5. Research and development expenses.   In the case of organizational expenses, the taxpayer must defer the expense and deduct it over a period of at least five years if he wishes to create a tax deduction. With research and development costs, however, the taxpayer has an *option* of either writing the expenses off in the year incurred or of capitalizing and amortizing them over the life of the project or if they do not relate to a specific project then on a straight-line basis only over a period of not less than five years.

Election to amortize these expenses over the five-year period requires a notification procedure similar to that described above for organizational expenditures.

There are several special rules in this area. *(a)* The option to write off research expenses in the year incurred does not apply to expenditures for depreciable property. *(b)* With costs incurred in oil or gas exploration, an operator may elect during the first year either to write off intangible exploratory costs (wages, fuel, rental expense) as they are incurred, or to capitalize these costs and recover them through depreciation or depletion. In the unlikely event the operator elects to capitalize intangible costs, he may expense those costs during the year that the well is abandoned.

6. Intangibles.   The cost of those intangibles whose productive usefulness is definitely limited in duration is usually depreciable (amortized) on a straight-line basis only. Examples of such *depreciable* intangibles are: patents, copyrights, licenses, and franchises.

On the other hand, intangibles whose period of usefulness is indefinite may not be amortized for tax purposes. Examples of such *nondepreciable* assets are: goodwill, brand names, and trade names. Although the write-offs are not tax deductible, the New York and American Stock Exchanges require that even these indefinite-duration intangibles be depreciated for the purpose of corporate accounting.

7. Corporate pensions. Amounts used to provide pension benefits are deductible as expense and are not taxable to the employee until he receives them so long as they are in accordance with provisions allowable under the Code. Generally, to be deductible such expenses must be paid by the company to a separate entity rather than simply accrued on the company's books. Thus employers frequently set up a pension trust, make contributions to the trust, and have the trust pay the retirement benefits; or make payments directly to an insurance company.

8. Corporate life insurance. An employee can exclude from gross income the premium on $50,000 of group-term life insurance provided by his employer. When a life insurance policy has been taken out on the life of an officer or stockholder of a corporation or a member of a partnership and the company is directly or indirectly a beneficiary of the policy, the premiums are not deductible, but the proceeds received upon the insured's death are tax-free.

C. Accounting period

1. Establishment. A new taxpayer may adopt either a calendar or a fiscal year basis on filing his first return. A new corporation may file its return on a fiscal year basis without applying to the revenue service for permission. A sole proprietor of an unincorporated firm may not figure his income from his business and his income from other sources on the basis of different tax years; e.g., he may not operate his business on a fiscal year basis and file his individual returns on a calendar year basis.

2. Change of period. The accounting period may be changed by application before the end of the short tax year (the period between the original and new accounting periods must be less than 12 months). The application will usually be approved if there is a substantial business reason for the change. The change will ordinarily not be approved if it substantially reduces a taxpayer's tax liability by shifting income or deductions.

D. Loss carryovers

1. Mechanics of computation. Nearly all taxpayers are allowed to carry back their net operating losses and apply them against prior income before taxes. This provision is applicable to corporations, individuals, estates, and partnerships. A net operating loss can be carried *back three years* and is first applied to the earliest of the three years; the remainder, to the second year preceding; and the second remainder, to the year immediately preceding.

A net operating loss may generally be carried *forward five years* following the loss year if the taxable income for the three years preceding is not sufficient to absorb the loss. When using this provision, the loss is applied to the years closest to the loss year successively until the loss is absorbed.

We can diagram this process of carrybacks and subsequent carry forwards as shown in *Figure 1.*

FIGURE 1

Year 0 (loss year)

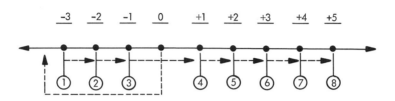

Thus, the fifth year in the future is the eighth and *last* year to which the current year's loss will be applied.

2. Constraints. To prevent traffic in loss corporations, there are restrictions against the preservation of carryovers in situations where there is a substantial change in ownership of such a corporation with a potential operating loss-carryover. In all cases, carryovers will be denied if the principal purpose of the acquisition was to avoid taxes. As a test of motives, this is a *subjective* standard. There are *objective* criteria as well. Thus, preservation of carryovers is denied when the following three circumstances occur together:

(a)   Fifty percent of the stock of the loss corporation has been acquired within two years by 10 or fewer persons;

(b)   the increase in holdings is due to purchase *or* redemption of stock; and

(c)   the corporation has not continued to carry on a trade or business substantially the same as that conducted before the change in the percentage ownership of the stock.

There are two additional rules regarding acquisitions:

(a)   *No carryback* of tax losses is permitted in any acquisition or merger case.

(b)   For the surviving corporation in a tax-free merger to be able to use the full value of the tax loss *carry-forward*, shareholders of the loss corporation must retain 20 percent or more of the common stock of the surviving corporation. For each percentage point below 20 percent, 5 percent of the net operating loss carry-forward becomes unavailable to reduce the taxable income of the surviving corporation.

E. Accumulated earnings tax

1. Purpose of the tax and its mechanics. The most common means of distributing a corporation's earnings to its shareholders is via dividends. But dividends are taxable at ordinary income rates. As a result, individual shareholders in closely held corporations in high tax brackets are tempted to avoid paying out dividends. Instead, accumulating these earnings within the corporate shell (and thereby eluding the individual income tax), these shareholders anticipate later dispositions of their stock (through sale, redemption, merger, or liquidation) which will retrieve those earnings at the lower capital gains rates.

To prevent this tax-avoidance procedure, the Internal Revenue Code provides for a special tax on undistributed corporate earnings in excess of $100,000 where such earnings are deemed to be for the purpose of avoiding personal income tax and are beyond the reasonable present or anticipated needs of the business. For a small, closely held company, the existence of a cash balance which is in excess of $100,000 and which is not drawn down below $100,000 during seasonal swings in the company's operations is a red flag to IRS investigators that the accumulation of earnings is excessive. The tax rate is 27½ percent on the first $100,000 (in excess of the allowable $100,000), and 38½ percent on additional amounts of unreasonable accumulation in any year. The accumulated earnings tax is especially important to the entrepreneur, because for all intents and purposes, it is only levied against closely held corporations, for it is with such corporations where the relationship between the corporate entity and the individual shareholder is so close, that corporate motives are most open to attack. The accumulation of cash in excess of $100,000 in a closely held corporation must be accompanied by bona fide and documented plans for the use of those funds in such activities as building new facilities, an acquisition program, and so on.

2. Criteria and examples. The *critical* provision of the accumulated earnings tax laws is the motive standard—i.e., the provision which points the finger at "a tax avoidance purpose" as the signal to invoke the tax. The "reasonable business needs" test was designed originally as only a procedural buttress to this one basic standard. Thus, the IRS's attack will always begin with an attack on the corporate motive for accumulating earnings. But because motives are subjective and difficult to prove, the actual cases in this area inevitably turn on the question of what is and is not a "reasonable present or anticipated business need." It is here that the defendant corporation will launch its defense. In other words, the establishment of a valid business need will "prove" a valid motive. This process is diagrammed in Figure 2.

The IRS will usually begin its attack on the corporate motive by examining three general issues or considerations:

FIGURE 2

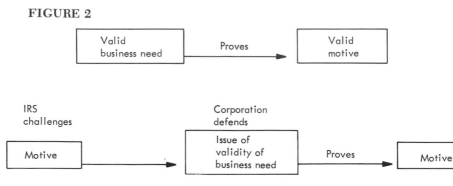

(a) The presence or absence of dealings between the corporation and its shareholders, such as loans or other distributions for the personal benefit of such shareholders. The presence of such dealings is indicative of an improper motive behind corporate accumulations, for if the earnings were available for shareholder loans, it is clear that no valid *corporate* business need existed.

(b) Whether the corporation has used its accumulated earnings to make investments in property or securities unrelated to the business. Again, the existence of such investments evinces corporate capacity to distribute its earnings as dividends.

(c) The dividend history of the corporation. A consistent history of dividend distribution will help the corporation to prove a valid purpose

As Bittker and Eustice point out, these three issues are not controlling. "Thus, corporations have escaped the penalty tax . . . despite poor dividend records, unrelated investments, and loans to shareholders, on establishing that the purpose of the accumulation was not to avoid shareholder tax"—once again proving that the motive standard is *the* bedrock test in this area.

In cases against the IRS, the burden of proof is on the taxpayer. Thus, the corporation will be forced to rebut the IRS allegations by showing a valid motive—almost always by proving the existence of a valid business need. While accumulations used to provide against *generalized* or *unrealistic* needs or hazards will not pass the test, the following examples, offered by Bittker and Eustice, constitute acceptable needs:

(a) Bona fide expansion of business or replacement of plant.

(b) Planned acquisition of a business enterprise through purchasing stock or assets.

(c) Retirement of bona fide business indebtedness.

(d) Working capital for inventories, etc.

(e) Investments or loans to suppliers or customers.

(*f*)   Need to meet competition.
(*g*)   Funding pension plans.
(*h*)   Reserves for *specific* risks such as strikes, loss of a a principal customer, or potential liability from litigation.

F. Personal holding companies

Like its cousin the accumulated earnings tax, the tax on personal holding companies is designed to deter wealthy (and consequently, high tax bracket) individuals who would incorporate their holdings and refrain from distributions in the form of dividends, relying on later dispositions of corporate stock to retreive any earnings at capital gains rates. Because the tax rate is so Draconian—*70 percent on the undistributed income* of a personal holding company (with the exception of long-term capital gains)—an individual businessman or investor is not likely to deliberately create a taxable personal holding company. Rather, it is normally through ignorance of the tax laws that a personal holding company situation is created.

What is a personal holding company? There are *two tests*, an income source test and a stock ownership test. It is important to note that an organization must satisfy *both* tests to be held liable for the 70 percent tax.

1. Income source test.   A taxable personal holding company is a corporation which receives *more than 60 percent* of its total adjusted annual gross income in the form of revenue classifiable under the Code as "personal holding company income." This circular definition is resolved by the Code's definition of personal holding company income as:

dividends
rents (except where (1) rents are 50% or more of gross income and (2)
   dividends paid are equal to or greater than the amount if any by which
   personal holding company income exceeds 10% of gross income)
interest
royalties
personal service fees (where (1) the customer can designate the employee
   [e.g., a athlete/entertainer] who is to do the work, and (2) the employee
   owns more than 25% of the company)

In general then, personal holding company income is either income derived from passive sources or income that would otherwise be compensation to an individual for his personal services.

2. Stock ownership test.   An organization is classified as a personal holding company if five or fewer individuals have a 50 percent or greater ownership in the company. For purposes of this second test, members of an individual's immediate family do not qualify as separate owners. Thus, it is difficult to avoid this test in closely held firms, where ownership of the company must be divided evenly among a minimum of 11 individuals to elude personal holding company status.

Finally, it should be recalled that the 70 percent personal holding company tax is a tax on only *undistributed* corporate income. Thus, even if a businessman should find himself in personal holding company status, he can avoid the penalty tax by simply paying out the corporation's earnings. As long as such complete distributions are contemplated, a personal holding company may be useful where an individual or family desires centralized control of a group of investments, such as real estate, stocks, bonds, copyrights, mineral rights, or a group of small businesses.

Certain organizations are exempt from the personal holding company tax. From the small businessman's point of view the most important are probably real estate and finance companies. But they must meet specific tests involving minimum percentages of net rent or interest income and minimum percentages of business expenses. In addition, in finance companies, loans to 10 percent stockholders may not exceed $5,000.

Foreign organizations classifiable as personal holding companies are beyond the reach of this law. However, U.S. shareholders in such companies are required to include undistributed foreign personal holding company income in their own personal gross income.

G. Capital gains and dividends received by a corporation

Net long-term capital gains by a corporation are usually taxed at a maximum capital gains rate of 30 percent. However, if the level of other corporate earnings is below $25,000, it is permitted, if it is advantageous to the corporation, to include capital gains as part of regular income and be taxed at the 22 percent rate on earnings up to a total of $25,000 and then at a 48 percent rate on the excess over $25,000.

To mitigate the effect of double taxation on corporate earnings, 85 percent of the dividends received by a corporation on stock held in most other domestic corporations are ordinarily exempt from tax. If a corporation receives dividends from a company in the same affiliated group (parent and 80 percent owned subsidiaries) and if an election is made, no tax is payable on the dividends. In electing to take this 100 percent deduction, however, each of the others in the group must forfeit its right to exempt the first $25,000 of earnings from the 26 percent corporate surtax and to exempt its first $100,000 of accumulated earnings from the accumulated earnings tax. To counteract the surtax exemption disallowance previously mentioned (see Section II, A, 2) which affects affiliated groups of corporations, the 1969 act permits a group to elect to increase its dividends received deduction from the present 85 percent to 100 percent at a rate of two and one-half percentage points each year.

H. Consolidated returns

1. Advantages. The basic advantage of filing consolidated returns is that profits of one corporation can be used to offset the losses of another, thereby allowing the taxpayer to take the losses in the same year without having to resort to the carryover provisions.

2. When consolidated returns may be used. The privilege of filing consolidated returns is limited to affiliated corporations. Such a relationship between corporations commonly results from an acquisition. There are two specific rules regarding when consolidated returns may be filed in the acquisition situation. *Both* must be satisfied.

(a)   To be said to have control over an acquired corporation, the acquiring corporation must own directly at least 80 percent of the voting and nonvoting stock (not including nonvoting preferred stock of the acquiree); and

(b)   Controlling stocks, as defined above, must directly rest in the hands of one or more of the includable corporations. The parent company need control directly only one of the affiliates.

Once the election to file consolidated returns has been made, such returns must continue to be filed in subsequent years unless (a) a new member joins the corporate group, (b) the tax laws are changed, or (c) the Commissioner grants permission to do otherwise.

I. Small business investment companies (SBIC)

Small business investment companies should not be confused with Subchapter S corporations or the provisions surrounding §1244 stock (see below), groups of tax advantages afforded *operating* companies. A small business investment company is equivalent to a venture capital firm—simply put, it provides capital to small business firms. To qualify for the various tax advantages available, an SBIC must comply with the provisions of the Small Business Investment Act of 1958 which, in effect, requires little more than that the SBIC be engaged in actively providing equity capital to small incorporated businesses. Once such compliance is achieved, the following tax advantages are open to SBIC's:

1.   An SBIC pays no tax on dividends received from corporations in which it has an interest. This 100 percent dividend deduction is an increase over the normal 85 percent deduction provided ordinary corporations.

2.   Any losses incurred by an SBIC on the purchase of the convertible debentures of a small business firm are treated as ordinary, rather than as capital losses. Such losses may be sustained through actual sale, exchange, or mere fact of the debentures becoming worthless.

3. An SBIC is exempt from personal holding company tax unless one of its stockholders owns 5 percent or more of a small business in which the SBIC is invested.
4. An SBIC is not subject to the accumulated earnings tax.
5. For the individual shareholders in the SBIC itself, all profits from the sale of shares in the SBIC are treated as capital gains, while all losses are treated as ordinary losses, and thus deductible from ordinary income.

J. Regulated investment companies

1. Definition. A regulated investment company is a corporation (e.g., a mutual fund or investment trust) whose principal source of income is from investments such as dividends, interest, and gains on dispositions of securities.

2. Advantages of qualifying as a regulated investment company. *(a)* The company is taxed only on *undistributed* income. (At least 90 percent of what would otherwise be taxable income must be distributed as dividends.) All dividends paid out constitute valid deductions. *(b)* Any capital gains are passed through to the shareholders, whether or not distributed. *Distributed* capital gains are taxed to the shareholders at capital gains rates depending on individual tax brackets, but *undistributed* capital gains are taxed at the maximum capital gains rate of 30 percent.

3. How to qualify as a regulated investment company. To qualify for the above advantages, a company must satisfy what Bittker and Eustice call "an elaborate network of conditions." For example, in addition to the 90 percent distribution rule the company must:

(a) Be registered under the Investment Company Act of 1940 or be a common trust fund.
(b) *Source of income.* 90 percent of the corporation's gross income must be derived from dividends, interest, and gains on the sale of securities; and
(c) *Diversification.* The company may not invest more than 5 percent of its assets in a single company in which they hold more than 10 percent of the voting securities. This requirement has been waived to some extent to permit venture capital companies to qualify as regulated investment companies. To so qualify, a venture capital firm must file with the SEC to the effect that its business is primarily furnishing capital to companies to exploit inventions, improvements, or products not previously generally available.

Finally, an unincorporated real estate investment trust (REIT) may elect to be taxed substantially similarly to a regulated investment company. But personal holding companies are specifically excluded.

K. Corporate tax returns

Every corporation not expressly exempt, or relieved from the requirement by the District Director, must file an income tax return, even though it has no taxable income, or has conducted no business in that tax year. Those corporations whose anticipated taxes are in excess of $100,000 are required to file a declaration of estimated tax. The tax-payment plan is scaled so that taxes in excess of $100,000 are partially payable during the current tax year. The Revenue and Expenditure Control Act of 1968 provides a transitional reduction of the $100,000 exemption to $5,500 over a five-year period, and an additional reduction over the following five years to $40. After 1978 corporations will be on a similar pay-as-you-go basis that individuals are presently under.

L. Reorganization and liquidation

The maze of rules regarding reorganizations and liquidations are particularly subtle, complex, and technical. As such, they are beyond the scope of this Note. Reference should be made to the more detailed discussion in the Note on acquisitions and mergers for entrepreneurs.

Briefly speaking, however, certain things should be kept in mind.

1. Reorganizations:
   - (a) The exchange of common stock of a company for common stock of the same corporation is nontaxable.
   - (b) Similarly, the exchange of a bond of a corporation for a bond of the same corporation is a tax-free transaction to the extent that the principal amount received does not exceed the principal amount of the bond surrendered.
   - (c) Most recapitalizations wherein the security holder receives a security with fewer rights than the security surrendered are tax-free events.
   - (d) The exchange involved in a statutory merger, where securities of one corporation are exchanged for securities of another, is a tax-free event at the corporate level, and also to the shareholder, with some constraints.
2. Liquidations:
   - (a) Generally speaking, the *corporation* itself does not recognize income on a partial or complete liquidation. Even though the corporation disposes of all or substantially all of its assets at a profit prior to the liquidation, no tax will accrue if the corporation is completely liquidated within a 12-month period.
   - (b) However, with the exception of the liquidation of a wholly owned subsidiary, a corporation *will* recognize ordinary income on certain items such as depreciation and investment credit recapture, and the restoration of bad debt reserves.

(c) When the *shareholder* receives *his* share of the liquidating distribution, he must compute long- or short-term capital gain or loss taxes on the difference between what he paid and what he received for his stock so long as he is not a dealer in securities.

M. Subchapter S corporations—taxing a corporation as a partnership

1. Purpose of Subchapter S. The announced purposes of Subchapter S, as revealed by the 1954 Senate proposal for the bill, were:

(a) to permit "small corporations which are essentially partnerships to enjoy the advantages of the corporate forms of organization without being made subject to possible tax disadvantages of the corporation," and

(b) to "eliminate the influence of the federal income tax in the selection of the form of business organization which may be most desirable under the circumstances."

2. Definition and criteria for qualification. The election of Subchapter S status allows the small corporation to be taxed as a partnership—i.e., the corporation exists to limit individual liability, but as a recipient of income, it is not taxed, acting only as a *conduit* to flow the earnings through to the individual shareholders. They include their pro rata shares of the corporation's income on their individual returns, whether or not such income is distributed. There are *four* principal tests which must be met in order to qualify for Subchapter S treatment:

(a) Must be a domestic corporation.

(b) Only one class of stock may be outstanding.

(c) Not more than 10 shareholders—and these shareholders must be individuals or estates, *not* other corporations.

(d) Not more than 20 percent of the corporation's income may be derived from passive investment sources such as interest, rents, dividends, royalties, gains on sale of securities—sources virtually identical to "personal holding company income." In other words, only operating companies need apply for Subchapter S treatment.

3. Advantages of Subchapter S status. The basic advantage of Subchapter S status is obvious—the qualifying corporation's shareholders retain the limited liability protection of the corporate form while avoiding the double taxation normally inherent in the corporate form of doing business. In its avoidance of double taxation, Subchapter S should be compared to such other devices as their capitalization (Section V, F below) and the payment of high salaries to shareholder-employees (Section II, B above)—both alternative means for minimizing the effects of taxation at both the corporate and individual level. But there are other specific advantages as well:

(a)   All long-term capital gains are passed through to the shareholders as individuals, and taxed at capital gains rates.
(b)   Other income is ordinary income, regardless of what it is at the corporate level. This means, of course, that ordinary losses at the corporate level are passed through to become ordinary losses at the individual level, and can therefore be deducted from the individual's ordinary income. A deductible loss, however, is limited to the cost of the individual's stock plus any indebtedness owed him by the corporation.
(c)   Carryovers are allowed at both the individual and corporate level.
(d)   Not subject to accumulated earnings tax or personal holding company tax.

Subchapter S is particularly useful for entrepreneurs engaged in risky activities. Early losses of a new enterprise can be used to offset investors' ordinary income in the year of occurrence of the business loss. When operations become profitable, the corporation could elect then to be taxed as a corporation. This election would enable the entrepreneur to utilize losses and also give stock to his children while the stock has a low value so that the children could receive the benefits of the increase in stock value. The entrepreneur could thereby lower both his gift tax (by virtue of the low stock value at the time of the gift) and his potential estate tax (since the heirs would already own the stock).

4. The future of Subchapter S.   Bittker and Eustice suggest that there is "a substantial likelihood" that changes in the near future will liberalize the eligiblity rules of Subchapter S. Of special interest are their predictions that:

(a)   The number of permissible shareholders will be raised from 10 to 15 in certain circumstances;
(b)   The one-class-of-stock requirement will be modified to permit other nonvoting equity issues such as preferred stock; and
(c)   The 20 percent passive income restrictions will be repealed.

The latter prediction is particularly significant given the close similarity between the forbidden passive income of Subchapter S and "personal holding company income." It would seem, in fact, that the repeal of the 20 percent passive income restriction for Subchapter S would make the personal holding company tax a dead letter since such personal holding companies could elect Subchapter S status (given 10 shareholders) and avoid the 70 percent tax.

N. Sale of mixed assets and installment sales

In any sale of depreciable and nondepreciable assets for an agreed-upon sum, the sum should be allocated to the different items sold even though separate prices were not at first set with the purchaser. This method of setting the prices of separate assets leaves the question of value of each to be agreed upon by the buyer and seller. With respect to assets like inventory, buildings, land, and equipment, the method allows buyer and seller to bargain about the problem of minimizing their respective taxes. The government may disallow the allocation under certain conditions but will usually accept any allocation which has been negotiated at arm's length by the buyer and seller.

The buyer usually wishes to allocate as much of the selling price as the Internal Revenue Service (IRS) will allow to inventory (to minimize profit on its subsequent sale) and to the depreciable assets (so maximum depreciation can be charged in the future against income over the depreciable life of the asset). The seller, on the other hand, wishes to allocate as much of the selling price as the IRS will allow to the nondepreciable assets, such as land and goodwill, so none of the depreciation previously charged against the depreciable assets will have to be declared as ordinary income; recapture of depreciation on equipment occurs when depreciable assets are sold at a price above their depreciated value. The effort in these negotiations between buyer and seller is toward minimizing their respective taxes. To be valid, the determined allocation of the price must be reasonable.

In sum: (1) *Buyer*—allocate to inventory and depreciable assets; and (2) *Seller*—allocate to goodwill and other *non*depreciable assets.

An installment sale of assets may permit income to be reported on an installment basis. A dealer in personal property may allocate the income attributed to the portion of the sales for which cash is actually received during the tax year. In real property transactions, gains can be allocated to the cash portion of sales (1) if there is no payment in the year of sale, or (2) if the payments in the year of sale do not exceed 30 percent of the selling price. If no interest rate is attributed to the notes involved in a transaction the IRS will impute an interest rate (usually 5 percent) which will be used in calculations of the 70 percent minimum non-cash portion of the transaction.

III. PARTNERSHIPS

The basic theory of a partnership is that the partners are taxed as individuals on their pro rata shares of the partnership's income or loss. The partnership as an entity is not taxed. It serves only as a conduit to pass earnings and losses through to the individual partners. On a partner's individual return, his allocable share of items such as partnership income or loss is reported *even though some or all may be retained in the partnership* rather than actually distributed to the partners in cash. This is in contrast to the corporation, where the shareholder reports as taxable income only the dividends actually distributed to him. There is *no accumulated earnings limitation* on partnerships. A separate partnership return is also filed.

A. Family partnerships

Partnerships are sometimes established among family members usually where securities are the primary asset of the partnership. Generally a family member donates shares in the partnership to other members of the family. The effect is to distribute income among several individuals rather than to have the income come to a single family member and be taxed at a higher rate. Family partnerships are eligible for such tax treatment even where states prohibit family partnerships.

Where the donor regularly contributes to the partnership a service significantly greater than the contributions of the other partners, he must be compensated above his proportional share of the partnership. The relationships between family members and their individual maturity is an important factor in establishing a family partnership.

B. Valuation, splits, and so on

The Code and later amendments define clearly the basis upon which depreciation allowances and other gains or losses shall be split; the basis for valuing partnership interests in the event of sales, liquidation, or death; and the tax basis for distributing property. (See Section 704 of the Code.)

C. Expenses

Many of the methods of handling business expenses, such as depreciation, mentioned previously in the discussion of corporation income tax, have application in partnership accounting.

IV. INVENTORS

Under the Code inventors or individuals who back an inventor with money before his invention is completed, get long-term capital gains treatment on transfer of a resulting patent, either outright or on a royalty basis if the patent is sold. (Such treatment is not available to the creator of a literary or artistic composition.) This treatment also applies to the sales of rights under patent applications, even if no patent is obtained. These rules do not apply to a relative (except a brother or sister) or employer of an inventor, nor to a corporation in which the inventor has a substantial interest. Under these latter conditions, the proceeds are usually treated as ordinary income.

V. INDIVIDUALS

A. Individual income tax rates

1. Rates on ordinary income.   Tax rates on individual ordinary income (as opposed to capital gains) vary from *14 percent* on the first $500 to *70 percent* on annual income in excess of $100,000. When the return is filed jointly by married taxpayers, the tax rates are based on double the income amounts given above.

The effect of taxes on ordinary income was reduced somewhat by the 1969 act's provision that a new maximum marginal tax rate of *50 percent* on *earned* taxable income is applicable for taxable years after December 31, 1971. For these purposes, earned income includes: wages, salaries, professional fees, and compensation for professional services. The maximum marginal tax rate for *unearned* income (generally defined as income from passive sources: e.g., dividends, rents, interest, royalties, annuities, and so on) remains at 70 percent.

2. Income averaging.   Individuals may elect to spread bunched or stepped up income over five years through income averaging, a device enabling the taxpayer to spread *all* his income (long-term capital gains, wagering gains, *earned* income, and the income earned by capital received as a gift or inheritance) in excess of 120 percent of his average income of the previous four years over a quasi-five-year period for purposes of computing tax. Averaging is *not* available unless the excess amount exceeds $3,000.

3. Capital gains and losses.   There are two classes of capital gains and losses.

(a)   *Short-term capital gains and losses* result from the sale or exchange of capital assets held six months or less. Net short-term gains are taxed in full as ordinary income. The treatment of short- term losses is more complex and will be discussed below.

(b)   *Long-term capital gains and losses* result from the sale or exchange of capital assets held more than six months. The tax on net long-term capital gains is at two levels:

  (1)   First $50,000 of long-term capital gains is taxed at either one half of the ordinary income rate for the individual in question *or* 25 percent, whichever is *less*. (For individuals filing singly,

capital gains rates will be *lower* than 25 percent for incomes up to about $22,000. For joint returns, the crossover point is roughly $44,000.)

(2)   Long-term capital gains in excess of $50,000 will be taxed at the new maximum capital gains rate of 35 percent.

(c)   Treatment of short- and long-term capital losses:

(1)   *Net short-term capital losses:* (net short-term capital losses) − (net long-term capital gains) = net short-term capital losses. Such losses may be applied as a direct deduction against ordinary income up to a total of $1,000 in one year. Any unused net capital losses may be carried forward indefinitely to reduce the short-term capital gains of succeeding years in the manner described above including the $1,000 deduction against ordinary income.

(2)   *Long-term capital losses:* (net long-term capital losses) − (net short-term capital gains) = long-term capital losses. Long-term capital losses may be applied as a deduction up to a total of $1,000 from the year's ordinary income, but are taken into account at only 50 percent (i.e., $2,000 of long-term capital losses are required for a $1,000 deduction against ordinary income).

(3)   Net capital losses retain their original character (short or long term) when being carried forward. Unused net long-term losses which can be carried forward from years prior to 1970 may be applied indefinitely at 100 percent. Those resulting since 1970 may only be applied at 50 percent.

4. Summary of maximum tax rates: By source

Earned income 50%
Unearned income 70
Capital gains 35

5. Tax preference items.   In response to what Bittker and Eustice refer to as "a public outcry" against tax shelter manipulations, the 1969 Tax Reform Act created a new tax of 10 percent (in addition to other taxes) on certain items of income and deduction for both the individual and corporate entity. There are two exclusions allowed (first, a basic exclusion of $30,000; second, the usual income tax for the year involved net of allowable credits). But after they are taken, the taxpayer has to pay a flat 10 percent tax on his preference income. For years in which a taxpayer had tax preferences in excess of $30,000 and also showed a net operating loss, special rules apply with respect to deferring payment of the minimum tax until tax benefit of preference items is realized.

In general, the taxpayer may be liable for the new tax on certain income or deductions received from any of the following sources:

(*a*)   Net long-term capital gains (added in at one half the total).
(*b*)   Excess investment interest until 1972 (individuals only).
(*c*)   Excess amortization of pollution control facilities and railroad roll-
        ing stock.
(*d*)   Accelerated depreciation on real property above the straight-line
        rate.
(*e*)   Accelerated depreciation on personal property subject to a net lease
        (individuals only).
(*f*)   Percentage depletion in excess of adjusted basis.
(*g*)   Restricted or qualified stock option.
(*h*)   Excess bad debt deduction of financial institutions.

Example.   Mr. A. has tax preferences of $70,000 from net long-term
capital gains (one half of a $140,000 net long-term capital gain) and
$70,000 excess investment interest. Mr. A. paid $90,000 in income taxes
and is entitled to the $30,000 deduction. Thus, he has preference income
of $140,000 minus deductions of $90,000 and $30,000.

This leaves $20,000 subject to the tax of 10 percent, and therefore Mr.
A. will have to pay an additional $2,000 in taxes.

For the great majority of investors, the enactment of the preference
income tax will not add to their tax liability. However, an entrepreneur
should be aware that this new tax could affect his raising money from
investors who would be liable for this tax.

B. Gift and death taxes

1. Gift taxes.   Gift tax rates vary from 2¼ percent on the first $5,000 to
57¾ percent on amounts exceeding $10 million. The base for the rates
is the *net* gift after the three available deductions—(*a*) a lifetime exemption of $30,000; (*b*) an annual exemption of $3,000 per donee; and (*c*) one
half of the value of noncommunity property (requirement would typically be met in more than 40 states) transferred to a spouse. The purpose
of the gift tax is to prevent a wealthy individual from being able to avoid
the majority of estate taxes by giving property away during his lifetime.
But because of the available exemptions, there is still a more significant
tax saving with transfers by gift as opposed to by estate.

It should be noted that the federal gift tax rates are applied to a donor's
cumulative lifetime gifts after the above two adjustments.

2. Estate taxes.   Upon the death of an individual, assets owned by him
are appraised and a tax is charged against the estate. Estate tax rates vary
from 3 percent on the first $5,000 to 77 percent on amounts exceeding
$10 million. The base for the rates is the gross estate less deductions and
an exemption of $60,000. The estate tax itself does not constitute a
deduction.

The basis for calculating gain when assets received by gift are sold is the donor's basis for those assets. However, the basis for assets received through estate is their appraised value upon which estate taxes were applied. In instances where assets have a low base compared to their appraised values, there may be substantial savings in achieving a stepped-up basis by allowing assets to pass through estate.

If in order to pay death taxes and funeral and administrative expenses, a corporation redeems its own stock, the distribution is subject to capital gains provisions (instead of being treated as a dividend and subject to ordinary income tax). *Two* requirements must be met:

(*a*) The redemption must be made within three years and 90 days after decedent's estate tax return is filed; and

(*b*) The stock redeemed must amount to either 35 percent of the value of the gross estate, *or* 50 percent of the decedent's taxable estate.

The executor of an estate which contains an interest in a closely held business may, in some cases, be allowed to pay the federal estate tax levied on that interest in equal installments over a period of up to 10 years.

If the *taxable* estate is:

Over	But not over	The tax is
$ 0	$ 5,000	$ 0 + 3%*
5,000	10,000	150 + 7
10,000	20,000	500 + 11
20,000	30,000	1,600 + 14
30,000	40,000	3,000 + 18
40,000	50,000	4,800 + 22
50,000	60,000	7,000 + 25
60,000	100,000	7,500 + 28
100,000	250,000	20,700 + 30
250,000	500,000	65,700 + 32
500,000	750,000	145,700 + 35
750,000	1,000,000	233,200 + 37
1,000,000	1,250,000	325,700 + 39
1,250,000	1,500,000	423,200 + 42
1,500,000	2,000,000	528,200 + 45
2,000,000	2,500,000	753,200 + 49
2,500,000	3,000,000	998,200 + 53
3,000,000	3,500,000	1,263,200 + 56
3,500,000	4,000,000	1,543,200 + 59
4,000,000	5,000,000	1,838,200 + 63
5,000,000	6,000,000	2,468,200 + 67
6,000,000	7,000,000	3,138,200 + 70
·7,000,000	8,000,000	3,838,200 + 73
8,000,000	10,000,000	4,568,200 + 76
10,000,000	—	6,088,200 + 77

* % is multiplied times the difference between the taxable estate and the figure in the first column.

Gift tax rates are equal to 75 percent of the rates on estates.

From the schedules of estate and gift tax rates, it can be seen that it may be advantageous to transfer property through a combination of gift and estate to benefit from the lower rates at the lower end of each scale. For example, $100,000 in taxable estate would have a tax of $20,000 [$9,500 + 28%(100,000 − 60,000)] whereas the same amount in gifts would have a tax of $15,525 [75% x $20,700].However, if $50,000 were used as a gift and $50,000 left to be part of an estate at death, the total tax would be:

$$\begin{array}{lll} \text{Estate} & \$4,800 + 22\% \ (50,000 - 40,000) = & \$\ 7,000 \\ \text{Gift} & 75\% \ \text{x} \ 7,000 & = \underline{\quad 5,250} \\ & & \$12,250 \end{array}$$

C. Stock dividends

1. In general.   The basic principle of the Code is that "gross income does not include the amount of any distribution made by a corporation to its shareholders with respect to the stock of such corporation, in its stock or in rights to acquire its stock." This rule, that receipt of stock dividends or rights is not taxable to an individual shareholder, can be traced back to the holding of the famous case of *Eisner* v. *Macomber*, that an income tax on such dividends is unconstitutional.

2. Exceptions and the 1969 act.   Prior to the 1969 act, there were only two exceptions to the general proposition that stock dividends were not taxable:

(a)   Stock dividends are taxable if the distribution is payable at the *election* of any of the shareholders in either stock or property.
(b)   Stock dividends are taxable to the extent that they are in lieu of preferred stock dividends.

The 1969 act went further in tightening up this area by providing for tax on all stock dividends that have the effect of distributing income to the shareholder. Thus such dividends are taxable where:

(a)   most importantly, the distributions are disproportionate—i.e., distributions that alter individual shareholder's prior proportionate interest;
(b)   distributions permit the shareholder to choose between cash and stock;
(c)   the distributions involve common stock to some recipients and preferred to others; and
(d)   the distributions involve preferred stock or convertible debentures.

D. Stock options

In the past, the granting of stock options was a classic method of providing high tax bracket corporate executives with compensation taxable at only capital gains rates. Similarly, an entrepreneur or other investor in a small company could use options to withdraw profits from the business at tax rates below those applicable to ordinary salary or dividend distributions. The typical scenario looked like this:

1. *January 1:*   The company's stock is trading at 100. It grants to its employee an option to purchase the stock at 50.
2. *January 1:*   Employee exercises the option, purchasing the stock at 50. Prior to 1946, no income is recognized by the employee.
3. *July 2:*   Having held the stock the requisite six months plus, the employee sells it. His profit is taxed at only capital gains rates.

To diagram:

```
              Holding period
          January 1          July 1
       Market value 100 .......... 100 Market value
       Option price   50 .......... 50 Cost basis
                                    50 Profit taxed at capital gains rates
```

The attack on this Golconda began in 1946 and continued through the 1964 Revenue Act. Now, for an option to be afforded capital gains treatment, the option plan must meet the Code's requirements of "qualified stock option plans." *If a plan satisfies these requirements:*

1. No income is recognized at the time the option is granted.
2. No income is recognized at the time the option is exercised.
3. Any gain on sale of the stock purchased via the option is taxed at capital gains rates.
4. Any profit made on the option is thus a capital gain, and not compensation income. Thus, there is no deduction available to the grantor company.

If a stock option plan does not qualify:

1. Usually the employee is taxed at the time of *exercising* the option. Such gain measured by the spread between the option price and market value of the stock at that point is ordinary income. Subsequent appreciation would ultimately receive capital gains treatment.
2. In some instances the option itself is treated as compensation. In this circumstance the option's fair market value is compensation taxed as ordinary income. Subsequent exercise would not then be a taxable event.
3. The employer corporation is entitled to a deduction in the amount of the compensatory income generated by the option plan.

Before listing the requirements themselves, something should be said about the general purpose behind them. There have always been two principal threats to an option plan's ability to deliver compensation: (*a*) fluctuations in the market price of the stock and (*b*) time. If a combination of these two variables causes the market price to drop below the option's exercise price, the option plan becomes useless as a vehicle for providing additional, capital-gains-taxed income.

Before 1946, these two threats could be handled very easily. A corporation was free to set the exercise price of an option as low as it wished, and the only time requirement on the employee was the required six-month-plus capital-gains-holding period. Thus, using our example of a corporation whose stock is trading at $100, the option price could be set as low as $.01, thereby virtually ensuring that the option would deliver at least some compensation.

But the rules have changed. The thrust of reform has been to expose the employee to the two variables of market fluctuation and time, thereby making his potential gain a function of the grantor company's overall success. As presented in the *Price Waterhouse Review* (Spring 1964), the new requirements include the following:

1. The option price must be at least 100% of the market price at date of grant. A lesser percentage does not necessarily disqualify an option plan, but may result in the increment being taxable to the grantee, upon exercise, as ordinary income.

2. Stock acquired upon exercise must be held for at least three years from receipt of the option, and at least six months from the acquisition of the stock itself. This new requirement subjects the employee's cash investment to the risks of the market over a longer period.

3. The option itself may run for no longer than five years. This halves the period previously permitted.

4. The grantee of the option must be an employee of the granting corporation, its parent or subsidiary, *continuously* from grant to three months prior to exercise.

5. Qualified stock options may not be granted to shareholders owning more than 5% of the stock except in corporations with equity capital below $2 million. If equity capital is $1 million or lower, 10% shareholders may qualify, and a proportionate increase is permitted in shareholdings for corporations with equity capital between $1 million and $2 million.

6. The option plan must be approved by the shareholders of the grantor corporation, and the granting period must run for no more than 10 years.

7. The option must provide that it cannot be exercised while a less favorable option granted earlier is still unexercised. This requirement was designed to prevent the scattergun issuance of options designed to guarantee a profitable one by the sheer law of averages.

E. Losses on small business stock (Section 1244 stock)

The general rule of the Internal Revenue Code is that investments in a corporation which become worthless are treated only as *capital* losses.

Such losses, of course, are not deductible from ordinary income beyond $1,000. On the other hand, an investor in a *non*corporate entity (e.g., proprietorship, partnership) can deduct operating losses directly from any other ordinary income he may have. Thus, many entrepreneurs choose noncorporate forms of doing business in the early, risky days of the business, thereby getting the maximum advantage of losses by providing themselves with the opportunity to deduct their losses from ordinary income.

But the drafters of the Code normally wish to avoid creating tax laws which will encourage an individual to employ *only* tax considerations as the criteria for critical decisions. Thus, in 1958, two important new sections were written to minimize the disparity between the treatment afforded investments in corporations on the one hand and proprietorships on the other. The first of these changes, Subchapter S, permitted certain corporations to elect to be taxed as a partnership, with the corporate tax avoided and the gains or losses passed through to the shareholder as ordinary gains or losses.

The second 1958 change is Section 1244, which permits an individual to treat a loss from investment in the common stock of certain "small business corporations" as an *ordinary* loss rather than as a capital loss. A "§1244 loss" includes any loss incurred in a sale or exchange, in complete or partial liquidations, in stock redemptions, and even in those situations where the stock simply becomes worthless. The stated purpose of §1244 is to "encourage the flow of new funds into small business" and to place small corporation shareholders "on a more nearly equal basis with . . . proprietors and partners."

The purpose is well served. Section 1244 is particularly useful to the entrepreneur in attracting wealthy investors since such high tax bracket individuals are the prime beneficiaries of the section. To illustrate, a man in the 70 percent income tax bracket who invests $25,000 in §1244 stock of a small company limits his *maximum* loss to 30 percent after taxes. On the other hand, should the company succeed, he will realize his profits as capital gains and retain 75 percent of such profits *after* taxes.

There are conditions and limitations involved in the use of §1244:

1. The taxpayer. Behind the rules defining the possible beneficiaries of §1244 lies one purpose: *to prevent traffic in this type of stock loss.* Thus, in order to restrict the advantages of §1244 to those who actually invested funds or property in the small business, the following limitations apply:

(*a*) The regular income loss feature of §1244 stock is available only to individuals—no corporations, trusts, or estates.

(*b*) The stock must have been issued to the individual claiming the loss (or to a partnership containing that individual)—i.e., vendees, donees, or transferees do not qualify.

2. The corporation. Section 1244's rules regarding qualifying corporations are concerned with timing, size, and source of corporate income.

(a) *Timing.* To qualify as a §1244 "small business corporation," the business entity must meet certain standards (1) when the original plan to offer the stock was adopted and (2) when the loss was sustained. The *first* hurdle contemplates conditions of size, the *second*, sources of corporate income.

(b) *Size. When the plan to issue common stock under §1244 was adopted,* the business entity must have been "a small business corporation." To qualify as such, *two* requirements must have been met, both having to do with capitalization.

   1. The amount offered under the §1244 plan plus the amount of contributions to capital received after June 30, 1958 (the date of adoption of §1244) cannot exceed *$500,000*.
   2. The amount offered under the §1244 plan plus the amount of equity capital of the corporation on the date of plan's adoption cannot exceed $1 million.

(c) *Source of corporate income: In addition* to meeting the two size tests at the time when the plan to issue §1244 stock was adopted, the business entity must pass *another* requirement *when the §1244 loss is sustained.*

   1. For the five years previous to the year of loss, the corporation must have received *more* than 50 percent of its gross income from sources other than royalties, dividends, interest, gains on sales or exchanges of securities, rents, and annuities. Notice that these sources are the type of "passive" income which will render a corporation a personal holding company. As Bittker and Eustice tell us, the purpose behind this source test is "to prevent a shareholder from enjoying a deduction from ordinary income under §1244 if the corporation was primarily engaged in investment activities which, if carried on in his individual capacity, would have produced [only] capital losses."

3. The stock. The rules regarding qualifying as §1244 stock are explicit. All are designed to insure that the beneficiary of §1244 is a real investor assuming the risks of a small business.

(a) Must be *common stock*, either voting or nonvoting. No convertibles.
(b) Stock must be issued for money or property, not for services or other stock.
(c) Must be issued pursuant to a plan adopted after June 30, 1958, and completed within two years.
(d) No portion of a prior offering can be outstanding.

4. Limitations on amount to be deducted. Again, the rules here are self-explanatory.

(*a*) Loss cannot exceed the amount of money or property originally paid for the stock.

(*b*) Maximum deductible loss is $25,000 per year, or $50,000 in the case of a joint return.

(*c*) Unused losses may be carried forward or back.

F. Thin capitalization

The tax laws afford two incentives for maintaining high debt-equity ratios: (1) interest on debt is a deductible expense whereas dividends are not; and (2) because the repayment of debt is considered a return of capital and therefore tax-free, shareholder-creditors cannot only recoup most of their original investment without incurring tax (as a repayment of debt), but can also receive corporate earnings on a capital gains basis by allowing such earning to accumulate undistributed within the business.

However, in instances of thin capitalization, the courts may disregard the announced *form* of the securities in question and rule that *both* debt and equity are to be treated as equity. Should the courts find that the debt was in effect a type of equity, (1) the repayment of debt would be considered *dividends* (as opposed to a return of capital) and taxed as ordinary income to the shareholder-creditor (as opposed to tax-free or capital gains), and (2) the "interest" would not be deductible to the company as an expense.

There is no generally accepted debt-equity ratio, the violation of which will cause the courts to regard the would-be debt as equity. Bittker and Eustice suggest that "a ratio of debt to equity that does not exceed 3 to 1 is likely to withstand attack." Far more important, however, than this imprecise rule of thumb is the 1969 act's sweeping delegation of authority to the Commissioner of Internal Revenue to issue regulations providing rules for distinguishing debt from stock interests in all situations arising under the tax law. The following factors may be used to establish such guidelines:

1. Whether there is a written unconditional promise to pay at a specified date a certain sum in money in return for adequate consideration, and to pay a fixed rate of interest. The presence of such a promise would suggest a debt classification.
2. Whether the alleged indebtedness is subordinated to or preferred over any other corporate indebtedness. The greater the degree of subordination, the more likely the indebtedness will be ruled equity.
3. The ratio of debt to the corporation's equity. Lower ratios, of course, lead to the award of debt status.

4. Whether the alleged indebtedness is convertible into the issuing
    corporation's stock. Ease of conversion renders a security more
    similar to equity.
5. The relationship between alleged debt and actual stock ownership
    in the issuing corporation, i.e., to the extent that the "debt" is held
    pro rata by the equity interests, the "debt" may be classified as
    equity.

VI. OTHER TAXES

In addition to the basic federal income tax structure there are numerous other taxes, federal, state, and local. Among these are excise taxes,
sales and use taxes, property taxes, transfer taxes, social security tax, and
employee's withholding taxes, to mention a few which will concern a
new business.

REFERENCES

Bittker, Boris I., and Eustice, James S. *Federal Income Taxation of Corporations
    and Shareholders*. Boston: Gorham & Lamont, 1971.

Kragen, Adrian A., and McNulty, John K. *Cases and Materials on Federal Income
    Taxation*. St. Paul, Minn.: West Publishing Co., 1970.

Smith, Dan Throop. *Tax Factors in Business Decisions*. Prentice-Hall, Inc.
    Englewood Cliffs, N.J.:1968.

Cases

Howard J. Forster

Early in February of 1968, Howard Forster was reflecting on his progress in the real estate business. While a student in business school he had come to believe that the level of financial sophistication in the real estate industry (specifically, regarding the ability to attract funds from the capital markets) was less than in other industries. Further, he saw that the industry was fragmented and had few participants who displayed the managerial abilities he had learned at business school and which were commonly associated with manufacturing industries. His classmates could rattle off the names of leading manufacturing companies but few could name more than two or three large companies in real estate. He also thought real estate offered a low cost of entry. With these observations in mind, Howard saw real estate as a desirable area for an entrepreneur.

It was Howard's intention to serve as a middleman between the real estate industry and the capital markets. His objective was to develop a company which had the ability to communicate effectively between developers and money sources. The company would need both the skills to evaluate real estate development projects in terms of marketing and construction feasibility and also the skills and resources to find and evaluate alternative sources of financing within the capital markets. He expected the company would pass through three phases: (1) startup—the assembly and development of a competent management group; (2) expansion of the equity base; and (3) maturity—the capability of attracting major equity investment.

Howard saw his first major real estate venture, a shopping center, as an opportunity to provide him with funds and the beginning of a successful "track record." But the venture was beset with problems. On one hand, he was intent on rescuing the situation from what appeared to be major difficulties in securing the site, getting financing, and finding another major tenant. He was also concerned, however, with his basic concept of being a real estate intermediary. Was such an activity viable? And, too, how much of his success would depend upon the outcome of this initial project?

Howard Forster

Howard was born in the Midwest. His father had never owned his own business, but he had, on occasion, built individual single-family houses. Howard had worked with his father on the actual construction of these houses, so he had concrete knowledge as to how a house is built. As an undergraduate, Howard had majored in liberal arts and had been active in student and local politics. At business school, he was particularly interested in economics and business-government problems, but he had been careful to include courses in real estate among his electives. At the end of his first year, Howard was elected president of the Student Association.

This office brought him to the attention of Don Harper, an alumnus and the founder of Holiday Stores, a regional discount chain in New England. In April of 1966, Mr. Harper had called Howard about working for him that summer. Howard had been actively working as a volunteer in the political arena and had hoped to work in Washington, D.C., in the summer for a political figure. However, at Mr. Harper's insistence, they met one evening in the library as Howard studied for exams. They appeared to hit it off, and Howard accepted a job to work with Mr. Harper. He thought it would be an opportunity to learn from a successful entrepreneur.

Urban renewal projects

In the course of scouting New England for store locations, Howard approached the Urban Renewal Office in East Greenwich, Rhode Island, for site information. The office was unable to help him with existing sites but did offer a site for a shopping center in an urban renewal area. In response to a similar request, the Urban Renewal Office in Leominster, Massachusetts, informed Howard of an additional potential site for housing.

Howard's interest in the possibilities of these projects was aroused, and by the end of the summer, he had contacted an architect and an attorney. To lend credibility to his proposals, he approached prominent individuals in the real estate field. Peter Galagher, reputedly one of Boston's largest apartment owners and managers, agreed to be a partner for 50 percent of the Leominster housing project venture. Mr. Harper and his partners also agreed to provide funds for expenses in developing proposals for both the shopping center and housing projects. Century Developers, Inc., a shell corporation, was formed. The company then entered into a joint venture agreement with Marcus Stern and Son, a firm experienced in commercial property management, on a 50-50 basis to develop the shopping center proposal.

The Stern company was attracted to the joint venture on the basis of a written proposal which Howard had prepared. The proposal, which included a market study based on census data and a survey of buying power done by *Sales Management*, indicated population and income characteristics, 1966 retail sales of the site area, and projected sales for the shopping center. For presentation to Stern, Howard prepared estimated costs for land, improvements, and construction which comprised the second part of the proposal. (See Exhibit 1. Also included in Exhibit 1 are lower cost figures which the group hoped to realize.) The proposal ended with pro forma statements based on expected lease terms (Exhibit 2), operating expenses (Exhibit 3), tax liability (Exhibit 4), mortgage potential (Exhibit 5), and taxable income and cash flow (Exhibit 6).

The Forum Shopping Center

In November 1966, while Howard was back at school for the second year of the M.B.A. program, the Leominster housing project was awarded to another bidder. However, the East Greenwich project was still potentially available. Although several parties in East Greenwich had expressed an interest in submitting proposals on the project there, only one other bid was submitted in addition to that of Century Developers, Inc. Mr. Anthony Caruso, a local home builder represented by Mr. Michael Pinza, an attorney influential in local politics, submitted a proposal.

The urban renewal site (Exhibit 7) was located on the east side of the city, adjacent to the main highway downtown, and in a heavily Italian-American working class area. On the site, but scheduled for demolition, were several local retail stores and Christopher Columbus Bank, the latter under the directorship of a group of elderly Italian-American residents. Started originally as a credit union to serve the limited English speaking Italian-American population, Christopher Columbus Bank had acquired a loyal following and had expanded its activities to that of a commercial bank. On a visit to the bank, Howard had observed that telephone callers were greeted in Italian.

Under urban renewal regulations a displacee has the right of first refusal on the renewal site but must submit a proposal to prequalify and then, if chosen, must submit a more detailed proposal. The directors of

Christopher Columbus Bank desired to remain at the site and had spoken informally to the urban renewal authorities, but they did not submit a proposal. Assuming even without a proposal that they would be awarded part of the site, they engaged Herman Cabot, an elderly architect specializing in bank work. Cabot prepared a plan for a bank which envisioned expensive construction. The bank paid Mr. Cabot $60,000 in fees. Mr. Caruso, aware of the bank's interest, had also retained Mr. Cabot to design the shopping center, so that it would be compatible with the bank's design. The bank's plan conflicted with Howard's proposal.

Prequalification proposal

On August 17, 1966, Century Developers, Inc., submitted a prequalification proposal prepared by Howard Forster. The 18-page proposal included: statement of purpose; design scope and extent of development; appropriateness of development; provisions for business displaced by the project; estimated cost of development; anticipated tax return; employment created; economic benefits to the locality; and individuals associated with the proposal. A summary of the proposal is shown in Exhibit 8.

Change in the joint venture

In April of 1967, Howard Forster was nearing the end of the M.B.A. program and undergoing job interviews. His time during the second year had been fully occupied with studies, outside political activities, and the Forum Shopping Center. Don Harper suggested he pursue the shopping center project full time. Although the Urban Renewal Office had not yet selected the winner of the prequalification bidding, for the past several months Howard had continued to contact likely tenants for the center. Up to this time, the shares of Century Developers, Inc., had not been distributed, but it was now agreed Howard would have a 50 percent interest and Don Harper and his partners would hold the balance. The Harper group would provide funds for expenses and a nominal draw for Howard of $8,000 a year (in contrast to $14,000–$15,000 job offers to business school graduates).

On August 5, 1967, Century Developers, Inc., was selected as the prequalification bid winner. By this time, however, Howard had become disenchanted with his partners. He had hoped to learn something about being an entrepreneur from Don Harper, but he had rarely seen him; nor had the Harper group or the Stern company participated actively in the shopping center project. As Howard saw it, he was doing all the work for only 25 percent of the deal and he had no control. He was never able to assemble all the participants for a meeting to consider decisions to be made. Whenever he needed a signature or a decision, he either had to track down each individual or had to make the decision himself without authority. With $600 in cash and $6,000 in debt, he informed Don that he wanted to leave in September. He suggested the Harper group buy him out. Don countered with the suggestion that Howard buy the interest of his group. This would have left Howard in a 50-50 deal with Stern. He would still lack control and be associated with a partner who was not providing active help. It was finally agreed that the Harper group would buy out Stern for $12,000 and that all the shares would be sold to Howard in return for a promissory note at 6 percent interest to cover the money expended by the Harper group. Howard felt Don Harper and his group had treated him fairly. Now he had 100 percent control of a venture which in effect had an option for a shopping center project.

Staying alive

With complete control of the shopping center venture the weekly draw supplied by Don ended. The office for Century Developers was now a cardboard box in the back seat of Howard's car. He no longer had the use of Don's office or his secretary to take telephone calls. He found the library at school and the Boston Public Library convenient as reference sources and office space when he wanted to escape his apartment. His apartment was in a shabby building in Cambridge where he paid a reduced rate of $80 per month in return for acting as the janitor.

To supply living funds while he pursued tenants for the shopping center, developed a final proposal, negotiated with contractors, and sought financing, he undertook "fill in" deals. Having obtained a Massachusetts real estate broker's license in the summer of 1966, he was able to earn a $1,500 commission for renting a store in a shopping center and a $2,000 commission from selling an apartment building to his landlord. Scouting around, he located two apartment buildings with basement space that was convertible into student apartments. On these, he acquired a purchase and sales agreement for $500 each, and then sold the agreement at a profit on the basis of his plan to increase the rental income.

Problems at the Forum Shopping Center

An important income source for the shopping center was a proposed restaurant tenant. The center "anchor tenant" was to be an 18,000-square-foot supermarket. Because supermarket managements realized the importance of a supermarket as a source of traffic and as a basis for mortgage financing, it had been the practice to negotiate leases at close to break-even rentals. Another expected tenant was a post office. The post office would also be an excellent traffic generator, but its

$1.25-per-square-foot rental was less than break even. The restaurant chain which had expressed an interest in locating in the center was needed to compensate for the low rentals from the supermarket and the post office.

Christopher Columbus Bank had been contacted by Howard about locating in the center. Informal talks had indicated some progress. Now, in February of 1968 he learned that the bank's plans for a bank building would eliminate the restaurant from the center. While he considered what to do about this turn of events, Howard learned from an attorney that the bank had written the local Congressman that it wanted ownership of part of the development site to implement the plans drawn by Mr. Cabot. Howard was told that the bank intimated to the Congressman that if he did not accede to their request, he would be confronted with an Italian-American constituency that opposed his reelection.

Though Howard had a contract to purchase the entire site from the Urban Renewal Authority, he believed it might be possible for the Congressman to delay the conveyance of title. Delay might jeopardize negotiations with prospective tenants and delay the start of construction. Howard debated whether he should fight the bank and rely on his legal position or should attempt to negotiate with the bank directors.

When he returned to his apartment from his disquieting day in East Greenwich, there was a letter from the supermarket chain with whom he had been negotiating. The letter stated that his proposed rental terms were not acceptable and that the chain was considering another site. It was not clear to Howard whether this was a negotiating tactic or whether he had best seek another tenant.

Howard thought that the loss of the supermarket as a tenant would seriously hamper his efforts to obtain a mortgage. In addition he was concerned about equity financing for the center as he had no equity funds himself and it did not seem possible to obtain mortgages greater than the cost of the project. He wondered how to proceed.

He was particularly concerned as to which problem he should attack first. Howard thought that the particular direction he decided to take might determine which investors would be interested in providing financing and could even affect the terms on which the money could be obtained. In addition he was concerned with his plans for establishing himself in the niche he saw between the real estate industry and the capital markets.

SUGGESTED QUESTIONS

1. What should Howard do now? Prepare in as much detail as possible a plan of action which will indicate an order of priority of steps to take, the possible outcomes, and contingent actions.

2. What is Howard's bargaining position with:
   a. Christopher Columbus Bank?
   b. Tenants?
   c. Financial sources?
3. What effects can the outcome of this venture have on Howard's long-range objective? Is Howard likely to become a successful entrepreneur? Why or why not?

EXHIBIT 1
The Forum Shopping Center
Projected cost

	Official figures	Internal working figures
Land..	$150,000	$150,000
Site work.......................................	115,000	80,000
	$265,000	$230,000
Construction (35,000 sq. ft. @ $11/sq. ft.)	385,000	367,500
Architect (approx. 8% of $385,000)	30,000	11,000
Interest (approx. 9% of $130,000)	11,500	11,500
Taxes	3,500	3,500
Insurance and bond....................................	4,250	1,000
Title search and recording fees	3,000	3,000
Legal, organization, and accounting	14,000	14,000
Financing fees (approx. 2% of mortgage)	10,500	—
Brokerage fees..	28,125	—
	$754,875	$641,500

EXHIBIT 2
The Forum Shopping Center
Terms of lease

Tenant	Sq. ft.	Rent/sq. ft.	Percent of gross sales	Term	Total rent
Supermarket............	18,000	$2.11	1.6	15	$38,000
Quick food franchise	1,600	4.25	4.0	5	6,800
Finance company	1,000	4.45	—	7	4,450
Restaurant..............	4,000	3.00	—	10	12,000
Holiday stores	3,000	3.50	—	10	10,500
Post office	4,800	1.25	—	3	6,000
Vacant	2,600	3.50	—	—	8,500
	35,000				$86,250
Plus parking lot maintenance ($.15/sq. ft. x 30,200 sq. ft.)					5,250
					$91,500

EXHIBIT 3
The Forum Shopping Center
Operating expenses

Building maintenance............	$ 1,405
Parking lot	2,720
Advertising and promotion	650
Real estate taxes	19,400
Insurance	1,200
	$25,375

Source: Urban Land Institute, "The Dollars and Cents of Shopping Centers, 1966"; and Tax Assessor's Office, East Greenwich, R.I.

EXHIBIT 4
The Forum Shopping Center
Anticipated tax liability

I. (A) Land $\dfrac{(\$150,000) \quad (58\% \text{ value}) \quad (\$75)}{\$1,000}$ = $ 6,525

   (B) Structures $\dfrac{(\$385,000) \quad (45\% \text{ value}) \quad (75)}{\$1,000}$ = 12,875

   (C) Total $19,400

II. Tax per square foot of GLA*
$$\frac{\$19,400}{35,000 \text{ sq. ft.}} = .554$$

III. Comparison with competitive shopping centers
1. Jericho
   GLA = 22,850
   Tax = $12,450
   Per sq. ft. = .544
2. Videri
   GLA = 85,500
   Tax = $36,363
   Per sq. ft. = .425
3. E. Greenwich
   GLA = 86,000
   Tax = $49,230
   Per sq. ft. = .572
4. Sears
   GLA = 91,796
   Tax = 61,150
   Per sq. ft. = .666

*GLA = Gross leasable area.

EXHIBIT 5
The Forum Shopping Center
Capitalized cash flow valuation

$$\frac{\text{Gross income} \quad - \quad \text{Expenses}}{\text{Capitalization rate}} \times 70\% = \text{Mortgage}$$

$$\frac{91,500 \quad - \quad 25,375}{.09} \times .70 = \$514,300$$

Comparison with cost
Total cost $754,875
Mortgage 514,300
Net $240,575

EXHIBIT 6
The Forum Shopping Center
Tax statement

	One	Two	Three	Four	Five	Six	Seven	Eight	Nine	Ten
Income available for debt	$66,125	$66,125	$66,125	$66,125	$66,125	$66,125	$66,125	$66,125	$66,125	$66,125
Less:										
Interest*	36,956	35,396	35,396	33,836	32,276	31,756	30,196	29,156	27,076	26,036
Depreciation †	16,500	16,500	16,500	16,500	16,500	16,500	16,500	16,500	16,500	16,500
Taxable Income	$12,669	$14,229	$14,229	$15,789	$17,349	$17,869	$19,429	$20,469	$22,549	$23,589
				Cash flow						
Income available for debt	$66,125	$66,125	$66,125	$66,125	$66,125	$66,125	$66,125	$66,125	$66,125	$66,125
Debt service	48,915	48,915	48,915	48,915	48,915	48,915	48,915	48,915	48,915	48,915
Before Federal Income Tax	$17,210	$17,210	$17,210	$17,210	$17,210	$17,210	$17,210	$17,210	$17,210	$17,210

*Assume a $520,000, 20-year, 7¼ percent mortgage (constant = .094068).
†Assume a 500,000 base, 3.3 percent per year.

EXHIBIT 7
E. Greenwich, R.I. shopping center site

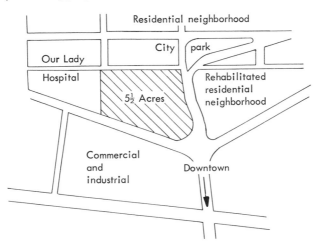

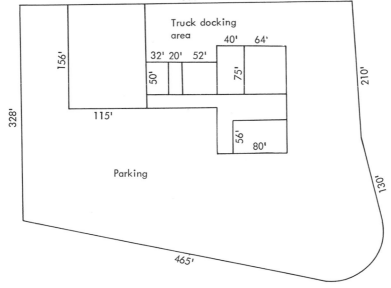

EXHIBIT 8
The Forum Shopping Center
Summary of prequalification proposal

Purpose
    Desire to undertake outstanding design and quality projects.
    Cooperate with Urban Renewal Office.
    Willingness of team of experts to work with local groups such as Christopher
        Columbus Bank and Our Lady Hospital.
Design, scope and extent of development
    35,000–40,000-square-feet shopping center.
    Maintain strict architectural control of planning and construction.
    Act as developers, owners, and managers of the property.
Appropriateness of development
    Fit with overall Urban Renewal Plan.
    Satisfy needs of the community.
    Contribution to community development.
Provisions for businesses displaced by the project
    List of present businesses for whom space will be available.
    Willingness to aid owners of displaced businesses to obtain other type retail
        operations if desired.
    Included copies of letters to present and prospective tenants and some
        replies.
Estimated cost of development
Anticipated tax return
    Contact with chairman of the Board of Assessors.
Employment created
    Breakdown of type stores with expected employment of 196 persons.
Economic benefit to the locality
    Creation of employment.
    Increase in residential values in eastern half of the city.
    Increase in tax return.
    Placement of short- and long-term financing with local banks—list of banks
        contacted and copies of interested replies.
Individuals associated with the proposal (See Exhibit 9.)

EXHIBIT 9
The Forum Shopping Center
Individuals associated with the proposal

Consultants
Mr. Donald Harper
6 Centre Street
Waltham, Massachusetts
President, Century Developers, Inc.
President, Holiday Stores, Inc.
President, New England Service, Inc.
Founder and Director, Chelsea Development Corp.
Founder and Director, New England Development Corp.
Founder and Director, New Horizons Development Corp.
Mr. Howard Forster
6 Centre Street
Waltham, Massachusetts
Vice President, Century Developers, Inc.
Developer
Mr. Marcus Stern
20 Lazlow Square
Boston, Massachusetts
Partner, Marcus Stern & Son
Legal counsel
Mr. Allen Harris
Lincoln, Lexington and Concord
60 James Street
Boston, Massachusetts

Mr. James Garland
Able & Grover
503 Rhode Island Plaza
Providence, Rhode Island
Architects
Mr. Joseph York
Jersey & York
Beacon Street
Boston, Massachusetts
Property management
Marcus Stern & Son
20 Lazlow Square
Boston, Massachusetts

Raymond W. Hill

In late May 1969, while in his second year at Midwestern Business School, Ray Hill was reflecting on his plans to construct apartment buildings in the Seattle area. He had spent a great deal of time thinking and planning this venture while at Midwestern and had made the idea the basis of his second-year research report.

It was Ray's intention to use apartment development as a vehicle to build a substantial corporate base, from which he could diversify and expand over the next 10 to 15 years. As the time neared when he would commit his time and personal resources to the venture, he was once again reviewing his plans and the data he had assembled.

Raymond Hill

Ray was born during the Depression in a small mining town in the Upper Peninsula of Michigan. His father was an iron miner, and the family income was meager. To supplement his small miner's income, Ray's father sold lumber and pulpwood, and Ray was cutting pulpwood by the age of ten.

Ray decided during high school to study electrical engineering and received a scholarship to study at Michigan Tech, in Houghton, Michigan, once the copper mining capital of the Upper Peninsula. During the summers between school years, he worked as a miner, a lumberjack, carpenter's helper, and foundry laborer. In 1957 he graduated with a B.S. degree, a fellowship to U.C.L.A., and $2,000 saved from summer jobs.

While pursuing a master's degree in engineering at U.C.L.A., Ray worked part time at Hughes Research Labs. He found little time to spend the money he earned there and had saved about $9,500 when he received his M.S. in June 1959. In May 1960, Ray left Hughes to accept an engineering position with a Seattle firm.

After leaving U.C.L.A. in 1959 Ray had lived on approximately one third of his salary and had managed to save the rest. After his marriage, living expenses had increased but his wife worked also and the savings program was not altered. By 1967 Ray was earning just under $20,000 a year. The average savings from salaries until Ray entered the business school was approximately $9,000 annually.

Soon after his arrival in Seattle, Ray began to develop an interest in real estate.

> Shortly after I arrived in Seattle I purchased a small, one-bedroom house. I had the bright idea of enlarging and remodeling this house while I lived in it, figuring I could sell it for a nice profit. After doing all the work except plumbing, I emerged three tired years later with a completely remodeled house, and a good lesson for myself. Never again, I vowed!

Later, he bought and managed several small apartment units in the Seattle area.

> During 1962, I made two acquisitions: a four-unit apartment house, and a wife, whom I met at a church social. We found the apartment rental business to our liking, so we added two more small units: a 6-unit apartment house was purchased in 1963, and an 18-unit building was added in 1965. Meanwhile, I was getting promotions in my job, which meant increased responsibility and consistent overtime, sometimes up to 30 hours a week. With three apartment buildings to watch over, along with my engineering job, I was a busy man. By late 1966 it suddenly struck me—there must be an easier way. Why not go to business school and learn to make money the easy way? I applied and was admitted in the fall of 1967.
>
> In preparation for the transition to business school, I sold my house and the four-unit building. We decided to keep the 6-unit and 18-unit buildings, and see if we could manage them at a distance of 2,000 miles. I left my job and its comfortable pay checks in July 1967, and entered school in the fall.

Ray felt these small ventures provided him with experience he considered valuable in his plans to enter into real estate development on a larger scale. He had become familiar with the Seattle area to which he planned to return. He had been exposed to many of the recurring problems in renting and managing apartment units. He had formulated certain policies on hiring and motivating resident managers. He had also become familiar with some of the nuances of real estate economics. Exhibit 1 presents the annual operating results and the capital gains (before taxes) on Ray's early investments.

Personal goals

In a discussion Ray gave the following response to a question by the casewriter:

> My basic financial goal is to increase my capital sufficiently within the next 10–15 years to enable me to earn at least $50,000 after taxes from investments without any significant input of personal time. This is important to me because I would like to be able to use my time for other interests: perhaps in leisure or charity work, but certainly in whatever fancies me at the time.
>
> It is also important to me that I have some flexibility in my time nitely want to avoid using the money of family or friends, that brings the financial objectives. I expect to be quite comfortable working essentially alone, as I like to do a lot of things myself. And finally, I want full personal ownership of the venture during its early years. Working with others' money means giving their views on operations an audience. And I definitely want to avoid using the money of family or friends; that brings the potential for all kinds of trouble.

Because of his experience with apartment development, Ray mentioned that he gave little thought to going into any other type of enterprise.

> I did consider starting a mutual fund; however, I finally decided I did not have sufficient experience in this area. The stock market still fascinates me personally, and I have had unusual success investing there in recent years. I believe I have the temperament to play that game, since I fully expect some losses in my portfolio. I also have whatever it takes to convince myself to sell after a 10 percent–15 percent gain, rather than hold, hoping for the rainbow. But I do not expect the extremely timely luck I have had to hold. Thus, while I will probably continue to follow the market closely as a private investor, I am more comfortable with my experience in the real estate business.

From 1959 until 1967 Ray's investments in the stock market had increased their savings by about $26,000.

Ray expected his plan to develop apartments to satisfy four long-run personal objectives. First, he wanted to found and build a personally owned company into a medium-sized public corporation. Second, he expected to develop a management team capable of continuing the corporation. Third, he expected to sell most of his personal investment in the company within 10–15 years. Ray explained one final satisfaction he expected from this venture.

> I am convinced developers can go a long way in improving the quality of apartment developing: in location, in design, and in construction. I have seen over 100 apartment buildings in Seattle; there always seems to be at least one major defect in them; usually there are several. One wonders how

so many eyesores could have been erected! I would derive a great deal of pleasure in developing apartment projects which would be aesthetically attractive, convenient, and functional for the tenants, and economically sound to me as the developer.

Market analysis

Based on the results of his research report, Ray considered the housing market in the Seattle area to be quite strong in the long run. Exhibits 2, 3, and 4 are extracted from his research report. Essentially Ray had found that population projections anticipated the entire King County area growing by 15 percent by 1975. The areas outside the Seattle city limits were expected to grow by almost 28 percent by 1975, with certain sections expected to grow by 40 percent to 50 percent or more during the same interval. Exhibit 2 highlights these projections.

Although he had confidence in the longer range potential, Ray had some reservations about the outlook for the shorter term: the next 12–24 months. Like residential construction in general, the apartment development business in Seattle was cyclical. Ray had expressed in his report that a period of low vacancy rates and high demand generally spurs a rush of construction activity, especially if fueled by readily available mortgage money. After a construction boom has satisfied the existing demand, rents and building prices stop rising, and vacancy rates begin to creep upward—especially in more remote areas. With rents and building prices stable, the developer has difficulty meeting the continually rising construction costs, and without evidences of unfilled demand, construction activity slows markedly. Purchase prices for existing buildings generally level off during this phase also.

Ray had several bits of data which implied to him that the Seattle area was just beyond the top of a construction boom, and several months away from a trough. Exhibit 3 highlights some of the indices he had collected during early 1969. The exhibit shows vacancy rates in the Seattle area in an upward trend since October 1967. While not included in this exhibit, Ray also had more detailed data which indicated that the newer, more modern, and better equipped buildings were not protected from this trend in vacancies, probably because they were generally located farther from the central city. Data from the local real estate board also revealed a dramatic rise through 1968 in building permits for multifamily structures. Ray commented on his evaluation of these trends.

> It seems to me the evidence shows we have just passed the peak of a construction cycle in the Seattle area. The housing starts are very heavy in 1967 and 1968. The fact that the three successive quarters of 1968 are high, but in a downtrend, indicates the possibility, however, that the peak is behind us.

Two other trends concerned Ray, and had a major impact on his final strategy for entering the selected market (discussed later). One was the reflection in the Seattle area of the national pattern of rising construction costs. The enormous jumps in these costs, particularly since 1967, had caused the final cost of housing to the consumer to skyrocket during that interval. Exhibit 4 presents this rise in terms of the Boeckh index.[1] Ray was concerned that the construction boom had brought supply and demand into better balance and that apartment dwellers might resist further attempts to pass on these costs through higher rents.

The final "red flag" in the short term Ray believed to be the steep rise in the cost of mortgage money. Rates in the first half of 1969 had returned to and surpassed those existing during the 1966 "credit crunch." At a level of 8 percent–9 percent, these rates were 35 percent–45 percent higher than those prevailing in 1964–1965. Unless this fixed annual payment could be offset by higher rents, the margin of profit (and safety) quickly vanishes in real estate projects which are by their nature thinly capitalized and heavily leveraged.

The timing elements of Ray's strategy were founded on: (1) these historic highs in construction costs and mortgage rates, both of which he believed to be temporarily in steep uptrends, and (2) his evaluation of the position of the Seattle market in cyclical swing.

> In order to build the kind of expertise I feel I'll need in the company, there are still plenty of skills I need to acquire. My experience has been only in buying and selling existing buildings. For several reasons I believe this is a costly way to get into the business; therefore, I plan to construct most of my buildings, rather than buy them. I will, however, keep my eyes open to potential bargains on existing buildings. Just as I expect the cyclical pattern of prices for completed buildings to allow me to sell at a "top" in prices, there will probably be some buying opportunities during "bottoms" when prices are relatively low and buyers relatively scarce.
>
> Now, given that (1) I need skills in planning and design, negotiating and supervising construction, obtaining financing, etc., (2) the situation at the moment in Seattle is inopportune, what do I do in the meantime? It seems to me a logical strategy to try and wait out the construction boom and begin any major projects at a slack time. In a slack period, construction bids may well be lower if construction firms want to keep their heavy equipment operating, and mortgage rates will be lower with less demand for funds. Hopefully, I would be able to be fully constructed just as demand begins to overtake available suppy and vacancy rates begin to decline. But I do not want to just sit and wait until the situation improves; therefore I have developed a three-phase plan for building the corporation over the next 10 years.

----

[1]The Boeckh index is considered a summary indication of all construction costs.

Strategic planning

Below is the plan Ray outlined to fulfill the following basic objectives for his firm.

1. By year 10, after-tax profits to be $100,000 annually (using straight line depreciation for reporting).
2. During the 10 years, a relatively stable earnings base, from which a successful public corporation would be launched.
3. In years 7–12, a 40 percent annual growth in earnings, to facilitate planned acquisitions through sale or exchange of stock at high multiples.

(Ray saw some flexibility in when to "take" earnings, by timing construction and sales, and by holding each building only as long as its shield was protecting other income, or its own income was protected by newer buildings with high depreciation charges.)

During Phase I, Ray expected to build one duplex and one eight-unit apartment building. He expected to use this time and these projects to learn the business of developing and constructing apartments, working with architects and financiers, and controlling contractors. After about one year, he expected to sell both the duplex and the first building and purchase a lot for a 30-unit building. This would permit him to move into Phase II.

> The initial steps will be designed to learn as much as possible. I expect to make mistakes but they will be on a scale small enough for the corporation to withstand them. Due to my inexperience in apartment building, I would be satisfied to break even during this phase, although I have forecast a small profit in my pro formas.

Phase II, years 2 through 5, were expected to be a period of "base building" in preparation for the rapid earnings growth expected in later years. Ray expected to construct two buildings of 30-units each during year 2, and one 30-unit building in each succeeding year through year 5. The intent was threefold. First, he expected to protect the cash inflows by double-declining depreciation, thus using the cash throwoff from constructed projects (plus possible refinancing and another personal investment of $50,000) to finance succeeding buildings. Second, tax losses would accumulate to protect the income of future years, and by reporting earnings based on straight line depreciation a modest but growing earnings record could be established. Third, the book value (using straight line depreciation) would be considerably understated since the market values are expected to grow 2 percent–3 percent per year. The potential of these understated assets will be carried into Phase III.

Phase II is the key to the overall strategy, and sets the stage for rapid earnings growth in Phase III. I expect to have cash "available" in the form of undervalued assets which will be sold, and tax loss carry-forward for the anticipated income growth during Phase III. Its success is somewhat dependent on a continuation of present tax rules for depreciation.

Phase III, years 6 through 10, were designed to take the company out of the apartment business and possibly out of Seattle. In years six and seven, two small acquisitions are expected to be made, using the accumulated cash flows and possible refinancing of the 150 units (five buildings of 30 units each) constructed during Phase II. Then another 150 units are to be built, and the original 150 units will be sold as their accelerated depreciation shield runs out. Two large acquisitions are planned in years 9–10, along with construction of another 150 apartment units. Sometime during years 9 or 10, Ray planned to offer 300,000 shares to the public; he planned to retain 250,000 shares.

My basic objectives during Phase III are several. First, I want to establish a public market for the company's stock. I hope to diversify through acquisition of existing firms and their management. It will be important to retain the existing management of these acquisitions, as we would probably not have the specific skills required. Probably most importantly, I will have to develop a capable management team. One of my resident apartment managers can probably take over the management of all apartment buildings. I will also need a financial manager to help in searching and financing the acquisitions.

Perhaps the usefulness of planning 5 or 10 years into the future is open to question, since the company is not yet even started. Perhaps new opportunities will present themselves, or changes in my present assumptions will require modification of these intentions. I still believe, however, that there is value in looking ahead; to see where one might be going, and what might be possible under a specific plan.

Financial planning

In order to fully understand the financial consequences of developing apartments, Ray had analyzed available sources for data on operating expenses and revenues, and market value determinations. The pro forma statements he developed are based on assumptions that certain features of the developer's environment would continue. The assumptions Ray made were:

1. Market value is generally computed at seven to eight times "full rental occupancy income."
2. Operating expenses average about 35 percent of full gross income. Vacancy usually takes 1 percent–2 percent of gross income. These

operating expenses do not include interest or depreciation; they include variable cash expenses only.

3. Development cost ratio[2] is expected to be about 85 percent–90 percent. This is a ratio of total development costs divided by market value. This figure is especially critical since it is the most sensitive indicator of profits.

4. Annual increases in rental income, operating expenses (direct expenses), and price appreciation of 2 percent.

5. Mortgage terms of 7 percent simple interest, 20-year loans. While rates in 1969 were 7.5percent–9 percent, Ray considered 7 percent a more reasonable figure for projections.

Ray believed the figures in Exhibit 5 reflected many of the points made in his research report: (1) the slowly growing reported earnings, resulting from reduced interest payments and rising rentals; (2) the tax loss carry-forward of $13,500 accumulated before a profit is earned (line 2); (3) a growing cash flow (line 3) for other use and as a cushion against vacancies; (4) the growing discrepancy between actual equity (line 4) and book value of equity (line 5) due to a constant depreciation and a growing market price of 2 percent.

Ray had also prepared detailed projections for the corporate financial situation as he expected it to unfold. Exhibit 6 shows the sources and uses of funds for the entire 10-year period and restates the corporate strategy discussed earlier in dollar terms.

Exhibit 7 presents Ray's pro forma income statement and cash flow projections. It shows the impact of the depreciation shield on income both from rental operations and from acquired companies. It also shows the growing amount of cash available as a partial cushion for contingencies.

Ray had calculated the value of his equity position in this venture in several ways. If the corporation were to be liquidated after five years, the apartment units then built would have a market value of 7.5 times gross rental income of $360,000, or about $2.66 million. Mortgage obligations of $1.96 million would be repaid, without penalty if the contracts were so written, leaving the value of his equity at about $700,000. His average investment during that period would have been about $150,000, yielding an average annual compound growth of about 48 percent.

He also calculated that at the end of 10 years, the liquidation value of the business would be the equity value in the apartment buildings if sold

---

[2]Mortgages are generally granted on 75 percent–80 percent of *market* value, which is seven to eight times full rental income. The mortgage commitment has little to do with *actual construction costs*. Therefore, the lower this "development cost ratio" can be pushed, the closer a developer can come to "mortgage-out"—that is, have the mortgage cover the entire cost of construction, and so on.

at their estimated market price, plus the value of the four acquisitions which might be conservatively valued at cost. This would result in an equity position of some $3.35 million, of which he would own some 45 percent (250,000 shares personally of the 550,000 shares outstanding). His equity position would then be worth about $1.6 million. If the corporation were still a growing concern in year 10, it would probably be valued as a multiple of earnings. With a four- to five-year pattern of earnings growth at 50 percent or better, the stock could carry a multiple of 20 and possibly higher. Ray had calculated the value of his investment with various P/E ratios. (See Exhibit 8.)

Operational problems

Ray Hill recounted to the casewriter his preliminary thoughts on some of the operational problems he might encounter. As he expected to be working almost alone during the early stages, many of his important relationships would be at arm's length, with architects, contractors, and financiers. Ray realized the impact his choice of legal organizational form would have, and he devoted a considerable portion of his research report to this consideration. He finally decided on a single corporation as the best vehicle to accomplish his aims. Partnership and proprietorship were ruled out because of the personal liability involved and limited access to additional equity capital.

In considering legal corporate forms, Mr. Hill discussed several possibilities. The real estate investment trust was discarded, despite the fact that it is one corporate form which avoids the problems of double taxation. Ray had found that if 90 percent of all income is paid out in dividends, the corporate profits are not taxed. However, to qualify, the trust must be held by at least 100 shareholders, and no more than 50 percent of the stock can be owned by five individuals. These restrictions made this vehicle unacceptable, as Ray wanted total ownership of the corporation. The chief disadvantage of the corporation for Ray's purposes was the problem of double taxation, an especially thorny problem in situations where one individual holds a controlling interest. In such cases, Ray found the IRS can classify the corporation as a personal holding company, and declare that profits are being retained to be eventually realized by the controlling stockholder in the form of capital gains through sale, rather than in the form of income through dividends. If so classified as a personal holding company, a tax of 70 percent on undistributed income would be levied on retained earnings which were not distributed as dividends; this tax is in addition to the normal corporate income tax.

Ray's research into the personal holding company and its effect on his personal plans led him to the following conclusions:

1. In determining "undistributed income," accelerated depreciation may be deducted.
2. All capital gains are excluded from the calculations.

Thus, Ray concluded that, even if the firm were to be classified as a personal holding company, it would *not* be likely he would ever pay the 70 percent tax. Accelerated depreciation would shield rental income, and capital gains on sale are not part of the calculation. Therefore, he decided in favor of the corporation as the ideal organizational form, accepting the possibility of being classified as a personal holding company.

Ray also rejected the notion of separate incorporation of the various projects for two reasons. First, with all projects under one taxable umbrella, depreciation shields from newer developments could shield the income flows from older buildings whose shields have been exhausted. And second, a single corporation qualifies for a 22 percent tax rate on income under $25,000, whereas each satellite of a multicorporation group would be taxed at 28 percent on this first $25,000. Ray had calculated that not until year 9 was there a taxable income at all, and it barely exceeded the $25,000.

With regard to marketing ideas, Ray had some rather general intentions. He expected to pick one particular segment of the apartment market, probably young marrieds, and create his apartments with their needs in mind. He expected to price in the mid-range of the probable income distribution of this group, feeling that each extreme offered too small a population. He also expected to include an array of amenities directed at the women in these households, since women play a large part in the decision to purchase or rent permanent housing.

In production, Ray expected to follow the established patterns of the industry. He would subcontract for most "production" services by hiring architects for the design, having contractors bid for construction, and search for locations himself. He expected to build a continuing relationship with an architect, while planning to have various contractors bid for particular jobs.

Ray indicated very clearly he did not want to become immersed in the day-to-day problems of managing the completed units; therefore, he planned to hire resident managers for each particular building or development. He would provide a set of basic guidelines based on his experience to date, but expected the managers to handle the operating situation themselves. He hoped to enlist married graduate students with two or three years of graduate work remaining. Compensation would be a combination of a free apartment, plus a rising percent of profits beyond a certain level.

Ray also expected to follow the traditions of the industry with regard to finance. He would personally negotiate for construction loans and permanent mortgage financing. He would attempt to develop a close and lasting relationship with a few key lenders, hoping that this would benefit him during periods of tight money.

After an intensive effort at researching and planning this venture, Ray was reasonably confident that he could make it succeed. He realized, however, that certain of the assumptions he had made were critical to his early plans. Before he went further in committing himself to the venture he wanted: to reevaluate his plans, to consider possible variances in the critical assumptions he had made, and to change direction where warranted.

SUGGESTED QUESTIONS

1. What should Ray do?
2. Evaluate the strategy Ray has outlined for his real estate ventures. What are his major risks? What do you anticipate will be his major problems?
3. Advise Ray about any changes you believe he should make in plans.
4. What does it take to pursue successfully a career in real estate as an individual?

EXHIBIT 1
Raymond W. Hill
Financial performance of early investments

		Building 1 (4 units)	Building 2 (6 units)	Building 3 (18 units)
A.	Capital Gain			
	1. Purchase price	$42,000	$68,500	$160,000
	2. Sales price..................	48,500		205,000
	3. Improvements	2,000		8,750
	4. Selling costs	1,000		1,250
	5. Capital gain	3,500		35,000
B.	Operating Results			
	1. Annual profit	$1,200–$1,600	$2,000–$2,700	$9,000–$9,700
	2. Average investment*	$12,800	$14,000	$45,000
	3. Annual return on investment.	10–12%	16–20%	20–22%

*The buildings were purchased with downpayments of from 15 percent to 25 percent of the full purchase price.
Source: Ray Hill's research report.

EXHIBIT 2
Raymond W. Hill
Population projections: Seattle area

Specific districts	1968	1975(E)	Percent change
Auburn	31,200	40,600	48%
Bellevue	83,300	102,900	25
Enumclaw	11,800	17,400	50
Issaquah	25,700	46,700	80
Kent	42,800	62,000	48
Lake Washington	53,000	77,200	44
Mercer Island	20,300	30,400	50
Seattle	587,000	602,600	3
Total County	1,230,000	1,415,000	15
Total County less Seattle	643,000	802,400	28

Source: King County Planning Department. (Contained in Ray Hill's research report.)

EXHIBIT 3
Raymond W. Hill
Selected indices of Seattle market

A. Vacancy rates (in percent)

	Oct. 1965	Apr. 1966	Oct. 1966	Apr. 1967	Oct. 1967	Apr. 1968	Oct. 1968
Total vacancies	5.2	2.5	0.6	0.9	0.3	1.2	1.7

B. Multifamily housing starts
Yearly

	Number
1964...................	3,043
1965...................	2,833
1966...................	5,835
1967...................	14,170
1968 (3 quarters)	11,460

Quarterly	1967	1968
1st	2,843	4,129
2d	4,222	3,955
3d	4,033	3,248
4th......	3,572	n.a.

Source: Ray Hill's research report.

EXHIBIT 4
Raymond W. Hill
Index of construction costs (1957–59=100)

Year	Seattle	Percent change	National average	Percent change
1958	99.0	—	99.2	—
1959	103.2	4.1	102.5	3.4
1960	105.4	2.1	104.2	1.7
1961	104.3	(1.0)	104.5	—
1962	107.7	3.1	106.3	1.8
1963	110.2	2.5	108.5	2.0
1964	113.4	2.8	111.6	2.8
1965	116.9	3.0	115.3	3.3
1966	122.3	5.8	120.2	4.2
1967	130.6	6.7	127.3	5.6
1968(E) ...	141.0	8.2	137.5	7.9

Source: Seattle Real Estate Board. (Contained in Ray Hill's research report.)

EXHIBIT 5
Raymond W. Hill
Pro formas for an average 30-unit apartment building

		Year 1	Year 2	Year 3	Year 4	Year 5
A.	Reported Income					
	Gross rental income	$ 69,100	$ 70,500	$ 71,900	$ 73,200	$ 74,600
	Operating expenses	25,600	26,100	26,600	27,100	27,600
	Interest costs	27,600	26,900	26,200	25,500	24,700
	Depreciation (straight line)	12,000	12,000	12,000	12,000	12,000
	1. Reported Income	$ 3,900	$ 5,500	$ 7,100	$ 8,600	$ 10,300
B.	Taxable Income					
	Income before depreciation	$ 15,900	$ 17,500	$ 19,100	$ 20,600	$ 22,300
	Depreciation (double-declining balance)	24,000	21,900	20,085	18,505	17,120
	2. Taxable Income	($ 8,100)	($ 4,400)	($ 1,000)	$ 2,100	$ 5,180
C.	Cash Flow					
	Income before depreciation and interest	$ 43,500	$ 44,400	$ 45,300	$ 46,100	$ 47,000
	Mortgage payments					
	Principal	9,600	10,300	11,000	11,700	12,500
	Interest	27,600	26,900	26,200	25,500	24,700
	3. Net Cash Flow	$ 6,300	$ 7,200	$ 8,100	$ 8,900	$ 9,800
D.	Equity					
	Market value of property	$522,000	$532,000	$543,000	$554,000	$565,000
	Less loan balance	389,400	379,100	368,100	356,400	343,900
	4. Estimated Actual Equity Value	$132,600	$152,900	$174,900	$197,600	$221,100
	Book value of property	438,000	426,000	414,000	402,000	390,000
	Less loan balance	389,400	379,100	368,100	356,400	343,900
	5. Book Value of Equity	$ 48,600	$ 46,900	$ 45,900	$ 45,600	$ 46,100

Source: Ray Hill's research report.

EXHIBIT 6
Raymond W. Hill
Pro forma sources and uses of funds for the company

	Beginning of year 1	Year 1	Year 2	Year 3	Year 4	Year 5	Year 6	Year 7	Year 8	Year 9	Year 10
Uses:											
1. Increase working capital	100,000				14,000		68,000	30,000	43,000	16,000	35,000
2. Build apartment buildings (in 30-unit packages)*		121,600	900,000	450,000	450,000	450,000			2,250,000		2,250,000
3. Purchase of acquisition							150,000	200,000		600,000	1,000,000
4. Reduction in mortgage debt										1,200,000	
Total Uses	100,000	121,600	900,000	450,000	464,000	450,000	218,000	230,000	2,293,000	1,816,000	3,285,000
Sources:											
1. Personal purchase of stock	100,000		50,000						100,000		
2. Decrease in working capital		49,400	13,000	21,000		22,000					
3. Earnings for year (straight line depreciation) (see Exhibit 7)		2,700	5,900	6,000	8,000	11,000	34,000	55,000	295,000	496,000	195,000
4. Depreciation (straight line)			6,000	24,000	36,000	48,000	60,000	60,000	120,000	60,000	120,000
5. Increase in mortgage debt		69,500‡	703,500‡	399,000‡	420,000‡	369,000‡	124,000‡	115,000‡	1,082,000‡		1,770,000‡
6. Sale of existing apartment buildings			121,600						696,000	1,260,000	
7. Sale of public stock (300,000 shares at $4)											1,200,000
Total Sources	100,000	121,600	900,000	450,000	464,000	450,000	218,000	230,000	2,293,000	1,816,000	3,285,000

*Except year 1.
† Available from new construction.
‡ Available from refinancing.
Source: Ray Hill's research report.

EXHIBIT 7
Raymond W. Hill
Pro forma income and cash flows for the company

	Year 1	Year 2	Year 3	Year 4	Year 5	Year 6	Year 7	Year 8	Year 9	Year 10
Reported Income:										
Net rental income		7,900	35,000	54,000	72,000	95,000	104,000	196,000	95,000	175,000
Net profit of acquired companies*						24,000	56,000	56,000	156,000	316,000
Overhead expense		1,000	5,000	10,000	13,000	25,000	45,000	55,000	70,000	100,000
Depreciation (straight line)		6,000	24,000	36,000	48,000	60,000	60,000	120,000	60,000	120,000
Net operating income before tax		900	6,000	8,000	11,000	34,000	55,000	77,000	122,000	271,000
Income taxes on ordinary income									9,000	76,000
Net extraordinary income (sale of buildings)		5,000						218,000	383,000	
Reported income (excluding extraordinary)	2,700	5,900	6,000	8,000	11,000	34,000	55,000	77,000	113,000	195,000
Taxable Income:										
Reported income	2,700	5,900	6,000	8,000	11,000	34,000	55,000	77,000	122,000	271,000
Extra depreciation (above straight line)	2,700†	6,000	24,000	32,000	38,000	33,000	30,000	74,000	50,000	105,000
Taxable income (before tax loss)	0	100	18,100	42,100	69,100	1,000	25,000	3,000	72,000	166,000
Cumulative tax loss						68,100	43,000	40,000		
Taxable income		0	0	0	0	0	0	0	32,000	166,000
Cash Flows:										
Reported income after taxes	2,700	5,900	6,000	8,000	11,000	34,000	55,000	77,000	113,000	195,000
Straight line depreciation		6,000	24,000	36,000	48,000	60,000	60,000	120,000	60,000	120,000
Cash from extraordinary sales								218,000	383,000	
Principal payments on mortgage‡		4,800	19,800	30,000	42,000	55,000	58,000	83,000	52,000	103,000
Net Cash Flow	2,700	7,100	10,200	14,000	17,000	39,000	57,000	332,000	504,000	212,000

*Assumes no improvement in profit performance.
†Construction writeoffs.
‡Interest payments charged against reported income.
Source: Ray Hill's research report.

EXHIBIT 8
Raymond W. Hill
Equity value in year 10 at various P/E ratios

1. Earnings in year 10 .... $195,000
2. Total value of company at .... P/E = 10 $1.95 million
                                              15   2.93
                                              20   3.90
                                              25   4.88
3. Value of Ray's 45 percent share ...... P/E = 10 $ .88 million
                                              15   1.32
                                              20   1.76
                                              25   2.20

Source: Ray Hill's research report.

Note

Aspects of real estate for entrepreneurs

I. PURPOSE OF NOTE

This note seeks to provide some background in the terminology, instruments, concepts, and scope of the highly diverse real estate business. This Note is not an all-inclusive treatment of the area. The reader will recognize that the almost infinite combination of instruments and concepts, limited primarily by the entrepreneur's ingenuity, makes "complete" coverage impossible in this Note and unlikely in any size text. It should also be emphasized that because the success of most real estate ventures depends on an advantageous merging of the legal, tax, and financial regulations with expertise in the use of a natural resource —land, and perhaps the use of construction and marketing skills, qualified counsel should be used in specific situations. However, because it is possible to undertake real estate ventures on varying scales and levels of sophistication, a general introduction to the field should be of use to the entrepreneur. In addition, nonreal estate ventures frequently have real estate as an asset, and it may prove helpful to the entrepreneur to increase his understanding of this asset.

Certain considerations such as depreciation, personal holding companies, unincorporated real estate trusts, and so on, are discussed briefly in other Notes. This Note will expand upon those areas only as necessary.

II. INTRODUCTION

The real estate industry contains a wide variety of subsectors: land sale, tract development, single-family residential building, apartment construction, industrial park development, shopping center development, commercial property development, and recreational facility development, to mention some of the major ones. Each subsector is characterized by different criteria for land selection and varying construction procedures, financing techniques, expected rates of return, and accounting practices. Some common characteristics of the various subsectors include:

1. Capital assets—land and improvements—tend to increase in value because of the essentially fixed supply of land and long life of improvements.
2. Highly capital-intensive industry, requiring large amounts of debt and equity capital long before a return is yielded. The assets may be somewhat unmarketable and the market is greatly influenced by local conditions. The debt to equity ratio is high with consequent high fixed costs.
3. Return on equity is the highest of any major industry, exceeding 50 percent per annum not infrequently, due to the high debt to equity ratio. Liquidity is a critical consideration and the high debt to equity ratio can exaggerate problems.
4. Technological obsolescence is not an important risk factor. Projection of the long-term operating environment (demographic and sociological trends) can be highly accurate. However, the industry—to a varying extent—is vulnerable to shorter term economic and monetary fluctuations. Changes in local market demand can be sudden, largely unpredictable and critical, for example, closing of a local plant employing a large portion of the immediately surrounding work force.
5. Low level of concentration with many small competing firms. There are few large, publicly owned companies. Uninformed, uneconomic competition can cause difficulties in a local market area.
6. Accounting practices vary widely with resulting misleading income and balance sheet data. Land development companies have often credited sales with the full purchase price of land sold on installment with a minimal downpayment.

The characteristics of the industry have caused abuses such as overbuilding, excessive land development, overextension of debt, syndicate failures, and excessive FHA loan guarantees relative to demand, to mention but a few. The lack of applicable data and poor management have contributed to the abuses. Tax benefits and government programs which provide incentives for real estate development can contribute to these kinds of problems.

III. THE DEVELOPMENT PROCESS

In addition to the common characteristics of the industry, the various subsectors may be viewed from a common process of development. This development may be considered to include five major subprocesses: economic study, preliminary decision, organizing the deal, marketing and investment management, and liquidation of the investment. This section will outline the components of the above subprocesses. The developer and/or investor should be aware that he may require professional expertise for all or portions of some components of these steps.

A. Economic study

The kinds of information and techniques useful to the developer in the early stages of a project before major commitment of resources include: appraisal, economic feasibility study, "highest and best use" study, land use study, market study, and marketability study.

1. Appraisal. The purpose of an appraisal is to estimate the value of a specific piece of property. The value is based on existing or proposed use for developed property and proposed use for undeveloped property. Large properties require for appraisal detailed market studies and "highest and best use" studies, together with estimates of likely absorption rates in marketing the developed property. To the developer of income-producing property, the value of the property means the capitalized value of the net income produced. The method of capitalizing net income will depend on the sophistication of the developer (capitalization rate × net income, discounted cash flow, present value, and so on) and his estimate of risk. Appraisals are often used as the basis for mortgage lending, and lenders are likely to place different values on a property depending on their preference and/or experience with that type of investment. The mortgage lender often compares the capitalized income value with the projected cost and uses the lower of the two as the basis for its loan.

2. Economic feasibility study. This type of study seeks to determine the likely rate of return on investment (ROI) of the project. The determination of ROI requires a particular development plan for a specific site to allow an estimate of total project cost and time for completion. A marketability study is also required to determine the land use and probable revenues. The ROI then compares the future income and investment costs.

3. Highest and best use study. The identification of the specific land use within the constraints of zoning and topography which will produce the maximum ROI. The study is concerned with a specific property under various concepts of land development. Obvious unsatisfactory uses are rejected with the reason for rejection stated. The remaining potential uses are screened to determine their marketability. Detailed economic feasibility studies are then made on the remaining possibilities. Whereas the site studied is limited to one, the variety of concepts of land use is limited largely by the creativity of the developer and/or his advisors, and thus the highest and best use study can be one of the most complicated economic studies.

4. Land use study. This type of study is a complete inventory of the land use of all parcels in a defined area such as a city. Since marketability and feasibility considerations are excluded, this study is not a highest and best use study. In effect, the study determines the potential land supply for various uses.

5. Market study. A generalized study of the present and future supply and demand for a particular land use in a specific geographic area. The rates at which supply and demand will change may also be analyzed.

6. Marketability study. A study of the present and future supply of competitive properties. The study determines: (*a*) sales or rental prices; (*b*) amount likely to be sold or rented per year; and (*c*) special factors such as financing, sales techniques, and amenities that will affect marketing.

B. Preliminary decisions

The various economic studies provide the information for the developer to decide whether to proceed with the development plan as is, modify it, or drop the particular site. It can be seen that the studies are to some extent interdependent. The developer in making his decision will in essence answer three subquestions: is the maximum project budget equal to or less than the expected development cost; is the estimated mortgage financing possible and desirable; and is the maximum equity investment equal to or less than the amount desired? The basic steps involved in testing the feasibility of the project are the determination of:

1. Gross rent ÷ Rent per net leasable square foot = Total leasable square feet
2. Net income = Gross rent less vacancy allowance and operating expenses
3. Cash flow before taxes = Net income less interest and amortization of mortgage
4. Maximum equity investment $= \dfrac{\text{Cash flow before taxes}}{\text{Return on equity desired}}$
5. Maximum project budget = Maximum equity investment and mortgage

Assuming the project is economically feasible and the developer is satisfied the project is marketable, he will then proceed to organize the deal.

C. Organizing the deal

The developer with a project that he deems feasible has to (1) bring together the equity investors and the development team; (2) assemble and/or acquire the land if he does not already own it, and (3) arrange the financing.

1. Equity investors and development team. These two groups may or may not be mutually exclusive. The equity investor may contribute land, services, cash, or credit in return for a share of the equity position. In terms of time sequence, the developer is likely to work on assembling the equity investors and the development team concurrently.

One of the first choices of the developer is the legal form to be used in creating the ownership interest. The two basic forms, corporate and partnership, offer different advantages. The corporate form limits the personal liability of the owners and allows: easy separation of ownership and management, easy transfer of all or part of an ownership interest, reduction of risk by holding more than one project. In addition, the corporation as a legal entity has a life span independent of its owners. Its main disadvantage is double taxation of profits. This disadvantage is minimized to the extent depreciation deductions result in tax-sheltered cash returns to the stockholder.

The partnership forms (general, limited, joint stock) are not taxable entities. The major advantage of the partnership is that income is taxed to the individual partners when received, and all the tax advantages from depreciation and interest deductions are passed directly to the partners. The limited partnership is the most frequently used legal form in land development deals. Most real estate syndicates are limited partnerships. The limited partnership must have at least one general partner who has management control, but has unlimited liability for the project. However, the general partnership may be a corporation, thus limiting liability for the individual but suffering a tax disadvantage. The limited partners may not participate in management and their liability is limited to their investment.

The real estate investment trust has been developed in recent years and is primarily used by large land developers, owners, or mortgage lenders to diversify risk among many projects and investors. The trust is treated for tax purposes much like an open-end mutual fund. Rent and other operating income of the trust are taxed as ordinary income to the investors, and there is no dividend exclusion permitted. Long-term capital gains distributed to the investor are treated as long-term capital gains. The trust cannot pass on losses to the investor. Earned income and capital gains which have not been distributed are treated by the individuals as if distributed for income tax purposes.

Prospective equity investors include the land seller, development team members, mortgage money lenders, investment trusts, and corporations, as well as the individual investor.

The development team members who should enter the development project as early as possible are the: market analyst, attorney, accountant, real estate broker, mortgage banker, construction manager, and planners. Each of these should be considered as categories of talent and not necessarily as separate individuals. The market analyst may be an economist, appraiser, or real estate broker who prepares the marketability and feasibility studies. The attorney is responsible for drafting, reviewing, and negotiating legal papers for construction, partnerships, debt financing, consultants' services, land purchases, sales and leases, corporations, and zoning changes. The accountant's advice on tax and financial considerations can be very important. The real estate broker may assist in testing the market, assembling the land, and marketing or managing the developed project. Permanent mortgage financing and interim construction financing are arranged by a mortgage banker. The construction manager may be a consultant or building contractor who can provide cost control during planning and design. The planners include architects, landscape architects, engineers, and urban planners. In addition to these major skill categories the developer may also require the services of others such as an insurance broker, public relations specialist, advertising manager, and property manager.

2. Acquiring the land.   The developer's objectives when acquiring land are likely to be to minimize his cash outlay and to delay carrying costs (interest, real estate taxes, and amortization) as well as to minimize the total purchase price. There is likely to be a long interval (perhaps years) before the developer realizes any income from his development and he may well be willing to trade off reduced cash outlay and delay in carrying costs for a higher price to the seller. There are obviously many ways to acquire property; some of the more common are:

a. *Deed and purchase money mortgage.*   This method is also called installment or deferred payment sale. The developer acquires ownership in return for a cash downpayment and a "purchase money mortgage" to the seller for the balance. If the total cash payment received by the seller (cash downpayment and amortization payment of the mortgage) in the year of sale is less than 30 percent and total payments extend over at least two tax years, the seller is required to pay income tax only on a portion of the profit (cash received less allocated cost basis) each year. The seller and purchaser both benefit from this arrangement: the seller defers payment of the full tax over several years and the buyer acquires financing. This method can only be used when the buyer is directly indebted to the seller. The terms of the mortgage, as well as the interest rate, will vary according to the sophistication of the parties involved, the preferences and tax status of the seller, and the traditional ways of doing business in the area. The ownership rights of the buyer: to divest ownership; to use the property as collateral for loans; to grant a right to use, i.e., lease; and to hold may be conditioned by the mortgage terms. The mortgage terms may also provide for such things as: release of portions of the land (usually with payment of a greater than proportional share of the mortgage), restrictions on removal and sale of top soil or minerals, and the granting of easements on the land.[1]

b. *Land contract.* In some states, the seller retains title (ownership) to the land until all payments (including interest) are completed. The purchaser gets full use of the land, and the arrangement will resemble the deed and purchase money mortgage situation. The advantage to the seller is that foreclosure is quicker and less expensive if the purchaser defaults on the mortgage terms.

c. *Option.* The developer may secure an option to purchase valid for a limited period of time or a series of options to give him time to raise the required cash and develop his plans. When a series of options are obtained the purchase price is likely to be greater for the later options. If the option lapses without the developer exercising his right to purchase, the seller retains the amount paid for the option. The use of an option reduces the developer's cash risk before he has an operative development, but he risks losing a parcel on which he has invested time and other funds if he is unable to complete his deal before the option expires.

d. *Ground lease.* Often, if the owner is unwilling to sell or if the developer wants to reduce his investment, he will secure the use of the land through the payment of rent. The developer may own the improvements placed on the land, or if the lease runs sufficiently long, the improvements may revert to the land owner. The concern of the developer is that he may enjoy the benefits of the return on the investment for a sufficient time.

e. *Joint venture.* The owner of the property may be willing to contribute the land to the partnership that will develop it in return for an equity position in the development. The share of the equity obtained by the landowner, the burden of paying property taxes during development, and restrictions on use of the land during development are all subject to negotiation.

f. *Exchanges.* It is possible that the landowner may not wish to sell because of the tax consequences or that the developer may own other

---

[1] An easement is a right granted a third party by the owner to use the property or a portion of the property. A common example is the granting of an easement to an electric utility to run power lines across a property.

property which the landowner finds desirable. In this case an exchange or trade may be possible without incurring a tax.

When the developer has acquired the land, he is ready to talk seriously with the mortgage banker about financing the project.

3. Debt financing. The mortgage banker's function is to secure for the developer the minimum loan amount and terms required for the development. A capable mortgage banker is familiar with the availability and terms of financing and the preferences of the various lenders. His knowledge and experience are also helpful in reviewing the feasibility of the project. For a fee, usually 1 percent to 1.5 percent, the mortgage banker will prepare, process, and negotiate the loan required by the developer, as well as obtain approval of loan guarantees from government agencies such as the FHA if the loan is to be made under a government program. The developer may be required to pay the mortgage banker's fee at the time a lending commitment is issued, or he may be able to delay payment of all or part of the fee until funds are initially drawn or until all the funds are drawn.

Basically there are two types of financing: permanent funds and short-term or construction funds. Generally the permanent loan commitment is secured first and then a construction loan is obtained from either the permanent lender or another source. When the same lender makes both loans, this is called a buy-sell agreement or conversion (of the construction loan to a permanent mortgage). The developer will likely reduce his financing costs (service fees, survey costs, title insurance costs) and minimize his problems of dealing with the lender if there is only one lender. In times of "tight money" the lender may discount the loan (charge "points") to increase his yield (for example, he might lend $980,000 on a loan of face amount $1 million). Lenders have in recent years sought an equity position in return for making a loan.

The construction loan is repaid from the proceeds of the permanent loan. (The permanent lender wants the construction loan which is secured by the property removed as a prior claim on the asset.) A construction loan is normally in an amount less than the permanent loan and is made available in installments as a percent of the value of construction completed to date. Lenders of permanent funds will generally lend more on a completed and income-producing building and thus may "hold back" 15–20 percent of the permanent loan commitment until a specified occupancy level is attained. The result is that the construction lender may not advance sufficient funds to pay for a completed building below the specified occupancy level. The developer may be required then to seek a second mortgage at a higher interest rate for a shorter term to close the gap or pay an additional fee to the construction lender to cover the gap.

When money is tight a developer may accept a permanent mortgage commitment with intentionally stiff terms, gambling that when he actually must take out the permanent mortgage he can obtain better financing. The lender is aware of this possibility but sees it as an opportunity to earn fees without actually committing funds, and if the loan is taken out, it is a higher yielding loan than usual. The developer in turn is able with a permanent commitment to secure construction financing and proceed with the project.

The prime institutional sources of debt financing are: savings and loan associations, life insurance companies, mutual savings banks, commercial banks, real estate investment trusts, and pension funds. These lenders, because of the varying legal restrictions, investment opportunities available to them, and the needs they are intended to serve, have different preferences for the type of financing and type of development they will generally consider. Savings and loan associations are the major source of individual home mortgages and residential construction. Typically they are restricted to initiating loans in their home area. Loans for residential properties may be for as much as 90 percent of cost, while loans for commercial properties may be restricted to 60 percent of value. Life insurance companies are the largest lenders on nonresidential properties. Usually they are not restricted to initiating loans to particular geographic areas. They may, however, restrict themselves to particular regions and alter their preference as to type of property they prefer at any given time in light of their view of the demand for such properties or the composition of their portfolio of loans. Mutual savings banks exist in only 18 states, primarily in the northeastern United States. Their loan preference is similar to that of the savings and loan associations, but their loan ratio may be more conservative. Commercial banks have been the primary source of construction loans and their activity is locally oriented to enable them to monitor construction progress. In recent years some have established mortgage banking divisions with a view to increasing their participation in permanent loans. The real estate investment trusts participate in both permanent and interim financing. Pension funds are an expanding source of permanent loans for all types of construction. The funds available in local market areas have been expanded in recent years through the sale of mortgages to lenders outside the area. The initiating institution frequently "services" the loan for a fee: collecting interest and amortization and seeing to it that property taxes are paid and that mortgage terms such as maintenance of the property and insurance coverage are fulfilled.

D. Market and investment management

The success of income-producing property depends on the production of the expected income. It is common practice for the developer to make a great effort to lease space during construction and even before construction begins. In addition to generating income as soon as possible after construction is completed, a pre-leased project can significantly lessen the developer's financing problem. Prospective tenants for properties such as office buildings and shopping centers lease on the basis of plans of the project. Residential properties such as rental apartments, condominiums, and houses are rented or sold using model houses or mock-up models. The developer may use his own staff or hire specialists.

For a rental property, typically, an independent management company will contract to handle the property for a minimum one-year period. The property manager's responsibility will usually include:

1. Periodic reports on changes in local rental markets, including rent levels and competitive practices.
2. Advice on rent schedules.
3. Advertising for and locating tenants.
4. Credit check of potential tenants.
5. Preparation and execution of leases.
6. Employ, train, and manage personnel as resident staff.
7. Contract for utilities and services.
8. Purchase materials and supplies for operation.
9. Specify and supervise repairs, contract for maintenance.
10. Pay all expenses.
11. Maintain a separate bank account for funds.
12. Monthly reports on income and expenses, and projected budget for the next quarter.
13. Maintain adequate insurance.
14. Review of local tax assessments and advise when appeals should be taken.

The fee for these services is usually three percent to four percent of gross rents. The owner's other operating expenses may total 35 percent of gross rents. As the property manager is the agent of the owner it is necessary to define in the management contract whether the owner or manager is responsible for individual expenditures made by the manager on the property.

E. Liquidation of investment

The owner of a property may liquidate his investment by selling or exchanging the property or he may make his investment liquid by obtaining a mortgage. In this case the owner borrows against the enhanced value of a property.

In most states only licensed real estate brokers or attorneys can sell real estate. Contracts of sale must be in writing. Though local real estate boards may set commission rates (which vary depending on the size of the sale, the type of property, and whether the broker is responsible for securing a mortgage for the buyer), commissions are negotiable. There are five basic methods of employing a real estate broker:

1. Open listing. A listing available to more than one broker. The broker who first produces a buyer who is "ready, willing and able" to meet the price and terms is entitled to the commission. The owner is free to find a buyer himself without paying a commission.

2. Exclusive agency. An agreement, generally in writing, employing a particular broker for a specified time to the exclusion of all other brokers. The owner may secure a buyer himself and no commission is due.

3. Exclusive right to sell. In this form of listing, a broker for a specified time period, to the exclusion of all other brokers and the owner himself, has the right to sell. The broker is entitled to the commissions no matter who else brings about the sale.

4. Conditional agency. The broker's commission is conditional upon particular events such as the complete transfer of the property in order to avoid paying a commission for work done by others.

5. Multiple listing. An exclusive listing with one broker who shares it with other brokers organized in a cooperative group. When the property is sold the commission is split between the listing and the selling broker.

In a sale the owner may avoid a large taxable gain in one year by selling under an installment sale as explained in Section III, C, 2 under Acquiring the Land. If the real estate is owned by a corporation in which the developer has stock he may preserve his capital gain by selling the stock or by liquidating the corporation. In either case he will pay a capital gains tax on the difference between the selling price and his cost basis (assuming a minimum six months' holding period). In liquidating the assets of a corporation under a plan of liquidation there is no tax to the corporation when the property is sold. If the IRS determines the corporation is "collapsible" (usually those liquidated within three years), a capital gains treatment will not be allowed.

A sale-leaseback is a transaction whereby the user of the property ends up as a renter rather than an owner. A developer may build-to-suit for a manufacturer. The manufacturer then sells the building to the developer who leases it to the manufacturer. The manufacturer thus avoids a capital investment and a mortgage as a long-term liability. In addition, the manufacturer has a tax deduction for the entire amount of his rent including the rental value of the land which would not have been a depreciable item for tax purposes. The developer, if he has a long-term lease (say 15 or more years) with a financially secure company, may be able to secure 100 percent financing of the costs.

When selling real estate, if the property has enjoyed accelerated depreciation, there will be a depreciation recapture due for a portion of the excess depreciation. The "recaptured" depreciation will be taxed as ordinary income. This topic will be further discussed in Section V.

Exchange as a method of disposing of a property is not usual for a newly constructed property. The basic reason for exchanging properties is to defer payment of a capital gains tax which would be due upon outright sale or because large tax liabilities would be incurred by retaining ownership of a largely depreciated property. Exchange is often referred to as a "tax-free exchange," but it is really a deferral of tax. The tax laws require that the property has been held for investment and not stock in trade and that it be owned for at least six months. The exchange must be for "like property," but the definition is broad and may include leases and partnerships. The tax basis of the received property is the basis of the old property plus any cash paid or mortgage assumed in excess of the mortgage transferred on the old property. Trades may be made between two owners or more than two. In a three-way exchange owner (A) may wish to sell property (X) for cash, owner (B) wants to trade property (Y) for property (X), while owner (C) wants property (Y). Either A and B may trade and A sells to C, or C may buy A's property and exchange with B. The services of a competent tax lawyer and real estate broker should be used to be sure all the parties achieve their objectives in a desired manner.

IV. FHA FINANCING PROGRAMS

The creation of the FHA (Federal Housing Administration) in 1934 revolutionized the housing industry through the introduction of mortgage insurance to protect against losses on funds advanced by approved lenders. With the reduction in risk, lenders have been able and willing to provide higher loan-to-value ratios, longer maturities, and lower interest rates. More borrowers were able to qualify for loans, and a mortgage instrument was created which could be traded nationally thus increasing available funds. The FHA required a level payment mortgage including interest, amortization of principal, accrued real estate taxes, and a mortgage insurance premium of one half of 1 percent of the outstanding balance of the loan. The use of the level payment mortgage (not including the FHA mortgage insurance premium) has spread to conventional (non-FHA) loans. Stability in the industry was also advanced by the development of minimum property standards with procedures for inspection.

The National Housing Act of 1934 which created the FHA also created the FNMA (Federal National Mortgage Association) to trade in FHA mortgages and the FSLIC (Federal Savings and Loan Insurance Corporation) to insure savings in savings and loan associations. If a lender under an FHA insured mortgage suffers a loss, the FNMA has the option of reimbursing him in cash or in government bonds. Over the years government action in housing has grown to include: 1937, the PHA (Public Housing Administration); 1942, the NHA (National Housing Agency—to include the FHA and the PHA); 1947, the HHFA (Housing and Home Finance Agency, as successor to the NHA); 1949, addition of the Slum Clearance Program; 1954, inclusion of rehabilitation and conservation in Slum Clearance, and the addition of the URA (Urban Renewal Administration) and the CFA (Community Facilities Agency); and 1964, extension of HHFA powers by the Mass Transportation Act. In 1965 the name of the HHFA was changed to HUD (the Housing and Urban Development Department) and elevated to Cabinet status. The nature of government action has altered from primarily mortgage insurance to aid private housing to include both subsidy and direct loan programs to aid elderly and low-income groups and to combat racial discrimination practices. FHA activity in multifamily units has increased as the need has increased and the programs have become more liberal. The FHA responsibility now includes mortgage insurance for land development; rental and private housing for low, moderate, and upper-income families, the elderly, and the handicapped; cooperative housing and condominiums; experimental housing; mobile home parks; housing at military installations; and long-term rehabilitation of housing.

The major private multifamily programs (Table 1) in 1969 were Sections 221(d)(3), 221(d)(4), and 236. The 221(d)(3) below market interest rate (BMIR) program, established by the Housing Act of 1961, is designed to aid private developers and nonprofit organizations to provide housing for low income and moderate income families in communities with a "workable program." A workable program is an official community program, approved by HUD, to use private and public resources to eliminate and prevent the spread of urban blight. Section 221(d)(3) limits the maximum annual income of eligible tenants, the maximum monthly rent, and the sponsor's profit. In addition the one half of 1 percent mortgage insurance premium is waived. The construction mortgage bears the current FHA interest rate ceiling, but the permanent mortgage is taken by FNMA at 3 percent interest. Section 221 was amended by adding subsections (i) and (j) which permit BMIR projects to be converted to condominium or cooperative ownership. Section 221 (d)(4) projects do not have to be built in an urban renewal area or in a community with a workable program, but occupancy priority must be given to families displaced by urban renewal. Sponsors can obtain up to 90 percent of replacement cost as a mortgage, whereas nonprofit sponsors can obtain up to 100 percent in the 221(d)(3) program.

Section 236 was added in 1968 and is intended to eventually replace the 221(d)(3) BMIR program. Under 236 a conventional mortgage is

TABLE 1

Privately financed nonfarm dwelling units started under FHA programs compared with total for United States—1969

Total United States	1,449,200	
Total FHA	240,497	
Percent FHA	16.6	
Home mortgage programs:		
203	136,368	
235	8,676	
221	7,675	
	152,719	
Total FHA		153,593
Project mortgage programs:		
221 market rate	27,328	
221 BMIR*	33,405	
236	10,168	
	70,901	
Total FHA		79,727
Rehabilitation projects		
221 market rate	500	
221 BMIR*-rental	3,862	
221 BMIR*-sales	1,897	
	6,259	
		7,177
Total FHA	229,879	240,497

*BMIR—below market interest rate.
Source: *1969 HUD Statistical Yearbook*, Table 2, p. 26.

obtained but the government can subsidize all but 1 percent of the market interest rate. A 236 project does not have to be in an area with a workable program. The maximum tenant income is lower than in $221(d)(3)$ but is still 135 percent of the public housing maximums. The mortgage insurance premium is waived and the sponsor's profit is limited. Groups eligible for participation are: nonprofit organizations; builders who will sell at a fixed 7 percent profit to a nonprofit group, nonprofit cooperatives; investor/sponsor who will sell to the cooperative at a fixed profit of 7 percent; and limited-distribution sponsors whose profit is limited to a cumulative return of 6 percent on 11.11 percent of the initial amount of the mortgage.

The 236 project sponsor, with prior FHA approval, must set for each dwelling unit: a basic monthly rent determined on operating with a 1 percent mortgage and a fair market monthly rent determined on operating with a mortgage at the FHA maximum interest rate, 7½ percent at present. The FHA computes the rental subsidy payment as the fair market rental, less 25 percent of the tenant's adjusted gross income, but the maximum subsidy cannot exceed the difference between the fair market rental and the basic rental.

Table 2 is illustrative of a project built under 236 and the determination of the rent and rent subsidy.

The effect of the lower interest rate on the rent is quite apparent. In addition, although the annual return to the limited dividend sponsor is 6 percent of the equity required (11.11 percent of the mortgage), there is a builders' and sponsors' profit of $126,875 included in the mortgage amount. This profit allowance, less 5 percent of the mortgage amount (2 percent working capital and 3 percent equity) can be applied to the

TABLE 2
Illustrative Section 236 project (limited dividend)

Estimated cost of 100 units

Land improvement	$ 55,000
Construction (includes 3% job overhead)	991,500
Fees—architect, general overhead, others	80,500
Total all improvements......................................	$1,127,000
Carrying charges, financing, FHA fees	123,000
Subtotal 1	$1,250,000
Legal and organization (1½% of Subtotal 1)	18,750
Subtotal 2	$1,268,750
Builders and sponsors profit (10% of Subtotal 2)	126,875
Total development cost, less land	$1,395,625
Land...	104,375
Total replacement cost	$1,500,000
Mortgage (90% of replacement cost).............................	1,350,000
Equity Required..	$ 150,000

Rent determination

	Fair market	Basic
Replacement cost	$1,500,000	$1,500,000
Mortgage...	1,350,000	1,350,000
Annual mortgage payment..........................	113,315*	40,963†
Total expenses	84,450	84,450
Reserve for replacement	6,000	6,000
Vacancy adjustment and collection losses,		
5% of gross market rent	7,443	7,443
Return to limited dividend sponsor	9,002	9,002
Total yearly rents	$ 221,210	$ 148,858
Average Monthly Rent per Unit	184	124
Maximum subsidy ....$184–$124 = $60		

*Derived by applying factor of 3.034273% to mortgage amount. Factor based on level annuity plan, 1% interest rate, 40-year term.
†Factor of 8.383673% for 7½% interest rate, 40-year term.
Source: "Homebuilding's Pocket Guide to Low Income Housing Programs," *NAHB Journal of Homebuilding*, Washington, D.C., Table II, p. IV.

equity requirement. The sponsor's return may be $9,002 per year on an out-of-pocket equity investment of $82,500. All other costs must be certified as actually paid. The penalties for borrowing more FHA-insured money than is actually spent can include criminal prosecution.

The procedure for applying for an FHA insured mortgage is similar for the various programs. The first step is a pre-application meeting of the local FHA and the proposed sponsor to determine the basic site and market feasibility. If the FHA feels the project is feasible it will by letter invite the submission of Form 2013 giving more specific details. A 221(d)(3) application requires also a request for reservation of mortgage funds from FNMA. An examination fee of 0.15 percent of the mortgage amount and preliminary architectural drawings and construction estimates must accompany the 2013 form. Upon acceptance, architectural working drawings are prepared and an FHA-approved professional estimator is hired to do a detailed construction estimate. The land value is determined at this time by the FHA. The FHA land value may exceed the sponsor's cost and provide a markup reducing the equity investment. The FHA has maximum values which it will allow under the various sections. The cost of site improvements will affect the land value, and the FHA will consider recent arm's-length sales of this or similar sites in the area. The next step is the submission of final drawings and the balance of the 0.3 percent examination fee for approval. Upon approval the initial mortgage closing can take place.

The developer during these steps seeks private lenders for the permanent mortgage, except for Section 221(d)(3) projects where FNMA makes the mortgage and for construction loans under all sections. The FHA allows a 1.5 percent financing fee to assist in compensating for interest rates above the FHA maximum and/or for points charged by the lender. Where FNMA takes the mortgage, an additional fee of 1 percent is required.

At the initial closing of the mortgage the developer may borrow 75 percent of the total architectural and engineering fees, all legal and organizational fees, and financing expenses. Except under Section 207 the developer can be paid for the land. Most of the out-of-pocket costs may be covered at the initial closing. The developer is required at the initial closing to put up a 2 percent working capital deposit, in cash, government bonds, or other acceptable security. This working capital deposit, except in a nonprofit 221(d)(3) project, is included as part of the mortgage. This deposit may be used for rental expenses or operating losses when the project opens.

Prior to closing the permanent mortgage, the developer must prove that in addition to the builder-sponsor profit allowance and the 2 percent working capital reserve he has at least 3 percent of the mortgage amount in cash. If he cannot prove this, he must place this amount in escrow for at least three years of operation after closing the mortgage to provide for possible operating losses. Funds not used at the end of the period are refunded.

The FHA exercises a number of controls upon a completed project. Rent increases above the authorized maximum require prior FHA approval. Management fees are controlled. A 7 percent vacancy allowance is permitted. Semiannual physical inspections are made, and compliance is required with report recommendations. Capital improvements from the replacement reserve funds deposited monthly require approval. The fund is transferred to the new owner when the project is sold. Prepayment of the mortgage carries penalties (frequent also with conventional mortgages) and a 221(d)(3) loan cannot be prepaid for 20 years. Distributions to the owner may be made only quarterly and only out of surplus cash, i.e., after-tax income plus depreciation less mortgage amortization and replacement reserve payments. Annual reports on a standard FHA bookkeeping system of accounts are required. Discrimination of tenancy based upon race, color, creed, or national origin is prohibited. The FHA must approve all transfers of the property or changes in control of ownership.

The major FHA home ownership programs are Sections 203 and 235. The 235 program is to help lower income families become homeowners with the assistance of federal subsidies in making mortgage interest payments. There is no requirement of a community workable program. Families eligible for assistance payments are encouraged, if possible, to provide "sweat equity," i.e., work done by the purchaser. The largest monthly subsidy which the FHA can pay the lender on behalf of the prospective mortgagor is the lesser of:

Principal + Interest + Mortgage insurance premium
  + Taxes + Insurance
less 20% of prospective mortgagor's income

or:

Principal + Interest + Mortgage insurance premium
less principal + Interest at 1%

If the monthly family income plus maximum subsidy does not equal or come close to the required monthly payment, the prospective buyer probably will not be qualified by either the lender or the FHA. As the family income increases, the subsidy will become less.

Section 203 under which the largest number of units are built under FHA programs has separate subsections. The 203(b) is the basic and most commonly used FHA loan insurance program. The 203(h) program is for replacement housing for disaster victims; 203(*i*) is for rural areas where all 203(*b*) requirements cannot be met; and 203(*k*) is for remodeling one–four family sales housing.

The maximum mortgage allowances are:

	203(b)	203(h)	203(i)
Single–family unit	33,000	14,400	16,200
2-family unit	35,750	n.a.	n.a.
3-family unit	35,750	n.a.	n.a.
4-family unit	41,250	n.a.	n.a.

The loan-to-value ratio varies as follows:

A. Approved by FHA or VA prior to construction or completed more than one year on date of application:

	Nonveteran	Veteran
First $15,000 of FHA value	97%	100%
Next $10,000 FHA value	90	90
All FHA value over $25,000 ...	80	85

B. Plans not approved prior to construction or completed less than one year on date of application:

	Nonveteran	Veteran
First $25,000 of FHA value	90%	90%
All FHA value over $25,000 ...	80	85

The mortgage term may be 30 years or three fourths of the remaining economic life, whichever is less, but it may be extended to 35 years if the mortgagor is not acceptable for a 30-year mortgage and the property is constructed subject to FHA (or VA) inspection.

The general processing schedule for a housing subdivision covers approval by the FHA of the site and the proposed construction as meeting FHA minimum property standards, inspection and approval as construction proceeds, and approval of individual mortgage applicants. The initial step by the developer is the submission of two sets of an Application for Subdivision Feasibility Analysis (ASP-1, Form 2250). Attached to this form are a location map showing the site relative to schools, recreation, shopping, churches, hospitals, and industry, a preliminary subdivision plan showing the layout of streets and plot sizes, and an Equal Employment Opportunity Certification (FHA Form 2010). If the FHA finds the subdivision is feasible it will respond by letter and request the submission of complete preconstruction exhibits. The second submission is done on ASP-7 Form 2256 together with two sets of a plot plan and grading plan and two sets for each house type of: a planting plan, heat plan, heat loss calculations, truss details by manufacturer, house drawings, kitchen cabinet details, description of materials (Form 2005), and a schedule of alternatives (Form 2439). At this time the following information on the proposed developer is required: names and addresses of all principals or officers, trade names previously used by the organization, location of past activities, and names of other FHA offices with whom the organization has dealt. The FHA will analyze the preconstruction exhibits, and upon issuance of a letter of approval, subdivision improvements may begin and applications for mortgage commitments on individual properties may be submitted. One set of preconstruction exhibits is returned with revisions, if needed, indicated to meet property and site standards.

Applications for mortgage commitments are submitted in triplicate on Form 2800 with exhibits showing any revisions from the approved set. The application is made by the developer and the mortgage lender. In addition the FHA requires a "record plat" or "filed map" which is the official subdivision of the land approved by the local planning commission and filed or recorded with the local government authority, usually the county clerk. Acceptance by the FHA and the issuance of a commitment signifies that the FHA will insure a mortgage for a qualified purchaser.

The developer as he proceeds with construction is required to call for inspection at various stages: upon excavation but prior to pouring footings for the foundation; the foundation; framing prior to enclosing the interior walls; and completion of the structure and the plot grading and landscaping. Note that in addition to FHA inspections, the builder is likely to be required to obtain inspections by the local building department and the prospective mortgage lender, at the same or additional stages. The building department is concerned with compliance with the local building code, while the lender, although concerned with the quality of construction, is also concerned with the value of the construction to date because the amount of construction loan that the builder may obtain is related to this value. The local building department issues the building permit allowing construction to begin and the certificate of occupancy when construction is satisfactorily completed and utilities are available to service the house.

The fourth submission to the FHA is an application for credit approval of a prospective purchaser. One set of Form 2900 and exhibits is required for each individual buyer. Included is a credit report from a recognized credit agency and a signed copy of the sales contract. The mortgage lender may or may not require an application for credit approval.

If a subdivision is large FHA approval may be obtained section by section. The subdivision may be divided into sections because the FHA wishes to approve a limited number of lots until marketability is established or because the developer may acquire additional land or for other reasons may not wish to submit the entire parcel at once.

The final submission to the FHA is a letter signed by the developer and a licensed civil engineer certifying that the streets, drainage, grading, utilities, and other site improvements are complete according to the approved plans and specifications and applicable published FHA standards. A similar letter will be sent to the local planning commission to request the release of the performance bond if the developer has been required to post such a bond for these improvements.

V. DEPRECIATION AND TAX CONSIDERATIONS

A. Depreciation

Depreciation is an expense deduction for recapture of capital invested in assets used for income production. To be depreciable the asset must have a determinable estimated life; thus land may not be depreciated. Needed for determining the depreciation expense to be taken are the cost basis, the estimated life, the salvage value, and the choice of a method for calculation. The methods for calculation generally used are "straight line," "declining balance," and "sum-of-the-years'-digits."

The cost basis is usually the actual construction cost of the property improvement. Included in the construction cost are not only bricks and mortar but also purchase commissions, costs of defending or perfecting title, and items not deductible as current expenses. When an improved property is bought, the allocation between land cost and improvement cost is usually done in the ratio of the assessed value of the land and the assessed value of the building, and the allocated cost of the building becomes the basis for depreciation.

The estimated life for depreciation is the useful life of the asset rather than the physical life. The useful life is the time over which the property is expected to be useful to the owner. This is determined by his past experience with similar property or the experience of others. Factors to be considered include age when acquired, obsolescence, wear and tear, repair and upkeep policy, climate, and changes in technology. The Treasury publishes guidelines for many commercial and industrial properties.

Salvage value is an estimate of the future value of a property after the owner stops using it. The salvage value may be reduced by the cost of removal. It is permitted to ignore salvage value if the owner expects to use the full value of the property or a declining balance method of depreciation is used.

Limitations on the choice of depreciation method permitted by the Internal Revenue Service include:

1. Used residential property with 20 or more years life and minimum of 80 percent of gross rent from dwelling units—maximum depreciation of 125 percent of straight line in the first year;
2. New nonresidential properties limited to a maximum 150 percent declining balance, other accelerated methods cannot be used;
3. Used nonresidential properties are limited to straight line or comparable;
4. Rehabilitated housing may depreciate rehabilitated portion by straight line over a five-year period and the shell or purchase price may be depreciated by any method permitted on residential rental housing.

The taxpayer is permitted to use a different method for each of his properties. Changes from accelerated methods to straight line are permitted at any time, but any other changes in method require IRS permission.

The importance of the depreciation deductions for the owner is that it is a noncash expense permitted in determining taxable income: an amount of revenue equal to the depreciation allowance is shielded from income taxes. The method selected for calculating depreciation does not alter the total amount of depreciation allowed for a specific property. The use of a shorter life and an accelerated method permits the owner to advance the time for taking the deduction and to defer the payment of taxes. This rapid depreciation provides the owner with cash for working capital or for investment in other income sources. The postponement of tax is equivalent to receiving an interest-free government loan. Note that the owner is permitted to depreciate the total value of the building including the portion financed by debt.

As there is no relationship between the depreciation allowance taken on a real estate property and the realizable value of the property, it is possible the property value may depreciate more slowly than the allowance taken or it may appreciate. In either case, upon sale the owner will receive a capital gain treatment of the difference between the selling price and the total costs of the property. The reference to "tax-free return" in real estate is based on the assumption that the property does not actually depreciate as fast as the tax depreciation rate. If a property did depreciate as fast as the tax depreciation rate, then the distribution above current income would be a return of the investor's own capital. The actual tax-free return is the difference between the depreciation rate and the actual depreciation.

B. Depreciation recapture

The 1969 tax law provides that *all* depreciation taken after December 31, 1969, on property held for 12 months or less will be "recaptured" upon sale, i.e., the gain includes the depreciation taken and is taxed at the ordinary income rates. The depreciation recapture provisions for properties held more than 12 months vary according to the type of property. For the period beyond the first 12 months the depreciation recapture refers to the taxation at ordinary income rates of the difference between the method of depreciation actually used and straight-line depreciation, with certain adjustments for the length of time the property was held. For residential rented property all excess depreciation is subject to recapture for a period of 100 months. Beyond 100 months the recapture is reduced 1 percent per month. If the property is held 200 months or 16 years and 8 months before sale, all income is taxed at the capital gains rate. The maximum gain subject to recapture is the lesser of the sales gain realized or the amount of excess depreciation taken.

For residential rehabilitation projects permitted a special five-year depreciation, the excess depreciation is subject to recapture if the property is sold before the expiration of the useful life of the improvement.

Residential rental property subsidized by federal programs such as 221(d) (3) or 236 programs is treated more favorably than nonsubsidized rental property. If the property is sold within 12 months all depreciation is recaptured. Up to 20 months all excess depreciation is recaptured. Beyond 20 months the recapture percentage is reduced 1 percent per month. Thus if a property is sold after 120 months, or 10 years, all income is taxed at the capital gains rate.

All excess depreciation on all commercial properties is subject to recapture regardless of the time held before sale. However, at some point annual straight-line depreciation will exceed the annual 150 percent declining balance depreciation, thus the excess depreciation subject to recapture will begin to decrease and eventually disappear.

The 1969 tax law provisions for depreciation recapture refer to all property regardless of age but it involves only the depreciation taken after December 31, 1969. Depreciation taken earlier is subject to the old tax rules. The old rules apply equally to all types of property: for up to 12 months or less holding period, all depreciation is recaptured; for more than 12 months and up to 20 months, all excess depreciation is recaptured: for more than 20 months, 1 percent per month reduction in excess depreciation is subject to recapture.

If a property has been held more than 20 months and less than 10 years and is sold after December 31, 1969, it may be necessary to calculate the depreciation recapture under both the old and new provisions. If the post-1969 depreciation recapture is greater than the gain on the sale the recapture is limited to the gain. If the post-1969 depreciation recapture is less than the gain on the sale, it is necessary to determine also the pre-1970 depreciation recapture. The two are then added and compared to the gain on the sale. The recapture limit is the lesser of the combined depreciation recapture or the gain on the sale.

C. Minimum tax on accelerated depreciation

A new tax of 10 percent on certain tax preference items for both the individual and the corporation was introduced in the 1969 tax law. Excess depreciation is considered a tax preference item. The 10 percent tax is imposed on excess depreciation in any one year above the taxpayer's basic $30,000 exclusion and the regular income tax paid.

REFERENCES

Arthur Anderson & Co. *Tax Sheltered Investments.* May 1970.

Beaton, William R., *Real Estate Investment.* Englewood Cliffs, N.J.: Prentice-Hall, 1971.

Smith, Halbert Co.; Tschappat, Carl J.; and Racster, Ronald L. *Real Estate and Urban Development.* Homewood, Ill.: Richard D. Irwin, 1973.

Case

Mark Olive

In February 1970 Mark Olive was preparing a proposal for the purchase of the Jadwin Precision Products Company, a manufacturer of jewelers' precision equipment and supplies located in the vicinity of Boston, Massachusetts. Mr. Olive considered the Jadwin company a likely prospect for purchase provided he could set a price, a method of payment, and a procedure for acquiring control which would be attractive to his associates and acceptable to the owner of the Jadwin company. As Mark Olive set out to accomplish this task, he was aware that he had specifically pointed his career toward acquiring and running a small company 14 years before. Thus, with this investment in preparation and with his future career at stake, he did not want to do a poor job of evaluating Jadwin and structuring a deal.

Background

In March 1969, Mark Olive at the age of 35 started to work on a project that had been planned 14 years earlier while he was a student in business school. On Thanksgiving Day in 1954, Olive was visiting at a classmate's home. Also present as a guest that day was an older man nationally known for his success in the financing and reorganizing of business enterprises. After listening to the experience and advice of the older man, the two younger men had a long discussion about their own career objectives. They decided that their goal would be to join forces and seek to take over the ownership and management of a small manufacturing company when they had reached an age of about 35. They agreed with the older man's advice regarding the desirability of having 10 to 15 years' business experience before endeavoring to take over such top management responsibilities.

Upon receiving his degree, Olive worked for three years in the industrial credit department of a large city bank. His work included surveys and on-site investigations of small and medium-size industrial plants. From 1958 to 1963, Olive served in the U.S. Air Force after which he was reemployed by the Algonquin National Bank in Philadelphia. His work was essentially the same as before his service experience. In October 1963, Olive accepted an offer at a subtantially more attractive salary from the Electric Appliance Corporation. This large company was going through extensive reorganization under its new management and was hiring a number of men who combined graduate business training with military experience. Mark's experience at Electric Appliance Corporation had concentrated in marketing and sales and his record had been excellent.

In the meantime, Olive's classmate had spent three years in a family wholesale business before going into the armed services. After the service he joined one of the country's larger manufacturing companies as a management engineer. He was assigned to headquarters organization in a staff capacity and in 1959 was made acting general manager of a small branch plant. His basic salary by 1969 was $25,000 and his annual bonus was estimated as approximately $5,000. Olive's own promotion opportunities and offers were such that he felt confident he could return to the Electric Appliance Corporation or to another large manufacturing company at an income level comparable to that being earned by his classmate.

By early 1969, Olive's classmate had accumulated some funds through his share of profits in the sale of his family's wholesale business and he was prepared to put some of the money into a mutual venture. Olive himself had received no inheritances, nor had he been able to save enough to make an appreciable equity investment. He had, however, won the confidence of a former employer who had substantial funds. This man had indicated that he was willing to invest in a new enterprise, provided the two younger men could establish such a venture through acquisition of a going concern on an attractive basis. He was an older man who had no expectation of participating in management other than as a director.

Olive resigned from the Electric Appliance Corporation in March of 1969. Through correspondence and conferences, he and his partners developed a mutually satisfactory plan of action. This plan involved Olive's devoting a minimum of one year and a maximum of three years full time to a systematic search for the kind of business opportunity desired. During this period, Olive would pay one third of his expenses and the other two men would each contribute a third. If they could acquire control of a good business on attractive terms, Olive expected to take over top management responsibility and would receive one third of the common stock acquired by the group. His third of the purchase price would be advanced by the older man who would then receive repayment out of Olive's share of the profits of the business.

Olive and his classmate decided that as a matter of personal preference they would like to live in the New England area. Accordingly, Olive mapped out a program which involved dividing his time between New York and Boston, with the greater part being spent in and around Boston. He then prepared the "Specifications for Purchase of a Business" shown in Exhibit 1. He had 500 copies made and left one with each business acquaintance and friend in the two cities that he thought might be helpful to his search.

Through his previous employment with the Algonquin National Bank in Philadelphia, Olive had a number of acquaintances in the New York as well as the Philadelphia financial community. Proceeding entirely on the basis of personal introductions, he first presented his objective to executives in the industrial departments of a number of New York banks, to numerous investment bankers, law firms, and accounting firms, and to several management consulting firms in the New York area. He also called on a number of business brokers, insurance agencies, and insurance companies.

After a month in New York, he spent another month "laying his lines" in Boston in a similar manner prior to making any effort to initiate purchase negotiations. During this initial period, he amassed a list of over 100 New England manufacturing companies that might be acquired from present owners. At the end of six months, his prospect list of companies for sale in New England had mounted to over 300. Fifty of these had appeared sufficiently attractive to merit careful personal investigation. In three instances tentative proposals had been submitted. None of these had been accepted.

In September 1969, Olive's classmate was considering taking a leave from his job to spend a few months making a similar investigation in the Midwest. He believed that conditions in the midwestern states might prove more conducive to location of an attractive opportunity. Accordingly, Olive prepared the following report to summarize his experience to date.

REPORT BY MARK OLIVE: September 1, 1969

This is to summarize my experience and to give you some suggestions as to how to proceed if you decide to make investigations in the Midwest along the lines I have been following here in New England.

First, I want to stress the importance of always working on the basis of personal introductions. The man you talk to will want to know not only why you are there, but who sent you. The degree of personal friendship and confidence between the man you are calling on and the individual who sent you can have a big influence on your reception. Usually the man you are seeing will telephone the mutual acquaintance immediately afterwards to find out how much he knows about you.

All my contacts to date have stemmed originally from family friends, classmates, former professors, former employers, and business associates. The number of leads I have been able to develop from these people and from their friends in turn seems almost inexhaustible.

Relatively few interesting leads, however, have come out of firsthand introductions from these personal friends. The effective pattern has been for them to introduce me in turn to friends of theirs who are top executives in financial and professional organizations. In particular, I have received my best leads from: (1) *Commercial bankers* (but not trust department officers who generally will not talk); (2) *Investment underwriting* firms; and (3) *Law firms* and individual lawyers having substantial estate or corporate practices. Altogether almost three quarters of my good leads have come from these sources. The fact that roughly an equal number have been obtained from each source probably reflects my own distribution of effort as much as anything else.

I shall continue numbering these general sources of leads here in rough order of their usefulness to me to date: (4) *Certified public accounting* firms and individual CPAs have not been used as extensively as the preceding three sources, but to date they have been equally productive when tried. (5) *Management consultants* have been very generous with advice, but have afforded only a few interesting leads. (6) *Insurance brokers and agents* who handle both estate and corporate policies do not have so many suggestions numerically but are likely to know when estate planning objectives make a business owner especially eager to sell. Incidentally, the insurance underwriting companies themselves unquestionably have their files loaded with good leads, but to date I have not found any way to crack this source.

The seventh source, in order of usefulness to date, has been the professional business broker who deals in the purchase and sale of established companies. The lack of results from these brokers may surprise you, as it did me. I had expected them to be far more fruitful. At least in this part of the country it looks to me as though the owner of a business does not list it with a broker until he has tried to peddle it quietly and found no takers. There was, however, one exception to this rule. One well-established firm in New York that concentrates on the purchase and sale of businesses did have a number of good leads.

At the bottom of my list in terms of specific leads, I put the venture capital firms. They gave me a lot of good advice on how to evaluate a business, but the few prospects they turned over to me proved to be ones they had dropped from their active list, and for good reason. None of them looked worth following up. In fact, I turned over many more leads to them than I received in return.

You will find no problem in picking up more suggestions than you could explore in a lifetime. I am finding that more and more of these prospects can be culled simply by keeping our own requirements and abilities clearly in mind. Too many times I have spent a full day exploring a situation only to find that some basic fact, which I could have determined by three minutes more discussion at the source of the suggestion, made the situation one we should not consider.

In particular, I would say we should stay away from companies having an annual sales volume much less than a million dollars. They generally cannot support much of a top management organization. Moreover, I am convinced that it takes just as much brains to make a 10 percent profit on $.5 million volume as it does to make the same profit margin in a company with $5 million sales. If anything, the smaller company is harder work for the top man who has to be Jack-of-all-trades.

I also think we would be smart to stay away from industries that are stagnant or that are moving out of a particular area. I have in mind a number of companies that are for sale in the textile, paper, and shoe industries in New England. Lots of plants and equipment can be bought cheap, and for a good reason. Often they are in distress and can be purchased accordingly.

At the same time, I think we might get burned even worse if we follow the crowd and try to buy into one of the currently popular glamour industries. If the word electronics can be stretched so that it in any way fits the product line of a small business for sale in the New England area now, you can be sure that the owner is asking 10 to 30 times earnings—if there indeed are any earnings. Tangible asset values are also generally small in relation to the asking price.

I have also seen a number of companies that we should shy away from because of personality problems. Most easily spotted are those companies that have been dominated by one or a few families whose relatives are packed throughout the organization. At first, it looks simple just to cut out the deadwood and thus build up the profits. If we do that, however, we are probably fooling ourselves about buying a going concern.

Another pitfall in the personality area is the small company with good earnings and a good financial record that depends excessively on the abilities and contacts of one top man. Too many times I have seen an opportunity to buy earning power which would provide an illusion once the former owner retired.

All in all you may be surprised and possibly discouraged at the number of interesting prospects that will blow up when you apply these tests. During the past six months, I have had approximately 300 companies called to my attention. In each case, my advisor had reason to believe that the company could be acquired and thought that it might meet our requirements. Simply by applying the general standards I have developed, about 250 were quickly eliminated.

Fifty of the companies seemed sufficiently attractive to merit my making more careful personal investigation. In each case, I visited the plant and had a conference with one or more of the officers. As you know, in three instances we later submitted tentative proposals. However, two of these situations were of sufficiently questionable value to us so that our proposed price was very low—so low, in fact, that we could have liquidated the operation without losing money if it did not pan out well after a year or two. The owners of these two companies could probably do better liquidating their companies themselves now.

It would be misleading to imply that only three companies out of 300 leads looked like a good business opportunity for us. In fact, the majority of the 50 companies that I selected for personal investigation were inherently attractive. In most instances, however, the owners' ideas of terms and prices seemed so totally unrealistic to me that there was no use wasting further time.

This inability to reach even a reasonable negotiating range is evidently not peculiar to us. In fact, I find that the venture capital firms who have large organizations constantly combing the woods and whose reputation brings in hordes of would-be sellers still locate very few they can buy.

Most commercial bankers seem to agree with our judgment and with the advice I have received from investment firms about not offering more than five times earnings for a well-established company together with all the assets necessary to produce those earnings. At the same time, the owners of established businesses are apparently being advised by their financial advisers that it does not make any sense for them to consider selling at less than 10 times earnings. This amount is usually greater than book value. I am sure the bankers and the financial advisors are not giving out double-talk, but sincerely believe in this apparently conflicting advice—depending upon the point of view and interests of the man they are advising. The pattern seems to be that most owners are holding out for about twice what most buyers will pay.

During the last six months, I have been maintaining a record on close to 100 companies being offered for sale in New England. During this period, only five of these owners were able to dispose of their businesses. Three liquidated their companies voluntarily, with facilities and equipment being sold at public auction. One was merged into a larger company in the same industry; the fifth was acquired by its own largest customer. I do not know whether this was accomplished simply by an exchange of securities—as I suspect—or whether it was an actual cash buy out. None have been sold to investors or to new investor-managers like us.

This is indeed a puzzling situation. There is no lack of capital seeking investment; on the contrary, there seem to be even more people and groups with capital looking for businesses to buy than there are companies available. Many prospective investor-managers are also in evidence. In fact, the competition from other prospective buyers is terrific. I would say there are 5 to 10 potential buyers for every business for sale. Why then are there so few sales?

I should like to swap ideas with you on this problem in the near future. Is something wrong with our timing, or have I been looking in the wrong part of the country? Please give this a lot of thought because I think the three of us should get together very soon to decide whether our present objectives are realistic.

Jadwin Precision Products Company

During the fall of 1969 the president of a commercial bank in Boston brought the Jadwin Precision Products Company to Mark Olive's attention. The banker pointed out that sale of the company by its present owner was of such obvious logic that he might be well advised to approach the owner, Mr. Carl Jadwin, even though the company was not ostensibly for sale. The banker warned that Mr. Jadwin might be difficult to approach on the subject. "Just last week, I understand that Jadwin virtually threw a smart young promoter from New York out of his office, when the subject of selling the company was raised." Further discussion of the violent reaction encountered by the promoter from New York indicated that his proposal had apparently anticipated either liquidation or resale of the company for a quick profit. The banker believed that an offer from a young man such as Olive who wished to come into the business and to make it his life's work would engender a totally different reaction.

The banker then telephoned Mr. Jadwin and explained briefly the nature of Olive's interest with emphasis upon the fact that Olive was interested in joining a company in the near future upon some basis whereby later he might be able to buy control. The question of immediate sale of the company was not discussed on the telephone. On the basis of this introduction, Mr. Jadwin said he would be willing to give young Olive a few minutes of his time.

At their meeting on November 8, 1969, Olive indicated early in the conversation that he had an interest in the possibility of acquiring the company if it appeared to be an attractive, long-term career potential for him. Mark also described the systematic approach he and his associates were using to find and purchase a business.

As the discussion continued, Olive learned that Mr. Jadwin at the age of 76 was a widower and had a niece who managed his household but had no other heirs. Nor did he have any individuals within his organization who he believed were capable of taking over the top management of the company. The bulk of his personal estate was represented by his equity ownership in Jadwin Precision Products Company. Accordingly, he was quite aware of the fact that he should be making plans for continuation of the company after his retirement or death. These arrangements would have to take account of the fact that he had no income other than his salary from the company.

Mark also learned that the management organization under Mr. Jadwin consisted of a sales manager, who had in recent years taken over most of the responsibility for customer relations, and a production manager, who carried complete responsibility for day-to-day factory operations. "The production processes are well organized and are now so routine," Mr. Jadwin explained, "that we have had no troubles and have had to make no changes for over 10 years. My production manager has been with the company almost 20 years and knows the business inside out."

Mark was told that Mr. Burke, the sales manager, had joined the company when it was started in 1935. He supervised the work of three resident salesmen who handled approximately 700 accounts with jewelry wholesalers throughout the country. Two of these men, ages 58 and 62, had been with the company for over 15 years. The third was the son-in-law of the older salesman.

Most of the selling activity during recent years had been confined to correspondence and to distribution of catalogs by mail. The company had attained a strong position in the trade during its first 10 years after being founded by Mr. Jadwin in 1935. During the last 15 years, it had maintained this position, but without further growth. Mr. Jadwin had said that sales volume could easily be tripled if the company wanted to exert an effort to enter the market with lower cost items. His policy, however, had been to adhere to the production of only high-precision, high-quality tools and accessories for jewelers. He had been content, he explained, to hold a leading position in the high-price segment of the market. Generally, sales had showed no seasonal patterns.

All questions dealing with finances and business policy were handled by Mr. Jadwin. Neither the sales manager nor the production manager were considered by Mr. Jadwin to be candidates for the long-range financial management of his business. Mr. Jadwin was, however, very proud of his organization which consisted of approximately 100 employees and was most desirous that the personnel have an opportunity to continue with a successful company.

The Jadwin Company had been stable and prosperous for a long number of years. Except for slight fluctuations of sales volume during the Korean War and World War II when shortages of material forced the company to accept a few government contracts for surgical instruments and other items which utilized the company's precision machinery, volume had been between $900,000 to $1,100,000 annual sales. During the last few years, Mr. Jadwin had been working shorter hours and had not made any effort to continue the development of new items to replace those which gradually lost competitive appeal.

Earnings since the Korean War had been remarkably stable ranging from $51,000 to $78,000 per year. The company had had no losses since it had incurred a $10,000 deficit during the 1938 recession.

Olive was particularly interested in the possibilities of utilizing the excess plant capacity and surplus working capital on other products. Mr. Jadwin estimated that current production could be handled with not more than half the available floor space and that it required not over one third the capacity of the key pieces of precision machinery. Olive believed that in many ways he was better equipped and more interested in dealing with industrial markets than in catering to retail organizations.

Accordingly, he saw in the Jadwin Company a possible opportunity to develop a line of general industrial instruments utilizing the precision machine tools and other equipment on hand.

In a subsequent meeting Mr. Jadwin showed Mark the company's most recent balance sheet and operating statement. (See Exhibits 2 and 3.) The company's excess of working capital evidently reflected the fact that Mr. Jadwin preferred to retain his earnings in the business he understood instead of investing in the securities of other companies. Olive estimated that current assets included at least $200,000 in excess of the amount required to conduct the business. An inventory of $150,000 appeared quite adequate to carry the current operations comfortably. The $100,000 excess above this amount had been invested in highly marketable precious metals which Jadwin stated he considered a method of investing his savings. The cash balance was also at least $100,000 higher than the business required. Moreover, rigid adherence to good credit practices might, Olive believed, permit reduction of accounts receivable by as much as $50,000. In his questions to Mr. Jadwin, Olive was largely able to substantiate his estimates.

The plant and equipment were carried at very conservative figures and had apparently been depreciated at the maximum rate allowed by the Internal Revenue Service. The plant itself was a relatively modern, well-maintained, two-story building containing 15,000 square feet of floor space. A recent appraisal by experienced industrial appraisers had resulted in the estimate that the plant and equipment could be sold on the current market for at least $160,000.

Over the next several weeks Mark tried to get information on the markets served by Jadwin Precision Products Company and estimates on its future potential and the potential of related industries which the company might also serve. Although he could find no industry data which he could match with assurance to the Jadwin Company's current lines, discussions with the industry association president indicated that Jadwin's current markets in aggregate were growing at an annual rate of about 10 percent per year. One company whose business was somewhat similar to Jadwin had averaged a growth rate of 30 percent per year for the past three years and had reached a sales level of $4.5 million.

Going after the industrial markets which Olive had tentatively identified appeared to have some longer term attractiveness. After some directed inquiry, Mark estimated that the market potential was at least as great as Jadwin's current business but the margins were more competitive.

As Mark Olive undertook his evaluation of Jadwin Precision Products Company and the structuring of a deal, he realized that if he were to be successful his effort should reflect both the qualitative and quantitative considerations of his group and the seller, Mr. Jadwin.

SUGGESTED QUESTIONS

1. Conceptually, what is the approach Mark Olive should use in evaluating his opportunities to purchase Jadwin Precision Products, Inc.?

2. How should the deal for purchase/sale of the company be structured?

$100,000

$100,000

$50,000

$250,000

EXHIBIT 1

~~Mark Olive~~

Specifications for purchase of a business

GENERAL

Established manufacturing concern engaged in production of industrial goods. Also will consider staple consumers' products.

Capitalization. $25,000 to $1 million. Preferably in $50,000 to $300,000 category.

Financial condition.   Working capital position adequate to maintain existing operations.

Will purchase company outright or buy controlling interest and will provide management.

LOCATION

Preferably in New England area, but will consider locations east of Rocky Mountains.

PRODUCT

Basic, essential product with established usage.
Relatively high unit volume with a broad market.
Product which lends itself to continuous technical improvement.
Typical examples—but not confined to following:

Control systems and equipment
Gauges, dial indicators, meters, and thermometers
Hand tools and small machine tools
Roller and ball bearings
Grinding machines and wheels
Light specialty machinery
Electronic equipment
Powdered metal products
Plastic molding, machining, and extruding operations
Precision instruments
Fluorescent lighting fixtures
Industrial fasteners
Containers, paper cups, and office supplies
Food processing and packaging operations
Drugs, cleaning and polishing agents
Metals processing and fabricating operations

EXHIBIT 2
Mark Olive
Jadwin Precision Products Company income statement (000)

	5-year average including 1968	1968	Nine months Sept. 30, 1969
Net sales	$1,042	$955	$661
Cost of goods sold	641	581	389
Gross Profit	$ 401	$374	$272
Administration and sales expense ..	252*	235*	181
Operating Profit ....:	$ 149	$139	$ 91
Federal taxes	74	67	44
Net Income	$ 75	$ 72	$ 47

*Salaries: Mr. Jadwin, $50,000; three resident salesmen (total), $45,000.

[handwritten] 15,000 / each.

EXHIBIT 3
Mark Olive
Jadwin Precision Products Company balance sheet summary, Sept. 30, 1969 (000)

ASSETS		LIABILITIES	
Cash	$231	Accounts payable	$42
Accounts receivable..................	104	Payroll taxes	9
Inventories	250	Federal taxes	83
		Miscellaneous	4
Current Assets	$585		
		Current Liabilities ...	$138
Plant and equipment..................	$122		
Reserve for depreciation	64	Capital stock	97
Net Plant and Equipment	$ 58	Earned surplus	414
Miscellaneous and deferred charges	6		
Total Assets	$649	Total Liabilities	$649

[handwritten notations: "400", "$ 511", "Mkt. Value $ 160,000", "No Debt!!"]

[handwritten: 600 / 250 / 350]

Note

The techniques of purchasing a company

There are several methods an entrepreneur may use to buy a company. For the buyer and for the seller, each approach has various advantages and disadvantages which relate to tax consequences, risk, cash requirements, and other aspects of the specific situation. This note will describe several methods frequently used for purchasing companies and will outline some of the more important aspects of each method. The first portion of the note deals with purchase methods which are appropriate means for an individual to buy a company. The second section deals with the traditional area of corporate mergers and acquisitions.

The actual mechanics of buying a company together with tax and legal consequences are far too complex and too important for an individual to pursue in depth without the help of an attorney experienced in this area. Developments in tax and related aspects can be the working knowledge only of someone continually engaged in these kinds of problems. On the other hand, it will be helpful for the entrepreneur to have a basic grasp of the area to aid him in working with his lawyer. Because this area is frequently critical to an entrepreneur he cannot afford to delegate it completely. Yet, the entrepreneur should keep in mind that in most instances the primary source of return on his time and effort will not come from tax angles but instead will come from the substance and viability of the venture he is buying and his ability to negotiate an attractive price and advantageous terms. He should not let the tax complexities and intricacies of structuring a deal unduly distract from the more fundamental concerns.

374

PURCHASE BY AN INDIVIDUAL

Purchasing for cash and/or notes

Purchasing the stock of a company for cash is a very simple means for changing ownership and it results in a minimal exposure of risk to the seller. This method permits the seller to free himself from most obligations and liabilities of the company and it provides him with a known, fully-liquid asset in return.

A frequent problem for the buyer in a cash purchase, however, is that he does not have the cash. Moreover, a loan for making the purchase may not be readily available to him from conventional lending sources. Therefore the buyer needs the seller to help finance the purchase; the seller will receive payments in the future from profits generated by the company. A disadvantage to the seller is that he will have to pay taxes in the current year on the profits he receives from the sale of his company—assuming that he makes a profit.

An *installment purchase* can frequently be used in this kind of situation and with some of the other approaches described below. This not only helps the buyer to finance the purchase, but it has tax advantages for the seller as well in *delaying* the payment of taxes. The tax laws permit the profit from the sale of property to be reported over the period of years during which payments are made, provided that payments received during the initial year of sale comprise not more than 30 percent of the total selling price. Notes or other debt are not included in figuring the 30 percent.

A note of caution should be made regarding the use of interest-free notes when the initial payment approaches the 30 percent figure. The IRS will frequently impute interest charges based upon the rate then provided in the applicable regulations, say 5 percent if the actual rate of interest is less than 4 percent simple interest with the result that the total amount treated as principal is less than the total amount to be paid and consequently the downpayment using these calculations may exceed 30 percent of that portion of the price recognized as principal.

Taxes

The classical problem of the entrepreneur who purchases stock is that he is subjecting himself to regular income taxes on funds which are earned by the company he buys and which he uses to pay off the note. Figure 1(A) and (B) illustrate this phenomenon. In purchasing the company, the Buyer gives the Seller cash and a note for all of the stock in the company. He can avoid a tax to the corporation by taking money out in the form of salary (a corporate expense and therefore deductible before corporate taxes) instead of taking it out as dividends (not a deduction to corporate income). But he still will be required to pay personal income taxes on what he receives and he is limited in the amounts he can deduct as a corporate expense in the form of salary. In the situation shown in 1(A), the Buyer must then pay off the note with money taken out of the Company as illustrated in 1(B).

FIGURE 1

Purchase of stock with maximum taxes

(A)

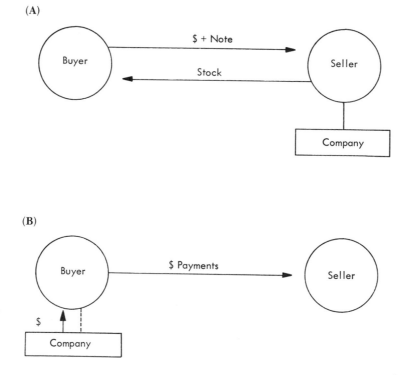

(B)

The personal tax problem can easily be avoided, however, if the entrepreneur first forms a new corporation and then has this new corporation buy the stock as shown in Figure 2(A) and (B). The Buyer sets up a new corporation and puts in cash in return for stock as in the prior example. The New Company then buys the Old Company for cash and notes.

Because the Old Company is now an affiliate of the New Company (more than 80 percent of the stock is owned by the New Company), dividends can pass through from the Old to the New Company without income taxes being imposed on the exchange. The New Company can then pay off the notes to the Seller without producing regular income for the Buyer. If the Old Company is liquidated into the New Company

FIGURE 2

Purchase of stock through a newly-formed corporation

(A)

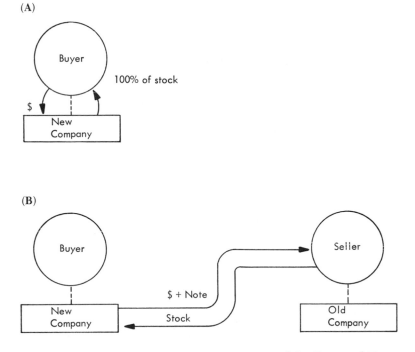

(B)

under a plan of liquidation under Section 332 of the Internal Revenue Code, the future earnings as well as the assets of the Old Company can be used to pay off the note. Moreover, such a liquidation can result in the "step up" of basis of the assets of the old company from their existing tax basis to the fair market value, often providing additional depreciation and other deductions. The wisdom of such a liquidation is, however, a function of many factors including the amount of ordinary corporate income to be realized on the liquidation from recapture of depreciation and investment credits.

A second method for buying the company's stock and avoiding most of the personal tax bite is what is known as a "seed purchase." (See Figure 3.) With this method there is no need to form a New Corporation. Instead, the Buyer purchases a small percentage of the shares from the Seller and the Company gives the Seller cash and/or an installment note. The result of these transactions is that for a relatively small amount of cash the Buyer owns 100 percent of the stock outstanding in the Company and the installment note is an obligation of the Company which can pay off the note with its own earnings and/or assets. The Buyer may guarantee payment of such a note without affecting the installment sale treatment of the Seller.

FIGURE 3

Seed purchase

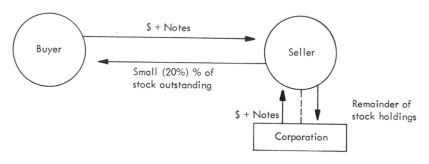

A drawback to a purchase of stock in either of the methods described above may occur when the buyer finds himself acquiring a company with depreciable assets whose fair market value is well in excess of their book value. He understandably would like to be compensated for the earnings shelter which the depreciation of these assets would provide if somehow he could write up their depressed book value. This can be accomplished by means of the liquidation of the Old Company as described above.

The most common direct problem arising from the purchase of stock for lump payment cash is that of unforeseen liabilities. A common solution, but one sometimes unacceptable to the seller, is for the buyer to withhold a portion of the purchase price for six months or a year. Even when this technique is agreed upon in general terms by the parties, strong disagreements may arise over whether interest-bearing notes should be given for the withheld portion, whether they should be secured, and how the price adjustment is to be determined (by whom, before or after tax effects, etc.). It is safe to say that, unless the entire purchase transaction is put in long-term escrow, or in the form of an installment sale, a significant portion of the purchase price should be withheld if possible, by the prudent entrepreneur, pending short-term developments. An *escrow arrangement* is one device by which this can be accomplished. Through this agreement a third party, such as a bank, holds the money and makes payment to the seller or returns money to the buyer when the conditions of the agreement have or have not been met. An escrow agreement is more frequently used to adjust a price rather than to determine an all-or-nothing transaction.

The Buyer's problems of unwittingly buying hidden liabilities or not being able to buy the stock of dissenting minority stockholders may be avoided by buying the assets of a corporation rather than the stock. The Buyer has an additional advantage in that he may have the New Corporation purchase only selected assets rather than all assets, some of which might be unwanted items of inventory, facilities, etc. (See Figure 4.) The New Corporation may also make use of an installment purchase agreement in buying assets; however, if the old company then liquidates, the seller loses the tax advantage and will be required to pay taxes on any profits although the cash will not have been received.

A problem arising out of a purchase of assets is the inevitable conflict between buyer and seller over allocation of the purchase price when the Old Corporation is not going to be liquidated. The buyer will want to allocate as much of the purchase price as possible to assets which can be expensed, depreciated, or amortized quickly, as long as this is consistant with his normal practices. He will want to allocate as little of the purchase price as possible to assets which cannot be expensed or depreciated at all. The seller, on the other hand, will want to assign the purchase price to capital assets held for more than six months so the company will realize capital gain or no gain if the sale is made pursuant to a plan of liquidation. He will also want to assign as little of the purchase price as possible to assets such as a non-compete agreement which will cause ordinary income. If buyer and seller agree on how the purchase price is to be allocated, the IRS usually will accept their position. However, if no

FIGURE 4

Purchase of assets through a newly-formed company

(A)

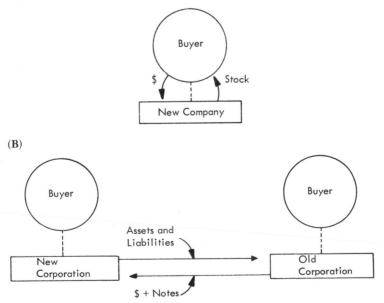

(B)

assignment is made, the IRS will make an allocation probably based on the fair market value of the assets.

One disadvantage to the Buyer in the purchase of assets arises from the fact that a tax-loss carry-over cannot be utilized. If the buyer plans to avail himself of such a carry-over he must, among other things, acquire the stock of the company in which the losses occurred. Another disadvantage to the buyer of assets is that he may not obtain certain leases, contracts, or franchises of value to him, without consent of the other contracting party, unless they were written to be specifically assignable.

It is possible for the unwary Seller in a sale of assets situation to subject himself to some Draconian tax problems. If the Old Corporation sells assets at a capital gain, the Old Corporation may be assessed a capital gains tax on these profits. If the funds are then paid out to the Seller as a dividend they will be taxed again, this time at personal rates. If the funds are retained in the Old Corporation and invested in securities or in other sources of passive income, the Old Corporation may be subject to classification as a *personal holding company* with a consequent 70 percent tax rate on undistributed income.

These problems for the Seller are easily avoided if the Old Corporation elects a plan of liquidation under Section 337 of the Internal Revenue Code which provides that under such a plan *the corporation* will pay neither regular income nor capital gains taxes on gains except for recapture of depreciation and investment credit, and the Seller will pay capital gains on his profits (assuming he has owned the company for more than six months).

Minority stockholders may present another problem. Frequently the entrepreneur will find that one or a small group of individuals with whom he has been negotiating owns a large majority of the shares of the company to be acquired but that the remaining shares are either widely held or are in the hands of persons who do not wish to sell. If the entrepreneur is not successful in acquiring these minority shares he may choose either to live with the dissenters or to take the following action: after obtaining controlling interest he can vote to liquidate and to sell the assets of the acquired company to a new company which he has formed.

A final warning may be helpful. Although the three basic forms of purchasing a company as described above are in fact fairly simple and straightforward, to the unsophisticated seller they appear to be more complex than the situation warrants. To some potential sellers, a proposed deal which involves a liquidation, an escrow agreement, or a more complex device can be seen as an untrusting or even a devious potential buyer. Consequently in some situations the entrepreneur may have to put together a less-than-optimal purchase plan because of limits or prejudices in the seller's understanding.

REORGANIZATIONS: CORPORATE MERGERS AND ACQUISITIONS

The term reorganization is used to describe any one of several forms of acquisition which are nontaxable both to seller and buyer. Stock in the buying corporation is the usual means of payment, but under certain circumstances cash or debt securities may be issued in addition to stock without jeopardizing the tax-free receipt of the stock involved. However, cash and debt securities are referred to as "boot," on which the seller must pay a tax; this tax is normally payable at current regular income rates since the boot is considered to be a dividend. Three types of tax-free reorganizations are briefly described here, together with related considerations of importance to the buying entrepreneur.

Type "A" reorganization

This includes the consolidation and the statutory merger. Consolidation refers to the fusing of two corporations into a new third corporation. Statutory merger refers to the process by which one corporation merges into and becomes part of another corporation (the survivor). These are the only forms of reorganization in which the stock issued by the acquiring corporation does not have to be voting stock to obtain tax-free treatment. In fact, debt or "boot" may also be issued (the seller pays ordinary tax rates on it) without affecting the tax-free status of the stock received. An outline of the transactions for a type A reorganization is shown in Figure 5.

In an "A" reorganization the entrepreneur has more freedom in selecting means of payment than in any other type of reorganization, but he must be wary of the so-called "continuity of interest" doctrine. This requires that a "substantial portion" of the consideration received by the shareholders of the acquired corporation be stock in the acquiring corporation. It is generally assumed that the IRS considers 50 percent of the total purchase price to be a substantial portion.

Type "B" reorganization

This is the "stock for stock" acquisition whereby one corporation exchanges *only* its voting stock in return for at least 80 percent of *each* of the classes of the stock of the acquired corporation. This method may be useful to the entrepreneur if he can convince shareholders of the company to be acquired that they will prosper as stockholders of his new corporation. This technique of acquisition is popular because detailed paperwork can generally be avoided, but it would of course be of little

FIGURE 5

Type A reorganization statutory merger and consolidation

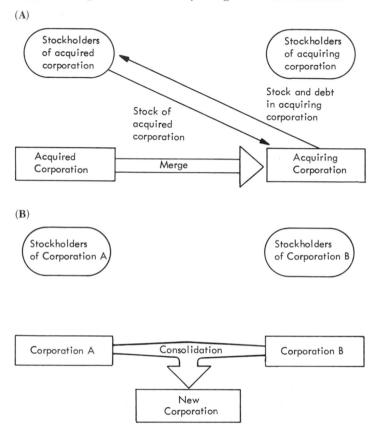

(A)

Stockholders of acquired corporation

Stockholders of acquiring corporation

Stock and debt in acquiring corporation

Stock of acquired corporation

Acquired Corporation — Merge → Acquiring Corporation

(B)

Stockholders of Corporation A

Stockholders of Corporation B

Corporation A — Consolidation — Corporation B

New Corporation

value when the acquirer wishes to obtain 100 percent of the widely-held stock of a corporation, because of the problem of dissenters. Figure 6 outlines the transactions comprising a Type B reorganization.

It should be remembered that in a "B" type reorganization the corporate entity of the acquired corporation remains alive. Therefore, for example, unless there is a subsequent reorganization, the acquiring company in a "B" reorganization will not be able to appropriate for itself any tax-loss carry-over which might exist in the acquired company.

Type "C" reorganization

This is the "stock for assets" transaction whereby *only* voting stock of the acquiring corporation is exchanged for substantially all of the assets of the acquired corporation. This can be a practical method for the

FIGURE 6

Type B reorganization (stock for stock)

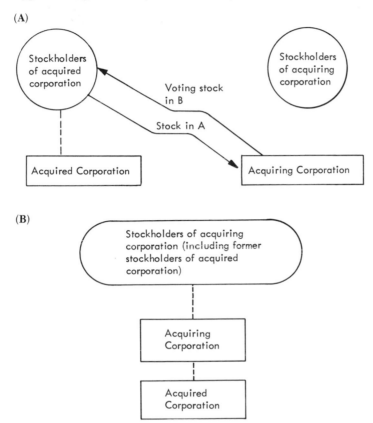

entrepreneur to acquire a business whose stock is widely held. One point worth noting is that whereas only voting stock may be used in obtaining substantially all the acquired company's assets, cash or other considerations such as the assumption of debt may be given for up to 20 percent of the market value of these assets.

The entrepreneur should recognize that, under the accepted court-made doctrine of "business purpose," every reorganization must have a bona fide corporate justification, apart from tax saving or postponement, in order to qualify for tax-free treatment, even though in form it may appear to meet all relevant tests. Likewise, the "step transaction" doctrine holds that a series of transactions, each one satisfying the appropriate reorganization laws, may still be disqualified from tax-free treatment if the integrated result is one which would be taxable if accomplished directly.

Finally, several additional comments on the utilization of tax-loss carry-overs in acquired corporations might be helpful. In an "A" or "C" type of reorganization, the carry-over will be reduced proportionately for any amount of stock under 20 percent which the stockholders of the transferor corporation receive in the surviving corporation. For every 1 percent under 20 percent received by the transferring stockholders, the amount of the carry-over which can be utilized is reduced by 5 percent. For example, if only 10 percent of the stock in the surviving corporation is distributed to stockholders of the acquired corporation, then only 50 percent of the loss carry-over would be available for use by the survivor.

It should be remembered that merely meeting these objective tests does not assure the availability of the tax-loss carry-forward. In taxable transactions the acquirer must also continue in substantially the same business (thereby precluding the acquisition of a "shell" corporation), and in all transactions must be able to demonstrate that the acquisition was effected for other than tax-saving reasons. This latter requirement has become increasingly difficult to meet in recent years because of the attitude of the Internal Revenue Service.

The entire subject of the utilization of tax-loss carry-forwards is a complex and disputed area of the law, and simple rules or guidelines are of limited value. The entrepreneur who is considering the acqustion of a loss corporation would do well to familiarize himself with sections of the Code prior to consulting with competent tax counsel.

FIGURE 7

Type C reorganization (stock for assets)

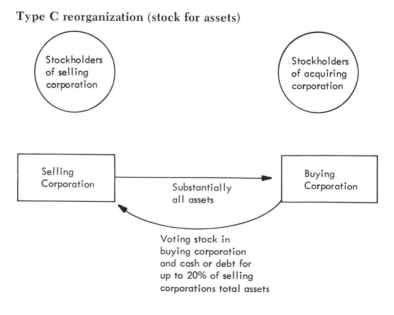

Cases

Tom Johnson and Jack Dresser

On Wednesday, April 17, 1963, Tom Johnson, a research associate at the Harvard Business School, was talking to three second-year students in his office. "Yes, eventually that's the kind of decision you're going to have to make. Presidents of big corporations may have to draw on more administrative skills than entrepreneurs, but I think there are some compensating challenges in hoeing your own row and creating something yourself. You're probably right, though, in that you might become somewhat unemployable if that makes you less able to adapt to the demands and rigors of a larger company."

Tom was interrupted by a sharp knock and Jack Dresser stepped into the room. "Excuse me, but it's four o'clock and we're going to have to catch that plane."

Tom got up but continued, "I think that an honest failure won't keep you from eventually being successful. A much greater fear to me is looking back on life and seeing what Robert Frost calls 'the road not taken.'"

As the students left, Jack grinned: "Let's go. It's raining in rivers out there and you know what that's going to do to traffic between here and Logan Airport."

As Tom was putting on his raincoat and rubbers Jack added, "I hope you're right about that failure bit."

Personal history and company background

Tom Johnson and Jack Dresser had been friends since 1954 and attended Amherst College together. In January 1963 they began discussing the feasibility of a company which would develop and operate cable television systems. At that time Johnson was serving as a research associate in the Management of New Enterprises course at the Harvard Business School. Dresser was employed by Concord Capital Corporation, a small SBIC which he had interested in the CATV industry and for which he was the nominee on the board of directors of a cable television system in Franconia, New Hampshire. In this way he had become familiar with what he was convinced would be a "real growth industry." Details on the background of the two men are presented in Exhibit 1.

Johnson and Dresser then joined in an exhaustive study of the CATV industry. They found the Harvard Business School library particularly useful, and it was convenient for Johnson. A great deal of information on the technical as well as marketing and financial aspects of the business was obtained (some of this material appears in the Appendix of this case). The two partners planned eventually to assemble a lengthy and detailed project plan for use in their search for capital.

The study, which they finished in February 1963, indicated that the industry had definite growth potential and that the risk of failure was apparently not very high. On this basis, Tom obtained a road atlas of the United States from a local service station and a copy of the "Television Factbook" from Baker Library. He and his wife then plotted on the maps of eight states all of the existing TV broadcasting stations and the then operating or proposed CATV facilities. The "Factbook" provided estimates for each broadcasting facility in the areas where good, clear pictures could be received. When these somewhat circular areas were shaded on the map, certain "holes" were left. Theoretically these "holes" would be good locations for a CATV system as they indicated where relatively few channels were being received and/or quite poor reception could be expected. One of the areas that appeared to be most promising was in the central part of Illinois.

Tom had pinpointed Appletown, Illinois, as a theoretically good location on which to make a serious study and had discussed the situation with Jack. A week later, leaving on a Wednesday to permit him to meet that week's scheduled commitments at the school, Tom flew out to Appleton to view firsthand the actual reception and to determine a course of action to pursue in establishing a CATV system there. Surprisingly, and with some concern over the validity of his approach, he found that most of the homes in Appletown were receiving fairly good pictures from Peoria and Springfield, which together provided viewing on six channels. As a result, he quickly decided to abandon Appletown and drove westward to the neighboring cities of Stanton (population 40,000) and Waterford (35,000), which were in the second-choice area.

In Stanton Tom was dismayed to learn that the Garner Broadcasting Company, a $15 million listed corporation, had already applied for a franchise to do business in those towns and had been actively involved in discussions with both city councils and the local utilities people for pole rentals. While it was conceivable that the partners could attempt to compete with Garner for a franchise, they decided over the telephone that night to look for an area where their success would not be threatened before they even got started.

The next day, Tom drove to the sister cities of Elmtown (22,500 population) and Roseville (16,500), Illinois, which were about 25 miles northeast of Waterford. As he came into Elmtown, Tom was impressed by its wide, tree-lined streets. To him it seemed to be a thriving community with a great deal of attention paid to the appearance of the storefronts downtown and well-kept lawns in the residential areas. Although there were a few empty stores on the main street, Tom's general impression of the business environment was a favorable one. He found Roseville to be similar to Elmtown in most respects, but with a more "bustling" atmosphere and a somewhat more industrialized environment.

In Elmtown Tom found several signs which he thought were encouraging. Cable television was virtually an unknown concept to the people with whom he talked, and no one had approached either town for a franchise to put in CATV installations. Johnson observed that TV reception was not generally of very high quality and that the choice of programs was quite limited because only two fairly clear signals were received from Chicago which was 50 miles away. That afternoon and the next day he contacted attorneys in both Elmtown and Roseville and discussed his and Jack's plans with them. He explained the principle of CATV and what it could mean to the people of those towns. He also discussed with the lawyers a concept that he and Dresser had for their company, which they wanted to have incorporated. He gave personal references to the two attorneys and that evening called Jack for a discussion of the day's events and a follow-up plan of action.

Tom knew that a franchise for such an operation typically required the approval of the governing body of the city or town; e.g., the city council in Elmtown. It would not necessarily be an exclusive right, but once granted, other companies would be discouraged from seeking a second franchise. Following the first reading of an ordinance by a council, a public hearing would probably be held. Then, if no objections were raised, a second and third public reading would be held and the ordinance would become law upon a majority vote of the council.

During the next three weeks Tom and Jack talked to each of the town council members at least once, and saw most members on several occasions. They attempted to sell the idea of CATV as a service beneficial to the community and personally to become better acquainted with the individual council members. At the end of three weeks Jack observed with a smile, "Until I found out that Jim Wenchel [the local barber in

Elmtown] was on the town council, I didn't think it was possible for a person to get a haircut every five days."

After a series of meetings with the councils in Elmtown and Roseville, with assistance from the local attorneys, Johnson and Dresser were granted permission to present an ordinance. (See Exhibit 2.) After the ordinance was given a first reading, representatives of the Garner Broadcasting Company immediately contacted council members and claimed that Garner could do the job better than "a couple of Eastern boys." They explained their plans for developing CATV facilities in Waterford and in a number of other towns near Elmtown and Roseville. The Garner management reminded the councilmen that Garner already had made a large commitment to the Elmtown-Roseville area, that J. MacMartin Garner, the company's founder, was the former Illinois governor who had run for president of the United States and that they had major newspaper and TV interests in various parts of the state. They pointed out that the boys from the East were totally inexperienced in the field.

During the week that followed, Tom and Jack had reviewed the Elmtown-Roseville situation and had drawn up a set of financial projections for the anticipated operations. A copy of these projections is shown in Exhibit 3. The two partners had calculated that the money that they could raise between themselves to invest in the venture would be less than $10,000. Exhibits 4 and 5 show additional data which had been put together during the library research conducted during January and February.

As Tom and Jack huddled at the end of Baker Library waiting for Tom's wife, Jack started the discussion which probably was going to continue until late into the evening. "We have got to get this franchise or some other one pretty soon or we'll be forever in getting a company started. And you know once we have a franchise there is going to be the real scramble to obtain financing and to get into operation."

Tom squinted in the rain. "Professor Tucker was around again today wanting to know whether or not I would be here to help him when he started teaching in the fall."

SUGGESTED QUESTIONS

1. What should Messrs. Johnson and Dresser do now? Be as specific as you can in defining how they should respond to their current situation.
2. Whether or not you think they should try to pursue either or both Roseville and Elmtown, how should they try to raise the financing for this kind of venture?

EXHIBIT 1
Tom Johnson and Jack Dresser
Personal background of the founders

THOMAS L. JOHNSON
Son of lawyer, Northampton, Massachusetts
Graduate of Deerfield; Amherst, 1956; Harvard Business
School, 1960
Married—One child
Six months in Army—1956

1957–58	Price and Anderson—public accounting firm
	Trainee and auditor
1960–62	Nestle and Prince—mutual fund distributor
	Salesman, sales manager, recruited and trained 50 salesmen
1962	Developed sales training program for large Boston real estate firm
1962–63	Research associate—Management of New Enterprise course—Harvard Business School.

In addition to these specific jobs he had done some consulting and had been involved in a variety of consumer sales activities.

JOHN E. DRESSER
Raised in Short Hills, New Jersey
Graduate of Pingry School; Amherst, 1958; Harvard Business School, 1961
Single
Six months in Army—1961

1958–59	International Power Company—U.S. and foreign developments
	Financial analysis and forecasting, operations analysis
1961–64	Concord Capital Corporation
	Business-Aid, Inc. Both small SBICs

General analysis; particularly pertinent was his investigation of the CATV industry, his being instrumental in involving both SBICs in the industry, and his serving as their nominee on the CATV companies' boards.

Dresser also had experience in the merging of five small CATV systems into a single company having assets in excess of $3 million.

EXHIBIT 2
Tom Johnson and Jack Dresser

ORDINANCE NO. 711-B

An Ordinance granting to Cablevue Inc., its successors and assigns, the right to erect, maintain and operate transmission and distribution facilities and additions thereto in, under, over, along, across and upon the streets, lanes, avenues, alleys, bridges, highways and other public places in the City of Roseville, Illinois, and subsequent additions thereto, for the purpose of transmission by cable and distribution of television impulses and television energy for sale to the inhabitants of said City, and other purposes, for the period of 20 years, and regulating the same, and declaring an emergency to exist.

BE IT ORDAINED by the City Council of the City of Roseville, State of Illinois:

Section 1. In consideration of the faithful performance and observance of the conditions and reservations hereinafter specified the right is hereby granted to Cablevue, Inc., a corporation organized under the laws of Delaware, its successors and assigns, hereinafter referred to as the "Company," to erect, maintain, and operate television transmission and distribution facilities and additions thereto in, under, over, along, across and upon the streets, lanes, avenues, sidewalks, alleys, bridges, and other public places in the City of Roseville, and subsequent additions thereto, for the purpose of transmission and distribution of television impulses and television energy in accordance with the laws and regulations of the United States of America and the State of Illinois, and the Ordinances and regulations of the City of Roseville, for a period of 20 years, from the date of the signing hereof.

Section 2. Wherever used in this Ordinance, the word "television" shall mean a system for simultaneous transmission of audio signals and transient visual images by means of electrical impulses.

Section 3. The poles used for the company's distribution system shall be those erected and maintained by Illinois Telephone Company and/or State Power Company, when and where practicable, providing mutually satisfactory rental agreements can be entered into with said Companies.

Section 4. The Company's transmission and distribution system, poles, wires and appurtenances shall be located, erected and maintained so as not to endanger or interfere with the lives of persons, or to interfere with any improvements the City may deem proper to make, or to hinder unnecessarily or obstruct the free use of the streets, alleys, bridges or other public property.

Construction and maintenance of the transmission distribution system, including house connections, shall be in accordance with the provisions of the National Electrical Safety Code, prepared by the National Bureau of Standards, the National Electrical Code of the National Board of Fire Underwriters and such applicable Ordinances and regulations of the City of Roseville affecting electrical installations which may be presently in effect or may be enacted by the City Council of the City of Roseville.

Installation and house drop hardware shall be uniform throughout the City, except that the Company shall be free to change its hardware and installation

EXHIBIT 2 (Continued)

procedure as the art progresses, provided such changes have been approved by the Director of Public Service.

Section 5. In the maintenance and operation of its television transmission and distribution system in the streets, alleys, and other public places, and in the course of any new construction or addition to its facilities, the Company shall proceed so as to cause the least possible inconvenience to the general public; any opening or obstruction in the streets or other public places, made by the Company in the course of its operations, shall be guarded and protected at all times by the placement of adequate barriers, fences or boardings, the boundary of which during periods of dusk and darkness shall be clearly designated by red warning lights.

Whenever the Company shall take up or disturb any pavement, sidewalk or other improvement of any street, avenue, alley or other public place, the same shall be replaced and the surface restored in as good condition as before entry within forty-eight (48) hours after completion of the company's work. Upon the failure of the Company to make such restoration within such time, or to begin such restoration within such time, if the restoration cannot be made within such time, or upon the Company's delay of more than twenty-four (24) hours in the continuation of a restoration begun, the City may serve upon the Company notice of the City's intent to cause the restoration to be made and, unless the Company within twenty-four (24) hours after receipt of such notice begins or resumes the proper restoration to be made, the City may cause the proper restoration to be made, including the removal of excess dirt, and the expense of same shall be paid by the Company upon demand by the City.

The Company shall at all times comply with any and all rules and regulations which the City has made or may make applying to the public generally with reference to the removal or replacement of pavements and to excavations in streets and other public places, not inconsistent with their use for the purposes contemplated by this Ordinance.

Section 6. All rates and charges exacted by the Company shall be fair, reasonable and just.

Section 7. The Company shall provide and make available to its customers a minimum of six (6) channels at any one time, provided satisfactory reception of a minimum of six (6) channels is available to the company in the area.

Section 8. The Company's distribution system shall conform to the requirements of the Federal Communications Commission, particularly with respect to freedom from spurious radiation.

Section 9. The antenna, receiving and distribution equipment shall be installed and maintained so as to provide pictures on subscriber receivers throughout the system essentially of the same quality as those received at the antenna site.

Section 10. Installation and maintenance of equipment shall be such that standard NTSC color signals shall be transmitted with full fidelity to any subscriber receiver.

Section 11. The distribution system of the Company to be hereafter installed shall not be abandoned, either in whole or in part, without the consent of the City Council. In the event of the failure of the Company to render community

EXHIBIT 2 (Continued)

television service to the City of Roseville as contemplated and provided for by this Ordinance within a period of one year from the effective date of this Ordinance, the City Council shall have the right, on reasonable notice to the Company, to declare this Ordinance and the rights and franchise granted thereunder forfeited; provided, however, that failure to comply with this stipulation by reason of causes beyond the reasonable control of the Company, which could not be anticipated at the time of its acceptance by the Company, shall not be sufficient grounds to declare a forfeiture.

Section 12. The Company shall indemnify and hold the City harmless at all times during the term of this grant from and against all claims for injury or damages to persons or property, both real and personal, caused by the construction, erection, operation or maintenance of any structure, equipment, appliance or products authorized or used pursuant to authority of this Ordinance.

The Company shall carry insurance in such form and in such companies as shall be approved by the Director of Public Service of the City of Roseville to protect the City and itself from and against any and all claims for injury or damages to persons or property, both real and personal, caused by the construction, erection, operation or maintenance of any structure, equipment, appliance or products authorized or used pursuant to authority of this Ordinance, and the amount of such insurance against liability due to damage to property shall be not less than One Hundred Thousand Dollars ($100,000.00), as to any one person, and Two Hundred Thousand Dollars ($200,000.00), as to any one accident, and against liability due to injury or death to persons One Hundred Thousand Dollars ($100,000.00), as to any one person, and Three Hundred Thousand Dollars ($300,000.00), as to any one accident.

The Company, upon receipt of due notice in writing from the City, shall defend at its own expense any action or proceedings against the City of Roseville in which it is claimed that the injury or damage arose from the Company's activities in the operation of its television system.

Section 13. Upon termination or forfeiture of this grant, in accordance with any of its terms, the Company shall, within a reasonable time, remove its cables, wires, and appliances from the City streets, lanes, avenues, sidewalks, alleys, bridges, highways and other public places within the City and subsequent additions thereto.

In the event of the failure of the Company to perform the obligation of the first sentence of this Section, the City shall have the right to make a written demand on the Company for such performance, and in the event of the failure of the Company to proceed to carry out the removal of such equipment within thirty (30) days from the date of such demand to proceed with such removal expeditiously, the City shall have the right to remove the same and retain it as the City's property, without accounting therefor to the Company, and the expense of such removal shall be charged to and paid by the Company, without credit for the value, if any, of the equipment removed by the City.

Section 14. If the Company shall fail to comply with any of the provisions of this grant, or default in any of its obligations, except for causes beyond the reasonable control of the Company, as provided for in Section 11 hereof, and shall fail, within thirty (30) days after written notice from the City to correct such

EXHIBIT 2 (Concluded)

default or noncompliance, the City Council shall have the right to revoke this Ordinance and all rights of the Company hereunder.

Section 15.   Should any Section, clause or provisions of this Ordinance be declared invalid by a Court of record, same shall not affect the validity of the Ordinance as a whole or any part thereof, other than the part so declared invalid.

Section 16.   This Ordinance is hereby declared to be an emergency measure, necessary for the immediate preservation of the public health, welfare, peace and safety.

The reason for such emergency lies in the fact that it will require considerable time to complete the necessary engineering and construction and the service should be made available to the residents of the City at the earliest possible time.

Therefore, upon the affirmative vote of two thirds (⅔) of all members elected to Council, this Ordinance shall go into immediate force and effect.

Passed this _____ day of _____ 1963.

_____

President of Council

ATTEST:

_____

Clerk of Council

Filed with me and approved by me this _____ day of _____ 1963.

_____

Mayor of Roseville, Illinois

EXHIBIT 3

Tom Johnson and Jack Dresser

Pro forma cash flow[*]

	1964	1965	1966	1967	1968	1969	1970	1971
Income:								
Connection income	$ 10,000	$ 40,000	$ 36,000	$ 24,000	$ 14,000	$ 10,000	$ 6,000	$ —
Service income	3,750	90,000	204,000	294,000	351,000	387,000	411,000	420,000
Total	$ 13,750	$130,000	$240,000	$318,000	$365,000	$397,000	$417,000	$420,000
Expenses:								
Installation	$ 10,000	$ 40,000	$ 36,000	$ 24,000	$ 14,000	$ 10,000	$ 6,000	$ —
Operations	32,500	79,500	84,500	91,500	94,500	101,000	101,500	104,500
Selling, general-administrative	32,500	56,250	62,250	64,500	66,000	64,500	63,000	63,000
From Operations:	(61,250)	(45,750)	57,250	138,000	190,500	221,500	246,500	252,500
Depreciation	40,000	60,000	60,000	61,000	61,000	62,000	62,000	62,000
Interest—senior debt	5,000	21,000	21,000	19,500	18,000	13,000	8,000	1,300
—junior debt	4,500	9,200	9,200	9,200	9,200	9,200	9,200	4,600
Net before taxes	(110,750)	(135,950)	(33,000)	48,300	102,300	137,300	167,300	184,600
Taxes	—	—	—	—	42,500	63,500	77,500	92,500
Net after taxes	(110,750)	(135,950)	(33,000)	48,300	59,800	73,800	89,800	92,100
Net Cash Flow (after interest and taxes)	(70,750)	(75,950)	27,000	109,300	120,800	135,800	151,800	154,100
Additions to net working capital	5,000	8,000	11,000	8,000	5,000	3,000	2,000	—
Additions to plant account	420,000	2,000	2,000	2,500	3,000	5,000	7,000	10,000
Systems Cash Generation:	(495,750)	(85,950)	14000	98,800	112,800	127,800	142,800	144,100
Equity	200,000	—	—	—	—	—	—	—
Junior debt	150,000	—	—	—	—	—	—	(115,000)
Bank loan	300,000	—	—	(37,500)	(75,000)	(75,000)	(75,000)	(37,500)
Cash Balance (end of period)	$154,250	$ 68,300	$ 89,300	$150,600	$188,400	$241,200	$309,600	$300,600
Number of Subscribers at Year End	500	2,500	4,300	5,500	6,200	6,700	7,000	7,000

[*]Prepared March 1963.

EXHIBIT 4
Tom Johnson and Jack Dresser
Average and extremes of percentage saturations of sample versus "minimum
expected" and "most likely" projections

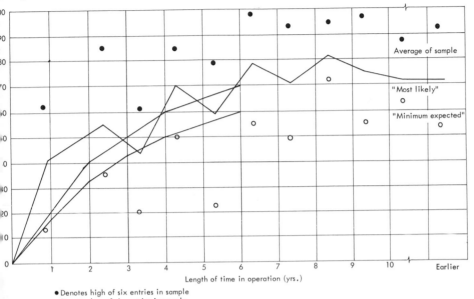

Length of time in operation (yrs.)

● Denotes high of six entries in sample
○ Denotes low of six entries in sample

Note: Average and extremes have been posted on the time scale at point of sample's median.

EXHIBIT 5
Tom Johnson and Jack Dresser
Growth of selected CATV systems*

Location	Service began	Number of free signals	Number of cable signals	Percent saturation at end of year					
				1	2	3	4	5	6
Johnstown, Penn.† ··············	1960	2	5	25	58	75	—	—	—
Keene, N. H. ·············	1962	2	5	32	—	—	—	—	—
Marietta, Ohio ·············	1957	1½–2	9	7	12	20	33	47	57
Pittsfield, Mass. ·············	1959	1½–2	5	10	17	35	50	—	—
Salisbury, Md. ·············	1957	2½	7	25‡	21	21	25	30	45
Winona, Minn. ·············	1960	1½	5	42	60	65	—	—	—
	1958	2	10	37	56	70	77	80	—
Projected Elmtown-Roseville									
"Minimum expected" ·············	1963	2	8+	17.5	32.5	42.5	50.0	55.0	60.0
"Most likely" ·············	1963	2	8+	20.0	40.0	50.0	60.0	65.0	70.0

*Chosen to demonstrate varying rates of subscriber buildup experienced by systems comparable to the proposed Elmtown-Roseville system in terms of free versus cable signals.

†Plant completed in 1960 passed 8,000 homes and had 2,000 and 4,650 subscribers at the end of the first and second years, respectively. At the end of the second year of operation (1962), 6,000 potential was added through plant expansion. Management estimates that 1,900 of the 7,900 subscribers on at the end of the third year were in the newly cabled area.

‡In 1958–59 the potential was increased by plant expansion from 4,000 to 6,000.

APPENDIX
Tom Johnson and Jack Dresser
THE CATV INDUSTRY

How a CATV system works

In simplified diagrammatic form, the accompanying illustration indicates the basic requirements for a CATV (community antenna television)
system.

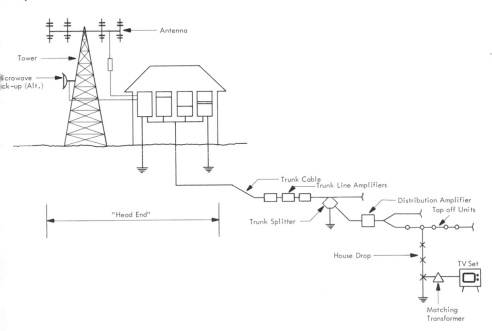

One of the most obvious items in the head-end section of a typical
CATV system is a tower, located on a plot of carefully selected high
ground in a good reception area. The height of the tower is dependent on
local conditions, the distance from the broadcast stations to be received,
FAA regulations, and the desirability of microwave pickup but usually
ranges from around 300 feet to 800 feet or more.

Signals are picked up by complex antennas on the tower (a separate
antenna is required for each channel received) and amplified by a channel preamplifier located on the antenna itself. Each signal is then sent
down the tower to the head-end equipment located in a concrete building.

In the head-end building, the signal is processed by a variety of
amplifiers, signal processors and mixers, traps and filters. Through use of
these units, the output from every channel is made as near perfect and

free from interference as possible, regardless of fluctuations, distortions, and disturbances that may have developed in the broadcast signal.

"Pure" signals then are usually sent out to the community in trunk line cables, although microwave links may also be used. This is the primary distribution link in the system and such cables are generally a 75-ohm coaxial type sheathed in aluminum to prevent weathering. One to four trunk amplifiers are usually needed per mile of trunk cable in order to maintain the desired power level.

The trunk line branches at various points to provide coverage to a community. A distribution amplifier takes a small fraction of the signal power out of the trunk for further distribution over smaller, thinner coaxial cables. Finally, tap off units and house drops bring the signal to subscribers over still smaller cables.

Each subscriber is provided with a "matching" transformer which is connected to the back of his set for the purpose of matching the 75-ohm coaxial cable system to his TV set, which normally has an impedance of 300 ohms. Where two or more sets are at a single location, special splitting devices are installed inside the home to divide the house drop into the desired number of lines.

Typically, a one-time connection charge of about $10 is made, and then a monthly fee of $4.50 to $5.50 is paid by the subscriber.

The cost of the equipment in any CATV system varies with the factors that are unique to that location. However, the following costs may be considered average for a typical system:

Head-end and tower:	
Tower 500 ft. @ $30 per foot	$ 15,000
Tower site preparation	500
Antennas—10 channels @ $400 per channel	4,000
Head-end building, fencing, air conditioning, 8 ft. x 12 ft. x 20 ft. concrete block	3,500
Head-end equipment for 10 channels	15,000
Antenna hardware, etc.	2,000
Miscellaneous	2,000
	$ 42,000
Office and other equipment (including vehicles)	30,000
Distribution system at about $4,000 per mile (assume 150 miles of cable)	600,000
Total	$672,000

Industry notes

CATV as a profit-making business had its inception in the fall of 1950 in Lansford, Pennsylvania. Since that time the industry has grown to include over 1,600 systems across the United States. The first systems were generally small (under 1,000 subscribers) and usually located in areas where, because of terrain or distance, the need was obvious. More recently, however, the pattern has been changing. CATV systems are being developed in larger population areas where there is a need for improving or supplementing the service already available.

In a recent study of the CATV industry by the Stanford Research Institute, the following points were highlighted:

1. Congress is likely to authorize FCC regulation to CATVs, but any resulting operational rules will probably allow owners considerable freedom. They may, however, have to pay copyright fees for programming picked up and restrict their duplication of local offerings.
2. Profits will shrink only moderately as a result of such regulations, leaving the return on investment at a very high level.
3. Despite increasing regulation, SRI sees CATV continuing to grow from the current level of over 1,600 systems serving over 2 million subscribers to 4,000 systems serving 8 million homes by 1975. (There were 650,000 subscribers in 1960.)
4. Total industry revenues are expected to quadruple by 1975 to over $460 million.
5. The current concept of a fee-based antenna service will predominate during this period, but pay TV and other experiments will increasingly be attempted.

It is anticipated that the level of technical sophistication will rise significantly between now and 1975. The consolidation of ownership and the interconnection of systems is expected to show a definite upward trend over this period.

Because of high demand and highly debt-leveraged ownership, most CATV systems have shown net return on invested capital rates in excess of 15 percent. In some cases, return on investment rates have been reported in excess of 50 percent. Depending upon the depreciation schedule used (usually five years), an established CATV system can show very high net returns after about five years. Also having appeal is the large cash flow generated almost from the start.

As CATV increasingly moves into large urban areas, the likelihood of regulation by some federal agency grows. In addition, as competition for franchises intensifies, many local governments can be expected to increase franchise fees and impose more stringent requirements on CATV operators. Quite often, locally powerful political elements, opposition by public utilities and existing radio and TV stations, and a general lack of understanding of CATV give rise to severe difficulties in the obtaining of a franchise to bring a system into a technically ideal area.

Despite the differences in the size and quality of CATV systems across the nation, Stanford Research Institute reports that virtually all of them make high rates of return and that, to date, only four are known to have failed. The basic success factors seem to be:

1. Continuing growing income from what can be a one-time investment.
2. Wide margin between income and normal operating expenses.
3. Accelerated depreciation (as little as five to seven years for full depreciation under current rules).
4. Highly leveraged ownership. Currently borrowed capital is often between 50 percent and 80 percent of total requirements and this is rising.
5. Virtual freedom from competition for the service provided.

While pressures on profits may come from increased costs of equipment per new subscriber, growing operating expenses such as program royalties, rental fees, and government imposed rate regulations, the attractiveness of the industry will continue at least through 1975. By that time, estimates Stanford Research Institute, the average payout is likely to reach 10 to 12 years rather than the 5 to 8 years common at present.

CATV systems have been sold in many cases at substantial capital gains for their owners. It is anticipated that this activity, as well as the gains being obtained, will increase in the future.

Cases

Robert S. Lewis

On a Tuesday late in May of 1966, Bob Lewis was sitting in his room in McCulloch Hall trying to figure out what to do about raising money for his new company, Computer Data Systems, Inc., which had been incorporated three weeks earlier. Bob had researched his ideas for a new enterprise during the past several months and had written a report for the Management of New Enterprises course. [The report is presented in its entirety as Appendix A of this case. Appendix B includes excerpts from the April and May 1966 editions of the First National City Bank of New York *Monthly Economic Letter* to provide current views on national economic conditions at that time.]

Personal background

Robert S. Lewis was graduated from Bowdoin College in 1959 with a B.A. degree in physics. A cum laude graduate, Bob had put himself through college with funds from a combination of scholarships, personal savings, summer jobs as an engineering trainee, and term-time work as a laboratory assistant and dining hall waiter. "I was always hustling for a buck," Bob recalled, "I had to. My father died while I was in college and I found I had to support myself. In retrospect, it was satisfying to know that I could and did put myself through." During the summers while in high school, Bob had had a variety of jobs including driving a laundry truck and working in a drugstore.

After college, Bob had gone to work for IBM in Boston as a systems trainee for $470/month. Soon afterward he had become a systems engineer where his work was primarily in public utilities and the airline industry. Then came a two-year military obligation in intelligence and

401

security, after which Bob had returned to IBM in the spring of 1962 to do much the same sort of work he had done before. Bob had left IBM and $530/month in the fall of 1963 to go to work for $700/month with Cutler Computer Associates (CCA), a computer consulting company in New York City. At CCA Bob worked as a consultant with IBM as his primary client.

In the spring of 1964 Bob had declined the suggestion of his boss to open a Boston office because he had not felt confident about his management and sales abilities. Having previously applied to the Harvard Business School, Bob left CCA to start the first year in September 1964.

At the business school, Bob had mixed success. He was elected social chairman of his section at the end of the second month. Among his courses in his first-year program he found the human relations course the most interesting. Managerial economics he found "less than good fun at best." Bob received a P+ in human relations and a low pass in managerial economics at the end of the year. "Let me be very candid with you although I don't mean to be unkind. I wasn't really sure about whether or not I could be a good manager before I went to the business school. But when I saw what my competition was going to be for jobs as the new leaders of American business, I figured I shouldn't have any trouble."

During the second year at the school, Bob had elected to write two research reports, one on his idea to start a computer software firm and the other on a marketing program for a newly designed gyrocopter, the first model of which was being assembled in a small machine shop in Cambridge. Bob had arranged his spring schedule to give him no classes on three days of the six-day class week, thus providing time for pursuing his reports and other interests. (Through IBM Bob had arranged to do some part-time systems work on some of those days when he had no classes. Funds from this source, together with about $8,000 in borrowed funds, financed his two years at the business school.) Bob finished the second year in the lower third of his class.

Development of ideas for starting a company

In the spring of his first year at the business school, Bob had thought about starting up his own computer software firm. To test some of his ideas he had tried them out on various people around Boston in different areas of the computer industry and related fields. Generally, he had found agreement that the market was growing, and people told him that there was an insufficient supply of software capability to meet the demand.

Early in his planning Bob had decided that part of his strategy would be not to get himself involved in the production side of his software operation. From what he had seen of moonlighters who wanted to go on their own in the software business, he had concluded that their growth was severely limited by their inevitable preoccupation with systems analysis and other phases of technical work. Bob had reasoned that his time should be used in the initial contact and sales activities and in recruiting qualified people to carry out the production work. To create a viable operation with growth potential he would need experienced personnel, an office, and working capital right from the start

While still in his first year at the business school, Bob had found an individual in New York who was very enthusiastic about his ideas and was willing to put up financial backing for the enterprise, which would be a source of computer technology for the manufacturing company which he owned.

In February of his second year at the business school, Bob calculated that $130,000 would finance a sizable initial operation and give some margin for unanticipated problems. Bob would put up $10,000 for 60 percent of the company's stock and he believed the New York investor would put up $120,000 for 40 percent. Several other people had rejected anything like this sort of a proposal as unreasonable because, as they evaluated the situation, Bob had not even begun to set up an organization, much less have a going business; yet he wanted to retain more than 50 percent of the company for only $10,000.

In the first week of March, Bob had talked to his financial backer in New York and was told that in the opinion of the investor and his lawyer, the proposed venture "just didn't make sense." They had said that Bob's ownership percentage had been the primary basis for their conclusion. Also they had pointed out that in Bob's proposed operation there would be no assets acquired to give some chance of equity recovery should the company fail. The next day Bob had recast his projections for a reduced start-up operation. This revised estimate became the basis for Exhibits C and D of Bob's report which appears as Appendix A of this case.

Bob had found enough tentative support from friendly sources (including two classmates at the business school) to raise close to the new sum of $50,000, although his company still had no people or contracts— nor any specific prospects for either—and Bob had only $10,000 in savings and readily available loans from his family. As he restudied his plans now, however, he wondered whether or not to change his plans regarding the financing. To proceed with approximately half of the amount originally planned would mean starting on a significantly smaller scale and would be allowing less margin for error in the projections of sales and cash income. Although Bob was confident from his discussions with friends and relatives that the $50,000 would cost him no more than 25 percent of the company, he knew that a slow start and consequent poor profit performance would have considerable effect on how much of the company he would have to give up should he then have to go for more

equity. On the other hand, Bob was uncertain about how much additional money he might be able to raise immediately and on what terms.
In any case, he would have to commit himself to the $50,000 sometime
within the next week as he had indicated earlier to his new backers that
his decision would be made at that time. Bob's own resources were
beginning to be drawn upon heavily (see Exhibit A of Appendix A) and
so far he was the company's only employee.

SUGGESTED QUESTIONS

1. What should Bob do now?
2. What risks do you see in the plan of action you suggest above? What is the
   upside potential for the venture? What are the key elements for making the
   venture successful?
3. Evaluate Bob's business plan as a proposal for raising capital.

APPENDIX A
MANAGEMENT OF NEW ENTERPRISES
RESEARCH REPORT*

This report consists of two parts—a description of my efforts involved in founding a new enterprise, and a prospectus used to raise equity capital from outside sources.

I am embarking on this venture with the expectation that it will form the cornerstone of my career. Basically, it is the satisfaction of being the master of my own fate which I find most appealing. My goals are long term in nature. I hope to grow at a rate which will justify a public offering within five years. This will require that the corporation progress rapidly and efficiently through a series of growth phases, expanding in range and depth of services offered. Once this stage is reached, additional challenge should be provided by the acquisition of related enterprises, geographic expansion, and possibly diversification.

One's choice of career plans is the result of numerous factors and influences.

The most significant determinant of my decision to found a new enterprise was my prior business experience. Upon graduation from college, I went to work for the International Business Machines Corporation as a systems engineer. I was to act as a consultant to users of IBM computers to help insure efficient utilization of their systems. The technical training I received in various IBM schools was thorough. However, as I spent more and more time in the field, I became increasingly dissatisfied with various aspects of working for such a huge company. I saw that people of differing capabilities and performance were all receiving similar recognition (or lack of it). Having previously spent two and a half years in the Army as an officer in charge of a few hundred men, I had a feeling for the degree of responsibility I could handle. I was impeded in my quest for more difficult tasks and challenging assignments at IBM. There was just so much that was expected of you and any additional zeal was a threat to your supervisor's job security. Another irritant was the constant pressure forcing everyone to adopt the corporate image. Individuality was not highly regarded (corporate policy statements notwithstanding), and I found myself constantly having to decide how far down the conformity continuum I would move from individual integrity to complete "organization man." In the end I decided that the type of environment was not suited to me or vice versa and I resigned. As a result of this experience and my knowledge of similar situations in other corporations, large and small, I was convinced that my requirements for work would only be met by starting a venture of my own, those requirements being:

A. Significant responsibility at an early stage in my career
B. Freedom to express my individuality
C. Opportunity to gain recognition based solely on my achievements
D. Involvement in a broad range of decision-making situations
E. Challenge requiring me to draw upon utmost of personal resources

*Robert S. Lewis, May 16, 1966

The next stop was an evaluation of my abilities and interests. My undergraduate degree was in physics, reflecting a long-standing fascination with the world of science. My enjoyment, however, of working in positions which required a high degree of personal interaction and my facility in that area had led me away from a career in research. Rather I choose to work in an environment where I can combine both of these interests (such as the technology-based consulting job at IBM). As for functional responsibility, I was anxious to move more toward sales and marketing where I could utilize my social talents and get away from overinvolvement in the technical side personally.

My search was rather short-lived. As I began to consider the various criteria I had established for the enterprise, my thoughts turned to a business I had been associated with for about a year. After my departure from IBM, I went to work for Cutler Computer Associates a data processing service company in New York City. At the time I started with them in the fall of 1963, there were four employees. At present (May 1966) two and a half years later they have a staff of 75. The nature of the business is fully described in the attached prospectus, but basically it consists of providing consulting and programming services to users of computers. The company has a full-time staff of systems analysts and programmers whose services are contracted out to client companies. In the case of systems analysts, the term of the contract could be anywhere from one day to many months in duration; programmers on the other hand would probably not be sought by clients unless the job required at least a few man-months. As for the economics involved, current billing rates for this type of service are approximately \$2,500–\$3,000 per month for systems analysts and \$1,800–\$2,200 for programmers. The salaries and expenses of these specialists come to about 50 percent of the billing rate.

In order to satisfy myself that the conditions within the industry were similar to those I had experienced almost two years ago, I contacted individuals in various smaller firms doing this type of work. Among those I spoke with were key executives from:

Computer Programmers & Analysts, Inc., New York
Research Applications, Inc., New York
MBI Systems, Inc., Boston
Clikeman, Swihart & Associates, San Francisco
Information Management Incorporated, San Francisco

In each case I was informed that business was booming and future prospects were even more encouraging with no slackening of demand in sight. The supply factor was, however, critical. There is a shortage of trained data processing personnel, and it is going to become more severe in the future.

I then investigated the situation of the giants in the industry by studying annual reports, stock prospectuses, and capabilities brochures. These firms included CEIR Corporation, Computer Sciences Corporation, Computer Applications, Inc., and Computer Usage Corporation. Here again the record of growth was impressive with prospects for a vastly expanding market. Finally, I met with executives of IBM and First National City Bank to seek their advice.

At this point, I was satisfied that an opportunity existed and I thought it worthwhile to examine, in more detail, the financial aspects of such a venture including risks and potential rewards. Like most service operations, this one is characterized by little or no fixed asset requirements and small fixed charges. Almost all of the costs are variable when viewed in a crisis situation, those costs being salaries. Minimum office space is required as company personnel perform their activities mostly at client locations. Office equipment and furniture can be leased. Secretarial services can be obtained as required from Kelly Girl or Man Power until volume builds up justifying a full-time secretary.

Based on the billing rates and salary scales mentioned previously, I estimate an average contribution (billings minus salary) per man per month to be $800. Monthly overhead and fixed costs will be in the range of $2,500–$3,000. Thus the breakeven point is achieved with three to four employees. With just 10 employees, monthly profit would be about $5,000 before taxes.

On the other side of the coin, the risks of financial disaster will be based on the demand of the marketplace for this service and the supply of adequately trained specialists to fulfill this need. With respect to demand, industry experts forecast a doubling to tripling of the number of computers installed over the next five years. Thus, the approximately 25,000 computers in the United States will increase to over 60,000 by 1970. This fact alone will create an increased need for these services. In the event of an economic downturn, the computer industry will tend to be less affected than other capital goods segments. Firms that have integrated computers into their operations cannot think of removing them. Since the switch to a computer is the result of a long-range policy decision, companies with computers on order or planning to order will most likely not change those plans. Thus, the data processing industry can be looked on as a hedge to protect against bad times.

The significant risk in this business revolves about the shortage of trained personnel. There are roughly 100,000 programmers in the United States at present. By 1970 an additional 175,000 will be needed—according to a McKinsey & Company estimate. The relative scarcity of systems analysts is even more striking. Any company in the industry must be prepared to compete for the limited number of people available. In many respects, a small firm has considerable advantages when it comes to attracting and holding members of this very mobile work force, since most of the highly qualified data processing specialists are working for the computer manufacturers (IBM, Honeywell), or large firms with a history of considerable computer experience. These companies are *the* source of talent, and pirating is a commonplace occurrence. I have spoken to numerous individuals in these categories and I was surprised at their willingness to discuss leaving present job security for a venture of greater risk. Among the attractions a small service company can offer is an environment which is more conducive to their creativity than exists in the giants: small working groups, high degree of individual freedom, challenging assignments in a variety of problem areas. Furthermore, there are numerous opportunities for managerial responsibility for individuals that have the desire and ability. Data processing has historically been a field of limited growth potential for these people with executive talents in addition to their technical competence.

The subject of salaries and benefits is naturally a concern for prospective employees. Increases of from $75 to $150 per month or higher will be offered as an initial inducement. A benefit program has been arranged with the Prudential providing for life insurance, hospitalization with major medical, salary continuation in the event of sickness or accident—all of the basic protection offered by the largest companies. Additional benefits, such as pension plan, tuition refund, and two weeks leave of absence with pay for military training, would be provided as the company grew.

One especially attractive incentive that will be made available is a profit-sharing plan and, to key personnel, a stock option plan. In this way, employees can financially identify themselves with the future of the company. At present stock options are available to only the highest executives in industry. The opportunities for a programmer or system analyst to participate in such a plan now are rare if not nonexistent.

Satisfied that I could attract qualified personnel, I then began to investigate the all-important revenue generating phase of the business—securing contracts. This, of course, is a difficult task for a new firm that has no success stories. The only thing it can promote are the accomplishments of the people who will be working for them. One of the contacts I had was at IBM where I had worked as an outside consultant when I was with Cutler Computer in New York. Based on their knowledge of my abilities and performance and the background of the people I had provisionally lined up, they were willing to try my firm as one of the number of contractors involved in a large programming project in New York City.

Thus armed, it appeared that most of the serious obstacles in my way were about to be overcome. My next thoughts turned to the financing requirements. Actually, very little capital is required to establish a business of this type. The lack of fixed assets and the low fixed costs make entry into the industry rather easy. Historically, the pattern has been one of a programmer or analyst who starts to moonlight—making extra money by handling outside jobs in the evening or on weekends. Finding this very profitable, he eventually leaves his job and starts free-lance work. In time he has one or two additional people join him, and a small data processing service company is created. Working capital is necessary, however, if the firm is to grow. For time and materials contracts, the company must be prepared to pay salaries for about two months before payment is received from the client. This amounts to over $2,000 per man. Other contracts may be written on a fixed fee basis where payment is made only upon completion and delivery of a total package requiring numerous man-months. In addition, it is desirable, if not necessary, to maintain a small inventory of people who are prepared to start working and are available for interview by prospective clients.

It was my intent to found a company which would grow to significant size in the industry within five years. With the initial contract calling for a total of 7 people, I felt that it was reasonable to project a work force of 15 at the end of six months of operation. Thereafter, I planned on a growth rate of 2 additional employees per month for the next 30 months, so that by the end of the third year I would have a total of 75 employees. At that time I would be in a position where earnings are high enough to justify a stock price of about $10 a share in a public offering. Such an offering would serve two purposes—place a market value on the stock so it can be more readily used for acquisitions and give investors and founder an opportunity to realize a capital gain. Of course, the longer a public offering is postponed, the higher the initial offering price assuming continuous growth. The timing of the offering will be contingent upon the status of the stock market and the needs of the firm.

Based on the growth estimates projected for the first six months, a cash flow was prepared (see prospectus) which shows a maximum net cash outflow of about $20,000 at the end of four months of operations. I then had to determine how much capital I should start with, including a margin for error. Since a majority of the equity funds was to be outside capital, it became a matter of a tradeoff between giving up too great a share of the company and starting with insufficient funds to support projected growth. I also had to consider what kind of a deal I would have to offer a prospective investor in order to make this an attractive opportunity. Considering the degree of risk, the fact that he would be "locked-in" for a period of years, and return on alternative investments, I concluded that an appreciation of 100 percent per year was both equitable and realistic. That is to say, for every dollar invested at the time of incorporation, an investor should be able to realize a capital gain of one dollar for each year he must wait before he is in a position to liquidate any of his holdings (public offerings).

With these considerations in mind plus the growth projections and subsequent cash requirements, I decided to attempt to raise $50,000 of outside capital which would purchase one quarter of the company. I would contribute $10,000 for a total capitalization of $60,000. There would be 200,000 shares issued and outstanding—initial investors would purchase 50,000 at $1 per share; I would hold the remaining 150,000. Within five years, investors would receive a handsome return (see prospectus-financing), and my equity would be worth approximately $1.5 million.

At this point, I felt it was time to seek competent legal and tax counsel. I contacted an uncle who is a tax accountant and partner of a large New York auditing firm and through him was referred to the law firm of Javits, Trubin, Sillcocks, Edelman, & Purcell, which was later retained. In my mind, it was important to establish an early and close association with a highly competent legal firm. Based on our discussions they recommended I incorporate in Delaware due to its model corporate code. My tax advisor suggested that we issue stock under section 1244 of the Internal Revenue Code—so-called small business corporation stock. This section offers some measure of incentive and protection to investors in small corporations providing that any losses incurred as a result of ownership of the stock are fully deductible as *ordinary* losses. This is especially attractive to investors in high tax brackets.

It appears that the desired outside capital will be raised in total, although I now think I can afford to sell less of the company and still continue with projected growth plans.

I am in the process of negotiating with a group of six very competent programmers with systems experience who are presently employed by one of the larger computer manufacturers. I hope to pirate them away and phase them into my starting contract with IBM. This would certainly solve my start-up problem, i.e., initial coordination of employees with contracts. Numerous other data processing personnel have been contacted, and I am about to advertise in the Sunday papers in New York, Boston, and Washington.

Corporate offices will open in New York on June 1, 1966.

PROSPECTUS FOR COMPUTER DATA SYSTEMS, INC.

The data processing industry

Background

Since its commercial debut in 1952, the computer has become one of the most efficient sources of energy ever harnessed, its logic power extending into almost every single segment of our economy. Electronic data processing (EDP) has irrevocably swept away methods that just five years ago were considered advanced and used by industry, government, and science to compile data for decision making. The computer's power lies in rapid-speed computation, extensive instruction storage capacity (the program), and its ability to make logical decisions.

The EDP industry is divided into two parts: those firms engaged in designing, building, and marketing computers and related equipment—the "hardware" companies—and those devoting their talents to the setting up of programs and techniques to help customers determine solutions to their particular business problems as rapidly as possible. This latter group—firms providing service—comprise what is commonly termed the "software" industry.

Growth potential

There is virtually unanimous agreement among members of the computer industry that a vast untapped market, where growth is limited only by the number of qualified personnel, lies ahead of the software industry. The overwhelming increase in computer applications to all phases of business, science, and government has created a proportionate rise in the need for problem analysis, programming, and related data processing activities, to the extent that by 1970 the industry will probably double its present size.

According to *Datamation*, a leading computer industry trade journal, software services in 1965 amounted to $1.95 billion or a substantial 30 percent of the $6.5 billion overall EDP market. With the introduction, in 1964, of "third generation" equipment (incorporating advanced solid state circuitry for vastly expanded computer power at lower relative costs), a new era of growth in computer usage is here. Accordingly, *Datamation* has estimated industry volume in 1970 to be $9.4 billion with software's share coming to $3 billion or 32 percent of the overall market. It is estimated that in five years, the number of computers installed will be triple the present figure. If these projections are accurate, the growth of the software end of this business is quite capable of eclipsing that of computers sometime during the next five years.

The personnel involved in the software segment include systems analysts whose job it is to assemble and evaluate the facts needed to reach the objectives of a particular client. The analyst determines the most effective procedure to employ in presenting the problem to the computer. A programmer then prepares a set of instructions—the program—telling the computer exactly how to go about solving the problem. The tasks of analysis and programming are an integral part of a computer installation, a necessary prerequisite for the efficient utilization of the computer system. At present, approximately 80 percent of computer software servicing is performed by well-trained, highly paid personnel who are employed by the computer manufacturers. The remaining 20 percent which amounted to $400 million in 1965, is shared by the independent software companies. Manufacturers, aware of the shortage of adequately trained programmers and analysts, are attempting to withdraw from continued overinvolvement in software. They will assist customers with the installation of new systems, but subsequent continued surveillance is too demanding of their key personnel whose services will be required on other new accounts.

The impact of this trend is a bright future for the independents. Within the next five years, the independents' share of software should reach 50 percent, up substantially from the 20 percent they now control. If they are ever going to make substantial inroads in the manufacturers' software business, the time is now.

Computer Data Systems, Inc. (CDS)

The company is incorporated in Delaware and will conduct its business initially in the metropolitan New York area. Contact with the International Business Machines Corporation has been established and assurance of a contract has been indicated. Competitive bids for the particular project are to be solicited in June, and formal notification of acceptance is expected early in July. The contract provides for five programmers starting September 1, 1966, and two more beginning November 1. The contract will be for the remainder of 1966 and renewable for the entire year of 1967. This contract will not only provide a substantial cash flow during the start-up phase of the company, but will also be used as an impressive referral to other prospective clients. In other words, the company will have personnel providing service to IBM, the established industry leader and standard of excellence. In addition, this contract and its projected accounts receivable cash inflow can be used as high-grade collateral for bank financing of working capital if required.

Staffing

Personnel to staff the company will be sought in Boston, Washington, and Philadelphia, in addition to New York. Newspaper advertisements will be placed in leading Sunday issues of those cities and interviews will be conducted. Starting salaries will be $75 to $150 a month higher than those presently being offered in the job market. Personnel who are dissatisfied working for a large organization, who would be attracted to a dynamic young company, who enjoy continued challenge, varied assignments, and responsibility, as well as capable individuals who have attended college but have not graduated, and are therefore ineligible for employment with many of our prospective customers, could be a potential source. The availability of stock options to key employees would also be used to attract capable personnel. Eventually the company itself would undertake to educate and train recent college graduates in the techniques of programming and systems.

Nature of the business

A professional service organization providing experienced data processing personnel on a contractual basis to organizations (clients) utilizing computers. Such personnel would supplement a client's resources or substitute for them on various projects. Among situations wherein this service would be sought by clients would be those cases where additional personnel are needed but a perpetual commitment is not desired, i.e., the handling of peak work loads, achieving forced deadlines, one-time projects, crash-programs, and so on. In addition, there are instances where clients require an expertise beyond their normal resources or seek the objectivity available through the use of an outside consultant. This service is also an efficient means of securing a scarce talent and eliminates all the costly administrative and overhead expenses associated with a work force other than a single check at end of month. Finally a factor not to be overlooked is the opportunity such a service provides for expenditure of budgeted funds for business entities which must relinquish any excess of budgeted over actual expense.

The services available to clients will initially consist of systems analysis and computer programming personnel who will have the capability to perform the following basic steps required of all computer projects.

1. *Definition*—What is the problem, what are the requirements, standards.
2. *System planning*—Selection of most efficient approach to solving the problem.
3. *Estimating*—Determination of systems, programming, and processing costs.
4. *Detailed planning*—the development of the complete system required for machine programming.
5. *Coding*—Preparation of machine instructions.
6. *Testing*—Preproving the system and machine instructions for the required results.
7. *Documentation*—Preparation of all machine and staff instructional forms.

Personnel

Systems and programming personnel will be classified according to their skills and experience in the following categories:

1. *Hardware*—Familiarity with specific manufacturer's products, e.g., IBM, Honeywell, RCA, and Univac.
2. *Software*—Knowledge of programming languages, e.g., FORTRAN, Algol, and Autocoder.
3. *Industry*—Experience with specific requirements of banking, retailing, distribution, and utilities.
4. *Applications*—Knowledge of accounts receivable, inventory control, payroll, and order processing.

With careful attention to the skills inventory in the hiring of company personnel, it is anticipated that a broad range of expertise can be acquired. Cross-training and exchange of knowledge is planned by varying the assignment of personnel to projects as well as periodic educational sessions so that a multidisciplined staff can be developed. The personnel hired will vary in degree of experience and capability.

Senior analysts have advanced degrees, outstanding professional experience, and at least nine years' experience in their fields of specialization. They:

--Conduct research into new and unexplored areas of data processing.
--Develop and evaluate program systems.
--Provide technical leadership for large or special programming projects.

Advisory analysts have at least five years' experience in data processing programming. They:

--Provide technical leadership for a programming group.
--Define large-scale problems to be programmed according to customers' objectives.
--Supervise preparation of final reports for large projects, including a summary of method and results, recommendations for future projects, general or detailed flow diagrams, program decks, and operating instructions.

Project analysts have at least three years' experience in programming. They:

--Supervise customer programming projects.
--Define problems according to customer specifications and prepare general system diagrams.
--Maintain customer communications on project progress and prepare final customer reports.

Program analysts have at least two years' programming experience. They:

--Prepare general and detailed flow diagrams according to customer specifications.
--Develop, code, debug, document, and test programs.

Programmers have at least one year programming experience. They:

--Code, debug, document, and test programs.
--Assist in defining problems and preparing general diagrams and prepare detailed flow diagrams.

Future expansion

As soon as resources permit, the company will expand its range of services to include those of increased sophistication and complexity, such as:

Data processing centers. Traditionally, the data processing center or service bureau has been set up to provide data processing services to various small and large companies on a time, project, or continuing program basis. Such services are of particular value to companies which either do not maintain their own equipment or, if they do have data processing equipment, need the help of an independent facility for peak-load processing.

Application services. Standarized programs to solve a specific problem developed by experts in their respective fields using a unique combination of knowledge of the problem and computing experience. The result is a highly effective total service available to solve a specific problem at a cost far below that for comparable results produced by custom computer programs.

Training services.   A variety of seminars and training courses for professionals as well as technicians who wish to acquire both basic competency and advanced programming skills.

Systems design and reliability.   In systems design, an entire process or problem is analyzed from beginning to end and a specific system, which is a combination of hardware and software, is designed and set up to achieve the most practical solution. In reliability and maintainability, a complex system is analyzed in terms of its many components so that procedures are developed to insure the most reliable performance possible from the system.

Systems development.   The field of programming systems pertains to improving the efficiency with which the human being can plan and implement solutions to his problems through the use of the computer. Along with the computer hardware, manufacturers of general purpose computers must make available to their customers certain programming systems, or "software"—including compiler systems, assemblers, sorting systems, and report writers. In addition, there are a variety of special purpose computers, or special application areas, unique to given customers, that very often require software development.

Management information systems.   The increasingly successful application of the computer to the routine processing requirement areas of business, industry, and government, along with the continually improving price/performance characteristics of successive generations of computer hardware, has made it possible and, in many cases, essential for management of these activities to plan for more advanced and encompassing data processing applications. Professional assistance is required by clients to develop and implement new techniques in the analysis of business data to produce timely, accurate, and concise management reports for important decision making.

Scientific and engineering applications.   In both industry and government, scientific research and engineering developments are ever increasing. Typical of some of the complex problems being encountered in these areas are the solution of partial differential equations representing fundamental problems in the space sciences, analysis of parts failure data, and the solution of differential equations involved in the evaluation of nuclear reactors. We will work in these areas and many others in which the accuracy and speed of computers can be applied to the solution of important problems in scientific and engineering fields.

Real time applications.   There are a variety of activities or physical systems which are sufficiently complicated in the amount or nature of the information to be processed to require an automated approach to the acquisition, processing, and dissemination of information within a time cycle that will maintain a stable or controlled operation. When the time requirement for the information acquisition, processing, and dissemination cycle is relatively short, and must occur simultaneously with the performance of the physical system, the computer application is said to be a real time application.

Some current examples of real time applications are reservation systems (such as are being used or planned by most of the major airlines), missile launch or tracking systems for space or weapons systems, and message switching systems used by common carriers or individual businesses. The ever-increasing requirements on speed of response, number of influencing variables, need for increased accuracy, cost, and other similar factors have made this a significant area of current activity, with even greater potential for future development.

The development of real time applications requires competence in a number of technical areas, such as computer language and compiler development, communications systems analysis, operating systems design, and file organization and management, plus complete familiarity with computer hardware.

Time-sharing. Through the medium of direct line or time-sharing, small businesses that cannot afford to take advantage of the services a computer offers may now share a computer that can be programmed to process the input data of a number of small businesses, each sharing in the costs of the service.

Developments in both time-sharing and teleprocessing foreshadow a portentous breakthrough in the information barrier that presently surrounds us. Through teleprocessing—an integral part of a management information system—a particular company's sales offices, warehouses, manufacturing plants, and so on, around the country will be linked with their computers into a single management information system. Computers will thus become independent of external input/output and will be able to communicate directly with each other.

In addition to expansion from within, as described above, CDS also plans to expand geographically, with offices in major cities across the country and ultimately through acquisitions and mergers.

Financing

The company is to be capitalized at $60,000. The founder is supplying $10,000 and an additional $50,000 is being solicited through the sale of 50,000 shares of common stock at $1 per share.

In total, 200,000 shares of common stock are to be issued. The founders will hold 150,000 shares and the initial investors, 50,000. An additional 100,000 shares will be issued for public offering at such time when earnings are sufficient to demand a price greater than $7.50 per share, approximately three to four years after the start of business.

It is anticipated that after-tax earnings will be between 12 percent and 18 percent. Billings are at the rate of $1,725 to $1,875 per month or approximately $20,000–$22,000 per man per year. With a work force of 75 projected at the end of three years, billings would total $1,500,000. Assuming only an 80 percent utilization factor due to time requirements for training and scheduling between assignments, revenue would total $1,200,000. To be conservative, an after-tax profit of only 10 percent will be assumed, or $120,000. With 200,000 shares outstanding, this equates to $.60 earnings per share. Historically, these service companies have gone public at a P/E ratio of about 20, based on earnings per share prior to dilution. In this case an offering could be made at 20 x $.60, or $12.00. Using a P/E ratio of 15 to be on the low side would yield a price of $9 per share. This would represent a capital gain of $8 per dollar invested. No dividend payments are anticipated prior to the public offering.

Sample notes for promotional brochure

CDS brings to these projects highly trained and imaginative programmers and analysts—people whose only job is to solve computer problems for others.

CDS is a rapidly growing computer programming analysis company headquartered in New York City.

A staff of professional and technical specialists who possess many man-years of data processing and analysis.

Broad and immensely varied experience available.

A high-level professional service organization with primary emphasis on the ability to plan and implement solutions to problems using computer techniques.

CDS offers a complete range of computing services on a unit cost of time basis; problems analysis, systems design, programming, data processing, machine usage, and training.

CDS provides the practical way to gain all the advantages of electronic data processing from problem formulation to final computer solutions. Equipment investment is not required, highly qualified personnel produce effective results, and costs are known in advance.

The total value of data processing results depends upon the experience and capability of the formulators and operators of the system as well as the computer used to produce the results. CDS makes a distinct and valuable contribution to this total value by providing long experience in data processing and computer technology. To customers, this means more effective results, better schedules, increased accuracy, and reduced costs.

With depth in data processing experience, machine facilities, and computer-oriented personnel, CDS offers every customer the advantages gained from solving thousands of data processing problems for scores of commercial, industrial, and government organizations.

CDS's programming services include problem definition and analysis by a multidisciplined staff of senior and advisory analysts. In addition to the company's regular staff, a number of outside consultants, who can bring the highest level of capability to bear on various problems, are members of CDS's consultant staff.

When a customer's problem is well defined or when system design is not required, skilled project or program analysts develop general systems charts from the customer's specifications and experienced programmers prepare the computer instructions necessary to process the work.

In doing this, the staff may use one or more of the many CDS library programs, or the project may require an entirely new program. Subsequent data processing may be done by either CDS or the customer's equipment. Computer users need not maintain as large or widely experienced programming staff as they ordinarily would if such a service were not available on an as-required basis.

The staff devotes their talents to the setting up of programs and techniques to help customers determine solutions to their particular business problems as rapidly as possible.

Service companies offer their clients a service rather than products. Companies, therefore, that provide the latest analytical problem-solving techniques in diagnosing their clients' data processing needs.

Staff is equipped to assist its business, scientific, and governmental clients in all phases of numerical and systems analysis and design, as well as programming necessary for the efficient and effective use of the latest integrated management information systems.

Prepares programming systems for the new equipment of various manufacturers and also develops program packages which are sold to the manufacturer who in turn will sell that particular program or set of programs to the purchaser of his equipment.

May supplement a customer's personnel or substitute for it on various projects.

The overwhelming increase in computer applications to all phases of business, science, and government has created a proportionate rise in the need for problem analysis, programming, and related data processing activities.

EXHIBIT A

Graph showing growth in data processing market shares—1965–70

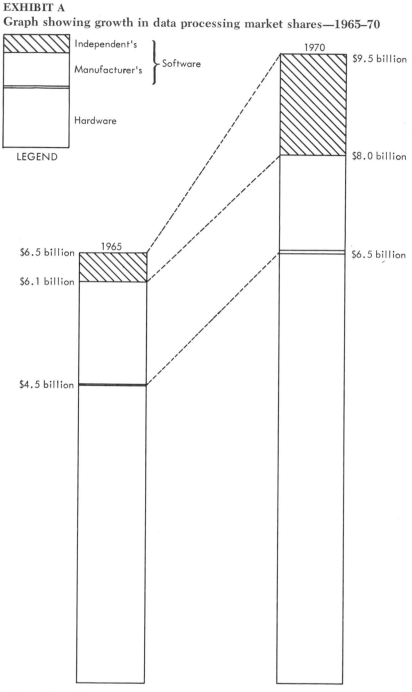

Source: *Datamation.*

EXHIBIT B
Organizational expenses (one time)

	April	May	June
Legal*	$500		
Accounting			$250
Advertising			500
Travel (recruiting N.Y., Boston, Washington)		$ 375	
Printing*		500	
Office supplies			100
Office space security deposit (3 months rent).......		1,200	
Telephone security deposit		100	
Office furniture security deposit.................		250	
Total	$500	$2,425	$850

*Additional fees deferred until 1967.

EXHIBIT C
Monthly fixed expenses

	June	July	Aug.	Sept.	Oct.	Nov.	Dec.
Office space..........................	$ 400	$ 400	$ 400	$ 400	$ 400	$ 400	$ 400
Secretarial service	250	250	250	400	400	400	450
Accounting	50	50	50	50	50	50	50
Phone and answering service	125	125	125	125	125	125	125
Office furniture—lease*	150	150	150	150	150	150	150
Office equipment—lease†	75	75	75	75	75	75	75
Office supplies	10	10	10	10	10	10	10
Periodicals, association dues	10	10	10	10	10	10	10
Executive salary	750	750	750	750	750	750	750
Sales promotion and travel	150	200	200	250	250	300	300
Insurance plans‡	100	100	125	125	125	175	175
Advertising	150	150	150	150	150	150	150
Employee meeting	50	50	75	75	100	100	100
Postage and messenger	20	20	20	30	30	30	40
Total	$2,290	$2,340	$2,390	$2,600	$2,625	$2,725	$2,785

*Desk, chairs, files.
†Typewriter, copier, calculator.
‡Corporate liability, key man life insurance.

EXHIBIT D
Cash flow

	April	May	June	July	Aug.	Sept.	Oct.	Nov.	Dec.
Expenses:									
Organizational	$500	$2,425	$ 850						
Fixed			2,280	$ 2,330	$ 2,380	$ 2,615	$ 2,640	$ 2,740	$ 2,800
Variable*..............			3,000	4,500	7,500	9,000	12,000	13,500	13,500
Total Monthly Expense .	500	2,425	6,130	6,830	9,880	11,615	14,640	16,240	16,300
Revenue†				8,750	8,750	17,500	17,500	17,500	26,250
Net Monthly Cash Flow	(500)	(2,425)	(6,130)	(6,830)	(1,130)	(2,865)	2,860	1,260	9,950
Cumulative Cash Flow	(500)	(2,925)	(9,055)	(15,885)	(17,015)	(19,880)	(17,020)	(15,760)	(5,810)

*Assumes hiring five personnel in June, and an additional five in August and October. Monthly expense per man is $900.
†Based on billing rate of $1,750 per man-month.

APPENDIX B
GENERAL BUSINESS CONDITIONS*

April 1966

The past month was marked by a rising chorus of proposals to tighten fiscal policy quickly to moderate the pace of economic expansion. Apprehension has intensified over the inflationary implications of higher capital spending plans, rising military procurement, growing labor shortages, strong demand for credit, and a sharp jump last month in the money supply. In addition, price increase announcements are proliferating, and public concern is mounting over the rising cost of living.

. . .

Some of the most pressing questions in the market now concern the ability of banks to expand loans and investments in coming months. Through their open market operations, the Federal Reserve authorities are evidently trying to moderate the expansion of bank credit in order to reduce inflationary pressures. Federal Reserve and other regulatory authorities have also been adjuring banks and other institutions to exercise restraint in lending.

May 1966

The economy has been expanding faster than expected in the early months of 1966. Gross national product rose at a rate of almost 10 percent a year in the first quarter, while industrial output shot upward at a rate of nearly 13 percent a year. Employment, incomes and consumer spending also climbed sharply. On a less happy note, average prices—as measured by the GNP deflator—rose at an annual rate of 3.6 percent.

While these first quarter figures depict the extraordinary strength of business for a period that is already behind us, other statistics point to further expansion. Backlogs of unfilled orders for durable goods have continued to lengthen. The latest survey of capital spending plans shows that business has again raised its sights for plant and equipment outlays. The substantial first quarter gain in profits—reported in detail in a separate article—undoubtedly has given a further lift to business sentiment. Also contributing to the expansive atmosphere has been the increase in the money supply, which has grown at an annual rate of 6.7 percent since mid-1965.

*From the First National City Bank of New York's *Monthly Economic Letter*. Used by permission of the publisher.

Charles M. Leighton

CML Group

Roger M. Davis

Introduction

In early June 1969, Roger Davis was reviewing the events of the last few months as he sailed out of the harbor for his first cup series of the year. Roger was group vice president of Dalton Corporation's leisure time division, which had grown under his direction to become the largest profit contributor in the company (see Exhibit 1). This accomplishment had earned substantial success and recognition for Roger and his management team within Dalton, and had enabled them to operate relatively free from corporate interference. However, by late 1968 they had begun to question their future direction, including any return from the stock option program, and the atmosphere that was developing within Dalton Corporation as a whole.

> The company seems to be passing through the inevitable stages of corporate growth. It just doesn't seem as lean and hungry for profit performance as it once was. It is more of a "corporate animal" and I find our performance becoming less of a factor relative to total company performance. And although options are granted on the basis of the division's performance, because the stock price reflects the operation of the company as a whole, we feel there is no direct relationship between our efforts and the value of the options.

Over the three years since he had joined Dalton, Roger had received options on 7,500 shares of stock, some at prices as high as $50 per share. As this was his chief incentive for performance the resulting action in Dalton's stock, as shown in Exhibit 2, had been extremely disappointing. At the same time, since his division's growth was largely based on an active acquisitions program, he thought that the downward performance of Dalton's stock could be a significant impediment to further growth. In addition, some of the executives from previously acquired companies

421

had received options and/or Dalton stock in exchange for joining the leisure time division. While they had produced on average a 25 percent internal profit growth since joining Dalton, the drop in Dalton's stock price from lower 1969 earnings in other areas was demoralizing.

In response to these developments Roger formulated a plan early in 1969 designed to counteract the situation that was occurring. The plan involved a partial "spin-off" of the leisure time division from the Dalton Corporation. Under this approach Dalton would sell a portion of the division's ownership to the public, but retain majority control for reporting purposes. Roger felt that this action would accomplish several things:

1. With Dalton's stock closing out 1968 at a multiple of 18 times earnings, the partial divesture would result in a substantial increase in value to Dalton shareholders as the leisure time division stock should command a substantially higher multiple on a portion of those same earnings. This idea was supported by the recent stock market performance of a similar but smaller company, the Leisure Group, Inc., which had closed out 1968 with its stock selling at $35 a share or approximately 65 times earnings. (See Exhibit 3 for The Leisure Group's operating results through 1968 and Exhibit 4 for a general description of their objectives and operating philosophy.)

2. By isolating the leisure time division in this fashion the current management team could be given stock options which would allow for a direct relationship between their performance and their incentive rewards.

3. The higher multiple and more attractive appreciation prospects that would be enjoyed by the division's stock would be a distinct advantage in pursuing the "growth by acquisition" strategy.

4. The greater independence resulting from corporate rather than divisional status would allow Roger's management team to establish its own mode of operation and corporate atmosphere.

Given the financial and legal (versus operating) orientation of Dalton's top management Roger felt that there was a good chance of gaining acceptance for the plan. However, he considered it necessary to test the feasibility of the plan and develop solid lower level support before presenting it to corporate management. His first step was to test the leisure time division's operating philosophy before the business community and gain external recognition for the performance of his management team and his division. This was accomplished in large part by an article he co-authored with a member of his staff, George Taylor, which appeared in a prominent business periodical. (See Appendix A.) Following up on this step he approached Dalton's investment bankers and major institutional lenders to sound out their reaction to the spin-off concept, as their approval would be necessary for the plan's execution. The response had been favorable.

In March 1969, Roger presented the plan at a meeting of the presidents of the division's subsidiaries. The response was enthusiastically in favor of the concept, giving Roger the support necessary to broach the idea at corporate headquarters. The next step had been a presentation to Dalton's president, who felt the idea should be discussed and set up a May meeting with Dalton's chairman and co-founder, Mr. Jasper. After listening to Roger's presentation Mr. Jasper responded by saying:

> That's what Jimmy Ling has been doing, and I've always said it wouldn't work. Besides you're asking me to spin-off one of our best groups.

At that point the spin-off concept died.

Roger's actions, however, did not seem to have jeopardized his position at Dalton. Shortly after his meeting with Mr. Jasper, he was asked to move his division's operations to corporate headquarters, where the possibility of a promotion at some future date to executive vice president was discussed. If and when promoted, Roger could make his current assistant, George Taylor, group vice president for the leisure time division. Before moving his family, Roger felt that he should consider other opportunities that might be open to him at this time. His group's track record had not gone unnoticed outside of Dalton, and he recently had been exposed to several interesting opportunities that required a decision in the near future. As he considered the prospects ahead of him, Roger also felt that he should explore the idea of forming his own company, a long standing interest that had been strengthened in the process of pursuing the spin-off plan.

Personal history

Roger M. Davis, 34, had received a B.A. in psychology from Colorado College in 1957, entered Stanford Business School that fall, and received his M.B.A. degree two years later. Before graduating from Stanford, Roger had studied the feasibility of starting his own sailboat manufacturing company. However, he reached the conclusion that he did not have the necessary experience and contacts to start such an enterprise on his own.

> Once I got into it I decided I just didn't have the tools to do it right. I was a liberal arts major as an undergraduate, and although I did have an M.B.A. from Stanford, I had little money or contacts in the business world and no experience. It seemed to me that I needed quite a bit of each of these if I was really going to make it on my own.

Instead of starting the sailboat company when he graduated from Stanford, Roger joined the marketing department of Industrial Safety Equipment Corporation (ISE), a company he had worked for between years at Stanford, at a salary of $7,200 a year. ISE manufactured and sold various devices designed to improve the operating safety of different kinds of automated equipment. Roger stayed with ISE for a total of four years, first as a sales engineer and then as a product line manager. At the end of this period, despite some success in the company, he began to question his long-term interest in industrial marketing and applied for a position with several consumer product companies in the New York and San Francisco areas. He felt that the marketing activities in these firms would be more challenging and more rewarding personally. However, potential employers advised him to stay in industrial marketing where he could capitalize on his experience at ISE. After several weeks with no success in his job search, he decided to return to Stanford as an instructor in the small business area. Roger had been teaching business management and marketing during the evenings while at ISE. In the process he accepted a salary drop from $13,000 to $8,000 a year.

The Dalton experience

Roger had first come in contact with Dalton while he was on the staff at Stanford. He had undertaken a consulting job for developing a tender offer for a company which Dalton acquired. In June 1965 Roger received an offer from Dalton to join the company as manager of the leisure time division. At that time the division consisted of recently acquired jewelry and boat manufacturing companies with total sales of $6 million and $600,000 in pre-tax contribution. Roger was to start at an annual salary of $18,000, with additional cash bonuses and stock options to be granted based on divisional performance. He would be responsible for building the division into a major operation of the Dalton group through acquisitions and successful operation of acquired companies. Roger accepted the job after finding someone to fill his Stanford position.

As division manager Roger made preliminary analyses of many firms in the recreational area and recommended suitable acquisition candidates to the corporate staff. Then, with members of the headquarters group, he became involved in the negotiations to purchase several of these firms, with special interest in how the acquired companies might best be integrated into his division. As companies joined the division Roger assumed responsibility for planning and control. He also provided general operating direction to the newly acquired managements. As a result he became familiar with all aspects of the internal operations of each subsidiary.

In July 1967 Roger hired George Taylor, 30, a graduate of Harvard Business School. Prior to attending Harvard, George had obtained an undergraduate degree in engineering from RPI, and had then gained experience in operations and production as a project officer in the U.S. Navy Systems Division and with the Cooke Chemical Company. George's responsibility with Dalton was to assist Roger in providing operating direction to acquired companies, especially in the manufacturing and operations areas. He worked without a staff and spent the great majority of his time working with management out in the individual companies within the division.

In July 1968 a third member was added to the team, Ronald Bowers, 34. Ron had received an M.B.A. from Amos Tuck School in 1962 and had worked for a major public accounting firm since graduation. Immediately before joining Dalton, Ron was small business department manager for a major accounting firm. With Dalton Ron was responsible for establishing an effective divisional control system and for helping the individual subsidiaries' controllers to establish effective operating controls and cost accounting systems. Like George he spent a good deal of his time in the operating subsidiaries.

Roger's objective had been to develop a three-man team with the broad range of skills necessary to manage the leisure time division as it continued its growth and expansion. His experience with these two people reinforced his opinions regarding the potential benefits available from this approach and the importance of establishing a good working relationship within a management team.

> We have been successful as a management team because we can make decisions quickly. And we make decisions quickly because each of us respects the other's special abilities and opinions. I don't think we've ever really had an argument at an emotional level.

The six acquisitions made by the leisure time division to date varied in size, in the form of the acquisition deal employed, and in terms of the valuation used. Although the average valuation was 11 times after-tax earnings, the prices paid by Dalton varied over a wide range. The division's dominant subsidiary, a pleasure boat and camper manufacturer, had been acquired outright for $23 million in cash, a little less than 10 times after-tax earnings. A smaller company with $200,000 in pre-tax earnings had been acquired for $1 million immediately and a potential additional $1 million to be paid if pre-tax earnings averaged in excess of $400,000 over the next five years. The other acquisitions had taken different forms including stock exchanges and stock earnouts.[1] To date

---

[1]The stock earnouts had taken two basic forms:

1. A specific amount of stock now plus an additional *number of Dalton shares* to be earned based on postacquisition performance against earnings bench marks.
2. A specific amount of stock now plus an additional *dollar value of Dalton stock* to be earned based on postacquisition performance. This approach allows Dalton to minimize future dilution if the stock price increases, but protects the seller in the event of a price decline.

In both of the above kinds of deals, no more than 50 percent of the intended number of shares was specifically stated.

postacquisition operating results of the six acquired companies had produced an average annual compound profit growth of 25 percent.

Roger's three years at Dalton had given him the opportunity to organize his thoughts on how he might best operate a company which was to grow rapidly internally and through acquisitions.

Roger's alternative opportunities

Given the nature of the alternatives seemingly open to him, the operating philosophy that he had developed, and the nature of the relationship he had formed with George and Ron, Roger considered it highly desirable to persuade them to join him should he decide to leave Dalton. He felt that there would be substantial value in maintaining the integrity of this compatible and highly successful team arrangement. However, he realized that Dalton would exert substantial pressure on these men to keep them with the company and he knew that he would have to offer them an attractive opportunity to get them to leave with him. Thus in examining the alternative courses of action he wanted to evaluate the prospects through their eyes as well as his own.

In late May Roger had been approached by the management of a large successful multi-industry company. The top officers of the corporation were approaching retirement, and they wished to discuss with Roger a position as head of their sporting goods division which had sales of $80 million. He was told he would receive a compensation package similar to what he currently received at Dalton, and if he could persuade George and Ron to join him they would also receive at least their current level of compensation. (Recent performance of the company is shown in Exhibit 5.)

At about the same time Roger had been approached by a well-known investment banking firm. They offered to assist him in assembling two or three small companies with total after-tax profits of about $500,000. The new company would then be taken public, and Roger's management team would receive from 10 percent–18 percent of the stock, depending on their success in completing the acquisitions. Under this approach professionals, investment bankers, would handle the financing, something with which Roger and his group had had limited experience. ·

Roger's talks with George and Ron had led him to believe that the above approach to getting into a company might be most appealing to them, as it removed most of the uncertainty from the process. He sensed that they might be more risk averse than he was because they seemed to feel that they would have less future flexibility than he would if the venture were to collapse or never get started. They felt that a future employer would tend to view the results at Dalton as Roger's track record, leaving them in a more vulnerable position if it became necessary to break up the group and each go his own way. For this same reason he felt they might consider the sporting goods company offer quite attractive.

In addition to the above opportunities, and despite the possible problems in attracting George and Ron to join him, Roger felt that they should seriously consider the possibility of forming a new company entirely from scratch. Although the investment banking firm's offer amounted to much the same thing, he was concerned over the implications for eventual control which lay behind large blocks of stock in the hands of outsiders, especially as most of them would have only short-term financial interest. He also felt that a greater share of ownership might be retained if he formed the venture himself.

In developing his thoughts on the shape that a new venture might take, if he pursued that course either on his own or with the assistance of the investment bankers, Roger had drawn heavily on his experience with Dalton's leisure group. His current thinking indicated that an approach which incorporated the following basic elements would offer the greatest opportunity for success.

——He felt that concentrating on developing a participation in the leisure-time recreational area seemed most appropriate in the short term because of his and the team's experience with and interest in that area, and also in the longer term because of the economic and life-style trends in the United States.

——He felt that his and the team's experience and expertise indicated a start-up and growth strategy oriented towards an acquisition program.

——Roger's analysis of the leisure-time recreational product buyer indicated that he attached great significance to purchase of this type of product and was often willing to pay substantially more money to gain even small marginal product performance advantages. Thus Roger felt that his acquisitions should be chosen from among those companies that had a reputation for quality and superior product performance in their respective fields.

——His experience indicated that this type of company often gained its position due to the creative strength of its entrepreneur owner/manager. He felt that it would be extremely important to retain and motivate this individual in order to perpetuate the product innovation required to maintain that company's preeminent position in its field.

——Finally, because his own management group would necessarily be fairly thin in numbers, and because he wanted to achieve rapid growth, he felt it would be important to restrict acquisition candidates to those companies that were currently operating reasonably successfully.

Roger estimated that he would need at least $2 million to finance working capital and for preliminary payments to acquisitions, until a sizeable cash flow could be achieved. With the SEC restrictions on a private placement, Roger knew that if he decided to go this route it would be extremely important to develop a sound strategy for raising the necessary funds. The problem of raising the money and the question of how much equity might be retained was compounded by the fact that he and his associates, if he could persuade them to join him, would be able to invest only $30,000–$40,000 personally. In addition Roger thought that it was important that all dealings with investors, bankers, and so on be restricted to those which had never dealt with Dalton Corporation, to avoid all possible conflicts in this area.

If the money could be raised, Roger felt he would also have to consider how he might best adopt the strategy developed at Dalton to the new situation. He was concerned that being a fledgling firm with only a fraction of the resources of Dalton might force radical changes in approach, and he wanted to ascertain what steps might be taken in the early stages to minimize these changes. He was also bothered by the question of how he should split up any equity available to the team members as founders, and recognized that this decision might be crucial to persuading George and Ron to join him, if they elected to pursue this alternative.

Other factors

Roger was concerned with the economic situation existing in the early summer of 1969. While he felt that it might have some impact regardless of the option he selected, he felt that general business conditions were especially relevant to someone seeking to start a new company, particularly one which planned to grow by acquisition. The prime lending rate had just been raised to 8½ percent, and Roger thought that many potential investors would be reluctant to sacrifice sizeable real interest dollars on a start-up venture until conditions improved. (See Exhibit 6 for an indication of the movement of interest rates.) Further, the Federal Reserve Board had recommended that the banking industry not provide money for the purpose of corporate acquisitions, and many banks and other financial institutions were taking this recommendation seriously. In fact the whole concept of growth by acquisition was coming under attack (see Appendix B), and the recent stock market performance of most conglomerates had been very poor. At the same time the acquisition game remained highly competitive, especially in the leisure industries area where big companies, like Dalton, were trying to develop a meaningful participation. Roger was concerned that these developments might seriously impact on his ability to raise money given the venture plans that he had formulated. Also he did not have specific companies which he could present to investors.

On the other hand, Roger felt that in terms of his personal situation now was the most opportune time to make a decision on what he wanted to do with his business career.

> I have spent considerable time laying the groundwork for an effort on my own. I have acquired certain skills, made various contacts, and produced a track record. These things all seem to be coming to a head now. People are bringing ideas to me on how to get started on my own, especially investment bankers. I have a distinct feeling that my track record will become less and less valuable over time, as people will forget how well the division has done—sales of $6 million and after-tax profits of $300,000 in three years to sales of $60 million and profits of $3.6 million.

Even the fact that his compensation had grown from $18,000 annual salary to $65,000 in salary and bonuses, plus company car and expense account, seemed to favor a move in the near future.

> Personally I am beginning to succumb to the urge to stay "fat and happy" with very attractive salary, fringe benefits, use of a company plane, and the like. I have thought for some time of wanting to leave the fat salary for peanut butter and equity sandwiches. It is getting to the point of now or never.

The other major area of concern for Roger was the impact that any decision he made might have on his family. To date his wife had lived through seven moves in eight years of marriage, and the oldest of his two children, now in the fourth grade, had attended four schools by the time she was through the first grade. Up to this point his family had lived in apartments except for one year when Roger was in Pittsburgh with Industrial. They now lived in a comfortable home north of an exciting metropolitan area.

Mrs. Davis had always taken an active part in his career whenever possible, as well as pursuing interests of her own. At Dalton she had helped Roger on several occasions, the most significant and enjoyable one being a business trip to Europe, during which she acted as interpreter for Roger in several acquisition negotiations. Her own current activities included a full-time (but unpaid) position as legislative assistant to a state senator, and she felt that there might be an opportunity in the near future to assume a similar position on the governor's staff.

In discussing the decision he faced with his wife Roger felt several significant factors had emerged that he should consider in arriving at any conclusions. First, both he and his wife placed great importance on their ability to retain control over their own life-style. Second, she expressed a strong preference for avoiding additional moves unless it meant that their own independence would be enhanced in some way. Finally, she expressed extreme confidence in Roger, and despite the above reservations was willing to support him in whatever decision he might make. In fact, if anything, she seemed to favor a decision for him to set out on his own, despite the income sacrifices and the risks that that might entail. However, Roger wondered if she fully appreciated the potential downslide implications of that decision and wondered how that decision would impact on their desire to control their own life-style.

Roger was aware that he probably had an excellent future with Dalton if he decided to stay. He was group vice president of one of the company's largest and most important divisions. He was also a possible candidate for corporate executive vice president, and recognized that it might be imprudent to give up his position now. In some ways, however, the sporting goods company opportunity might offer even more along these same dimensions, and he felt he had to give that alternative serious consideration. Against this background he had to consider how much the prospects of starting a small new company might hold for him if he should pursue that course with or without the help of the investment banker. He knew that the others would face the same dilemma. George, whom Roger especially wanted to join him, would be the logical candidate to replace Roger as group vice president if Roger left. This would mean a sizeable jump in compensation from his present $20,000 annual salary and a chance to operate on his own. This type of inducement might well override the strong personal relationship and mutual respect that had developed between the two men, regardless of what Roger decided to do or could offer George as an inducement to come with him.

SUGGESTED QUESTIONS

1. What should Roger do now?
2. How should he try to evaluate his alternatives? What specific guidelines would you give him?
3. What does Roger Davis have to sell? What has been his performance to date? How significant should he consider his team?

EXHIBIT 1
Roger M. Davis
Performance of Dalton Corporation's leisure group 1965–68 (fiscal years)
($ millions and % of total)

	Sales							
	1965		1966		1967		1968	
Leisure time division	$ 6.5	6%	$ 11.2	8%	$ 25.9	16%	$ 60.6	24%
Textile division	31.8	31	58.3	44	63.1	39	76.5	30
Industrial product division	21.2	20	33.2	25	38.0	24	37.1	14
Transportation division	17.1	17	16.9	13	17.1	11	16.4	6
Public safety division			12.8	10	16.5	10	23.2	9
Other*	26.2	26					45.1	17
Total	$102.8		$132.4		$160.6		$258.9	
	Profit contribution							
	1965		1966		1967		1968	
Leisure time division	$1.2	20%	$ 1.7	15%	$ 2.6	20%	$ 7.2	33%
Textile division	1.8	30	3.6	32	3.5	27	3.3	15
Industrial product division	1.3	22	2.1	18	2.5	20	1.8	8
Transportation division	1.6	27	0.9	8	0.4	3	.1	1
Public safety division			3.1	27	3.9	30	6.6	30
Other*	.1	1					2.8	13
Total	$6.0		$11.4		$12.9		$21.8	

*Includes sales/profits from discontinued operations in 1965.
Source: Dalton Corporation annual reports.

EXHIBIT 2
Roger M. Davis
Price movement of Dalton Corporation common stock (monthly)

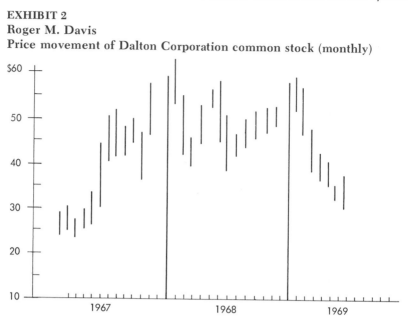

EXHIBIT 3
Roger M. Davis
The Leisure Group, Inc., financial highlights ($ thousand)*

	Fiscal year ended October 31			
Operating results	*1968*	*1967*	*1966*	*1965*
Net sales	$30,427	$22,161	$19,069	$10,234
Net income	1,053	571	191	89
Earnings per share	.54	.36	.14	.10

*Taken from The Leisure Group, Inc., annual report.

EXHIBIT 4
Roger M. Davis
The Leisure Group, Inc.*

GENERAL HIGHLIGHTS

The Leisure Group, Inc., (TLG) manufactures and markets a broad line of leisure-time consumer products on a nationwide basis. Principal product groups are sporting goods, youth recreation products, and lawn and garden equipment. The company operates 18 plants in the United States and one in Canada. Total employment is approximately 3,100.

Operating results are in line with performance levels established as objectives when TLG was formed. Since that time, the company's stated goal has been to build a major business enterprise engaged in the manufacture and marketing of leisure-time products. Specifically, the firm's long-range plan continues to call for the following:

−−15 percent annual sales increase through internal growth, starting one year after acquisition in the case of new product lines.
−−50 percent annual sales increase through acquisition of new product lines.
−−Net income equal to 6 percent of sales.
−−Minimum annual increase in earnings per share of 25 percent.

To achieve these goals, TLG has adopted three basic business strategies:

−−Concentrate and expand activities in the leisure-time market, which is growing rapidly as a result of increased affluence, more disposable income, and growing leisure time.
−−Capitalize on the changing pattern of distribution for leisure time products—a change that parallels the evolution in food marketing from small independent grocery stores to large supermarkets.
−−Apply professional management techniques to the operation of all phases of the business.

ACQUISITION POLICIES

Since The Leisure Group was organized, it has followed specific criteria for growth by acquisition. These criteria are divided into four major areas:

Distribution

Compatible integration of acquired product lines into TLG's distribution system is a basic requirement. This is because TLG consolidates marketing with a single nationwide sales force handling all products. The company's concept is

*Taken from The Leisure Group, Inc., annual report.

EXHIBIT 4 (Continued)

to concentrate largely on fast-growing mass merchandisers, servicing them at all levels from major buyers to retail store managers.

While all product lines continue to be sold through traditional retail outlets, the bulk of the marketing effort is aimed at large, retail chains. The objective is to upgrade sales of acquired lines by professional marketing oriented to large-volume operations.

Products

TLG looks for products with strong brand recognition, because a well-established consumer franchise is essential in mass merchandising.

If a product does not enjoy strong identity, then at least it should easily lend itself to being marketed under a TLG brand name. An example of the latter is Werlich toboggans, a name associated with quality and well known in Canada, but not in the United States. These products, however, are now being sold successfully under TLG's popular Flexible Flyer name.

In addition to brand recognition, TLG looks for other desirable product characteristics: patent coverage, specialized machinery to manufacture the product competitively, and technological know-how. The reason for the last two requirements is to avoid extreme price competition, particularly over products easily copied or sold as commodities.

Industry position

Size of acquired firms is less important than their relative position of leadership. TLG's strategy is to move into markets only with a lead product. This does not necessarily mean the acquired product line must have the largest share of the market, but it does require a leadership brand image. TLG's Ben Pearson archery line, for example, achieved stature in the field in terms of both size and product quality, whereas Flexible Flyer, while not the largest, enjoyed a long-standing position of leadership.

Once TLG has established major leadership positions in specific markets, it applies a second set of acquisition criteria. These relate to accessory products. One example is sporting firearms. With a basic leadership position established by the High Standard line, TLG can add companion products such as the recently acquired Sierra line of reloading ammunition. Similarly, the Black Magic line of indoor plant care products was added to TLG's established lines of lawn and garden products, whereas the same line would not have been acquired on its own.

Operational characteristics

In analyzing operations of potential acquisitions, TLG concentrates on three major areas: cost of goods sold, manufacturing methods, and technologies that capitalize on the company's design know-how. These areas are particularly

EXHIBIT 4 (Concluded)

pertinent because of TLG's policy of total integration of acquired companies. Because of this policy, earnings history is not relevant as an acquisition criterion.

Cost of goods sold. TLG prefers operations that exhibit a high manufacturing overhead and a high labor content as they represent the greatest potential for improved gross margin.

Manufacturing methods. Acquisition prospects which have not applied professional management techniques in the areas of inventory control, production planning, work simplification, and value engineering provide the best opportunity for TLG to make significant improvement.

Design and manufacturing technologies. Inasmuch as each acquired plant is considered a center of specific manufacturing capability, instead of a producer of specific products, TLG is always interested in acquiring new technologies that might subsequently be applied to existing product lines.

EXHIBIT 5
Roger M. Davis
Price movement of sporting goods company
common stock (monthly)

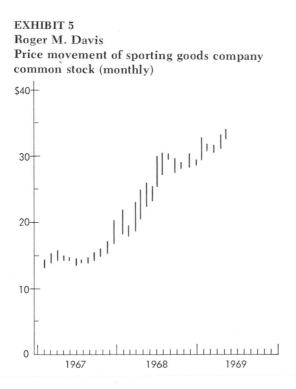

EXHIBIT 6
Roger M. Davis
Selected interest rates

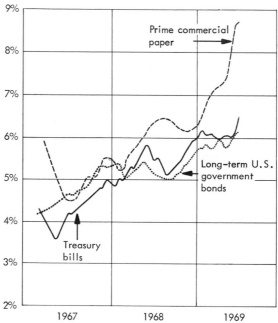

APPENDIX A
ROGER M. DAVIS
After the Acquisition: Continuing Challenge*

The acquisition route to corporate growth has long been championed by the captains of industry, and certainly the acquisitions business is lively today. Once the dust has begun to settle on an acquisition agreement, however, the picture that emerges is all too often a somber one. Judging from what we have seen and heard, more than half of all acquisitions consummated fail to live up to the expectations that buyer and seller alike had for them. The late Jerome S. Hollender, formerly Shearson, Hammill & Co.'s vice president of mergers and acquisitions, succinctly stated the major reasons why acquisitions go sour:

"Most acquisitions are consummated too hastily. Then, too, there's an overdependence on intuition. Another reason is that frequently the acquiring company doesn't know enough about the potential of the company it is buying. There is also the lack of management compatability and, finally, an unawareness of the motivations of the seller."[1]

We strongly agree with this statement. To put it another way, most buyers, although they are willing to explore at length the *legal* and *financial* aspects of an acquisition, fail to consider thoroughly, and in advance, how the new company will be *operated* and *managed* after the acquisition agreement has been signed. One need only refer to the many press notices of management shake-ups in the postacquisition phase and of declining profits and P/E ratios to appreciate how true this is and how grave the consequences of poor planning (or no planning) in this area can be.

As members of a team that is responsible for managing a group of our company's acquisitions, we have had the opportunity to develop an approach to postacquisition management that offers vital benefits to both partners of an acquisition.

To understand this approach, it is necessary to understand something of the environment in which it has evolved. To begin with, our company has a policy of allowing its group management teams a high level of autonomy and therewith a high level of responsibility. Because we are responsible for the results, it seems clear to us that we should have some say as to how each acquisition agreement is framed, inasmuch as it will be the framework within which we shall have to operate as managers. Indeed, we feel that we should have some say as to whether a particular company is acquired in the first place, since we are the ones who will be "stuck" with managing it in the long run.

Our top management recognizes the fact that it has given us responsibility, and consequently listens to what we have to say on these points. Accordingly, our thinking about postacquisition management tends to focus on the negotiation and settlement phases as well as on the postacquisition phase itself; and the approach and planning techniques we have developed reflect this fact.

Thorough advance planning pays a rich reward in two important areas. First, it

---

*Used with permission of the authors.
[1] Paul J. Keil, "Expert Stresses Need for Planning," *California Business*, July 5, 1966, p. 8.

is valuable in helping to consummate the deal itself. It is worthy of mention that of the five companies approached in the past three years, we have succeeded in acquiring four—in each case without the aid of a broker or the expense of finder's fees. This compares favorably with the industrywide average of one company acquired out of ten wooed. Second, all our acquisitions are operating successfully. They comprise, in fact, our company's largest profit group.

Our system is far from foolproof. If one thing is clear in this business, it is that no one has all the answers; and we have made our share of mistakes. In recent years, however, we have refined our management plan to a point where our batting average is relatively high.

Our system also has a certain scope and locus. It is suited to companies of a size roughly comparable with ours, and hence to a fairly compact management group. Our team consists of three men: a group vice president, a manager, and a controller. Structurally, presidents of acquired companies report to the group vice president, who heads up the group management team and who himself reports directly to our corporation president. Our team is currently responsible for seven acquired operating companies, each of which was worth $25 million or less at the time of acquisition.

We make no claim to unique or remarkable expertise. However, the literature on how to manage an acquisition is as meager as the literature on how to acquire a company is voluminous; and we shall therefore try to pinpoint the strategies that are working well for us and to identify the pitfalls we have learned to avoid.

MANAGEMENT PLANNING

Our basic approach to acquisition management planning is simple, and it can be stated in nine rules of thumb. The assumption is, of course, that the acquiring company has a carefully developed, detailed acquisition strategy and that it has highly reliable financial and legal evaluations available. In general, furthermore, a key ingredient for a larger company's success in acquisition is the possession of its own flexible and creative acquisition staff. It is when these conditions are fulfilled that our rules of thumb begin to apply.

The first three rules deal primarily with the preacquisition phase, but they also have a definite long-term value as political and diplomatic guidelines:

1. Get group management in at the outset.
2. X-ray the candidate.
3. Minimize anxieties.

The remaining six apply more directly to substantive problems in the continuing management of an acquisition:

4. Fight the prima donna urge.
5. Sell yourself as the helmsman.
6. Motivate to the hilt.
7. Humanize management controls.
8. Cross-fertilize aggressively.
9. Make the group manager a "man for all seasons."

1. Get group management in at the outset

Wisely, most expansion-minded corporations develop a well-defined strategy for both screening and selecting acquisition candidates. More often than not, the strategy centers around legal and financial considerations. This is all to the good. But, except in rare cases, this usually means that operating objectives and procedures are not spelled out until after the acquisition agreement has been signed. In our view, this is a mistake.

For group management to manage *successfully*, it must get into the act long before the deal is made. For one thing, as we have stated, it is group management that will be held responsible for the successful operation of the acquired company. In fact, under most incentive compensation systems in force today, group management's income is strongly influenced by the profitability of the companies for which it is responsible. Also, once again, decisions and agreements reached in the early stages of negotiation often have a strong bearing on the future policies and operations of the acquired company and on the basic buyer-seller relationship as well. Thus the group management team has an important stake in what takes place in the early stages.

Composition & functions. Each company must decide for itself what its requirements are so far as the composition and organization of this team are concerned. In our team, one man has a strong financial background, and the other two are generalist-specialists with knowledge-in-depth of the industry in which acquired companies operate. This mix of personnel seems to work well for us. The three-man team is by no means sacrosanct, however. Group management may consist of as few as one person or as many as four or five. More than this is not recommended: the team tends to become unwieldy, and close liaison and control are more difficult to achieve.

Actually, the roles that group management will have to play determine the scope of talent that must be included within it. In our company, for example, group management does not have responsibility for screening and negotiation; as in many multimarket companies, this task is assigned to the acquisition staff. The team is mainly responsible for operations, and takes over after the agreement has been signed. The team can provide assistance to the acquisition staff, especially because of its detailed knowledge of the industries in question—assistance that can play a major part in ensuring a smooth transition and successful operation.

What *are* the roles that group management should play in the early stages? There can be no preset formula. "Necessary" functions will vary according to corporate structure and degree of decentralization. They will also be influenced by the nature and purpose of the proposed acquisition, the parent company's past experience in buying and operating companies, and the styles and personalities of the seller's management. Certain points are clear, however.

Role as intermediary. One major concern of group management is the fairness of the acquisition agreement. If it is too favorable for the buyer, it will be difficult later on for group management to motivate the seller to perform at his top productivity. If the seller wins too great an edge, on the other hand, group management will be hard-pressed to achieve its financial objectives, such as return on investment. Thus group management is in the middle. It can, indeed *must*, participate as a neutral party who has the interests of both buyer and seller at heart.

Once our negotiators presented a particularly complicated payout formula to a potential seller. Viewing the presentation objectively, our team could see that the seller's president lacked the financial sophistication necessary to understand the arrangement. Instead of leaving him and his aides to wrestle with what was to them a perplexing riddle, we worked with them patiently to clarify the arrangement. This paid off later on. When the time came for final negotiations, they understood the formula and had confidence in its application. Our session together had convinced them that the formula had been tailored to their needs. In particular, they clearly saw how its incentive factors had been designed to induce them to remain in their jobs. This gave them the kind of reassurance they had been anxiously seeking.

This matter of incentives is of central importance to group management. If the acquisition candidate is a well-managed company with an excellent reputation in its field, it is desirable to keep the president and his executive team at their present jobs whenever possible. The time to make this clear is during the negotiation stage, and no one is better equipped to do so than the group management team.

Involvement & rapport. If group management gets to know the score by participating right from the outset, it is much more willing to accept responsibility for profit goals. The same principle of commitment applies to the seller as well. He needs to have objectives clearly identified, methods of attaining them explained to his satisfaction, and rewards for success plainly spelled out in the contract. If the group management team coaches him a bit, future misunderstandings will be minimized, and an operating climate will be developed in which all parties to the contract feel they are moving in the same direction. This process will also help the seller's management to absorb the facts of group management life.

This point brings up a further benefit that accrues from the team's early participation. To a large degree, successful postacquisition operation depends on the rapport established between the group management team and the acquired company's president. The best time to start laying the foundations of this relationship is right at the outset of negotiations, *before* the hectic and trying period of transition from independent to divisional status takes place.

This period is *always* a trying one for the president, no matter how advantageous the deal may be for him. As Carborundum's president, William H. Wendel, puts it:

"When such a man is brought into a larger corporation, he may be overwhelmed by the broader concepts and the more sophisticated approaches that are essential to the operation of a large, multidivisional company. No longer strictly his own boss, he must now defer to the new top man. His ego may understandably be bruised. If he is flexible and is guided enough, he will adapt to the new environment. Every effort must be made to help him do so, to make the personnel problems in the acquisition easier to cope with."[2]

The seasoned and sensitive group manager can help immeasurably here. He is in a position to drive home the fact that, indeed, his own interests and those of

---

[2]"The Big Business of Buying Businesses," *Dun's Review and Modern Industry*, April 1967, p. 82.

the president are basically the same. He thus has an opening to sell himself, the group management team, and the corporation to the president.

One obvious way for him to do this is to arrange meetings between the president and the presidents of previously acquired companies that are already operating successfully. The principle here is that what has worked for the other sellers can also work for him. Presumably, if a company is being seriously considered as a candidate for acquisition, there are points of compatibility between its management, the corporate management, and the managements of the other companies in the group; and the group manager should call the president's attention to them. Experience shows that as these points of compatibility come to light, anxieties are relieved, a more amicable frame of mind is generated, and financial negotiations can begin in a more relaxed atmosphere. The establishment of warm human relationships inevitably serves as a soft presell. It not only helps pave the way to more effective management later on, but greatly boosts the chances of bringing negotiations to a successful and mutually agreeable conclusion as well.

2. X-ray the candidate

Too many acquisitions are based on an attractive-looking balance sheet and earnings statement plus a quick trip to the plant. The buyer is impatient to act quickly, lest somebody else grab up the prize, and he makes the deal with "details to be ironed out later."

Later, unfortunately, may be too late. As Textron Corporation's L. A. Casler points out:

"The reasons why a company is up for sale can be complex in the extreme. And if the would-be buyer is wise, he will take the trouble to unwind the complexities. Ideally, before he makes a decision on a particular proposition, the buyer will know at least as much about the company as he would had he been an employee. Of course he may not know every executive by his first name, but he will have a picture in depth of the firm, its management, the details of its operation and its prospects."[3]

Someone ought to be charged with a general responsibility that extends beyond the purely legal and financial considerations. Someone must be able to ask, "How good are the products? The quality control? The marketing operation? The manufacturing facilities? The research program? The management team? New capital needs?"

No one recognizes this need for broad scrutiny more fully than the financial community. As Edward A. Weinstein of the accounting firm of Touche, Ross, Bailey & Smart has written:

"In most cases unsuccessful mergers result from defects which might have been detected before the merger took place had the information flow between the parties been adequate."[4]

Knowing the president is vital. Company assets, P/E ratio, and synergistic

---

[3]"The Pitfalls of Acquisitions," *Dun's Review and Modern Industry*, June 1966, p. 89.
[4]"Let the Buyer Beware!" *The Journal of Accountancy*, June 1965, p. 53.

potential notwithstanding, it is people who make a deal and people who will make the acquisition succeed or fail. Willard F. Rockwell, Jr., the chairman of North American Rockwell Corporation, has emphasized that in buying a company, "what you acquire first of all . . . is its people. They are the precious asset that can keep it imaginative, aggressive, inspired, and dynamic."[5]

We cannot overstate the importance of getting to know the president and his key personnel. Evidence indicates that the more fully group management understands their emotional and personal needs, their weaknesses and strengths, their fears and apprehensions, the more effectively it will be able to help with the acquisition and to manage the company later on. This is particularly true when the acquiring company approaches a candidate directly rather than through a broker. In the cold-call approach, we have achieved our greatest success by discussing personal benefits, personal needs, and operating philosophies before getting into financial considerations.

In one case we were competing against a larger corporation for the acquisition of a manufacturing company. Our competitor offered a more attractive security, but he showed less personal interest in the company and its management team. When the president stated he might wish to resign for reasons of health, the larger company was agreeable. Our team had gotten to know the man and to respect his abilities, and therefore we advised our corporate management to take an opposite stand, and our negotiators informed the president that our offer was contingent on his continuing in his job. It was this stand that clinched the deal, we subsequently learned. The president's pride had been hurt by the larger company's willingness to exclude him; our refusal to do so, on the other hand, convinced him that we wanted him as well as his company.

Before acquiring a company, we make every reasonable effort to become acquainted with the president with whom we will have to deal. We visit his office and speak with his associates. We ask questions (without, of course, prying into matters that are none of our business). We engage him in personal discussion. We inquire as to the extent of his participation in civic and community affairs, and so on. In short, we do our best to determine what kind of person he is and what his true interests and ambitions are.

What we learn is usually revealing. In one case we ran into a president who was the rigid, dictatorial type, a man who had never reported to anyone and was not about to start doing so now. This individual, we were convinced, was not amenable to change. Further discussion would have been a waste of time, and we recommended that our corporation cut negotiations short. Our alternative would have been to replace this man after acquisition. This alternative was a particularly unsatisfying one, for the following reason: our experience has taught us that when it is necessary to bring a new president in, it is dangerous to do so right at the time of acquisition. It is much better to persuade the outgoing president to remain active for six months or so, if this is feasible. In this case it was not feasible, and this compounded the difficulty out of reasonable bounds.

In another case the president was in his early sixties and had no backup man behind him. His track record was excellent, but, as we recognized prior to

---

[5]"How to Acquire a Company," *Harvard Business Review* September–October 1968, p. 132.

acquisition, he could not continue in office indefinitely. We were able to convince him of the need to groom a successor, and we offered our assistance, which he accepted.

The key point is this: when you get to know a president's problems and needs, you are in a better position to lay the foundation for change. You can review various possibilities with him and give him a chance to say *yes* or *no* to them. This prepares him for living with you, and coexistence later on is simpler, pleasanter, and more productive.

3. Minimize anxieties

It is critical to deal with the anxieties of everyone concerned immediately after the acquisition: those of the seller, the parent company personnel, the suppliers, the customers, and the community. The best strategy is for the acquiring corporation and the seller to join together in formulating a plan for allaying anxieties, and to do this well in advance of the signing. Because of its position as intermediary, the group management team is in an ideal position to work out the details of this joint plan and then implement it. We have found the following general scheme to be successful:

––The acquired company's president sends a letter to all his employees on the day of the signing. This letter explains why the company has accepted the offer and outlines the benefits and growth opportunities he expects to accrue from the merger; and plainly states that in the president's view, the acquisition is in the best interests of the company. We believe it is important for seller personnel to be informed of the agreement in a personal way such as this, rather than having to read about it in the local paper or get information via the rumor mill.

––The acquiring corporation sends a letter to the press which announces its management plans and explains that, in line with its customary acquisition philosophy, the president will stay on as head of the acquired company. This will allay a major presidential concern; in most cases, more than anything else, the president wants assurance that life for him and his employees will not take a turn for the worse as a result of the sale. He and his employees want assurance that his authority, responsibility, and status will not be diminished in any way.

––The acquiring corporation's president sends a letter to all employees of the acquired company and encloses an annual report. In his letter he explains why he feels the company and its personnel are outstanding, and he cites the major *nonfinancial* benefits he expects from the acquisition.

One time we acquired a prestigious family-owned company in New England. The sellers' main anxiety was that the organization's superb reputation for product excellence be preserved. The company's quality image was, in fact, one of the main reasons we wanted to acquire it, and stressing this fact in the letter made a significant difference in their ultimate attitude and outlook.

––A joint announcement is sent to suppliers, major customers, and the business press, giving highlights of the agreement. This move has the same effect as a "business as usual" sign, but on a much greater scale.

––Within the first week after the signing, a dinner is scheduled for managerial and supervisory personnel of the newly acquired company. Both presidents speak, outlining expected benefits in more detail and stressing the importance of people to the success of the merger and the new opportunities for growth.

――In cooperation with the company president, the group management team sponsors discussions between key corporation personnel and key personnel of the acquired company's service organizations—its bankers, lawyers, accountants, and so forth. These discussions give real reassurance in many cases. In one acquisition, for example, the president wanted to know if he would be required to change the bank with which he dealt. We assured him that this was strictly up to him, explaining that it is our policy to respect the wishes of the seller so far as his relations to service organizations are concerned. As well as reducing seller anxieties about authority and self-determination, these discussions give group management valuable additional background.

――If possible, the community is reassured that the acquisition will not disrupt the local economy and will, in fact, produce new opportunities for growth and employment. This is frequently of special importance. If the acquired company is to continue to operate successfully, the community's cooperation and goodwill can be essential. In one acquisition, the team arranged for our corporation to take an option to buy 25 acres of land for expansion space, a move that convinced both the company and the community that our focus was on growth and not relocation. The town fathers were so pleased that the community agreed to pay for the grading of the land.

Once again, we should emphasize that group management organization can be useful in applying the first three rules only if it has been in on the proceedings up to the signing of the acquisition agreement and is fully aware of all the details of negotiation. The remaining six rules touch more closely on the team's primary function—managing the acquisition.

4. Fight the prima donna urge

A few years ago our team visited a newly acquired company in the Midwest. The weather was poor, and our plane landed at the airport two hours late. The president, a venerable, white-haired multimillionaire much older than any of us, was waiting for us in his car. We resolved on the spot, "Never again!" It has since been our stated policy to blend as naturally and harmoniously as we can into the seller company's pattern of doing business, to take no special advantage, and to ask no special favors.

A group manager should not expect to be treated as a visiting dignitary, and the one impression he ought to avoid giving is that he is an inspector general. In other words, don't make a visit into a visitation. Let the seller know early in the game that you don't want to be picked up at airports, escorted on night club tours, or given any other kind of preferential treatment. Make your own arrangements for transportation. And if, at times, you decide to work into the night, do so at your hotel, not on the company premises, where others may feel obligated to stay with you. If the seller feels uncomfortable about this, tell him that it is more important for him to be running his company than playing host on your behalf. Let him and his personnel understand that they are no more obligated to entertain a member of the group management team than they are to entertain associates in their own company.

Such matters, of course, must be handled with tact and finesse. On the one hand, you must convince people that you are not a prima donna. On the other, you do not want to convey the impression that you are snubbing them socially.

5. Sell yourself as the helmsman

In theory, the president of a group company will run it in line with the objectives that have been explicitly agreed on. Group management's function is to see to it that these objectives are met as specified and on schedule. Thus, in a very real sense, both parties are at the helm, the president as administrative head, and the group management team as manager and coordinator. If they are to work effectively together, group management must win the complete confidence and respect of the president. This is no easy task—it takes time, effort, and patience; and there are two major hurdles to overcome.

First, the president is generally older than the group manager. He has already "made it," and is probably prosperous. He knows his business and is accustomed to deferential treatment from his associates and subordinates. Moreover, as often as not, he is operating an enterprise that he or his family has built, and he will have strong proprietary feelings about it.

Second, a president is used to dealing with men at the top. At the outset he is apt to resent having to work with a group vice president rather than the present corporation's chief executive. Our experience proves that overcoming these obstacles requires a concentrated effort on the part of group management.

We have suggested that early in the game, during negotiations, group management should introduce a candidate's management to group company presidents who already are operating happily and profitably. This tactic is important in the present context because success sells itself—when a candidate sees that others are effectively managed, his respect for group management's professional competence will automatically rise.

One main task is to convince the president that you are there as much on his behalf as on the behalf of the parent company—that you are a direct embassy, an official mission from the top management at corporate headquarters to him, and as such can be of real use to him. Corporate headquarters can help immeasurably in getting this point across, and in our company we receive their full cooperation. In their contact with a group company, by policy, members of our top management work only through us. They do not even visit such a company without clearing their plans with the group management team.

Under such an arrangement, group management takes on its proper significance for the group president, and he quickly comes to understand its great potential usefulness to him. For example, should he make a request for additional capital, the request might stand no chance of being approved if he were to put it through directly. But a justified request stands *every* chance of approval if it is recommended by the group management team. This kind of thing is of extreme importance: it serves to build up the stature of the group management in the president's eyes, and this makes it easier for him to work with the team. He does not feel that he is "losing face" in any way.

Another good way to promote respect from the president is to convince him you are there to help him on a no-charge basis and, equally important, that your assistance is of real value. This sometimes requires aggressive group management action.

In one recent acquisition we did a comprehensive survey that analyzed in a unique way the sale of a group company's products by state. The study, a relatively sophisticated one, produced valuable information that the company had neither the facilities nor the experience to generate. This information proved to be an eye-opener for the president, which is exactly what we had in mind. As a result, he has since hired a much-needed market-research man. Prior to this he had taken our offers of help with an obvious grain of salt; today he comes to us regularly for assistance with a variety of projects and studies.

Details of physical setup can also help to convince the group company president that the management team's efforts are directed toward him specifically. For example, there are good reasons to separate physically group management offices from the offices of the corporate staff. To begin with, it reassures the company president that group management will not develop what might be called the "corporate staff personality." Also, it makes him aware that group management's concern is exclusively with companies it manages and not with other corporate activities. Third, it makes group management more easily accessible when problems arise.

Putting across group management's usefulness to the acquired company is a continuing job. Each time it visits a company, for example, a team should make it a point to bring something of value to the president, to remind him constantly of its help, and to maintain his esteem. Once his respect has been gained, the president will frequently consult group management on matters of production, marketing, personnel strategy, and so forth. The president will reciprocate the team's efforts, in other words, by providing full cooperation in the achievement of corporate objectives.

6. Motivate to the hilt

The·surest way to achieve corporate objectives after the acquisition has been made is to effectively motivate the management of the new company. The key man to work on is the president. Experience shows that if the president is properly motivated, he can generally be counted on to spark his own people in turn.

Motivation takes many forms, but it starts with compensation. Incentive compensation systems for group company personnel range from return on investment schemes to complicated agreements predicated on sales, profits, or on both. If an incentive compensation plan is to be effective, three conditions must be fulfilled:

––The terms of the acquisition agreement must be fully understood.

––The goals which it sets must be clear and attainable.

––Rewards for achievement must be sufficiently attractive.

An effective arrangement in some situations is a system which permits the president's income to rise over a predetermined period of, say, five years in direct proportion to his company's profit growth. Under this setup, usually, the year just prior to sale serves as a base for determining growth, and provisions are made as well for specific return on assets and on new capital expenditures. Where the growth potential is real, this can be an attractive incentive—one that ensures an aggressive attitude toward profit goals for at least the term of the agreement.

In structuring a motivational compensation plan, it is also useful to place both the acquired company management and group management under the same kind of plan. This serves as a unifying bond and makes it clear that both parties are moving toward the same goal. What is more, group management, because it is operating under the same profit incentive, will be in a better position psychologically to sell new programs, concepts, and strategies to the group company president.

Direct compensation, of course, is not the only way to motivate men financially. Another is the "growth opportunity" route. Thus, we try to stay alert to possible intercompany arrangements that can produce extra growth, and we encourage key personnel in the various group companies to seek out such possibilities themselves. We also encourage group companies to suggest acquisition candidates who would fit with their own operations. Presidents of group companies particularly appreciate this opportunity for external growth.

What really serves to motivate a president? This is an intriguing question. In one operating company, the president, a self-made millionaire, was recently given a 12% salary boost. Soon afterwards his top aide remarked, "The boss is pleased as punch. You should hear him crowing about that raise."

Is the money the motivation? We doubt it. We believe, rather, that the president lives in a lonely world. He is expected to be continuously cognizant of his duty to appreciate the good work of his people, but personal recognition for himself is not easy to come by. Money often means little to the millionaire—far more important to him is the fact that the parent company thought enough about the job he was doing to give him a raise.

It is, of course, no great revelation that in many cases the explicit recognition of a man's personal status can equal or surpass financial compensation as an effective motivator, but this fact is particularly relevant for group management. The most seemingly trivial action can take on deep personal significance for someone in a group company. Some months ago, for example, the president of a division was promoted to chairman. We announced his elevation to the press but reserved to him the right to announce the appointment of the new president. This was a small and subtle action, perhaps, but one of special importance to him.

7. Humanize management controls

Many smaller companies have inadequate accounting systems. It is thus doubly important to make sure that well-structured financial monitoring exists which will enable the group management team to take an accurate reading of results achieved by the group company's personnel. Otherwise, corporate headquarters may easily lose control of an operation, especially in the period of rapid growth which usually follows a transfusion of capital and management assistance.

We learned this the hard way. One of our early divisions doubled its sales (from $3 million to $6 million) within two years after acquisition. A final reckoning quickly took the sunshine out of the picture. It revealed an actual reduction in profits, which could largely be attributed to flimsy internal controls. We had made the mistake of building a powerful marketing organization and *assuming* that the financial house was in order just because the president had hired a new controller. It was anything *but* in order. Inventories were badly overstated; no one knew costs; financial controls were inefficient; an excess of uncollectible accounts receivable was on hand; and so forth.

It is an error we take great care not to repeat. Today we patiently explain our financial-reporting requirements and make clear *why* they are needed. This is important because small companies are usually not accustomed to preparing comprehensive, in-depth reports. The best period to start this spadework is in the preacquisition stages; then when the time for implementation comes, personnel of the acquired company will be prepared for reporting requirements. What if they offer resistance? This sometimes occurs, but it is almost invariably melted down by the offer, "Don't worry; we'll do it *for* you for the first couple of months." The trick here is to use the *sell, not tell* approach—to convince them of the benefits of such reporting. They will catch on quickly enough when they begin to understand the benefits.

One important control function, especially in larger acquiring companies, is performed by an internal auditing staff which visits each group company once or twice a year, or when something seems out of line. This staff in most cases reports directly to the corporate financial officers, and it provides an excellent outside check on the company's progress and financial controls. It is no substitute, however, for a good accounting system inside the group company.

The aim of any good control system is to prevent surprises. Hence the group management team should include an experienced controller if at all possible. He too will be cognizant of the importance of good communications, for however well structured the financial-control system may be, it will be difficult for him to take punctual and accurate soundings of progress and development unless the system is supplemented by effective human relationships.

Corporate service and overhead costs relating to an acquired company raise another issue. Some say they should be allocated to the group company. We disagree. This practice can trigger antagonism for the simple reason that the acquired company has no control over these costs. They are, after all, only paper charges, and can be added after the group income statements arrive at corporate headquarters. They are by no means essential to control, as such.

It must be stressed, furthermore, that figures alone cannot control an operation. They must be supported and reinforced by person-to-person communications. Group management ought to visit each acquisition at least once a month and maintain frequent telephone contact. We have found it advantageous to go to them rather than to ask them to present their problems at the corporate offices; group management is then in a better position to monitor on-the-spot performance. In reviewing our records, in fact, we find that last year our team spent 42% of its time visiting its group companies, and we do not see how we could have maintained effective rapport and control with any lesser expenditure of traveling time.

8. Cross-fertilize aggressively

How do you synergize successfully? The expansion of two plus two into five doesn't just happen—it must be managed. For the most part, synergizing boils down to a process of dovetailing the resources and abilities of different organizations in such a way as to create new sources of profit. The specific problem that faces group management here is to identify "fits" and to cash in on them by aggressively encouraging cross-fertilization. Because of its excellent vantage point, the group management team has a key responsibility to help spark and keep alive a never-ending flow of ideas.

We have developed a number of techniques for doing this. One is to make certain that there is continuous interaction among the management personnel of the group companies. For example, group management can sponsor informal meetings (for luncheon or dinner) for key group company personnel and personnel from related industries. A trade show is an ideal occasion for such meetings. In addition to encouraging exchanges of information and news of innovations, these meetings give the hard-working personnel a "day in court," which is an obvious motivational plus. If there are no convenient occasions for get-togethers of this kind, group management would do well to create a few.

Within the family, group management should also arrange meetings of controllers periodically at the corporate level. At the group level, the presidents, marketing personnel, purchasing agents, production personnel, and R&D personnel should be brought together from time to time. Again, these meetings will serve a dual purpose: to disseminate information and ideas and to supply psychological motivation.

Concomitantly, the team should also see to it that group companies have the authority and responsibility to follow up sound ideas generated by the cross-fertilization process. To accomplish this, the team may have to help spell out the benefits of a venture and establish its ground rules; and while this can be a slow and difficult process, the team's vantage point once again makes it the ideal unit for the task, and the results are often well worth the effort required.

We should like to mention four specific areas in which systematic cross-fertilization has substantially increased our profit.

Marketing. We hold two special meetings a year for the key marketing executives of our group companies. At the first meeting, they outline their companies' programs for the year ahead and comment on recent successes and failures. This exposes each company to the others' programs, which is extremely helpful to their efforts at self-evaluation. It also develops a constructive, competitive spirit among them, and gives them a variety of approaches and thus a better understanding of the total market.

At the second meeting, the group management team presents creative marketing concepts. Our aim here is to generate interest and thought about long-range problems and strategies, as well as to help educate and broaden the viewpoint of marketing personnel.

Purchasing. Several of our companies manufacture products using similar materials. Because of our decentralized operating philosophy, these group companies had no obvious way to cash in on the economies that centralized purchasing arrangements can offer. We came up with what has proved to be a simple and effective solution: we ask each group company to submit a summary of materials purchased each year—by volume, source, terms, specifications, and so forth. We, in turn, cross-tabulate the individual summaries into an overall summary for distribution to all the companies in the group. This does two things:

1. It provides a guide for the individual purchasing manager that enables

him to evaluate objectively his own buying policies and performance. Thus corporation-wide comparison spurs him to strive more vigorously to improve his relative performance.

2.   The factual documentation gives the purchasing manager a strong lever to use in negotiating with suppliers on items for which other purchasing managers have obtained more favorable deals than he has. As a result, group companies are able to achieve substantial cost savings without the authority and responsibility of individual purchasing managers being watered down.

Production.   Promoting visits of one company's production and management people to other group companies can be most effective. In one company, for example, we observed that it took the plant 120 hours to manufacture a specified number of items. Another company did a similar job in only 80 hours. We suggested that Company A's production people pay Company B a visit. They did so, and were introduced to a more efficient tooling setup which they have since adopted in their own operations with outstanding results.

R&D.   One of our larger acquisitions invested considerable capital and engineering expertise in the development of certain molds and vacuumforming machinery. Our knowledge of operations told us the development might be useful to some of our smaller companies in their own production processes. We brought in the presidents and production people from these companies to observe the innovation. Some of them found it beneficial to duplicate the innovation, which could have cost them a considerable sum if they had initiated it on their own.

Experience shows that the benefits generated through cross-fertilization of ideas can be an important factor in meeting the profit objectives set for group-companies. But it must be stressed again that these benefits do not come automatically; they depend largely on group management's effectiveness as a catalyzing agent. The process cannot be forced. It must be carefully planned and discreetly nurtured.

9. Make the group manager a "man for all seasons"

Group management must wear a variety of hats. First and foremost, it must never divorce itself from the actions, good or bad, taken by individual companies, since it has the authority, as an ultimate expedient, to change programs or personnel that it thinks will impede the achievement of objectives. Hence it must never lose sight of its final responsibility for the acquired company's failure or success. Group management treads a fine line between its function of motivator on the one hand and responsibility center on the other.

To sustain this delicate balance, the group manager must indeed be versatile—a "man for all seasons." Most of all he needs the human understanding and the flexibility required to fulfill in a professional manner a variety of roles that range from consultant, catalyst, and coordinator to innovator, ambassador, and boss. And he must play these roles with infinite care, or he will give the impression that he is trying to become a satrap.

We shall discuss some of these roles and illustrate how we have played them.

Consultant.   To act as a professional consultant, the group manager must possess a thorough knowledge of the group company's strengths and weaknesses and its relative position in the industry as a whole. If he has a strong background, he can often offer sound advice. But as a consultant per se, he must be content to *advise,* and not try to *impose* his ideas.

We recall a good case in point. A group company urgently needed a finance plan for its dealer network, and we volunteered our services to help devise it. The plan we developed was sophisticated and superior, well tested and well proved. Group management, we feel bound to add, did an outstanding job of presenting the plan at a joint meeting of company and dealer personnel. In the absence of opposition, we assumed that the arrangement was acceptable to all. This was a mistake.

The plan was a complicated one. And because it was *our* plan, the group company's marketing personnel did not extend themselves to understand it fully. As a result, they were not qualified to administer it properly; and, much worse, they did not assume a personal commitment for its success. Needless to say, the plan failed.

It can be a great mistake for group management to bluntly impose ideas, methods, or systems on group personnel. If the idea "belongs" to the team, they may rely on the team to make it work. Among other things, this can provoke the company president, since it is his job, not group management's, to run the company. And if the program fails, the blame is certain to fall on group management's shoulders, not the company's.

Ambassador. Group management represents the parent corporation to the family companies; but it is also part of group management's job to represent the acquired company to the parent—when capital expenditures are needed, for example, as we have already mentioned. This has two benefits: *(a)* it heightens group management's status in the eyes of the group companies; and *(b)* it makes it advantageous for the acquired companies to work closely and harmoniously with group management, to keep it abreast of requirements, to make sure it fully understands their problems and goals, and to ensure that their needs are effectively represented.

In one company, a $400,000 expansion move was suddenly required to meet sales commitments. The problems involved were complex, but having been in on their development, the team fully understood the reasons for the move and approved of it. Within 24 hours the required sum was forthcoming, an action which left the president with a deep respect for group management's influence at headquarters.

Coordinator. In addition to promoting cross-fertilization, group management must at times resolve an intercompany conflict. This becomes a vital service when the conflict threatens to injure profits—where two acquisitions are competing in the same market, for example.

One such situation was potentially explosive. Studying the problem, we determined that the facilities of one company were ideal for production. The other company's marketing setup made it better suited for distribution. The solution suggested itself. We helped establish a third, jointly owned, corporation that combined the production capabilities of the first company with the second company's distribution system. This new corporation produced and marketed a profitable line more economically than either company could have done on its own.

Innovator. The wise group manager uses the *sell, not tell* approach to put his innovations across.

For example, one of group management's major concerns is the development of well-qualified personnel in acquired companies. Sometimes this means suggesting that a key executive be hired from outside, a suggestion that is commonly resisted. In one situation we saw the need for a competent controller to modernize a company's financial system. The president was dead set against our suggestion to hire one. We could have forced the mandate on him, but preferred to win him by persuasion if possible. With this in mind, we agreed to bring in a man and pay his salary for six months. At the end of this time, we told the president, we would relocate the new man if he didn't work out. When six months had rolled by, the president thanked us for our help and put the new controller on his own company payroll.

Boss. In any enterprise, the leadership role is the most critical, the most difficult to establish, and the one requiring the most courage and imagination. As we understand it from the point of view of group management, the boss role involves *(a)* giving strong personal support to company management, *(b)* accepting responsibility for failure as well as for success, and *(c)* removing roadblocks that may impede progress toward profit objectives. In fulfilling his responsibility as a leader, the group manager, like any other manager, must often weigh long-term gains against short-term ones.

We recall one case that makes our point about leadership responsibility by perhaps overstating it. Several years ago the president of a newly acquired company requested a $50,000 capital expenditure to develop a new product. On reviewing the situation, our team decided that the idea stood little chance of success. On the other hand, our personal relationship with the man was still in the formative stage, and we concluded that turning his request down might dampen his motivation and shake his confidence in our willingness to go to bat for him. Also, his record of achievement was good. Therefore, although we expressed our doubts, we approved the request.

Later, when failure did occur, we assumed responsibility for it. The president never forgot this incident, and his subsequent performance made up for the loss many times over. Moreover, when we felt we had to reject requests from him from time to time, the president did not balk. It cost $50,000 to establish the president's confidence in our judgment, but it is one of the best investments we ever made.

What happens if corporate objectives are not achieved? First, group management should make every effort to determine what is wrong. If exhaustive investigation shows that what is wrong is the president himself, group management has no choice but to replace him.

We remember one case in which the culmination of months of unsatisfactory profit results was a personal confrontation with the president. Investigation revealed beyond any doubt that the potential for excellent profit performance existed in the operation, but to bring it out would require substantial replanning and a fresh approach. Repeated dealings with the president convinced us that he was unable to cope with the task and that a change therefore had to be made. Unpleasant as this kind of responsibility may be, group management must face it squarely.

What about this president's own men? How did they react to a new president? This was less of a problem than we expected. Most of the key personnel were sharply aware of the boss's shortcomings. *They* knew (even better than we) that he was holding back the company and limiting their own earnings and growth. When the change was made, the general feeling was one of relief.

FINAL WORD

A group management force must be carefully designed to meet the responsibilities that are to be assigned to it. Its members ought to be persuasive, sensitive to human needs, quick to learn, flexible and imaginative in action, with a thorough understanding of the companies with which they are dealing and the corporation that they represent. If they are given the opportunity to participate early and to take the reins firmly in hand after the acquisition agreement has been signed, they can successfully perform a new kind of role in the business world by adapting common managerial techniques to the special challenges of group management.

APPENDIX B
Roger M. Davis
"Want to get rich"*

Dear Jack:

Thanks for your letter telling me that you'd decided to become a conglomerate. It's about time you wised up and resolved, as they say, to flourish and make megabucks instead of knocking yourself out trying to keep the earnings of your crummy foundry from going down.

You ask how to do it. Brains, guts, funny money, a smile and a shoeshine ought to be a sufficiency. It's really not much harder or very different from promoting one of those chain-letter games we used to play when we were kids. And don't kid yourself, it may end the same way. But you make a lot more money.

Those Meistersingers

Anyway, the first thing to do is get hold of the speeches and annual reports of the real savvy swingers, who know the lingo and can make it sing. Guys like Duke of Whittaker, Singleton of Teledyne, Stone of Monogram. The Gulf & Western guys are too crude; they call movies "leisure time" and talk about feeding the world with sugar, but it doesn't grab. As for Textron, they run a good 19th Century conglomerate by Graham and Dodd, thinking about archaic concepts like assets, book value and working capital per share.

Actually, for my money, a cat out on the West Coast has the real psychedelic line—it's too bad you're not a doctor of something like he is. This doctor stuff and a research-technology background goes over very big with the security analysts. Anyway, read his stuff. He's got all the moves.

Like productizing

He made a speech to the San Francisco security analysts, where he talked about "advanced material systems," "productizing R&D" and "the tools of growth: nucleation, replication, and working the synergies." He told *Business Week* the aim of his acquisition program was to provide "rivers of marketing into which we can feed the higher technology materials and products," and yaks about "the point of nucleation for a large scale market penetration."

And this from a cat with about two-thirds of sales in defense parts, valves, actuators, structures and metals brokerage-and-distribution. At least the last time I looked that's the way it read, but at the rate he's making deals, it's hard to stay current on earnings, much less product mix.

In the presentation at San Francisco, the Whittaker guys must have talked at least an hour about technology, philosophy and the future, and hardly mentioned their present business except to repeat that they were a growth company "in the area of advanced materials systems." Duke bought a fishing rod company, Shakespeare, and convinced the analysts he had integrated forwards into materi-

---

*This article by John Wall was reproduced with permission from *Barron's*, February 5, 1968.

als usage. Next it will be further forward integration with a string company, and, of course, with that he's got the perfect hook for a move into oceanography—a very high-multiple area, incidentally.

That foundry of yours could be used, in Whittaker jargon, as your "nucleus for growth" in the apocryphal fields of specialty metals and materials technology.

But to go on, I think in general it's a mistake to admit that your acquisition program is mostly opportunistic—although realistically it has to be. Jim Ling of LTV pretty much concedes that he's opportunistic and the market doesn't like it. Analysts and investors want conceptually oriented conglomerates, preferably in high-technology areas. That's what they pay the high price-earnings ratio for, and life is a lot less sweaty with a high multiple.

But you've got to be more articulate and convincing about your concepts than those Gulf & Western guys, who say, about chemicals, fertilizer, auto parts, movies, etc., that the rationale "has to do with population and great growth." That's no good. Analysts are only analysts, but even they know that everybody's got population growth going for them.

Now G&W—there's a perfect case of conglomerate in dire need of sophisticated promotion. They must have doubled their earnings in the last year and the stock hasn't moved. The best thing they've done on the P-E front is to take out the ampersand and put in the plus between Gulf and Western. Gulf + Western?

The interface with change

The point is that you have to project the right image to the analysts so they realize you're the new breed of entrepreneur. Talk about the synergy of the free-form company and its interface with change and technology. Tell them you have a windowless room full of researchers with genius IQ's scrutinizing the future so your corporation will be opportunity-technology oriented, so it will fashion change rather than merely respond to it like stupid old GM. Copy Roy Ash, who wrote the book, soliloquize about flexibility, mobility, and the importance of pace, whatever that means.

Always talk "bottom line" and "earnings per share" so they know you're interested in the price of your stock. And don't be afraid to project earnings for next year, five years out, even 10. Nobody's going to remember those forecasts in 1972. Tell them you and your young team are dedicated to internal growth of 15% to 20% annually, and external growth from acquisitions of another 20%, so that for the next five years you can grow at least 35% to 40% a year.

Guys like Stone, Duke and "Automatic" Sprinkler's Harry Figgie make projections like that all the time. Figgie even says it in his quarterly reports to shareholders. The analysts? They swallow it without even chewing. They'd much prefer you make the projections for them rather than to have to do it for themselves.

That certain smile

And when some wise guy asks you how you can get 15% to 20% growth from a foundry or a meat packer or an auto parts company that has grown at a 2% rate historically, give him that smile and show him that shoeshine and tell him how your efficiency experts have isolated millions of dollars of excess costs; your market geniuses have found four fresh, uninhabited markets; and besides you can triple the margins in the next three years.

Another thing, never use a little, simple, understandable word when you can use a big complex one. Talk about market matrixes, core technology fulcrums, modular building blocks, and the "nucleus theory of growth," a la Mr. Figgie. Sprinkle your language with scientific and electronic terms like bionics, electromagnetics, fiber optics. No one from Wall Street may know what you mean but everyone gets that nice warm feeling of being in the mainstream of the thrust of technology.

And learn how to describe the business you've bought: ship-building is marine systems, zinc mining goes into the minerals division, a steel company is materials technology. A lighting fixture or lock company, that fits into your protective services division. (Crime prevention is a high-multiple growth industry these days.)

The in crowd

But you have to be alert. Styles change and you may have to flip nomenclature and maybe even businesses. A few months ago supplemental airlines were very in; now they're way out and several conglomerates (the best known being Transamerica) got stuck. Poor LTV took over its airline just as Wall Street got disenchanted with the group.

Incidentally, be sure to tell the analysts you look at 20 to 30 deals for every one you buy. Makes you sound discriminating. And talk about breakfast and Sunday meetings to build that go-go-atmosphere.

Some of the big hitters claim they can walk through a plant and tell whether it's profitable or not. You might go them one better by saying you can do it blindfolded and decide from the noise and smell. This is important, too. Never, never mention balance sheets. They're out, old fashioned, even chicken—and besides, yours is likely to be far from robust.

But don't overdo the materialistic stuff. The "modern manager" is supposed to be a renaissance man—a humanist concerned with his own, and his corporation's, role in society. So be a man for all seasons. Talk about the problems of the times—air pollution, water, the ghettos, poverty, integration—and explain how you want to evolve a systems approach to their solution. Later on you probably should collect art.

One other point on analysts. You've got to have the right setting when you see them. Don't forget you're supposed to have charisma, to be a man on horseback. My idea would be to have a modern, functionally luxurious (but not opulent) office. Lots of papers and notebooks around and a sheaf of wall charts. Have a blackboard full of mathematical formulas. And have at least three secretaries in your suite—suggesting it takes that many to handle your output. They should be real lookers but demurely dressed.

If you can, I think it's a good practice to affect the clipped, precise, McNamara style and have your coat off and maybe even your sleeves rolled up (if you've got manly arms). Exude charm and animal vitality. As your conglomerate gets larger, it's wise to have a straightman around to tell the analysts how magnificent you are and how you work 20 hours a day and sleep only four.

Name the game

Next you've got to get a new corporate name. As I see it, you can go either of a couple of ways. Get a flamboyant, high-technology name like Teledyne or Electro-Laser-Optic Instrument Corp., or low-key it with a classy moniker that's descriptive of nothing, like Litton, Monogram or Whittaker. Obviously something like Textron with its textile association is dreadful; they have no one to blame but themselves for the fact that it took years before they were selling at over 15 times earnings.

A complete name change is much better than a partial. For example, White Consolidated Industries is too close to White Sewing Machine. And that initial stuff like LTV or FMC leaves me cold. It sounds cheap, low-multiple, but that's just a personal prejudice.

O.K. Now after all the preparation, you're ready for your first public announcement, which is to tell the analysts that you're going to become a conglomerate and expound your acquisition concept and philosophy of modern management. In Wall Street parlance this means you're an "emerging conglomerate," and that statement alone will put at least 10 points on your stock—fast. (Be sure you get your options program set up before the announcement.)

After a little while you can announce your name change, which will give the stock another jab, and about the same time you've got to grab somebody away from Litton. It doesn't much matter who he was or what you have him do, but the mere announcement of a Litton guy to work on your acquisition program will put another 10 points on the stock and it gives the analysts something to say in their reports. Actually so many Litton people have defected in the past year that it's getting very tough to acquire one with any real experience. But that doesn't matter just as long as he's from Litton.

Beards and slide rules

Eventually you've also got to get some intellectual-looking creeps, maybe with beards, to be your long-range planning staff. The odder they look, the more impressed the security analysts will be. Then you'll need some bright-looking slide-rule types out of Arthur D. Little to form the team that goes out and doctors sick divisions, and a couple of accountants from Arthur Andersen to run the accounting controls section at corporate headquarters which will monitor the divisions' financial performance.

Wall Street is very sensitive to early-warning accounting systems which can alert headquarters to trouble, ever since the Evans Products' fiasco. So every presentation must include a section on corporate controls. It's boilerplate, but you've got to have the language on variance accounting, exception reporting with red circles, inventory input analysis, burden deviations and triple-early-warning systems. The other standard line is that you control and motivate by having the profit center at the lowest possible level.

Of course, these are the same techniques every well-run major corporation has employed for years, but it will give you the free-form management, people-depth aura that you've got to have to sustain a 20-plus multiple.

As Lammot DuPont Copeland put it: "Running a conglomerate is a job for management geniuses, not for ordinary mortals like us at DuPont." You wonder how all the different divisions will run themselves, since you don't know anything about the businesses they're in. Relax—and hope. Hope, hope, hope that we keep having prosperity, that only one or two go sour at a time, that you can make deals big enough to paper over their bad figures, and that if the whole thing falls apart you can get out before the deluge.

Don't own up to it

Incidentally, one thing I forgot. Never, under any circumstances admit you're a conglomerate. Kidee is just about the only one that concedes it's a conglomerate. Whittaker? "We're no conglomerate," says Duke, "we're a product-oriented growth company." Litton? No. "Litton is a large and growing group of creative people." City Investing? Scharffenberger told the New York Society of Security Analysts: "Please, whatever you say about City, don't call us a conglomerate." Gulf & Western? Bluhdorn says he doesn't know what a conglomerate is, but he does know that G&W is a company in motion—"a moving picture, not a snapshot." "Automatic" Sprinkler? Figgie hates the word "conglomerate" and prefers to be called a free-form company.

You get the idea. Those other guys are dirty, deal-doing conglomerates, but you're a nice, clean, free-form growth company.

Acquisition gimmicks

Now about acquisitions. It's always been a chain-letter game where you swap your funny-money preferreds or high price-earnings-ratio common for lower-multiple stock. The trouble is that now there are so many people who want to play, competition has created new gimmicks. For example, a conglomerate's stock is selling at 75 and it buys a company for a million shares. To sweeten the deal the conglomerate agrees that if the stock isn't worth $100 million in a year, it will issue enough additional shares, regardless of the earnings of the acquired company, to bring the value to the selling company up to $100 million.

At first glance that may look a little hairy, because if the conglomerate's stock is selling at, say, 50 instead of the anticipated 100, it obviously will have to issue twice as many shares. But that's the way the game's being played, and modern management doesn't think about its stock going down.

Another new twist is a variation on the old technique of issuing additional shares if the earnings of the acquired company have increased. Some conglomerates now will issue additional stock if the earnings of the acquired company stay the same in the year following acquisition, still more if the earnings go up based on a complex formula that includes the future market price of the conglomerate's stock.

Paying the piper

The other problem on acquisitions is that it's a seller's market with a vengeance. In the old days—five years ago—Textron and Litton were virtually alone and had things all their own way. Today Litton has to pay 20 times top-of-the-cycle earnings for a machine tool company and over 30 times for a restaurant and frozen food company that it would have sniffed at paying 15 times for in 1961.

So don't have any illusions. Everybody's paying up for earnings that are often inflated and maybe even buying a lot of obsolete inventory, worn-out plants and unfunded pension plans in the bargain.

Obviously, there's a big difference between buying a good, growing company at 10 to 15 times earnings when you're selling at 25 times and buying a problem company at 20 times that you've got to put management and money into to turn around.

Bottom of the barrel

In other words, the whole acquisition area has been picked so clean in the last few years that there are no more bargains around. Every hick manager knows or thinks he knows what his company is worth, and when you try to get tough and make a tender, some other conglomerate will boom in and top your bid. Certain conglomerates now are grossly overpaying for second-and third-rate companies, but you and everybody else will have to keep running because acquisitions are what make the earnings and stock prices go up. And if the acquisitions ever stopped, and you had to rely on the internal growth of your junk collection, you and the stock would be headed south.

Of course, there are a few things you can do with accounting to make your acquisition look better—you know capitalizing stuff that used to be written off, sale and leasebacks, stretch depreciation schedules, that kind of thing. You have to get a real savvy accountant who knows all the angles. Pooling of interests, purchase of assets, combination; he'll show you the best way. He can make the comparative figures look good, at least for awhile. But by all means, never show goodwill or the premium above book value of acquisitions on your balance sheet. Those things really bug Wall Street.

Art of reporting

In my next letter I'll tell you more about annual and quarterly reports and how to write them. Remember, though, they've got to have thick rich prose, sort of like *Fortune,* and be full of glossy photographs of plants and products to lend substance and credibility. It's real art. You want emphasis on concepts and imagery, but some guys get carried away. LTV had one called "Building Lasting Values from the Golden Age of Greece" that was full of urns, chariots, and pictures of great men from Socrates and Thomas Edison to Jim Ling.

But Litton's the past master. This year they featured a stained glass overlay with the allegory that "the responsive corporation like Litton in a challenging environment calls upon a similar respect for vision joined to enterprise." Pure baloney on vellum, and expensive to produce, too, but it's all part of the game. Incidentally, if Litton's stock keeps going down, Ash and Thornton are going to be facing a challenging environment of their own. A high multiple is their staff of life, the magic wand that makes acquisitions and earnings come true.

So that's it for the first installment on forming a conglomerate. Just remember you're not trying to build General Motors. You're pasting together with words and music and acquisitions a corporate hodgepodge whose parts may or may not have some common bond of affinity. In any case this polyglot is going to have massive operating and financial leverage, and be so diverse that not even Adam Smith or Alfred Sloan could really manage it.

If you pull off some good deals, and if the economy stays strong and your luck holds, you'll make a fortune, become a Captain of American Industry, and your stockholders will make some money too. If you pull off some bad deals or the economy goes sour at the wrong time—well, at least you ought to know enough to get out fast.

Anyway, keep the faith baby, and I'm buying some of your stock today. There's nothing like an "emerging conglomerate" to get action in this market. Charisma and conglomerates forever,

Yours,

Charlie

Note

Venture capital: What it is and how to raise it

INTRODUCTION

There exists a spectrum of definitions of venture capital investing, including the following:

1. Investing in any high-risk financial venture.
2. Investing in unproven ideas, products, or start-up situations; that is, providing what is called "seed capital."
3. Investing in going concerns that are unable to raise funds from conventional public or commercial sources.
4. Investing in large and possibly controlling interests in publicly traded companies where uncertainty is significant.

This Note concentrates on the venture capital activity which lies in the middle of the above spectrum and typically involves investments of $50,000 to $5 million. Interestingly enough, seed capital situations are considered by some individuals or firms as too risky to be described as suitable for venture capital and by others as the only form of "pure" venture capital investment opportunity. This Note first includes a discussion of the seed capital stage as background for the more common venture capital situation. Although many of the principles discussed apply to raising funds for almost any investment opportunity, the primary emphasis is on the financing of industries involving manufacturing operations rather than those in real estate, entertainment, retail, or service ventures.

VENTURE CAPITAL SOURCES

The range of venture capital sources is broad when one considers that any entity with funds is, at least, a potential source of venture capital.

461

However, this Note considers venture capital investors to be those sources that are frequent suppliers of such capital and that seek profit primarily through realization of capital gains. A description of the various types of venture capital investors and their objectives is fundamental to understanding this type of investing.

1. *Wealthy individuals* are a prime source of venture capital, especially for seed capital. When relatively small sums ($5,000–$100,000) are involved, individuals are inclined to accept greater risks than institutional venture capital investors, especially when the individuals are in a high personal income tax bracket. They are also inclined to be less formal and less thorough in their investigation and examination of the situation. Their involvement in an investment may range from an arm's-length relationship to a complete domination of the venture. Quite often commercial and investment bankers have wealthy clients who desire to make investments that offer the potential for substantial capital gains. Doctors and other professional men are other good sources of seed or the more risky type of capital.

2. *Small business investment companies (SBICs)* are privately or publicly owned, government chartered suppliers of capital to businesses. They were formed specifically to increase the availability of venture capital throughout the country. There are over 300 SBICs today with assets from roughly $300,000 to around $20 million. There is, however, tremendous variation between the operations and objectives of different SBICs. It is possible to categorize SBICs, but it must be remembered that within these categories there exist many differences.

Captive SBICs are usually guided by the objectives of the parent organization. The most common example is the bank SBIC where emphasis is more often on grooming future bank customers than on making a capital gain. Other SBICs may be associated with larger venture capital outfits or even industrial concerns.

Noncaptive SBICs are independent; however, the nature of their ownership also determines their philosophy. Some are privately held by a few individuals, some partially by institutions, and some by the public through widespread distribution of their stock. These SBICs are usually more oriented toward capital gains and are more flexible than captive SBICs.

In both categories of SBICs there are those that tend to specialize in a particular industry, area, or type of risk. Most SBICs are interested in some form of equity participation; however, there are some that concentrate solely on lending money at interest rates up to 15 percent.

A total of 324 actively operating SBICs are located throughout the country, down from a figure of over 600 in the mid-1960s. They are restricted to making loans within the United States and its territories such as Puerto Rico and the Virgin Islands.

Most SBICs are oriented toward 5- to 20-year long-term investments. They are limited by law to a minority shareholder position except in situations where some covenant of the original purchase agreement has been violated. Under these circumstances, they may have the stock placed in a voting trust. These covenants typically relate to the profit-making ability of the firm, specifying a certain level of profits to be reached at a set time. Another restricting regulation prohibits SBICs from investing in more than 20 percent of their capital in any one venture.

Because of limitations upon the types of nonportfolio investments they can make, SBICs are also limited by their size in the amount of staff they can afford to support. In fact, many SBICs are run part time by one individual. The limited staff curbs the effectiveness of these smaller SBICs in consulting with their investments on business problems. Because of the aforementioned factors, the size of an SBIC greatly determines its suitability for financing certain ventures.

It can be said that SBICs, in general, are more apt to come in contact with the more "mundane" business ventures rather than the "glamorous" ones often referred to in literature about the field. Many SBICs limited in geographic area and management talent, invest in the smaller businesses located in their area. Their chief advantage is an intimate knowledge of local businessmen and local sources of capital. They are often forced by their stockholders to invest in less risky ventures to show a return on their investment.

3. *Private venture capital firms* are usually related to family fortunes. However, a few publicly held firms exist in the field. Family firms are especially interested in ventures that will relate to a contribution to industry, technology, or society. For example, sea water conversion, air pollution control, and mass transportation are currently considered very promising fields. Nevertheless, these firms are often forced to seek investments of a less glamorous nature to keep their funds actively invested.

One of the more dominant characteristics of these institutions is the maintenance of the reputation of the family name connected with the firm. Night clubs, liquor stores, or brassiere manufacturers are usually unacceptable as investments. The opinion was expressed, however, that if the family's name were not directly connected with the firm's name, greater freedom existed in making such investments. A large firm, as an example, recently sold its investment in an underwear manufacturer at a sizable gain.

The extent to which these firms become involved in the management of the venture varies greatly. However, they are most likely to cast themselves in a role somewhere between that of a director and that of a management consultant.

Because of the caliber of men they can afford to have on their staff, these private venture capital firms are apt to be more sophisticated investors than the other sources except for the larger SBICs. For this same reason, they can also be of great assistance to a new company. The investment opportunities they prefer are those involving $100,000 or more; nevertheless, they do make smaller investments upon rare occasions.

4. *Corporation venture capital activities* have been set up in some large industrial companies to make investments usually in related but noncompeting fields—several of the larger manufacturing companies, oil companies, and insurance companies are quite active. At present these represent the most rapidly growing segment of the venture capital sources. Their objective is usually to cultivate a potential merger candidate, a potential supplier or customer, or to provide a service to society. Some firms with large research and development budgets emphasize spin-offs of internally generated patents, products, or going businesses. However, because venture capital and related activities are such a minor part of a corporation's overall activities, quite frequently top management attention is not oriented in this direction. As a result, corporate venture capital investing falls below its potential.

5. *Public offerings.* From time to time it is possible to raise start-up funds from public markets which happen to be particularly receptive to highly speculative new issues. Usually, however, some amount of seed capital is required prior to raising public money. The types of investment banking firms which take new ventures public frequently are not the types of firms with which the entrepreneur would want to develop lasting relations. Also he may find that public stockholders and related government reporting requirements during the early, uncertain years of a company's life may be a considerable expense and nuisance.

6. *Miscellaneous.* There are other potential sources of venture capital which do not fall into the previous categories. Frequent sources are "idea brokers" who seek funds for an investment from their many contacts when a suitable venture is found rather than already having a fixed pool of funds. Such brokers either make their profit by investing some of their own funds or by charging a finder's fee. Other sources are private foundations, investment or management companies, investment groups, and investment banking firms. The activities of these latter groups are not predominantly in the venture capital field; nevertheless, they are always potential venture capital investors.

There are several other aspects to venture capital investing which are important for an understanding of the venture capital investor and how he operates. First of all, the cost of maintaining a staff to evaluate and administer venture capital investments is a serious limitation even for the larger firms. As an example, there are only 10 active management personnel in a large venture capital firm with portfolio investments of over \$20 million. For this reason, it is not surprising to find that the venture capital community is a very small one. Most of the prominent venture capital investors, whether they operate regionally or nationally, know or have worked with each other. They are all in on what might be described as the "deals flow" or off the mainstream in one of the many regional deal flows. As ventures grow or mature, many of the venture capital investors move from these fringe areas into the mainstream. This close-knit community has produced several phenomena of interest to the entrepreneur:

——Venture capital investors often go in on ventures together in order to minimize their investment and to share the risk.
——Venture capital investors have high ethical standards in most cases. Those venture capital investors who do not abide by the ethics of the financial world are quickly discovered and excluded from deals. The reputation of a highly regarded venture capital investor is his most important asset.
——As soon as a venture is turned down by one venture capital investor, other venture capital investors often become wary of it, but venture capital investors often will recommend ventures they have rejected to other venture capital investors who might find it more to their liking.

As one moves away from the main deals flow, one must become increasingly careful with whom he is dealing: the high level of ethics found among the prominent venture capital firms, unfortunately, does not always exist outside the mainstream.

RAISING THE INITIAL SEED CAPITAL FOR A NEW VENTURE

The first venture capital is needed when the talk and ideas of a venture begin to move into the active planning stages. The initiator of the venture, the entrepreneur, might be one or more inventors, scientists, engineers, promoters, or businessmen.[1] Except in those cases where the entrepreneur has sufficient resources of his own, he must raise the initial seed capital for the venture from some other source.

A seed capital situation arises whenever a new venture is of such a nature that the investor is essentially the first to put money into the project. Seed capital might typically be used to make a feasibility study, develop a new product or idea into the prototype stage, or start up a new company. Thus, in cases where either the venture or the founder has little or no track record with which to evaluate its possible success, a

---

[1]The term *entrepreneur* will be used throughout this Note as meaning the man or group of men who are trying to establish a new venture.

special form of higher risk venture capital, seed capital, is usually called for.

There are many reasons why most venture capital investors, especially those that are institutionalized, tend to shy away from investing in seed capital situations. These reasons typically are:

Risk

--The entrepreneur has no track record of proven business experience.

--Until the idea or business is fully developed or in operation it is almost impossible to assess its feasibility.

Cost

--It is uneconomical to invest money in many small ventures because the cost of thoroughly studying each of them often is between $3,000 to $4,000.

Price

--Even for only $20,000 the venture capital investor must receive something sufficiently large to make the risk worth his while. This may mean that he would require a seemingly large part of the company for that amount. When seed capital investments are successful, the entrepreneur is apt to think that the venture capital investor took advantage of him. He usually fails to understand that the venture capital investor took a high proportion of the equity in order to compensate for the greater uncertainties inherent in a start-up situation.

For these reasons, the entrepreneur should not use up his goodwill early in the life of the venture by asking venture capital investors for money before he has exhausted the more common sources of seed capital.[2] These sources frequently are:

--Personal savings and income.

--Family, friends, and close acquaintances who are apt to supply money on very favorable terms.

--Past employers who have confidence in the entrepreneur and his project and are willing to invest in both.

--Reasonably well-to-do individuals (especially doctors and lawyers) who have funds to invest.

--Industrial companies that are interested in the development or purchase of new products or ideas. (If personal independence is not a predominant factor, these may be the most appropriate sources.)

--A few "brokers" and firms established to provide capital for seed situations.

---

[2] In approaching seed capital sources, most of the procedures described later in the report for approaching a venture capital investor are applicable to seed situations and should be followed.

In raising this seed capital from the above sources, there are many pitfalls an entrepreneur should avoid. Problems that arise most frequently when raising seed capital are:

--The investor who desires to make a fast profit and is not really concerned with what is best for the entrepreneur or the long-range success of the venture.

--The investor who is unethical in any manner.

--The investor who expects or has been promised a quick profit (often this is the fault of the entrepreneur) and who becomes easily disenchanted when the gains do not materialize in the expected time.

--The "investor" who promises money but dispenses the cash very slowly, in a piecemeal fashion, or not at all and causes a disruption in the operation of the venture and in the entrepreneur's plans.

--The investor who desires to run his own business and begins to move the entrepreneur aside if the venture succeeds.

Consequently, in seeking seed capital the entrepreneur should use those financial sources with which he is best acquainted and with whom he thinks he can best get along.

The handling of the seed capital stage by the entrepreneur gives a venture capital investor a record of performance on which he can base his analysis of the venture. In his evaluation, a venture capital investor will typically be interested in the following areas surrounding the seed or incubation state of a venture:

--Did the entrepreneur go about raising seed capital in a logical and effective way?

--Has he been able to sell himself and his venture to other people?

--Did those who knew the entrepreneur have faith in him?

--Has he utilized the most logical sources of seed capital available to him?

--Has the entrepreneur been perseverant? Has he been and is he now fully committed to the venture? Has he made personal financial sacrifices?

--How has he handled his setbacks and disappointments so far?

--Has the entrepreneur been realistic in his projections to date?

--Has he been able to budget his use of time and money?

The sophisticated venture capital investor is looking for initial evidence of qualities in the entrepreneur that will be essential to the future of a venture. Because of this factor, the entrepreneur should be extremely careful in the seed stage. If he handles the incubation period of his venture poorly, his future ability to raise funds will be severely jeopardized. If the entrepreneur cannot give affirmative answers to most of the questions above, then he most likely is not personally ready to go to a sophisticated venture capital investor in search of funds.

There are certain types of situations where venture capital investors will go into a venture in what is considered the seed capital stage. Nevertheless, even in the following examples of such seed investments, there is usually some evidence of an earlier commitment of capital or time by someone.

--A group of four scientists with a well-thought-out plan and a professional consultant's study of a certain industry (for which the group spent $10,000 of their own funds) succeeded in raising $40 million for a start-up situation.

--A man had devoted four years part time and one year full time to developing an idea. He was able to raise additional seed money from a venture capital firm to fully develop his product and start a company.

--A venture capital investor invested money to help a group continue an economic feasibility study of a hydrofoil transportation system. (It is very infrequent that money is committed for such a truly seed situation. The investment in the study may pay off if its findings indicate a profitable venture is possible. It is important to note that the funds were committed only to the preparation of the study itself.)

The above examples tend to illustrate the type of seed capital situations that might interest the more sophisticated venture capital investor. One can see that in these examples there has been *some form of prior commitment* by the entrepreneurs involved. When the entrepreneur has exhausted most of the logical sources of seed capital available to him and when the investment required is of a reasonable size, a venture capital firm is more apt to invest additional seed or venture capital.

The timing of the entrepreneur's search for additional capital is often crucial to his success. The best time will most likely be when he sees that he will exhaust his present source of funds, has a developed product, and has operated his business successfully (not necessarily at a profit) for a period of time. To raise money successfully from the venture capital investor, the entrepreneur needs to have a method of searching for and approaching these sources of capital.

SELECTING THE PROPER VENTURE CAPITAL INVESTOR

In searching for and deciding upon what investors to approach, the entrepreneur should first seek advice from people who know the financial community—bankers, lawyers, accountants, investment bankers, and others. These individuals should be able to refer him to and provide introductions to potential investors that can be trusted. Hopefully, they can also familiarize the entrepreneur with the operations and ethics of the financial community. Unfortunately, many entrepreneurs do not understand that reputable investors will not steal his idea for their own gain.

It is helpful for the entrepreneur to learn as much about the venture capital investor as possible from these outside sources before asking for capital. If the venture capital investor is not one of the better known organizations, it is crucial to investigate others' views of his methods of operations and ethical values. Available sources of information are public records and talks with individuals connected with presidents of portfolio companies of the venture capital investor. There are several things in a potential investor that the entrepreneur should be looking for at this time.

--An investor that can give more than money by providing contacts, management assistance, legal advice, financial services, and moral support.
--An investor with whom the entrepreneur is personally compatible.
--An investor whose ethics and reputation are of high caliber.
--An investor that will be compatible with the type of venture proposed.

In order to assess fully whom to approach, the entrepreneur might ask himself such questions as:

--Is this a glamour venture? Will this be a gigantic industry in the future?
--Is this just an idea for a small business with no great potential?
--What type of image does the venture have? Does it have philanthropic overtones or does it have connotations of financial manipulation?
--How large an investment will the venture require now? In the future?
--What is the degree and nature of the risk?

Having answered these questions the entrepreneur can compare them with the objectives, resources, and method of operations of the venture capital investors available and eliminate those that are not suitable or would not be interested in the venture proposed.

After getting outside help to make his own assessment of a venture capital investor, the entrepreneur should go to the venture capital investor and sound out his interest in the entrepreneur's type of venture. This does not involve an in-depth presentation. It is only a brief inquiry to determine whether or not the venture capital investor wants to consider this kind of situation. He may already have an investment in a competitive company or he may have decided as a policy matter that his group will not invest in certain industries. For whatever reason, if a venture capital investor indicates at this point that he is not interested, do not argue or object. It is a waste of time on both sides. Even if the individual could be persuaded to investigate the venture in detail, he would start off with a negative attitude, a handicap unlikely to lead to a financing, especially one attractive to the entrepreneur. It is to the advantage of the entrepreneur not to be rejected by a venture capital investor who has investigated the situation. With no investigation, lack of interest generally has no negative connotations.

The entrepreneur should keep in mind that there is a wide range of criteria and interests among venture capital investors and that one may find very unattractive a deal which another would see as very exciting. Therefore, the entrepreneur should not be discouraged by initial rejections during preliminary discussions as long as the major reasons are because the venture capital investor cannot evaluate or for other reasons has no interest in ventures within that industry.

It is sometimes suggested that the potential entrepreneur start his search for capital long before he needs the funds. He should be constantly alert for potential investors and keep a record of contacts made. By becoming familiar with the sources of capital before needing to ask for funds, the entrepreneur can avoid part of the time problem in raising capital by eliminating that time necessary for the investor to get to know the entrepreneur personally. He should be careful to realize that an expression of interest by an investor and a promise to invest "if things look good" is, by no means, a guarantee. *Until he has cash in hand or a signed agreement, the entrepreneur should not consider his search completed.*

It is also suggested that one actively contact various sources prior to seeking funds to learn about their methods of operations and objectives and to assess the venture capital investors' personnel. The entrepreneur should not be asking for money but rather should be making an effort to become acquainted with the venture capital investor. No detailed plan need be presented at this time *provided* the entrepreneur does not attempt to ask for any funds during the meeting.

Most SBICs and venture capital firms make a practice of talking with most, if not all, visitors. Because most venture capital investors are usually extremely busy, the entrepreneur should be careful not to wear out his welcome with unnecessary visits.

Many venture capital investors, likewise, are actively seeking deals themselves. If an entrepreneur has an interesting project or company underway, he is quite apt to be approached by some venture capital investor. This is especially true if it is known that the entrepreneur is working in one of the popular fields such as pollution control or oceanography. If an entrepreneur is approached by a venture capital investor, he should follow the same procedures he would were he to approach the venture capital investor himself.

Venture capital investors use a variety of sources to locate these ventures and opportunities. Several of these sources are:
-- Investment bankers, commercial bankers, and business brokers.
-- Technical journals, financial publications, and trade journals.

--Lawyers, professors, engineers, scientists, auditors, and other personal contacts.

--Suppliers, customers, managers, and directors of the venture capital investor's present investments.

Depending on the amount of uncommitted resources and the interests of the venture capital investor, he may be very active in searching for ventures while others may be quite passive. Some venture capital investors say that the best deals are always the ones that they have drawn together themselves.

LEGAL ASPECTS OF RAISING MONEY

In his search for capital the entrepreneur must avoid inadvertently "going public" or be subject to refunding stockholders' money sometime in the future—usually when the money has been spent—at their request. Although the Securities and Exchange Commission has proposed a rule (Rule 146) which attempts to clarify the area, unfortunately, as of now the activities and conditions which determine whether or not one goes public have not been given any clear definitions.

Going public according to the federal security laws and regulations means that the entrepreneur has *offered securities* to an *unsophisticated* investor or that he has offered securities to *more than a few* sophisticated investors (25 is an unofficial guideline number). The term *offer* has been interpreted to mean any form of direct or indirect solicitation, specifically stated or implied. Note that the number determining whether or not there has been a public offering is under the present laws the number of *offerees*, not the number of those who actually invest.

The term *securities* has been defined broadly. Court rulings have included certain types of franchises, limited partnership interest, pyramid sales schemes, scotch whiskey warehouse receipts, and real estate investments in this category. It is not likely that even the most imaginative entrepreneur could avoid the regulations by using a particular form of investment for raising funds.

At least in theory, just one unsophisticated offeree causes the financing effort to be a public offering. The sophistication of the investor has generally been interpreted in terms of that individual's general knowledge and skills for understanding the business and other aspects of the investment situation. If we use this concept of sophistication, a venture capitalist would be considered sophisticated; a musician would not unless, of course, the nature of the business were something in which the musician was knowledgeable and he understood the financing. Recent court rulings, however, have extended the meaning of sophistication to the point that no one is considered sophisticated in the abstract. Instead, to be sophisticated regarding the financing of a venture, one must be knowledgeable about that specific situation. In other words, without the material information about a venture, not even a venture capitalist is sophisticated. This forces the entrepreneur to be diligent and open in informing potential investors about the important aspects of the company and the industry.

The figure of 25 offerees is arbitrary but is particularly significant when dealing with individuals. If one were to contact only venture capital firms, one could probably approach perhaps twice that number without undue concern.

In trying to prove that an unregistered stock offering was really a public offering because of the number of offerees, the Security and Exchange Commission and the disgruntled stockholders frequently have the problem of finding out who the offerees were. It is very difficult to retrace the steps of an entrepreneur in his search for financing. However, some acts are obvious offerings and relatively easy to ascertain: the number of actual investors gives the minimum number of offerees (the courts have ruled that investing is proof that an offer was made), all present at a meeting where the venture was described to determine interest are offerees, and so on. The mere duplication of a number of offering circulars can be strong circumstantial evidence that this number of offerings was made.

Many states have regulations regarding the registration and offering of securities which closely follow the federal guidelines and interpretations. Some, however, do not and it is imperative that the entrepreneur know the regulatio: s in his state before he tries to raise money. In the state of Ohio, for example, one to five investors in a venture requires a registration. Five to fifteen requires a description of the business and more than fifteen requires extensive reporting. Moreover, the authorities in Ohio, as in several other states, rule not only on whether or not there has been the proper disclosure of facts, such as required in federal regulations, but also whether or not in their opinion the price to investors is "fair."

In addition to the pitfalls related to going public, the entrepreneur must also beware of the possible interpretations which might be given to what he tells investors verbally and in his business plan. In particular, he must be careful to disclose all material facts related to the business and its history and he must not say that he will do things which he cannot do or later decides not to do because of changing circumstances. For example, what could be interpreted as a promise, "The final version of the prototype will be completed by the end of December," is better stated as a best guess, "Management believes that the final version of the prototype will be completed by the end of December." Then, in the event February comes along with the prototype design not yet finished, the new investors are less likely to feel misled by what they were told.

Should the entrepreneur misrepresent the situation to investors in soliciting money, he is risking having to repay those funds should the investors become dissatisfied.

EVALUATION CRITERIA USED BY VENTURE CAPITAL INVESTORS

In evaluating any proposal, the typical venture capital investor is primarily concerned with making a profit through equity participation and capital gains. Therefore, the investor's evaluation is oriented toward assessing not only the potential profitability of the venture, but also the probability of being able to realize a substantial capital gain.

It must be said that there are almost no fixed decision rules in the venture capital field. However, it is possible to compile a set of composite criteria used by many investors. The entrepreneur should be fully aware of these criteria in preparing his campaign to raise funds.

The evaluations of an investment opportunity can be broken down into two areas: the people involved and the concept of the venture itself. Most venture capital investors agree that the people concerned are far more important than the idea behind the venture.

Evaluating the people

1. Integrity and reliability. The venture capital investor will always check the entrepreneur's background and history to judge his integrity and reliability. If anything disreputable is uncovered, the entrepreneur's likelihood of raising money is very small. Likewise, if the entrepreneur attempts to hide or fails to mention a significant part of his past, such as being fired from a job, the venture capital investor will usually conclude that the entrepreneur is not trustworthy enough to warrant a business relationship.

Except for obvious cases of dishonesty and deception, making evaluations in this area is very difficult. It is easy to review the past record but quite another thing to predict how the entrepreneur will act in the future. Often those qualities of stubbornness and strong-mindedness that are necessary for success as an entrepreneur may have been the reason for an entrepreneur's clash with a past employer. Similarly, in some cases the very qualities that have made a man beyond reproach in the past make it hard for him to accept losses and defeats should the venture run into difficulty.

——For months a venture capital investor had put pressure on a company president to reduce material wastage. After trying in vain to do this, the president created a fictitious inventory to solve the problem and satisfy the investor. A year later the inventory proved to be grossly overstated on the financial statements.

—A man of extremely high caliber, a pillar of the community, was pressured by his wife to take large amounts of company money and donate it to charity in the family's name to increase their prestige in the community. When this was discovered by the venture capital investor, the man shot himself rather than face the disgrace of exposure.

—A housebuilder claimed he had been completing houses and closing out the financing when in actuality he had not. The mortgage money, of course, never materialized. Suddenly, a business that had been reporting large profits was bankrupt. This man had also been considered to be above such activity, but rather than face the fact that his business was unsuccessful, he altered the books.

These cases indicate that even when a man's past record is impeccable, there can be substantial risks. For this reason, anyone with less than an attractive record or who has been involved with someone of questionable business ethics is apt to find it difficult to raise money from a reputable venture capital investor. The potential entrepreneur should, therefore, be extremely careful as to whom he "gets in bed with" either in previous employment or in the seed capital stage.

2. Abilities and demonstrated competence. The venture capital investor wants to investigate the entrepreneur's areas of competence. Technical ability is of concern, but more important is an awareness of business operations and an ability to manage a growing organization. All too often, the ideal entrepreneur is not the ideal manager for the business once it becomes a going concern. Most investors prefer to see a *group* of individuals with various complementary abilities and goals. With a group, the investor is more assured of getting a broad range of skills and is also reducing the venture's dependence upon any one individual. The importance of an awareness of all areas—technology, manufacturing, finance, and especially marketing—is crucial.

—Before the electronics boom was really recognized, three men were able to raise $1,500,000 from investment bankers to buy an electronics firm and eventually to acquire other companies to build an integrated electronics firm. The three men had complementing industry experience which lent credibility to their ambitious scheme.

The ability of the entrepreneur to be flexible and meet unforeseen challenges is necessary. In many instances, the original idea or product that a venture is founded upon does not work out. Investors like to feel that the entrepreneur is not so personally wedded to an idea that he will pursue it in a blind manner.

--A successful electronics firm was founded to make a certain type of electronic component. It soon became obvious that there was no market for the product. The founders quickly began to work on a new product which was successful. Since that time, their product line has changed completely several times.

The potential investors will always evaluate carefully the competence and performance of the entrepreneur in his past employment and activities.

--A sales manager of a toy company had an idea to combine four toy companies and achieve great economies of scale by consolidating the sales force. He was considered the top salesman in the industry. Three large venture capital investors liked the venture and went in on it together.

The investors will also look to see if the entrepreneur is committed to the venture and has made sacrifices. They will want to see how he has reacted to pressure and disappointments. This, again, points to why the seed capital stage is so crucial to the investors' evaluation of the entrepreneur. Demonstrated competence and a good track record can be the most important factors in an entrepreneur's ability to raise money.

Virtually all venture capital investors make a great effort to avoid ending up in a management role in one of their ventures. If the entrepreneurs who originate a venture do not look as if they can manage the business, an investor will almost invariably turn the deal down no matter how promising the venture itself may appear. Venture capital investors, however, have added new men to a group of founders to strengthen weaknesses.

3. Attitudes and ambitions. It is important to both the venture capital investor and the entrepreneur that their goals and methods are mutually compatible. Factors of "body chemistry" and personality are of primary importance. One of the theories expressed was: "If you cannot work with a man, then you have no real basis to cope with the situation when things go wrong." There must be a working relationship between the investor and the entrepreneur regardless of whether the venture is a success or failure.

--Failing to establish a working relationship was the fallacy in the toy company example. The president, his lawyer, and the comptroller felt they knew how to run the business. The president had been an excellent sales manager but proved to be a poor company president. The management would not listen to their venture capital investors and built up huge inventories in anticipation of the fall demand. The venture capital investors realized the danger and sold out when they had an opportunity.

In most ventures, the venture capital investor must come in with more funds at some later date, either to finance growth or to save the company. Therefore, regardless of the success or failure of the venture, there must be a working relationship between the parties and a capacity on the part of the venture capital investor to come in with additional funds.

There are extreme case examples where, because of the personality of the entrepreneur, the venture capital investors have had to decide between turning down the opportunity or writing a "blank check" for the entrepreneur. These cases are rare and occur only when the venture is so promising that it far outweighs the inability of the venture capital investors to work with the individual.

Most investors like to see a little humility in the entrepreneur. When the entrepreneur has limitations, it is essential that he be aware of them and be willing to accept some assistance and suggestions from the investor. The individual who "knows it all" is considered dangerous regardless of the talent he shows. Although aggressiveness and confidence is desired to some extent, investors are easily scared away by "hot shots" who try to make the venture look too easy.

−−A man had worked in the paint industry as a protege of a very successful executive who had built an empire by acquiring small paint companies. This man claimed he had learned all the techniques used by his former boss. He had a blueprint for success and already had set up the initial deals. He was *too* sure, and the investors did not provide the money. He probably would have done better had he been less sure and had pointed out some of the potential problem areas and how he planned to attack them.

It is also extremely important that the long-range objectives of the entrepreneur and investor be compatible. The investor is usually concerned with whether or not the entrepreneur is flexible in his goals; wants the business to grow; is agreeable to giving up a portion of the equity; and is amenable to a future merger, acquisition, or public offering. The man who just wants to own his own business usually has goals that are incompatible with those of the investor.

−−A man had a sound manufacturing business with sales of about $2 million. There was no great potential in the product line or in the man. The business was considered to be an excellent "practice" but not an attractive investment. The venture capital investor would not be able to get a good return and would have had no way out of this investment because of the low return. On the other hand, a really attractive investment would have existed if the man had been willing to find a new product line to increase profits.

−−Another man became so captured by the idea of owning his own business that he could not bear the idea of giving up control to obtain new funds. Expansion was, therefore, held back. He would rather have had 100 percent of a $2 million operation than 45 percent of a $10 million business. This man was more motivated by the idea of being president of his own company than he was about making money for himself as an investor.

The investor must evaluate the entrepreneur's ambitions to avoid such situations. Venture capital investors would like to see the man have a realistic plan for what he would like to be doing 1, 2, 5, and 10 years in the future. Because the investor is usually going to be able to realize his profit only in the long term, the compatibility of the entrepreneur's ambitions and the venture capital investors' objectives is of paramount importance.

Evaluating the venture itself

1. Suitability of the venture for the venture capital investor. Probably one of the initial factors that an investor investigates is the general suitability of the venture for the particular venture capital investor. The following is a list of the factors that are frequently relevant in the decision making:

––If the investor tends to specialize, is this opportunity within his geographical areas, technical area of competence, or size of investment desired?
––Does this fit the image of the venture capital investor or is it "distasteful" for nonfinancial reasons?
––Is this an area where the venture capital investor can contribute something more than money to the venture? Does the venture capital investor have unique skills that will contribute to the success of the venture?

2. Potential economic gain. The investor also assesses the potential return on his investment offered by the project. Depending upon the goals of the venture capital investor and the degree of risk he is willing to assume, a wide variety of rules of thumb might be used in this evaluation. Some typical rules are:

––15 percent–25 percent annual return as a minimum.
––Double the investment every three to five years as an overall goal.
––Earn three times your investment in five years, if all goes moderately well; and fifteen times, if all goes very well.
––At least a return better than that of the New York Stock Exchange's average return.

3. Assessing the probability of success. If a venture capital investor expects to have his overall portfolio perform as above, it is imperative for him to minimize his failures. Nevertheless, the performance of most investments is strikingly poor. A sample of a relatively successful venture capital investor's investment portfolio of 20 investments might look roughly like this:

1 project —very successful
3 projects —fairly successful
6 projects —break even
4 projects —very poor
6 projects —complete losses

Often the unsuccessful firm is the one that has not been fortunate enough to have the one real winner. This gives some indication of the degree to which the investor must study and analyze investment proposals before making a commitment. At first, the venture capital investor often finds the venture deceivingly promising. He must be a "devil's advocate" in the evaluation of the venture. One of the things he must avoid is being carried away by the overenthusiasm that most entrepreneurs have for their ideas.

Assuming that the project looks feasible, the venture capital investor usually is concerned with how much money he must invest and how long it will take to get an indication of whether or not there will be success. No investor wants to get into the situation of "throwing good money after bad." This is why most investors tend to shy away from investing seed capital, especially in new product development.

As a counterpart to assessing the gain, most investors also look to some extent at the downside risk of the investment. Some venture capital investors, typically SBICs, tend to look more at the security aspect of their investment, while other venture capital investors seem to be more concerned with what they stand to gain and not with what they stand to lose.

The investor also likes to see something unique in the venture that tends to make its success more likely. Such things as a special skill, a technical advance, a market name, a proprietary product, or a patent are factors that add credibility to the venture's success.

--There are many electronics firms producing semiconductors. In many instances these firms have a highly specialized talent that enables them to gain a niche in an otherwise very competitive market.
--An inventor with a patented technique for a special machine tool successfully obtained financial backing. This patent prevented many other established manufacturers from producing this advanced product and competing for the large demand.

Investors have also learned that patents themselves do not insure success. They are considered nice to have but they are not a major criterion in many situations. In far too many instances, it has been possible for competition to improve on an individual's patent and to come out with an even better product on their own.

Most experienced investors realize the importance of motivating the entrepreneur to put his best effort into a venture. In cases where the entrepreneur is primarily motivated by financial reward, investors like to see that he has an opportunity to get rich if the venture succeeds. For these reasons, the past financing of the venture is carefully examined. If the entrepreneur has already given away so much of equity that he is completely dominated by those who initially invested in his venture, a venture capital investor will hesitate to back him unless they can arrange a plan with the other investors to give the entrepreneur some incentive (for example, stock options, bonus schemes, and so on).

With these general criteria in mind, the entrepreneur is in the position to prepare his presentation to prospective venture capital investors.

Presenting a proposal to a venture capital investor

The presentation of a proposed venture to a venture capital investor is one of the most crucial aspects of raising capital. As important as the actual facts and ideas expressed is the entrepreneur's method of presenting them. Because the tone and manner of this presentation can reveal a great deal about the entrepreneur, the venture capital investor looks for such things as:

--Is he organized? Has he thought out his program? Does he have a proper time perspective? Does he have a plan? If he cannot organize his presentation, how can he organize a company?

--Does the man admit to the pitfalls, risks, and problems likely to be encountered? If he does not discuss these problems, either he is trying to conceal them or he has not thoroughly thought out his proposal.

--Does the entrepreneur admit his own personal weaknesses? A man who does not admit or volunteer any faults may be difficult to work with and may have trouble organizing and building a company.

--Has he logically sought advice and counsel in preparing his presentation, or has he gone rushing ahead with his campaign to raise money? If he isn't the type who has sought advice and assistance in these matters, he may not be receptive to a venture capital investor's efforts to work with him in the future.

--Is the entrepreneur a good salesman and does he present himself well? To be successful in almost any venture he must be a salesman to some extent.

--Is he realistic and down to earth in his dealings with the venture capital investor? Has he tried to find out about the venture capital investor before approaching him? Is he oriented towards giving the prospective investors the facts they want? If he is oblivious to the venture capital investor's point of view and methods of operation, he may not alter this attitude when the investment is made and disagreements arise in the future.

——How is his presentation and outlook oriented? Is he concerned just with technology, production, finance, or marketing? What areas does he leave out? By allowing the entrepreneur to have complete freedom in making his presentation, the venture capital investor can evaluate his awareness of what will make the business operate. When major areas are not discussed in detail, it indicates that the entrepreneur is either inexperienced or unconcerned with such areas. This has profound implications on how he might operate his business. Most venture capital investors stress the importance of an awareness of the profit motive, cost control, and especially the *marketing* area. Entrepreneurs are too often not aware of how crucial these areas are.

——Has he shown a proper time perspective? Has he prepared to seek funds well in advance of his actual needs? A lack of such foresight suggests a potential managerial weakness in the areas of budgeting and allocation of resources.

In addition to evaluating the general tone of the presentation, the venture capital investor looks for specific items and areas which should be covered in the actual presentation:

1. Format. The entire presentation should be neatly prepared in written form that includes all pertinent information and parallels the oral presentation given. It is often helpful to have the presentation reviewed by specialists such as lawyers, accountants, financial men, and relevant consultants. A qualified impartial critic can add a great deal to a presentation. As in any sales presentation, mistakes are best made where they do not count. Having specialists attend a presentation is often helpful for providing both moral and technical support to the entrepreneur.

2. Plan. A well-thought-out plan for the venture's future (½, 1, 2, 3, and 5 years) is desired. This plan should contain, when applicable, the following information and projections: complete financial information including cash flows, pro forma income statements and balance sheets, and financing requirements; detailed marketing information; production schedules; and relevant technical factors. In addition, the entrepreneur should state his own personal objectives for the future. Preferably he should make a sensitivity analysis indicating the critical factors and assumptions and outlining contingency plans.

3. Realism. Plans should be realistic rather than extreme. Many investors are skeptical of entrepreneurs with grandiose ideas, whether they be financial or technical in nature. Grossly overoptimistic profit projections will usually scare investors away rather than attract them. Similarly, very few investors seem to possess the "vision" that most entrepreneurs claim to have. To prevent the venture capital investor from becoming too skeptical, the entrepreneur is advised to tone down his ideas to a level where they will seem feasible to the potential investor.

——A group seeking funds to buy an electronics firm in the early 1950s sold their idea on the future of electronics. They were, however, very careful not to mention that "space" was one of their future markets. To have done so would probably have ruined their chances of raising money at that time.

4. History. A detailed history, when available, of all the facts relevant to the venture should be available, including descriptions of key personnel, financial information, production data, product lines, marketing programs, management techniques, customers, suppliers, bank and investor relationships, and past and potential problem areas. It is important that the entrepreneur reveal all the facts for it will make the investigation easier for the investor and will shorten the time required to evaluate the venture.

5. Unique strengths. A careful analysis of what it is that has made or makes the venture unique is advisable. It is important that the entrepreneur himself know what his competitive advantages are. In many instances, success to date has been made possible because of factors that will not continue in the future, such as limited competition due to a temporary market advantage. The entrepreneur must show clearly what makes his venture competitive.

6. Weaknesses. The entrepreneur should admit what his weak areas are. The entrepreneur should show where he needs assistance or must correct a deficiency, such as locating a good production man, getting someone with management experience, or establishing trade relations. It is important that he understand how involved the particular venture capital investor likes to get in the venture. Some venture capital investors will want to help the man solve these problems whereas others, who do not like to get involved in management, will be more concerned with how the man himself intends to solve these problems. Needless to say, if the entrepreneur can correct any of these weak areas before giving his presentation he will be more persuasive, especially if he can tell the prospective investors how he has solved or is solving his problems.

7. Product(s). If the venture involves a new product, venture capital investors like to see a working model, if at all possible. In most instances they would also like to see actual sales of the product or a definite order to buy it. Market studies, promises to buy, or expressions of interest are generally not considered to be reliable. The farther removed the product is from the marketing stage, the less interested the investor becomes. A detailed plan of how the product is to be sold is essential. Too many entrepreneurs think that a good product will sell itself—this is usually a serious fallacy.

8. A reason for acting now. If the entrepreneur actually has a need for funds in the near future, he should be able to explain why now is the time the investor should come in on the venture. It is natural for an investor to have a "wait-and-see" attitude. (This, incidentally, is one reason why an entrepreneur should make early contact with venture capital investors and presell them long before he actually presents them with a proposal.) An entrepreneur, however, must be careful not to pressure a venture capital investor into acting quickly. If a deal is "hot" the venture capital investor will want to know why time is crucial or else he will shy away from it. In many instances it might be best for the entrepreneur not to stress the fact that he is in a rush for he stands a better chance of getting the money if the investor does not feel pressed.

––The group that was raising funds to buy the electronics firm for $1,500,000 realized that this would probably be their only opportunity to get in before the electronics boom. Although they were in a hurry to raise the money, they did not tell the venture capital investors how much of a hurry they were in. They were able to raise the money in three months

After the entrepreneur has completed the stage of making a formal presentation, he has arrived at the beginning of the investigation and negotiation stage.

INVESTIGATION AND NEGOTIATION

In a fairly short amount of time, the venture capital investor should be able to give the entrepreneur an indication of whether or not he is interested in the venture. Typical patterns for the investigating of 100 proposals presented to a venture capital firm or an SBIC might be:

50 discarded immediately within five minutes.
30 eliminated within several hours.
10 eliminated after a close study of a week.
5-8 eliminated after a detailed study of several weeks or months.
2-5 accepted after a detailed study of several weeks or months.

After receiving indications of interest following an in-depth presentation of the venture, the entrepreneur should get from the venture capital investor an estimate of how long investigations should take. On the one hand, the venture capital investor who has sufficient interest in a situation to take on the task of investigation has the right to expect the entrepreneur not to make a deal with another investor while his research and examination is underway. On the other hand, the entrepreneur is probably pressed for time and cannot afford to wait very long. The entrepreneur should also realize from the outset that the venture capital investor usually stands to gain from delays in commiting funds to the venture. It is to his advantage to get better acquainted with the entrepreneur and to see how he works with the other members of his group. Additional time also permits further investigation and study of the industry. Obviously, at some point further delays in the financing can seriously hamper the progress of the venture and the entrepreneur must press for a decision and, if necessary, begin looking for other potential backers if the delays become protracted. Most venture capital investors understand this kind of response and know that they will have to go ahead if they find the venture attractive or risk losing part or all of the deal to another investor.

It is usually possible for the entrepreneur to ascertain early whether or not the venture capital investor would want all or only part of the deal. The entrepreneur's risk of delay may be decreased if he can present his situation in depth to a number of venture capital investors while the first pursues the investigation. Then, all may invest if they wish or some may decline without stopping the financing entirely. Among reputable venture capital investors there is little chance of one of the firms trying to run away with the deal.

The venture capital investor will quite often use outside consultants in the investigation stage when he does not have the expertise in a particular area. This is especially true when scientific ventures are involved. Sometimes it may be that the entrepreneur brings in the consultants in order to verify the feasibility of a venture.

--A man decided to start a new manufacturing company in the Midwest. After hiring a consultant to make a market and feasibility study for the project, he was able to take the study to an investor and obtain funds.
--A venture capital investor attempting to evaluate a new transistor had a group of scientists at a university analyze the technical aspects of the item. The scientists later joined the venture capital investor in investing in the company.

Investors also like to have time to observe the entrepreneur in action. If the investment involves a going concern, the venture capital investor will usually send someone to the plant to observe operations and see how the management handles daily problems. On such visits many things not otherwise evident are often observed about the business and the people involved.

--An SBIC was looking at a small manufacturing firm. By observing the antagonistic and argumentative manner of the manager under stress in a plant, a characteristic they had not seen when he had visited their office, the managers of the SBIC decided not to invest as they felt that they could not work with the individual.

The investor will also seek information about the company from other outside and inside sources. Suppliers, customers, distributors, and employees are among these often contacted.

The investigation stage will begin to blend into the negotiation stage as the venture capital investor feels he has been able to verify the entrepreneur's presentation and has convinced himself that it is a potentially attractive investment opportunity. It is in this stage that the investor begins to suggest certain changes that will make the deal more attractive. One venture capital investor reported that in all but the most straightforward ventures the actual deal that evolves is quite different from the proposal as it was first presented. Often unforeseen obstacles have to be overcome before the deal can be made. Changes in the internal or external environment of a company or a deal may make the proposal suddenly seem either attractive or unattractive. Depending upon the complexity of the situation, negotiations can take quite a while—a rule of thumb might be an average of two months within a normal range of from one week to two years.

The negotiations usually center around creating a "package" that will satisfy both the entrepreneur's need for capital and the venture capital investor's desire to realize a capital gain. A few venture capital investors are, however, more concerned with other aspects of the venture. A bank SBIC may want to create a potential customer, a large corporation may want to follow the development of a new technology in an emerging industry, a foundation may desire to invest in projects that will be partially philanthropic in nature, or a lending SBIC may want to make a high return on its loans. In the negotiations, both parties should attempt to discover whether or not their interests are compatible and whether or not there is mutual understanding between the parties.

Aside from the actual amounts of money involved, the three primary controllable factors in most deals, especially when there is a loan and equity package, are:

--Percentage of equity given to the investor.
--Debt covenants and the amount of security given to the investor.
--Interest rates and conversion privileges.

Aside from the usual mechanics and techniques pertaining to financing a small business,[3] there are certain aspects of these three factors that are especially relevant to venture capital.

---

[3]On this subject there is a great quantity of material available which the entrepreneur should study.

Percentage of ownership. The distribution of the equity in any deal depends largely upon a measure of the total contribution of the parties involved and the amount of risk assumed by each. Generally, the further along the venture is from the initial seed capital stage, the greater the share of equity the entrepreneur should be able to retain. Most of the venture capital investors like to make certain that the entrepreneur will be motivated to make the venture succeed, and consequently, they either leave him with an attractive portion of the equity or else give him options or warrants to buy additional shares if the venture succeeds. Typical ranges of equity for different stages are roughly estimated to be:

——10 percent–20 percent for the entrepreneur when the venture capital investor puts in all the funds and the venture is still in the seed capital stage.
——30 percent–80 percent for the entrepreneur when the seed capital stage is over, depending upon the amount invested by the venture capital investor.
——10 percent–50 percent for the venture capital investor in a mature venture where substantial capital has already been invested and the funds are to permit additional growth.

A strategic question for the entrepreneur is whether or not to make the terms and structure of the financing a part of the written presentation and early discussions or whether to wait until the potential investor is hungry to do a deal. If the entrepreneur takes the initial step in proposing terms he can make his ensuing arguments along the lines, "And look at the very attractive return an investor stands to make on his investment." If no terms are mentioned, the potential investor, once he decides he likes the venture and the entrepreneur, can try to base the terms on the argument, "We should divide the pie according to what each of us is bringing to the party." And in these situations his dollars almost inevitably appear large and certain relative to the entrepreneur's contribution of the idea, his commitment to the venture, and his progress to date. On the other hand, if the potential investor is going to have to look at the situation in some detail before he can become seriously interested, he may be put off by what in the early stages of discussions appears to be an expensive deal.

Some very wise individuals have pointed out that it is foolish for an entrepreneur and a potential investor to quibble over a few percentage points of ownership when they both want the deal to go through. This is true. However, the venture capital investor's objective of seeing that the entrepreneur is sufficiently motivated by ownership does not necessarily mean that the investor is being generous or that he is taking only as much as he would be willing to take to do the deal.

At some point in negotiations one party is likely to discover that the other side is more anxious to do a deal than he is. This gives one side a decided advantage in pushing for a greater part of the ownership. The party with this kind of power, however, should be careful not to push his position too far. He may discourage the other side and wind up with no deal at all. Or he may antagonize the other party and reduce his eagerness to push the venture along even if the deal is done. In those cases which end in a deal but with one party dissatisfied, unhappy, or otherwise feeling that he was put upon, at the next negotiation—and there is *always* a next negotiation—the aggrieved party will have his turn. It is likely that these kinds of adversary relationships between investor and entrepreneur will be very detrimental to the progress of the venture.

It is quite possible for an entrepreneur and a potential investor to disagree in good faith over the potential of the venture and therefore the terms to the investor. The entrepreneur simply sees a better future for the company than the investor. In such instances it may be appropriate for the deal to be structured to enable the entrepreneur to improve his ownership position if the venture progresses in sales and profits as he predicts.

— — An entrepreneur claimed he would make $200,000 profit the first year and $600,000 the second on sales of $1 million and $3 million, respectively. The investor thought that profits of $150,000 the first year and $350,000 the second would be more realistic. The covenants in this situation were made according to the investor's estimates of profits and included a stock option which became attractive to the entrepreneur if profits exceeded the investor's expectations.

— — A highly speculative standing-start situation was financed with the investor, a manufacturing concern, being required to buy out the founder interests at the end of five years at a price mutually agreed upon or otherwise determined by outside arbitration.

The issue of control, which is closely tied to equity, is one that varies with each venture capital investor. As a general rule, most venture capital investors prefer a minority interest provided that the entrepreneur appears receptive to advice and that there are sufficient protective covenants in the agreement.

Covenants and degree of security. Most venture capital investors insist on having some means of protecting their investment if things go wrong. This is especially common in start-up situations where the entrepreneur has had little business experience. It is less common where the entrepreneur and the venture have a track record sufficient to give the investor confidence in the management. The usual convenants are similar to those on a bank loan. Typically, the venture capital investor has the power to take control under the following circumstances.

— — Working capital falls below certain limits.
— — Sales are not at a specified level.
— — An agreed upon profit has not been realized.

--Net worth is below a certain amount.

In most instances, the entrepreneur is willing to agree to such covenants for his expectations usually exceed the levels that the investor believes are realistic. The entrepreneur should be aware, however, that control, essentially absolute control, can more readily be obtained by an investor through default of loan convenants than through ownership of a majority of the equity shares.

Many venture capital investors would prefer to give the entrepreneur the amount of money they think is necessary rather than the amount he has asked for. The amount may be either more or less than what was requested. A common covenant, however, is to earmark these funds for specific areas. For example, the venture capital investor might allocate the amounts to be used for marketing, production, or increasing working capital. He might also insist that the funds spent in other areas be limited to prevent excesses in such things as inventory buildups, investment in plant, or promotion expense. These types of covenants are most frequently used where the venture capital investor notices that the enterprise needs strengthening in one area or that the entrepreneur is prone to get carried away with certain types of expenditures.

--In one highly speculative situation, the venture capital investors initially paid over only 20 percent of the investment they had committed with the remainder to be paid only when certain clearly definable milestones had been reached.
--In the case of the toy company, the venture capital investors had no such covenants and the management of the firm built up huge inventories. The investor was helpless to prevent this allocation of funds.
--In another example, the entrepreneur spent excessive amounts on promotion and advertising. He later required additional funds for working capital.

Securing the debt with inventories or receivables is more frequent with the SBIC investor than with other venture capital investors. In many new ventures there is very little one can use to provide adequate security. Most venture capital investors, however, are not preoccupied with the negative side.

Interest rate and conversion privilege. In addition to straight equity investments, most venture capital investors use some form of debt, usually in the form of convertible debentures or bonds with warrants. Interest rates on these debentures range upwards to 16 percent, with the usual rate between 6 percent to 10 percent. In many instances where the venture would be unable to cover the fixed charges, the interest rate will be low since the investor expects to realize his profit later through conversion into stock and capital gains.

An entrepreneur should be skeptical of any proposal to obtain funds on a straight loan basis. In most cases, an entrepreneur underestimates his need for funds. If he borrows money at high interest rates, he has not got an investor but rather has incurred large liabilities which may involve high fixed charges and a very unsympathetic financial partner.

In the final stages of the negotiations, it is imperative that good legal counsel be present. The legal advice not only protects both parties, but also insures that the venture's legal structure is on a sound footing from the start. Once a firm is incorporated with a cumbersome legal structure, it is often quite difficult and expensive to rewrite the structure years later when the firm is larger and desires to go public.

OPERATING PERIOD

Seldom is the relationship between the venture capital investor and the management of one of their investments a distant one. Although the vast majority of venture capital investors want to avoid becoming involved in the daily operations of one of their investments, they usually take an active interest in the affairs of the venture. Venture capital investors' activities are primarily oriented towards:

1. Helping the company succeed.
2. Preparing the firm to merge, go public, or sell out.

In order to increase the company's chances of success, investors may provide a variety of helpful functions. One such function is simply to be an interested person outside the company in whom the entrepreneur can confide about his problems. Often when employees find out that the firm is having difficulties, their morale drops and the problem is further aggravated. The investor can sometimes help provide solutions to these problems and bolster the entrepreneur's own morale. The wrong attitude by the investor, of course, can make things worse in this regard by applying too much pressure on the entrepreneur at just the time when he needs assistance and encouragement.

The venture capital investor also can serve as an informal mediator and help resolve conflicts within the organization. Such conflicts often occur in cases where several men have started the enterprise together. A disagreement between the scientific partner and the commercial partner is a typical example. Having an interested investor as a mediator has often held many ventures together when they would otherwise have fallen apart.

Contacts with banks, industrial firms, investment bankers, and consultants may be provided by the investor. The presence of a respected venture capital investor will increase the prestige of the company. Because of a venture capital investor's interest in the firm, banks often will make loans to a company which they normally would not have considered.

Venture capital investors are also able to effect necessary personnel changes. One investor estimated that in one third of the ventures in which his firm had invested the original president was not capable or did not want to face the increasing pressures put on him by the growth of his company. Through its many contacts, a venture capital investor is often able to help locate personnel to fill important positions in a company.

--One SBIC provides semiretired businessmen that "live-in" as part-time consultants to each of its investments. The normal cost to each company for this service would usually be about $200 to $300 per month.
--A venture capital firm located a controller for a small portfolio company that was in desperate need of an accounting and cost control system.
--When a technical man trying to manage an electronics firm realized that he had neither the time nor the ability to handle the business aspects of the company, the investor helped find a man to become president so that the original entrepreneur could continue to pursue his technical interests.

Many investors, possessing a capable staff of marketing, engineering, and finance men, can and often do provide a wide variety of consulting services in areas such as production control, reporting systems, compensation plans, personnel procedures, and organizational problems associated with growth. Because of their experience with growing companies, most venture capital investors have seen many of these problems before and are well equipped to solve some of them.

--One manufacturing firm had virtually no accounting system; receipts and records were chaotic and literally were stuffed into the safe. A partner of one of the venture capital investor firms spent six weeks in the plant straightening out the records.
--A small manufacturing company was growing very quickly. The scope of the firm's operations had expanded beyond the managing capabilities of the president who wanted to be a part of every decision in the firm. After pointing out the abilities of the other men in the management team and the possible consequences of not being able to solve all the problems personally, the venture capital investor convinced the president that he should delegate some responsibility to these men.
--A president of a small technically-oriented manufacturing firm continually developed and tried to introduce new products before the markets were ready. The venture capital investor involved with this company helped the man concentrate on developing his existing markets more fully by bringing in a new experienced marketing man.

Not all venture capital investors are willing or able to provide these types of services. In many instances, the investor becomes involved only when conditions are such that action is necessary to save the company.

In addition to helping the company succeed, venture capital investors usually are active in making the company a more attractive and liquid investment. One step is to prepare the entrepreneur for a possible future public offering by introducing him to investment bankers. The reporting system will usually have to be revised to provide more adequate information to satisfy regulations of state and federal securities regulatory groups. The entrepreneur must also be familiarized with the SEC regulations. The biggest part of this process is teaching the entrepreneur the difference between dealing with one to five investors and dealing with the public market.

During this same period, the small law and accounting firms that have been serving the company for many years, often since its inception, usually have to be replaced by the larger and better known firms. This is, of course, a difficult transition for most entrepreneurs because of the personal relationships he has developed with his lawyer and accountant.

Orienting and convincing the entrepreneur/manager and his company that they should merge, go public, or sell out often requires a long period and a great deal of preselling on the part of the investor. As the venture matures, the investor turns toward actually realizing the profit on his investment.

HOW THE INVESTOR REALIZES HIS GAIN OR LOSS

Regardless of the performance of a venture, the investor must at some time come to a decision as to what he should do with his investment.

Usually one or more of the following events eventually happens:

—Bankruptcy occurs.
—Liquidation is initiated and the company goes out of business.
—The company is either merged with or acquired by another company.
—The company is sold to another investor.
—Stock is sold to the public.

The typical non-SBIC investor may look for a payout of three to five years. Once this period has passed, he desires to get out of his investment unless it looks as if the next few years will produce additional growth in capital. If the investor has misjudged the attitudes and ambitions of the entrepreneur, he often finds that the most profitable way out for him is blocked by a stubborn manager. This situation most frequently occurs when the venture is not too successful and the investor wishes to liquidate his investment by merger, sale to another company, or even liquidation of the business since public sale of stock is not possible, given the company's past performance. The entrepreneur, on the other hand, is often content with the status quo and is usually unsympathetic to any scheme that would alter his position as the manager of his own company.

The venture capital investor will usually allow a company to remain in business as long as it is profitable or has a chance for profit in the future. The investor will continue to seek ways of getting his capital out of the venture if the future is unattractive. Frequently, the venture capital investor searches for another investor who finds the venture attractive.

––In the toy company case, the three venture capital investors became alarmed when management kept building up the inventory for the fall season. The venture capital investors sold out to an investment banking group for their initial investment plus interest. The investment bankers claimed that the venture canital investors did not have enough "imagination." The anticipated demand for the toys did not materialize, and the investment bankers lost their entire investment.

When a venture is on the verge of bankruptcy, the investor's bargaining position is quite strong despite the amount of equity he possesses, for he is often able to convince the entrepreneur that drastic action is warranted. In cases where the situation is not so serious, the investor's position is often quite weak because he may have difficulty in selling the entrepreneur the idea that the status quo should not be continued. This is especially true in cases where the entrepreneur is essential to the firm's success and where the investment without him would be of little value.

By going public, a venture capital investor is able to create a market value for its investment which is especially attractive for reporting the status of its portfolio to the stockholders. The public market also enables the venture capital investor to gradually liquidate its investment as desired.

The importance of this final stage is why the venture capital investor, before making an investment, analyzes the entrepreneur and the venture for factors that may create difficulties in the long run. Unless a capital gain on the investment can be realized at some point in time, a venture capital investor has not made a successful investment regardless of how successful the venture may be from the entrepreneur's or an outsider's point of view.

––A recent Broadway show was considered a great success, but the backers made nothing on their investment due to the high cost of producing it.

This same situation often arises when manufacturing companies, whose products have very successful sales records, show no profit because of high costs.

TRENDS IN THE VENTURE CAPITAL FIELD AND THEIR IMPLICATIONS FOR THE ENTREPRENEUR

There are trends in the venture capital industry today that will influence the future availability of funds for the entrepreneur. These trends are generally applicable to the overall venture capital market, but exceptions must still be made for the peculiarities of each individual venture capital investor.

The original concept of many prominent venture capital firms was that profits were to be made from financing men with ideas and helping start new businesses. As these investment firms gained experience, their interests have moved away from this type of venture. Experience proved to many venture capital investors that providing such seed capital involved great risk and was not as profitable as originally anticipated. Accordingly, many venture capital investors are now more interested in finding the mature ventures that involve less risk, require larger investment, and still offer an attractive capital gain.

Several investors have expressed the opinion that the institutionalized investors appear more conservative for several additional reasons. When many venture capital firms (especially the SBICs) were formed, large reserves of liquid venture capital became available all at once. In an effort to put this cash to work, venture capital investors, inexperienced and under pressure to get this money invested, rushed to find investments, most of which were not successful. As a result, many venture capital investors became disillusioned and overly conservative. On the other hand, whenever substantial gains are actually realized on an investment, the principals or the stockholders may tend to pressure a firm into protecting its gains by investing it in, or keeping it in, less risky ventures. As more of a firm's money is invested in new ventures, there is also a tendency to diversify its portfolio into more conservative, income-producing investments to be able to report some earnings. The real problem is that a balanced portfolio of venture capital investments can take up to 10 to 15 years to build up due to the length of time required for the initial ventures to mature.

The trend away from start-up situations is compounded by the increased competition created by the industrial firms that are also seeking out ventures and by the increasing investment required to finance many of today's ventures. Some of the electronics and defense firms founded in the 1950s required relatively little initial capital investment; it is becoming more and more difficult to find such industries today.

There is a continuing trend toward the syndication of deals among venture capital investors—they seem to have become accustomed to working with each other and to relying on each other's judgments. Syndication also serves to spread the risk and provide larger capital reserves for future investments in the larger projects. For ventures which are large relative to the venture capital investors' resources, syndicates will be the rule.

Less reliance is being placed on waiting for deals to "walk in the door." Because of the increased number of venture capital investors and the difficulty that they seem to have in making entrepreneurs aware of their services, most venture capital investors must actively seek out ventures in which to invest. A few venture capital investors are becoming increasingly convinced that it is the ventures they create themselves that are the most profitable. Typical examples of such activity might be:

——Locating a promising field, finding a good company, employing a top manager, and expanding the operation.
——Finding a promising area of technology, recruiting top people in the field, and starting a company.

By creating a venture themselves, these venture capital investors find they can avoid many of the pitfalls involved in investigating someone else's proposal, insure that the people most qualified for the jobs are recruited, and tailor the entire venture to their own requirements.

Much less emphasis is being placed on technology ventures today than was the case several years ago. After the popularity of the "scientific growth companies" in the 1950s and early 1960s and subsequent fall in the stock market in 1962 and 1973, investors have become somewhat disillusioned with such ventures. Nevertheless, some investors seem to be recovering from that scare, and scientific ventures are again becoming popular. This time the investors seem to be more aware of the potential pitfalls and more realistic in their expectations. For these reasons, it is doubtful that scientific ventures will be quite as fashionable as they were a few years ago.

Complementing this lessening in the relative importance of scientific ventures is an increasing interest in leisure and service industries. Although many venture capital investors previously avoided the service industries due to the characteristically high risk from the heavy reliance upon one man's abilities, there is evidence that they are now taking a second look at such investments. For some the low capital investment and high potential return makes them attractive. The following are examples of recent investments in service organizations.

——Many groups establishing CATV companies have been able to secure capital from venture firms.
——A number of franchised fast food, tax service, and other service industries have received venture capital financing.

The SBIC program is no longer viewed as today's major source of venture capital. Despite their wide geographical coverage and combined resources (potentially $1 billion), they are no longer the dominant force in the field. On the other hand, the SBICs have been able to attract and invest in many ventures that, before the SBIC program was conceived, went to other venture capital firms and private investors or else received no funds at all. Since the first years of the SBIC program, many inexperienced SBIC managers have been replaced, smaller SBICs have been merged with other SBICs, and a great deal of collective knowledge has been gained in lending to small and new businesses.

Several problems of the SBICs arise from the fact that certain activities are regulated by the Small Business Administration, the Securities and Exchange Commission (if their securities are publicly traded), and the Internal Revenue Service. These agencies often have conflicting objectives and make the SBICs' activities more difficult. This has caused SBICs to decline in popularity as a venture capital vehicle; from over 600 firms in the mid-1960s, their number is now just over 320.

In terms of dollars, large manufacturing companies, oil companies, and insurance firms are in the position to provide the greatest amounts of capital. However, because of their lack of experience in the field and reluctance to hire expertise with compensation based upon performance, these organizations usually participate with the more traditional venture capital firms which act as lead investors at earlier stages in the venture.

Although this report did not consider the international aspects of venture capital, it should be noted that this type of investing is presently being institutionalized abroad. Several well-known venture capital investors in the United States have been instrumental in the organization of similar firms in Canada and Western Europe. Other firms either have made direct investments in foreign ventures or else have created subsidiaries to do this investing. The trend in venture capital abroad also seems to parallel the trend of the financial community toward more internationally-oriented activities.

REFERENCES

Baty, G. *Initial Financing of New Research-Based Enterprises in New England.* Boston: Federal Reserve Bank of Boston, 1964.

Rubel, Stanley. *Guide to Venture Capital Sources.* Chicago: Capital Publishing, 1973.

Sinclair, Leroy, ed. *Venture Capital.* New York: Technimetrics, Inc., 1973.

Note

Securities regulation—a businessman's guide

INTRODUCTION

A large portion of business financing and acquisitions as well as other types of business transactions are regulated by state or federal securities laws. Federal securities laws are administered principally by the Securities and Exchange Commission (SEC) and state securities ("Blue Sky") laws are administered principally by the securities administrators of the respective states.

Securities laws apply to private business transactions as well as to public offerings and the stock markets. Like tax laws, securities laws are complex and not always grounded in logic. The consequences of violation (even technical violation) can be vastly disproportionate to the harm inflicted and can impose severe personal liabilities on management (including innocent management) as well as preclude present and future business financings. Treatment and cure of violations, when possible, can be time consuming and expensive. To complicate matters, securities regulation has changed dramatically over the past several years—partially in response to the speculative abuses of the late 1960s—so that accepted practices of a few years ago are at best hazardous today. In addition to the federal and state agencies charged with administering the securities laws, there has arisen a group of lawyers whose practice specializes in the bringing of private "class actions" against companies, their management, and principal owners on behalf of all members of a class of investors allegedly harmed by violations of the securities laws. Courts have awarded these lawyers substantial legal fees upon successful adjudication or settlement of the claims as an incentive to bring such actions as private protectors of the public. The consequences of violations of the securities laws are considered in greater detail below.

Statements contained in this Note are of necessity general in nature and become outdated with the passage of time, and therefore they should not be relied upon in formulating definitive business plans but rather as an indication of the nature and extent of securities regulation that may be applicable in various circumstances. In this regard, it should be borne in mind that in addition to the federal securities laws, there are securities laws in each of the 50 states—many of which vary substantially from state to state. Financings and other business transactions involving securities also may be subject to the rules and regulations of self-regulatory bodies, such as the National Association of Securities Dealers, Inc. (NASD) and the various securities exchanges.

DEFINITION OF A SECURITY

The securities laws are applicable only if a "security" is involved in the transaction. The statutory definition of security includes common and preferred stock, notes, bonds, debentures, voting-trust certificates, certificates of deposit, warrants, options, subscription rights, and undivided oil or gas interests. In fact, the definition is broad enough to encompass just about any financing transaction, whether or not a certificate evidencing the investor's participation is issued, so long as the investor's participation in the business is passive or nearly so. Generally, a security is involved whenever one person supplies money or some item of value with the expectation that it will be used to generate profits or other monetary return for the investor primarily from the efforts of others. Thus, a limited partnership interest is a security. So is a cow—if purchased together with a maintenance contract whereby someone else will raise, feed, and sell the cow without the participation of the investor. Similarly, an orange grove is a security if coupled with an agreement to maintain, harvest, and sell the orange crop; a condominium unit is a security if coupled with an agreement to rent the unit to others when not occupied by the owner; and parcels of oil property may be securities if sold with the understanding that the promoter will drill a test well on adjoining land. A franchise may or may not be a security, depending upon the extent of the participation of the investor. A commodities future is not a security, since the efforts of another are not involved; however, a discretionary account to trade commodities futures may be a security, since the skill of the broker is involved, and a participation in a pool for the purpose of commodities future trading certainly is a security if the investor does not make or participate in the trading decisions.

Generally, there must be an expectation of a "profit" or monetary return; the expectation of some other benefit may not be enough to cause a security to be created. However, in some jurisdictions the so-called risk capital theory would cause a security to be involved where benefits other than profits are expected if the money or item of value invested is used to start up the venture. Thus, a membership in a country club may be a security in California if the proceeds from the purchase of the memberships are used in the startup of the club.

Despite the broadness of the above generalizations, there are some financing transactions that are deemed not to involve securities merely because they traditionally have not been considered to involve them. Thus, a note given in connection with a long-term *bank* loan is generally not considered a security although it falls squarely within the statutory definition.

In addition, there are many securities which are exempt to varying degrees from some or all of the various provisions of the securities laws. These include government securities, bank securities, commercial paper, securities issued by charitable and religious institutions, and those issued by common or contract carriers.

BUSINESS FINANCING DISCLOSURES

The financing of a business frequently involves the investment of money or some other item of value by a person who is not a part of management or otherwise familiar with all of the material aspects of the business. In order for an outside investor to make an informed investment decision, he must be made aware of the material factors that bear upon the present condition and future prospects of the business and of the pertinent details of his participation in the business and its profits. The securities laws thus impose an obligation upon a company and its management to disclose such information to a potential investor together with the factors which at the time of the investment materially adversely affect the business or which may reasonably be foreseen to do so in the future. In addition to financings by a company, these laws impose similar disclosure requirements whenever a member of management or a principal equity owner sells his personal security holdings to an outsider.

In financings involving outsiders, it is common practice (whether required or not) for management to prepare a prospectus, offering circular or memorandum describing the nature, condition, and prospects of the business and the nature and extent of the investor's participation in it. In this manner the pertinent disclosures are set forth in a permanent written record so that there can be no argument as to whether or not the disclosures have been made or what they were. Such a document traditionally discloses the terms of the offering, the use of the proceeds, the capitalization of the business (before and after the financing), contingent liabilities (if any), the operations of the business, its sources of supply, marketing techniques and market position, its personnel, government regulation and litigation, its management and management's remuneration, transactions between the company and management, the principal equity owners of the business, and balance sheets and earnings statements of the business and, where pertinent, its predecessors.

Despite the fact that disclosure documents are often prepared and reviewed by attorneys and accountants, the law imposes the primary obligation for complete and accurate disclosure upon the company, its management, and principal equity owners. If an underwriter or securities sales agent is involved, the law requires him to exercise "due diligence" to verify the accuracy and completeness of the disclosures. As a safeguard, the underwriter will usually require the attorneys to give opinions and the accountants to give "cold comfort" letters concerning the disclosures. To support the opinions and cold comfort letters, the attorneys and accountants will undertake certain verifications of the disclosures by review of underlying business records and documents. If the attorneys and accountants overlook or fail to uncover some item which should be disclosed, the primary liability for the inaccurate or incomplete disclosure still falls upon the company, its management, and principal equity owners and at best they may have an action for malpractice against the professional if the professional is particularly sloppy.

It thus is essential that each member of management and each principal equity owner be satisfied that the information in the disclosure document is accurate and complete, based upon his own personal knowledge of the company and its records. He must be satisfied that the disclosures accurately and completely portray the myriad of existing and possible problems which do or may materially adversely affect the properties of the company or its results of operations. Like the underwriter, he will be protected if he exercises "due diligence" in verifying financial disclosures, but this standard is a high one and his obligations may not be delegated to someone else. However, unless they know something is wrong, management and principal owners need not independently verify the disclosures in audited financial statements, as the accountants have presumably done this in connection with the audit. Nevertheless, the financial statements are generally deemed to be the company's disclosures, not the accountant's, and the company itself remains principally responsible for their accuracy, even when an audit has been performed. In fact, in a federally-registered offering, the company itself has no "due diligence" defense at all and is absolutely liable if any material misstatements or omissions occur anywhere in the prospectus.

A disclosure document which satisfactorily meets these disclosure standards often appears "negative" in its presentation. Such a document need not be unduly so in order to provide the necessary protection, and, in any event, what appears "negative" to management may not necessarily appear negative to the financial community, which is accustomed to reading disclosure documents of this type.

Federally registered offerings

All public offerings must be "registered" with the SEC under the Securities Act of 1933 unless an exemption from registration is available. The most commonly applicable exemptions are the private, intrastate, and Regulation A offering exemptions discussed below.

The registration process involves the preparation by management of a carefully worded and organized disclosure document called a "registration statement," which includes a "prospectus" to be provided the potential investor. The registration statement is "filed" with the appropriate securities administrator, which for federal registrations is the SEC. The various items of disclosure which must be discussed in a registration statement are fixed by law, and in addition, there must be set forth any other material matter which affects or may affect the company or its results of operations. The SEC staff reviews the disclosure documents and (unless a special "cursory review" procedure is used) makes detailed comments on the method and quality of disclosure, and the disclosure documents are revised by amendment as appropriate as a result of the comments. If the staff is satisfied with the revisions, the SEC enters an order declaring the registration statement "effective," and selling of the offering may commence. The SEC order in no way constitutes an approval by the SEC of the accuracy of the disclosures or the merits of the offering, and any representation to that effect violates the securities laws. At the time of the effectiveness of the registration statement the underwriters will usually place a "tombstone" advertisement in the financial press announcing the offering. A copy of the final prospectus must be distributed to persons purchasing company securities of the type sold in the offering for up to 90 days after the effective date, or until the offering is sold or terminated, whichever last occurs. During this period, if any material event affecting the company occurs, it must be disclosed by a sticker "supplement" to the prospectus. The disclosure documents become outdated after approximately nine months from the effective date and may not be used thereafter unless updated by post-effective amendment to the registration statement.

Federal registration is expensive and time consuming. A first federally registered public offering using an underwriter frequently takes six months to accomplish and costs in excess of $100,000, exclusive of underwriting commissions. A typical cost breakdown is as follows: printing, $30,000; legal fees, $40,000; accounting fees, $25,000; and Blue Sky and miscellaneous costs, $15,000. (These figures are rough and may vary considerably from offering to offering.) In view of the amount of the costs involved, federal registration of a first offering using an underwriter is generally not feasible unless more than $2 million is involved in the financing.

The cost of a public offering depends as much upon whether or not an underwriter is used as upon whether or not federal registration is required. This is true because the agreement between the company and the underwriter usually requires the company's attorneys and accountants to undertake detailed and costly verification of the disclosures in the prospectus at the company's expense. Underwriting commissions typically run from 7½ percent to 10 percent of the gross amount of the offering in first equity offerings. Because placement of a large amount of securities often involves market price stabilization and other sophisticated and highly regulated techniques, an attempt by a company to place a large amount of securities without a professional underwriter or selling agent usually involves an unacceptable amount of risk. Also, it may be extremely difficult for a large amount of securities to be placed without the assistance of a professional underwriter or selling agent who has a number of investor customers that rely upon his investment advice.

Underwritings are of three types—"firm commitment" underwritings in which the sale of the entire offering at an established price is guaranteed by the underwriters; "best efforts" underwritings in which the underwriter uses his best efforts to sell as much as he can of the offering at the offering price; and "all or nothing" underwritings, which are like best efforts underwritings except that the company and selling security holders need not sell any of the offering unless the underwriter can place all. The type of underwriting used is usually determined by the size and strength of the company and of the underwriter.

The first step in an underwritten offering is usually the entering into of a nonbinding "letter of intent" between the company and the managing underwriter. Although not a legally binding document, the letter of intent is one of the most important documents in the offering, as it establishes the basic terms of the underwriting, including usually the price range—perhaps as a range of multiples of the company's most recent earnings. (If multiples of per share earnings are used, it should be clear whether the per share figures are to be calculated using the number of outstanding shares before or those after the offering.) After the letter of intent has been signed, the disclosure documents (including the prospectus) are prepared for filing with the SEC.

From the outset of an underwritten offering, the managing underwriter and the company (or selling stockholder) commence subtle negotiation of the price of the offering, which negotiation is usually culminated by the setting of the price on the evening before the offering. During the course of the registration, the company is incurring substantial offering expenses, which (as both parties well realize) will to a large extent be unrecoverable if the financing is postponed or aborted. In addition to the problems a firm-commitment underwriter has in guaranteeing sale of the entire offering when the price is at a high level, a managing underwriter has an incentive to negotiate a low price for his customers and for those of his underwriting and selling syndicate, with which he usually has an established business relationship. (A broker with unhappy customers soon has no customers.) He often does this by subtly threatening to abandon the deal after the company has expended substantial unrecoverable funds in preparation for the offering and after it has terminated negotiations with competing underwriters. It is thus important for the company, if possible, to require the underwriter to bear his own expenses (including those of his attorney) so that any abandonment will result in some loss (although a lesser one) for the underwriter. This arrangement should be set forth in the letter of intent. The offering price should not be set too high, on the other hand, or the price of the securities may suffer in the aftermarket to the detriment of future financings and the value of the remaining securities holdings of the principal owners.

Throughout the period of registration, including the prospectus delivery period following the effective date, the company must carefully monitor statements of its management, its public relations advisors, and its advertising program to assure that no optimistic disclosures concerning the company's condition or prospects are disseminated to the investing public. If, for example, an article on the company appears in *Forbes* or *Business Week* during registration, it may be deemed to be part of the company's selling effort (to the extent it is grounded upon information supplied by management) and the disclosures in the article subject to the rigid disclosure standards of the securities laws. Disclosure during the period preceding the initial filing of the registration statement with the SEC (the "prefiling period") is particularly sensitive, as such disclosure might be considered to be an attempt to precondition the market ("gun-jumping"). Even the information to be contained in an announcement of the filing of the registration statement is regulated by SEC rule. After the effective date certain types of supplementary selling literature may be used if preceded or accompanied by a final prospectus.

The registration statement as initially filed contains a preliminary prospectus with a "red herring" legend printed in red sideways on the cover page. While the SEC staff is reviewing the registration statement and preparing its comments (the "waiting period"), the preliminary prospectus will be used by the underwriter in the formation of its underwriting and selling syndicate. Although the various members of the underwriting and selling syndicates often have an established business relationship with the managing underwriter, a new syndicate is formed for each deal. The preliminary prospectus will be used by syndicate members during the waiting period to solicit "indications of interest" from the investing public. The reception of the investing public to the preliminary prospectus will affect the price of the offering, which, as noted above, is usually established immediately prior to the effective date.

As a result of registration with the SEC, a company becomes subject to the periodic reporting requirements of the SEC and, in the case of a first public offering, must report the actual use of proceeds to the SEC three months after the offering so the SEC can compare the same with the disclosures in the prospectus. If there is a discrepancy, the company can expect SEC inquiry.

Offerings registered with the SEC generally must also be registered with the securities administrators of each of the states in which the offering is to be made. A simplified registration by "coordination" with the federal registration is usually allowed under state law. If an underwriter or selling agent that is a member of the NASD is used, the terms of the underwriters' or sales agents' compensation must be reviewed by the NASD.

Regulation A offerings

If the financing involves a public offering on behalf of the company of $500,000 or less, and if the company's management, principal equity owners, or other persons whose securities require registration before resale, seek to publicly offer not more than $300,000 of securities (with a maximum of $100,000 for each person), the offering may be made under SEC Regulation A rather than pursuant to full registration. Only the company may sell securities under the Regulation A exemption if the company is not at least one year old and has had profitable operations during one of its last two fiscal years. The Regulation A offering procedure is similar to full registration except less complex and faster. Filing and review of the offering materials are made at the SEC regional office level rather than at the national office level. Unlike the full registration procedure, the prospectus (or "offering circular") may not be distributed to the investing public until SEC comments have been received and the offering materials amended accordingly. A 90-day prospectus delivery period exists for Regulation A offerings. Within six months of the commencement of the offering, the company must report the status of the offering and the use of proceeds to the SEC.

As a result of simplified disclosure requirements and processing procedures, Regulation A offering costs are usually substantially less than those for fully registered offerings. Also, because of the smaller size of a Regulation A offering, management or the selling stockholders often attempt to place the offering directly without the use of an underwriter or selling agent. Typical costs of a nonunderwritten offering under Regulation A might aggregate approximately $20,000 and be broken down as follows: printing, $2,000; legal fees, $10,000; accounting fees, $5,000; and Blue Sky and miscellaneous costs, $3,000.

Like fully registered offerings, Regulation A offerings must be registered (usually by "coordination") with the securities administrators for the states in which the offering is to be made. Use of an underwriter that is a member of the NASD requires NASD review.

State-registered (intrastate) offerings

If a local business seeks local financing exclusively, registration under the federal securities laws is not required, and the financing may be made pursuant to a long-form ("qualification") registration under state securities laws. More accurately, if all of the "offerees" in the offering are bona fide residents of the state under the laws of which the company is organized (e.g., the state of incorporation, if the company is a corporation), if the company's business is principally conducted and the company's properties principally located in that state, and if the proceeds of the offering are to be used in the state, federal registration is unnecessary and only state registration is required. Under recently adopted SEC Rule 147 the intrastate offering exemption will be deemed available if 80 percent of a company's gross revenues are derived from, 80 percent of its assets are located, and 80 percent of the offering proceeds are used within, the state in which the offering takes place.

Historically, the intrastate offering exemption has been abused and erroneously relied upon in many instances in which a local financing by a local company has not actually been involved. Also, disclosure requirements and review of offering materials by state securities administrators are generally less thorough than by the SEC, so that the quality of disclosure has been less reliable in state-registered offerings than in federally registered offerings. For this reason, the staff of the SEC has sought to restrict the applicability of the exemption as much as possible. In so doing, the SEC staff has applied a so-called integration doctrine to combine intrastate offerings with interstate offerings that may have been made by the company prior to, coincident with, or after the intrastate offering, so that the intrastate offering exemption is lost. The most common way in which the integration doctrine destroys the exemption in a preported intrastate offering is by combining it with a private or Regulation A offering that occurs within a few months of the intrastate offering. The second most common way is by combining the separate intrastate offerings of a series of separate companies set up by the same promoter in different states to conduct the same kind of business. Under Rule 147 legal offers and sales of securities six months before and six months after an intrastate offering will not be integrated if no offers or sales of the same or a similar class of securities occur within either 6 month's period.

The intrastate offering exemption is delicate and vulnerable to attack. Large offerings which appear to require more than local financing are prima facie suspect. Like all exemptions from federal registration, the burden of proving the availability of the exemption is upon the person claiming it. (This means that all a complaining person needs to do to make out a prima facie case of violation of the registration provisions is to prove that the securities were sold and that they were not registered— the defendant must prove that an exemption is available, which means that he must prove each of the elements of the availability of the exemption.) Generally, the company must prove that all *offers* in the financing have been made to bona fide residents of a single state and that *no* offers have been made to nonresidents. If even a single offeree is a nonresident, the exemption is forever lost as to the entire offering. This is true even if the offeree has misrepresented his place of residence. In this regard, the term *offer* encompasses more than formal invitations to invest. In fact, any discussion concerning the company and its prospects by a person involved in the financing with a person who might be a potential investor may be deemed an "offer" for purposes of the exemption. It follows that a great deal of control must be exercised over an intrastate offering to preclude loss of the exemption by improper offers. Rule 147 requires that a written representation be obtained from each purchaser as to his residence.

To prevent bona fide residents of the state in which the offering is made from serving as conduits in the distribution of the securities by resale to nonresidents, thereby destroying the exemption, subsequent transfers of securities sold in an intrastate offering must be restricted for 9 months to transfers to other bona fide residents of the state in order for Rule 147 to apply. These limitations on the resale must be disclosed in writing to prospective purchaser. Also, certificates evidencing the securities are required bear a legend reflecting these transfer restrictions.

Registration-by-qualification requirements vary so much from state to state that no estimate of costs can be made. Such costs are generally somewhat less than are those for Regulation A offerings however. As in the case of other offerings, NASD review is required if a NASD member serves as underwriter or sales agent.

Private offerings

Federal securities laws and most state securities laws recognize that some potential investors are sufficiently sophisticated in business investment matters to be as able to investigate a business and assemble relevant data as are management and regulatory authorities. Preparation of an orderly and systematic discussion of the business in a formal prospectus and the review of this presentation by government agents is deemed unnecessary in these circumstances if the amount of the proposed investment by each offeree is large enough to warrant his own investigation. Under these circumstances registration is unnecessary, and the company and its management and principal equity owners may rely upon the so-called private offering exemption from registration (except in California, where most private securities transactions are reviewed by the securities administrator).

Like the intrastate offering exemption, the private offering exemption has been much abused, and certain types of offerings commonly made in reliance upon this exemption a few years ago cannot safely be made today.

The principal criteria for the availability of this exemption are business acumen or "sophistication" of the offeree and access to material information concerning the company. The degree of sophistication required is dependent upon the complexity of the business and the financing transaction. The proverbial little old lady may have sufficient sophistication to understand a neighborhood restaurant business but be totally unsophisticated in evaluating a high-technology venture. Similarly, a simple common stock financing is more readily understood than one involving a combination of convertible debentures with springing and detachable warrants.

The level of sophistication required in order for the private offering exemption to be available is quite high. Failure to make a thorough investigation and verification of the books and records of the company and its major contracts suggests lack of adequate sophistication. Similarly, acceptance of the company's first financing offer without negotiation suggests lack of sophistication. In this regard, use of a prospectus that fixes the terms on which the financing is to be carried out also suggests that the offer is to be made to unsophisticated offerees. (Knowledgeable management uses instead a "private placement memorandum" that discloses all material information concerning the business, schedules the pertinent business records and their location so that they may be inspected by the offerees, and leaves the final terms of the financing for negotiation.)

A person that is able to "fend for himself" rarely enters into a substantial investment without face-to-face negotiation personally or through an agent, and lack thereof also suggests an absence of sophistication. For this reason, a "private placement" through an intermediary such as a broker-dealer without face-to-face negotiation between the parties is prima facie suspect.

If the offeree's potential investment is sufficiently large to justify his hiring a sophisticated agent to investigate and evaluate the investment, and if the offeree in fact does make a *complete* investigation and evaluation, the sophistication of the agent will be substituted for that of the offeree for determining the availability of the exemption. The agent must truly be the offeree's agent and not the company's. In this regard, an investigating agent recommended by the company is presumptively the company's agent and not the investor's. A sophisticated agent that is so closely related by blood or marriage to the offeree that the agent has a strong incentive to protect the offeree would also cause the sophistication test to be met.

Access to material information concerning the company must be complete as to each offeree or his investigative agent and must arise by virtue of the relationship of the offeree to the company as a member of management or by virtue of negotiating power arising out of the amount of the potential investment and the company's need for the financing. In this regard, two or more offerees may act in concert in the negotiations, so that their respective potential investments are combined to create the bargaining power necessary to be able to compel the company to provide access to all of its material contracts and books and records. If management does not make full disclosure to each offeree of all materials information concerning the company and its prospects, the access test may be deemed not to be available, so that the exemption fails and the financing violates the registration provisions of the securities laws as well as the antifraud provisions discussed below.

The access requirement cannot be met merely by the company's voluntary furnishing of information to potential investors, as this would undermine the registration requirements of the securities laws, which require administrative supervision of voluntarily furnished information. For the access test to be met, there must be verification by or on behalf of the investor based upon access to records arising out of a special relationship with the company or bargaining power. (The SEC has recently proposed a new rule that would allow the access test to be met by the company's voluntary furnishing of certain types of information to potential investors, but at the time of this writing this rule has not been adopted.)

As in the case of the intrastate offering exemption, the private offering exemption is forever lost for a particular financing if even *one offeree* does not meet the sophistication or access tests, *even though that offeree does not invest.* In this circumstance, a sophisticated investor who well understood the risks involved when he made his investment decision may successfully sue the company and its management to recover his investment.

The number of offerees is not as important to the private offering exemption as the sophistication and access criteria. However, there comes a point at which the number of offerees becomes so large that the offering must be deemed "public" irrespective of the sophistication of the offerees or their access to information. The limit to the number of offerees is not fixed; however, when the number of offerees exceeds 25, the offering begins to appear public. Generally, the more sophisticated the offerees, the greater the number of offerees allowable without loss of the exemption. (Under the recently proposed SEC rule, a numbers test of 35 *purchasers* (not *offerees*) is used.) Advertising of the financing in public media for the purpose of making contact with potential investors is inconsistent with the spirit of the private offering exemption and probably renders the exemption unavailable.

As in the case of the intrastate offering exemption, it is necessary to restrict resales by investors to prevent their serving as conduits to noneligible offerees and expanding the scope of the offering. The investor traditionally respresents in writing to the seller by an "investment letter" that he is acquiring the securities for his own account without a view to distributing them to the public. It is accepted practice to place a stop-transfer order upon the transfer books of the company precluding transfer pending receipt of an opinion of counsel, concurred in by counsel for the company, that such transfer will not violate the registration provisions of state or federal securities laws. A legend indicating the existence of this restriction is set forth on the certificate evidencing the securities. The SEC has indicated that the absence of such transfer restrictions raises doubt as to the availability of the exemption.

As in the case of the intrastate offering exemption, the integration doctrine may be used to destroy the private offering exemption by combining a private offering with a public intrastate offering or another private offering.

The burden of proving the availability of the private offering exemption is upon the person asserting it. In order for the risks of nonavailability of the exemption to be reduced to an acceptable level, positive and compelling documentary proof that each of the prerequisites to the availability of the exemption must be compiled during the course of the offering. One approach is to keep a log of potential offerees. Their sophistication should be thoroughly investigated *before* they are approached, and a memorandum setting forth their background and the reasons for their sophistication placed in the log. In making the initial presentation, use of a private placement memorandum, as discussed above, should be made, each such memorandum being numbered and containing a legend that it is not to be reproduced or disclosed to outsiders. The number of the memorandum and the date on which it is submitted to the offeree should be set forth in the log. If the offeree becomes an investor, the date on which he or his representative reviews the books and records of the company, the books and records so reviewed, and the date on which he or his representative engaged in face-to-face negotiation should be recorded in the log. At the end of the offering, a memo should be placed in the log stating that no persons other than those set forth in the log were contacted or offered any of the securities, such memo reciting the definition of "offer" discussed above to indicate that it is understood. The log should be placed in the company's permanent files as evidence of the availability of the private offering exemption as to the financing.

Resale of securities acquired under the private offering exemption, or held by a member of management or a principal equity owner of the company (no matter how acquired, and whether registered or not) is severely restricted unless the securities are registered under the Securities Act of 1933. For this reason, it is common practice for private placement investors, management, and such owners to obtain an agreement from the company to register the securities upon demand or to include them "piggyback" in any other SEC registration that the company might undertake.

If the securities are not registered or covered by Regulation A when they are resold, as a practical matter the resales must be made either under SEC Rule 144, SEC Rule 237, or the private offering exemption, or they may not be resold at all. If the securities are transferred without consideration—by gift or upon death, for example—the restrictions generally apply to the recipient.

Securities cannot be sold under Rule 144 unless a public trading market in the securities exists, and then they can be sold only in limited amounts in ordinary brokers' transactions without any solicitation by the broker or the seller. In order for Rule 144 to apply, the securities must have been fully paid for and held for two years, and a Form 144 must be filed with the SEC. In any six-month period the seller, and certain persons closely associated with him, or the securities, can sell no more than 1 percent of all such securities of the company then outstanding. If the securities are listed, the amount that can be sold is further restricted to the average weekly trading volume of the four calendar weeks immediately preceding the filing of the Form 144. Rule 144 is not available unless certain types of current information are publicly available. This requirement is met when the company makes periodic reports to the SEC under the exchange act (see discussion below); otherwise, whether or not the proper information is publicly available is determined by the SEC on a case-by-case basis.

If Rule 144 is unavailable, small amounts of securities may be sold under Rule 237. Rule 237 is not available to the company, its management, or a broker-dealer, however. The seller must have paid the purchase price and have held the securities for at least five years, and the resales must be made in negotiated transactions without the use of a broker-dealer. The amount of securities sold under Rule 237 during any 12-month period cannot exceed 1 percent of the total amount of such securities outstanding or $50,000, whichever is less. Also, a Form 237 must be filed with the SEC at least 10 days prior to the sale.

The problem with the use of the private offering exemption in resales of securities is that the access requirement of the exemption is difficult to meet. Under present law, voluntary disclosure by the company is not sufficient. When the investor negotiates directly with the company, he can extract the type of information he needs from the company by direct bargaining pressure. When resales are involved, the investor is not dealing directly with the company and presumably has no bargaining clout to extract information from the company. Access by the prospective investor to material company information must thus arise by virtue of some special relationship between the company and the potential investor. Management of the company and existing large equity owners of the company presumably have access as a result of these relationships, and if so, they would qualify. Other relationships would have to be scrutinized with care to see if they truly give rise to the type of broad access necessary for applicability of the exemption. If the resale occurs soon after the original private placement, it should be deemed integrated with the original offering for purposes of determining the number of offerees.

The foregoing notwithstanding, shares acquired under the private offering exemption and fully paid for prior to April 15, 1972, by a person that is not a member of management, a major equity owner, or a broker-dealer may be freely resold without restriction if they have been held for at least three years without any indication of their having been originally acquired with a view to public distribution.

Restrictions upon subsequent resale must be disclosed to potential investors in a private placement or the financing will be deemed by the SEC to violate the antifraud provisions of federal securities laws. This disclosure is often recited as part of the "investment letter."

TRUST INDENTURES

If a financing involves a public offering in excess of $250,000 in any 12-month period of debt securities not issued under an indenture, or a public offering in excess of $1 million in any 36-month period of debt securities issued under an indenture, the financing must be qualified with the SEC under the Trust Indenture Act of 1939. This act requires that an independent trustee be appointed and granted certain rights and duties for the protection of the holders of the debt.

ACQUISITIONS

Securities used by a company in the acquisition of another company must be registered under federal and state securities laws unless exemptions from registration apply. Despite the form of the transaction and the number of separate steps it may involve, its overall effect and the ultimate recipients of the securities must be considered in determining the availability of an exemption. Most state securities laws provide registration exemptions for acquisition by statutory merger or stock for assets. Under federal law, if the intrastate or private offering exemptions are not available, full registration is required in all acquisitions. Under the law as it existed prior to January 1, 1973, SEC Rule 133 (now abolished) provided for exemption from registration for statutory mergers and stock-for-assets acquisitions.

Under present law, solicitation of the shareholders of the acquired company to execute proxies to vote on the acquisition is deemed to constitute an offering of the securities of the acquiring company to be issued to the shareholders in the acquisition. If the private or intrastate offering exceptions are unavailable, registration is required. A somewhat simplified registration procedure is available under SEC Form S-14, pursuant to which SEC staff review is less strict than for registration under the more conventional Form S-1. The prospectus under a Form S-14 registration statement is made up of a proxy statement conforming to SEC rules, to which a cover sheet setting forth the terms of the offering has been added—the combination sometimes being referred to as a "wrap-around" prospectus. When Form S-14 is used, the company must undertake to update the offering materials by posteffective amendment upon resale of the securities by the management and principal equity owners of the acquired company. Form S-1 may be used instead of the S-14, and in such event no such undertaking is required. Form S-14 may not be used in a stock-for-stock acquisition. If 25 percent or more of the security holders of any class of equity securities of the acquired company are residents of California, the transaction must be registered with the California securities administrator.

Resale by the acquired company's management or principal equity owners of the securities of the acquiring company received by them in the acquisition is restricted and can only be effected by registration or under the provisions of Rule 144 (without, however, the necessity of a holding period or having to file a Form 144). Resales under a registration statement are particularly hazardous to such management and owners, however, because they may be held personally liable for misstatements in the prospectus concerning the *acquiring* company as well as any concerning the acquired company, which presumably is the only company with which they are intimately familiar. Resales by such persons that acquired their shares under old Rule 133 may still be resold under the "1 percent rule" of Rule 133, which is similar (but not identical) to that for Rule 144.

Acquisitions of equity securities of public companies for either cash or securities is further discussed below in connection with tender offers and takeover bids. See also the section on "Investment Companies" for regulation under certain circumstances.

DISCLOSURE OF MATERIAL INSIDE INFORMATION

In any purchase or sale of a security, whether public or private, if one of the parties has any nonpublic material inside information that relates to the present or future condition of the company's business or its properties, he must disclose it to the person on the opposite side of the transaction or be personally liable under the antifraud provisions of the securities laws for any damages that may result. Similar liability will accrue to any person that aids and abets the misuse of inside information by tipping others or otherwise. In this regard, both "tippors" and "tippees" are liable under the law.

This simple principle is at the heart of all securities laws and yet is perhaps the most abused. The liabilities can be enormous in scope, however, as discussed below under "Consequences of Violation."

One emerging area of the law in this area deserves special mention because of the magnitude of the exposure involved and the ease in which violations may occur. In any public pronouncement by a public company (whether by press release, report to stockholders, or otherwise) contains a statement concerning the company's condition or prospects that is erroneous or misleading in a way that is material to an investor, so that the price of the company's securities in the securities markets is affected (either up or down) the company, its management, and its principal owners may be personally liable for any ensuing loss to *all* persons who trade in the company's securities to their disadvantage in the open market, regardless of whether or not management, the company's owners, or the company are concurrently trading in the company's securities in the market. Cases decided in this area so far indicate that management must have some ulterior purpose for the misinformation in order to be held liable; however, this purpose need not include any intention to violate the securities laws.

MANIPULATION

The securities laws broadly prohibit use of fraudulent or manipulative devices of any type in the purchase or sale of securities whether in private transactions or in the securities markets. Specifically, market manipulation of securities prices up or down or at any level (except in connection with stabilization in a public offering, as to which special rules apply) or falsely creating the appearance of security trading activity by the use of fictitious orders, wash sales, or other devices is prohibited. Again, violation can lead to substantial liability.

REGULATION OF PUBLIC COMPANIES

Companies of significant size that have a large number of security holders and companies that are listed on a national securities exchange are regulated under the Securities Exchange Act of 1934. This regulation attaches when the company files a registration statement under the Exchange Act as a result of being listed or of having in excess of $1 million in assets and in excess of 500 holders of a class of its equity securities at the end of one of its fiscal years. (Such a registration statement should not be confused with a public offering registration statement under the Securities Act of 1933.) Registration under the Exchange Act submits the company to the periodic reporting, proxy, tender offer, and insider trading provisions of that act. Once registered, the number of equity security holders must drop below 300 before the company may be deregistered.

Periodic reports

In order to maintain a constant flow of reliable information to the SEC and the financial community, companies registered under the Exchange Act and those that have previously undertaken full registration under the Securities Act are subject to the periodic reporting requirements of the SEC. Under these requirements the company must file with the SEC annual reports (containing audited financial statements) on Form 10-K, quarterly reports on Form 10-Q, and current reports on Form 8-K. These reports are generally available to the public through the SEC.

Proxy solicitation

In order that security holders of companies registered under the Exchange Act be fully advised of proposals (including the election of directors) to be acted upon at meetings of security holders, such companies must use proxy or information statements that conform to SEC rules and have been reviewed by the SEC staff. Such proxy or information statements must be transmitted at least annually and upon each proxy solicitation to the company's voting security holders. The form of the proxy itself is also regulated.

Tender offers and takeover bids

Tender offers by persons other than the company to acquire securities registered under the Exchange Act must conform to the SEC tender offer rules. These require certain information to be filed with the company and the SEC not later than the date the tender is first made. Securities tendered are recoverable by the tenderor within the first 7 days of the commencement of the tender offer and after 60 days. Acceptance of less than all of the shares during the first 10 days of a tender offer must be on a pro-rata basis. Of course, if the tender is being made using securities of the acquiring company rather than cash, they must be registered under the securities act prior to the offering.

In order for the SEC and the management of a company to be aware in advance of the acquisition of securities of a company that could result in a change of control, a person that acquires any equity security of an Exchange Act registered company which results in his owning in excess of 5 percent of the outstanding securities of that class must within 10 days after the acquisition file with the SEC and transmit to the company certain information concerning the acquiring person, his purpose in making the acquisition, and his method of financing the acquisition. This requirement applies even if the shares are received as a result of an acquisition by the company or some other company by the issuance of equity securities. If two or more persons who together own in excess of 5 percent of a class of equity securities of an Exchange Act registered company enter into a mutual arrangement to acquire control of the company, such information must be filed within 10 days after the entering into of the arrangement.

If either of the above transactions results in an appointment of directors for the company other than by vote of security holders, there must be transmitted to all security holders that would be eligible to vote for the election of such directors if elected at a meeting of security holders, at least 10 days prior to the appointment, information equivalent to that contained in a proxy or information statement under the proxy rules.

The securities laws for the state of Ohio contain tender offer provisions designed to discourage takeover of Ohio corporations and those whose principal business and substantial assets are within the state. Minnesota recently has adopted, and other states are considering the adoption of, similar legislation.

Insider reporting and trading

Management and 10 percent equity security holders are deemed "insiders" of an Exchange Act registered company and must report their transactions in the company's equity securities to the SEC. The SEC publishes these transactions quarterly.

The insider trading provisions of the Exchange Act contain an arbitrary and absolute six-month trading rule designed to preclude any incentive for insiders to make use of insider information to gain for themselves short-term profits by trading in the company's securities.

If both a purchase and a sale of such securities by an insider fall within any six-month period, any security holder of the company may sue on behalf of the company to recover for the company the profits thereby obtained. The word "profits" has a technical meaning in this context and does not necessarily refer to any benefit obtained by the insider—in fact the insider may have incurred a net overall loss in a series of such transactions and still be liable to the company for substantial sums. The formula used by the courts in measuring the recovery is to match the highest sale with the lowest purchase in any six-month period, then to match the next highest sale with the next lowest purchase, and so on, so that the largest possible amount of profits from any given set of trades is thereby computed. Since theoretical losses incurred are not offset against theoretical profits, the liability of the insider can be substantial even though he sustains an overall loss.

That an insider in fact is not trading on inside information is no defense to an insider-trading suit. In fact, if an insider purchase and sale have both occurred within six months, there is virtually no defense to a timely and properly prosecuted insider-trading suit, and the best course of action is usually to pay the profits to the company as quickly as possible to minimize the ample legal fees that are usually awarded by the courts to plaintiff's counsel in such actions.

CREDIT REGULATION

In order to compel lenders to prevent the pyramiding of credit in the purchase of securities, which can have a disastrously depressing effect upon securities prices in a declining market, the federal securities laws empower the Federal Reserve Board to establish margin requirements in the purchase of securities which must be adhered to by lenders. A lender that, for the purchase of securities, extends credit secured by the securities may be liable to the borrower if the FRB margin requirements are exceeded as a result of a decline in the market price of the securities and the securities are not timely sold. In such a situation, the amount of damages would be the difference between the value of the securities, or the amount for which they are eventually sold, and the price at which they should have been sold at the time the margin was exceeded. The borrower may recover against the lender even though the lender foregoes selling out the borrower because the borrower pleads to the lender for more time to raise additional collaterial or not to sell him out.

THE SECURITIES INDUSTRY

The securities laws establish a broad system of regulation of the securities industry. Federal securities laws provide for registration of national securities exchanges, registration and regulation of broker-dealers and investment advisors, and the establishment and administration of a pool of funds within the securities industry to offset losses by customers of brokerage firms that fail. State securities laws generally provide for registration and regulation of broker-dealers and their salesmen. Details of this regulation are beyond the scope of this Note.

INVESTMENT COMPANIES

A company whose principal business is investing or trading in securities is subject to regulation under the Investment Company Act of 1940, unless it has not made and is not making a public offering and has fewer than 100 security holders. Although this act is primarily directed toward mutual funds, it also regulates companies that inadvertently fall within the statutory definition of "investment company." Thus, if a public company sells a major portion of its assets and, rather than distributing the proceeds to its security holders, holds and invests the proceeds in other than government or commercial paper while exploring alternate business activities, it may be deemed to have become an investment company. "Hedge funds" and investment clubs that rely upon the private offering exemption become investment companies when the exemption is lost and the offering becomes public.

Discussion of the mechanics of investment company regulation, which is all-encompassing (and for companies that are not mutual funds burdensome and expensive to comply with), is beyond the scope of this Note.

CONSEQUENCES OF VIOLATION

The majority of securities laws violations have not been investigated or litigated. However, the possibility of nonenforcement provides but uneasy comfort to potential defendants when commercial transactions of any size are involved. Moreover, many of the transactions of today are potential lawsuits five years from now, when investors may be more aware of their rights under the securities laws and more inclined to enforce them.

The consequences of violation of the securities laws in connection with a company's prior financing are rarely serious so long as its operations continue to be successful and this success is reflected in the price of its securities. If public estimates of a company's success have been too conservative, however, an investor who has sold his securities too cheaply may complain. Investors and regulators tend to scrutinize company disclosures in minute detail when a business turns sour, with the hopes of discovering some technical or other securities law violation to use in unwinding a financing or holding management responsible.

The most serious consequence of violation of the securities laws is potential civil liability that may be incurred by those persons deemed to have violated such laws or to have aided and abetted violations. Where a corporation or other business entity is involved, management (i.e. officers and directors, general partners, and so on) and the company's principal equity owners may be held liable as controlling persons. In this regard, the corporate entity, which serves as an effective shield from liability in other situations, affords no protection from securities laws violations. The magnitude of the liabilities that may thus be incurred can be enormous. If management is aware that an outsider is manipulating the company's stock, management and the company may be liable as aiders and abetters if the violations are not reported to the appropriate securities administrator. If a violation involves improper disclosure, the applicable statute of limitations is generally tolled until the person harmed discovers or reasonably should discover the improper disclosure. Furthermore, agreements to indemnify management and owners from liability for securities laws violations are apparently void as against public policy. Insurance from these liabilities is expensive and often difficult to obtain.

Suit under the securities laws by damaged investors or others is relatively easy to maintain. Such suit may be brought in federal court in any jurisdiction in which any defendant is found, lives or transacts business, or in which any act constituting the violation occurs, and service of process may be made anywhere in the world. A single plaintiff may bring a class action on behalf of all persons similarly situated, and courts liberally award attorneys fees to successful or settling plaintiff's attorneys as an inducement to bring such suits as private guardians of the public.

A company that makes an offer to an ineligible offeree in a nonregistered offering in which the private or intrastate offering exemption is relied upon is thus subject to a contingent liability to all investors in the offering for the aggregate amount of their investment. Under past practice, this contingent liability was deemed by the SEC staff to be cured by a subsequent registered or Regulation A offer to the investors to repurchase the shares sold in violation of the registration provisions. Subsequent financings without either the offer to repurchase or a disclosure of the contingent liability violate the antifraud provisions of the securities laws. Under recent SEC staff interpretations, even a registered offer to repurchase may not remove the contingent liability, and the contingent liability must be disclosed in subsequent financings until the three-year statute of limitations has run, or else an antifraud violation will occur.

Uncorrected securities laws violations can preclude subsequent Regulation A or registered financings. The SEC may take administrative, civil, or criminal action, which can result in fine, imprisonment, court order requiring restoration of illegal gains, order suspending or barring activities with or as a broker-dealer, or other sanctions reflecting the nature and seriousness of the violation.